Praise for *Captain Sir Richard Francis Burton* . . .

"**First class.**"—*New York Times Book Review*

"**An amazing story.**"—*Washington Post Book World*

"**Fascinating . . . A masterpiece.** Rice gives us the definitive work on Burton, a book so full of fascinating historical scholarship and yet so exotic and exciting that I read late into the night and started again at dawn."—Jonathan Kirsch, *Los Angeles Times*

"**Engrossing.** Explorer, swordsman, linguist, scholar, writer, lover of women and pursuer of hidden knowledge, Burton was par excellence the Victorian version of Renaissance man. Rice delivers a book worthy of Burton's fierce spirit and protean accomplishments."—*Publishers Weekly*

"**A splendid and exciting work.** Rice handles the complexities of Burton's story with immense skill, organizing the wealth of detail with admirable finesse and bringing people and places to life with striking images and lively anecdotes."—*Kirkus Reviews*

"**A fresh, thorough and detailed treatment of Burton's extraordinary life.**"—*Booklist*

"**A welcome biography of a man who refuses to be forgotten.**" —*Chicago Tribune*

"**A sturdy, fascinating biography** . . . if you spent many childhood hours staring at maps . . . lamenting our increasingly unadventurous age, this book makes it vividly clear just what, for better or for worse, you missed."—*Entertainment Weekly*

"**Definitive and compellingly written,** the sort of wonderfully crafted tale that befits a life so colorfully lived . . . the best biography of Burton yet written."—*Baltimore Sun*

CAPTAIN SIR RICHARD FRANCIS BURTON

The Secret Agent Who
Made the Pilgrimage to Mecca,
Discovered the *Kama Sutra*,
and Brought the *Arabian
Nights* to the West

EDWARD RICE

HarperPerennial
A Division of HarperCollinsPublishers

A hardcover edition of this book was published in 1990 by Charles Scribner's Sons. It is here reprinted by arrangement with Charles Scribner's Sons.

First HarperPerennial edition published 1991.

Library of Congress Cataloging-in-Publication Data

Rice, Edward.
    Captain Sir Richard Francis Burton : the secret agent who made the
pilgrimage to Mecca, discovered the Kama Sutra, and brought the
Arabian nights to the West / Edward Rice. — 1st HarperPerennial ed.
      p. cm.
    Reprint. Originally published: New York : Scribner's, c1990.
    Includes bibliographical references and index.
    ISBN 0-06-097394-3 (paper)
     1. Burton, Richard Francis, Sir, 1821–1890. 2. Explorers—Great
Britain—Biography. I. Title.
    [G246.B8R46 1991]
    910'.92—dc20
    [B]   90-56099

91 92 93 94 95 CT/MPC 10 9 8 7 6 5 4 3 2 1

To Susanna

Contents

vii

Contents ix

Illustrations

(between pages 172 and 173)

The Burton children (from Thomas Wright's *Life of Sir Richard Burton*)

Burton and his sister, Maria (from Wright)

Burton's India (from Edward Forster's *Arabian Nights Entertainment*)

Nautch girls (courtesy of the British Library)

A Tantric initiate (from *Vikram and the Vampire*)

A Qādiri Sufi (from John P. Brown, *The Darvishes*)

Burton about 1848 (source unknown)

Isabel Arundell, age seventeen (from W. H. Wilkins, *The Romance of Isabel Burton*)

Edward Burton (from Wright)

Burton in Arab dress (from *Personal Narrative of a Pilgrimage to El-Medinah and Meccah*)

The Magic Mirror (from Edward William Lane, *An Account of the Manners and Customs of the Modern Egyptians*)

The chemist's shop in Cairo (from Lane)

The Gypsy dancers of Egypt (from Lane)

The Sufi ṭarīqa (from Lane)

Burton as a pilgrim (from *Personal Narrative*)

Acknowledgments

Few books are written in isolation, and authors must often rely on the assistance of many individuals and institutions, assistance often given unknowingly but generously, such as that I received from the Anglo-Indians (Eurasians), names now lost, who supplied details of the history of those born of British or Portuguese fathers and Indian mothers; the Sufi rickshaw wallah in Baroda who took me to his mosque; the book dealer in Karachi who found me a copy of Burton's *Sindh*; people who directed me along roads previously unknown, such as that which led to the discovery of the Āghā Khān Maḥallātī's escapades in Persia and India in the 1830s and 1840s. And—one wishes the names could be recalled!—the bodyguards in Somalia who kept an enraged nomad from disemboweling me and the UN representative who persuaded a Bedawin chief in the Arabian desert not to execute me for innocently violating tribal laws. Most of all I must thank relatives and friends who did a lot of hard work in helping the book progress, among them Edward Rice III, who located some rare works on Sufism and was responsible for much of the photo laboratory work, Christopher and Liza Rice, who generously made photocopies of the many versions of the book

and gave editorial suggestions, Jan Elizabeth Strance, who helped pre-
pare the manuscript, and most of all, Susanna Franklin, who was an
invaluable friend and confidante in many ways. Special thanks are due
Constanza Clarke, Joan Ford, and the staff of the Hampton Library
(Bridgehampton, New York) and the staff of the Suffolk County, New
York, Library Association for locating a variety of works dealing with
Burton and his age; Peter White for the use of an original edition of
Burton's *Book of a Thousand Nights and a Night*; Frances Colley for
material on the British in Ceylon; and Frank Monaco and Lavinia Jones
in London for unlimited help in finding books and photographs.

A Note on Sources

The sources drawn upon for this biography are many—a full list is given in the bibliography—but the most important must be identified here.

The primary source for any book about Burton is, of course, Burton himself. His works are amazing in their range, detail, insight, erudition, complexity, and caustic humor. There is much biographical information buried in unexpected places and often disguised as an anecdote about "an officer of my acquaintance" or in dialogues with imaginary people—"Mr. John Bull," for example—all ways in which Burton gives the reader information about himself or reveals states of mind or attitudes, telling stories about men who in the end are no other than Lieutenant Burton himself. The reader is referred to the bibliography for a complete list of Burton's books.

The next major source is Isabel Burton's biography of her husband, the work upon which all others, for good or bad, must draw, *The Life of Captain Sir Richd F. Burton, K.C.M.G., F.R.G.S.*, published in 1893. Lady Burton's work is huge, rambling, and disorganized, and she repeatedly fails to give sources and dates. ("Lady Burton was not a suitable person to write her husband's biography," snapped Norman Penzer,

Burton's bibliographer.) But the book is a gold mine for those who would dig. Lady Burton has not only included three short autobiographical chapters by Burton himself but almost "everything" else—not only the "true" facts but the facts as she saw them, somewhat askew, and also personal opinions, observations, irrelevant anecdotes, stray thoughts and afterthoughts, letters, newspaper cuttings—whatever was on her desk at the moment and seemed appropriate.

Burton's three autobiographical fragments are unfortunately a skimpy source for what is known of his early years. The first and longest was dictated by Burton to his wife in the languid days aboard ship on their trip to India in 1876; it covers the period from his birth in 1821 to the end of his Indian years in 1849. Isabel claims to have reproduced it exactly as dictated, but one might question not only her accuracy (she seems to have erred on certain Indian and Persian names, which leads the reader to suspect other material) but also her reliability, for she was known to delete or rewrite what she disliked of her husband's work. However, much of this material in the autobiographical fragments is barely more than an outline. Burton's account of his initiation into the Nāgar Brāhmins needs fleshing out from other sources, as does his involvement with the renegade Persian nobleman the Āghā Khān Maḥallātī, his joining the Isma'īlīs, his initiation into the Qādiri brotherhood, the practice of the ecstatic Sufi sword dances, and the accounts of brothel life in various ports of call in India. The second section is a summary of the same material written for a friend, Francis Hitchman, who did the first full-length (but uncritical) biography of Burton. The third is a self-portrait of Burton (in the third person) as a secret service agent in western India. (This material originally appeared as an appendix in Burton's *Falconry in the Valley of the Indus*, 1852.) From the period 1843 onward there is a profusion of autobiographical material in Burton's own works, from his mystical searches to his addictions and obsessions.

Burton's niece, Georgiana Stisted, the daughter of his only sister, Lady Maria Stisted, gave the world a brief but still significant biography, *The True Life of Capt. Sir Richard F. Burton* [etc.], published in 1896. This work is rather short and is in part a refutation of Isabel Burton, whom she disliked intensely. Miss Stisted was able to draw upon her mother's recollection of Burton as a child and young man, and she writes openly of the great passion in her uncle's life, the mysterious

"Persian girl," whom Isabel ignored. Miss Stisted has other material that Lady Burton also ignored, or saw differently, primarily on the matter of Burton's religion. As a Roman Catholic, Isabel liked to think her husband was one, too, though of erratic sincerity. Miss Stisted was certain her uncle was a staunch but nonpracticing member of the Church of England. (His close friends believed he was either an agnostic or an atheist.)

Thomas Wright's *The Life of Sir Richard Burton* (1906), written after both Lady Burton and Miss Stisted had died, contains anecdotes and information lacking in the previous biographies and is useful in filling out otherwise blank episodes in Burton's life, although one must watch for possible errors. Wright interviewed many of Burton's friends and had access to letters and other unpublished material. However, unlike his subject, Wright was a prude: "As regards Burton's letters I have ruthlessly struck out every sentence that might give offense." Today, many of Burton's letters (and much other material) are sequestered in private or government collections and remain unread and unexamined.

Isabel Burton had begun her own autobiography in collaboration with W. H. Wilkins but died before it was completed. Wilkins published the book in 1897 as *The Romance of Isabel Burton*. Norman Penzer, always critical, states that "Wilkins' participation . . . was not due to genuine admiration for Lady Burton but for reasons more personal"—he was apparently hoping to gain control of Burton's literary estate.

The nineteenth-century biographers deserve much credit for what they said of this amazing man, although they have their faults. However, all present a whitewashed version of Burton, the kind of man Victorian mothers would like their daughters to marry. Isabel and Georgiana passed over what might have been truly embarrassing—not only sexual episodes but political opinions as well.

The first objective work about Burton was not a biography but a bibliography, Norman Penzer's *An Annotated Bibliography of Sir Richard Francis Burton, K.C.M.G.* (1921), with not only descriptions and prices of Burton's works but much incidental information. Penzer's comments and opinions and the fact that he could draw upon the memories of people who knew Burton, such as his personal physician, Dr. Frederick Grenville Baker, are of particular interest.

During this and the next few decades, biographies of Burton tended to the "that Blackguard Burton" type and are not to be considered seriously. Fawn Brodie's *The Devil Drives* (1967) stands as the first attempt at a scholarly biography of Burton. Mrs. Brodie has unearthed material previously unpublished, lost, or unknown. The book can be seriously criticized for applying twentieth-century Freudian analysis to an individual of another century whose world was not West Coast suburban and academic America but revolutionary Europe, colonial Asia, unknown black Africa, and a Muslim Levant in turmoil.

Lastly come the two volumes by Burton's associate in the exploration of East and Central Africa, John Hanning Speke, who began as a friend and companion in danger and ended as an unyielding enemy. Speke's two books, *Journal of the Discovery of the Source of the Nile* and *What Led to the Discovery of the Source of the Nile,* cover the same ground as Burton's works on the same expedition but sound as if they were written about another part of Africa and about a different venture. Yet for all their anger, misjudgments, and errors, they are an essential commentary on a part of Burton's life.

Alphabets and Currencies

The transliteration of words and phrases from other alphabets—Arabic, Hindustani, Persian, etc.—is a problem that has baffled scholars for centuries. Burton's contemporary, E. B. Eastwick, pointed out that in English there were thirteen ways in which to spell Muḥammad (Mohammed, Mohamet, Mahammad, etc.). Burton spelled by ear, and, one suspects, by whim. Thus, in his writings, the Indian province where he served appears as Scinde, Sindh, Scind, and Sind. He was as likely to write Paunjaub as Punjab or Panjab. He was also as likely to use a Persianized version of a word as the Arabic—*wuzu* for *wudu* (properly *wuḍu*), and so on. The simplest method in quoting seems to be to use the spelling of the original writer but to follow contemporary academic spelling elsewhere. Thus, Burton's *Takiyyah* is otherwise written *ṭaqīya*, etc.

So far as pronunciation is concerned, scholarly rules are complicated and tongue twisting. The simplest is an approximation. In any transcription in this work, short *a* is "uh" and long *ā* is "ah"; short *i* as in "it" and long *ī* as in "ee." Short *u* as in "uh" and long *ū* as in "oo." Finally, *o* as in of and long *ō* as in "good."

The transposing of nineteenth-century currency into late-twentieth-century terms is also a problem. In the 1840s—Burton's period in India—the rupee was worth 47¢ U.S., and the British pound was equivalent to $4.48 U.S. Burton often put money into terms of the Spanish dollar, a coin roughly equivalent to the American dollar. In the 1840s cotton weavers in the Manchester area of England earned an average wage of 9s. 6d. per week, about $2.28 U.S. In the United States, $1.00 per day was a good wage for "common laborers." The influx of work-hungry immigrants soon reduced that figure by about one-fifth. In the 1980s an unskilled laborer in the Texas oil fields earned $4.00 per hour for a ten-hour day. Is multiplying wages, prices, and money by a factor of forty a satisfactory way in which to figure? In some cases the ratio should probably be more like eighty to a hundred. Burton's father paid £500 for his son's army commission: $25,000 on today's scales might be a fair though not necessarily accurate guess, and $100,000 (a factor of forty) seems exorbitant but possible. Burton estimated that the gold-wrapped cannons of the ruler of Baroda were worth £100,000 each, a figure almost beyond computation. Modern writers dealing with Burton's time are usually content to leave figures as they were then reported. But this begs the issue to the detriment of the reader. When necessary, I have tried to make informed guesses, with, I hope, some degree of accuracy.

CAPTAIN
SIR RICHARD
FRANCIS
BURTON

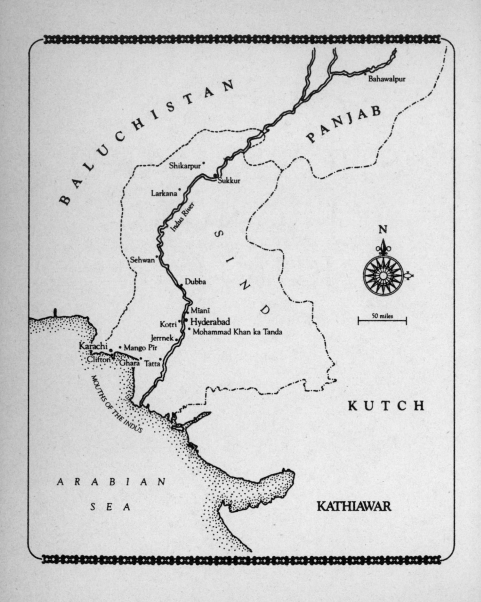

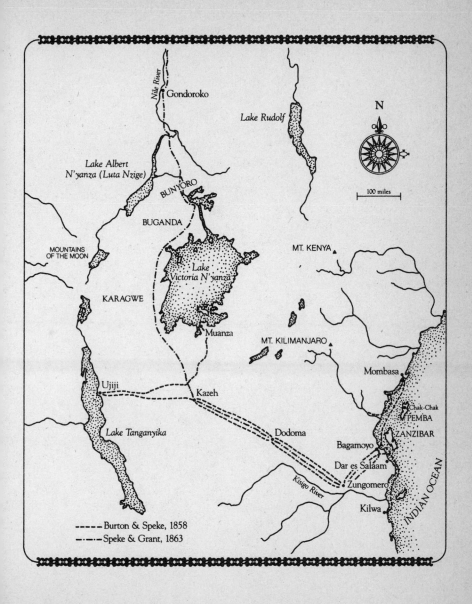

Introduction

I f a Victorian novelist of the most romantic type had invented Capt. Sir Richard Francis Burton, the character might have been dismissed by both the public and critics in that most rational age as too extreme, too unlikely. Burton was the paradigm of the scholar-adventurer, a man who towered above others physically and intellectually, a soldier, scientist, explorer, and writer who for much of his life also engaged in that most romantic of careers, undercover agent.

Burton was born in 1821 and died in 1890, a crucial period in the history of his country. Queen Victoria was his sovereign and Karl Marx a fellow searcher in the reading rooms of the great institutions of London. The Industrial Revolution was in full bloom, turning the verdant countryside of the English poets into slag heaps of human misery; the European powers had divided the world rather raggedly into colonies, protectorates, and spheres of influence; inventions that daily changed the tenor of ordinary life arrived in an avalanche, and as literacy became widespread, ideas of all sorts—revolutionary, intellectual, scientific, and political—percolated throughout the world with the force of an epidemic.

Burton was unique in any gathering except when he was deliberately working in disguise as an agent among the peoples of the lands being absorbed by his country. An impressive six feet tall, broad chested and wiry, "gypsy-eyed," darkly handsome, he was fiercely imposing, his face scarred by a savage spear wound received in a battle with Somali marauders. He spoke twenty-nine languages and many dialects and when necessary could pass as a native of several Eastern lands—as an Afghan when he made his famous pilgrimage to Mecca, as a Gypsy laborer among the work gangs on the canals of the Indus River, and as a nondescript peddler of trinkets and as a dervish, a wandering holy man, when exploring the wilder parts of Sind, Baluchistan, and the Punjab for his general. He was the first European to enter Harar, a sacred city in East Africa, though some thirty whites had earlier been driven off or killed. He was also the first European to lead an expedition into Central Africa to search for the sources of the Nile, a venture as daring and romantic then as going to outer space a century and a half later.

Such exploits reflect only the "surface" Burton and obscure the inner man, a man of extraordinary complexity, sensitivity, and intelligence. Although he was one of the best-known individuals of his age and was especially popular with the public, there were times when he was almost an outcast among his own people. His opinions on various subjects—English "misrule" of the new colonies, the low quality and stodginess of university education, the need for the sexual emancipation of the English woman, the failure on the part of Government to see that the conquered peoples of the empire were perpetually on the edge of revolt—were not likely to make him popular at home. Nor did his condemnation of infanticide and the slave trade endear him to Orientals and Africans. His scholarly interests often infuriated the Victorians, for he wrote openly about sexual matters they thought better left unmentioned—aphrodisiacs, circumcision, infibulation, eunuchism, and homosexuality. He had some private opinions that angered his wife, Isabel, normally a tolerant person, for he passionately believed in polygamy as a means of reinforcing family stability, alleviating the household burdens on a single wife, and lessening the evils of prostitution.

In India, because of his odd beliefs and strange practices, his fellow officers of the army of the Honourable East India Company called him the "White Nigger" and "that Devil Burton." (His own description of himself was "Amateur Barbarian.") He learned early to keep certain opinions and interests to himself and became a master of the Shī'a Muslim practice known as *taqīya*—dissimulation or concealment—in which one's private religious beliefs are kept hidden. And he had his unpleasant side, unfortunately all too public—he could be harshly intolerant of other men and brutally sarcastic, reflecting to an extreme the popular prejudices of the age against blacks, Jews, and Asians. Yet he understood the evil effects of Westernization on native people and warned against its threat, and he had a great sympathy for the Arab race in general as well as for the desert peoples loosely called Bedawin. There was also a strong touch of snobbery in his remarks about fellow Englishmen, when class consciousness was an open and cruel fact.

Burton's adult life was passed in a ceaseless quest for the kind of secret knowledge he labeled broadly as "Gnosis," by which he hoped to uncover the very source of existence and the meaning of his role on earth. This search led him to investigate the Kabbālah, alchemy, Roman Catholicism, a Hindu snake caste of the most archaic type, and the erotic Way called Tantra, after which he looked into Sikhism and passed through several forms of Islam before settling on Sufism, a mystical discipline that defies simple labels. He remained a more or less faithful practitioner of Sufi teachings the rest of his life, seeking the mystical heights denied all but the elect, what certain Muslims define as Insān-i Kāmil, the Perfect Man, who has attained the most profound spiritual goals.

Burton erected such a formidable barrier around himself with *taqīya* that his religious interests have been virtually ignored. He passed several years among a Shi'a sect, the Isma'īlīs, a once-formidable messianic movement whose excesses in the past gave the world the term "assassin." But it was his more sensible lifelong commitment to Sufism that deserves acknowledgment and study. Judging by the bibliographies of scholarly works dealing with Islam, Burton was the first Westerner to write popularly but as an insider about Sufism, yet this commitment remains a blank in biographies of both this and the previous century. Islam dominated his writings in the last fifteen years of his life, and he made several elegiac statements about what he called "the Saving Faith" that cannot be ignored today.

Even then he found other esoteric interests to investigate: spiritualism, Theosophy, the doctrines of Hermes Trismegistus, and extrasensory perception. (Burton was the first to use the term "ESP.") Despite his private searches, however, he was often a scoffer and skeptic, particularly of organized religion, and wrestled constantly with the problem of "God and No-God."

Beyond this, there were his investigations of the mores and customs of primitive and semibarbarous peoples, who in some cases have already disappeared from the earth, and his vast comprehension of native life. He was a pioneer in ethnological studies and might be ranked with the great American Lewis Henry Morgan (*League of the Iroquois*, 1851), although Burton's contribution to the science has only recently been recognized. Perhaps as important as any other preoccupation was his role in what was later called the "Great Game," a phrase Rudyard Kipling popularized in *Kim*.

The Great Game absorbed much of England's energies in the nineteenth century. The competition between the European powers for control of Asia and the Levant—the reasons were primarily economic—narrowed down to a struggle between Britain and Russia, mostly undercover, sometimes military, for the domination of large areas of the world east of Suez.

Burton's role in his country's colonial policies was important but ill defined. He never wrote openly about it but left clues scattered throughout his works—notably in his cryptic references to the use of "Secret Service funds" in the overthrow of certain native princes and to the "shady side" of great military victories. Some of his exploits had major implications at the time, such as his involvement in the 1840s in a plot to overthrow the Shāh of Persia. And he was one of the agents who helped put the Indian provinces of Sind, Baluchistan, and the western Punjab firmly under British control. (They now form the modern state of Pakistan.) Under the pretense of amateur archaeological investigation, he explored areas of Palestine, Lebanon, and Syria that his government considered worthy of expropriation. There were other areas that, sometimes virtually alone, he scouted out for England and then suggested taking. In his somewhat acerbic entry under "Burton" in the *Encyclopaedia Britannica* (eleventh edition, 1911), Stanley Lane-Poole, one of Burton's most energetic "unfriends," tried to point out without actually revealing state secrets that Burton's "East African pioneering coincided with areas which have since become peculiarly interesting to the British Empire" and that his later explorations "on the opposite side of Africa, at Dahomey, Benin, and the Gold Coast . . . have also entered among the imperial 'questions' of the day."

In the East, religion and sex are not incompatible, as they have been so often in the West. In his writings, Burton opened sexual vistas that Victorian England dared not enter. He was adamant that women enjoy sex as well as men, this at a time when Victorian brides were told at marriage, "Lie still and think of the Empire." Burton translated a number of books that today stand as classics in their field and helped bring about new attitudes toward sex in the Western world. His versions, given substance by his own opinions and experience and heavily annotated, of erotic works like the *Ananga Ranga*, the *Kama Sutra* (which he discovered), *The Perfumed Garden*, and even his *Arabian Nights* lead the reader to see that in Burton's view sex, for women as well as men, was not an uncomfortable duty for the propagation of the race but a pleasure to be enjoyed with enthusiasm and vivacity.

Underlying Burton's relentless physical and intellectual energy was an inner turmoil. He suffered frequently from severe bouts of depression, and he was a drug addict. Cannabis and opium were his principal escapes, and he experimented with rare narcotics like khat, which is said to have a priapic effect. During his early middle age he became such an alcoholic that his career was threatened. He worked his way out of his addictions and dependencies and was able to pass the last years of his life free of narcotics and alcohol, though by this time his health had deteriorated seriously. His interest in sex was at one point virtually an uncontrollable obsession, yet when he married, he seems to have remained faithful to his wife.

His marriage is another matter that has not been studied fully. At a time in England when Roman Catholics were considered second-class citizens, even though laws had been passed for their emancipation, he married an English Catholic, Isabel Arundell. To his family and his contemporaries, he might as well have married a woman from tribal Africa. His marriage was thus the forcing of barriers more formidable than the deserts and Bedawin nomads he encountered on the way to Mecca or the miasmic swamps he crossed in Central Africa. Victorian England was scathing about Lady Burton, and the prejudices that surrounded her then echo still in some of today's writings about her husband. But this marriage, seemingly so perilous to both Burtons, was happy and solid and needs to be considered afresh.

Burton was a great raconteur but wrote very little about himself except in cryptic terms and in a curiously detached way—he was in actuality a very "private" person—as if the very intense adventures he had undergone were to remain in oral tradition and not to be written down for the public. Sadly, very few of these stories were collected and put on paper by his friends. Isabel Burton remarked that she wished her husband had written a novel about his life, but he never did. "First he thought that [it] would never suit Mrs Grundy [the mythical censor of British morals], and though he could retain a crowd of friends around him till the small hours of the morning, to listen to his delightful experiences, in print he could never be got to talk about himself."

Despite this, Burton has been a popular biographical subject and also the basis for fictional characters. Rudyard Kipling used him at least twice, once as Strickland in the short story "Miss Youghal's Sais" and rather vaguely as Colonel Creighton, the mysterious unattached British agent in *Kim*; there are also shades of Burton in the strange shopkeeper Lurgan. *Kim* is filled with anecdotes that sound as if Kipling had heard them directly from Burton or from Burton's friends, and his description of Strickland in the short story is Burton down to the last characteristic and is based on a portrait of "a young English officer" (as Burton often referred to himself) in Burton's travel book *Goa, and the Blue Mountains*, from notes he had made in India in the 1840s.

Kipling's description of Strickland is virtually Burton in his Indian days—"a quiet, dark young fellow—spare, black-eyed— and when he was not thinking of something else, a very interesting companion." Strickland "held the extraordinary theory" that an officer in India "should try to know as much about the natives as the natives themselves."

Following out his absurd theory he dabbled in unsavory places no respectable man would think of exploring—all among the native riff-raff. He educated himself in this peculiar way for seven years and people could not appreciate it. He was perpetually "going Fantee" among natives, which, of course, no man with any sense believes in. He was initiated into the Sat Bhai [the Seven Brothers, a Hindi and Tantric cult] at Allahabad, when he was on leave; he knew the Lizzard Song of the Sansis, and the Hálli-Hukh dance, which is a religious can-can of a startling kind. When a man knows who dance the Hálli-Hukh, and how, and when, and where, he knows something to be proud of. He has gone deeper than the skin. . . . He had helped once, at Jagadhri, at the Painting of the Death Bull which no Englishman must even look upon; had mastered the thieves' patter of the *chángars*, had taken a Eusufzai horse-thief alone near Attock; and had stood under the sounding board of a border mosque and conducted services in the manner of a Sunni Mollah.

His crowning achievement was spending eleven days as a *faquir* or priest in the gardens of Baba Atal at Amritsar, and there picking up the threads of the great Nasiban Murder Case. . . . The Nasiban murder case did him no good departmentally; but after his first feeling of wrath, he returned to his outlandish custom of prying into native life. When a man once acquires a taste for this particular amusement, it abides with him all his days. It is the most fascinating thing in the world. . . . Where other men took ten days to the Hills, Strickland took leave for what he called *shikar* [the hunt], put on the disguise that appealed to him at the moment, stepped down into the brown crowd, and was swallowed up for a while.

And in summary, "Natives hated Strickland; but they were afraid of him. He knew too much."

1

The Gypsy Child

Richard Burton's father, Joseph Netterville Burton, was a gentleman in an age when being a gentleman was a proper calling. By rank he was a lieutenant colonel in the British army, with several years of active service to his credit. Though English by ancestry, he was born in Ireland, where his father, the Reverend Edward Burton, was rector of the Anglican church at Tuam and a landholder. This led to Richard's often being called Irish, but in fact he lacked any traces of Irish blood. The Reverend Burton married Maria Margaretta Campbell, who, if the romantic stories of the family are true, was descended from an illegitimate son of the French Bourbon king Louis XIV, through his mistress, the beautiful Comtesse "La Belle" Montmorency.

The Burton family tree included a bishop and an admiral. For some years there was also a baronetcy, but the title fell into abeyance and could not be revived. Though the name Burton was common in England, it was also a Gypsy or Romany name, and everyone agreed that Richard Burton had the general appearance associated with Gypsies. His endless wanderings were taken by admirers, who would not have tolerated the presence of a true Gypsy for a moment, as a sign of his Gypsy blood.

Joseph Burton's military career was passed in relatively pleasant and uneventful surroundings. He entered the army as a teenager, when volunteers were called to fight Napoleon; those who brought with them a certain number of men for the ranks received commissions. "Thus my father found himself an officer at the age of seventeen, when he ought to have been at school," said Burton. The young officer was sent to Sicily, where from 1806 to 1814, much against the wishes of the local people, a British garrison kept a tottering Bourbon dynasty alive by subsidies and its own dominating presence.

In 1814 the British moved on to the mainland, invading Leghorn with the aid of Sicilian troops, and continued on to Genoa. Here Colonel Burton was made town mayor. He entered wholeheartedly into the city's social life. One of the stars around whom the British officers gathered was the unfortunate Princess Caroline, wife of the Prince of Wales, later George IV, infamously profligate and known as "the most accomplished blackguard in Europe." The marriage was not a happy one, and Caroline was sent to Italy, to become the star of a group of society people whose behavior was said to be "scandalous." Caroline herself was rumored to be adulterously involved with one Bartolomeo Bergami. In Genoa, as Burton wrote, "her kindness to the officers greatly prepossessed them in her favor." When George succeeded to the throne in 1820, he gave orders that Caroline was not to be accepted as queen and initiated divorce proceedings against her in the House of Lords, the charge being adultery. Colonel Burton was called as a witness against the queen, but he refused to testify. This act of gallantry was costly to Joseph Burton. He was removed from active service by the Prime Minister, the Duke of Wellington, and placed on half pay. The Colonel's refusal to compromise a woman's honor affected even his sons: Richard complained later that he had to begin life as a lowly East India

Company cadet, and his brother, Edward, could get a marching regiment only, while their cousins were taken into the more fashionable Guards and other crack corps of the queen's army.

During the proceedings against Caroline, Colonel Burton had gone to Ireland to check on the family estates. He found them in a frightful condition. He called the tenants together and, after being duly blarneyed, as his son put it, told them that from then on the rents would have to be paid more regularly. The only regular result was that he was shot at frequently. With that, the Colonel decided to give up the game and let matters take their own course.

But the Colonel's return to England was not a total loss. He found a bride for himself. Her name was Martha Baker, and the rites were duly celebrated. "As handsome men generally do," said Richard Burton of his father's marriage, "he married a plain woman," and "the children favoured, as the saying is, the mother." It was not merely filial reticence, this modesty about his mother. Someone else said she was "accomplished but plain." Another view was that she was "a thin, delicate woman of good family."

Whatever the ancestry and looks of Martha Baker, her family had money. She brought to her marriage a dowry of £30,000, an extremely large sum at the time, but her father had tied up the money so that it was paid out in installments. This proved to be a fortunate move, for the Colonel was a heavy but careless speculator in various risky ventures.

The marriage produced a child within the expected time. The baby was christened Richard Francis Burton after Martha's father and her husband's brother. The date of the child's birth was March 19, 1821—"Feast of St. Joseph," noted Richard Burton later. The baby had red hair, blue eyes, and a fair complexion, but as he grew older, these traces of Anglo-Saxonism disappeared into the famous "gypsy looks, gypsy eyes."

Life in England did not appeal to the Colonel after his troubles with the Irish tenants and reduction in pay. Since his wife had a regular income and there was not much to do except dabble in chemistry as a way of passing the time, the Colonel, who was an asthmatic, decided to move abroad shortly after the birth of his first child. The clear, dry air of France was tremendously appealing. Packing up his household, Colonel Burton moved with his wife and baby to the Loire Valley and took an old château at Tours, where there was a small English colony and an English school. The city was picturesque and attractive, as Richard Burton recalled later, the climate healthy, the hunting good, the living cheap, and the local people, despite Napoleon's loss at Waterloo, friendly.

In Tours, Joseph Burton's lungs improved rapidly. Two more children were born to the Burtons, Maria Catherine Eliza in August 1823 and Edward Joseph Netterville in August 1824. For Edward's birth the family returned to England, and both he and Maria were baptized at Elstree parish church.

Life for the Burton children in France was at first all play and plenty of childhood pleasures: apple puffs ("admirable," recalled Burton) at Madame Fisterre's pastry shop; grapes from the garden; in warm weather, play with Noah's ark animals under the box hedges; climbing the tails of horses, collecting snail shells and cowslips in the lanes, playing with three black pointer dogs, Juno, Jupiter, and Ponto.

The children were left more or less to the servants while their parents enjoyed the society of the English colony. There were no snobs then, Burton recalled in later years, but the Tours community was intensely and patriotically English. Besides being strongly Protestant in a Catholic country, the English were very nationalistic. "Any Englishman in those days who refused to fight a duel with a Frenchman was ostracized," said Burton. "English girls who flirted with foreigners, were looked down upon by those English who have lived in black countries. White women who do these things lose their caste."

Education came haphazardly. Colonel Burton had but a smattering of this and that, and though he expected more for his children, learning was never so diligently pursued as parents in later generations would have demanded. However, little Richard was started on the fundamentals of Latin at three. At four he was given a Greek grammar. (He thought he was intended to be "that wretched being, the infant phenomenon.") Then the pleasant years of play ended abruptly. One morning the children saw their schoolbooks fastened with little straps. Richard and Edward were bundled into a carriage, and off they went to a school in town run by an expatriate Irishman named Clough. It seems to have been a very small school, with English and French boys at hacked, ink-spotted desks and a schoolmaster who was pleasant only when parents were on hand. One day Mr. Clough ran away because of his debts, to be replaced by his sister, and this was all the formal schooling the Burton boys were to experience abroad. Next came a tutor, John Gilchrist, who was adept at caning, to teach drawing, dancing, French, and music, all necessary accomplishments for nineteenth-century English gentlemen and women. But the favorite study for both boys was arms, almost from the time they could walk, when they were given popguns and spring pistols and tin and wooden swords.

Richard early showed a streak of violence. At five he wanted to kill the porter for making fun of his toy weapons. The Colonel hired various young men and women to keep discipline among his children, a thankless job. "We boys became perfect devilets, and practiced every kind of trick despite the rattan. We boys beat our *bonnes*, generally by running at their petticoats and upsetting them." When one newly hired nursemaid took the young Burtons for a walk, they knocked her down and jumped on her with their tiny boots.

There was an air of violence everywhere. At times, Gilchrist beat their hands with a ruler. Fighting among children was forbidden, but the English children and the French children, usually the sons of peasants, fought constantly. The Burtons fought the French gutter boys with sticks and stones, fists and snowballs. "Our father and mother had not much of an idea of managing their children," said Burton. Richard had a vile temper; he was rough in manner, and, said his niece Georgiana Stisted, "mischievous as a monkey," but, "he adored his mother." Despite his roughness, "there was a gentle side to his nature. He loved pets of all kinds and would try to rescue the maimed and the dying." In short, wrote his niece, his relatives often thought him "most troublesome and disagreeable" but "one of the most warmhearted boys that ever breathed."

Gilchrist was not without a streak of sadism. One day he took his three young pupils to witness the guillotining of a woman who had poisoned her children. He told the Burtons to cover their eyes when the blade fell. Naturally, no one did, and at first the image of the severed head produced not nightmares but play guillotining.

But nightmares there were to be. Burton was haunted by several, which continued into adulthood. In Sind, in the wild country near the Beloch hills, he came across a spot haunted by a Giant Face, "the remains of some pagan magician whose head was spared whilst his form was consigned to the flames below," and this reminded him of the persistent nightmares of his childhood.

Did you ever . . . when abandoned by your nurse to the horrors of a big black bedroom, see a grinning face advance towards you from the distant apex of a huge cone which lay before your closed eyes—advance gradually, but unavoidably, till in spite of your struggles, its monstrous features were so close to yours that you could feel them; then, almost suddenly, start back from you, flit away, diminish till nothing but the dark eyeballs remain in sight, and disappear presently to return with all its terrors? If you did, you may understand what I mean by calling this [the Giant Face] a strong superstition.

And even later, when he was fifty-nine, in his elegy, *The Kasîdah*, he spoke of the "Black phantom of our baby-fears."

As a child, Burton prided himself on his stoicism. He could endure a toothache without complaint, the problem being noticed only by the swelling of his face. He had ambiguous ideas about self-restraint. Could he stare at sugar and cream and not eat them? How strong was his self-control? He would look at the food for minutes, asking himself, Have I the courage not to touch them? He had, but with greed conquered, the experiment was finished, and down went the objects of the test.

The young Burtons were liars, too, not ordinary run-of-the-mill liars trying to avoid unpleasant situations like beatings but liars for the sheer pleasure of lying. "Resolute and unblushing," said Burton of himself as a child liar.

> I used to ridicule the idea of my honour being in any way attached to telling the truth. I considered it an impertinence being questioned. I could never understand what moral turpitude there could be in a lie, unless it was told for fear of the consequence of telling the truth, or that one would attach blame to another person. That feeling continued for many a year, and at last, as very often happens, as soon as I realized that a lie was contemptible, it ran into the other extreme, a disagreeable habit of scrupulously telling the truth whether it was time or not.

By the age of nine Richard was virtually a hard-core delinquent. Having filched his father's gun, he used old monuments in the graveyard for targets and shot out stained-glass windows in the church. With others his age ("all Anglo-French boys were remarkable young ruffians"), he stole from shops and made obscene remarks to the French girls.

At last, the Colonel reached the breaking point. Early in 1830 he came to the conclusion that other English children in this foreign atmosphere had turned out badly, and with mounting evidence of delinquencies staring at him, he feared for the future of his own. Moreover, by 1830 anti-British feeling was rampant. "Things began to look black," said Burton. Anti-English remarks were heard on the streets, and incidents took place. "A French officer of the line who . . . associated with English girls, was insulted and killed in a dastardly duel by a pastrycook." It was time for the Burtons to return to England.

The household was dissolved, and the family set off by coach to Dieppe to embark for "the cold plunge into English life."

2

Dark and Sooty
England, Sunny France

"Landing in England was dolorous," said Burton. To the children, the air of Brighton, full of smoke and soot, was unfit for breathing. The cold gray skies made them shudder. "In the town everything appeared so small, so prim, so mean, the little one-familied houses contrasting in such a melancholy way with the big buildings of Tours and Paris." The children revolted against the coarse and half-cooked food; accustomed to the wines of France, they found port, sherry, and beer "like strong medicine." Worse was the bread, "all crumb and no crust." The milk seemed to be chalk and water. "The large joints of meat made us think of Robinson Crusoe, and the vegetables *cuite à l'eau*, especially the potatoes, which never heard of *'maître d'hôtel,'* suggested the roots of primitive man."

Now ten, Richard could see the crevices and cracks of English life. Later, in his fragment of autobiography, he condemned the whole lower class society which seemed to be governed by the fist. The national temper, fierce and surly, was a curious contrast to the light-hearted French.

The little children punched one another's heads on the sands, the boys punched one another's heads in the streets, and in those days a stand-up fight between men was not uncommon.

And the men beat their wives.

Colonel Burton planned university educations for his sons. Although Eton was the ideal preparation for Oxford and Cambridge, a friend Burton described as "blundering" suggested instead a school run by one Reverend Charles Delafosse. A heavyset, bluff man who took a prodigious amount of snuff, Delafosse seemed like a character from a nineteenth-century novel—perhaps, Burton thought, from Dickens. "He was no more fit to be a schoolmaster than the Grand Cham of Tartary." Delafosse had some redeeming qualities: he spared the rod and at times returned from dining half-tipsy. The school was run in a tightfisted manner by the thin-lipped Mrs. Delafosse, who skimped on meals. Richard would sometimes scrape the butter from several slices of bread until he had enough on one corner to make a decent mouthful. Lean and bruised from constant fighting—he found himself in daily battles—he went to bed hungry night after night.

Fighting was inevitable. Richard had a short temper, he was sensitive and proud, and he received enough slights, he recalled later, that at one point he had thirty-two affairs of honor to settle. The fights were held daily after classes among the hacked, scarred benches and ink-stained desks of the schoolroom, with the older boys as referees. Edward, less inclined to take offense, had fewer fights. At Delafosse's the Burtons' principal acquisitions were "a certain facility of using our fists, and a general development of ruffianism." More than their bodies suffered at the school. Instead of learning anything, the brothers lost much of what they already knew, especially French.

Burton's memory of the period at the school was so painful

that he could not recognize a school chum whom he met in India years later. In fact, the school and college years, which Burton believed most boys liked to recall with the greatest pleasure, were "a nightmare to us."

Before the term was finished, measles broke out, several boys died, and the school was closed. Richard came down with the measles but recovered. The Colonel could easily persuade himself that education in England was a failure. Besides, he longed for the shooting and boar hunting of the French forests. It was time to return to the Continent. As was common among many well-to-do English families, the Burtons hired tutors, a Miss Ruxton, red-faced and stout, for Maria, and for the boys, a Mr. H. R. Du Pré, a clergyman's son and an Oxford graduate. Later, Burton had halfhearted regrets about this rejection of his mother country, for he felt that families raised abroad lost all the friends who might be useful in the future. "In consequence of being brought up abroad, we never thoroughly understood English society, nor did society understand us." The man brought up outside his country and especially outside his village and parish was "a waif, a stray . . . a blaze of light without a focus."

The question was where to live. Colonel Burton had been very happy at Tours but for reasons his son never revealed was reluctant to return. He now dragged his family in a wandering search for the perfect place to settle. They passed through Orléans, but everything seemed to smell of "goose and gutter." They drifted to Blois, where there was a substantial British colony. "When one describes one colony, one describes them all," said Burton, leaving the details blank.

At Blois, Miss Ruxton, with no reluctance, resigned her post, leaving the burden of teaching to Mr. Du Pré. He set up a small school with a staff to aid him—a professor of Latin and Greek, a French master, a dancing master, and best of all, a fencing master who had lost a thumb in the Napoleonic Wars. Fencing became the favorite subject of both boys, and they used real, not wooden, foils and swords.

And so life ambled along, filled with activity but with no major demands, with no stresses, but becoming boring. Meanwhile, the parents were "imperceptibly lapsing into the category of professional invalids," like people living a negative, neurotic existence who have no business in life "except to be sick."

Restless and asthmatic, the Colonel yearned for Italy and its sun. "You'll kill your wife, sir," said Grandmamma Baker, who had come to care for her daughter. She was sent home, and the Burtons packed and left to wander through Provence. Years later, Burton could still remember the impression the landscape made on him. Everything "seemed to fall into a picture . . . like a sun that burst upon the rocks. . . . It was quite a sensation."

From Marseilles they sailed to Leghorn, a city swarming with bandits and vermin—even the washerwoman's head appeared to be walking off her shoulders with lice—and "utterly unfit to inhabit." The Colonel moved the family to Pisa, where he found lodgings on the shady—wrong—side of the Arno. "The dullness of the place was something preternatural," and the climate was "detestable." The discomforts were considerable. In the chill ("Icelandic") the only heat came from a brazier in the center of the room. "The servants were perfect savages."

The job of education continued, with an Italian teacher added to the staff, and to teach a hated instrument, a violin master, who pushed his oldest pupil too far by saying that the other children were beasts but Richard was an archbeast. "In a fury of rage I broke the violin upon my master's head."

The wandering never stopped. Colonel Burton, in a frantic search for some kind of peace, was now moving without reason, hoping that over the horizon there might be a city more hospitable, with a better climate, a more congenial English colony. At Siena, "almost all the English . . . were fugitives from justice, social or criminal." The family passed through Perugia, then on to Florence, where Burton had his now familiar mixed recollection of the city: "Colonies go on as they began, and the Anglo-

Florentine flock certainly contained, contains, and ever will contain some very black sheep." However, old Colonel de Courcey had "some charming daughters."

In Rome for the Holy Week, the Colonel took apartments in the Piazza di Spagna, where the English colony was centered. The children ran wild in the ancient city, then still an unexcavated, unrestored ruin. They found unexpected treasures, going from Vatican to Capitol, from church to palazzo, from ruin to ruin. They haunted the coin and curio shops, saw the old Forum and the ruined Colosseum, all unrestored and unretouched, and took excursions into the countryside.

Then came two weeks at Naples. At Sorrento the boys practiced pistol shooting and delighted in cockfighting with unarmed birds. They drank furtively, then openly. "We were getting too old to be manageable, and Mr. Du Pré, taking high grounds on one occasion, very nearly received a good thrashing." The Colonel returned to his chemical experiments, filling the house with "abominations of all kinds." Aunt G. arrived with a friend, Miss Morgan, who was "the only one who ever spoke to us children as if we were reasonable beings, instead of scolding and threatening." The kindly "Miss Morgan could do with the juniors what all the rest of the house completely failed in doing."

They left Sorrento and settled in Naples ("perhaps the most dissolute city on the continent"). Of the English visitors, Burton recalled: "Their morals were unspeakable," but "the girls were beautiful." Then cholera broke out. The Burtons had seen it before, in France and at Siena and Rome. "At Naples it only excited our curiosity." With the help of the family's Italian manservant, Richard and Edward got the necessary clothing, "and when the dead-carts passed round in the dead of night, we went the rounds with them as some of the croquemorts," helping remove the bodies from the pauper houses and taking them to the pits outside the city. "Into these flesh-pots were thrown the unfortunate bodies of the poor, after being stripped of the rags which acted as their winding sheets. Black and rigid, they were thrown down apertures like so much rubbish, into the festering heap below."

And then there were the prostitutes in a house on the next street. Richard and Edward signaled to one of the girls from their balcony, and a party was planned. "Being abundant in pocket money . . . the orgie was tremendous, and we were only too lucky to get home unhurt, before morning, when the Italian servant let us in." But Mrs. Burton discovered letters "of extreme debauchery" from the girls. "A tremendous commotion was the result." The Colonel and Du Pré tried to horsewhip the boys, who took to the roof until they were pardoned.

Because his army service had interrupted his own education, Colonel Burton was determined that neither son would enter the military. "Some evil spirit, probably Mr Du Pré," suggested that the boys be sent to Oxford, an idea both detested. However, in order to crush their pride, they were told that they would enter Oxford as "sizars, poor gentlemen who are supported by the alms of others. Our feelings may be imagined." But the Colonel was determined that his fencing, shooting, whoring, delinquent sons would become clergymen and carry on the family tradition that only he had broken. Visions of his sons enjoying a luxurious life in fat country parishes filled his head. Both boys protested. Each had repeatedly expressed a desire to enter the military. But the Colonel was adamant. There were also practical reasons: It cost money to buy a commission, and the pay was not good; army men were not noted for their brains, and the Burton boys clearly had outstanding talents. With his mind made up, the Colonel told his sons that they were to attend those two ancient centers of religious learning, Richard at Oxford and Edward at Cambridge.

It was time to move again. Colonel Burton decided to return to France. The usual mountain of baggage was packed in the enormous boxes of the period, and the family boarded one of the English coastal steamers that, as Burton said in a disparaging tone, "infested the Mediterranean" and in due time reached Marseilles. They wandered through Provence, where anti-English feelings were rife, to the Pyrenees and took up an extended residence in Pau. Here the boys were tempted to join a party of smugglers, but now Burton's mind was centered more on women than on high adventure, remembering the L'Éstranges ("one of the daughters was a very handsome woman") and old Captain Sheridan, with "two good-looking daughters." However, the children's studies were kept at with unremitting attention. An emphasis was placed not only on the classics but on drawing and painting. "It was lucky for me that I did. I have been able to make my own drawings, and to illustrate my own books," Burton recalled. He added a thought that, fulfilled, would have been of benefit to the world: "And I never ceased to regret that I had not practiced sufficiently to be able to write down music at hearing. Had I been able to do so, I might have collected some two thousand motives from Europe, Asia, Africa and America, and have produced a musical note-book which would have been useful to a Bellini, or Donizetti, or a Boito."

The brothers were now young men, and tensions mounted in the home. The Colonel moved the family, both sons unruly, to the Baths of Lucca, where the inevitable breakup of the family began. The boys were impossible to manage. "I do think," said Burton, "that we were not pleasant inmates of a household." The Colonel's temper had permanently soured. He could no longer beat his sons, but he could make himself very unpleasant with his tongue. Du Pré was thoroughly cowed. The boys threw their books out the window if he attempted lessons in Greek or Latin and went off to the countryside to shoot pistols and fence. "We made experiments of everything imaginable, including swallowing and smoking opium."

In the middle of the summer of 1840 the final breakup came. "It was comparatively tame," said Burton. Instead of the wonderfully emotional partings of Italian families, which he seemed to admire, "the British mother," after the habits of fifteen years, can "easily part with her children at the cost of a lachrymose last embrace."

Mrs. Burton and Maria were left at Lucca, while the Colonel and his sons made their way to England. "We lads cast longing eyes at the charming country which we were not destined to see for another ten years. . . . How melancholy we felt when on our way to the chill and dolorous North!"

3

Among the Grocers

Colonel Burton and his sons arrived in England during Oxford's long vacation. Edward was placed in the care of a country parson, a Dr. Havergal, for a year of tutoring before going on to Cambridge. Havergal wrote to the Colonel that "Richard must not correspond with his brother." Richard was sent to one Dr. Sholefield, a professor of classics, and put through his paces. He was "lamentably deficient" in Virgil and Homer. Worse still

> it was found that I, who spoke French and Italian and their dialects like a native, who had a considerable smattering of Béarnais, Spanish and Provençale, barely knew the Lord's Prayer, broke down on the Apostle's Creed, and had never heard of the Thirty-Nine Articles —a terrible revelation!

The man who was to tutor him to repair his deficiencies was Dr. William Alexander Greenhill, who had just married Laura Ward, a member of a prominent intellectual family. "Mr Du Pré vanished and was never seen again," said Burton with relief. Greenhill was one of half a dozen men who were to have a profound influence on Burton's life and help steer him, then unknowingly, into his interest in the Orient. Greenhill was not only proficient in Latin and Greek but knew Arabic as well. He was then involved in a study of Arabic and Greek medical works and a few years later published an English translation of an Arabic work on smallpox; he was also a specialist on Sir Thomas Browne; his edition of *Religio Medici* was for decades the standard version. He wrote biographies of several individuals long forgotten, translated various spiritual works, was a member of the Oxford Movement, in which issues that had long ago lost the attention of the Anglican church were being reexamined, and was a close friend of Dr. John Henry Newman's, to whom he introduced Burton. Though only seven years older than Burton, Greenhill was the first genuine scholar he had ever met. Greenhill not only got his unpromising student tutored in Latin and Greek but filled out the gap in his religious background and introduced him to a noted Arabist, Don Pascual de Gayangos, a Spaniard.

But aside from meeting Greenhill and his circle, Burton's introduction to Oxford was not happy. "The first sight of Oxford struck me with a sense of appal." As he passed through the portals of the university a couple of collegians laughed in his face for his foreign appearance. Having been insulted, and accustomed to Continental decorum, Burton handed the taller boy his card, expecting a duel. Instead, nervous explanations were given, "and I went my way sadly, and felt that I had fallen among *épiciers,*" said Burton, using the French term for grocers.

Oxford would get no better. His college porter warned him of practical jokes played by upperclassmen and told him to keep his door locked. Burton left the door open but kept a red-hot poker in the fireplace. "This was part and parcel of that unhappy education abroad." Expecting serious studies, he was confronted with practical jokes, drunkards and gamblers, hazing by his elders, and withdrawn, nervous dons.

Alone for the first time in his life since his short year at
Delafosse's school (and then Edward was with him), Burton felt
pangs of abandonment. He missed even his father, stern though
the Colonel had been about his son's educational lapses. He was,
he confessed later, too lonely and miserable to get into trouble.
He quickly made up his deficiencies with Greenhill's help, and
thanks to his inquiring mind, excellent memory, and uncanny
ability to learn, he was soon on a level with the majority of the
other students. But he had no enthusiasm for college life. In
contrast to the riches of his boyhood and youth on the Continent,
Oxford offered little to attract him. He described even his rooms
as a "couple of dog holes." Chapel, which was compulsory, was
a bore, and the lectures that formed the core of his education
were either incomprehensible or useless.

Oxford in the 1840s, Burton believed, was undergoing great
changes. It had once been a Benedictine monastery, and the
older fellows retained a kind of monklike innocence. Their scholarship was of the most primitive sort. One remark, which must
have annoyed Burton, for he referred to it several times (notably
in *Vikram and the Vampire*), was that of the university fellows,
who, seriously, as a matter of philosophical inquiry, "were capable of asking you if 'cats let loose in the woods would turn
into tigers.' "

Among a student body of mediocrities, Burton's special talents
had no challenges. The university was, with a few exceptions,
"a hotbed of toadyism and flunkeyism." There was more than
the sons of grocers, dull gray walls, boring hours in chapel, and
unedifying lectures to annoy him. The first day at Trinity brought
him face-to-face with another of his favorite abominations, bad
food. His "foreign stomach" began to revolt. He complained of
stodgy puddings, malt liquor in place of wine, heavy beers and
ales, and the endless drinking at table after meals.

Aside from his own varied intellectual pursuits, Burton found
that he was leading "a dull and monotonous life." He had a few
classes in the morning; then his day was free. He could not afford

to keep horses, so his amusements were "walking, rowing and the school-at-arms." His walks had a purpose. There was an encampment of Gypsies in the dense forests of nearby Bagley Wood, where they found a sanctuary from the general prejudices against them. Here Burton met an attractive Gypsy girl named Selina, who, "dressed in silks and satins, sat in state to receive the shillings and the homage of the undergraduates." From this time on Burton had an intense attraction to Gypsies. One can surmise that these encounters with Selina have sexual connotations, but Burton in later years spoke several times of "the rigid chastity of the Gypsy girls in England and Spain. Indeed in Europe generally, where a lapse would lead to certain death." From the Indus to Gibraltar corporal chastity "has ever been a distinctive characteristic." Whatever the relationship with Selina, Burton picked up some of the type of Romany spoken among the Bagley Wood Gypsies, for when he was stationed in India, he was able to connect it with various tongues common in Sind and the Punjab.

One of the few fortuitous experiences of the year for Burton came when Dr. Greenhill introduced him to Don Pascual de Gayangos, the Spanish Arabist. Weary of a concentrated study of Latin and Greek, Burton had "attacked Arabic" and tried to teach himself the alphabet, using the famous Arabic grammar of Thomas Erpenius, a sixteenth-century Dutch Orientalist. But Burton had failed to pick up one of the most basic points of Arabic: in his ignorance he wrote the characters of the alphabet from left to right, though the words were read from right to left. "Gayangos, when witnessing this proceeding, burst out laughing, and showed me how to copy the alphabet." Burton hoped to be able to attend regular classes in Arabic, but "in those days learning Arabic at Oxford was not easy." The one professor who might have taught Burton would not work with a single student, so Burton was forced to continue his struggle alone. His frustrations with Oxford were echoed in later years when he complained that the richest university in the world was too poor to afford the

host of professors needed for proper instruction: moreover, Oxford could not even teach Cornish, Gaelic, Welsh, and Irish,
the original languages of the islands.

After the fall term ended ("and very long it seemed"), he went
down to London to stay with Grandmamma Baker and his aunts.
The household was not lively—"a household full of women only,
rarely is"— so he and Edward took other lodgings and passed
the winter vacation enjoying themselves. Then it came time to
return to the university. Burton was decidedly unhappy at Trinity. He felt the general run of collegians "highly disapproved of
my foreign ways, and my expressed dislike to school and college,
over which I ought to wax sentimental, tender and aesthetic; it
appeared little short of blasphemy." But this seems to have been
an extreme opinion from later life, contradicted by his closest
friend at Oxford, Alfred Bate Richards, who wrote long afterward
that he thought Burton was "brilliant, rather wild, and very
popular," but "none of us foresaw his future greatness."

However, he wanted to be educated according to his own
standards. He stirred the bile of the dons by speaking real—that
is, Roman—Latin instead of the artificial type peculiar to England, and he spoke Greek Romaically, with the accent of Athens, as he had learned it from a Greek merchant at Marseilles,
as well as the classical forms. Such a linguistic feat was a tribute
to Burton's remarkable ear and memory, for he was only a teenager when he was in Italy and southern France.

Not only languages but philosophy and mysticism attracted
him in the turmoil of this year at Oxford. He began to investigate
what he called "odd by-ways of learning," seeking out some kind
of arcane knowledge, what he was to call "Gnosis," which he
was to search for passionately in India and the Middle East in
later years. In London during his winter vacation he had met a
man named John Varley, a practitioner of occult sciences. Varley
was an artist by profession but, "miserably poor," had taken up
"practical astrology" and made it a second profession. When
Burton met him, he had just published a curious work called

Zodiacal Physiognomy, which stated that after a fashion every man resembled the astrological sign under which he had been born. Varley cast Burton's horoscope and "prognosticated that I was to be a great astrologer." This set Burton off on a study of occult works, and he retained a lifelong interest in astrology and related subjects. Another occult interest as Burton defined it was "Falconry"—the falcon was a symbol in Muslim mysticism of the "soul exiled among ravens," as Burton thought he was among the *épiciers* of Oxford.

Varley seems to have been the instigator of Burton's involvement in the Kabbālah, a medieval Jewish esoteric discipline. Proper study of the Kabbālah requires a teacher, or "guru," and Varley may have played that role for Burton. One of the key figures in Burton's readings of Kabbālistic texts was the famous Christian Kabbālist Heinrich Cornelius Agrippa von Nettesheim, a sixteenth-century Germanic counterpart of the Portuguese soldier-poet Camões, who later became a literary preoccupation of Burton's. Cornelius Agrippa was not only a Kabbālist but by repute a magician, a man of "wonderful and varied genius"—a wanderer and ex-mercenary who never lacked for employment in the best courts of Europe.

Although he was a firm, lifelong Catholic, his outspoken views earned him the enmity of the Inquisition; at Metz he defied the Church by defending a woman accused of witchcraft; at Pavia he taught the doctrines of Hermes Trismegistus ("the Thrice-Blessed Hermes"), a legendary Egyptian sage whose disciples, the Hermetists of the first three Christian centuries, followed his teachings in a secret quest for mystical experience. Years later, in one of those spasmodic inquiries that he hoped would bring him to the mysterious "Gnosis" he sought, Burton turned briefly to Hermetism. Burton apparently also read Cornelius Agrippa's most famous and controversial work, *De occulta philosophia*, kept from publication for twenty-one years by the Inquisition, a defense of magic "by means of which man may come to the knowledge of nature and of God."

The Kabbālah probed hidden and obscure meanings in the sacred Hebrew writings, exploring layer upon layer of text for emanations of the Holy Presence through the mystical interpretations of words, letters, numerals, and sounds. But more than Hebrew texts was drawn upon. A pivotal figure in the study of mystical works was the early-thirteenth-century Provençal scholar Isaac the Blind, who studied not only Jewish but early Greek and Christian Gnostic writings and certain works by a mysterious Sufi brotherhood at Basra, the Brethren of Sincerity, whose "Epistles" were also indirectly to influence Burton shortly in India.

One of the most articulate exponents of Kabbālistic doctrines whose works were in manuscript form at Oxford was the four-teenth-century Spanish scholar Abraham Abulafia of Saragossa, a mystic of messianic pretensions, who had traveled to the Middle East and North Africa and had returned with certain Hindu yogic techniques of sitting, breathing, and rhythmic prayer that he and his disciples introduced into Kabbālistic ritual.

Although Burton probably could not read Hebrew at the time, the Oxford library had at least one of Abulafia's works in manuscript. This was the *She'eloth ha-Zaken* ("Questions of the Old Man"), in which detailed instructions were given for the creation of a *golem*, an artificial clay creature that, although it could not speak, served as a kind of house servant and helpmate until it grew so large that it had to be destroyed, lest it overwhelm its creator. More than Hinduism influenced Kabbālistic ritual, and thus subtly Burton. There were themes of the secret meanings of words, names, and letters derived from the Sufis, the undefined mystics of Islam, and even more complicated numerologies, formulas, and incantations that supposedly, for the initiates, removed the veils that shielded the "Great Face," the image of God denied all but the elect. One of the important influences on Kabbālistic numerology was the strange Islamic sect the Isma'īlīs, who were known as "Seveners" because they not only followed a line of seven sacred imāms, or leaders, but made the number seven the key to their ritual and beliefs. Two years later, in western India, Burton was to come across the long-obscure Isma'īlī imām and be drawn into the sect.

The Kabbālah was perhaps the most important intellectual influence in Burton's early life and was his introduction to works that might lead him to a secret knowledge. At this point he was merely a dilettante, a curiosity seeker, but the little he learned served to prepare him for deeper, more complex forms of esoteric inquiry in India and the Middle East.

Spring term passed without notable events but for Burton's realization that he had no interest at all in continuing at Oxford: "The fellows at Trinity were nice gentlemanly men, but I had by no means wished to become one of their numbers." Burton's parents and sister were now in Germany, his mother ill with a heart complaint, his father wheezing and puffing as usual. The summer holidays commenced, Richard and Edward went to join them, and the inevitable wandering began, from one pleasant little town to another. "Bonn, somehow or other always managed to show at least one very pretty girl, with blue porcelain eyes and ginger coloured hair." The young Burtons danced endlessly, and Richard and Edward tried but failed to enlist in one of the student fencing brigades at Heidelberg. But there was more pressing business at hand, a traditional encounter between generations. Both boys approached the Colonel on the matter of their future. They were not quite suited for the Church, each could argue, and all their current interests pointed to careers in the army. Richard pleaded for permission to enter the military— "the Austrian service, the Swiss Guards at Naples, even the Legion étrangère." Or he could emigrate to Canada or Australia. Edward, too, having finished his tutoring under Dr. Havergal, said he would prefer the lowest rank in the army to entering Cambridge. But the Colonel stood firm, visualizing luxuriant livings as clergymen for his sons rather than his own ragged military career on half pay. Defeated by his father's inability to understand, Richard returned to England "determined to leave Oxford, *coûte que coûte.*"

"Of course my action was one of boyish thoughtlessness." He got drunk, wrote parodies of sacred subjects, did caricatures of the heads of houses, improvised obscene rhymes, and made up epigrams and epitaphs at wine and supper parties. His object was to be "rusticated," not expelled, to be sent down temporarily from the university as a punishment. For the present the authorities ignored him.

In London, over the winter holidays, Richard and Edward had what proved to be a memorable encounter. They met the three sons of a Colonel White of the Third Dragoons. The Whites were preparing for service in India, and they stirred the Burtons' interest in that country and the East. England had just experienced a massive defeat in Afghanistan at the hands of native forces—some sixteen thousand troops had been lost. Since so many officers had perished in the unhappy war with the Afghans, it was, the young men agreed, a propitious time to gain rapid advancement in the Indian armies. However, Colonel Burton would hear nothing of his sons' latest wishes. He was still determined to turn them into clergymen.

The crisis came in the spring when a celebrated steeplechaser named Oliver appeared at the local races at Oxford. Unwisely, the university authorities forbade the students to attend. Burton defied the ban and went to the races. The next day, he was called up before the college authorities. His companions were humble, but Burton argued that there was no moral turpitude in going to a race, that college men should not be treated as children, and that "trust begets trust." The other students were temporarily suspended, but Burton was expelled. With another rusticated student, he rode off atop a coach, blowing a yard-long trumpet, driving over flower beds, and kissing his hand to the pretty shop girls while the lines of a poem ran through his head.

"I leave thee, Oxford, and I loathe thee well,
Thy saint, thy sinner, scholar, prig and swell."

In London, Burton was received by Grandmamma Baker and his
women relatives, somewhat astonished by his sudden appearance,
for they knew that the term was not finished. In order to have
some peace before the inevitable reckoning with the family,
Burton told his aunts that he had been given an extra vacation
"as a reward for winning a double first." A clergyman dropping
by for dinner nailed down Burton's evasions by saying, "Rusticated, eh?" Rusticated he was. A horrendous scene followed
when the Colonel learned the truth.

One gone, it seemed wise to give the other formal approval
to go also. The Colonel wrote to Edward that he need not
continue with an ecclesiastical career; not that his second son
was dutifully plodding his way into the ministry. Asked what he
now intended to do, Richard answered that he preferred to enter
the army, but he favored the Indian service, as it would show
him more of the world and would give him a better chance of
active duty. There were two choices in the military in India,
one with the regular armed forces of the English government—
the Queen's service—the other with the armies of the Honourable East India Company, the mercantile venture that had exclusive rights to trade in India and elsewhere in the Orient.

It was not difficult for Burton's family to arrange for the purchase of a commission in the Company's army. "My conviction,"
said Burton, "is that the commission cost £500."

It seemed like a foolhardy and dangerous choice, to join the
ranks of this vast, octopuslike commercial organization, but
Colonel Burton's gallant refusal twenty-two years earlier to testify
against Princess Caroline still cast a shadow on the possibility of
regular military careers for his sons. Edward, however, was more
fortunate than his brother, receiving as a gift a commission in

the 37th Regiment from Lord Fitzroy Somerset, afterward Lord Raglan of Crimea fame.

It was arranged that Richard would sail in the late spring of 1842. He had an opportunity to learn an Indian language from a "dirty, smoky" Scotch linguist named Duncan Forbes. Hindustani became so important to Burton that he gave up boxing and fencing for the while.

He could not have found a better teacher to introduce him to both Hindustani and the cultural riches of India. As a young man, Forbes, who grew up speaking Gaelic and was educated at Perse Academy, had got a post in the newly founded Calcutta Academy. Here he was introduced to the Oriental language studies that the English were developing for the benefit of their soldiers and clerks. The Eastern classics the English were translating from various native tongues were not pedantic dry-as-dust debris from the literary morgues of India. The English were mostly young men with a keen eye and ear for the bawdy, the erotic, the picturesque, and the novel. Among the works they discovered were those known as "Parrot Books," an Indian forerunner of the *Arabian Nights* (which are in part derived from Indian sources) and distantly similar to Aesop's *Fables* and other such apologues. They also had come across some of the openly erotic works of the type that Burton was to translate later, such as the *Ananga Ranga*, a popular marriage manual.

Ill health forced Forbes to return home after three years in Calcutta. He joined the faculty of King's College, London, and advanced rapidly in Arabic, Persian, and Bengali as well as Hindustani. Forbes gave Burton long hours in the latter tongue, and soon it was time for formal acceptance in the army of the East India Company.

Burton was sworn in at the Company's offices, "a wonderful dull and smoky old place." So great was the need for soldiers and officers after the Afghan disaster that the Company was willing to take almost anyone.

The excess of demand explained the curious appearance of the embryo cadets when they met to be sworn in at India House. They looked like raw country lads, mostly dressed in homemade clothes. . . . Colonel White's son, who was entering the service the same day, and I looked at one another in blank dismay. We had fallen amongst young Yahoos. . . .

Then he got his outfit, complaining that the cadets—or their parents—were always victimized by the outfitters in England who loaded them down with unnecessary uniforms, guns, pistols, swords, and saddles of the most useless type, plus boots of no value, dictionaries and grammars of Hindustani, Wellington's dispatches, army regulations, Mill's ponderous *History of India*, and whatever else the unwary could be sold.

Burton also bought one item ignored by the others. Early in life, presumably during the hot days in Italy, he had learned the advantages of shaving his head in order to keep cool. So he got a wig for times when a head of hair was required. And he bought an Oxford bull terrier bitch, a veteran of many dog fights and tussles with rats. The animal was old when Burton got her, and why he did not select a younger dog he did not explain. At last he was ready to set off for India, for a land he knew only by hearsay, rumor, and myth. He had no idea where he was to serve or what he was to do. He expected to fight Afghans, but otherwise his future was a blank. When he sailed, he did not have a definite assignment, but while he was aboard ship, the commander in chief's office in Bombay assigned him to the 18th Regiment, Bombay Native Infantry. What he was to make of his life during the coming years would be in part dictated by military necessity and the vagaries of history, but mostly determined by his very strong will and unlimited curiosity.

4

The Great Game

What Burton was heading for—unaware and naively—was a role in what came to be called "the Great Game," a game of secret intelligence that was as deadly as it was sporting and was one phase of the shadowy war between England and Russia over native territories in Central and West Asia. By Burton's time the Portuguese had long ago faded away as active competitors in the East, the Dutch had retreated to Indonesia, and the French, having lost the Napoleonic Wars, had also failed in India, though they held on to some very small, isolated territories on the southern coasts. In British eyes the subcontinent was very well divided and ruled, but to the west lay great prizes of inestimable worth. Although the English Parliament had said in its regulating act of 1784, "To pursue schemes of conquest and extension of dominion in India are measures repugnant to the wish, honour and policy of this nation," half a century later the Court of Directors of the East India Company, forgetting previous hypocrisies, stated that its representatives in India should overlook "no just and honourable accession of territory." The early nineteenth century revealed three great areas that demanded immediate and concentrated attention: Sind, the Punjab, and Afghanistan. Farther west was the very rich, war-loving land of Persia, whose shahs had invaded and sacked India with ease in the past and which was a peripheral prize not to be ignored. In fact, at that very moment the British were financing and secretly aiding uprisings against the rule of the Qājār Shāh. Beyond these lands lay the mountainous Himālayan states, the northwest frontier, and beyond all, the vast steppes of Central Asia, still not under Russian domination but ruled by various princes of unparalleled and legendary cruelty. For the moment a general unease pitted Sikhs, Sindhis, Baluchis, Afghans, Persians, and a dozen other tribes, subtribes, and princely states against each other, a situation that the British sought to profit by.

The Honourable East India Company—popularly known as John Company—was still at the height of its powers when Burton was accepted into its armies, but decay was already rampant. The government, alarmed at the excesses of the Company and its merchant employees ("gentlemen" were specifically excluded as members), had for over half a century been forcing restraints upon it. In 1813 the Company's trading monopoly in India was abolished, though it would remain the "ruler" of India, working as the private agent of the Crown in both mercantile and administrative fields, and it was allowed to retain the very profitable trading monopoly with China, the chief item of which was opium, and the second, cotton. However, almost two and a half centuries of exploitation of the Indians, of misrule and greed, corruption and chicanery, had so undermined the Company's effectiveness that it had only fifteen years left when Burton signed on.

The heart of the Company's success was opium, which was so important to its balance sheet that the directors were willing to go to war to maintain their markets, waging the so-called Opium

War with China in 1839–42 to force an open market despite the wishes of the Chinese, with the result that "at no period of the history of this article has the trade in it to China been carried on so successfully and so extensively. . . ." The port of Bombay alone, in 1844, exported £1,800,000 of Malwa opium, a leading variety, to China and £500,000 of Indian cotton—China, after severe famines, had turned its cotton lands to food crops. In the same year the combined total of legal exports to and from England was only £2,000,000.

But more than commercial traffic concerned the Company. Russia was an unseen—and occasionally visible—enemy. By 1832 the English were fully convinced, to the point of para-noia, that the major threat to West Asia and their hold on India was no longer the faraway French or the native princes of the Punjab and the surrounding territories—Sind and Persia in particular—but Russia alone. The wily hand of the czar was seen behind every minor uprising, behind every rumor out of a bazaar. The Russian thirst for India was sensed in Calcutta by the servants of John Company and in London by the Crown. Strange and irresponsible figures added to the specter. David Urquhart, who has been called a "sort of Messiah type" and who had made a career out of promoting Turkish interests over Russia and served in both open and secret missions to the sultan, warned day in and day out of the Russian threat and kept the people at home alert to the danger. Urquhart had a special credibility—was he not the man who introduced the hot-air Turkish bath to London and also kept a harem, Turkish style, of women from various parts of the sultan's empire? In Persia the chief of the English mission, Dr. John M'Neill, thought it was in that country that "the danger to British interests is greatest and most immi-nent. . . . The Moscow Gazette threatens to dictate at Calcutta the next peace with England." And so it went, with one voice after another raised against the threat. But the Russians saw it otherwise: Count Nesselrode, the Russian Secretary of State, complained in October 1838 to his ambassador in London of the "indefatigable activity displayed by British travellers [agents] in spreading disquiet among the peoples of Central Asia, and in carrying out agitation, even in the heart of the countries bordering our frontiers, while on our part we ask nothing but to be admitted to share in the fair competition in the commercial advantages of Asia."

In Afghanistan a dynastic battle between two brothers offered John Company an excuse for invasion and occupation, thereby thwarting the Russians, whose "generals" had been active in directing the armies of various native princes against each other or against the Persians; opposing armies were in many cases officered by English, French, or Italian mercenaries, often men who were veterans of the Napoleonic Wars. The legitimate Afghan ruler, Shāh Shuja, had been forced into exile by his younger brother, the very ferocious Dost Muhammad al-Mulk. After a temporary refuge at Lahore, where he was relieved of a rare collection of jewels, including the famous and much-traveled diamond the Koh-i-noor, or "Mountain of Light," by the wily Sikh leader Ranjīt Singh, the Shāh found protection under the East India Company at Peshawar, an old and romantic city on the eastern side of the Khyber Pass. The Company saw the exiled Shuja as a means of gaining control of Afghanistan. By now Dost Muhammad was welcoming Persians and Russians at his court in Kābul, and the Czar's agents were operating openly. Meanwhile, the English were actively moving about Sind at the lower end of the Indus River and then upstream to the Punjab, where Ranjīt Singh assured them of his support in an invasion of Afghanistan.

The key figure in these operations was the brilliant young political officer Alexander Burnes, who had violated treaties forced upon the Sindhis by going up the Indus to Lahore, where he worked out agreements with Ranjīt Singh and the Sikh warlords. Burnes had then gone on to the great steppes of Central Asia to spy out the khānate of Bokhara and to look over other potential prizes, an act of daring exploration that made him the lion of London society when he returned home, after which he rejoined his unit in western India.

The warlike maneuvers of the English, especially in Sind, despite all the disclaimers about peaceful "mercantile" interests, had stirred the native courts into a state of anxiety, and the presence of so many English, openly and in disguise, on the plains and in the passes and valleys, in Afghanistan itself, and even as far as the Central Asian khānates, was disquieting to the court at Kābul. But, "my friend," the English Governor-General of India, Lord Auckland, told Dost Muhammad, "you are aware that it is not the practice of the British government to interfere with the affairs of other independent nations."

However, the invasion of Afghanistan took place in February 1839, when the British assembled an army of several white and native contingents and marched up the Khyber Pass, taking Kābul, the major city, with considerable ease. The army was composed of 9,500 British and some 6,000 native troops, many of them Punjabi Muslims raised by Shāh Shuja, and the amazing number of 38,000 camp followers. There was little resistance: Dost Muhammad did not oppose the invaders, and the defense of Ghazni, one of the legendary cities of Asia, was, Burton wrote, conducted by a "rabble." Shuja was installed as ruler.

Unexpectedly, down on the baking Punjab plain, Ranjīt Singh began to fade away of mysterious causes, possibly a series of strokes exacerbated by his luxurious manner of living, and soon died, leaving the British flank exposed, for all the supplies for the army in Afghanistan had to pass through the Punjab and now the many powerful and newly independent Punjabi chieftains who had been controlled by Ranjīt Singh's iron will began to menace the British lines of communication.

The old Lion of the Punjab was cremated in the ancient and traditional sacrificial rite known as *satī*, a term meaning "faithfulness" and which denoted the devotion of a man's women even in his death. Ranjīt Singh's four wives perished in the flames along with five favorite dancing girls, one of whom was the beauteous Lotus, a woman known throughout West Asia for her grace and charm and an especial favorite of the English officers at the court. "They are dead—nine living beings having perished together without a shriek or groan," lamented a young English officer, Captain W. G. Osborne, when he heard of the cremation.

That the tragedy that followed might have been avoided is possible. It was not until 1861 that it came to light that some of Alexander Burnes's dispatches from Kābul had been altered to convey "opinions opposite to his." But no matter. In November 1841 Burnes and his brother Charles were cut down by a street mob near their home and their bodies hacked to pieces. The British commander, Sir William Macnaghten, did nothing. More violence continued, with further English deaths. Shāh Shuja, now a virtual prisoner of the mob, "lost all his self-possession," according to Lady Florentia Sale, wife of one of the ranking English officers, "and told the 860 females of his zenana [harem] that if the cantonment fell to the enemy, he would poison them all." On December twenty-third Macnaghten and three other officers went on horseback to meet Akhbar Khān, son of the now-exiled Dost Muhammad. Macnaghten and one officer were shot down, the other two taken prisoner. The heads of the two murdered men were hung on hooks in a butcher shop in the bazaar.

Soon uprisings began among the more outlying tribes, and by the end of 1841 the unrest had spread to Kābul. With total chaos now reigning and with armed gangs running through the streets, the remaining British leaders decided that the only solution was to retreat. A handful of officers were turned over as hostages, along with the wives of the higher officers. Some of the wives of the lower ranks of the British abandoned their husbands, put on Afghan dress, and joined the enemy. After negotiating what they thought was a safe-conduct for leaving Afghanistan, the English set off on January 5, 1842, for refuge on the warm plains of India, some sixteen thousand people, English and native troops, and camp followers. The entire force—all sixteen thousand—was destroyed in that famous retreat through snow-covered passes under constant Afghan attack by tribesmen armed with knives and swords. There was one survivor, Dr. William Brydon, whose name became a household word in England as a symbol of Victorian bravery.

Such, in brief, were the tangled events and the great tragedy that brought young Richard Burton to India to play a role in the Great Game.

5

The Griff

On June 18, 1842, having been "duly wept over," Burton set sail from Greenwich aboard the *John Knox* on a four-month voyage to India, leaving home "with the scantiest regrets," missing no one except his relatives, and looking forward to serving in the campaign that would retake Afghanistan and avenge the tragic defeat of the army of occupation. With him aboard ship were twenty other ensigns (they were commonly called griffs, or griffins, in the current military slang) as eager as he for active service. What pleased him most about the *John Knox* were the three native servants who spoke Hindustani. During the voyage Burton boxed with the captain, taught the art of the sword to his fellow griffs, bathed alongside the ship in a sail to fend off sharks, and shot some "unhappy birds." The chief part of his time, he said, was passed in working at Hindustani. He read all the Eastern books on board, but best of all, he had the servants to talk to. The *John Knox* rounded the wintry Cape of Good Hope, "and a wonderful scene it was," as "waves measuring miles in length came up from the South Pole." Four months passed in a dreamlike haze of play and work, of boredom and momentary flashes of excitement. Meanwhile, events had changed radically in India, and great campaigns, which would affect Burton's life, had already begun to roll ahead with the profound momentum of armies at war.

On the night of October twenty-seventh the *John Knox* made its way through the nets and fishing stakes of the shallows off the Bombay coast and anchored among the pattymars and other native craft to await the dawn. For miles offshore the griffs had noted "that faint spicy odour, as if there were curry in the air, which about the abodes of man seems to be crossed with an aroma of drugs, as though proceeding from an apothecary's store." On the morning of the twenty-eighth, as the rising sun showed the silhouette of Bombay lying low and romantically across the harbor and the day's heat began to burn with that special intensity of the tropics, the government pilot came aboard. He was immediately plied with questions about Afghanistan, the dream of all the griffs and the concern of the other passengers.

"What of the war?" he was asked. At his answer all hopes fell to zero. Lord Ellenborough had succeeded Lord Auckland. The avenging army had returned through the Khayber Pass. The campaign was finished. Ghuzni had fallen, the prisoners had been given up. Pollock, Sale, and Pratt had been perfectly successful, and there was no chance of becoming Commander-in-Chief within the year.

A "wretched shore boat" landed the griffs at "unclean" Appolo Bunder. Burton was quick to notice that "Appolo Bunder" was an English misspelling of the Marathi word *apalawaya*. As to the name Bombay, he preferred the Indian claim that it was a corruption of the ancient Mombadevi, a local tribal goddess, rather than the more reasonable and possible Portuguese, *Bom Bahia*, Good Bay.

Burton and his companions shook hands and, "not without something of soreness of heart," went about their business. On the Bunder, Burton had an immediate and pleasurable success: The language lessons with Forbes and the running conversations aboard the *John Knox* enabled him, when he broke into Hindustani, "to land with *éclat* as a raw griff and to astonish the throng of palanquin bearers that jostled, pushed and pulled me in the pier head, with the vivacity and nervousness of my phraseology."

In first setting foot on Indian soil, Burton encountered squalor and dirt unlike anything he had seen in the slums of Naples and Rome or anywhere else in Europe. The rains had ended, but the sky was never clear. Even when favorable, the weather worked against him, and "the sun seemed to burn all the colour out of the landscape." Disappointments mounted rapidly. Burton had envisioned Bombay in poetic terms:

> Thy towers, Bombay, gleam bright, they say,
> Across the dark blue sea.

He thought the sentiment absurd. "The bay so celebrated was anything but beautiful." The waters of the once-magnificent harbor were filthy. There were no towers except the stunted spires of the Anglican cathedral, which he said resembled a village church, already scarred by the rigors of the tropics— "splotched and corroded as if by gangrene." The old Portuguese fort—useless for defense—he described as "dingy." He was also appalled by his first sight of a sepoy, an Indian soldier, "with dingy face, greasy hair and arms like broomsticks, and a body like a mummy." Could this be the kind of man he was to command, the type of soldier upon whom his life might depend in battle? Later he came to appreciate the sepoy as a soldier, but now he was offended by the sepoy uniform, a faded scarlet coat and blue dungaree trousers.

Even so, despite these momentary disappointments, there was a romantic, exciting city at his feet. In the 1840s, Bombay was rough and raw, a long narrow island made of smaller islands slowly being tied together as the creeks and channels between were filled in. The city showed traces of its earlier occupants, the Hindu rājas, then the Muslims, who ceded it to the Portuguese, who in turn transferred it to the English as part of the dowry of Catherine of Braganza when she married Charles II in 1662.

At first, Bombay's dirt, odors, and unabashed crudity offended Burton. Should he return to the *John Knox*? He and the other griffs were lodged in a run-down tavern, the British Hotel, "not only filthy but exceedingly expensive . . . all uncleanliness at the highest prices." That officers of the Company's army were expected to pay for their lodgings wherever they served was one of Burton's constant complaints.

However, the British Hotel had a pleasant surprise for him. Waiting in the lobby for the incoming griffs was a *munshī*, a teacher, in this case of languages, one Dosabhai Sohrabji, a Parsi, white-bearded and shrewd and known as the best teacher in Bombay. Sohrabji taught Gujarati, Hindustani, and Persian ("the latter the usual vile Indian article," said Burton). Sohrabji "managed to ruin his reputation by publishing a book in English and these three languages, wherein he showed his perfect unfitness." But the *munshī* was "very good when he had no pretensions," and he gave Burton the *Akhlāq-i-Hindī* and the *Tota-Kahāni*— books Forbes had already introduced him to—as basic texts. Burton was to remain friends with the old Parsi, and as he said often, the *munshī* "always used to quote his pupil as a man who could learn a language running."

Aside from his language lessons, Burton found life in the hotel intolerable. The building reeked of curry. As in many such places in the Orient even today, the walls of thin muslin did not reach the ceiling. Drunken officers, standing on chairs, looked into neighboring rooms. The lack of privacy made Burton "sick with rage."

After a week at the British Hotel, Burton came down with diarrhea and through the kindness of the fort surgeon, Paddy Ryan, got himself moved into what was euphemistically called the Sanitarium. Ryan prescribed good port as a cure, so Burton reasoned that if port was a cure it might also be a preventative and ever after made it a part of his dietary regime.

Work seemed to be the only anodyne. Burton threw himself into his language studies. Sohrabji worked with him on his increasingly fluent Hindustani and started him on Gujarati and Persian, taking his mind off the dismal lodgings ("unfit to house an Englishman's dog") and the depressing odors wafting from the cremation grounds next door—"the smell of roast Hindu was most unpleasant."

Burton realized he had exchanged exile in the English colonies of Europe and the dull gray life of Oxford and London for exile in Bombay's Little England. It was a difficult, narrow society, and Burton could not avoid its restrictions. "In 1842," he said, "there were very few white faces in Bombay." A contemporary, a Mrs. Elwood, noted that there were fewer than "five hundred respectable" Europeans in the city. There was nothing but an endless round of social activities to keep people busy. "But," said Burton, "indigestible dinners are not pleasant in a Turkish bath; dancing is at a discount in a region of eternal dog-days. . . . Visits become visitations."

He could not stand Bombay society. "I stood perfectly aghast at its presence." The small English group was not a colony but a garrison, he complained, where everyone knew everyone else's business. Moreover, "the children were hideously brought up, and, under the age of five, used language that would make a porter's hair stand on end."

However, there was another, more enjoyable side to his life than suffering through social gatherings with prudish memsahibs and the sons of clerks and businessmen. In the sanitarium by the sea Burton entered into what he called the "roystering and rackety life" of the other inmates, one of whom led him into "all kinds of mischief, introducing me to native life of which the less said the better." He was referring to Bombay's brothels, where the women stand in the doorways of cagelike stalls fronted with iron bars, soliciting visitors. He complained at first about the uneventful days: "Life was confined to a solitary ride (at dawn and dusk), a dull monotonous day"—but at night he found

> some places of dissipation—to put it mildly—such as the Bhendi bazar, whose attractions consist of dark young persons in gaudy dress, mock jewels and hair japanned with coca-nut oil, and whose especial diversions were an occasional "row"—a barbarous manner of town and gown.

The Bombay bazaars were exciting places at night. In a passage from his easy and flexible translation of the *Kama Sutra* (1883), in which he did not hesitate to add from personal experience what was missing in the original, Burton wrote what he thought was as true of the sixth century when it was written as of the nineteenth.

> A courtesan, well dressed and wearing her ornaments, should sit or stand at the door of her house, and without exposing herself too much, should look on the public road so as to be seen by the passersby, she being like an object for sale.

It was at this time that he began his first journals of ethnological notes and observations that he was to draw upon for future work. Angry as he might have been with his fellow English, he quickly came to believe that Bombay—in fact, whatever he saw of India and later of other parts of the Orient—was marvelously exciting, for every moment was charged with the picturesque and the unusual. Despite his endless complaints, this was India, huge, complex, swarming with people of all races, colors, languages, and religious beliefs.

Before he had passed six weeks in Bombay, Burton received orders from the Company that he was to be sent to the 18th Bombay Native Infantry at Baroda, a city in Gujarat. With this assignment Burton was at last made a full and formal member of the ruling class and caste of India. He organized his equipment. A horse was a necessity. "I had utterly rejected the so-called

Arab horse—bastard brutes from the Persian Gulf," for they were the kind of mount the average officer was persuaded to buy from the native dealers at extravagant prices. Burton got himself an Indian horse, a Kattywar.

This was a bright dun, with black stripes and stockings, a very vicious brute, addicted to all the sins of horseflesh, but full of spirits as a thoroughbred. Master and horse got along thoroughly well.

And since every officer, every Englishman, and every white family had a staff of servants, as many as one could afford, he engaged a household of Goans, presided over by one Salvador Soares. Salvador became a useful foil in Burton's writings, serving as the mouthpiece for various anecdotes about a young English officer, which the sharp-eyed reader would recognize as Burton himself. *

With his Kattywar, his retinue of half-caste servants, his bull terrier, and an endless number of trunks, a solid command of Hindustani, and a good supply of port, Burton boarded a two-masted sailing ship, a pattymar, for the voyage north to Gujarat. It was a leisurely trip, covering seventy to eighty miles a day through fair seas, and one that could only delight Burton, now completely enamored of India. This was the first time he had been fully alone, among Indians, with no white faces to remind him of the land and people he did not care for with any deep sentiment. The voyage was one he was to repeat many times during the next few years, either to Gujarat or to the western province of Sind, and every sailing was enjoyable, with stops rarely visited by Europeans.

---

* Burton preferred Goans as servants, as "they were less troublesome than the Hindus and Mussulmans," for as vegetarians the former disliked working for casteless meat-eating Europeans and the latter believed that their own Islam was superior to the whites' Christianity. The Goans were a mixture of low-caste Indian and Portuguese from the Portuguese enclave on the Konkan coast south of Bombay.

The pattymar first put in at the sacred Hindu city of Dwarka in Cutch, "guarded outside by sharks and filled with fierce and fanatic mercenaries," and then sailed eastward along the coast to Surat, the first home of the Honourable East India Company and the womb of the British Empire in India, where Burton's "half-piratical countrymen" were followed by the Portuguese, Dutch, and French. Magnificent tombs of the Europeans who died at Surat testified to their success as traders in the short lives the tropics had allowed them. "The old graveyard," Burton wrote in the first of many such tributes to valiant forebears, was "not devoid of some barbaric interest," but he could not find the tomb of Thomas Coryat, a man he had long admired. Burton had a peculiar fascination for the graves of men with whom he felt a special kinship, men who were wanderers, linguists, adventurers, scholars, men of both daring and intellect, in whom he saw his spiritual and scholarly ancestry. The individual here—"Tom Coryate of the Crudities," as Burton called him—was Thomas Coryat, an Englishman born in 1577. After a wandering tour through Europe, he published an account of it in 1611 as *Coryate's Crudities, Hastily gobbled up in five Moneths travells.* . . . He set off for Asia on foot, begging his way through Greece, the Holy Land, and Persia, and after a visit to the Grand Mogul, he settled down in Surat, a holy beggar and a mystic.

Search as he would for Coryat's tomb, Burton could not find it. Only later did he learn that his native informant had led him astray and that Coryat was buried farther downriver.

At last, saturated with sights unimaginable in the gloomy, frustrating days at Oxford, Burton disembarked at Tunkaria-Bunder, a mud bank with a mooring stake on a beach in the Gulf of Cambray. Not willing to endure his skittish Kattywar nag for the three or four days' ride ahead, he rented some native carts and spread a mattress for himself in one "comfortable enough for young limbs and strong nerves." He set off through countryside "green as a card table, and just as flat." All teemed with "sights and sounds and smells peculiarly Indian." The barking of the monkeys, the braying of the conch shells calling the faithful in the evening to the village temples, the "peacocks screaming their good-night to the sun," struck him as much as the aromas of the cow-dung cooking fires. And the air, after Bombay's stenches, was "soft and pleasant."

Then, suddenly, he was at Baroda, and he found the road that led up to the British cantonment, sprawled in apparent disorder on a slight rise half a mile west of the native city, whose towers and turrets and minarets he could see glimmering above the palms and banyans and pipals.

6

The Black Wife

On arriving in Baroda, Burton found his corps in skeleton condition. One wing, with the majority of officers, had been sent to Mhow on the Malwa plateau, about 160 miles away, to guard John Company's opium crop. A few officers were on staff duty, and some were working in the Company's civil service. Only eight officers of the 18th Bombay Native Infantry were present to welcome Burton and his retinue.

He was brought to the traveler's bungalow, "a dismal place," he complained later of the ramshackle building maintained for the Europeans who passed through Baroda. Here he was inspected by his brother officers, led by a Major James, then in command of the regiment. James, seeing Burton's discomfort, immediately gave him temporary lodging in his own quarters. At mess that night, Burton was formally presented to the other officers.

The regimental mess, with its large cool Hall and punkahs [fans], its clean napery and bright silver, its servants each standing behind

55

his master's chair, and the cheroots and hookahs [water pipes] which appeared with the disappearance of the 'table'-cloth, was a pleasant surprise, the first sight of comfortable home-life I had seen since landing in Bombay.

With his instinct for alienating himself unnecessarily from more conventional people, Burton immediately set himself apart by refusing beer and got off to a bad start with his messmates by bringing out his diarrhea-resisting port: "The first night at Mess was an epoch, and the old hands observed that I drank no beer. This was exceptional in those days. . . . 'Drink beer, think beer' was the practice at the time in India."

When he got his quarters, he found them a great disappointment. In one account he called his bungalow a "dog-hole"—the same term he had used to describe his rooms at Oxford; in another, "a thatched article not unlike a cowshed," which kept out the sun but let in the rain. Settled in his bungalow with his household of servants, his bull terrier, and his new horse, he could finally take stock of his situation. It was possible that he might be in action soon, for despite the retaking and leveling of Kābul and Ghazni and the liberation of the prisoners, "the ominous words 'tail of the Afghan storm' were in many men's mouths." Afghanistan was still a topic at mess, although it was being replaced by the increasingly unstable situation in Sind as a subject for speculation. Meanwhile, there was more to occupy Burton than idle talk about future campaigns. Before him was Baroda, a true Indian city, his first—feudal, primitive, old as history, a sharp contrast to Bombay, with its dense Portuguese and English imprint. Baroda was India, with all the exotic finery, pomp, tawdriness, dirt, smells, decadence, and danger.

Aside from the presence of the cantonment outside the city, Baroda had been spared much of the anguish of the rest of India, for the English had invaded it only forty years before and the occupation did little to alter the life of the inhabitants. Except in extreme cases, such as infanticide, they allowed the Gaekwars, the rulers, full liberty to follow their own ways. The Gaekwars, however, were not Gujaratis but Marathas, originally village toughs whose military genius gave them control of several Indian states, and were thus outsiders. The Maratha princes at Baroda gave themselves the honorific of Gaekwar—roughly "Cow-keeper"—because of their profound devotion to the herds sacred to their Hindu deities. They were patrons of the great god Śiva and practiced forms of phallic worship, engaged in by male and female devotees alike in very wild and primitive rites.

By Burton's time the Gaekwars' humble origins had been forgotten. Now they were rulers possessing great power and wealth, wealth of a type and shown in a manner that offended English sensibilities, although Burton was most appreciative of certain ways in which it was expressed. The current Gaekwar had two great guns to which *pūjā* or adoration was regularly offered: "They were of massive gold, built around steel tubes, and each was worth about £100,000," said Burton.

Despite the presence of the English, Baroda at heart remained a medieval, barbaric state. In the eyes of the rulers, as in the eyes of the gods, people ranked below cattle, and kindness to one did not necessitate kindness to the other. Excesses of all types were common, and punishments were cruel. Criminals might be tied to the hind legs of an elephant and dragged through the streets. If the victim failed to die, his head was placed on a stone, and the elephant crushed it. The wives and daughters of honest men could be taken on the streets and sent to the ruler's harem. Not only were there fights between animals for the benefit of the people in a public stadium; so, too, were there battles to the death between male wrestlers, intoxicated with opium and marijuana, with claws of sharpened horns strapped to their wrists; they fought until one or the other collapsed in a mass of bloody strips of flesh. Female infants were disposed of by an overdose of opium or by drowning in a hole filled with milk, for among Hindus girls were a liability.

In later years Burton was to take a more callous view of life in the Orient, with its brutality, tortures, poverty, sorrows, and death. But at the moment there was the city of Baroda, walled, medieval, lying compactly on the banks of the river Vishwamitra ("Good Water," said Burton). It was not an easy city to survive in. Dense jungles surrounding the walls trapped the heat. Temperatures of 105° were to be expected, and Burton noted days of 120. Then there were the monsoon rains, when a full three feet of water dropped like overturned lakes and all was damp, rotted, and limp in the tropical ooze. The rains, said Burton, were "torrential, sometimes lasting seven days and seven nights, without an hour's interruption."

Along with the menace of the heat and rain there were the people. The population was "mostly hostile, and eyed us with hateful eyes, and seemed to have taught even their animals to abhor us." Over and over again Burton warned that sooner or later the Indian people would rise against the English, and when they did, particularly in the rebellion of 1857, he could only regret his prophecy.

Hostility or not, Baroda—"a mélange of low huts and tall houses, grotesquely painted, with a shabby palace, and a Cauk, or Bazar"—was always intriguing, enticing, and dangerous. It was an exciting place for a young officer who wanted to break away from the routines of the cantonment. Few of the English ventured into the crowded streets, searched the stalls in the bazaars for manuscripts and books, or visited the women in the tenements that lined the thoroughfares and alleys.

It was those crowded streets, so narrow that a man and a sacred cow had barely room to pass each other, that became an obsession with Burton. Accustomed as he was to non-English cities, to life in French and Italian towns, and to the slums of Rome and Naples, he found Baroda an even more exciting, exotic—and erotic—city than any he had known before.

In Burton's day, even though the ruler was Hindu, Baroda's streets and alleys, crowded, mysterious, were filled with the sights and sounds of Islam: the calls of the muezzins to prayer, the faithful dropping to their knees in the mosques and in the streets or at the shrines of saints and pīrs, the holy men. All the tenements, which ran to three and four stories in height, had balconies where the Muslim courtesans would sit idly singing, composing poetry, chewing betel nuts, chatting with their friends, calling to people on the street, serving cool sherbets and sweets to their admirers. The floors of the apartments were spread with rich carpets and covered with clean white sheets: the balcony tiles were sprinkled with fresh water and the parapets lined with fragrant clay water pots smelling of new earth. Then there were the flowers. Flowers garlanded everything, the doorways and rafters, the cots and piles of cushions, and the women wore them in their hair and draped their lovers especially with the *mogra*, the flower known as *rāth-kī-rānī*, "Queen of the Night," which would be spread on the beds when the couple united, to be crushed in the moment of passion. Over all wafted the sweet smell of the hookahs, and incense, opium, and hemp.

For most of the white officers, Baroda city, half an hour's ride from the cantonment, was a faraway place. Their lives were centered on their base and their pastimes, especially hunting. His fellow officers, Burton thought, lived rather handsomely. "Each had a horse or two, part of a house, a pleasant mess, plenty of pale ale, as much shooting as he could manage, and an occasional invitation to a dance . . . or to a dinner party where a chair unexpectedly falls vacant." Life was pleasant and easy, and except for the ordinary discomforts of India, it was, for most, a life of fun. "But," said Burton, "some are vain enough to want more and of these fools was I." And a certain self-delusion ruled: "There was not a subaltern in the 18th regiment who did not consider himself capable of governing a million Hindus."

At Baroda, the cantonment, like all cantonments, was surrounded by encroaching native hutments, shacks, and stalls— "a huge dirty bazar [they were called *lāl bāzārs*, "red bazaars," after the red coats of earlier troops], full of shopkeepers and servants, soldiers and sepoys, ladies of no virtue to speak of, naked children and yelping curs—a scene strictly in the eastern low-life style."

In the officers' quarters along the edges of the cantonment there was a noticeable hierarchy, starting with the fine white tall-arched mansions of the superior officers. Next came "the small, neat building with carefully curtained windows . . . an apology for a garden kept up in the face of many difficulties, [which] points out the married captain, or field officer."

Finally, there was what is clearly Burton's own house:

> Another bungalow, jealously trellised round with bamboo-work, a gaudy palanquin lying near the dirty huts, and two or three jaunty, debauched looking "darkies," dressed in the height of black dandyism, show manifest traces of the "Búbú."

Later, Burton clarified or censored (or his wife did) these paragraphs, pointing out that the married captain or field officer had a "white wife," and, finding the term "Búbú" unclear, substituted "black wife."

But búbú (or booboo, as Burton sometimes spelled it) was a common word known to Old India hands. Burton explained that it was a western Indian corruption of bíbí (or beebee), a lady in the highest social sense, though bíbí came to be used for white women in general and for high-ranking native women and búbú for brown, a shorthand identification that allowed no ambiguity about the woman who shared the officer's bed.

So we find Burton at home with a native "wife," a woman from Baroda city, perhaps a Hindu but most likely a Muslim found for him (as for the other white officers) by the hawaldār, the grizzled old regimental sergeant major, who knew the tastes of white men and what kind of woman from his own people would be likely to please. Burton's regiment was composed of high-caste Hindus, so the hawaldār would have been a Hindu, but he would have found women among the most likely groups, and here they came largely from the Muslim courtesans.

The custom of the búbú had developed slowly over the years

of English rule. Originally, the white soldiers in John Company's armies had been encouraged to marry Indian women and were given a subsidy to do so. Some of the higher-class officers and administrators married into the nobility, taking wives from the ruling Hindu and Muslim families, but gradually, as color prejudices came to dominate, formal unions were looked down upon, and the common courtesan served as a temporary "wife."

This was a heavily sexualized society, the English in India. While many men avoided entanglements with the native women and the missionaries eloquently condemned sexual expression outside marriage and with the natives, there were many opportunities for liaisons. One of Burton's contemporaries, Samuel Sneade Brown, rotting away in a post as district magistrate in the Punjab, expressed a common point of view. He thought the native women were "so amusingly playful, so anxious to please that a person, after being accustomed to their society, shrinks from the idea of encountering the whims or yielding to the furies of an Englishwoman."

What was there to occupy a man's time in the long hours after drill? Burton mentioned that when supper was finished the officers would play whist, but he thought there were too few men present for good games. On special occasions there was a nautch, an erotic dance performed by the courtesans from the city. However, Burton's recollection in mature years was anything but favorable.

> The scene has often been described in its picturesque aspect [Burton told his wife in 1876]. But it has a dark side. Nothing could be more ignoble than two or three debauched and drunken musicians squealing and scraping the most horrible music, and the *figurantes* with Simiad or apish faces, dressed in magnificent brocades, and performing in the most grotesque ways. The exhibition gave one a shiver, yet not a few of the old officers, who had been brought up to this kind of thing, enjoyed it as much as the Russians of the same epoch, delighted in the gypsy soirees of Moscow. . . .

That was his "Victorian" point of view, recollected in late middle age. Or he may have been dissembling for his wife's benefit. But in *Scinde; or, The Unhappy Valley*, published in 1851 from notes he had made during his life in India, he gave a very different view of the nautches. A Sindhi Hindu named Hari Chand has secured the services of a group of dancers headed by "a celebrated lady of pretty name, Mahtab—the 'Moonbeam.' " The troupe arrived in litters on camels.

> But stop, Mr. Bull [Burton is addressing an imaginary countryman], at this rate you will be falling in love with the Moonbeam: —I tremble to think of the spirit in which your lapse would be received-by the bonneted, well curled, be-mantled, strait-laced, be-petticoated partner of your bosom. I would almost engage you to say nothing of the scene when you return home; it would grieve me even to dream of "minx" and "savage" in connection with yonder masterpiece of prettiness.

The dancers drink something which looks like water but "which I believe to be something stronger."

> Mahtab floats forward so softly that trace of exertion is imperceptible: slowly waving her white arms, she unexpectedly stands close to you, then turning with a pirouette—it has no other name—, but its nature is widely different from the whirligig rotations of a Taglione—she sinks back, retires and stands motionless as wax-work, and again all *da capo*. . . . The guitar [sitar] is in the seventh heaven of ecstasy, the pipe [flute] is dying away with delight, and the kettledrums threaten to annihilate their instruments. The lady's sisters or rather sisterhood are too completely under the spell to feel envious. . . .

The other dancers fail to interest Burton except for one, Moonbeam's sister Nūr Jān—"Mademoiselle Radiant Light"—who was to become one of his mistresses in Sind.

The musicians were by now completely drunk. "They would fall under the table but there is no such article in the tent." The troupe, except for Moonbeam, put on costumes and danced a "charade" of a lover stealing the wife of an old husband. "The pipe is going fast, and extraneous aid is necessary to the drooping form of Nūr Jān, the Moonbeam's youngest and prettiest sister."

The nautches were not merely dances. A high pitch of sexual arousal was certain to develop as a result of the music and the throbbing voices of the singers, the erotic lyrics, the drugs and alcohol, the flashing jewelry, the jangling anklets and bracelets, the bare midriffs, flashing smiles, unloosened hair. Streams of women, of wine and music, flowed not only in the royal courts and in the cauks and bazaars but even in the cantonments.

The English were fascinated, condemnatory, anxious—attitudes that continued but were never resolved. There were, after all, very few white women in India at the time, and they were usually married and confined to the larger cities, where amenities were better.

> The Bíbí (white woman) was at this time rare in India [said Burton in his fragment of autobiography]; the result was the triumph of the Búbú (coloured sister). I found every officer in the corps more or less provided with one of these helpmates.

For some officers the solution to sex in India was the pastime known as "peacocking," or "poodle-faking"—calling on other officers' wives. But peacocking in the heat "soon beat off the most ardent admirers of the white fair sex."

> The latter revenged itself of anything like neglect in the most violent way, and the consequence was that, in those days, most men, after their first year, sought refuge in the society of the dark fair. Hence in the year of grace 1842 there was hardly an officer in Baroda who was not morganatically married to a Hindi [Muslim] or a Hindu woman. This could be a fertile ground for anecdote, but its nature forbids entering into detail.

"These irregular unions were mostly temporary, under agreement to cease when the regiment left the station," he said. "Some even stipulated that there were to be no children." The native mistress had "an infallible recipe to prevent maternity, especially if her tenure in office depends on such compact."

The system had its advantages and disadvantages. It connected the white stranger with the country and its people, gave him an interest in their manners and customs, and taught him thoroughly well their language [although, he pointed out, some men learned only the feminine forms from their "wives"].

However, these liaisons had their dark side. "These unions produced a host of half-castes, mulattoes, 'neither fish nor fowls, nor good red herring,' who were equally despised by the races of both progenitors."

The guarantee of the native mistress against conception was a vague and airy promise. Contraceptive methods differed widely from those used even then in the West. Mantras, prayers, and charms were popular but ineffective, as well as cow dung, leaves, the juice of citrus and other acidic fruits, natron (a natural form of sodium carbonate), and (it was reported), among tribal women, a stone. Abortions were common. Many Englishmen were surprised to learn that they had sired a child by the "black wife." Burton himself seems to have been the progenitor of a line of half-castes, for there is a family in western India today bearing his name who have a tradition that they are descended from an Englishman in Baroda, a "sir" and a "Major," the younger members of the family showing a striking resemblance to Richard and Maria Burton in the dual portrait painted by François Jacquard in 1851 in Boulogne.

"I had a fine opportunity of studying the pros and cons of the Búbú system," said Burton.

Pros: The "walking dictionary" is all but indispensable to the Student, and she teaches him not only Hindostani grammar, but the syntaxes of native life. She keeps house for him, never allowing him to save money, or, if possible, to waste it. She keeps the servants in order. . . . She looks after him in sickness, and is one of the best nurses, and, as it is not good for a man to live alone, she makes him a manner of home.

"The disadvantages are as manifest as the advantages," he added, somewhat vaguely, and at this point the explanation faded away, for whatever he told Isabel (who was writing it down) has not survived. Whatever the problems of communication thirty-four years after the event, it is clear that Burton was enamored of Indian women. He was to become involved with others, whom he mentions with many circumlocutions, but in ways that Old India hands would understand and that Isabel, who was no fool, could pretend not to.

During the Baroda period, Burton, with the pleasant memories of Dr. John Henry Newman and the vibrant new Catholicism at Oxford, began to attend the Roman Catholic chapel. He must have been a great prize for the priest, a half-caste Goan. The Church was then making a great effort to convert Gujarat, which had been placed under the protection of the Virgin Mary. Burton's "conversion," when it was known, touched off a battle with family and friends. "I left off 'sitting under' the garrison Chaplain," he said in the *Life*, "and transferred myself to the Catholic chapel of the chocolate-coloured Goanese priest, who adhibited spiritual consolation to the buttrels (butlers and head servants) and other servants of the camp."

The white Protestant chaplain may have come to terms with the affairs of the young officers, but the Goan priest saw Burton's relationship in a different light. Was not this young Englishman preying on another Indian, no matter how immoral she was? Burton soon found the priest lecturing him about his conduct. "I had to suffer the protestations of the Portuguese [Goan] *padre*, who had taken upon himself the cure and charge of my soul, and was like a hen who hatched a duckling."

That brown- and black-skinned women were an especial favorite of Burton's, not only during his India years but for long afterward, is clear. Burton never hinted openly of a serious relationship with a white woman in India. In fact, he was quite negative about his countrywomen, for he seems to have suffered their criticism.

Even during my day, married men began, doubtless at the instance of their wives, to look coldly upon the half-married, thereby showing mighty little common sense, for India was the classic land of cicisbe-ism [gigoloism], where husbands are occupied between ten a.m. and five p.m. at their offices and counting house, leaving a fair field and much favor to the sub[altern] unattached. . . . The confirmed hyp-ocrite and the respectable-ist, when in power, established a kind of inquisitorial black mark to the name of the half-married. At last the Búbú made her exit and left a void.

Shiploads of unmarried—and unmarriageable—women, known as the "Fishing Fleet," began to arrive from England in search of husbands, and shortly the native wife was replaced by women who often boasted the most rigid views of life and family duty and propriety.

Burton's all-but-indispensable "walking dictionary" was not only his teacher in sexual techniques but also his most effective introduction into native life. In such households as Burton's there was a wide ambience of native society surrounding the Indian mistress—the mother or older female relative who ran the es-tablishment and made sure the girl got her rewards, the brothers, sisters, cousins, and other vaguely defined people, who were learning the tricks and customs that enabled them to use the white officers as their introduction to Western life. And in the chaotic households of the *búbús* there was more than sexual enjoyment. There were foods and customs, superstitions, poetry and music, and above all, religion, for the women who made up the courtesan classes, the Muslim nautch girls and the Hindu *devadasis*, were then virtually the only educated women in India, and they were the ones who knew the religious texts, the Persian Sufi poets, and the Indian *bhakti* mystics and sang their music with that deliberate ambiguity that encompassed both the Divine and the erotic.

The Indian women Burton lived with during his seven years in the subcontinent furnished him with the material he was to work into his books through introductions, footnotes, commentaries, and the elucidation of passages in the original texts, where he was trying to make it clear to his European readers that there was an inner state of erotic possession, the long sequences of caresses, kisses, scratches, bites, love cries, and various positions that led to an extended state of sexual gratification and excitement, which was to be enjoyed with abandonment by man and woman alike. He was concerned that not only were Englishmen in general inept in sex; so were "most English women," who "never really learned the real delight of carnal copulation," an ignorance "to be remedied only by a constant and intelligent study of the Ananga Ranga Scriptures," a work he "translated" over thirty years later.

In his notes to the various erotic texts he was to turn out, he gave a series of what might be called homilies about techniques, advice for both the man and the woman. He believed that "many men utterly ignore the feelings of the woman, and never pay the slightest attention to the passion of the latter. To understand the subject thoroughly, it is absolutely necessary to study it. . . . A woman must be prepared for sexual intercourse, if she is to derive satisfaction from it." Speaking from his own experience, he noted that

> men who are well acquainted with love are well aware how often one woman differs from another on her sighs and sounds during the time of congress. Some women like to be talked to in the most loving way, others in the most lustful way, others in the most abusive way, and so on. Some women enjoy themselves with closed eyes in silence, others make a great noise over it, and some almost faint away. The great art is to ascertain what gives them the greatest pleasure, and what specialties they like best.

In all of this, though he was talking to—lecturing—the average Englishman and woman, Burton was not talking about "love" in the Western sense. Romantic love was not an issue in the kind of relationships he was recalling from his Indian days. They were "business" arrangements. In such an alliance, much as the woman might profess her undying love for the man, she was in fact not expected to have any truly sentimental feelings. "A courtesan in love?" asks the nineteenth-century nautch woman Umrā'o Jān Adā in her autobiography. "It is always the lover who was undone."

> Men were consumed with jealousy and these girls deliberately played one against the other. And the irony of it all was that their feelings were not involved because they considered all men worthless. Their affection was mere affectation. If any wretch fell to their wiles, they were the first to pretend they were in love.

Should a courtesan act foolishly, there was always her mother or aunt or the madam or her "sisters" to remind her that she was in the alliance to gain wealth. Burton was quite aware of this, saying that the Indians "have ever had the good sense to recognize courtesans as a part and portion of human society." And he spoke with appreciation of their "subtlety . . . their wonderful perceptive powers, their knowledge, and their intuitive appreciation of men and things."

7

The Snake Priests

The weather had been still pleasant when Burton arrived in Baroda, but shortly it began to change and quickly became unbearable. By March the hot season had begun, and April and May made it clear that they were the hottest months of the year.

Now the sun blazed down in full fury from a brassy sky; the air was dry, and all became parched—men, animals, the land; the streams and rivers dried up, the soil cracked and groaned, and there was not a breath of air except along the coasts, where late-afternoon breezes blew in from the sea, giving false hope that tomorrow would be better. When the heat struck with full force, the temperature, Burton complained, stood at 120°. Life moved slowly in such heat: people tended to sit about languidly, and the servants had to be goaded to activity. This was the period when the wealthy English and the high-ranking administrators and military officials went off to mountain resorts like Simla, where in May the temperature was still in the sixties.

In such heat the schedule was not demanding for the young

officers. At the first glimmer of dawn, in the black almost starless sky, they arose, dressed, and had a cup of tea brought to their quarters by the bearers. Their horses, already saddled and brushed, were led up by the syces, or grooms, and off to the drill grounds they rode for the morning's exercises.

In the exciting moments before the dawn, when the crows were beginning to break the silence of the night and the odors of the newly lighted cow-dung cooking fires drifted across the field to mingle with the steam of the hard-packed earth and the air was still cool with the night's dampness and gentle breezes, everything, said Burton, "looks and sounds intensely military." In the distance, a squad with glistening fixed bayonets was drilling in close column; nearby a troop of horse artillery wound along the road.

Finally, the sun's rays broke across the tree tops with the first hint of the coming heat. For a few moments more drill would continue, then the officers and men went to their respective breakfasts. Here, as in so many other things, Burton could not resist the temptation to stand apart. For his fellow officers, tea, café au lait, biscuits, bread and butter, and fruit formed the first meal of the day, but Burton contented himself with a glass of the inevitable port and a biscuit. Then, while the other subalterns dribbled away their time with billiards or shooting or pig sticking, he went to his studies with his *munshī*, for he was now preparing to take the government examinations in Hindustani.

Life at Baroda was not all drill and concentrated language studies for Burton. He could take time off from regimental duties to hunt. In the 1840s, Baroda was still surrounded by heavy jungle. In the dense bush the officers found tigers, black buck, antelopes, and such birds as adjutant crane and snipe. Elephants could be hired for the hunt, and sometimes the Gaekwar would take the English out on his own elephants. At first, Burton would hunt and kill anything but monkeys, but he eventually gave up shooting entirely. One of his greatest regrets was shooting a monkey. "It cried like a baby," he said, "and I can never forget it." He was appreciative of the near-human qualities of monkeys, how they chattered and warned each other of the presence of humans. Later, in Sind, he got a collection of monkeys from the bazaar and set about studying them, giving each a title and a rank: there was a doctor, a chaplain, a secretary, and an aide-de-camp, among others. Isabel Burton said that "one tiny one, a very pretty, small, silky-looking monkey, he used to call his wife, and put pearls in her ears." The monkeys sat on stools and ate at table as Burton kept order with a whip and the Goan servants waited on them. He was able to collect sixty "words" from the monkeys before his interest faded. Unfortunately, his notes were destroyed in a warehouse fire in 1861.

It was an exciting life, and a full life. On his Kattywar nag Burton was skillful enough to win the regimental horse race against the Arabs of the other officers. He learned wrestling in the Indian manner and taught his troops gymnastics and the use of the sword according to European practice. He had a minor tragedy when his dog died. But all in all, Burton felt he had been set down among men of lesser sophistication and knowledge, with few interests beyond the cantonment and with no insights into pursuits that might profitably and enjoyably occupy time and place. Burton's work was his escape. "I threw myself with a kind of frenzy upon my studies," he said, "I kept up my little stock of Arabic that I had acquired at Oxford and gave some twelve hours a day to a desperate tussle with Hindustani." Here he was being modest, for he was making great strides with the language. Then, in March 1843, came astounding news. "The whole of the little cantonment was electrified by the report of the battle of Meeanee." The English under General Charles Napier had invaded the province of Sind in force and after several skirmishes had defeated the local rulers, the amīrs (or mīrs), in two great battles, the first at Mīanī, the second five weeks later at Dubba. "After a number of reverses truly humiliating to British self-esteem, the Sun of Victory had at last shone upon her bayonets." Mīanī was "the crowning achievement of the season."

With the news of General Napier's victories in Sind there came reports of a tragedy, the murder of two English secret agents, Stoddard and Connolly, in Bokhara. They had been disguised as Uzbeks but were eventually detected and beheaded. Burton was sure another war would follow, but the excitement died down, his depression lifted, and he returned to his Hindustani studies. By the end of April he felt sufficiently a master of the tongue to ask for two months' leave so he could go to Bombay to take the government examinations.

Now accustomed to survival in this fiery land of heat, insects, disease, noise, torpor, and prying natives and wanting to be alone, Burton avoided the British Hotel and the Sanitarium and pitched a tent in the area known as Strangers Lines on Back Bay, facing the Arabian Sea. With the assistance of his former *munshī*, Dosabhai Sohrabji, he crammed to the moment of the examination.

The examiner was a famous character, Major General Vans Kennedy, an excellent Orientalist, who had been in India since 1800, having come out at the age of sixteen. He had become a great linguist, specializing in Hindustani, Gujarati, Sanskrit, Persian, and Arabic and was as well a noted jurist and an expert on military law. Kennedy lived in what Burton described as a "tumbledown bungalow in a tattered compound," surrounded by books and Oriental manuscripts and the inevitable household of natives. Kennedy did not accept a candidate on the basis of a brief talk. In a rigorous test Burton had to translate two books from Hindustani and a sample of native handwriting, write a short essay in the language, and carry out a conversation in it. He finished first out of twelve candidates. He became a close friend of the general's and always visited him on his trips to Bombay, until Kennedy's death in 1845.

After his examinations, Burton spent a week in Bombay, his purpose unspecified—did he return to the Bhendi Bazar to visit the japanned young ladies in the cages? As he arrived back in

Baroda after a leisurely voyage by pattymar, the southwest mon-
soons broke, and from that time onward, for the entire summer,
it was a constant effort to survive rains that showed no mercy.
Night and day he was soaked. The air was alive with insects,
which settled on food and drink and one's person and crawled
across the pages of books. Between cloudbursts the winds stirred
up swirls of dust so dense that candles were lighted at midday.
At times the rains fell seven days and seven nights like some
Biblical plague. To reach mess and dine in comfort, Burton had
to wrap his clothing in a waterproof and send it on ahead by
bearer and then in a macintosh gallop at full speed through waters
that never seemed to abate but ran like rivers across the road.
There was no duty for the troops: the parade grounds were like
a lake.

> The monsoon . . . completely changed the tenor of Anglo-Indian
> [that is, white] life.* . . . I have seen tropical rains in many a region
> near the Line [the Equator], but never anything that rivals Gu-
> jarat. . . . This third of the year was a terrible dull suicidal time,
> worse than the gloomy month of November.

His bungalow was constantly flooded. He moved to another,
bigger building, a house very much in the native style. "The
floor was washed with one of the five venerable products of the
cow"—cow dung—he said archly. Cow dung was believed quite
correctly to have antiseptic properties. The second bungalow was
an unlucky place:

> An English officer had been wounded in it, and the lintel still bore
> the mark of the sabre which some native ruffian had left, intending
> to split a serjeant's head. . . . The rule of the good Company was,
> however, not a rule of honour, but of expediency, and the safety of

* In Burton's time "Anglo-Indian" referred to the British who served in
India. Later, the term was applied to those born of European fathers and Indian
mothers and their descendants, replacing the derogatory "Eurasians."

its officers was little regarded; they were stabbed in their tents, or cut down by dacoits [bandits], even when travelling on the highways of Gujarat.

For Burton this period of rain and dust and military idleness was not wasted. He had turned to Gujarati, like Hindustani one of the Prakrits or vulgar tongues of India. He also began to study Sanskrit, the classical language of the priests. For Gujarati he had a teacher named Him Chand, who was, said Burton, a "Nagar Brahmin." But he did not explain why he mentioned Him Chand's specific caste. His Sanskrit teacher was the regimental Brāhmin priest, who tended to the sepoys. Through both teachers, especially Him Chand, Burton "soon became as acquainted as an outsider can be with the practice of Hinduism." The same relentless energy that he had put into other studies Burton now applied to the pursuit of the ancient faith of Hinduism—primordial, complex, pregnant with contradictions and ambiguities. "I carefully read up Ward, Moor, and the publications of the Asiatic Society," he said—Ward and Moor were experts on Hinduism at a period when it was still unaffected by the West—and he studied the *Tota-Kaháni*, one of the parrot books, and the *Baital-Pachisi*, a story about Tantrism that was to lead to his *Vikram and the Vampire*.

Through such works and from Him Chand, Burton became knowledgeable about Hindu worship and practice on the most primitive and archaic levels, the lives and practices of people untouched by outsiders, their folklore, prejudices, superstitions, occult practices, saints, and holy men. He learned of the rite of *satī*, in which widows sacrificed themselves on their husbands' pyres, and of such yogic practices as control of the breath and of the semen and the circulatory system, practices he himself was shortly to emulate, mainly through the celebration of the underground observances known as Tantra, which was common in the Baroda area among the Nāgar Brāhmins and other castes.

In his highly imaginative translation of *Vikram and the Vampire* Burton described Tantric practices that apparently were not in the original text but which he learned from personal experience, including the intense forms of meditation followed "in order to see Brahmin," the Hindu god-head, and to "do away with the illusion (Maya) which conceals all true knowledge." Writing in the third person about himself,

> He repeated the name of the deity till it appeared to him in the form of a Dry Light. . . . He attended much to Pranayama, or the gradual supression of breathing, and he secured fixedness of mind. . . . He practiced the eighty-four Asanas or postures . . . till he felt no longer the inconvenience of heat or cold, hunger or thirst. He particularly preferred the Padma or lotus-position of sitting . . . and he practiced Prityahara, or the power of restraining the members of the body and mind [until he] resembled the unruffled flame of the lamp [and was] enabled to ascend from gross images of omnipotence to the works and the divine wisdom of the glorious original [that is, union with the god Brahma].

After these intense studies in Hinduism, "my Hindu teacher officially allowed me to wear the Brahminical thread." Thus, Burton received the *janeo*, the sacred three-ply cotton cord that meant the wearer was a member of the highest caste. This was a rare and unheard of honor for a young man from another culture, a culture that bore much enmity to Hinduism and everything it represented. The *janeo*, Hindus emphasize, is a privilege *never* given the outsider, for to be truly Hindu one must be born a Hindu. There are no short cuts, though in orthodox Hindu theology all people ever born are Hindus: in Hinduism one must pass through an inevitable cycle of births and rebirths to enter Hinduism and work one's way upward through the maze of castes and subcastes.

The Brāhmins are the most exalted of the four major castes and the two or three thousand subcastes. Even among Brāhmins there are numerous divisions and clan groups, the latter identified by the term *gotra*, "cowpen," for in ancient times that sacred beast, the cow, formed the focal point of the exogamous* clan unit, and specifically of the patriarchal family. The type of *gotra* depends on the area, occupation, traditions, and family and household. There are roughly six hundred types of Brāhmins, many of them mutually exclusive and hostile to one another, so strict that certain Brāhmins will not talk to other Brāhmins, eat with one of another *gotra*, or even use another's kitchen or toilet facilities for fear of ritual pollution.

Him Chand was a member of a *gotra* that stood apart, though the Nāgar Brāhmins had their very definite and necessary place in Indian society. They had very ancient roots in the fertile and moldy soil of the subcontinent, but they could be called into question by orthodox purists, for they were what might be called colloquially "snake priests." Nāgar Brāhmins were not only associated with snakes but particularly with cobras, the snake so symbolic of India. (A common term for snake is *nāga*, which also means cobra.) In the old Hindu epics like the *Mahābhārata* and the *Rāmāyana* and the Buddhist *Jātaka* collections, the snake, the *nāga*, and the forest-dwelling indigenes, the *Nāgas*, are identical. The *Nāgas*, human or reptile, are the possessors of the earth and guardians of its treasures and the repository of a secret wisdom not shared with others. *Nāga* temples could be seen everywhere, and where the cobra did not have his own temple, he had his images and was often portrayed intimately entwined around certain of the deities, especially those from the most archaic past. A cobra encircles the waist of the three-eyed phallic god Śiva; a cobra is a necklace around the black goddess Kālī, whose rites Burton was to enter into, even though he was in theory an untouchable born outside caste, yet to be purified through an indefinite number of births and rebirths.

---

*Not endogamous, as might be assumed. "There are innumerable *gotras* in seven main divisions of the brahmins, each of which must marry outside its own *gotra*, which corresponds to the Latin [*Exogamous*] *gens*."—Damodar Dharmanan Kosambi.

If a young man in search of the Infinite, questing for God-knows-what mysteries in this ancient land that is all mystery, enigma, illusion, all veiled and wrapped in secrets of impenetrable density, wished to touch the heart of a people so intimately denying themselves to others not of their caste and color and *gotra*, would he not try to delve deep into the most sacred and archaic of all the sects? Why try to become a Brāhmin of a *gotra* that founds its sanctity on the purity of the food it eats, food untouched by untouchable hands, undefiled by low-caste shadows, while here in the dust and heat and dirt of India were the Nāgar Brāhmins, with the secret lore and wisdom of the hoary past? One need not share meals with a Kulin Brāhmin or chant mantras with the priests of the dead or read the Vedas with a Sārasvat elder, when the worship of the Great Snake transports the adept across millennia, to the primeval ages when the black-skinned, small-nosed *Nāgas* swarmed the land, unaware that thousands of miles away, on the Asian steppes, were a nomadic white-skinned people who would be propelled by unknown forces to migrate to the fierce heat of the Indian peninsula to conquer and who would remain, now enslaved to the enveloping coils of the *Nāgas*.

Somehow Burton, by charm, persuasion, and a display of his for-the-moment sincerity, convinced Him Chand and the Nāgar Brāhmin elders to accept him into their *gotra*, leaping aeons of caste, metempsychosis, and reincarnation.

That he made a deliberate effort to enter the Nāgar Brāhmins hardly seems questionable. If he merely wanted to become a Hindu, he might have been able to persuade his Sanskrit teacher to accept him into one of the more conventional *gotras*, although from what is known about Brāhminic anxieties over pollution and the impurities emanating from untouchable whites, it seems most unlikely that he could ever have been allowed to enter an "ordinary" caste. Since he was a meat-eater and had other habits objectionable to Hindus, the question of untouchability always hovers over his initiation and presents a formidable obstacle that only a *gotra* like the Nāgar Brāhmins could surmount. They were so set apart from other Brāhmins that they would not necessarily lose face by taking in a *mleccha*, as non-Indians have been called for some 3,500 years. Though the Nāgar Brāhmins can boast of a solidly established role in the traditional caste system, their questionable origins make them suspect to other *gotras*. Most Brāhmins refuse to eat with the Nāgars, and in Baroda the caste's women are called *Nāg-kanya*, "snake-maidens," for it was commonly believed by other castes that they were not born in the normal manner but of a union of a snake with a jar, a supposition of great antiquity.

So pervasive is the cult of the *nāga* that virtually all of India celebrates a festival of snakes called Nāg-pancami in the Hindu month of Śravana (roughly June-July). The feast, which means "Fifth Day of the Snake," is sacred to the demigods in the form of serpents. Doors of homes are smeared with cow dung and the leaves of the purifying nimba plant as a preservative against poisonous reptiles.

It is possible that it was the joyous and widespread observances of Nāg-pancami that attracted Burton to the Nāgar Brāhmins, for the festival is celebrated all over Baroda and the sect plays a leading role in the rites. Burton had arrived back in the city after his first language examination just in time to observe Nāg-pancami, and it did not take him long to become deeply involved with the *gotra*.

There are ambiguities in Burton's account of his conversion to the Nāgar Brāhmins, but certain details are clear. He specifically mentions the "Nagar Brahmin" Him Chand (and later in the *Arabian Nights* even recalls the parchment-yellow skin of his guru). However obscure this passage in his life may be, the fact remains that he was formally initiated into the *gotra* by one of the priests, after being accepted by the elders, and received the sacred cord, the *janeo*, that is the special sign of the twice born. In the hoary past, initiation had taken weeks or months, but by Burton's time the ceremonies were reduced to a few days. ("Five or six days preliminary fasting, with other signs of mirth, as at a marriage," Burton wrote of such rites.) The ceremony, called *upanaya*, was preceded by a day or more of purification. The candidate was isolated, often in a small hut of branches, and fasted and prayed. On the morning of the initiation he bathed, a barber cut his fingernails and shaved his head except for the famous Brāhminic tuft, the *śikhā*, and he received a clean garment, a simple cloth of cotton that was wrapped around his waist, the torso being left bare. During the ceremony the candidate was perfumed and anointed with oil and turmeric and sometimes sandalwood paste.

Thus, Burton was made a Brāhmin and given the privilege of reciting the special Brāhminic prayer, the Gāyatri mantra, the saying of which was denied to women and lower castes. As a good Brāhmin, he was to pray the mantra three times a day, at the sacred hours of sunrise, high noon, and sunset, moments known as *sandhi*, the "junction of time," periods according to yogic belief that are especially efficacious for meditation, when the mind is calm and refreshed and in a "sattvic" state, that is, "harmonious, pure and luminous." The prayer is said in Sanskrit and is one that Burton knew intimately. He left a translation, adding, as was his wont, to the original to give it clarity and substance. The hymn is to the sun, Savitur, and is prefaced and closed with the word *Oṁ*, the most sacred of sounds.

> Let us meditate on the supreme splendour
> of that divine ruler
> who may illuminate our understandings.
> Venerable men, guided by intelligence,
> salute the divine sun with oblations and praise.

If he were conscientious, Burton would recite the mantra 108 times on each occasion, that number being sacred and mystical (and without explanation), and also magical.

Being a "snake priest" was more than an honorary role in a private brotherhood. The Nāgar Brāhmins took an active part in the daily life of the people. In a land where snakes were found everywhere and often in situations—certain rites and rituals, for example—where a slip could mean death, the Nāgar Brāhmins were widely called upon to treat snake bites. Victims who died were not normally given cremation but had to be buried; a person dying of a snake bite could expect to be reborn as a snake in the next life. In Gujarat, Nāg-pancami continued in a special form every month in the observances of childless women or those afflicted with some misfortune or other caused by a perhaps unsuspected injury to a snake. For periods of a year to three years, on the bright fifth of each Hindu month, barren women worshiped an image of the snake, *nāga*, and on the final observance of the rite, the woman and her husband, dressed in clean white clothes, offered *pūjā* to the snake demon. So important was the snake in certain aspects of Hinduism that snakes were cremated with the same rites given a Brāhmin, and everywhere snakes were venerated, and for the tribal peoples of the jungle, the snake was the standard by which oaths were sworn.

Burton was now a fully practicing snake priest. It was his privilege to handle snakes, particularly cobras, under the tutelage of Him Chand. He seems to have believed that this initiation would bring him into the depths of some secret knowledge, what he constantly referred to as "Gnosis," into the archaic roots of the human race, for it was commonly believed that snakes preserved a "hidden doctrine" to be transmitted to certain adepts through the masters to their pupils. But of arcane knowledge there was nothing, merely the handling and care of some highly dangerous reptiles. Burton's initiation into the Nāgar Brāhmins and his wearing of the *janeo* were hardly a secret, for his brother officers began to call him the "White Nigger." Later Burton tried to make light of it, but the term stuck to him throughout his years in India. The fact was that even before the end of his first year in India he had separated himself as far from the English world as he could without actually quitting his regiment and going *jungli*, as the term was for those Europeans who went native.

Burton had been fascinated by the many facets of Hinduism, but the opportunism and chicanery of the Hindu priests he saw all around him, added to his general dislike and distrust of the clergy of all religions, soon gave him doubts about what he had done. Initiated quickly into Brāhminic *nāga* Hinduism, Burton just as quickly left. The cobra is not a house pet, and he had the good sense to realize it instead of turning it into a challenge to be mastered. His search into the primal depths of mankind could have brought him not enlightenment but extinction had he been bitten. Then the strange character of Hinduism lost its appeal. His later references to it are not sympathetic. The great number of deities—thirty-three million by tradition—the strange tenor of Hindu worship, custom, and practice, the unreal, cruel, and immoral behavior of the gods and goddesses—their very earthy habits, sexual excesses, thievery, lying, deception, and other forms of rascality—plus the confusion of beliefs manifested by the large number of strange cults and sects within Hinduism, the differences and contradictions among the philosophers, and the necessity to suspend rational judgment, common sense, and proportion—all make it difficult for an outsider to believe as a Hindu. The practical, skeptical, and hardheaded young Burton did not believe for long. The very important mystical release gained by rigorous discipline, study, and mental and physical training seems to have been the one aspect of Hinduism that attracted Burton, and even here he next got himself into one of the most extreme and underground of all Hindu practices, that of Tantric Yoga. Again he sought arcane, subterranean knowledge, hoping to find some key to the mysteries of life in the worship of the primitive deities, the phallic king Śiva, and the all-embracing female power Śakti, who is known under an endless number of names and appears in a multitude of forms in Hinduism. But Burton had not quite abandoned the *nāga*, at least in the abstract. In the fine amalgam of beliefs that distinguishes folk Hinduism, the cult of the snake, *nāga*, has been since time immemorial associated with the worship of both Śiva, the yogic nature deity, and especially the great female deities, all forms of the Great Goddess Śakti, the eternal and Supreme Power, manifest energy, the substance of the All-Pervading, the expression of the creative principle.

In the folk iconography, Śakti, in various aspects, often as Kuṇḍalinī, the Serpent Power, is primarily associated with Śiva, here the Lord of Sleep. In this aspect he is passive and white (Kuṇḍalinī is jet black) and lies on his back with an erect penis. The god is awakened only by the energies of the goddess, who mounts him to produce the paroxysm that creates the universe. This divine coupling is celebrated again and again in the widespread folk practice of Tantra, usually observed secretly, loosing the primeval forces of the universe through sexual symbols and yogic sexual rites, and is based on what is forbidden to the higher castes of Hinduism.

The rites, Burton wrote, point out that the Tantric is

> not to indulge shame or adversion to anything, nor to prefer one thing to another, nor to regard caste, ceremonial cleanness or uncleanness, but freely to enjoy all the pleasures of the senses.

And while the orthodox high-caste "holy men, holding that the subjugation or annihilation of the passions is essential to final beatitude," accomplish this by "bodily austerities and by avoiding temptation," the Tantric blunts "the edge of the passions with excessive indulgence." While the pious ascetics are "safe only in forests, and while keeping a perpetual fast," the Tantric could "subdue his passions in the very presence of what they most desired."

In *Vikram and the Vampire*, the collection of ancient Sanskrit folk stories, which Burton felt obliged to enlarge upon with personal material—"I have ventured to remedy the conciseness of their language, and to clothe the skeleton with flesh and blood"—he added numerous descriptions of Tantric and yogic rites that seem to have come out of his own experiences. In one story he describes a Tantric rite enjoyed by one of the minor

characters, a low-caste youth, who, having inherited considerable wealth from his father, "leads a villainous life." The young
man is deformed, "with a face like a monkey's, legs like a stork's,
and a back like a camel's." Nevertheless, "he made love to every
woman, and despite his ugliness, he was not unsuccessful." Burton then describes, without much detail, the Tantric rite.

> The hunchback, moreover, became a Tantri[c], so as to complete
> his villainies. He was duly initiated by an apostate Brahman,* made
> a declaration that he renounced all the ceremonies of his old religion,
> and was delivered from their yoke, and proceeded to perform in
> token of joy an abominable rite. In company with eight men and
> eight women—a Brahman female, a dancing girl, a weaver's daugh-
> ter, a woman of ill fame, a washerwoman, a barber's wife, a milkmaid,
> and the daughter of a land-owner—choosing the darkest time of
> night and the most secret part of the house, he drank with them,
> was sprinkled and anointed, and went through many ignoble cere-
> monies, such as sitting nude upon a dead body.

This is all very much standard Tantric worship, but Tantra is
not primarily an excuse for sexual release, although men will use
it for such. Sometimes there is but one woman, who is passed
about from lap to lap, the participants sitting in the normal yogic
posture, the *padmāsana*, or lotus position, with the woman
astride. Or the eight women may be passed from man to man.
Often there will be but a single man and a single woman. Sex
is the central act of the rite, but not as the West might think
of it. The woman represents—is literally—the Goddess Śakti
and is known as *śakti*. The man—the *sādhaka*—must first go
through a ritual of purification with mantras and *pūjā*. The area
of celebration is laid out in a circle, a kind of yantra or mandala,
according to the custom of the particular group, and is a sacred
ground, a cosmic center. The *śakti*, one or several, is, like the

* This passage raises the possibility that Burton was initiated by an apostate
Nāgar Brāhmin, but since there is no information the question has to be left
unanswered.

sādhaka, purified with mantras and *pūjā*. She is anointed and massaged from head to foot with sweet-smelling oils and perfumes, with special attention to the pudenda. A dot, the *bindu*, is painted on her forehead to symbolize the Third Eye, and a line, to symbolize the ascent of Kuṇḍalinī, the Serpent Power, is drawn from the genital area to the *bindu*. The time of consummation of the rite is usually midnight or later, and the *śaktis* are loosely covered in thin purplish or violet silk, and the scene is lighted by a faint lamp; castor oil is preferred, for it gives a violet flame believed to stimulate the sexual organs.

The description Burton left of the typical devotee seems, as so often, to be almost a self-portrait.

> He was clad in the ochre-coloured lion-wrap of his class; from his head streamed long tangled locks of hair like horsehair; his black body was striped with lines of chalk, and a girdle of thigh bones encircled his waist. His face was smeared with ashes from a funeral pyre, and his eyes, fixed as those of a statue, gleamed from this mask with an infernal light of hate. His cheeks were shaven, and he had not forgotten to draw the horizontal sectarian mark. . . . He was playing on a human skull with two shank bones, making music for the horrid revelry.

But such activities were not to the liking of the normally rational young Burton. Hinduism faded away in his mind, and he turned to still another faith. When he seriously took up Roman Catholicism is not clear. No matter how deep or how trivial his interest in Hinduism had been, he seems to have been far more emotionally involved in Catholicism. In his references to his *búbú*, he had pointed out that he "had to suffer the protestations" of the "Portuguese" *padre*, who had "taken upon himself the cure and charge of my soul." Would a priest, an Indian Catholic from Goa—a native—have dared protest the very common actions of a young white man who was not a practicing member of his congregation? No one doubts, however, that Burton, during his months at Baroda, attended the Catholic chapel.

Even Georgiana Stisted, who was adamant in her claims that her uncle was not a Catholic, grudgingly admitted that he attended Catholic services from time to time.

> It is said that our versatile soldier occasionally varied his Sundays by attending a Romish chapel served by a berry-brown Goanese padre; and it is possible that he did profit by this opportunity of studying the affect produced by the Church of Rome on the semi-civilized people around him.

But she immediately tried to set to rest the possibility that her uncle had become a convert.

> But the foolish tale that the said chocolate coloured divine received him into the communion in question was utterly refuted by the fact that at his marriage nearly twenty years later, the presence of a register was required in the chapel; a functionary called in only when the contracting parties belong to a different religion.

Determined to keep her uncle out of the Roman Church, Miss Stisted, in her biography, got him out of all. In his last years in India, she wrote, "as often happens with deeply read and widely travelled men, Burton found the views of his youth no longer tenable." In studying "alien faiths" in India—Hinduism, Islam, and Sikhism—"Christianity dwindled in his mind to what he considered her true proportions—not the one religion, but one amongst many religions."

She continued to emphasize that

> towards the Church of Rome he had a positive aversion. . . . While believing our own [the Anglican] the purest form of Christianity extant, he had lived so long amongst the teeming populations of the East, that he was disposed to award the palm to El Islam as the faith best fitted to civilize the wretched creatures known under the comprehensive name of heathen.

Burton's religion, or religions, for he formally converted to Islam and Sikhism not too long afterward, offered much for relatives, friends, critics, and biographers to argue about. He was not a theologian, a philosopher, or a very deep thinker in religious matters, though he had all the marks of a man who was *searching*—for what he did not know. He wanted Gnosis, the secret knowledge that unlocked the mysteries of the universe, and if it came in his teenage investigations of the Kabbālah or a Bombay cage or a Catholic chapel in primitive Baroda or the Arabian desert, it did not matter.

In the hectic summer of 1843, surviving the rains, joining the Nāgar Brāhmins, studying Gujarati and Sanskrit, becoming involved in Catholicism, performing his regimental duties, enjoying his búbú, Burton was still able to learn enough of his second Indian language to be able to take another official examination. Again he traveled down to Bombay by pattymar for the tests in Gujarati under Vans Kennedy and passed with the highest marks of all the candidates, having surpassed another young officer of the same age, Christopher Palmer Rigby, a most remarkable man, who already had mastered four Indian tongues and knew Somali and Amharic as well and was considered the most outstanding linguist in the Indian army. Despite their common interests, or perhaps because of them, Burton and Rigby in after years became enemies rather than friends.

Burton was appointed regimental interpreter, with a slight increase in pay. He returned to Baroda for the celebrations of the 18th Bombay Native Infantry, which had just been ordered to Sind to serve under General Charles Napier. His autobiographical fragments say nothing of heartbreak or of relief or loss at leaving Baroda and his búbú. He referred to her at this point as his "morganatic wife," but apparently she was left behind— he does mention one woman aboard the troop ship that took his regiment to Karachi. He does not identify her, but, curiously, mentions in the *Life*—dictated thirty-three years after the event—that she was a "native." Why did this detail remain in his mind? Was she one of the Indian women with whom he had lived?

He was clearly happy to leave Baroda, for he twice referred to November there as a "suicidal month." The 18th Bombay Native Infantry got itself packed up and on the move—"the usual slow march," Burton complained, for he liked to travel alone or in small mobile groups, lightly and swiftly. The regiment finally arrived at Bombay, having made the trip by land, to be loaded aboard the steamship *Semiramis* bound for Karachi and great adventures in the war against the Sindhis.

8

Young Egypt

It was, said Burton of the *Semiramis*, with its "freight of 600 negro souls," a "Shippe of Helle." The heat, he added, promised to set the *Semiramis* and its passengers afire. There was no place in which to keep cool. The gun room stank of dinner and sour bread, the decks burned "with the fury of the deities." It was too hot to read. The sepoys, who were Brāhmins, threatened to drive Burton out of his mind with the sound of their voices. "How they chatter, squabble, blow the conch, sing hymns to the sea-god, and smear themselves with oil of coconut." As usual, the food annoyed Burton. He complained about "milkless tea, tincture of coffee . . . sour bread, passenger pickles so hot an ounce lasts a year, blueish red boiled-to-tatters mutton." Even more insulting, the officers had to pay a pound a day for their passage and food.

In a land where sunstroke was common, so also was moon-stroke. "You omniscient English gentlemen may laugh," said Burton, but, he claimed, one could arise with one side of the face so discolored that it would take a year to recover from the effects of moonblow. Burton dressed in native clothing, a loose cotton shirt and the floppy cotton drawers he explained were called "pajammas."

Boredom. But an interesting character appeared among the maze of faces so fiercely crowded into the broiling ship. Here was a man of Burton's own interests and instincts, lanky, blondish, bearded Capt. Walter Scott, all too often identified first as a nephew of the celebrated novelist. Scott was a surveyor and engineer and was coming to join the Sind Survey to work on the immense complex of uncontrolled waterways that centered around the Indus. General Napier had the commendable dream of making the peasants of Sind truly self-supporting, of taking control of the Indus and its waterways away from the mīrs, who kept its exotic banks and swamps as private hunting preserves. Scott had the assignment of turning the endless desert into canal-fed oases of greenery, farmland, and paddy. Burton and Scott became fast friends, for Scott was also a scholar and an amateur archaeologist, "a truly fine character" who "never said a disagreeable word or did a disgraceful deed."

There was also a young German, Dr. John Steinhauser, a surgeon in the Indian army, a scholar, and something of a linguist—he knew Persian and Arabic. Burton favored as close friends self-sufficient scholars of proven consistency and good humor. Of Scott he said, "We never had a divergent thought, much less an unpleasant word; and when he died, in Berlin, in 1875, I felt his loss as that of a near relation." Of Steinhauser he said much the same: "No unkind thought, much less an unfriendly word, ever broke our fair companionship. . . . He was one of the very few who, through evil as well as through good report, disdained to abate an iota of friendship, and whose regard was never warmer than when all the little world looked its coldest." Still, Steinhauser is curiously shadowy in Burton's recollections, although he and Burton were to conceive the idea of translating that amorphous collection of stories, legends, homilies, poems, and didactica generally known as the *Arabian Nights*. Burton seemed to consider Steinhauser almost a brother; they often traveled together, and when the doctor died suddenly of apoplexy in Berne in 1866 on his way home, Burton had a strange experience.

> At that time I was wandering about Brazil, and a tooth suddenly fell to the ground, followed by a crash of blood. Such a friend, indeed, becomes part of oneself. I still feel a pang as my hand traces these lines.

After four days at sea the *Semiramis* cast anchor off Karachi while the pilot boats came to pick up the passengers. Burton had arrived at "Young Egypt"—the official proclamation on the taking of Sind, wrote Burton in *Scind Revisited*, was that the new conquest was "equal to Egypt in fertility."

In the 1840s, Karachi was nothing more than a village, with a population of 6,000 souls. Though Sind was three-quarters Muslim, the dominant religious group in the town was Hindu, largely of the *banya*, or business, caste, and a few Goan Christians.

Karachi, the only workable port in Sind (the others, all small fishing villages, had silted up from the debris brought down by the Indus), had been in English hands only since February 1839. In an overwhelming display of Company arrogance, an expedition under General John Keane had sailed into the harbor, such as it was, and demanded the surrender of the garrison of Fort Kalhora. Burton was sarcastic about the "battle." The defenders replied, "We are Sindhis and will fight!" When the walls were battered down by the British bombardment, the defenders were found to be an old man, a woman, and a child.

What the invaders saw before them was a vast, broiling, often hateful province with a great marshy delta into which the Indus River emptied. Enemies threatened Sind from all sides. The Afghans and the Sikhs had long taken tribute from that unhappy land. Starting in 1832, the British had forced treaties upon the

Sindhi amīrs, who granted trade and travel rights in exchange for a guarantee they would not use the Indus for military purposes. Then, in 1838, the Company informed the Sindhis that "contrary to the articles of the treaty between the two powers, the Indus must be used for the passage of military stores"—the Company was preparing for the invasion of Afghanistan. "The conduct of the native princes on this occasion seems to have been peculiarly Asiatic," wrote Burton, apparently with a straight face, for the Sindhis protested. But control of the Indus was essential: Beyond all the Asian powers lurked the Russians, who might at last attain their long-cherished dream of moving down to India. British control of Sind and of the Indus was now taken for granted as an imperative. The river, leading into the rich lands of the Punjab—the "Five Rivers"—was a route by which trade into Central Asia could be developed. Moreover, war rather than infiltration would give an excuse to loot and plunder the vast treasures of the mīrs, believed to be overflowing with gold and silver coin, rare jewels, swords and armor, and all the other prizes so valued by an aggressor. The land itself seemed worthy of exploitation as well. The term "Young Egypt," so grandly applied to this vast, sandy, steaming province, was a token of that expectation.

Events in Sind under the British were so ambiguous and contradictory during Burton's time that one treads a shaky line in sorting out unreconcilable versions of what actually happened, who was at fault, who was the hero, why one amīr was preferred over another, and why the English, who always seemed to pride themselves on their honesty, were involved in chicanery so extreme that the thieves and knaves among their enemies seemed, in contrast, like saints.

The key figure in the manipulations that involved both sides, English and native, was the leading prince, the Talpur chieftain Mīr Rustam, then about eighty-five, somewhat feeble in strength, but clearheaded and still in perfect health. Rustam was then being challenged by a very junior brother, 'Alī Murād, who was scheming for the throne. English assessments of Rustam were not consistent—Napier said he was "effete through debauchery," while E. B. Eastwick, the chief political officer in Sind, stated that Rustam from the very first had "shown the strongest inclination to be on friendly terms with the British." In fact, all the amīrs with the exception of 'Alī Murād were as a group sympathetic to the English. In the decades that followed there were bitter arguments over the vexing question of whether the right or the wrong amīr—'Alī Murād over Rustam—had been supported.

The summer of 1842 saw the beginning of the tragic events that were finally to give the province to the British. Eastwick, a key figure for stability in the province, fell ill and had to retire. He had been a moderating force, trying to temper the greed of "the avaricious, grasping, never satisfied Faringi," the English. Then the harsh and brutal superior officer, Ross Bell, died unexpectedly and was replaced "by the abler hands of Major [James] Outram." "Had [Outram] been suffered to continue at his post," wrote Eastwick, "the plains of Sindh would never have been drenched with the blood of thousands of its inhabitants slaughtered on the fields of Mīanī and Dubba."

To complicate and confuse the situation, 'Alī Murād and others had been involved in a massive forgery of documents purporting to show that his brother Mīr Rustam was conspiring against the English. Some of the younger English officers began to challenge the authenticity of the various documents that turned up so surprisingly. The papers were written in Persian, the court language, which few of the English understood with facility. All of this material was sent on to the new Governor-General, Lord Ellenborough, who was easily convinced that the Sindhi amīrs were preparing for an uprising against the English garrisons. Meanwhile, Outram was under attack by his own people, and his powers were undermined so completely that his effectiveness in Sind was negated. The loss of his services following Eastwick's resignation added to the tragic turn of events.

Both men were trusted by the amīrs, and each, though he would never have betrayed the interests of his own people, however he might question them vociferously and intelligently, continued to believe in the good faith of the native leaders. Burton, no friend of Outram's—each man was a good hater, and their animosity was lifelong—pointed out that

> during the fearful catastrophe that occurred at Kabul, the Sindhis and their chiefs took no part against us, a circumstance generally attributed to the honourable and sagacious line of policy adopted by Major Outram, the resident.

But then, tragically, Outram's "political appointment in Sindh had been abolished." In London the strange and unsettling reports being received from Afghanistan, followed by the disaster there and the disturbing reports from Sind, alarmed the Court of Directors of the East India Company, and in an effort to find a superior officer who would be able to handle what appeared to be a coming crisis, they approached General Charles Napier, a career soldier, to go to the Bombay Presidency. The General was a man devoted to the military life who kept his private views to himself and did not let them affect his work, although he could be critically outspoken afterward and would show little interest in the sensibilities of the conquered, though he liked it known that his life was "one long protest against oppression, injustice, and wrong-doing." Thus, Napier, at the advanced age of sixty (far too old by Indian standards), was given the task of consolidating the amorphous situation along the Indus. After almost a year of acclimatizing himself in the mountains of southern India, Napier landed in the Sind delta on October 25, 1842. This was three days before Burton went ashore at Bombay; their paths were not to cross until sometime in 1844.

In India, Napier, like other military men, would have to serve the Company as well as the Crown. As a lifelong professional soldier, Napier despised and hated the Company, calling the

Directors "a parcel of shopkeepers" and "the shopocracy," but he had no money and had three daughters, the result of an alliance with a Greek woman, to worry about. During his service in India the General denounced the Company in terms that were both accurate and virulent.

> The English were the aggressors in India, and, although our sovereign [Queen Victoria] can do no wrong, his [sic] ministers can; and no one can lay a heavier charge upon Napoleon than rests upon the English ministers who conquered India and Australia, and who protected those who committed atrocities. . . . Our object in conquering India, the object of all our cruelties, was money . . . a thousand million sterling are said to have been squeezed out of India in the last ninety years. Every shilling of this has been picked out of blood, wiped and put in the murderers' pockets; but, wipe and wash the money as you will, the "Damned spot" will not "out."

Eastwick, in commenting upon this passage, asked, "Can these be the words of the man who waded through blood to the treasures of Haidarābād?" and remarked that the Directors had in fact "pronounced the war in Sindh uncalled-for, impolitic, and unjust." To highlight the hypocritical cast of the war in Sind for all the parties concerned, despite Napier's professed sorrow over the invasion and the Company's shock over what the General had done, the Directors awarded him, as Burton claimed, £60,000 in silver rupees for taking Sind for John Company. Outram was awarded £3,000 but refused to accept it. Of the Company's pious and ambiguous attitude, Eastwick asked, "But when did a nation ever give back a profitable acquisition, however wrongfully obtained?"

Burton has always been made out to have favored Napier, and previous biographers accept him as one of the General's protégés. Certainly Napier could appreciate Burton's talents and daring and often used him on dangerous missions. But a close reading of Burton shows that he favored Napier only to the extent that

Napier became an enemy of Outram's, who was his enemy. Burton was most critical of Napier on the question of the prize money and dashed off some doggerel that did not please the General.

> Who, when he lived on shillings, swore
> Rupees were stained with Indian gore,
> And, "widows' tears" for motto bore,
>   But Charley?

> And yet who, in the last five years
> So round a sum of that coin clears,
> In spite of "gore" and "widows' tears,"
>   As Charley?

Napier was placed in control of both upper and lower Sind, and Major Outram was shortly reduced to a very subordinate position under him. Eastwick wrote:

> How much this step must have alarmed the Amirs is too obvious to require remark. The officers with whom they had been accustomed to transact business were at once either removed or degraded into inferior positions, and in their place appeared a stern and rough soldier, ignorant of their manners, language, history and resources, filled with a furious, persecuting spirit, hateful and hating them.

By the end of 1843, Napier, with his troops ready for battle, wrote Eastwick, "with savage and indecent haste declared that the whole country, from Rohrī to Sialkot, confiscated." Napier had come to Sind with "a pre-determination to find hostility or to make it." Then followed a "tissue of errors, cruelties, and extravagances which now, wave upon wave, succeeded each other." Napier had some inkling of the injustice of the invasion, for he said, "We have no right to seize Sind, yet we shall do so, and a very advantageous, useful and humane piece of rascality it will be."

Ignorant of India and the people, Napier was able to carry out his commission oblivious to the fact that several fair and sensible treaties forced upon the Sindhis by the Company had been abrogated when greed demanded. Not only did the General fall into 'Alī Murād's schemes—which Outram had tried to warn him against—but, wrote Eastwick, he said "he saw the only chance of goading the amirs into war would be by persecuting Mir Rustam." Coastal Sind and a strip of land on either side of the Indus were taken "in perpetuity" from the mīrs—"as a punishment for their former hostile intentions," wrote Burton in *Sindh, and the Races that inhabit the Valley of the Indus.* Mīr Rustam, though he had been pro-English but not sufficiently so, was deposed and replaced by 'Alī Murād, so thorough and obvious a scoundrel that no one in any of the English factions now had a good word for him.

Mīr Rustam fled into the desert, pursued by Napier. Meanwhile, with Sind barely in the General's control, Outram was sent back to Sind from Bombay to serve directly under Napier. As with so many situations in India, the present one was hopelessly entangled, and Outram had orders to try to simplify it. The short of it was that though a state of war existed, Outram was able to visit Mīr Rustam and other amīrs and persuade them to affix their names to one more treaty, with the promise that Mīr Rustam's case would be considered in the highest circles of the Company and the Crown. But their hopes were in vain. When Napier continued his advance into Sind, and Mīr Rustam his retreat, the lesser chiefs, contrary to advice from the amīrs, decided to fall upon Outram, then at Hyderabad, as the more vulnerable of the two English forces in their land. After a heroic resistance, Outram's small army managed to escape the Sindhis' savage attacks, with the loss of only two officers, and get aboard a steamer to go up the Indus to join Napier. Two days later, on February 17th, at Mīanī, in a battle famous in British military annals, "Sir Charles Napier and his little army," to quote Burton's summary, "by admirable conduct and desperate valour, obtained a decisive victory over a vast host of the enemy." That was his opinion in *Sindh*, when he was still young, not too cynical, and not beyond hoping to impress his superiors, the Directors of the Company.

There is no denying that Mīanī was an impressive victory. Whatever his faults, Napier was a skilled and experienced general. The Sindhis had 22,000 troops in the field, while he had but 2,800, six hundred of them engaged in guarding the baggage or scouting the enemy under Outram. Only five hundred of Napier's forces were white; the rest were natives whose loyalty and reliability under fire were always a source of concern to the English. On the seventeenth, as the morning mists lifted, Napier saw the enemy close by. Seeing a gap in the Sindhis' hastily built fortifications, he ordered a Captain Tew into it, with orders to seize and hold it, and, if necessary, to die there. Tew and his detachment were cut down immediately.

The Sindhis advanced wave upon wave, to be mowed down by Napier's superior firepower. The lesser number of Company troops were able to outflank and encircle the enemy, and, unable to escape, the Sindhis marched relentlessly into the English cannons. "No fire of musketry, discharge of grape, or push of bayonet could drive them back," wrote one of the General's biographers. "Leaping at the guns, they were blown away by scores at a time, their gaps being continually filled from the rear."

There was bitter hand-to-hand fighting, and then the surviving Sindhis fled. In the frightful carnage Napier lost twenty officers and 250 troops. Six thousand natives died or lay wounded on the field. Hyderabad surrendered, and its treasures were in Napier's hands.

Hot weather was quickly setting in: The daytime temperature had already reached 110°. Napier received reinforcements, and on March 24 he attacked Shir Muḥammad, "the Lion of Mirpur," at the hamlet of Dubba, where he sent his five thousand men against the Sindhis' 26,000. Again Napier crushed a numerically superior foe: Five thousand natives were killed or wounded to Napier's 270. That was the end of Sindhi resistance. And now the controversies broke out.

Brilliant as the victories had been, Napier had to face criticism from enemies and friends alike. The new English humor magazine, *Punch*, barely a year old, published a cartoon of Napier striding through the carnage of the battlefield with the caption "Peccavi"—"I have sinned," as indeed he had.

Some of the more bloodthirsty among the military and the Company directors thought Napier's reward for the victory was too much for a battle that cost so few English lives—"the Butcher's bill" was not justified in their eyes, wrote Burton. In his *Life*, in a reversal of his admiring passage in *Sindh*, Burton infers that the reason for the easy victory was not what was publicly stated. The account by Napier's brother Sir William was "a work of *fantaisie*," charged Burton, speaking from later knowledge and the bitterness of middle age. "The story was admirably told, the picture was perfect, but the details were incorrect."

> Neither of our authorities tell us, nor can we expect a public document to do so, how the mulatto [Eurasian] who had charge of the Amir's guns had been persuaded to fire high, and how the Talpur traitor who commanded the [Sindhi] cavalry, openly drew off his men and showed the shameless example of flight. When the day shall come to publish details concerning disbursement of "Secret service money in India," the public shall learn strange things. Meanwhile those of us who have lived long enough to see how history is written, can regard it [William Napier's account of the battle] as little better than a poor romance.

The "mulatto" and the "Talpur traitor" who had betrayed the Sindhis in the heat of battle had been approached and bribed by one Mirza 'Alī Akhbar, recently arrived from Persia. He had served first as *munshī* or personal secretary to James Outram and then to Napier. 'Alī Akhbar, Burton said, served with special bravery at the Battle of Mīanī and then at Dubba. Napier had remarked later to Burton that the *mirza* "did as much towards the conquest of Scinde as a thousand men," for as a fellow Muslim he was able to enter the enemy camps and bribe some of their best forces to desert the battlefield. Thus, added Burton, "he did his best to save as many unfortunate Beloch [Sindhi] braves as possible."

To impugn British victories, British valor at the height of Victorian passions, when a certain Arthurian code of chivalry was at its peak, was an act of heroism itself. But Burton's words did not reach the public until after his death, and by then the Empire had passed through numerous crises at home and abroad, and such charges about the use of "Secret service money in India" were ignored.

Dubba was the tragic climax of the Sindhis' struggle to maintain their freedom. "By this second blow," wrote Burton, "the tottering throne of the house of Talpur irretrievably fell." Napier was appointed governor of Sind, as well as commander, and English officers were nominated to administer English (rather than native) justice throughout the newly conquered province and, most important of all, to collect the revenues that the amīrs had previously taken for themselves.

The defeated amīrs, added Burton with perhaps a touch of compassion for men who were outwitted at the treaty table and on the battlefield alike, "were sent in captivity to Bombay; whence, in 1844, they were moved to Bengal, where a few of them still exist in a kind of state prison, the melancholy spectacle of fallen greatness."

Two parties developed among the English, one called Outramists, after Major Outram and his supporters, who favored a firm but peaceful course, giving the remaining amīrs the most freedom consistent with peaceful administration, and the Napierists, who took a harsh, even cruel hand with the amīrs and made it clear that it was the British who ruled in Sind, not the natives. Napier was to govern with bayonets and the hangman, and soon there was little opposition and little crime. "The pacification of the new province was marvellously brought about by the enlightened despotism of the Conqueror," Burton wrote in *Sindh*. "Sir Charles made it safer than any part of India within a year. . . . In 1844, when leveling down the canals, I was loudly blessed by the peasants, who cried out, 'These men are indeed worthy to govern us, as they work for our own good.' "

A final word might be Eastwick's:

> We accepted a mass of falsehoods as evidence against a family of princes, our allies, stripped them of their all, hunted them from place to place, and thrust them into prisons, with but one deliverance— the grave.

Almost from the beginning Napier had to suffer a barrage of criticism, having inherited not so much the successes of his predecessors in Sind, the Punjab, and even Afghanistan but their sins. Napier would tolerate no views other than his own either among the conquered peoples or from critics among his fellow English. Despite the magnificent award he received from John Company, he immediately got into a quarrel with the Directors. One of his favorite targets was Sir James Hogg, extremely influential at home, rich from his early years in India, and a spokesman for the Company in the House of Commons. Napier referred to him as "that Hogg" and called him by the Hindustani word *suar*, pig, one of the most insulting terms in the language. One of Napier's obsessions was the talented Dr. George Buist, a onetime preacher who had become a noted journalist, taking over the post of editor of the Bombay *Times* in 1839. Buist was something of a Renaissance man, for he was also a scientist and served as the unpaid inspector of the astronomical, magnetic, and meteorological observatories of Bombay. He had been outspoken in condemning the government for the massacres committed against the Afghans in the retaking of Kābul in 1842 and was equally vocal about Napier's seizure of Sind. Buist continued to criticize the General and his officers, especially in the matter of their morals, for they were believed to have appropriated certain of the mīrs' harems instead of setting them free. Napier went on a crusade against Buist and the *Times*, a war that was to continue not only past Napier's retirement but for a decade afterward. Napier called the editor "the blatant beast of the Bombay Times," reported Burton, and "declared war to the knife" against enemies "real and imaginary." "To answer the Enemy at the Gate, and to reply to 'the base and sordid Bombay fiction, headed by Rampant Buist,' " Napier's friends, with the strong backing of officials who preferred to remain anonymous, began a lithographed sheet called the *Karachee Advertiser* filled with "the most spicy articles" devoted primarily to fighting the Outramists and defending Napier and describing "the vices of the Sind amirs in language the reverse of ambiguous." Burton stated that the general was "utterly deficient in prudence, he did not care a fig how many enemies he made, and his tongue was like a scorpion's sting." On his side Buist was no calmer or more factual than his attackers. He declared that Sind would be found to drain the lifeblood of India; in fact, providence already appeared to be stepping in to punish the "Gigantic deed of spoliation."

These battles were tragic distractions from the serious business at hand. Throughout 1844, Napier had been trying to establish some kind of order under abysmal conditions—"with two other Commanders in Chief . . . two governments [Company and Crown] to correspond with; an enemy on the borders; a people to keep quiet," he complained in a letter to his sister at home. "All this in a sun so debilitating that no young man even pretends to do much!"

The simple machinery of ruling made overwhelming demands on Napier and his officers. There were all the minutiae of governing—judicial cases with the natives, courts-martial, commissions, the commissariat, the work of the military engineers, barracks to be constructed, pipes to be obtained for wells still to be dug (many of which produced contaminated water and had to be abandoned), roads to be laid out and based, reservoirs to be excavated. On top of such routine chores were the heat and the sun, about which not much could be done except to be "sensible," advice the energetic English were not likely to follow and were to suffer from continually. And underlying all was the possibility of native "treachery": Would the amīrs revolt, would the Sindhis, forgetting traditional enmities, ally themselves with the Sikhs, the Persians, the Afghans in a massive uprising? What native agents and who among his own officers could be counted on to bring back information that would forestall a revolt, a mutiny, or even a full-blown war?

Though the government liked to claim that the new conquest was a rich province, anyone who landed on its shores was bound to have mixed reactions. "Oh, the barren, barren shore!" wrote Burton when he arrived. He found "a regular desert, a thread of low coast, sandy as a Scotchman's whiskers; a bald, dismal glaring waste, with visible and palpable heat playing over the dirty-white, dirty-yellow, and dirty-brown surface." Sind was "a get-between a dust-bin and an oven."

Only the "noble Indus" offered hope for riches. The river was the life force of the province. All depended on its whims and vagaries.

> Deserts spring up, cities, ports and towns fall in the space of time which it takes the Indus to shift its bed for a few miles, or a native prince to remove his capital. . . . It is at once the great fertilizer of the country, the medium of transit for merchandise, and the main line of communication. . . . It is difficult even for a European, to view that noble stream without admiration, not unmixed with awe: the Oriental goes a step beyond . . . to adoration.

The land was cursed by its climate. Burton spoke of the "almost total absence of rain" and "the want of trees." The temperature in the coastal areas was "seldom less than 92° Fahrenheit; when at Sukkur [a town 250 miles inland] it would not be lower than 112°. The delta lands were at all times a hot-bed of miasma."

The new capital of Sind, Karachi, lacked even a hotel for visitors. The native town was a miserable collection of wattle huts and mud houses clustered around the ruined walls of a native fort. Mud was the common building material: Town and garden walls, foundations, houses, tenements, all were built of mud, which dried and crumbled and blew away in the offshore breezes and collapsed in the monsoon rains. "The Eye, the Nose and Ear" were offended, Burton wrote, by "the steady beat of drums, the squealing of native music, the roaring, bawling, *criard* voices of the people, and the streams of hungry gulls fighting over scraps of tainted fish." This "odour of carrion was varied, as we approached the bazars, by a close-faint, dead smell of drugs and spices." He had discovered the opium dens, the *dhaira*.

A little outside all the large towns there are several Dhaira, as they are called, walled gardens, planted with Bhang, and the Nazbu (a kind of Ocynum, supposed to excite mirth), and containing an Otak, or hall, for the convenience of the company. There, about five or six o'clock, P.M., the Bhangi, or hemp-drunkers, congregate. At first there is a scene of washing, pressing and rubbing the plant; and the prospect of their favorite enjoyment renders it an animated one. The potion is drunk in solemn silence, after which some smoke, and others eat sweetmeats, or dried and parched grain. Presently, one begins to sing, another calls for music, a third amuses himself and his friends by talking in the most ridiculous way, and a fourth will fall asleep.

A man inclined to dissipate need not confine himself to opium and cannabis and odd forms of wines and brandies. (He mentioned "the peculiar prevalence of intoxication.") Did one want an affair with a married woman, the wife of some respectable citizen? Sindhi women were notoriously unchaste—"the amativeness of the female here appears to be stronger than that of the male." And they were "most indecent in their language, especially in abuse and deliberately select the worst words used by the men. They are fond of drinking liqueurs and different preparations of hemp: intoxication is always the purpose." And, "Intrigues" were a favorite pastime.

The ordinary prostitutes he visited were of two kinds. One

was a low courtesan of the Jatki race, a type of Gypsy, who "inhabit villages close to the main roads, and support themselves and the males by the contributions of travellers." The second was the kanyari, the nautch girl, who "unites the occupation of dancing with the more immoral part of her trade."

> The Kanyari is, generally speaking, well dressed and clean in her person, she seldom drinks more than other women, and, like the lower orders of the frail sisterhood, is scrupulously obedient to the injunctions of her religious teachers.

What particularly intrigued Burton among the tremendous variety of races, sects, and social groups in Sind were the Sīdīs, the descendants of black slaves brought from the Somali coast of Africa and the Arab state of Muscat.

> In disposition they are at once cheerful and surly, merry and passionate . . . as revengeful as camels, and subject to fits of sulkiness so intense, that nothing but the most violent corporal punishment will cure them. . . . Brave and remorseless, they are also the most daring and treacherous of villains; nothing, in fact, except the certainty of death can deter them from robbery and bloodshed.

But an unexpected tragedy struck the Sīdīs. "One day Napier took it into his head to manumit the slaves, who were at once turned out of house and home. . . . There was general wailing and gnashing of teeth; few, however, starved, because life is easy in these latitudes."

An excursion to a shrine supposedly of great antiquity, sacred to both Hindus and Muslims, brought him some interesting insights into the practices of the people, who mixed the beliefs of two contradictory and hostile faiths in an easy amalgam, an odd synthesis in this most Muslim of Indian provinces. "In the hills to the northeast of Kurrachee, a great Haji [pilgrim] turned a flower into an alligator, whose descendants still wallow in the mire of a marshy pool," filled with hundreds of alligators, from two to twenty feet in length. Burton was one of the first Europeans to recognize the significance of Mango Pīr, as the shrine was popularly called; it has since become an object of study for scholars and ethnologists. Among the Muslims of India and Sind, Burton wrote, "The superstitions of the Hindoos have been adopted as points of practical faith."

> The dancing of the Nautch girls at the tombs of the holy men, the adoptions of sacred places from the heathen, and the respect shown by the Muslims to certain Hindoo saints and devotees, are abominations in the eyes of the old stock of the [Muslim] faithful; at the same time they are acceptable acts of religion here.

During the month of Ramaḍān, the great Islamic period of fasting and mourning, there was a large fair at the shrine. "The courtesans, who here as well as in India, are, generally speaking, the most strict in their devotions, flock to it in numbers." At the fair Burton's companion was an Arab, who, "after looking at the scene, declared that Satan was clearly at the bottom of all that was going on, and opined that Katl Am, or a general massacre, was the only way to purge the land of such abominations." However, Burton had a different interpretation. He immediately noted that the Yezīdīs, the "devil worshippers" of Kurdistan, called Satan "Melek-Taus," the Peacock King, and that the Sindhis were likely to call the chief alligator "Mor Sahib," Mister Peacock. He was subconsciously on the threshold of an important ethnological and mystical discovery involving the Yezīdīs—the Peacock Angel cult—an association that haunted him for years. The sect would appear frequently in his life, until he finally exorcised it in his meditative elegy, *The Kasîdah*.

Not everyone was as respectful of the sacred alligators as were the nautch girls. The young officers from the garrison found them a diverting sport. After making advances to the women pilgrims, mostly kanyaris, the subalterns found it fun to poke up the alligators, "a quasi-sacred animal in young Egypt" as they were in old Egypt, Burton remarked.

The poor devils of alligators, once jolly as monks or rectors, with nothing in the world to do but to devour, drink, and doze; wallow, waddle, and be worshipped; came to be shot at, pelted, fished for, bullied, and besieged by the Passamonts, Alabasters, and Morgantests of Karachi.

The officers were "accompanied by a scratch-pack of rattish bull terriers, yelping and dancing their joy at escaping the dogboy at the camp." When "Trim, Snap or Pinch got eaten, they would futilely salute the murderer's eyes and mouth with two ounces of shot." The faqīr who guarded the tank warned the griffs of the danger, but a Lieutenant Beresford proposed to test the warning by hopping across the tank on the backs of the alligators. The faqīr was given a bottle of brandy to go away, and Beresford—"the very model of a guardsman"—took a running jump onto the back of an alligator, then to another and another, dodging snapping jaws and lashing tails to reach the other side of the tank, a hero. No one else dared follow him, but Burton proposed another test of adolescent masculinity. He muzzled a crocodile with a rope and dangled a chicken on a hook before its nose. As the beast rushed forward for its prey, Burton leaped on its back for a short, erratic ride. But is his telling of the story the truth or a young man's boasting?

Then the 18th Bombay Native Infantry was transferred to Ghara, an outpost some thirty miles east of Karachi, where, on a quiet evening, Burton could hear the sunset gun at the capital. "Gharra was purgatory, but Karachi was the other place." Conditions were abysmal. The previous regiment had not bothered to build permanent houses for itself, so the newly arrived officers and troops had to live in tents. The heat was formidable, an almost constant 115° in the sun and 125 in the tents. It was a settlement Allāh forgot: Sindhi bungalows in the native town, built of reed mats covered with mud, lying along a saltwater creek, bone dry at the moment and to remain so until the fall monsoon rains arrived, when it would flood. On all sides was a vast waste of a salt flat, barren rock, and sandy plain, punctuated by barren hillocks subject to frequent gales from the sea. "Oh the hideous landscape!" moaned Burton.

Not only was there no formal housing at the post, there was no prospect of any being built. For the first months, the 18th B.N.I. survived under canvas, weathering heat and winds. Burton was fortunate enough to be alone in his own single-poled tent, where, in his off-hours, he wrote endlessly. To escape suffocation, he covered his worktable with a wet cloth and sat underneath it for the better part of the day. During a dust storm his pen would clog and the paper become covered with one layer of dust, then another. Sweat ran down his reading spectacles and dropped on the paper. His duties were not demanding; because he was so much more fluent in Indian tongues than the other officers, he was often assigned to court-martial duties, but what he had to do somehow seemed to fall into his search for languages. Of the many open to him at the time he preferred Persian, having already had a smattering of it in Bombay under his old *munshī*. Burton and another subaltern together "leased" a Persian *munshī*, Mirza Muḥammad Ḥosayn of Shīrāz, and "we jointly laid the foundation of a lengthened course of reading in that most elegant of oriental languages."

From this period in Ghara on, Burton was immersed in a Persian milieu. His closest associates, aside from the English officers with whom he was working in the field and friends like Scott and Steinhauser, were Persians and men of importance. From early 1844 to the late summer of 1846, when he became so ill he had to go on leave in southern India, he was surrounded by Persians and so heavily influenced by them and their culture and religion that he soon began to refer to himself as an "Ajami."[*]

---

[*] "Ajam" to Arabs and to Sunnī Muslims, the most "orthodox" of the Faith, means a non-Arab land and usually denotes Persia. "Ajami" is a Persian and, as Burton was to learn, a pejorative term used by Arabs for Muslims they considered inferior or heretical.

Among the Persians Burton associated with during the period were the *munshī* 'Alī Akhbar, who had served Napier so successfully as a secret agent, and the *munshī*'s fellow countryman Mirza Daúd. The pair shared a newly constructed bungalow outside Karachi. Mirza Daúd, Burton said, was "a first-rate Persian scholar," a quality he found most appealing in native acquaintances. However, the other Persian, 'Alī Akhbar, was under a shadow; he had become suspiciously rich on his small army pay and was facing the first of many inquiries from Bombay about the source of his income. "My life became very much mixed up with these gentlemen," Burton said. For the moment he was quite Persian in his thinking and way of living, almost uncritically so. But learning an elegant language seems upon examination not the primary reason for Burton's extended association with Persians.

> Mirza Hosayn* was a brother of the Agha Khan Mahallati, a scion of the Isma'iliyah, or "Old Man of the Mountain," who, having fled his country, Persia, after a rebellion, ridiculous, even in that land of eternal rebellion, turned condottiere, and with his troops of one hundred and thirty ruffians took service with us and was placed to garrison Jarak [a town on the Indus near Hyderabad]. Here the Belochis came down upon him, and killed or wounded about a hundred of his troops, after which he passed on to Bombay and enlightened the Presidency about his having conquered Scinde.

Burton's Persian teacher, Mirza Muḥammad Ḥosayn, was a member of a somewhat obscure heretical Shī'a sect, the Isma'īlīs, and his older brother was its leader, the Prince-Imām Āghā Khān Mahallātī, the first of his clan to bear that soon-to-be-distinguished name. The Mirza now brought his pupil into the orbit of a controversial family, once famous but in Burton's time just one of many branches of Islam that thronged the Eastern world,

---

* Although Burton calls the Mirza "Hosayn," other sources give his name as Ḥasan.

though its leaders, the imāms, had for centuries been regarded by the faithful as virtual divinities, bearing within themselves a luminous, otherworldly character that made them sparks of the Godhead on earth.

Ḥosayn referred to himself as a Shīrāzī, a man from Shīrāz, one of the ancient and respected centers of the mystical discipline known as Sufism and a city his family, who were alternately favored and exiled by the royal court at Tehran, had from time to time held among its many scattered domains. The city was especially noted as the birthplace of the great mystical poets Sa'dī and Ḥāfiz, whose works were soon to be found in Burton's saddlebags in his travels in Sind, Baluchistan, and the lower Punjab. Sa'dī was connected with the Isma'īlīs through the secret society of savants, the Brethren of Sincerity, a group about whom little was known, though in the eleventh century they had published an encyclopedia of mystical and practical character, *The Epistles of the Sincere Brethren*. It was this work that influenced certain of the Kabbālists Burton had studied at Oxford. The brotherhood had many enemies, who referred to it as "subterranean," meaning dangerous and heretical to other Muslims. Nevertheless, their teachings, however derived, seemed to offer Burton, through the Isma'īlīs, a guide in his search for "Gnosis," the inner knowledge that he had been pursuing since his Oxford days but which had escaped him among the Nāgar Brāhmins.

All about Burton were similar cults and sects, many showing traces of the ancient Persian faith, Zoroastrianism, with its dual powers of Good and Evil and an "overseer" who stood aloof. In many sects there was a theme of a Primal Light—"God created the Light of Muhammad from His own Light," and after many aeons "He created from it the whole universe." This Light was embodied in the figure of the fourth khalīf of Islam, 'Alī ibn Abī Ṭālib, from whom an almost uncounted number of sects descended, each offering arcane Ways and Paths.

And then, 'Alī was incarnated in the Āghā Khān Maḥallātī, the Prince-Imām, to whose court General Napier had assigned

Burton not only to gather intelligence but in the hope that the Isma'īlī leader might be persuaded to return to Persia, "that land of eternal rebellion," to continue his war against the current ruler, the Qājār Shāh. For the next two and a half years Burton was very much a part of the Āghā Khān's court, learning the language and flattering, cajoling, and perhaps even bullying a very reluctant Imām to reenter the battlefield.

9

The Assassins

The Āghā Khān's background was one that could only be fascinating to a man like the young Burton, so enamored of the exotic, the unusual, and the dangerous, even though he was to develop an incorrigible dislike for the Prince-Imām. For a long period the Isma'īlīs, an offspring of the powerful Fatimid dynasties of Spain and Cairo, had disappeared into the mists of history, existing for nearly five centuries in a foggy obscurity through which a few shadowy figures could be glimpsed. Then, early in the eighteenth century, inquisitive Europeans found scattered groups of Isma'īlīs in Syria and Persia who gave allegiance to the sacred presence of a spiritual leader, the Imām, who was believed by the faithful to be a direct descendant of Islam's fourth khalīf, 'Alī. The Imām was said to be living in central Iran* and

* Burton was vehement about the correct pronunciation of Iran and Irani (not Iranian): not "Eerahn" and "Eerahnee" as commonly pronounced by Europeans, but "Eeroon" and "Eeroonee."

the news aroused scholars, who believed the sect and its Imām had long since vanished.

The Isma'īlīs had once been known as the Assassins, for they had developed special techniques for eliminating religious and political enemies, but assassination had probably not been practiced for several centuries. Though various very extreme Isma'īlī doctrines had been softened or changed, the sacred character of the imām had not diminished. He was not only supreme in religious matters but was also a person of great power and wealth—yearly the Isma'īlī faithful, generally known as Khōjās, came from as far away as India with tribute, the Islamic *zakāt*, or tithe. This tribute filled the strongboxes of the Prince-Imāms and gave them that wealth so common among certain classes in the Orient, uncounted and spent with abandon.

Finally, in 1812, in a village near the sacred city of Qum, in the province of Mahallāt, an Isma'īlī stronghold, the then-current Isma'īlī Imām, a man named Khalīlullāh, was discovered by a wandering Frenchman. Khalīlullāh was very much detested by rival sects but enjoyed the considerable protection of the Persian Shāh, Fath 'Alī, of the nomadic Turco-Persian Qājār dynasty, and shortly he became a subject of interest to John Company in its plans to seize Iran as a bulwark against the Czar.

Khalīlullāh was revered "almost as a god by his followers, who attribute the gift of miracles to him," travelers reported. Then, in 1815, Khalīlullāh met his death at the hands of a mob in Yezd, a town in the south, after a riot in a local bazaar. A rival sect, the Twelvers, seemed to be the instigators. The leading Twelver mullah was brought in disgrace to Tehran, bastinadoed, and—a most degrading insult—his beard was plucked out, but he was not executed.

Khalīlullāh's seventeen-year-old son, Ḥasan 'Alī Shāh, became the new Isma'īlī Imām, and the boy's mother, a vigorous and powerful woman, petitioned Fath 'Alī Shāh for the return of ancient domains. With the family in royal favor, the Shāh bestowed the grandiose Turco-Persian title of Āghā Khān Mahallātī upon the new Isma'īlī Imām—"Aqa" (also Ahgha* and Āgā) was a Tartar term meaning dignitary or lord, and "khān" was the equivalent of sovereign and emperor, both terms now degraded from overuse. Mahallāt and other lands were returned to the young lord, and the Shāh gave him a sister in marriage, supposedly ensuring his loyalty to the throne. But one of the most important Isma'īlī lands, the rich province of Kerman, noted both for its bounty and its religious fervor and significance in Isma'īlī tradition, was kept by the Shāh.

The unexpected discovery of the Isma'īlīs, led by the youthful Āghā Khān Mahallātī, reestablished them as a force in Islam still to be reckoned with, though in a different perspective from the remote past. Though not numerous, they soon became of great help to the English, for the young Prince-Imām was an opportunist of unsurpassing shrewdness and skill. He had before him the choice of two patrons: the Shāh, who could be a dangerous rival, and the English, who might be friendly.

Before long, English agents and the Āghā Khān were holding secret meetings. The Qājār Shāh, Fath 'Alī, died in 1834 and when his successor, Muhammad Shāh, was crowned in 1835, the Imām and the new English chargé d'affaires, John M'Neill, became fast friends. The country was in turmoil at the time. Popular expressions of dissatisfaction with Qājār rule were rampant, and wandering ascetics preached an otherworldly doctrine that God was immanent in all things and that the imāms, the elect of God, were personifications of the divine attributes. Food was scarce (barley sold for ten times the normal price), and the Shāh's troops took to plundering the countryside. English offers of friendship were rejected by the Shāh, who turned to the Russians. Was Persia at last to be lost to the feared enemy to the north? The new ruler's campaign into Afghanistan, where he attempted to take Herat, ended disastrously. Meanwhile, the young Āghā Khān had petitioned him to be made governor of

---

* As Burton sometimes spelled it.

Kerman, that province of intense religious and emotional significance to the Isma'īlīs; there were many Isma'īlīs in the area,
and its nearness to India made it an easy journey for *zakāt*-bearing
Khōjās. The entire province was now in a state of civil war. The
English sent up native troops from Bombay in an attempt to
stabilize the situation. In the end, after several years of incon-
clusive warfare, the Āghā Khān had to suffer the indignity of
capture and imprisonment by forces loyal to the Shāh. During
his eight months' incarceration in a provincial jail, the faithful
Khōjās came from India to pay their divine leader their annual
tribute and homage. The Imām was finally released with the
understanding that he go into retirement on the family estates
at Maḥallāt. But Kerman was still on his mind. One might
question his judgment, for throughout his life he was generously
given by loyal subjects what established rulers had to force by
the way of taxes, taxes given under the pressure of the tax farmer
and the knot.

Meanwhile, the English were planning their invasion of Afghanistan and were nibbling away at the amīrs' lands in lower
Sind. John Company needed a diversion in Iran that would
prevent Muḥammad Shāh from again pressing claims to Afghanistan at an inopportune moment. To John Company the
entire area was a unit: Control of Afghanistan, southeastern Iran,
Baluchistan, Sind, and the Punjab—a massive territory—would
not only open up Central Asia but slow the Russian drive to the
south and also warn the French not to meddle again. It would
also stop the Shāh from further attempts to invade neighbors.
Thus, one more secret alliance—John Company and the Āghā
Khān—was forged, one that history slights in the tangle of secret
alliances of the time and which now matters little except that
it was to involve young Richard Burton.

In presumed exile in Maḥallāt, the Āghā Khān was doing
anything but admiring his gardens. He gathered an army of
Isma'īlīs, including five hundred horse and hired mercenaries,
and in October 1840 set off for the south en route to Kerman,

without the Shāh's knowledge or permission. Forged documents, a *sine qua non* for success in such a venture, appointing him governor of Kerman, enabled him to proceed through dusty rural towns without opposition. But at Kerman the forgeries were discovered. A battle broke out with the legal governor, one of many that were to engage the Isma'īlīs during the next two years.

Accounts from different sources naturally fail to agree on essentials. The Āghā Khān always declared that he had been properly appointed to Kerman and that after he was legally in power the former governor rebelled. Burton's considered opinion after coming to know the Prince-Imām was that it was nothing but "a most ridiculous attempt at rebellion against the reigning sovereign, Mohammad Shah," a view that he published at least twice.

Subsequent battles showed the Imām to be no genius on the field even though he was now receiving weapons in quantity from John Company, including at least two heavy field pieces that had a devastating effect on the lesser-equipped government troops. But battles were being lost; one of the Shāh's generals could report to Tehran that he had captured "a number of cannons with British markings." Kerman slipped again and again from the Imām's grasp. Retreat seemed the clear and inevitable course. Amid the madness of war and the defeat and flight of their Alid incarnation, the Khōjā pilgrims again found their living Imām and pressed their *zakāt* on him for their spiritual and his material benefit.

Mass desertions followed the collapse of the Imām's campaign; even one of his brothers, Sardār Abul Ḥasan (or Ḥosayn) Khān, who was to become Burton's Persian teacher at Ghara, was among those who abandoned him. Afghanistan, now in the hands of the English, his secret allies, seemed to be the only haven. With the remnants of his army, the Āghā Khān fled into Afghanistan, arriving on December 20, 1842, at Qandahar, where the famous Major Henry Rawlinson was ruling through a puppet governor. Rawlinson immediately granted him not only safety but also an allowance of one hundred rupees a day, a worthy sum at the time and more than a token of thanks for past and expected services. The Prince, always opportunistic and telling the major that the English were "*khalq 'ullah*," "the People of God," offered to take over as governor of Qandahar, and why should he not seize Herat also for England's ally, Shāh Shuja? But the time was most unpropitious for such adventures. A few days later, at Kābul and elsewhere, the Afghanis rose against the British garrisons, creating the tragic events that were to lead Burton to enlist to go to India.

Sind was the next haven for the Āghā Khān. Here he was faced with a difficult choice. Should he throw in his lot with the Sindhi amīrs as fellow Orientals and Muslims, or should he aid the People of God in absorbing Sind? Sending messengers on ahead, the Āghā Khān, speaking as a friend of the People, advised Mīr Nasīr Khān of Hyderabad to allow the Company to annex Karachi, advice that went unappreciated—the English already had it. Switching allegiance again, the Prince-Imām decided to abandon his new allies and take up the Sindhi cause as his "Muslim duty." Mīr Nasīr Khān, in no need of such a turncoat, was also determined to avoid bloodshed with the English if he could. But unrest was paramount: "The assembled clansmen, irritated to the highest degree, determined to fall upon Major Outram and those who accompanied him," wrote Burton of the event. Then the Imām, no opportunity too disgraceful to embrace, threw in his lot with Outram "for the sake of God's pleasure" and in a meeting at Hyderabad disclosed what he knew of the Sindhian plan of battle, by which act he saved the major from a nighttime attack. This was the Āghā Khān's version of events. Burton gives another side. "Mir Nasir Khan, feeling that he had lost power over his infuriated subjects, sent messages and letters to Major Outram, warning him of his danger, and entreating him to retire from the vicinity of Hyderabad with the least possible delay." Outram withdrew from the area, but three days later came the celebrated victory at Mīanī, to be followed by that at Dubba, and the end of Sindhi resistance.

For services true or imaginary Napier awarded the Āghā Khān an annual stipend of £2,000 and honored him with the title of "Highness," an honor liberally awarded the native princes, giving them a false dignity that enabled the English to manipulate them more easily. The Prince-Imām continued to aid his new friends and was instrumental, he claimed, in the taking of Baluchistan. (Of this Burton snidely remarked how the Āghā Khān "enlightened the [Bombay] Presidency about his having conquered Scinde.") On the Indus the Āghā Khān stopped to await the expected tribute from the Khōjā pilgrims (it was the Irani new year, March 21); the faithful as usual were able to locate their Imām even in the midst of another battle. Here—Burton was remiss in not giving details—a raiding party of Baluchis, who had been bent merely on disrupting the wood and coal supplies for the English steamers on the river, captured the treasure and killed a large number of the Isma'īlī forces. The Āghā Khān pressed his new friends to help him get his money back; they replied that he should have taken better care of it. A few months after this loss the Prince-Imām and his entourage, which now included women and children along with the remnants of his army, moved into Sind and settled in the desert east of Karachi, close to Ghara, where the 18th Bombay Native Infantry was to be located, a haven far removed from hostilities.

10

The Royal Court

The Āghā Khān had established a vast camp outside the mud
huts of Ghara and the orderly British cantonment, with
hundreds of huge tents in clusters, each group being surrounded
by high canvas walls decorated with floral designs on the inside.
From the encampment came the bustle of daily life, the chatter
of voices, snatches of songs, the sounds of quarrels and fights,
the muezzin's five-times-daily call to prayer, screams from women
and slaves being beaten, the bleating of sheep led to the slaughter, the clatter of messengers rushing to the Prince-Imām's tent,
the arrivals of caravans and secret agents, of high officials and
dancing girls. It could not but enthrall Burton, much as he was
coming to dislike the Prince, a strongly built man with a pock-
marked, cruel face and overbearing manner and a vanity that
was unquenchable. As a youth, the Āghā Khān had been attracted to Sufism and came to believe that he was the highest
of all beings, the *insān-i-kāmil*, "the primordial man of fully re-

alized spiritual qualities." And in his short autobiography, *'Ibrat Afzā*, in which he disclaimed any desire for worldly power, the Prince-Imām wrote: "Through the grace of God and the blessings of my immaculate forefathers and ancestors, I am able from the wide and lofty expanse of dervishhood, to disdain and despise all monarchy." Such false and self-deprecating modesty could only infuriate Burton.

Among people to whom the exotic was normal in both life and religion, the Isma'īlīs had a long and dramatic history that led back to the tumultuous decades after Muḥammad's death in A.D. 632, for their leaders were directly descended from 'Alī ibn Abu Ṭālib, the Prophet's cousin and son-in-law and the fourth khalīf or successor. Throughout his life Burton favored 'Alī over the first three khalīfs. 'Alī was a "proselyte worth a thousand sabres." Burton thought him more of a scholar than the other khalīfs, an important qualification, for he "wrote poetry, indited proverbs, and, according to some, improved the [Arabic] syllabarium by the invocation of vowel points."

When 'Alī was elected khalīf in the face of much dissent, his supporters, the Shī'a (roughly "partisans"), were opposed by the more orthodox group, the Sunnī (the "Followers of the Path"). Civil war broke out, and Islam was irrevocably splintered.

But not even the rallying point of the House of 'Alī held the Shī'a together: they split into numerous divisions and sects, often as much at war with each other as with the Sunnī. The Alid schism hardened and assumed an otherworldly character with the development of the doctrine of the Divine Imām, the spiritual leader of supernatural character and qualities. The poorer people, especially the non-Arabs and above all the Persians, seized upon the conviction that a descendant of 'Alī would guide every age, in person or absentia, until the end of time. The Shī'a sects soon equated their Imāms with God Himself, the Imāms sharing His attributes and powers. They were consequently living proof of 'Alī, always the same numinous Being that incarnated Itself in different forms, the soul of each Imām passing into the body of his successor.

By the time of the seventh Imām a further split developed among the Shī'as. A major group believed that the Imām Isma'īl went into *ghayba*, or occultation, having disappeared from the world to await the coming of the Madhī, the "Expected One," who would appear at the end of time. Despite his absence in *ghayba*, the seventh Imām, however, lived on spiritually in each successor and was very much alive in the Āghā Khān Mahallātī, hardly sinless or a messiah in the eyes of the young Lieutenant Richard Burton. Those Shī'as who did not become Seveners (there are also Fivers, among other types) continued their line to the Twelfth Imām and are consequently known as "Twelvers." There is much bitter rivalry among all the sects.

A key tool in the growth of Isma'īlianism was the use of devotees, the *fida'is*, whose role it was to propagandize and convert and also to murder opponents as a final act of dedication to the Grand Master. Many legends developed about their skill and secretiveness in attaining their goals, one being that they were given the best of all material lives, with fine foods and their pick of nubile young women, and were drugged on hashish— Indian hemp or *cannabis*. The Syrian Arabic term for these *fida'is* was *hashshashin*, hashish takers, and it was not long before the Crusaders, who faced them in the Levant, had turned the word into "assassins," now common in many languages. Throughout the Middle East, religious leaders and other divines, generals, prime ministers and wazirs, and heroic warriors, including the great general Saladdin, of views other than those held by the Seveners, faced death at the hands of the Assassins. Men took to wearing chain mail under ordinary clothing and employed bodyguards, who, in some instances, were *fida'is* in disguise awaiting their chance to kill.

To survive reprisals and to avoid detection among orthodox Muslims, the Isma'īlīs and other extremist sects had developed the practice of *taqīya*, dissimulation or concealment of belief.

Under the Sunnī princes, their enemies, the Shī'as, could be forced under pain of death to denounce 'Alī and the Imāms. The hiding of one's true beliefs by taqīya came to be not only a matter of survival but of religious ordinance. The tenth-century Shī'a divine, Ibn Babūya al-Sadūq, stated, "Our belief concerning taqīya is that it is obligatory. . . . God has described the showing of friendship to unbelievers" as being possible only "in the state of taqīya."

Taqīya seems to have been adopted by Burton as a sensible practice—naturally he could not admit to taqīya—and the result is that often his feelings about the faith of Islam are obscure, though never negative: questioners were not likely to get a clear answer from him, and in print he was very circumspect. Taqīya, especially among the Seveners and the Āghā Khān, was still as common in Burton's time as it was in the earliest centuries of Isma'īlī history.

> It was to be remembered that the Shieh branch of the Moslem creed whenever settled among anti-religionists [that is, among the Sunnīs], always hold as a tenet, and rigidly adhere to the practice called Takiyyah, i.e. . . . the systematic concealment of anything that concerns their faith, history, customs, and in a word, any peculiarities the disclosure of which might be attended with unpleasant circumstances.

But in the thirteenth century an enemy appeared who could not be diverted by assassination or taqīya. "The Ismailiyeh heresy," wrote Burton with a certain relish in Sindh, was "severely treated by Holoku Khan." The Mongols had overrun the Assassin fortresses in Persia. Some twelve thousand Isma'īlis, simple believers as well as Grand Masters, were slaughtered in the central fortress of Alamūt alone. The Seveners in Syria lasted less than a century longer. This appeared to be the end of the sect and of the Assassins, so far as the world knew, until the fortuitous discovery of Khalīlullāh.

When he found a group of Khōjās in Karachi, Burton immediately began a brief study but was not able to probe deeply —all the Khōjās practice *taqīya*, and information obtained from them was at best "inaccurate." The Karachi Khōjās were not at all popular, he wrote, but were "thoroughly despised." He noted that they were called "Tundo," meaning "handless" or "maimed," by their enemies, the Sunnīs, an insulting allusion because among Muslims the right hand is used for handling food, the left for "sanitary" purposes. A man who loses his right hand (as punishment for theft, for example) is thus forced to eat with his left, a disgrace that automatically means his banishment from the community of the faithful. The Sunnīs refused to eat with the Khōjās, and, wrote Burton in *Sindh*, "the Sunni, if a religious man, would always suspect that a dish offered him by one of these heretics contained some impurity," probably pork or scaleless fish, both anathema to pious Muslims.

No doubt the Persians were charming, intelligent, witty, highly educated, and entertaining (Burton's annotations in the *Arabian Nights* recall many anecdotes, often bawdy, from this period), but he did not take the Imām's claims to divinity at all seriously. There were other issues at stake. The Āghā Khān still hoped to gain Kerman, and it was to the advantage of the English to keep these expectations alive. Thus, recently arrived in Sind, Burton found himself not only studying the common administrative tongue of Muslim India—Persian—with the royal Mirza Ḥosayn, but also assigned to keep close watch on a very slippery Prince-Imām, who might be of use to the Company in helping dismantle the very unpopular pro-Russian Qājār dynasty in Tehran. *

The details of the situation at Ghara are foggy, especially the role of the *mirza* Muḥammad Ḥosayn, Burton's Persian teacher.

---

* The Qājārs were not deposed until 1925, when Reza Shāh seized the throne.

He was a leading member of an important family, and he had been a general of some repute in the battles against the Shāh, commanding with special glory in campaigns first against the Baluchis and then in a fourteen-month-long defense of a citadel at Bam that the Āghā Khān had seized from the Shāh. The family had spectacular wealth and a steady tribute from the Isma'īlī faithful as well as a solid stipend from John Company. That an important member of the royal family descended from the sanctified 'Alī was reduced to teaching two young English officers had to have another reason. Burton's fellow student is unnamed and disappears in his recollections after but a single mention, but Mirza Hosayn surfaces time after time, not only in the *Life* but in *Falconry in the Valley of the Indus* and elsewhere. The stipend of £2,000 per year was a very large sum to allot to a renegade, untrustworthy nobleman of exotic religious beliefs. That the Āghā Khān expected to regain his holdings in Iran as well as control of Kerman was obvious. But how was this to be done? The Persians seemed to be using Burton as their tool, just as he was trying to maneuver the Prince-Imām into taking positive action. For the next thirty months Burton stuck close to the Isma'īlī leaders, traveling with Mirza Hosayn and studying the Isma'īlī communities in Karachi when he was not on secret missions in Sind, Baluchistan, and the lower Punjab for Napier. He was often disguised as a Persian, possibly even as an Isma'īlī, and he began to absorb some of their doctrines.

Aside from the Mirza and 'Alī Akhbar and Mirza Daúd, Burton did not find the royal family particularly congenial. Hatred could run deep and long in Burton. What slights he received from the Āghā Khān or what traits the Imām unwarily exposed to the highly critical young Burton are unknown. He had an unrelenting enmity to the Prince, who, from the scattered fragments of information that have survived embedded in accounts of more important events, was hardly a likable figure. Not only was the attempt at rebellion "ridiculous" to Burton, but so was the Āghā

Khān's ability as a military leader. In a world where prowess on the battlefield was a key to successful rule, he was inept. Burton thought the prince's title was due more to his "religious position as head of the Ismailiyeh heresy." Though he did not like the Khōjās, he wrote in *Sindh* that the Āghā Khān, "for years a pensioner of the British Government in India, has done much to injure the tribe by his rapacity and ill-judged extortion" and that his people in Bombay objected to "his too great predilection for drinking and intriguing with females."

Despite his resentment of the Āghā Khān and the Khōjās, Burton became absorbed in Isma'īlī doctrines. He could now see a relation to some of the Kabbālistic beliefs he had come across at Oxford, especially in the mystical use of numbers. The inner core of Isma'īlī belief has baffled scholars, for many of the sect's works were burned by enemies and the substance is known only in excerpts quoted by opponents in order to refute them. The Isma'īlīs did not receive the nickname of "Seveners" only because of their last Imām. Seven was a ruling number in their eschatology. Not only were there seven imāms; so were there seven cycles of history, identified with the seven Nāṭiqs (literally "Utterers")—Adam, Noah, Abraham, Moses, Jesus, Muḥammad, and lastly, the unknown Imām who was to consummate the cycles. Between each Nāṭiq was a series of Seven Mutes or Silents who completed his work. Seven also was applied to exoteric interpretations, especially of the Qur'ān, the first words of the sacred work being written in Arabic with only seven characters, which are taken to refer to the Seven Nāṭiqs; from these letters are derived twelve others, which signify the twelve descendants of each Nāṭiq. There are seven verses in the first Qur'ānic *sura*, or chapter, symbolizing the seven degrees of religion. The gloss is inexhaustible.

As with the Nāgar Brāhmins, Burton had again allied himself with a special—and very unorthodox—sect of a major religion. Despite his consuming passion for knowledge, for facts, for information, he was more a collector than an analyzer, and what he saw of the Isma'īlīs seemed to have led him not to a careful consideration of their beliefs and practices but to a desire to enter Islam no matter what. From this point on there is no appreciation in his writing of any faith but Islam.

11

The Smell of Death

Burton and the 18th Bombay Native Infantry had arrived in Ghara just when, in late January, the Isma'īlīs began their commemoration of the dark tragedy of 'Āshūrā, the great Shī'a passion play, one of the most important feasts on the calendar, for it marked the martyrdom not only of the Khalīf 'Alī (who was assassinated in A.D. 661 on his way to the mosque) but also of his sons Ḥasan (who was believed to have been poisoned) and especially Ḥusayn, the direct ancestor of the Āghā Khān. In 680, Ḥusayn and his retinue, a mere two hundred people, were led into a trap by a rival, the usurping khalīf Yazīd. The group spent ten days without water fighting off the enemy in the heat of the Iraqi desert near Karbala, until all were killed, an event that was recalled yearly in intense purgatorial passion plays in which the Shī'a faithful throughout the world faced the mystery of suffering and death. In the lamentations of 'Āshūrā, as the search for water and the battle was recalled, the men beat their naked chests until the blood ran, chanting, moaning, and wailing, working themselves into a frenzy, their flesh becoming as raw as beef. Shrieks and wails rent the air; men and women fainted in mystical ecstasy.

The climax of the festival came with the reenactment of the events leading to Ḥusayn's death at the hands of his archenemy Shimr—the martyr's "death" took place offstage—when a bier with his headless corpse was brought out, the head to be carried off to the usurper Yazīd, a great insult in Shī'a eyes because Ḥusayn was the Prophet Muḥammad's favorite grandson. The faithful, ravaged by real tears and unable to control their emotions, shouted the saint's name over and over again. It was a highly affecting spectacle that had an impact on Burton and aroused his interest in the Isma'īlīs.

A few months later, in 1844, Burton's nagging and bullying of the Āghā Khān to return to Persia to carry on the uprising against the Qājār Shāh brought some results, and a campaign to put pressure on those wavering or independent Baluchi chiefs in the eastern hills of Persia who had not submitted to the British was mounted in the hope of ensuring a safe flank when a full-scale invasion of Iran was begun. Earlier the chiefs had been attacked from the Sindhi side with the aid of the Prince-Imam. Now they were to be squeezed from the west as well. Thus, the Company was using the Isma'īlīs to solve its problems with the troublesome local khāns, while the Isma'īlīs were making the most of the English to get a base in Makran Province, on the way to Kerman. The Āghā Khān's brother, Muḥammad Bāqir Khān, landed on the Makran coast from bases in Sind, and while his forces attempted to gain a beachhead, the local chieftains were bombarded with messages from the Prince-Imam, now well supplied with British arms, who was to claim that he had pacified the tribesmen. Muḥammad Bāqir became entrapped in two years of desultory fighting while the Āghā Khān withdrew to his encampment at Ghara to mull over other plans.

Despite the attractions of the Āghā Khān's court, with its esoteric religious beliefs and arcane practices and practical jokes of extreme bawdiness, life at Ghara was often one of boredom for Burton. Shortly he was able to get away from the post and, during the years of 1844 and early 1845, go out on a series of missions for Napier, all the while keeping an eye on the Isma'īlīs. He made numerous trips into other parts of Sind, into the Indine delta, up the river itself, north to the edges of the Punjab and through the Baluchi hills, where the Āghā Khān was doing more bragging than fighting. He could pass himself off as a trader or a laborer, or, what particularly pleased him, as a dervish, for among the natives Burton was now acting out the role of a Muslim, not only externally but in inner belief, for sometime during this period he seems to have converted to Islam, though it was to the heretical Isma'īlī Shī'as with Sufi influences rather than to the orthodox Sunnīs.

> He was sent out amongst the wild tribes of the hills and plains to collect information for Sir Charles [said Isabel Burton in the *Life*]. He did not go as a British officer or Commissioner, because he would see nothing but what the natives chose him to see: he let down a curtain between himself and Civilization, and a tattered, dirty-looking dervish would wander on foot, lodge in mosques, where he was venerated as a saintly man, mix with the strangest company, join the Beloch and Brahui tribes . . . about whom there was nothing then known. Sometimes he appeared in the towns; as a merchant he opened a shop, sold stuffs or sweetmeats in the bazaar. Sometimes he worked with the men in native dress, "Jats" [Gypsies] and Camel men at levelling canals.

Cut loose for long periods from the conventional living of the garrison outposts, adrift in a sea of dust, Burton became more and more of an outsider to his own people, though he remained close to Scott and Steinhauser. In the formidable heat it seemed sensible to wear native clothing, and it brought him nearer to the people. He put on the loose cottons that protected one from the sun, usually wearing the ample, flowing muslin shirt he called the *pirhan*, and for trousers a pair of blue silk *salwars* "wide enough without exaggeration," he wrote in *Scinde; or, The Unhappy Val-*

ley, "for a young married couple, the baby and all, tight around the ankles." Over the shirt was a kind of coat—more like a second shirt—of cotton. Around his waist he tied a "shawl" as a wide belt or cummerbund, with a small ivory-handled Persian knife stuck in it—"equally useful for cutting your mutton and defending yourself from your friends." In the brief cold months of December and January even Lower Sind can be unpleasant, with occasional frosts, so he would put on a *kurti*, or jacket, of whatever kind of cloth one could afford ("from cloth of gold to cloth of frieze"), padded with cotton, with shirted sleeves, and on top of that an Afghan *chogheh*, a long cloak lined with sheepskin or Astrican wool, "the leather tanned to a wonderful softness, and then intricately stitched and embroidered." On his head he wore a cotton skullcap called an *arachkin* ("perspiration catcher"), around which he wound twelve yards of ornamental sprigged muslin to form a turban. When he went riding, he wore a pair of boots of softened yellow cordovan; at other times, a soft slipper worked with silk flowers. In short, though Burton often passed himself off as a dervish and a faqīr, a poor wandering holy man, he was something of a dandy in his guise as a Muslim.

But dressing as some kind of follower of the Prophet was not sufficient. Clothes marked a man's religion, for the Hindus wore different clothing from that of the various Muslim sects, and Christians as part of their conversion took up Western dress. When Burton visited mosques and brothels, sat around the bazaars with the merchants, and stayed in the caravanserais, he was not passing himself off as an English officer in native clothing for the mere convenience. He was a wanderer from another Islamic land, rootless and unattached—the Holy Prophet had said, "Be in the world as of a stranger or a traveller"—often a half-breed, part Persian, part Arab. He tried disguises endlessly, like an actor working out the shadings of a character. But this was no act for Burton. If he said he was a Muslim, then he was one. He would not have survived for long on a mere pretense of being a Muslim in a land so fiercely devoted to its faith. Other

English officers got caught, like Connolly and Stoddard in Bho-kara. Burton was so immersed in Islam and in Sind—he claimed he hated Sind and perhaps he did, but that was another matter—that to live and work on a day-to-day basis he had to become a Muslim in the fullest sense and it would have been impossible to pass himself off as a native of any type in a Muslim country if he did not have that distinguishing mark of the Muslim that was circumcision.

Circumcision is the identifying mark of the Muslim, though other races and other religions also practice circumcision of var-ious types. Among Muslims the mark is crucial, often one of life and death. Just to urinate in public is to make a religious state-ment and to go to a prostitute in a Muslim land, as Burton often did, meant another religious proclamation. Many Muslim pros-titutes will not engage uncircumcised men except in those broth-els catering to foreigners. Since nineteenth-century Englishmen were not normally circumcised, there has been some speculation about Burton's circumcision, some of it ribald, most of it unin-formed, but circumcised he would have to be, as he so carefully pointed out in various works. He mentions circumcision fre-quently, especially in those of his books that are concerned with Islamic and Arab themes, and he was most adamant on its ne-cessity for those who would travel in Muslim lands. In *Personal Narrative of a Pilgrimage to El-Medinah and Meccah* he quotes a Mr. Bankes as saying early in the nineteenth century, "Even to travellers in Mohametan countries, I look upon the safety of their journey as almost impossible, unless they have previously submitted to the rite."

Burton's comment was that "the danger is doubled by non-compliance with the custom. . . . In bigoted Moslem countries, it is considered a sine qua non." He pointed out in the same volume that to make the pilgrimage to Mecca "it must be un-derstood that it is absolutely indispensable to be a Mussilman (at least externally) and to have an Arab name." "At least ex-ternally," of course, meant to bear the identifying mark of the

Muslim normally incumbent upon every Muslim, male and female alike.

In the case of a convert to Islam for whom the operation may be a cause of physical suffering, it can be dispensed with, but for someone like Burton, who was traveling in "barbarous" Muslim lands and was to make the pilgrimage into the heart of Arabia to Mecca, circumcision was expedient. He left a description of the rite as practiced in Sind. The ceremony was known as Sathri or Toharu, the latter an Arabic term meaning "purity," and was generally performed on the male when he was in his eighth year. As with similar ceremonies of initiation in every religion, there was much celebration, with feasting, music, and fireworks. The initiate

> dressed in saffron-coloured clothes and adorned with Sihra [a paper or flower garland], is mounted on horseback, and led round the town to the sound of instruments, singing and firing of guns. When he returns home the barber performs the operation in the same way as done in India, but not nearly so skillful. Clarified butter, wax and the leaves of the Neem tree [considered to be an antiseptic], are used as a dressing to the wound, which is expected to heal in eight or ten days. . . .

Here Burton added a note, most likely based on his personal experience.

> No evil results are expected from the circumcision of adults; it has often been tried in the cases of African slaves. The cure, however, is generally protracted for the period of at least six weeks.

A few years later Burton expressed a different opinion about the physical results of adult male circumcision, with possible regrets for lost pleasures.

> Male circumcision makes love slow and difficult. For the softness of the gland is hardened by friction, hence coitus is painful, slow, and not energetic enough. Perhaps in some nations a local cause

[for circumcision] also exists: a small piece of flesh growing beyond bounds, the necessity for amputation arises.

Such an intimate part of the male as the foreskin had to be protected carefully. Burton noted that the Pathans buried the foreskin in a damp part of the house where the water jars were kept, possibly in the hope that it would grow and add to the boy's virility. In other areas of the Punjab it was tossed on the roof of the house or tied to it by a straw. The Muslims of Delhi tied the foreskin to the boy's left foot with a peacock feather so that no evil shadow would fall on him. The Brahuis, a Dravidian people of the north who attracted Burton's interest, either buried the foreskin under a tree so that the boy would be fruitful in generation or in damp earth to cool the burning pain of the wound.

To be initiated into Islam is one thing; to live as a Muslim was something more demanding. Islam is not only a religion; it is the very heart of existence, of daily life, a way of speaking, of thinking, eating, sleeping, defecating, of attitudes and outlook. Even the mention of the name of the Holy Prophet Muḥammad demanded the addition of the phrase "Peace be upon him!" Otherwise, the speaker would be thought to be impious. And such simple an act as quenching one's thirst became an involved ritual.

> Look, for instance, at that Indian Muslim drinking a glass of water. With [the English] the operation is simple enough, but his performance includes no fewer than five novelties. In the first place he clutches his tumbler as though it were the throat of a foe; secondly, he ejaculates, "In the name of Allah the Compassionate, the Merciful!" before wetting his lips; thirdly he imbibes the contents, swallowing them, not sipping them, as he ought to do, and ending with a satisfied grunt; fourthly, before setting down the cup, he sighs forth, "Praise be to Allah"—of which you will understand the full meaning in the Desert; and, fifthly, he replies, "May Allah make it pleasant to thee!" in answer to his friend's polite "Pleasureably and

health!" Also he is careful to avoid the irreligious action of drinking the pure element in a standing position. . . .

There were even more formal customs to follow, many of which went back to the Holy Prophet himself. In general, Muslims shave their heads, as Burton had done even before coming to India, but leave the beard and mustaches, which must be properly trimmed—Burton wore heavy mustachios and a slight beard in the Shī'a style then current. Males shave under the arms and shave the pubic area every forty days or so. Some men prefer to remove the hair by plucking. Women let the hair of the head grow long but remove the pubic hair, usually with a depilatory or by vellication, a custom believed to have originated with Bilkis, the queen of Sheba, who was told by King Solomon, one of the greatest of the Islamic prophets, that he would not marry her until the hair of her legs was removed with a depilatory. It was a custom sanctioned in sacred tradition. Burton noted that "at first vellication is painful, but the skin becomes used to it. The pecten is shaved either without or after using depilatories. . . . Not a few Anglo-Indians [meaning himself] have adopted these precautions."

Such practices were standard throughout the Muslim world, and their use by women fascinated Westerners. Burton's contemporary, Gustave Flaubert, in Egypt in 1849 and 1850, wrote "These shaved cunts make a strange effect—the flesh is as hard as bronze. . . ." In the Orient, women of communities other than Muslim shave the pubes for erotic reasons.

And then there was the practice of urinating that Burton had to follow even more automatically. Muslims, like most Easterners, urinate squatting, and when finished, the man wipes his penis with a stone or clod of earth or clay, one, three, or five pieces, whatever local custom demands. There is a frequently repeated story that during his trip to Mecca Burton was observed absentmindedly following the call of nature in a non-Muslim manner by urinating standing, the Western position, and had to kill his discoverer in order to save his own life, a legend he tried to deny, pointing out the difficulty of urinating in cumbersome Arab robes while erect. Still, Burton obviously enjoyed the notoriety of having killed a man in cold blood; however, his detractor Stanley Lane-Poole liked to point out that Burton "confessed rather shamefastly that he had never killed anybody at any time."

Then defecation also meant a religious and cultural act, for practices differ from those of the West. A Muslim should enter the lavatory on his left, not right, foot, and he cleanses himself with water (or sand or earth if there is no water) with his left hand. The two heirs of Europeans in India, the half-caste Anglo-Indians and the half-caste Goans of Portuguese antecedents, were divided on the issue of toilet custom. The former followed English practice and used toilet paper after defecation; the Goans washed themselves with water, using the left hand, as did other Indian communities. The Anglo-Indians derided the Goans as "washers" and the Goans castigated the Anglo-Indians as "wipers."

Then there was the matter of prayer, both public and private. Ordinarily, the good Muslim prays five times a day. The prayers are preceded by a ritual of purification, the *wuḍū* (or *wuzu*, as Burton called it in his Persianized pronunciation), which must be so ingrained in a Muslim's life that it is performed automatically. During the prayers the Muslim takes various positions, standing, bowing, sitting, turns his head from side to side, and at one point, after saying *Allāhu Akhbar*, "God is Most Great," touches the ground with his forehead in the position known as *sadja* in token of his submission—Islam—to God. The proper observance of these rituals is demanding—one does not make mistakes or shirk the full observance—and if Burton erred in a word or gesture, it would have brought suspicion upon him as a true believer. Acting outwardly as a Muslim, however, was not sufficient. Each step, each act, gesture, and thought, had to come out of the depths of his heart and be totally and naturally "Muslim."

Thus, he was circumcised, and made a Muslim, and lived like a Muslim and prayed and practiced like one. Was the pain of initiation worthwhile for a man who merely wanted to disguise himself as a native in order to engage in undercover missions on behalf of his commander, or was there some other, deeper, more secret reason, more than masquerade and sham? Burton was indeed a practicing Muslim and was to remain one, with many shades of interest for what he called the Saving Faith. Whether or not he erred in his initial choice of the Isma'ilis, he began to conform to more orthodox Islam after the abortive Isma'ili attempt to invade Persia through Makran. However, much as he might profess to the claim that the Sunnis were the correct community, his sympathies lay with the "heterodox Shieh" and, when he had advanced further in his studies, with the Sufis, whose allegiance is to neither party but to the Mystical Path. A Muslim he would be throughout his life, and often a devout one, but still with many backslidings and failures. His works have some harsh things to say about Muslims, but it is difficult to find a negative word about Islam.

Burton was now very much immersed in playing out the Great Game, and the surface show of merchant or dervish was a very skillful way of amassing information. As a wandering trader riding a camel, Burton—and other agents—had an excellent means of measuring distances. Unlike the horse, whose pace was irregular, the camel had a steady stride, nearly as regular as a metronome, and made an almost predictable number of paces per hour, depending on whether it was crossing sand or hard soil. Thus, distances in previously unknown areas could easily be mapped. Such information was important, for a surveyor or a war party, for example, could predict even in an uncharted area, as the Sind deserts were, how much ground had been covered.

Burton had a touch of paranoia and hostility about him during his Sind days, perhaps caused by the loneliness and danger of his work. A beast of such magnificence as the camel did not escape his notice as a means of criticizing someone else. His calculations showed that a camel covered 3,600 yards per hour on level ground, while Alexander Burnes had set the distance as 3,700—but, said Burton, that was over soft and sandy soil—and as 2,833 at other times. Obviously, to Burton, who could be annoyingly pedantic and uncharitable, his earlier rival was not only inaccurate but dangerously misleading to those whose lives might depend on the stride and pace of a camel.

The disguise of dervish was ideal for Burton and the other players of the Great Game since religious mendicants were a commonplace and were not usually questioned except for the efficacy of their cures and the miracles they could deliver. Often the "dervishes" were attached to a Survey—Burton was a member of the Sindh Survey and his fictional counterpart in *Kim*, Colonel Creighton, of the Indian Survey and was "a man without a regiment." The agent disguised as a peripatetic holy man—Muslim, Hindu, Sikh, or Buddhist—usually carried a staff and a rosary suitably modified (the Tibetan "lamas" also had a prayer wheel), instruments that, in the hands of a trained man, could be used as rough surveying tools, measuring hills and mountains, valleys, wadis, rivers, and other geographical landmarks. (The technique was copied by Sir Baden-Powell's Boy Scouts in later years.) These "mendicants" wandered all over West Asia and even into Tibet, the Forbidden Land. One of the best and most famous agents, Lt. Edmund Smyth, crossed many times into Tibet and had the temerity to paddle about the sacred lake, Mānasarōvar, in a rubber boat. It was Smyth who initiated the Corps of Pundits, a team of native surveyors, Indians, who mapped what they could of Tibet with rosaries and prayer wheels.

At times, Burton seemed to be in the company of other officers, probably disguised as a servant, or with Muḥammad Ḥosayn, dressed as a wandering holy man—he fudges details in *Scinde; or, The Unhappy Valley* and other works from this period. But as a traveler his ear was sharp, his eye keen. The scene before him had little to recommend except to the geographer, the linguist, and the scientist. "Oh, the howling wastes," Burton complained, and he added elsewhere, "The Persians say of Sind—'The smell of death is in our noses.' " But in this vast wilderness he found much to entertain him. He wrote of the wild life in the marshes of the riverbanks—glossy ibis, gray crane, the stork, the spoonbill, the noble demoiselle, and the flamingo, standing amid fat sedges, tall grass, and matted reeds in every stage of vegetable existence, from germination to decay, growing amid the black mud and torpid sheets of water. He was a born naturalist, and if he had pursued this line alone, with his charming sketches, so few of which have survived, he might have ranked among the greatest.

But not all was so idyllic, for there were the insects—insects that got into nose and mouth, swarms of them, wasps, centipedes, scorpions, gigantic hornets, sandflies, mosquitoes, and "other bed fellows" in spite of boiling the bedding every second day. There were also locusts, and white ants that produced a finely powdered gray dust out of books, boots, boxes, and valuables, along with large and small white ants "who allow themselves to be cut in two rather than relax the stubborn hold of their pincers upon our skins," and large red ants and small red ants that walked on his mustache. Then there were prickly heat, boils, and blains—"ulcers, rather malignant ones."

Equally annoying were the bandicoot rats. Writing in the third person in *Scinde*, he complained how they would "drop upon him from the boards above, race vigourously over his person, playfully pat him with their cold paws and sniff him with their damp, uncomfortable snouts."

The desert, the Indus Valley, and the great delta were deep in history. Not only were there remnants of the passage of Alexander the Great through the area in 326 B.C. but vestiges of even earlier peoples, known and unknown. Sind was awash with myths and stories. Burton was told of djinns and spirits, the Seven Headless prophets, corpses that rise and speak prophetic words of warning, emperors and Moghul warlords, saints and holy men and women. All was dusty, perishable magnificence. Tattah, once a flourishing center of half a million people in the Indus delta, had by Burton's time declined to an outpost of a few thousand, a bedraggled, hostile place of ruins and hungry beggars. The great mosque of the Moghul emperor Aurengezeb, with its towering walls and huge arches, still stood, but now it was surrounded by squalid and half-ruined tenements in blocked-up streets of fallen masonry. He dined at the Travellers' Bungalow, the rest place kept for officers on missions. It had huge, high rooms, but many were in ruinous condition, with holes in the floors and ceilings. Burton went up to the roof to escape the heat. On a roof across the street were some young prostitutes, bareheaded, in short, loose chemises, playing ball; on another roof was a housewife preparing the bedding for the night. Nearby was a small group of young people sitting on a rug at prayer. An old white-bearded man was teaching them to "chaunt the Koran." "It is a very devotional spectacle, and the voices of the juniors are very soft and pleasing." In this relaxed atmosphere Burton was again a man in love with the East. He could rail at the gross, the absurd, the criminals and cheaters, the vanity of the people, but he also saw their humanity. Of the young learners he remarked:

> Not one of the party understands more than a parrot would of what is being thus gravely presented—but that is part of their education: some will learn; others will merely repeat by rote, no worse than the practitioners of any faith from Tokyo and Benares to Plymouth Rock. And here is a Hindu Scindee performing his ablutions stark naked.

One must not stare too much, Burton said—"see a pair of fiery eyes fiercely glaring at our inquiring countenances. . . . There is nothing this people hate so much as to be overlooked: it is considered an outrageous violation of their domestic castles."

On a ride to Killian Kot, a site near Tattah believed to have been a fortress built by Alexander the Great, he was infused by an overwhelming sense of the ancient, archaic religion—Hinduism: "Almost every celebrated place in Scinde still displays distinct signs of original Hinduism." He found it even in the Mekli (Mecca-like) hills among a six-square-mile area, with the tombs of some million Muslim saints, where there were "some places of Hindu pilgrimage: certain upright stones stained with vermillion, and decked with huge garlands of withered flowers, upon the margin of a small deep tank. . . ." These were *lingas*, the sign of the great god Śiva, and the tank was the representation of the vulva of the Great Mother, Śakti. Then he was off on further exploration. He was disgusted by the dirt—worse than native dirt ("Tattah is a mass of filth") was English dirt.

> You could scarcely mistake the place, even were I not to point it out. Look at the thousand fragments of black bottles, in these regions the unmistakable token of the white man's presence, and we will not wonder at a cut hoof.

He was constantly annoyed that the generals were not concerned to secure the good health of their troops. At Karachi, "within a few hundred yards of the cantonment, the corpses of fifty camels are allowed to lie and fester, and feed the jackalls, and poison the air, as if a little more death were really wanting." Hyderabad had a "miasma-breeding pool close to the walls. How to impress upon this Anglo-Indian mind the paramount importance of drainage and cleanliness? . . . Were I to command a station, no Dutch village . . . should be more scrupulously, more priggishly clean."

He had equally firm opinions about the people. He liked the Baluchis and the hill tribes but thought "the Scindian is constitutionally a paltroon. . . . They deceive because they fear to trust; they lie because truth is not to be told with impunity or without an object." He had a special and vitriolic dislike of a certain Hari Chand, a Hindu, who must have caused him more than an unusual amount of trouble. The aide-de-camp to the "foxy" amīr Ībrāhim Khān, Hari Chand appears several times in the Sind books. He was

> a portly, pulpy Hindoo, the very type of his unamiable race, with a catlike gait, a bow of exquisite finish, a habit of sweetly smiling under every emotion, whether they produce a bribe or a kick; a softly murmuring voice, with a tendency to sinking; and a glance which seldom matches yours, and when it does, seems not to enjoy the meeting. How timidly he appears at the door! How deferential he slides in, salams, looks deprecating, and at last is induced to sit down! Might he not be considered a novel kind of automaton, into which you transfer your mind and thoughts—a curious piece of human mechanism in the shape of a creature endowed with all things but a self.

But "you would start could you read his thoughts at the very moment you are forming such opinions of him." The rascally Hari Chand, Burton explains, likes to boast that an English-woman is "desperately enamoured of him." This, Burton adds, he says to himself, will irritate the fool white man beyond mea-sure.

> Envy, hate and malice are the seeds which the Oriental loves to scatter about as he passes over life's path—not for sheer diabolicality, but with the instinct of cunning weakness.

Burton had arrived in Ībrāhim Khān's court in company with some other officers. After boasting of his own conquest, Hari Chand informed his visitors that his master, the Mīr, had been to Hyderabad, where he drank two sahibs under the table and made love to every white woman in the place. "Hari Chand is determined to excite our ghairat, or jealousy, by perpetually hammering at it." But later Burton may have owed Hari Chand his thanks, for it was the pulpy aide-de-camp who secured the services of "a lady of pretty name, Mahtab—the Moonbeam" for a nautch, where Burton met her younger sister, Nūr Jān, and took her as his mistress.

Though he found the Sindhi men, both Hindu and Muslim,

obsequious, overbearing, and dishonest, Burton had a different view of the women. Indeed, he liked women in general, whatever the race or color, and wrote that he rejected the theory that beauty is subjective, that, for example, the blackest of the black in a race with the flattest nose would be the model of beauty only for the men of her own race. "My experience is distinctly the reverse: wherever in the four quarters of the world, I saw a pretty woman she was generally admired." And so he admired the Sindhi women, even to their skill at picking up objects with their toes. Their skin appealed to him: he had great praise for Indian cosmetics and the beneficial effects they had upon a woman's skin, as opposed to European unguents. He approved of the Oriental use of depilatories, not then common in Europe, and stated that because the Eastern woman wore no stockings or tight undergarments she was free from "callousities and other complaints."* And how could any man resist the beauty of the Sindhian woman?

> Her eyes are large and full of fire, black and white as an onyx-stone, of almond shape, with long drooping lashes, undeniably beautiful. . . . The nose is straight and the thin nostrils are delicately turned.

He was troubled by the general corpulence of both men and women in the East, where, he remarked, "beauty, male and female, goes by hundred-weights. . . . Thinness is considered not only a personal defect, but also a sign of poverty." People would ask Burton if he hadn't had enough to eat. "You see now the reason for my adopting the Arab costume," he wrote. "Arabs are allowed on sufferance to be thin without being hungry."

---

* Burton complained frequently about the "unhealthy" and confining undergarments of European women. In nineteenth-century England it was common among the well-to-do classes to enclose girls as young as four in tight-fitting whalebone or steel canvas corsets so they would develop hourglass figures as they grew, a practice that not only affected their intestines and skeletal structure but their general health as well.

The children entranced him. "In few parts of the world do you see prettier children than those of the higher classes in Scinde." He thought that the children, in simple shifts and skullcaps and a waist shawl with a tiny dagger, contrasted "most advantageously" with the "dancing-dog costumes" in which English women dressed their own children. Moreover, "as a boy he is a little man, and his sister in the harem is a little woman."

But he had no illusions, however, about the people he was traveling among. Those beautiful, well-mannered children would grow up to be pulpy Hari Chands and foxy Ībrāhim Khāns.

> The native of India, and the adjacent parts of Central Asia, parcels out his brethren into two great bodies—knaves and fools; and what is wiser still, he acts upon the conviction that they are such. The division, you must own, is remarkable for a pregnant simplicity, and eminent adaptation for practical purposes.

Unfortunately, his own people fell into the category of fools, and Burton's many strictures on the subject served not to educate but to annoy. He complained over and over again that the English failed to understand how the natives thought. The matter of punishments was a prime subject, for Napier and his officers tried to make punishment humane, not cruel, and the result was that they were ineffective.

> How contemptible they must appear to the ferocious barbarians that encurred them. The Affghan is detected stealing; he expects to have his right hand chopped off: we lodge him for a few months in what he considers luxurious retreat, where he can eat, drink, doze, smoke his pipe, and abuse the Frank [the foreigner] in plenary animal satisfaction.

And the acts of the English toward their so-called allies and friends also infuriated and distressed him. What happened to the amīrs in Sind who sided with the English? he asked.

> Tortures and death await the traitors, who, after we left, remained in their native country, and all the miseries of exile, poverty and

neglect, pressed heavily upon those that followed our steps, have, I fear, done much to disperse throughout India a most pernicious suspicion that the English are not staunch friends: that they will use a man when they want him, and are ready to cast him off, heedless as to what becomes of him.

Sometime during his first or second year in Sind, Burton took advantage of a popular Shī'a custom, temporary marriage. In Goa he mentions a certain young English officer—himself—who is adept at passing himself off among the natives.

> Lieut. ----, of the --- Rgt. was a very clever gentleman, who knew everything. He could talk to each man of a multitude in his own language, and all of them would appear equally surprised by, and delighted with him. Besides, his faith was every man's faith.
>
> He chaunted the Koran, and the circumcised dogs considered him a kind of saint. The Hindoos respected him, because he always ate his beef in secret, spoke religiously of the cow, and had a devil (i.e., some heathen image) in an inner room. At Cochin [where there was a very ancient colony of Jews] he went to the Jewish place of worship, and read a large book, just like a priest. . . .

Most significant is a detail previously overlooked: "In a certain Mussulmanee country he married a girl, and divorced her a week afterward."

At the time that Burton wrote Goa, the only "Mussulmanee" country he had lived in was Sind. A temporary marriage was known as mut'a. It was a legal marriage, performed before witnesses, the time for which is contracted for and agreed upon in advance. Mut'a was a survival of early Arab custom, at first allowed by Muḥammad but afterward prohibited. The Shī'as, however, still consider mut'a perfectly legal, finding sanction for it not only in their version of sacred Tradition but also in the Qur'ān. Burton gave his mut'a but a bare mention and went on to other affairs. One of the most serious was that involving a Persian woman, about whom there is much mystery.

The woman in question is known in various biographies as

"The Persian Girl." Burton mentions her rather early in *The Unhappy Valley* and again in *Scind Revisited*. As with much in Burton's early years in India, the affair is shrouded in ambiguity. His own account makes the relationship only a brief encounter that failed even a face-to-face conversation, but the Burton and Stisted families, according to Georgiana Stisted, had a different tradition. On a mission in the desert, possibly in Baluchistan, Burton encountered a family of Persians encamped nearby, an "array of striped tents . . . scattered boxes, neglected bags, and heaps of camel litters, in whose glaring shade repose some dozens of long-bearded individuals, with huge conical caps of lamb's wool, fierce eyes, thick beards, loud voices, and a terrible habit of profane swearing." He added, "They are Persians, escorting one of the prettiest girls ever seen to her father's house, near Kurrachee."

Burton called to a slave boy from the caravan and questioned him. The boy told him, when asked about his employment, "I serve the Beebee [lady], in the house of the great Sardar, A•••a Khan."

"A•••a" is clearly Burton's early spelling of "Ahgha"—the sardār or nobleman was none other than the Āghā Khān Maḥallātī. The young woman was possibly one of his daughters, or at least a member of the Prince's extended family—Burton was about to fall in love with a noblewoman of the Isma'īlī royal family. After bribing the boy with a rupee, Burton sat down to write the Beebee a letter in the most lush phrases—"the rose-bud of my heart . . . the fine linen of my soul." He told the young woman that "woe is me! the garden lacketh its songster, and the simooms of desire have dispersed the frail mists of hope," and other such flowering (and rather empty but poetic) phrases.

He finally finished his letter—it was on bright yellow paper —and sealed it with yellow wax and sent it to the Beebee with the boy.

Eventually, the slave returned with a message from the lady. Did he have any Ferengistan (foreign) medicines? There was not a word about a meeting. Burton brewed up a mixture of coarse gin and powdered white sugar, simmered it over a slow fire, flavoring it with "an idea of Eau de Cologne," and turned out "as dainty a dram, sweet and strong, as any liquor-loving oriental queen could desire." Peeping through his tent flap, Burton could see the lady.

> Is she not a charming girl, with features carved in marble, like a Greek's, the noble, thoughtful, Italian brown eyes deep and lustrous, as an Andalusian's, and the airy, graceful kind of figure with which Muhammad, according to our poets, peopled his man's paradise?

In his own version of the story Burton was rejected without meeting the Persian woman. Her "grim" guardian entered her tent, but Burton was still hopeful.

> The fair one comes forth muffled and wrapped; the beast, her dromedary, kneels, she mounts, turning her latticed face toward us; I hear a tiny giggle; she whispers a word in the ear of the slave girl that sits besides her; the auditor also laughs; they draw the little curtains; the camels start—

That, in Burton's account, is the end of the Persian girl. Georgiana Stisted, drawing upon family tradition received from her mother, has preserved a more romantic—and tragic—version. Miss Stisted was convinced that there was a real and deeply rooted relationship that ended unhappily. "Even in Burton's own family," she wrote, "only his sister knew of his passionate and ill-fated attachment in Sind, a love which occupied a unique place in his life."

> During one of his romantic rambles in the countryside . . . he met a beautiful Persian girl of high descent, with whom he had been able to converse by means of his disguise. Her personal charms, her lovely language, the single-hearted devotion of one of those noble natures which may be found even amongst orientals [!], inspired him with a feeling little short of idolatry. The affectionate young soldier-student, separated by thousands of miles from kith and kin, expended

the full force of his warm heart and fervid imagination upon his lustrous-eyed, ebon-haired darling; never had he so loved before, and never did he love again.* She worshipped him in return: but such rapture was not to last. He would have married her and brought her home to his family, for she was as good as she was beautiful, had not the fell foe that lurks in ambush to strike or divide when for a while we dare to be happy, snatched her from him in the flower of her youth, and the brightest hours of their joy-dream, her untimely end proved a bitter and enduring sorrow. . . .

No matter what romantic notions his niece had in her head, Burton would not have had an easy time with his fellow English if he had brought a Persian wife home. "Her untimely end" was taken to mean that the girl was killed rather than let go to Burton, a not uncommon event in the Orient when a woman —property—has in some way been "damaged," as the term is, by someone outside the community. The murder of a woman— a wife, a sister, a mother, or a daughter—for a sexual trespass was a commonplace in Sind, as elsewhere in India and the Orient. Eastwick wrote that it was "the cruel Baluch custom" to put women to death for the bare suspicion of unfaithfulness. "Women were constantly found hanged, having ostensibly made away with themselves." After Napier conquered Sind, wrote Burton, "he issued an order promising to hang anyone who committed this species of legal murder." But "any man who endured his wife's or mother's adultery was tabooed by society and became a laughing-stock and a disgrace to family and friends." Napier's solution was to black the offender's face, shave her head, and lead her seated backwards on an ass through the bazaars, to be pelted and hooted.

It was tragic that Burton and the woman attempted to defy custom, for both were aware of the implications and knew they were flouting a very rigid social code. She did not fade easily from Burton's memory. He mentioned the affair both in *The*

---

* This snide remark is probably aimed at Isabel Burton.

Unhappy Valley and also years later, in a more polished form, in *Scind Revisited*, and earlier than any of his Sind books, in an unpublished poem that speaks of the death of a woman in India. She had been killed by poison, and the verses tell how the author of the poem in turn killed her murderer, followed by the melancholy scene of her burial. The woman has been taken to be Burton's Persian love. A few lines describe their passion:

> the rounded form of her youthful charms
> heaved in my encircling arms.

But then—

> Little I thought the hand of death
> So soon would stay that fragrant breath . . .
> Or that soft warm hand, that glorious head
> Be pillowed on the grave's cold stone
> Leaving my hapless self to tread
> Life's weary ways alone . . .
> Adieu once more fond heart and true
> My first my only love adieu
> The tortures of the poisoned bowl
> Cast the gloom of death around my soul . . .
> Spirit of my own Shireen Fate heard my vow
> Neer was a maid so fair so loved so lost so 'venged as thou.

The poem, which gives a very strong basis for the Stisted version, was found in a notebook that dates back to Burton's days in India. The paper is watermarked 1847, and the handwriting corresponds to other pieces by Burton known to have been written in the same period. (His later handwriting changed into near illegibility.) Consequently, the poem would have had to have been composed, or at least transcribed, about that time, though it may have been drafted earlier and later copied into the notebook, which contains other material from the Sind years.

Despite some poetic license, the poem appears to be autobiographical. The woman in it was killed presumably for having violated the accepted strict social code, which dictates no sexual relationships, even in marriage, outside communal boundaries except in those rare dynastic alliances of profit for both parties. Burton certainly could add nothing to the stature of the Isma'īlī royal family, and so his love for the woman was illicit and unwelcome. And having loved her and seen her sacrificed for profaning the code, he had to avenge her murder. This is where poetic license enters: there is no way in which Burton's phrase "so 'venged as thou" can be corroborated.

A final word about the tragic affair was Miss Stisted's:

> Years after when he [Burton] told the story, his sister perceived with ready intuition that he could hardly bear to speak of that awful parting, even the gentlest sympathy hurt like a touch on an open wound. From the day of the death of his best beloved he became subject to fits of melancholy, and it seems as if the conception of his fine, but pessimistic poem, the "Kasidah," dated from the great grief of his life.

There is another woman somewhere during these Sindhi years whom Burton, in a very obscure work entitled *Stone Talk*, called a "goddess" and described as a "Pariah's widow," which meant she was a member of the lowest of all Hindu castes and, as a widow, was even more of an outcast. *Stone Talk* was not published until 1865, but Burton could still recall the charms of his paramour.

> I loved—yes, I! Ah, let me tell
> The fatal charms by which I fell!
> Her form the tam'risk's waving shoot,
> Her breast the cocoa's youngling fruit;
>
> Her eyes were jetty, jet her hair,
> O'ershadowing face like lotus fair;
> Her lips were rubies, guarding flowers
> Of jasmine dewed with vernal showers.

And that is all that is known of still another of Burton's many loves in India.

From time to time Burton served, as did the other young officers, at courts-martial, but since he was the only man in the 18th Bombay Native Infantry who knew the native tongues, he got more than his fair share of work. Who was being court-martialed for what offenses is not known, though years later, in the famous "Terminal Essay" in Volume X of the *Nights* Burton mentions one case that passed before him. A sepoy, a Brāhmin, had a sexual relationship with a low-caste soldier, a pariah. The sepoy finally killed the other man. The problem was not one of passion, of homosexual jealousy, of guilt or shame or some other Western abomination, but of caste, and it was this fact that attracted Burton's interest.

> The dirty heap of mud-and-mat hovels which represented the adjacent native village, could not supply a single woman; yet only one case of pederasty came to light and that after a tragic fashion some years afterwards. A young Brahmin had connection with a soldier comrade of low caste and this had continued till, in an unhappy hour, the Pariah patient ventured to become the agent. The latter, in Arabic, Al-Fa'il = the "doer," is not an object of contempt like Al-Maful = the "done"; and the high-caste sepoy stung by remorse and revengeful loaded his musket and deliberately shot his paramour. He was hanged by court martial at Hyderabad and, when his last wishes were asked, he begged to be suspended by the feet, the idea being that his soul, polluted by exiting "below the waist," would be doomed to endless transmigrations through the lowest forms of life.

But after much activity there would be periods in which nothing happened. There would be no courts-martial, no trips into the countryside; there was, in fact, nothing to do but to survive, when the heat set in more fiercely and the sun burned, as one visitor complained, as if there were two suns together. The generals could plan no campaigns, and the Āghā Khān gave up even his race horses. What was an officer to do when he was not egging on the Isma'īlīs to risk all in an attempt to invade Kerman except sit under his worktable with a wet cloth over it and write, write, and write some more, scribbling down notes that few others could have taken in so short a time in this so desolate wilderness. On and on he wrote, like some lunatic trying to fend off collapse by sheer attention to minutiae, to details. He made lists of tribes and clans, of words, fragments of tongues scraped up in this vast dustbin of empire. He noted water tables and water levels, the shifting course of the Indus (But—"The geography and history of the province in ancient ages are equally obscure"), the system of taxation, the types of education; he made notes on demonology, magic and alchemy, the Book of Fate, the epics (in four languages—Belochi, Jataki, Persian, and Sindhi), "Extracts from Tales of Sasui and Punhu, Marui and Umrah the Sumrah," which tell of Sindhi saints and warriors of other ages, and then he wrote another chapter: "The same subject continued." Everywhere he dove into languages, dialects, derivations, languages that piled up in him as if he were some great multilayered polyglot walking dictionary, and that would pour out of him in the future, as if he, Richard Francis Burton, alone were the source of the Ur-tongue, primordial, agglutinative, and inflected to seventeen cases. And he tried to squeeze into a few pages, a few paragraphs about everyone, everything, as if no future investigator would ever appear to record what he missed. Here were saints, castes, the outcast tribes, prostitutes, gymnastic exercises and games, religious mendicants, "The Amil Class: its Origins, Office, and Character for Fraudulence," funeral obsequies, crimes and their punishment. The mind staggers at the sheer immensity of his curiosity and knowledge.

But he was unhappy. He despised Sind—"The Unhappy Valley" had many meanings for him—so much so that he took up Marathi, the major language of the Bombay Presidency, in hopes of getting transferred back to peninsula India, with its better living conditions. He absorbed enough Marathi to be able to get leave to go to Bombay in October for the fall examinations, which, as expected, he passed with honors. Back in Sind, he found he was there to stay, having been appointed to serve immediately on the General Staff under Napier, and he buckled down to making the best of it. During this boiling, dusty year he said he came to have "Persian at my fingers' ends, sufficient Arabic to read, write and converse fluently, and a superficial knowledge of that dialect of Punjaubee which is spoken in the wilder parts of the province." He had also picked up a working knowledge of Sindhi, though at first, after an initial bout with it, he had rejected it; finally in *Sindh*, he was able to give as concise and appreciative a summary of the tongue as anyone could wish in twenty-one pages, with various other references, a most impressive example of his powers of concentration.

Burton's reference to picking up Punjabi as "spoken in the wilder parts of the province" meant that not only had he gone into the wild and rough hills west of the Indus plain on secret missions but also that he had penetrated the ferocious back country of Ranjīt Singh's former kingdom, where a new generation of Sikh leaders was busily planning anti-British activities of a most hostile nature. So it seems that Burton was ranging far and wide and, from the brief references that continually surface in his writings, often under cover.

Exactly when Napier took Burton into his immediate circle of trustworthy officers who bore the brunt of civilizing western India is one of those details no one can agree on. It was probably Scott who told the General about Burton's qualifications. Stisted writes that "the old Commander-in-Chief like most clever men, admired genius in others, and kept his eye on his promising young soldier," and at the end of the first year in Sind posted him to the Sind Survey. Burton writes from a somewhat different point of view. It is a known fact, he said in the *Life*, that "a Staff appointment has the general effect of doing away with one's bad opinion of any place whatever. So when the Governor of Sind was persuaded to give me the temporary appointment of Assistant in the Survey, I began to look with interest on the desolation around me."

> The country was a new one, so was its population, so was their language. My new duties compelled me to spend the cold season in wandering over the districts levelling the beds of canals, and making preparatory sketches for a grand survey. I was thrown so entirely amongst the people as to depend on them for society; and the dignity, not to mention the increased allowance, of a Staff officer, enabled me to collect a fair stock of books, and to gather around me those who could make them of any use.

It would now appear that Burton was given his head and a free hand by Napier by being appointed to the Survey, which, for most of the time, was but a façade for his work in the Great Game. He could pass himself off as a mere officer of no special importance if he wished, as when he went to pay formal compliments to Ībrāhim Khān and Hari Chand, or he could pose as a native servant in Scott's entourage and slip out of the encampment to visit the native quarters, or he could drop out completely from the Survey and wander away into the countryside, into territory not only uncharted but hostile, where he could match nerve and wit against Baluchis, Sindhis, and Punjabis. Thus, after roundly condemning Sind, the people and their tongue, he was sent out to face all. On December 1, 1844, Burton, with a party of six camels—he mentions the number of camels but not the number of officers and men, if any (he may have been alone)—set out for the Phuleli and Guni rivers.

Riding northward with his camels, he came across village after village of people known as Jats, and with his usual pedantic passion for accuracy, he had to make it clear that there were not simply "Jats" but that "under the name of Jat no less than four races are involved."

Then he made an important find:

It appears probable, from the appearance and other peculiarities of the race, that the Jats are connected by consanguinity with that peculiar race, the Gypsies. *

The "curious expression" he saw in the eyes of the Jats was the so-called "Gypsy eye" that intrigued Burton whenever he wrote about the Gypsies, for he, too, was said over and over again to have the same eye.

The Asiatic Gypsy has also that peculiar indescribable appearance and expression of eye, which is so strongly developed in the Roma [Gypsies] of Morocco and Moorish Spain [and he quotes an unnamed source]: "a feature which, like the brand on the forehead of the first murderer stamps this marked race over the whole globe, and when once observed is never forgotten. The 'Evil Eye' is not the least of the powers with which this people is superstitiously invested."

When he met Gypsies later in Syria, Burton was again drawn to the eye.

The long, coarse, lank hair, with the duck-tail under curl, the brown-white eyes, whose peculiar glance is never to be mistaken, the prominent Tartar-like cheekbones, and the irregular-shaped mouths, suggested Hindu origin and physiognomy.

The Spanish Gypsies

preserve the characteristic eye. The form is perfect, and it has an especial look to which is attributed the power of engendering grandes passions—one of the privileges of the eye. I have often remarked its fixity and brilliance, which flashes like phosphoric light, the gleam which in some eyes denotes madness. I have also noted the "far-off" look which seems to gaze at something beyond you, and the alternation from the fixed stare to a glazing or filming over of the pupil.

* Burton was adamant that the word be spelled Gypsy, not Gipsy, and that it be pronounced with a hard G.

After Burton's death, *The Gypsy Lore Journal* of January 1891, in its obituary, remarked about

> the singular idiosyncrasy which his friends have often remarked—the peculiarity of his eyes. "When it (the eye) looks at you," said one who knows him well, "it looks through you, and then, glazing over, seems to see something behind you. Richard Burton is the only man (not a Gypsy) with that peculiarity. . . ."

Though he could record the universally bad opinion of the Jats ("Throughout the eastern parts of Central Asia, the name Jat is synonymous with thief and scoundrel . . . occupying a low place in the scale of creation"), Burton was not critical of them, as he was, for example, of most Orientals. In fact, he empathized to some extent with their presently low position: once a ruling class, "now not a single descendant possesses anything like wealth or rank."

Scott had a Jat in his service, "and the rough old man's peculiarities afforded us abundant diversions." But Burton's connection with the Jats was not merely through a peculiar old man. Apparently he cut loose from Scott and the Survey team and for a time became a Jat himself, joining the Jat work gangs cleaning and digging canals for Napier. He was half-scornful, half-distressed by the manner in which the work was done. The people were poor—"in the winter they will do anything to save themselves from semi-starvation." The head man lay drunk under a sheet, while those who were not squatting torpidly on their haunches

> lazily scrape up the cake with dwarf hoes. . . . Every half hour they all smoke, and at a certain time each man takes something which he has been dreaming about all morning. . . . Without constant attention the canals will not be full again, and upstream some rascally landowner will block off the canal so as to monopolize the water for his Persian wheel.

Perhaps Burton's slight note of antagonism toward these unfortunate people came from the fact that this particular winter was for the most part spent alone and he was most conscious of the arrival of Christmas. It was a miserable, lonely existence, "riding in heathen garb, spear in hand, over a scorched plain, or down a sandy canal, burned by the sun upon the chills of morning, and with a breakfast in posse not in esse." His mind played a strange trick: He heard the ringing of church bells—it was Christmas, he realized. The bells were "the twanging of some over-excited nerve—the mere revival of things obsolete and forgotten." The sun set, and darkness fell upon him "like a shroud." In a lonely, ill-lit tent, dinner was "a boiled barn-door, with a biftek of goat." He lay awake for hours, rolling restlessly from side to side as each new thought left a sting in him. "In a moment you are severed from yourself. . . . Again you hear the dead familiar voices of family and friends ringing upon the typanum of your soul. . . . You sink back, mournfully acknowledging that you are and must be where you are."

During this trek to the north he found time to engage in some falconry, and out of this sport came one of his minor works, *Falconry in the Valley of the Indus.* What was more important than the subject was the postscript to the book, which gives one of the few pictures by Burton of the way in which he lived and worked among the natives. The first difficulty, he said, "was to pass for an Oriental, and this was as necessary as it was difficult."

The European official in India seldom, if ever, sees anything in its real light, so dense is the veil which the fearfulness, the duplicity, the prejudice and the superstitions of the natives hang before his eyes. . . .

After trying several characters, the easiest to be assumed was, I found, that of a half Arab, half Iranian, such as may be met with in thousands along the northern shore of the Persian gulf. The Scindians would have detected in a moment the difference between my articulation and their own, had I attempted to speak their vernacular dialect, but they attributed the accent to my strange country, as naturally as a home-bred Englishman would account for the bad pronunciation of a foreigner calling himself partly Spanish, partly

Portuguese. Besides, I knew the countries along the Gulf by heart from books, I had a fair knowledge of the Shieh form of worship prevalent in Persia, and my poor Moonshee [Mirza Muhammad Hosayn] was generally at hand to support me in times of difficulty. . . .

His hair fell to his shoulders in the approved Shī'a manner, he had a long beard, and his face and hands, arms and the soles of his feet, were stained with a thin coat of henna. He called himself Mirza Abdullah and claimed to be from Bushire, an important trading post on the northern edge of the Persian Gulf. He was a "Bazzaz," a vendor of fine linen, calicoes, and muslins.

Such chapmen are sometimes admitted to display their wares even in the sacred harem by "fast" and fashionable dames;—and he had a little pack of *bijouterie* and *virtù* reserved for emergencies.

However, wrote Burton, he displayed his stock only when absolutely necessary. "Generally he contented himself with alluding to it on all possible occasions, boasting largely of his traffic, and asking a thousand questions concerning the state of the market." Thus, Burton could enter houses even if the master objected and even penetrate the harems, where, while showing his stock, he could pick up the latest gossip for Napier. He claimed that several fathers offered him their daughters in marriage and he "won, or had to think he won, a few hearts; for he came as a rich man and he stayed with dignity, and he departed exacting all the honors."

When he entered a strange town, he would engage a house in or near the bazaar.

Now and then he rented a shop and furnished it with clammy dates, viscid molasses, tobacco, ginger, rancid oil and strong-smelling sweetmeats; and wonderful tales Fame told about these establishments.

He gave the best weight for the money to the ladies—"particularly the pretty ones"—and when he wasn't acting as a tradesman, he became a dervish.

Sometimes the Mirza passed the evening in a mosque listening to the ragged students who, stretched out at full length with their stomachs on the dusty floor, and their arms supporting their heads, mumbled out Arabic from the thumbed, soiled and tattered pages of theology upon which a dim oil light shed its scanty ray, or he sat debating the niceties of faith with the long-bearded, shaven-pated, blear-eyed and stolid-faced *genius loci*, the Mullah. At other times, when in a merrier mood, he entered uninvited the first door, whence issued the sounds of music and the dance;—a clean turban and a polite bow are the best "tickets for soup" the East knows. Or he played chess with some native friends, or he consorted with the hemp-drinkers and opium eaters in the estaminets, or he visited the Mrs. Gadabouts and Go-betweens who make matches amongst the Faithful and gathered from them a precious budget of private histories and domestic scandal.

Burton seems to have been a confirmed addict, not only of hemp or *cannabis indica* but of opium, taking both drugs in all their many forms. "And of course the more habituated a man becomes to the use of drugs, the more pleasurable he finds the excitement it produces," he wrote in *Scinde; or, the Unhappy Valley*. "Opium taken in moderation is not a whit more injurious to a man than alcohol and brandied wine," he said from the depths of his personal knowledge. "And for some it seems to act beneficially, if the doses are regular, not increased," as it was by those addicts who enjoyed "smoking themselves screwed." With bhang, a mixture of *cannabis* and milk, "your thoughts become wild and incoherent, your fancy runs frantic," and he quotes a nonsense verse written on a wall.

The teeth of the mountain were set on edge by the eating of betel Which caused the sea to grin at the beard of the sky.

Unfortunately the details of this dramatic life in the Great Game were to be denied his readers. More surfaces about drugs and prostitutes than about dangerous escapades or simple espionage. Said Burton continuing in the third person, "What scenes he saw! What adventures he went through! But who would believe, even if he ventured to detail them?" Only a vague outline remains of his life in the back country, the towns and villages and the bazaars, and what he experienced is now lost.

12

The Secret Path

Burton's twenty-fourth birthday, March 19, 1845, was passed in the field. In April he returned to Karachi, where his corps was now stationed. A new phase of his life began, and for a short period he spent more time with his fellow officers, though the Persians, Mirza 'Alī Akhbar and Mirza Daúd, as well as the omnipresent Mirza Muḥammad Ḥosayn were his regular companions.

"Karachi was, for India, not a dull place in those days," he said. There was first a lot of office work—"daily work of planning and mapping the surveys to be carried out in the cold season, and practising latitudes and longitudes till my right eye became comparatively short-sighted." He was able to have his own bungalow built, and he had his mess in the survey compound with five other officers—"local society pronounced us all mad," though he does not say why, and adds, without explanation, "I cannot see that we were more whimsical than our neighbors."

This association with his fellow English did not last long. Burton preferred the Persians. Either he was foolish, had no regard for the opinions of possible enemies among the other officers, or he was under Napier's instructions. "My life became much mixed up with these gentlemen, and my brother officers [again] fell to calling me the 'White Nigger.' " Unfortunately, 'Alī Akhbar's troubles with Bombay over his finances had by now come to a crisis. He was charged with having acquired property worth a hundred thousand rupees, which he was found to have sent to an agent in Bombay from Sind in 1843. He claimed that the money came from a patrimony and the rest was trade—he produced affidavits so testifying—but it was against regulations for a government employee to have engaged in commerce while in service. Napier stood by his *munshī*, certain that the attacks on 'Alī Akhbar were one more example of Bombay's malice toward the army in Sind.

Napier soon had work for Burton other than mapping canals. With the assistance of Muḥammad Ḥosayn, Burton opened "on the sly" three shops in Karachi "where cloth, tobacco, and other small matters were sold exceedingly cheap to those who deserved them." Again, the gossip was passed on to Napier. Now something in another vein appeared. Napier was told, said Burton,

> that Karachi . . . supported no less than three lupanars or bordels, in which not women, but boys and eunuchs, the former demanding nearly a double price, lay for hire. . . . Being then the only British officer who could speak Sindi, I was asked indirectly to make enquiries and to report upon the subjects; and I undertook the task on express condition that my report should not be forwarded to the Bombay Government, from whom supporters of the Governor's policy could expect scant favor, justice, or mercy.

Napier had thought the brothels were corrupting his troops, white and native alike. In what frame of mind Burton took the assignment is not known. He was a skilled observer, and while some officers might merely have reported that the houses were indeed as rumored and were infecting the troops, Burton gave precise information. In the *Nights*, he described how boys were preferred over eunuchs because "the scrotum of the unmutilated boy could be used as a kind of bridle for directing the movements of the animal." Various of Burton's enemies, and some of his biographers, have taken for granted that he participated actively in the brothel life. There is no evidence one way or the other, and in later years, when he might have taken a "neutral" or a scholarly attitude, he was sarcastic and denigrating about "Le Vice," as he called it in the popular term of the Victorian age, and he used words and phrases like analist, pathic, abuse, the evil, pathological love, "a race of born pederasts," and anus beater. Homosexuality is forbidden in the Qur'ān, as Burton pointed out, and there were many instances of the most severe punishments for its practice, including death, but in Sind, Burton wrote, "Le Vice is looked upon almost as a peccadillo, and its name crops up in every jest book."

Napier immediately had the brothels destroyed and sent Burton off on other missions. The General wrote in his diary that he had improved public morality "by putting down the infamous beasts who, dressed as women, plied their trade in the Meers' time openly."

At this point one might wonder if Burton, with his denigratory remarks, might be dissembling over what had become an embarrassing and even painful experience, one that had been undertaken under orders but one that he may have made the most of. He had said he "passed away many an evening in the townlet and visited all the porneia and obtained the fullest details." Napier's conversation might be bawdy—"salty" was a popular term used to describe it—but at heart he was so straitlaced that if he thought Burton had any homosexual proclivities he would not have been likely to order him to investigate something he might have favored; it would have been easier to assign another officer. Certainly, if the brothels were catering to British troops and officers, it would not have been difficult to order someone else, native languages or no, to visit them and make a report. And certainly, after receiving Burton's report, Napier lost no confidence in him and continued to use him as an agent. But whatever had happened, Burton's enemies, of whom he had many, found they could use the episode against him, and he was shadowed the rest of his life by the rumor that he had participated actively in the Karachi brothels. In the *Nights* Burton wrote:

> . . . the Devil's brother [Napier] presently quitted Sind leaving in his office my unfortunate official [the report on the brothels], this found its way with sundry other reports to Bombay and produced the expected result. A friend in the Secretariat informed me that my summary dismissal from the service had been formally proposed by one of Sir Charles Napier's successors, whose decease compels me parcere sepulto.

But there is something amiss here. Burton's other reports from the field were apparently given to Napier verbally—at least no written versions of any have been turned up by various researchers—so why was this most sensitive subject committed to paper? But even this report, supposedly in the secret files, has not been found. Fawn Brodie, who has been among the most diligent to seek out the odd byways in Burton's life, searched hard and fast to find it. She writes: "The original of this report seems hopelessly lost," and gives the names of various officials in London, Bombay, Karachi, and Lahore who searched the old files at her request. So there is a mystery about why the matter of the Karachi brothels was written down, whereas other material concerning Burton's many missions was apparently given verbally to Napier. But in fact did Burton actually write out a report about the brothels? Is he trying to find some excuse for the troubles he encountered during his last years in India? Or is his memory at fault some forty years later, and he thinks he had written out a formal report, when he merely made notes, which were destroyed when no longer needed? Or did Napier himself write down Burton's verbal report and leave it in his files? Whatever the known facts, something is not quite right, and we are not likely ever to learn the truth.

Napier shortly ordered Burton off to Hyderabad in central Sind, to go in disguise with no connection at all with the English—there was a garrison outside the city—to a place known as Mohammad Khan ka Tanda.

By now the summer of 1845 was coming on, and the heat, after the usual rainless spring monsoon winds, was becoming unbearable. In the company of Mirza Muḥammad Ḥosayn, Burton wandered up the Indus, along the vast, dusty, sultry valley of tamarisk and camel thorn, where "the fierce rays of the sun, combine to render the atmosphere essentially insalubrious." Hyderabad lay on the Phuleli, a byway of the Indus, bringing some small charm to this otherwise unlovable town by flowing through "beautiful gardens of palm, mimosa, pomegranate, mango, and other trees," and this was the best Burton had to say of Hyderabad. The city was once the old capital of Sind, and though it had faded tragically, it was still an important center, especially for the Baluchi chieftains, who might reasonably be suspected of plotting against the English. When he arrived, Burton found Hyderabad "a squalid mass of ruins, with here and there a lofty brick house or a glittering minaret. . . ." Fever and ague racked the city.

Now quite at home as an Oriental, Burton found an excellent position in which to enjoy himself and at the same time gather information for Napier. Abandoning his role as a merchant, he took up the guise of a *mirza*, a scholar and student, whose "favorite school for study," he wrote in *Falconry*, "was the house of an elderly matron on the banks of the Fulailee River, about a mile from the Fort of Hyderabad." The matron was known as Khanum Jān, a common title applied to the madam of a brothel. She had as a companion her lover and pimp, an aging man known as Muḥammad Bakhsh. Khanum Jān's house, like most of the buildings in the old city, was, said Burton, "a mud edifice occupying one side of a square formed by tall, thin, crumbling mud walls." When the brothel was active—"The respectable matron's peculiar vanity was to lend a helping hand in all manner of affaires de coeur," wrote Burton coyly—"it often happened that Mirza Abdullah [himself] was turned out of the house to pass a few hours in the garden."

> There he sat upon his felt rug spread beneath a shadowy tamarind, with beds of sweet-smelling basil around him, his eyes roving over the broad river that coursed rapidly between its wooded banks and the groups gathered at the frequent ferries, whilst the soft strains of mysterious, philosophical transcendental Hafiz [the Persian poet] were sounded in his ears by the other Mirza, his companion Mohammed Hosayn—peace be unto him!

During this period Burton seemed fond of Ḥāfiẓ—or Muḥammad Ḥosayn was—and the poet's phrases sunk deep into his memory, deep enough so that in *The Kasîdah* he quoted quatrains either whole or paraphrased. Burton was very much influenced by Ḥāfiẓ, though he was not in the mainstream of Sufi religiosity, being, as Burton liked to call him, a "licentious Anacreon"— Anakreon was a Greek lyric poet of the sixth century B.C. noted for his "triple worship" of the Muse, Wine, and Love—"who disguised his grossness . . . under a garb of mystical double entendre." This was a later view; earlier, in *Sindh*, he spoke of Ḥāfiẓ in more favorable terms, numbering him among a handful of "the most striking specimens" found in the Sufi mystics, though they too were "Anacreontic poets."

Sufism seems to have become Burton's major preoccupation during this period, and the chapter he wrote about it in *Sindh* is a remarkable presentation at a time when Westerners knew virtually nothing of the discipline—Burton was the first European to publish knowledgeable and accurate material about Sufism in the popular press. His writings show not the outsider's casual glance but the insider's hard-won knowledge and training, gained first under the tutelage of Mirza Muḥammad Ḥosayn, and then, after the Mirza returned to Persia, under an Afghan, an old *munshī* whom he did not name, then an Abyssinian, and finally another *munshī*, either a second Persian or perhaps an Arab. "A system of belief such as Tasawwuf," wrote Burton, using the term preferred by many Sufis, which attracts the best minds in Islam, "must be supposed to possess some intrinsic value."

> The merit of Tasawwuf [Sufism], is its beau ideal of goodness as connected with beauty, and universal charity and love as flowing from the source of all goodness. . . . The Koranic idea of the human soul or spirit, for instance, is similar to [the Christian]; but the Sufi, deducing the doctrine of the soul's immortality from its immateriality . . . and convinced by reason that nothing can be at once self-existent, immaterial, and unbounded by time except the Deity, concludes that the spirit of man is nothing but the breath, the particle of the Divine soul lent to mankind, the noblest of God's works.

Burton identified Sufism as the modern form of Gnosis, the secret knowledge passed down from the ancients, the Zoroastrians, the old Hindu yogis, the Platonists, and the Essenes, the followers of the Secret Path having continued "up to the present time, under diverse mystical appellations, with tenets modified by the ages in which they live. . . . They formed from the 'archetypes' of existence, a regular system of spiritual creation anterior to the material." However, he was not ready to divulge whatever secrets of Gnosis he may have learned, if any, for he seems to have bound himself by the precepts of *taqīya*, concealment and dissimulation, that he had learned from the Isma'īlīs.

By the late summer the heat had become unbearable. "The stagnation of atmosphere," wrote Burton, was "peculiarly distressing." The summer of central Sind lasts eight or nine months, with no break but an occasional cloudiness or a passing shower. Desert winds and dust storms build up in frequency and violence. It was now time to leave this pestilential hole and return to the cooling sea breezes of Karachi. Burton was able to express some pleasure with the summer.

Of all economical studies this course was the cheapest. For tobacco daily, for frequent draughts of milk, for hemp [hashish] occasionally, for the benefit of Khanum Jan's experience, for four months' lectures from Mohammed Bakhsh, and for sundry other little indulgences, the Mirza paid, it is calculated, the sum of six shillings. When he left Hyderabad, he gave a silver talisman to the dame, and a cloth coat to her protector: long may they live to wear them!

The next few months seem to have been ones of leisure and study, time with his friends and fighting his cock Bhujang. But suddenly and unexpectedly he was taken away from his indolent days. "The careless life broke up in November"—a crisis had arisen in the Survey Department and Burton was called upon to do his duty. So short was Napier of capable men that he could find only one, Burton, to send out in a new team under Scott in a concentrated effort to put the entire operation of clearing the canals, which had to be done every year, completely into British hands, for the General had come to the conclusion that the minor native officials who supervised the work did it "at a wild cheating rate, to which no check could be put." Scott protested the amount of work his small force was being assigned, for he had only ten British subalterns and twenty British and four Indian surveyors to do the same work that a hundred or more native officials had done previously. Also, few officers— Burton being the major exception—knew any Sindhi, and only Scott and two others were qualified engineers.

Burton and Scott set off on a three-month tour, their final destination the extreme western frontier where the Baloch tribesmen were "in their wildest state." There was no doubt that at this time the canals, not espionage, were Burton's primary duty. They rode up the banks of the Indus, then went eastward to Hyderabad, where the 18th Bombay Native Infantry was temporarily stationed; Burton had a "jolly week" with his regiment. He found that in the short time since he had left Hyderabad some unexpected competition was challenging Khanum Jān. "A new class has lately appeared," he reported in *Sindh*, "composed of women who are half respectable, half prostitute; they devote themselves to Europeans and the Sepoys. At Hyderabad the courtesans have complained that their occupation was gone, in consequence of the loose conduct of the married women."

Burton and Scott headed westward again, on a ride that was more uncomfortable than interesting. Sehwan, which was believed to have been a former campsite of Alexander the Great's, was "a hot, filthy, and most unwholesome place, remarkable for the rascality of its inhabitants . . . and the abundance of its beggars, devotees, and courtezans." Sehwan was among Burton's many baneful experiences.

> Everything in this place seems to hate us. Even the pet tiger, as he catches sight of our white faces, shakes off the purring little cats that amuse themselves by walking over his broad flanks, springs up, glaring at us with bloodthirsty eyes. . . .

The Burton children, in
a portrait from Wright

Burton and his sister,
Maria, in the portrait by
Jacquard, Boulogne,
about 1851

Lieutenant Burton's India

The India of Burton's period—
a time before massive
deforestation and exploitation
of the land—was lush,
romantic, exotic, with waving
palms and pipals and crumbling
castles and forts.

Nautch girls of the type that
served as Burton's mistresses in
Baroda and Sind. In the
background are their
attendants.

A Tantric initiate, surrounded by vampires and other evil spirits, drums on a human skull in the celebration of forbidden rites. The drawing is from Burton's *Vikram and the Vampire*. Burton spent much of his first year in India among the Tantrics, until he was transferred to Sind, with its Muslim environment.

A Qādiri Sufi, a member of the mystical brotherhood into which Burton was initiated in Sind. This is how he would have dressed on his journeys into the backcountry.

Burton about 1848, wearing the turban and robes of a half Arab, half Persian from Bushire. He had just returned from sick leave in Goa and was preparing for further undercover work.

Isabel Arundell, age seventeen, in an unfinished sketch, done before her family went to Boulogne

A rare photograph of Edward Burton, taken before the tragic year of 1857, when he gradually lost his mind and had to be confined to the Surrey County Lunatic Asylum

Burton in Arab dress, on the pilgrimage to Mecca

The Magic Mirror—actually a drawing usually sketched on a patient's hand—was a favorite device of Burton's for treating his neighbors' illnesses when he was practicing as a doctor in Cairo. The Arabic numerals in the sketch are

$$4 \quad 9 \quad 2$$
$$3 \quad 5 \quad 7$$
$$8 \quad 1 \quad 6$$

and add up to fifteen in any direction, including diagonally. The spot in the center is a drop of ink, in which the practitioner sees the patient's future.

The chemist's shop in a side street in Cairo—"a perfect example of Nilotic queerness"—where Burton studied Islam under the old shaykh Muhammad al-'Attār, the "Druggist"

The Gypsy dancers of Egypt, the Ghawázis, "whose personal beauty makes them dangerous." Burton got syphilis from the Ghawázis. He referred to them as practitioners of "Al-Nahl," the "Bee-dance," and also called them Walid Nahl.

In the Sufi *tarīqa*, or oratory, that Burton attended, the celebration of rites often went to extremes, including the use of fire and swords and the handling of snakes. Here the master of the chapter rides his horse over the faithful.

Like so many Westerners abroad, Burton could not resist leaving graffiti behind. Written on the wall of a mosque in al-Medina, this gives his Arabic name and says, "Abdullah, the servant of Allah, [A.H.] 1269."

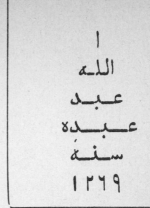

ا
الله
عبد
عبده
سنة
١٢٦٩

Burton in the pilgrim's costume, the *ihrām*, which consists of two six-foot-long pieces of cloth, one tied around the waist, the other tossed over the left shoulder. The female pilgrim wears conventual clothing, which must be clean. The straw "veil" is not supposed to touch the face.

Shortly after the pilgrimage to Mecca, Burton, in the company of three other officers, one of whom, Captain John Hanning Speke, was to be his traveling companion over the next several years, entered the coast of Somaliland. On the last day of the expedition, the officers were attacked by nomads. Here Speke, severely wounded in eleven places by Somali spears and knives, runs for his life.

Burton was to return to Africa many times after the Somaliland expedition.
This photograph (from Isabel Burton's *Life*) was taken during one of his
visits. *Left*: Both Burton and Speke relied heavily on the service of a former
slave, Sidi Bombay Mubarak (*seated*), who was the general factotum of the
two Nile expeditions and the man who held them together by sheer hard
work and great intelligence.

13

Searching for Camões

After the death of Ranjīt Singh in 1839, relations with the Sikhs, once friendly, started to disintegrate. The chieftains began to quarrel with each other, and lawlessness spread rapidly throughout the Punjab. Moreover, the barbarism practiced during Ranjīt Singh's time became even worse: "Princes and generals fell in quick succession and almost everyone of them was accompanied by his wives and concubines. Three women died with Maharaja Kharag Singh, five with Basant Singh, eleven with Kishori Singh, seventy-two with Mira Singh and 310 with Suchat Singh."

The single effective power in the Punjab by 1845 was the well-trained Sikh army, the Khalsa, numbering some 89,000 warriors and a formidable artillery. The Sikhs, with some justification, suspected the British of planning annexation of the Punjab. On December 11, 1845, a force of Sikhs crossed into British-held territory in the eastern Punjab. The British brought troops into position and on the seventeenth declared war.

In a series of artillery and infantry battles in the eastern Punjab both sides lost heavily. By the middle of February 1846, the British were able to force the Khalsa to meet at Lahore for a treaty. The Sikhs agreed both to limit the strength of their army and to pay indemnities. An amended treaty with the Sikh leaders in December made the English the true rulers of the Punjab. But the Sikhs were not happy with their new masters, and the *sardārs*, the noblemen, continued to agitate for action.

Even before the first move by the Sikhs, the bazaars, as Burton wrote, were rife with reports of coming war. "The news made me wild to go." He persuaded Scott, much against the Major's wishes, to release him for active duty. Finally, after fighting through bureaucratic red tape, Burton and other officers eager for action were released and allowed to join their regiments. The 18th Bombay Native Infantry, with Burton ready to fight, marched off for war on February 23, 1846. They went up the Indus Valley and entered Bahawalpur, once the center of a Gypsy kingdom and in Burton's time the capital of the largest of the Punjabi states. Here they got the "heart-chilling order to retire and march home," and after a few weeks of slogging through the deserts, Burton and his regiment were back in the old quarters in Mohammad Khan ka Tanda on the Phuleli. "But our physical trials and mental disappointments had soured our tempers, and domestic disturbances began," Burton said. He got into rows with his colonel, Henry Corsellis, an India-born Englishman. "Neither his colour nor his temper were in his favour. The wars began on a small matter." One evening at mess Burton had been amusing his fellow officers by improvising doggerel rhymes on their names. He knew Corsellis was touchy and passed him over, but the colonel demanded his verse. "Very well," said Burton, "I will write your epitaph."

> Here lieth the body of Colonel Corsellis;
> The rest of the fellow, I fancy, in hell is.

Corsellis was annoyed, and he and Burton began to quarrel.

I shall say no more upon the subject; it is, perhaps, the part of my life upon which my mind dwells with least satisfaction. . . . And to add to my regimental troubles, there were not a few domestic disagreeables, especially complications, with a young person named Nur Jan.

She was the young woman Burton had met at the Moonbeam's nautch in Larkana. Nūr Jān was a moody and temperamental person. At one point the police came to the house, for what reason Burton did not say—perhaps their fights had aroused the neighbors, or he may have been beating her—it was not, however, the kind of incident that would have been of concern to neighbors—or he was under suspicion as a foreigner. Whatever the cause, when the police arrived, Burton hid his mistress under a pile of straw until they left.

Living with Burton at the time—he seems to have avoided going back to Scott's survey team—was an old Afghan *munshī*, unfortunately not named. Many Afghans had settled about Hyderabad and northern Sind, and Burton liked them, remarking that "they are a large and uncommonly handsome race of people. . . . The women are not inferior to the men in personal appearance, and display all the fondness for, and boldness in, carrying on intrigues that characterize them in their native land."

The Afghan was serving as his *munshī* and religious instructor. He and Burton were reading a famous Afghan mystical poet, the great 'Abdu'r-Raḥman, affectionately known as Raḥman Bābā, "Daddy Rahman."

Abd el Rahman, or Rahman, as he is familiarly termed, is a perfect specimen of the rugged race which preserved the independence of the Affghan hills. The Pushtu, a dialect more barbarous than that of Sindh, becomes in his hands a very tolerable vehicle for poetry stern and gloomy as his. He abounds in fierce invective against the world, its falseness and treachery, its passing good and permanent evil: his content of life is scarcely tempered by devotion, and he seems to indulge in an occasional pleasant thought with regret. I have never heard an Affghan read one of his odes without a sigh.

That year the monsoon struck with a great fury. Rain fell all night. By the morning, what had been dry mud had become thoroughly soaked. Not dreaming of any danger, Burton was sitting in his drawing room—"an apartment comparable to nothing but a gravel pit roofed and furnished"; he rarely had a good word for his housing—reading 'Abdu'r-Raḥman in the company of the old Afghan *munshī*. The subject, he said, was "a pathetic dole concerning the melancholy uncertainty and empty vanities (De da dunya—'Of this world') when, plump! half a ton of water-soaked walls without the least warning fell into the living room floor." Burton and the *munshī* rushed through the door—not a word of Nūr Jān here—and escaped in time to see the entrance hermetically sealed behind them. Three neighboring houses also melted away in the next few hours. Burton's foot was injured in the accident. Nothing seemed right for him during this dreadful year. He had missed a brief opportunity to see some action, he was in trouble with his commanding officer, he had been fighting with his mistress, and now he had lost his lodging.

After the early rains, the summer was one of unusual heat. Burton was returned to Karachi, where in June an epidemic of cholera broke out in the native town. It quickly spread to the cantonment, affecting first the British, then the Indian troops, who had some slight resistance to the disease. It raged furiously for four days. The medical staff was "overwhelmed." Napier, himself in poor health, twice a day made the rounds of the hospitals—there were seven—trying to give some comfort to the ill and the dying. When the epidemic was over, eight hundred soldiers and some seven thousand civilians had died. Even the rugged and indestructible Burton was hit. He went into sick quarters in early July, after the epidemic had supposedly abated. Though he claimed to have "a strong case," one might question the authenticity of his cholera. He did show some kind of fever, but he did not evidence the usual clinical symptoms, which almost always follow a long-observed, virtually classical pattern in which the victim manifests initial symptoms of nausea, vomiting and diarrhea, abdominal cramps and fever, along with muscular weakness. The severe dehydration that follows brings the patient close to death, and if he or she can survive this crisis and the next three to five days, recovery is almost certain. Burton reported little or none of the standard symptoms. He had a fever, but in that area of Asia fevers beyond count strike daily and are a part of life—fevers, said Burton, "one kind of which strikes you down in a matter of hours, the other kind takes days of prognosis."

Whatever he had, he was not recovering as he should. By early September, still ill and debilitated, tired and depressed by his ordeal and the hard life of western India, Burton closed down his house in Karachi, said good-bye to his Persian friends, and went down to Bombay. His *munshī*, Mirza Muhammad Hosayn, had just gone back to Iran to join his brother Baqīr Khān in the attempt to overthrow the Qājār Shāh. Supplied with arms from John Company and using British-held territory in Sind as his base, the Mirza left for eastern Iran by ship. "Determined to attack Persia via Makran [the easternmost province], he managed so well that he found himself travelling to Tehran lashed to a gun carriage," Burton wrote with mixed emotions of his *munshī*'s capture and humiliation by the Qājār armies. But that was not the end of the tragedy. "Poor fellow," added Burton, "after passing through the fires of Scinde unscathed, he returned to die of cholera in his native land."

The Āghā Khān, finding it wiser to embrace his British protectors in the safety of urbane, civilized Bombay rather than in the chaos of Sind, had closed down his encampment in December 1845 and also left, moving majestically with his retinue through Kutch, Kathiawar, and Gujarat. He was welcomed along the way by adoring crowds of Isma'īlīs, who, as believers converted from Hinduism, took him as an avatar of the solar god Vishnu, and in Bombay he established permanent headquarters.

Also in Bombay, Burton found that the Presidency had its hands full with the slippery Prince-Imām. Although his brothers were attempting to steal southern Iran from Muḥammad Shāh, the Āghā Khān importuned for clemency, thus upsetting British negotiations with Tehran; in return the Shāh demanded that his enemy be extradited to Persia. The Āghā Khān's reply was, as Burton wrote, to introduce the Shāh's representative to "the pleasures of the race track."

Burton was now comfortably entrenched in Bombay, from time to time trying to egg on the Isma'īlīs to a greater effort in Persia—the final attempt at rebellion was a total disaster—and filling out the papers that would get him an extended convalescent leave. He passed the five winter months in Bombay with little hint in his written works of what he did at the time. Then the "ancient gentlemen of the Medical Board, who will never think you are sufficiently near death to meet your wishes," finally certified him for leave. He had done what he could to instill a warlike spirit in the weak-spined Isma'īlīs, the only result being that the Presidency decided to move the Āghā Khān to a place where he could cause little trouble; he was sent to Calcutta to join the imprisoned Sindhi chiefs in exile, the same men he had volunteered to help overthrow.

Ahead for Burton was "the delightful prospect of two quiet years during which you may lie in bed half the day if you prefer it. . . ." Five months in the burning humidity of Bombay was a long period for a man who claimed to be seriously ill, but now he was ready to leave for the southern Indian town of Ootacamund, a recently founded resort and convalescent home in the Nilgiri mountains for British officers and their families. But Burton was not going directly to Ootacamund. He had just become interested in the Portuguese poet Luis Vaz de Camões (Camoens in Burton's spelling), who had spent most of his adult life in the Far East and India as a soldier in the Portuguese garrisons and had composed a major, though relatively unknown work, Os Lusiadas, which now absorbed Burton's attentions. There was nothing like an intellectual quest to revive a feverish Burton. We hear not another word about cholera and few about "fever," if he ever had one. He was hot on the trail of Camões. And if he were actually sick, he spent an unusually long time in reaching the salubrious refuge of Ootacamund. Illness may have been an excuse to get out of Sind in order to escape to the Portuguese colony of Goa to investigate Camões *in situ*.

In *Goa, and the Blue Mountains; or, Six Months of Sick Leave* (the two years granted him have now shrunk to a quarter of that time), Burton makes it sound as if he were traveling alone. In fact, he had his usual entourage with him: his Goan servants, including Salvador, and to replace Mirza Muḥammad Ḥosayn, "an Arab coach," Haji Jauhur, a young Abyssinian Muslim who had made the pilgrimage to Mecca. Jauhur was married, and he and his wife, Burton wrote, spoke "a curious Semitic dialect" and were "useful in conversational matters." Even his Kattywar nag was brought along. Finally, he was ready. He had a pattymar, and on February 20, 1847, he set off on the pellucid sea.

Departure was preceded by the usual confusion. The *tindal*, the captain, was drunk, as was the crew—"the last nigger, in a manifest state of full-blown inebriation"—so Burton established order by kicking the *tindal*, a Hindu, in the head and calling him "Suar ka sala," brother-in-law of a hog, the standard vile insult. "One small touch of our magic slipper upon the region of the head" is how Burton phrased the kick.

At last, after a peaceful voyage, the pattymar sailed up the mouth of the river Mandovi to Panjim, the town of New Goa. Dawn was breaking—"most beautiful was the hazy tone of colour"—and Burton quickly found a house, which he rented for about a third of what the normal charge would be for an Englishman.

Despite its passionate Iberian influences the colony made few demands on those who were accustomed to challenges, and though Burton filled *Goa, and The Blue Mountains* with numerous observations, he quickly worked up an unappeasable fury against Goa and the Goans, his anger being dumped impartially with sarcasm and indignation on whatever he encountered. Panjim was a town of "yelping curs and officious boatmen." "That Panjim is a Christian town appears instantly from the multitude and variety of the filthy feeding hogs, that infect the streets. The pig here occupies the social position that he does in Ireland." He visited the local library, hoping to find some rare old books and manuscripts, but "the library disappointed us." He seems to have visited the brothels. He commented on the dirt of the streets and the unpainted houses and found men beating their wives. He met the "Governor-General of all the Indies," as the Portuguese commander was called, but the interview "did not last long enough to be tedious." Burton and His Excellency had nothing to say to each other. A meeting with a celebrated former brigand, "a wee, ugly, grey, thin, old and purblind Maharatta," was equally disappointing.

Panjim was not the primary object of his visit. He wanted to go upriver to see Old Goa, where Camões had passed some years, and he got a canoe to take him. The city of Old Goa, once the prize of the East, had been established by the Muslims shortly before the arrival of the Portuguese under Albuquerque in 1510. The conquerors turned it into a great cosmopolitan center of some 200,000 souls, larger than Lisbon itself. But now it was all in ruins, having been ravaged by fevers and a change in climate; the Jesuits, who had been the heart and soul of the religious life, were expelled, "and their magnificent convents and churches were left all but destroyed." It was a most unhappy land. Burton decried Albuquerque's advocating marriage between white and Indian: "Experience and stern facts condemn the measure as a most delusive and treacherous day dream." The half-castes—"in plain English," he wrote ferociously, "mongrels"—"it would be, we believe, difficult to find in Asia an uglier or more degraded looking race. . . . During the whole period of our stay in Goa we scarcely saw a pretty half-caste girl. . . . They marry early, begin to have a family probably at thirteen, are old women at twenty-five, and decrepit at thirty-five." And the Goan men were largely drunkards. The Goan half-castes, he said in summary, were "a strange mélange of European and Asiatic peculiarities, of antiquated civilization and modern barbarianism."

But Goa was the land of his hero, and after a cathartic release of his angers and prejudices, he turned to Camões. The Portuguese poet, an adventurer, scholar, and poet, must be placed alongside those other strange figures who peopled Burton's psychic life: Cornelius Agrippa, Coryat, Forbes, and other similar heroes. Camões was the wayward son of a poor noble family; he was born near Lisbon about 1524, destined to lead an epic life, a life that was, wrote Burton, "one of the most romantic and adventurous of an age of adventure and romance." It was a life that Burton felt almost his own.

> Opening with the fairest and brightest promise; exposed in manhood to the extremes of vicissitudes, to intense enjoyment and 'terrible abysses'; lapsing about middle age into the weariness of baffled hope: and ending comparatively early in the deepest gloom of disappointment, distress, and destitution, the Student, the Soldier, the Traveller, the Patriot, the Poet, the Mighty Man of Genius, thus crowded into a single career, the efforts, the purpose, the events of half a dozen. . . . Considered in such a light the Portuguese may be looked upon as unique; never was such a spirit so maltreated by Fortune.

Burton was almost sixty when he wrote this paragraph, after thirty-five years of studying Camões, and it applied as much to him as to his predecessor.

Though his family boasted "noble blood," Camões was sent to a college in Coimbra for "honourable poor students." Here he was urged to enter the clergy. "He was unwilling to swell the number of priestly drones, who regard more the goods of life than the cure of souls" and refused to become a priest, preferring to write poetry, which even then was of some competence. Unlike other scholastics and intellectuals, who wrote in Latin or Greek, Camões preferred Portuguese, which he sprinkled liberally with neologisms of classical origin—Burton himself was prone to the same practice.

While attending church on Good Friday, 1544, Camões saw the thirteen-year-old D. Caterina de Ataide, daughter of the high chamberlain to the Infante D. Duarte. A formal introduction was made, and Camões entered into the "high passion" of his life. This infatuation continued unabated, but Caterina was dominated by indecision and coyness, with only occasional love for her suitor. The poems from this period, Burton wrote, are marked with that particularly untranslatable Portuguese quality known as *saudade*. "This word," said Burton, "has no English equivalent. It is . . . a mixture of melancholy and longing."

Because of the strictness of the times it was dangerous for the couple to meet. Camões got into a duel with Caterina's brother and was exiled. On his return to Lisbon in 1546, he got into more trouble over Caterina and was exiled again, this time to Africa. He joined the army as a common soldier; on the voyage to Africa he lost his right eye in a battle with pirates. Back in Lisbon, unsuccessfully wooing Caterina, Camões was denied the honors he had expected for his military service. He had returned, said Burton, "poor as a poet." Seriously disfigured, he was spurned by the women of the court. "Fair dames diverted themselves by dubbing the disfigured one *Diabo* and *Cara sem olhos*," the Devil and the Eyeless Face. A street fight on Corpus Christi Day, 1552, landed him in prison; he was pardoned on the condition that he go to India to serve the Portuguese empire. He was now almost thirty. He saw Caterina for the last time on Palm Sunday, 1553, the day he set sail, hoping to make his fortune in the fabled East. During the six-month voyage, during which time he did not touch shore, Camões conceived the idea of *Os Lusiadas*, an epic work extolling the conquests of the Portuguese and their great exploits in the Indies. It was this romantic, dramatic, heroic theme that so entranced Burton, written by a man, who, as he himself was doing, actually lived the life he wrote about. But dream for Camões, as it sometimes was for Burton, was to be different from reality. "As is generally the case," said Burton, speaking all too obviously from his own personal experience, "Camoens landed with pleasure in India," but he soon began to complain "loudly of the dreary world about him."

India did not produce the wealth Camões had expected, although other men were making more than their share. Two years later he was sent to China. His "so lucrative an appointment, which allowed the Poet to raise himself from the slough of poverty, was the strangest of punishments"—his new wealth did not produce happiness. He continued to work on the *Lusiadas*. In 1558, on his return to India, his ship was wrecked off Cambodia, and he "lost all at the mouth of the River Me-Kong," saving only the manuscript of *Os Lusiadas*, by now having six of the seven proposed cantos. It was during this period that Camões was informed of Caterina's premature death. In Goa he was thrown into jail for "malversion of office." The next few years were a mélange of prison and freedom, freedom and prison. Jailed on false charges, Camões would always manage to gain his liberty. Life continued in this manner, sometimes in luxury and acclaim, sometimes in poverty or prison. He never married, but there was always a native woman, Chinese or Indian, to assuage his sorrows and manage his household. Whatever his circumstance, Camões continued to work on his poems. In 1567 he was finally given a high post as Inspector of Public Works in Goa but, Burton wrote, "never had the talent of success. When Fortune smiled on him, he began to cry like a child for home. . . . The profoundest melancholy gathered on his once joyous temper. *Saudades* overwhelmed him."

Camões came to hate Goa. He had left Portugal with high ideals, but the corruption, injustice, and rascality he found in the colony had disgusted him. To him, Goa was Babylon, "the mother of villains and the stepmother of honest men." Wrote Burton, "The idea of dying in India became intolerable; his spirit was broken. Sixteen years of wayfare and warfare in his gorgeous tropical exile had done their work. He must go home." When he got as far as Mozambique, he was thrown into jail for debt. He finally reached Lisbon in April 1570. "The world of Lisbon had no room for the Poet, who returned a pauper from the land whence so many had brought back fabulous riches." Camões was now aged, reduced to crutches, and dependent on public charity for food. "According to some," Burton wrote, "he was occasionally supplied with victuals by a mulatta woman named Barbar" who "begged food for him during the night-time." He died "either 1579 or 1580, age 55 or 56 . . . unmarried and the last of his line after a 'life that had been distributed in pieces about the world.' "

Here at Burton's feet were the streets of Goa where Camões had walked, before him the churches where he had gone to Mass, and even the ruined walls of the prison where he had from time to time been incarcerated. How closely Burton identified with Camões at this period one can only speculate—the poet was reckless, outspoken but at times craven, dissolute and monastic, penurious and a spendthrift, and unsparing in his comments on the rich and powerful.

Burton had left Nūr Jān in Sind, and apparently, he had not replaced her on his convalescent leave. Now he was tormented by not having a regular partner. *Goa* refers to several attempts to "abduct" nuns from local convents. One was at an orphanage where he pretended he was looking for a wife. "We . . . do not keep a naughty house," said the mother superior, who saw through Burton's lies. In another attempt, he tried to rescue a "very pretty white girl" from Saint Monica's convent one night, but in the darkness Burton went to the cell of the wrong nun and, when he realized his mistake, pushed her into the river. The story is told in *Goa* by Salvador about a "young English officer," who is generally assumed to be Burton, and is accepted as true by biographers. Despite the time spent following the trail of Camões, he seems to have been driven to desperate lengths for something to do and to satisfy his sexual urges, the prospect of moving on to Ootacamund appearing less and less inviting.

With two friends encountered in Panjim, he set off for a town down the coast said to have many houses of beautiful young women "enchanting to novelty-hunters and excitement mongers." The town, Seroda, turned out to be an overnight trip by boat. It was, wrote Burton, "intensely a Hindu town." A pimp steered the officers to the house of "the most respectable matron in town," and the three Englishmen settled down to watch an extended nautch and to enjoy its attendant pleasures. Ever the collector of information, even in a brothel, Burton noted the ages and colors of the girls, their cost as slaves, their dialects and voices, the fact that several were able to read, and that the matron could recite Sanskrit verses and knew some of the classics. The highlight of the trip to Seroda for Burton seems not to have been the nautch but a visit to the former house of an Englishman, Major G——, who had gone native, married a nautch girl, and died more or less a Hindu of a low caste. The Major struck a sympathetic note in Burton's heart, for he was also a scholar, and Burton noted the surviving contents of his library, mostly books on magic and occult knowledge of the type he had investigated at Oxford, along with works on dreams, geomancy, astrology, osteomancy, oneiromancy, and divination. "The relics of this library still stand side by side there, to be eaten by the worms," he wrote.

A visit to the Major's tomb moved Burton most forcibly, as had similar pilgrimages to the burial sites of other respected predecessors.

> It is always a melancholy spectacle, the last resting-place of a fellow-countryman in some remote nook of a foreign land, far from the dust of his forefathers—in a grave prepared by strangers, around which no mourners ever stood, and over which no friendly hand raised a tribute to the memory of the lamented dead. The wanderer's heart yearns at the sight. How soon may not such fate be his own!

In the morning there was a frightful row with the matron over payment. The officers were taken advantage of by their boatman ("native Christians, as usual. . . . It is strange that these people must tell lies, even when truth would be in their favour"). "Periodical chastisements" to their guide relieved their tempers, and shortly, "hungry, thirsty, tired, and sleepy, we found ourselves once more in the streets of Panjim."

Finally, he had explored all the minor treasures of the colony and had absorbed everything he could of Camões's exile. He called together his crew and servants, got his horse aboard the pattymar, and after the usual arguments with the perpetually drunken captain about getting under way—"a rapid succession of small double taps on the Tindal's shaven and cocoanut-like pericranium"—at last the vessel was again sailing through the tranquil waters of the Arabian Sea. Four days of languid cruising brought them to Calicut, a once-great city—Camões had called it *"Cidade—nobre e rica"*—formerly a trading center for Portuguese, Dutch, French, and Danes but now declining into a tropical backwater, where even animals were in short supply. "There are no horses, sheep, or goats, and the cows are scarcely as large as English donkeys," Burton observed. Among the populace there was "an abundance of sore eyes." There was not much to see in this lackadaisical port, and as always, the natives were definitely nasty. "The populace apparently regards us with no friendly feeling, Moslem and Hindoo, all have scowls upon their faces, and every man, moreover, carries a knife conveniently slung to his waistband. . . . The Hindoos generally in this part of the world are accustomed to use their knives with scant ceremony."

Everywhere Burton went he was aware of how much the whites were hated—information he had picked up in disguise in the bazaars or in uniform as an English officer sensitive to other people's feelings. Over and over again he mentioned this intense dislike. He felt it in southern India. By this time he was so experienced in India and had attained such an understanding of the mind of the people, great and small, soldier, ruler, peasant, merchant, serf, Hindu and Muslim, that he believed great calamity faced the English in India. "Everyone knows that if the people of India could be unanimous for a day they might sweep us from their country as dust before a whirlwind," he wrote in *Goa*.

A visit to a local raja was unrewarding. For once, Burton had language problems. "The Rajah understand little Hindoostani, and we less Malayalim." He received Burton in a room filled with Western bric-à-brac, "with the effects of an old curiosity shop." The courts were crowded with "diminutive, but seemingly most pugnacious cows," but the harem aroused his attention. "The ladies were young and pretty—their long jetty tresses, small soft features, clear dark olive skins, and delicious limbs" pleased him. What was more, "their toilette in all save the ornamental part of rings and necklaces, was decidedly scanty," and much in the manner of the South Seas—"all naked above the waist, and barefooted."

Finally, he had delayed too long and had to complete his journey. In May 1847, on his rugged little Kattywar nag, he reached his goal, the hill resort of Ootacamund, taking so long to do so that it is obvious that he dawdled deliberately, for at Ootie he would come face-to-face with people he had not cared for much since childhood and even at times despised, his fellow Englishmen, for Ootacamund—popularly known as "Ootie"— was Little England personified, callow and cliquish. There were two routes up to the resort from the coast. Burton took the longer, more than double in length than the shorter. He was still not feeling well. "In a perpetual state of low fever you cannot eat, drink, or sleep; your mouth burns, your head throbs, your back aches, and your temper borders upon the ferocious."

At first it looked as if Burton might relax and enjoy himself at Ootie. He didn't. He came down with an eye infection, possibly picked up in steamy Calicut, which he termed "rheumatic ophthalmia," probably a form of conjunctivitis. Burton blamed it on "the sudden change from dry Scinde to the damp cold mountains." The affliction was rampant among the English. Burton was now to be handicapped by eye problems for almost two years, until he left India in March 1849. He tried special diets and darkened rooms. He moved to more congenial surroundings and was given "blisters of sorts, and the whole contents of the Pharmacopeia," but nothing helped. At intervals he was able to work, and he did some sightseeing. Meanwhile, he wrote letters to the Bombay *Times*, studied Telegu and Toda, both South Indian tongues, and worked away at perfecting his Persian and Arabic.

For a few weeks all was "excitement, joy, delight." The air was cool, and his appetite improved. "The mutton had a flavour which you did not recollect in India. Strange, yet true, the beef was tender. . . . You praised the vegetables, and fell into ecstasy at the sight of peaches, apples, strawberries, after years of plaintains, guavas, and sweet limes." He noted the attractiveness of the young English women at Ootacamund, for the mountain air and the fresh climate gave them a wonderfully brilliant look. There was a freshness in everyone's complexion, he noted, in contrast to the "cadaverous waxy hue which the European epidermis loves to assume in the tropics."

But after his health improved, Burton began to get bored and restless. He took boat rides, horseback rides, and walks until every pebble on the road was "deadly familiar." The blue mountain air, the cool breezes, paled. The company of English memsahibs began to bore him. His pampered palate lost its taste, and he came down with diarrhea from too many fresh vegetables. The two libraries had no books of consequence. There was no theater, no concert room; tennis, racket, and fives courts were all lacking. The officers from the two Presidencies, Bombay and Calcutta, did not mix.

But among the complaints there were some bright spots. He found a copy of one of the Indian classics he had studied earlier, the *Akhlāq-i-Hindī*, "Indian Morals," rummaged in his trunk for his *Hindostani Grammar*, bought a copy of Duncan Forbes's *Hindostani Dictionary*, and set about translating the work, neatly copying it into a ninety-six-page booklet, with the text on the right-hand page and his notes on the other. Unfortunately he was never able to get it published. E. B. Eastwick, his predecessor in Sind, was more successful with a version from Persian, *Anvār-i-Suhaili*, which appeared under the title of *Fables of Pilpay*.

Accustomed to easy access to native women, Burton found himself at a loss in dealing with the intricacies of courtship among the English. It was as if he had come from another world, and he was not aware of how men and women flirted and played one against the other. He talked about going riding with "Miss A----," who, he feared, "will assuredly confer the honour of her company on your enemy, Mr. B----, if you keep her waiting five minutes." At the moment he was afraid of losing her, he was nervously standing before the commanding officer arguing about a servant who had accused him of withholding his pay, while Burton was charging the servant with stealing.

"What a detestable place this Ootacamund is during the rains," Burton complained. Unnerved by the incessant rain and the dampness, Burton decided to leave Ootacamund. He persuaded the officer in charge that he was "fit for duty long before the expiration of his leave granted at Bombay," having come to the conclusion that life with Charley Napier in the wastes of Sind was better than the muggy, damp, and showery London-like climate of the Nilgiri mountains. What he did not know was that Napier had resigned his post in July and was to leave India on October first, before Burton could get back to Karachi. In a farewell rainstorm Burton set out for the coast and a steamer to Bombay. On October fifteenth he passed in Persian at the Town Hall, coming first of some thirty candidates. "This was succeeded by something more substantial, in the shape of an 'honorarium' of RS. 1000 from the Court of Directors."

Disgruntled and restless as he had been at Ootie, Burton's convalescent vacation had not been wasted. He had begun work on a translation of *Os Lusiadas*, though it and the accompanying two-volume commentary were not to be completed and published for another thirty-three years, had translated the *Akhlāq-i-Hindī*, had assembled copious notes for *Goa, and the Blue Mountains*, had learned Telegu and the rudiments of several tribal languages, and had brushed up his Arabic and polished his Persian. But he had more ambitious and challenging ideas than merely being proficient in Oriental tongues. He had been mulling over two major steps—going further into Islam by formally becoming a Sufi and making the sacred pilgrimage to El-Medina and Mecca, not as an Englishman in disguise but as a true and practicing Muslim.

Before he left Bombay, he found a *munshī* to replace Mirza Muḥammad Ḥosayn, one Shaykh Hāshim, "a small half-Bedawin," who was to help him with his Arabic and would direct him on the path to Sufism.

"My return to the head-quarters of the Survey was a misfortune to my companions," wrote Burton. "My eyes forbade regular work, and my friends had to bear my share of the burden." He was still suffering from ophthalmia and could not read, but that did not prevent his working on languages and studying Sufism. And since technically he was still on medical leave—that would not end until early 1849—he was more or less free to follow his own inclinations for the coming year.

A friend of Burton's from this period, Walter Abraham, left a description of Burton at the time. After his return to Karachi, Burton shared a bungalow with a Dr. J. E. Stocks, an assistant surgeon from the Bombay Presidency and "Vaccinator in Sind." Burton and Stocks were then collaborating on papers that were not published in the Bombay Government Record until 1853, "Brief Notes Relative to the Division of Time" and "Articles of Cultivation in Sind; to which are appended Remarks on the Modes of Intoxication in that Province." Said Abraham of Burton in 1847:

He was on special duty, which in his case meant to perfect himself for some political duty, by mastering the languages of the country. When I knew him he was master of half a dozen languages, which he wrote and spoke so fluently that a stranger who did not see him and heard him speaking would fancy that he heard a native. His domestic servants were—a Portuguese, with whom he spoke Portuguese and Goan [Konkani], an African, Persian, and a Sindi or Belochee. They spoke their mother tongue to Sir Richard as he was engaged in his studies with moonshees, who relieved each other every two hours, from ten to four daily. The moonshee would read an hour and converse the next, and it was a treat to hear Sir Richard talk; one would scarcely be able to distinguish the Englishman from a Persian, Arabian or a Scindian.

His habits at home were perfectly Persian or Arabic. His hair was dressed à la Persian—long and shaved from the forehead to the top of his head, his eyes, by some means he employed, resembled Persian or Arabian.

Abraham did not realize that Burton applied koh'l to his eyes following the custom of the Prophet Muḥammad, thrice to the right eye and twice to the left, beginning with the right—the disparity between the number of applications was for the sake of having the sum total odd in number because, according to al-Ghazzālī, "odd numbers are superior to even numbers," and "God Himself is unique and prefers odd."

Even in his dress and customs, Abraham added, Burton was thoroughly an Easterner.

. . . he used the Turkish bath and wore a cowl; and when he went out for a ride he used a wig and goggles. His complexion was also thoroughly Persian, so that Nature evidently intended him for the work he afterwards so successfully performed, namely, visiting the shrine of the Prophet Mohammed—a work very few would have undertaken unless he was a complete master of himself.

Abraham describes a scene in which Burton, dressed as a poor Persian traveler (probably a dervish) fooled even his own *munshī*, 'Alī Akhbar, who was seated one evening before his bungalow in Karachi, enjoying the evening breeze and chatting away "as Persians are wont to do." After the usual polite exchange of compliments, at which he was a master, Burton inquired for the traveler's rest home and then talked of people the *munshī* knew, "with a long rigamarole of his travels and of people." "Then as he had gone a few steps he called back in English to 'Ali Akhbar if he did not know him. The moonshee did not know where the English voice was coming from."

Burton's separation from his own people had its negative side, notably in his relationship with white women. Aside from the two attempts at connecting with young European girls in Goa and his frustrations at Ootie, his writings from his Indian years never mention anything but relationships with Indian women of the courtesan class or with the Persian girl. In the notebook in which he had written the poem about his lost Persian love, there is also a fragment of a poem that speaks of "fair Margaret the far famed Clifton maid . . . loved & courted, wooed in vain." Could "Clifton" be the same beach resort outside Karachi where the English relaxed and recuperated from their labors? Could Margaret have been a member of an English family stationed in Sind? And could Burton have escorted her on rides along the shore? If such speculation has some basis to it, Margaret would be the only white woman known to have been associated with Burton in his seven years in India. But his wooing was, of course, "in vain." Burton, with his shaved pate, long hair, dark skin, and generally Oriental appearance, could hardly have made other than an odd impression on an English girl of presumably normal Western interests and prejudices. "The final pages [of the journal] are ripped out altogether, most certainly by Isabel Burton," said Brodie, guessing without evidence. But Burton himself is the more likely culprit. Considering Lady Burton's tendency to destroy wholesale, a selective destruction of a few pages seems unlikely; Lady Burton could be expected to destroy the entire journal, Persian girl and fair Margaret together.

Though his eyes continued to affect him, they did not prevent Burton's studies in Sufism. As a Sufi *murīd*, or novice, he would not have been required to read—in fact, the *murshids*, the masters, make a point of the *murīd*'s not reading. Sufic teaching is first and foremost oral, for the masters believe that the pupils are all too likely to wander off if they take up Sufi literature alone, without guidance, since the texts are so highly ambiguous and couched in allusions and obscurity. Burton was intensely serious about his studies: hard work, concentration, and a rigorous regime are essential for the novice in Sufism, as in other disciplines. Under Shaykh Hāshim, said Burton,

> I began a systematic study of practical Muslim divinity, learned about a quarter of the Koran by heart, and became proficient at prayer. It was always my desire to visit Mecca during the pilgrimage season: written descriptions by hearsay of its rites and ceremonies were common enough in all languages, European as well as native, but none satisfied me, because none seemed practically to know anything about the matter. So to this preparation I devoted all my time and energy: not forgetting a sympathetic study of Sufi-ism, the *Gnosticism* of Al-Islam, which would raise me high above the rank of a mere Moslem. I conscientiously went through the *chillá*, or quarantine of fasting, and other exercises, which by-the-by, proved rather over-exciting to the brain.

He interrupted the narrative at this point to state: "At times when overstrung, I relieved my nerves with a course of Sikh religion and literature; and, at last, the good old [Sikh] priest, my instructor, solemnly initiated me in the presence of the swinging 'Granth,' or Nanah Shah's scripture." This excursion into Sikhism had almost nothing to do with Burton's religious enthusiasms. The bazaars were filled with rumors that the brilliant Sikh queen Rāni Jindan and her chieftains feared further English expansion into the Punjab, and war seemed imminent. Burton apparently hoped that by studying Sikhism at this time he would be able to go in disguise into the Punjab as an agent. His initiation into Sikhism smacks solely of political opportunism. Sikhism had begun in the early sixteenth century under the brilliant mystic Guru Nānak, who drew upon the best of Islam, especially Sufism, and on the Hindu devotional movement known as *bhakti* to forge a monotheistic religion of great spiritual intensity. Numerous vicissitudes turned the Sikhs from pacifists into a warlike nation, whose ideal was the warrior-saint. By Burton's time they were respected as much for their ferocity as for their sanctity. The Sikhs accepted any sincere petitioner—Muslim, Christian, or Hindu of any caste—and so Burton was not forced to pretend that he was anything but an Englishman seeking the "pure" religion.

After a ritual bath of his entire body, Burton was brought into the Sikh temple, the *gurudvāra*, where its most precious object, the Sikh scripture, the *Adi Granth* (or Primordial Book), lay on a low cot; the work was not a mere symbol but enshrined the mystic personalities of the Ten Gurus of the Sikhs. Burton approached it with covered head and bare feet, rubbing his forehead on the ground in obeisance. He was then given some sweetened water, *amṛt* or nectar, in his palms and told to recite a mantra, the *Jap-ji*, in praise of the Almighty. The *amṛt* was stirred by a double-edged dagger, *khanda*; next he was given a new name with the suffix *Singh*, lion, and swore to wear the five K's—unshorn hair and beard (*keś*), a comb in the hair (*kangh*), a steel bangle (*karā*) on the right wrist, short drawers (*kacch*), and a sword (*kirpān*). Four rules of conduct (*rahat*) were also enjoined: Burton had to refrain from cutting his hair, from tobacco and alcohol, from adulterous relations with Muslim women, and from meat not slaughtered according to Sikh practices, all proscriptions he could not have followed too long. This "conversion" meant not only an intense period of studying some very difficult mystical writings but a new name (which he did not mention) and a promise to follow some very strict, formal rules. That Burton might have had serious intentions at first is possible. Sikhism promises serenity and repose, meditation on God's name, purification, and yearning for the Eternal Formless One. But little remained in Burton's memory of his conversion except to recall that the bangle, *karā*, "made of Amritsar iron . . . is supposed to have the property of causing sleep."

Thus his period as a Sikh was short-lived and opportunistic, and he passed it by offhandedly in various autobiographical fragments except to say that "my experience of Eastern faiths became phenomenal" and quickly, returning to Islam, "I became a Master-Sufi." From the vague references in the *Life*, he was still living in Karachi, and the time of initiation would have been late 1847 or 1848.

14

The Mystical Rose

Sufism penetrated the most obscure facets of Sindhian life. "There is nothing more remarkable in Sindh than the number of holy men it has produced," Burton wrote in *Sindh*, "and the extent to which that modification of Pantheism, called Tassawuf [Sufism] throughout the world of Islam, is spread among the body of the people."

But the prevalence of Sufis and the influence of a debased Sufism was not for the good of the province. That once magnificent Path had degenerated to an alarming degree. The initial purity of Sufism had given way to a kind of popular superstitious religion that stood in opposition to orthodox Islam, itself becoming moribund in Sind. "As might be expected from a semibarbarous people," said Burton, ". . . an immense superstructure of falsehood is built upon a slender foundation of truth," and he mentioned "the miraculous lie" that after a generation or two "becomes universally known to the people in the shape of a legend or tradition." And he gave a page of examples attributed to various holy men.

> Curing complaints and diseases, such as impotence, madness, deafness, dumbness, blindness, ophthalmia, issue of blood, epilepsy (especially), lameness, wounds, the bites of serpents, &c. . . . Changing female into male children . . . compelling inanimate objects to act as if they possessed life and volition . . . making youths' beards grow, and *vice versa* restoring juvenality to worn out old men; raising the dead [etc.] . . .

Burton divided the Sufis of Sind into two major groups, the Jelalis (their "immorality and debauchery are known to all") and the Jemalis ("a much more respectable class"). Though he was to become a Jemali, the Jelalis were far more interesting ethnologically. The most humiliating rites prepared the candidate for the kind of life he was to lead—all the hair on his body was shaved, his face blackened, his shoulder seared with a hot iron, and he was stripped and smeared with cow-dung ashes. Then he went out into the world to survive as he could, "a sturdy, irretrievable beggar, unfit for any useful occupation in life, sure of Heaven, and, meanwhile, permitted to make earth as pleasant a place as he can, by the liberal use of hemp or spirits, and the pursuit of a most degrading sensuality."

There were four great Sufi brotherhoods, the Qādiriyya (or Qādiris), Naqshbandiyya, Suhrawardiyya, and Chistiyya, each with numerous subdivisions and affiliates, and many independent orders—the membership of the brotherhoods ran into millions. When Burton became a Sufi, he joined the Qādiris, the most powerful and widespread order, founded on the teachings of the great twelfth-century mystic and saint 'Abdu'l-Qādir Gīlānī. The order was known from North Africa to Indonesia, with branches everywhere, at which Burton would always be most welcome.

The rose was the great Qādiri symbol, and a story of its meaning was often repeated among the dervishes. When the shaykh approached Baghdad, he was greeted with a cupful of water sent by another shaykh, meaning that "Baghdad being full of holy men, there was no room for him."

Whereupon 'Abd-u'l Qādir put a rose into the cup, which meant that Baghdad would find a place for him.
Then all present exclaimed, "The shaykh is our rose!"

The rose might not only be red but green, "because the word *Hayy* (the Living One, *i.e.*, God) was manifested in green." In the center of the rose was the seal of Sulaiman (Solomon), a mystical figure greater in Islam than in Judaism or Christianity.

The period of training as a member of a brotherhood was, and is, unhurried, and stresses withdrawal from the world and an eschewing of mundane affairs.

In addition to prayer and fasting [said Burton], the Jemali Sufi is recommended penance and seclusion; silence; meditation in dark and gloomy spots; perpetual devotion; abstinence from food, sleep and carnal enjoyments; perfect love and obedience to his Shaykh, or religious superior; abnegation of self and all worldly ties, and, finally, the strictest attention to the rules and regulation of his order.

Burton had written that he "conscientiously went through the *chillá* or quarantine of fasting and other exercises," but he did not elaborate, and what he experienced was then unknown to all but a few Islamic scholars among his own people. *Chillá* means a retreat of forty days' duration with fasting, prayer, and recollection; it was based on the forty-day fast of Moses, when, as the Qur'ān says (Sura 7:143), he received a vision of God. In actual practice *chillá* may be extended for longer than forty days and embody more than a fast, at times requiring six, eight, or ten months, or even longer, according to the disposition of the candidate and his instructor.

The practice of *chillá* was an especially Indian Sufic custom and showed the influence of yoga—the *chillá ma'kusa*, for example, required the candidate to hang upside down in a well while engaging in the prescribed prayers and meditations for forty days. As a novice or *murīd*, Burton went into seclusion, leaving his place of retreat, the *chillakhāna*, only for common prayers with the other novices of the convent that he had entered. During the *chillā* he devoted his time to reading the Qur'ān. Burton learned about a quarter of it by heart and was entitled to call himself a *hāfiz*, one who can recite the Qur'ān from memory—a good *hāfiz* can move an audience to tears, as Burton did later in Somalia. Meditation and self-examination were a part of his practices and especially the remembrance of God's name through *dhikr*, which Burton, using the Persianized term he preferred, *zikra*, identified simply as "a formula repeated aloud."

Dhikr is basically the constant repetition of a sacred word or phrase, aloud or silently, perhaps hundreds of times. Each order has its own particular *dhikr*, though the famous prayer, sometimes known as the "Testification"—"*La ilāha illā-Allāh*," "There is no God but God," said or chanted rhythmically to the devotee's inhaling and exhaling—is widely practiced, followed by the second part of the prayer, "*Muhammadun rasūlu*"—"and Muhammad is His Prophet."

This kind of repetitive prayer was common throughout the Asian religions and had even passed into Christianity as the famous "Jesus Prayer." Burton thought it originated in Hinduism, though the Sufis denied any but an Islamic origin. In all— Hinduism, Sufism, Christianity (and also Buddhism, Sikhism, the shamanistic faiths, and others)—the practice of such prayer centered on hundreds of repetitions and regulated breathing, the mind being focused on a mystical center in the body— "making the spirit descend into the heart," as a Greek mystic wrote in a phrase that could have been said by a devotee of any faith.

Initiation into a Sufi brotherhood was not a precipitous act for any novice. Burton already had several years of training and study, and he was as expert as any *murīd* could be, perhaps more so, for he had studied doctrine and practice with his accustomed thoroughness. The shaykh who was to receive him had prepared himself with prayer—dreams, visions, and "manifestations" of spirits were vital to both master and *murīd* as guides to initiation.

When he was at last ready, Burton was brought into the convent, the *tauhīd-khānah* (meaning "the house of unity"), and into a large whitewashed hall carpeted with rugs and mats. Seated in a large circle on the floor was the assembly of Sufis, with the shaykh at the center, sitting on a clean prayer rug (which Burton said in *Sindh* was called the "Musalla"), facing the direction of Mecca (which here was to the west). Burton now sat on the same carpet, on his knees, with his heels under his buttocks, the position known in Islamic ritual as *jalsa*. The shaykh took Burton's right hand in his own, thumbs touching (this was a sign of repentance). Next came a long series of prayers, private meditations, readings from the Qur'ān on God's mercy and on the Prophets, homilies and exhortations that took about an hour, slowly absorbing Burton into the great *tarīqa*, the Mystical Path of the Sufi brotherhoods, and producing a profound transformation that infused his thinking for the rest of his life and which he could never shake off.

In his essay "El Islam," begun a few years after his initiation as a Sufi and never completed, and unpublished until after his death, Burton summarized what led him to Islam and Sufism and to the rejection of other faiths, not only Hinduism and Judaism but particularly Christianity. He wrote of Christianity that over the centuries "the Religion of Love was dishonoured by malice and hate, persecution and bloodshed." And what he considered necessary for a well-ordered religious life, "The founders of Christianity had neglected to insist upon daily prayers at stated times [as Muslims did], and ceremonial cleanliness, which is next to godliness." Also, they forgot the dietary regulations so necessary to the East and allowed "the use of inebriants, together with impure and unwholesome meats as pork and rabbit's flesh." Then, "about the sixth century of its era the Christian world called loudly for reform. When things were at their worst, Muhammad appeared upon the stage of life." From this statement onward, Burton could only praise Islam, "the Saving Faith," for in short, from its dietary prescriptions to its highest moral, ethical, philosophical, and mystical beliefs he thought it was the only faith for man, guiding him through the perils of life:

> "The world is the Muslim's prison, the tomb his stronghold, and Paradise his journey's end." . . . To the Muslim, time is but a point in illimitable eternity, life is but a step from the womb to the tomb. . . . He has no great secret to learn. The Valley of Death has no shadow for him; no darkness of uncertainty and doubt horrifies his fancy. . . . As in Christianity as in El Islam, eye hath not seen, nor hath ear heard, nor hath fancy conceived the spiritual joys of those who in mundane life have qualified themselves for heavenly futurity.

As a Sufi, Burton had a point of view that was anything but opportunistic and selfish.

> The whole practice of the Sufi consists of seeking the Divinity, not as the "popular prudential and mercenary devotee," but from fervency of love to God and man. He "proclaims the invisible truth above visible comfort"; his entire resignation can face the horrors of eternal death inflicted by divine Will; "he has something higher even than everlasting gain."

During the ritual Burton entered his own meditation "with closed eyes upon the appearance of his religious instructor," seeing him in a mystical light that went back first to 'Abdu'l-Qādir and then to the Prophet Muḥammad. While Burton was meditating, the shaykh entered into the mystical state known as "Fanah fi'llah," which Burton translated as "merging the creature into the Creator," that is, the master, as "a holy traveller in the desert of existence," effaced himself in the Deity. After some five minutes the shaykh emerged from his meditative transport and, raising his hands in prayer, said the Fātiḥah, the first chapter of the Qur'ān and the expression of Muslim belief in God's unity, a prayer that is said on numerous occasions, religious and secular alike. Burton repeated the prayer after the shaykh.

"Lastly," said Burton in *Sindh*, "the instructor, placing his hand on the candidate's breast, mutters a few words, 'God bless and save Mohammed and his descendants' and finally blows in the direction of his disciple's heart." The shaykh then touched Burton's hand and breathed three times into his ear, saying, "*La ilaha ill Allah*," and commanded him to repeat it daily 101, 151, or 301 times, though in Burton's case, in his "Murid's Diploma," he was instructed to repeat it 825 times each day. With this, the ceremony was ended, and Burton was now a fully initiated *murīd*; he might also be called a dervish, a holy wanderer, and a *faqīr*, a poor man devoted to the religious life.

He had also been invested with the *khirqa*, the patched robe, or mantle, a garment symbolic of the new Sufi's willingness to accept the embrace of poverty, a type of symbol also found among the Buddhists and Zoroastrians. The *khirqa* contained that luminous quality known as *barakā*, "blessing," for usually it had first been worn, or at least touched, by a holy man of great sanctity and possessed certain mystical and even magical powers, and thus its blessings were passed on to the new member of the brotherhood. The shaykh had also given Burton "the high sounding name of Bismallah-Shah, 'King-in-the-name-of-Allah,' " and now he was ready to go out into the world as a true dervish, a *faqīr*, a Muslim to the bone but also an agent of John Company.

Initiation into a Sufi brotherhood was merely the first of a long series of steps, each more demanding than its predecessor, which the devout believer would follow to the end of his life, starting what were called *shugls*, or practices. Each *shugl* lasted forty days, a *chillá*. There was, to start with, a daily emphasis on *dhikr*, recollection, with some prayers said a thousand times, then four thousand, concentrating on Allāh as "He Who is" and on the Prophet Muḥammad. More advanced *shugls* focused on certain mystical centers in the body, a practice probably derived from Hinduism, all the while breathing slowly and rhythmically and invoking the name of Allāh.

Burton not only practiced the exercises faithfully but felt he profited by them.

> The moral effects . . . are said to be exaltation and attraction towards the Deity; purification of the heart, even as a room is swept by the broom;* intense love for, and "desiderium" [spiritual yearning, a Catholic mystical term] when separated from, the Supreme Friend; and finally, a total abnegation of self and the world.

After working his way through several *shugls*, each more demanding than its predecessor, the new Sufi, Burton wrote, was now called a "Salik," Wayfarer, a popular term. In a kind of self-hypnosis the *sālik* was able to move the name of Allāh throughout his body, from below the navel to the brain, to the shoulders and finally to the heart, again an exercise reminiscent of certain yogic techniques. The Sufi now has "complete mastery over his senses" and "an increased intensity of affection for the Supreme being."

At this point, if he has survived the rigors of his training and has mastered his craft, the Wayfarer on the spiritual Path may be considered a *murshid*, or master. Sometimes, said Burton, he is called "Sahib Irshad," roughly, "Master of Bliss," and is capable of directing others. The twentieth and last exercise "enables the Gnostic to arrive at 'fana fi'llah,' or absorption into the Deity."

How far Burton progressed in the various stages of a very demanding and complicated religious discipline he never said, though he left the impression in various works that he was not a mere novice but a master. Certainly he got a good grounding in Sufism, to the point where he could make a most outrageous

---

* Pilgrims from the Indo-Pakistan area still go to the tomb of 'Abdu'l-Qādir in Baghdad, to walk around the sanctuary sweeping up the dust with little brooms. To clean the threshold of a holy man or saint is considered spiritually very rewarding work.

claim and not be challenged for well over a century. In his autobiographical fragment in the *Life* he boasted that after his Sufi initiation, "I became a Master-Sufi," and in his *Pilgrimage* he wrote:

> A reverend man, whose name I do not care to quote, some time ago [in Sind] invited me into his order, the Kadiriyah [Qādiri] under the high-sounding name of Bismallah Shah, and after a due period of probation he graciously elevated me to the proud position of a Murshid, or Master of the mystic craft.

And in a note he added that "a Murshid is one allowed to admit Murids or apprentices into the order." In proof of his rank he reproduced an English translation of the so-called diploma given to Sufi masters.

"As the form of diploma conferred upon this occasion may be new to many European Orientalists, I have translated it."

But Burton was exaggerating. The diploma, which is most impressive even in English, contains some mysteries. In Islam the chain of attestation, from the master to *his* master to *his* master, and so on back, is important in establishing the credentials and credibility of a claim or a tradition. In Burton's diploma the names of the shaykhs who passed on their powers to the new "murshid" were "here omitted for obvious reasons"—a most suspicious remark: The reasons are not obvious to anyone but Burton. In place of names, initials A, B, and C are used. His bibliographer, Norman Penzer, states that the diploma was "received from the Shaykh El Islam," but the person in question is nowhere identified in Burton's works, and the date Penzer gives for the bestowing of the diploma, 1853, and the place, Mecca, are puzzling, for Burton always claimed to have been made a Master Sufi or murshid in Sind after he returned from Goa. That would have been between November 1847 and March 1849, when he left India. The most important point, however, is that the diploma, contrary to what Burton claims, does *not* testify that "the owner has become a master in the craft of Sufism."

One must, perhaps, expect occasional lapses from Burton's normally rigid probity in personal matters. All that the document states, despite its impressive appearance (it is four feet five inches long), is that Burton was taught "the Saying of Unity [the prayer *la ilaha illa llah*, as Burton transcribes it]" and was ordered to recite it 165 times after each of the five required daily prayers, "and on all occasions according to his capability."

Consequently, Burton's claim to an advanced rank as a Sufi must not be taken too seriously. The average Englishman had no idea what a Sufi was, and "Master" sounds better than novice. What is important is that Burton was one of the first Westerners to convert to Islam and then to follow it deeper into a religious brotherhood. He certainly was the first European to write about Sufism, not as an academic but as a practicing Sufi. He gained a sufficient grasp of the inner knowledge, the Gnosticism he mentioned so often, to be able to preach in various mosques in Sind and Baluchistan ("in the manner of a Sunni Mollah," Kipling was to write) and later in Somalia. And he had realized a good part of that honored Muslim practice, the memorizing of the Qur'ān.

But there was more to being a Sufi than a robe and a new name and a series of demanding spiritual exercises. One of Burton's favorite practices was the sacred dance, the *samā'*, in the *tauhīd-khānah*, where, after praying silently for half an hour, seated in a circle on sheepskins on the floor, swaying in rhythm to the *dhikr*, the dervishes would begin the first movements of the dance and then, on their feet, enter the majestic cadences.

> They uncover their heads, take off their turbans; form a second circle with the first; intertwine their arms; lean their shoulders against each other; raise the voice; and unceasingly utter—*Yā Allāh! Yā Hu!* They do not stop till strength is exhausted. Each one leaves when he pleases.

They chant *Allāhu Akhbar*—"God is Great"—and the *Fātihah* until they reach the stage of *hālat*, ecstasy. At this point two dervishes would take cutlasses down from the niches in the walls and heat them red hot and present them to the shaykh. Breathing over them in prayer, the shaykh would impart the mystical presence of 'Abdu'l-Qādir Gīlānī and return them to the dervishes.

Transported by frenzy, the dervishes seize upon the glowing irons, gloat over them, lick them, bite them, hold them between the teeth and cool them in their mouth!

Others stick cutlasses into their sides, arms, and legs.

If they fall under their sufferings they cast themselves, without a complaint or a murmur or a sign of pain, into the arms of their brothers.

After the dance the shaykh treats each dervish for his wounds, rubbing them with his saliva, saying prayers, and promising them a speedy cure. "It is said that twenty-four hours afterwards, nothing is seen of their wounds," states the Sufi manual, the *'Awārif-u'l-Ma'ārif*, a handbook of the brotherhoods.

When Burton's body was prepared for burial after his death in 1890, it was found to be covered with scars, the wounds of innumerable swords, which have never been explained, "the witnesses of a hundred fights," thought Thomas Wright in his biography. What seems likely is that Burton, in engaging in the *samā'* with the other dervishes, did not hesitate to enter fully into the ritual of the swords, suffering cuts on his torso and limbs with the same abandon as the other dervishes.

Now there was a war in the offing to distract Burton. The Sikh chieftains were restless. Throughout the spring of 1848 rumors of an armed uprising flooded the bazaars, and it appeared but a matter of time before war broke out. Finally, in what seemed like a testing of British nerve, the Sikh general at Mūltan, a hot, dusty city in the southernmost Punjab, murdered two English officers. The incident inflamed both sides. Because of the heat, which was rapidly overwhelming the Punjab, the English took no immediate action, but on August eighteenth, aided by some turncoat Sikhs, they laid siege to Mūltan. By the fall months the campaign against the Sikhs had increased in intensity, and officers were called up from all the various branches, including the Survey. In a letter begun in mid-November to his cousin Sarah Burton—one of the few to have survived from this period—Burton said, "A furious affair has broken out in Moultan and the Punjaub and I have applied to the General commanding to go up on his personal staff." Burton had applied for a post as an official translator. He had already passed the official examinations in six native languages and was studying two more and was eminently qualified. "A few days more will decide the business of going on active service—and I am not a little anxious about it, for though still suffering from my old complaint—ophthalmia—yet these opportunities are too far between to be lost." In this letter he mentions his brother, Edward, now in Ceylon, where a native uprising, known as the Kandy Rebellion, had just been crushed. It had been a short but brutal war, and the bitterness that resulted was to affect Edward Burton directly. The rebellion had come about after a series of riots when the British imposed heavy taxes on the people, having already devastated large sections of the forests for coffee, tea, rubber, and coconut plantations: the people saw their very sources of food disappearing. The Singhalese could respond only with anger and frustration: civil disturbances broke out. The 78th Highlanders, who had suffered grievously from cholera in Sind, were transferred to Ceylon to put down the disturbances. One of their young officers, Captain John MacDonald Henderson, wrote that the taxes were "most foolish and unjust . . . and I may add, impracticable." And, "The wildest rumors arose . . . Among others that the women were to be taxed in proportion to the girth across their breasts." The riots were stopped, but, added Henderson, "the government proceeded to go berserk." For two months English troops roamed the countryside teaching the "rebels" a lesson. The hatred of the Singhalese for their oppressors continued to smolder, and a few years later Edward Burton fell to the unappeased anger of the peasants. He was a great hunter, unlike his brother, and elephants, tigers, cheetahs, and other game fell before his gun. About 1855, during an elephant hunt, he was attacked by villagers—"Buddhists all," wrote Georgiana Stisted, "animated by bigoted feeling towards one who openly violated the precepts of their religion by taking beast life wholesale, fell upon him and inflicted serious wounds on his head with sticks and stones." Edward seemed to regain his health—in fact he served two years later in India during the Sepoy Rebellion—but "his mind slowly gave way and never recovered." From then on, Edward Burton passed his days in silence, unmarried, never responding to questions, confined most of the remaining forty years of his life to the Surrey County Lunatic Asylum.

Burton held the letter to Sarah for ten days longer; then, in a postscript dated November 25, 1848, he wrote, "I am not going up to the siege of Mooltan, as the General with whom I had expected to serve is recalled." That was not the full story. For other reasons, Burton, who was so proficient in so many languages, was passed over in favor of a man who spoke only one (probably Hindustani), certainly not the most important one for the post, Panjābi. Years later, in the "Terminal Essay" of the *Arabian Nights*, he claimed that the reason he was turned down was that his "Official" on the male brothels in Karachi had been sent on to Bombay after Napier's retirement, and here his enemies—he had many of them at this point—had brought it out when he had applied for the post of translator in the Sikh campaign. Whether this was actually so, or he was trying to explain to his own satisfaction an episode that bothered him throughout life, the fact is that with all his talents he was bypassed in favor of a man definitely his linguistic inferior. He was abrasive, witty, caustic, daring, heroic, highly intelligent, literate, independent, scornful, and always sure he was in the right, and none of these characteristics helped him in the eyes of Company and army bureaucracy.

Six years of hard work, of studying and risk taking, had ended in nothing but the "blackness of darkness." His ophthalmia was worse; he seemed to be shriveled with some unknown disease, perhaps a fever. By now it was the end of the year. He was confined to quarters in Karachi, isolated, a "White Nigger." By the beginning of 1849 he decided to go home, seven years now behind him, work, sport, women, languages, dangerous expeditions into places where no white man had ever ventured before, among people who flayed enemies alive, put out the eyes of brothers, sons, and fathers in their dynastic quarrels, kept women in a kind of prison (and where the women were given captives to castrate, slowly)—all part of an experience no man had ever had before, and so far as anyone can learn, no one has repeated and is not likely to.

He was racked by fever and chills, his eyes ached, his eyes were red rimmed, and ached and ached and itched unbearably. He felt

> qualmish upon the subject of desert districts, dusty roads, tamarisk jungles, mud mausolea, lean Hindoos, puny Scindians, mosques, bazaars, and clay towns with tumble-down walls.

His friends urged him not to wait too long, for his frame was shrunken and tottering, his voice without sonority, and his eyes—his eyes got worse and worse. He packed his treasures— "Specimens of sugar and sugar-cane, opium and hemp, tobacco and sulphur, indigo leaves, unknown dyes, échantillons of cotton in every state . . . Tattah shawls, isinglass prepared from the lungs and air vessels of an Indus fish . . . Scinde mosaic work . . . cigar-cases, worsted boxes," and so on, for a collection of bric-à-brac that undoubtedly seemed fascinating and important once but at home was to be but one more collection of oddities such as almost every Anglo-Indian brought back.

He could not await the sight of familiar faces and familiar places. Shipped down to Bombay, he seemed like a man at the end of his rope. His friends were sure he was dying. There seemed to be little hope that he would reach home alive. He wrote a farewell letter to his mother. "In a well-nigh insensible condition," he said later, "I had to be carried aboard the brig *Eliza.*"

He settled down for the months ahead of sailing, attended only by his Afghan servant, Allahdad. By the time he reached England, he was in much better shape, thanks to the bland and health-giving ocean breezes and the assiduous care of the Afghan. Health, strength, and vitality had returned, and when he disembarked, he had all the natural bounce and verve of men of his age.

Burton now regarded the seven years in India as time wasted. He had achieved prodigious feats but had gained no rewards: the record did not favor him at all, and the opinions of officers who had never known the dangers of the field and the Great Game remained in his file to shadow him for decades. Daring, intelligence, talent, and a cool head in danger had been negated by Burton's own insensitivity to and scorn of army politics. Still, it was in Bombay, Gujarat, the Punjab, Baluchistan, and Sind and southern India that he had slipped into the secret life of the religious and sexual mystic and had begun to collect the material that would lead to the *Arabian Nights* and the publications of the Kama Shastra Society, with their amazing notes and commentaries and their revelations of a world so much different from that of England. And most of all, he had gained a vision of Islam through personal experience that was to lead him to Mecca.

15

Daisy

As Burton regained his health and the *Eliza* scudded before favorable winds, he turned his thoughts to his family. In his seven years in India he had been unable to see Edward, stationed with the Queen's Thirty-seventh Regiment in Ceylon. Both parents were in poor health, but not seriously, with the complaints that kept them in a halfhearted malaise in France and Italy. In 1845, Maria had married a young army officer, Henry William Stisted (later to become a lieutenant general), and already had two daughters, Georgiana Martha and Maria. It was the late summer of 1849 when the *Eliza* landed at Plymouth. Burton immediately went to see his aunt, Georgina Baker, and other relatives ("notably two pretty Burton cousins," Sarah and Eliza) and finally set off for Pisa with his servant Allahdad; the Afghan began to fight with the family's Italian servants and was sent home.

The mild climate and comparative luxury of Pisa brought a further advance in Burton's health, but he was not to make a full recovery for many months. At the end of the year he returned to England. Here, still on sick leave, he continued to be plagued by the problems that had developed in India. He had a wan look on his face, indicative of more serious ailments. Liver trouble, bronchitis and other pulmonary diseases, and "internal inflammations" sapped his energies and kept him a walking invalid. He went from one health resort to another without great success, to Leamington for its saline springs and baths, to Dover, which was noted as an exceptionally healthy locality and a pleasant resort town, and to Malvern for the hydropathic treatments. He thought briefly of returning to Oxford to complete his university requirements, but he was now of an age when college life seemed puerile, and he abandoned the plan. He was not happy in England. All the old complaints returned, and the dull gray monotony began to depress him.

About a year after his return, Burton went over to France. The exact date is moot—Isabel Burton says 1850, while Georgiana Stisted and Thomas Wright believe it was 1851. Burton settled down in Boulogne, an old port town of mixed charm, only twenty-eight miles by sea from England. It was a popular English resort, being appreciated for its "change, quiet and economy." It was this last quality that had the most appeal for the majority of the expatriates. The town had developed a marked English ambience, having several English churches and boarding schools and many English shops. The port's charms came from the Haute Ville, the old medieval section perched atop a hill, surrounded by thirteenth-century ramparts, which the English favored as a strolling place and where they could meet friends. And the young men found the Ramparts ideal for making the acquaintances of previously unknown young women.

Burton took rooms in an old hotel in the Haute Ville. John Steinhauser was with him at least part of the time—the doctor "looked as if his face was carved out of wood," said Isabel Burton after meeting him—and Colonel and Mrs. Burton arrived from

Italy, and his sister Maria and her daughters—Stisted was then in India—also came to keep him company. Always eager for strenuous physical activity, Burton began a rigorous schedule of fencing, with all the intensity that a mastery of the art demanded. This was the beginning of an exhaustive study of the sword— "The Queen of Weapons," as he called it—upon which he was to work throughout his life. "The best of calisthenics," he wrote later in *The Book of the Sword*, "this energetic educator teaches the man to carry himself like a soldier. A compendium of gymnastics, it increases strength and activity, dexterity, and rapidity of movement. . . . Swordsmanship engenders moral confidence and self-reliance, while it stimulates a habit of resource. . . ."

Unfortunately for Burton, the sword had virtually disappeared both as a weapon and as an article of military dress. Nevertheless, under the aegis of a M. Constantin, a famous master, Burton earned the prestigious *Brevet de Pointe*. By now he had overcome the various illnesses that had accompanied him home from Sind, and his eyes were clear and sharp. His mastery of the sword became legendary not only among the English but also among the French, and when it was known that he was about to put on an exhibition at Boulogne's Salle d'Armes, dozens of onlookers would come to watch. A friend from this period, Lieutenant Colonel Arthur Shuldham, wrote to Georgiana Stisted after Burton's death to describe a typical encounter.

In the year 1851–1852 I met the late Sir Richard Burton at Boulogne, and he asked me to accompany him to the Salle d'Armes where he was going to have a fencing bout with a sergeant of the French Hussars, a celebrated player. The sergeant donned his guard to protect his head, and a leather fencing jacket, while Burton bared his neck and stood up in his shirt sleeves; on my remonstrating with him, he said it was of no consequence. They performed the customary salute and set to work. It was a sight to see Burton with his eagle eye keenly fixed on his adversary, shortly followed by a very rapid swing of his arm and a sharp stroke downwards when the Frenchman was disarmed. He did this seven times in succession, when the sergeant declined any further contest, saying his wrist was nearly dislocated by the force with which this Englishman struck his weapon. The spectators, mostly French, were astonished at Burton, who with the exception of a prod in the neck, was otherwise untouched.

But his activities were not confined to fencing. Burton had two other pursuits, one writing, the other women. He finished the manuscripts of books he had started as early as 1844 in Sind and continued working on in England during his convalescence. On his worktables at this time were *Goa, and the Blue Mountains; or, Six Months of Sick Leave*; also, *Scinde; or, the Unhappy Valley; Sindh, and the Races that inhabit the Valley of the Indus; Falconry in the Valley of the Indus*; and *A Complete System of Bayonet Exercise*. These manuscripts, though often covering different aspects of a subject, represented a massive amount of work—Burton had started early on his practice of writing several books at the same time—and within the space of a few years more were to follow. But this enormous flow of creativity had its dark side. He began to suffer from melancholia. His relatives received frequent letters complaining of "dulness and low spirits." This was the start of a depression that affected him from time to time for the rest of his life. He would try to disguise it, but it was easily apparent to those close to him. Part of his depression came from the fact that energetic and prolific as he was and new and important as his books were, they failed to sell. Critics were generally hostile. The prestigious *Athenaeum* said that *Goa*, published in 1851, was "at once a very good and a very bad book." The same year's *Scinde* was written off as "smart, rattling and clever," and the very important second Sind book was denigrated for "extreme opinions." Such comments infuriated Burton, and when he made a reply in *Falconry in the Valley of the Indus*—a work that by 1877 had sold less than half of the original five hundred copies printed—he got in return some unpleasant remarks from reviewers about his predilection for living like the natives. But Burton trod on virgin ground and had opened up matters that were reserved for the scholar and the pornographer. Probably no one before him had discussed seriously in works meant for the general public such subjects as, for example, aphrodisiacs, as he did in *Sindh.*

Our ignorance of aphrodisiacs is considered the most remarkable phenomenon: there being scarcely an oriental work on physic that does not devote the greater part of its pages to the consideration of the question which the medical man in the East will hear a dozen times a day.

And he wrote frankly and openly about the Búbú system, prostitutes, and brothels. Whereas his contemporaries were likely to use phrases like "Mohammedan superstition and bigotry," he spoke of Islam in neutral if not favorable terms.

At this period in Boulogne, Burton fell in love with Elizabeth Stisted, one of his cousins. It seems to have been a congenial relationship between Burton and the young woman. She was lively, amiable, well dowered, in short, an excellent choice. But Burton, handsome, dashing, and intelligent as he was, failed as a match, for everyone knew he was but a lieutenant in the East India Company's native army, on half pay, would likely have to spend the rest of his life in India, and had no great financial prospects. "He reluctantly bowed to the wise decision of her nearest relations," wrote Georgiana Stisted, "who, sincerely as they cared for him, could not sanction an engagement." Miss Stisted was always fascinated by Burton's romance with the young Persian woman, and here she mentions it, saying, "His affection for his cousin lacked the intensity of his love for the dead girl in Sind." Burton fell in love again a year later—this, too, seems to have been a serious romance, but, reported Stisted, it was "a very evanescent one, which, like the last, came to an untimely end."

There was no avoiding romance in this cloistered English colony. The Stisteds, the mother and later the two daughters, seemed to know more about Burton's heart than did Burton himself. Isabel Burton was to gloss over his romances in the *Life*, though some receive passing mention as minor events in his youthful years. But Burton was now close to thirty; marriage was a social, physical, and economic obligation, and the Stisteds were aware of Burton's flirtations. "That Burton had a great many *affaires de coeur* is no secret," Miss Stisted wrote. "They were mostly of an ephemeral nature." Burton, she said, had nothing of the hermit about him, he enjoyed women, and "he found a fair face an irresistible attraction."

> As he was not merely a handsome but a powerful magnetic man, women fell in love with him by the score, often careless whether their affection was returned or not. It is certain that many of his amours were not originated by himself; and in these cases, some of a delicate and troublesome nature, he was at a distinct disadvantage.

But the right woman did not appear, though Burton never lacked for feminine companionship. "So long as a girl was handsome it never seemed a matter how narrow, how vain, how supremely silly she might be." Here Stisted is all too clearly referring to her uncle's future wife, Isabel Arundell, whom he was to meet in Boulogne. In *The True Life*, Georgiana Stisted never mentions Isabel at this point but condemns in broad terms: "While keenly appreciating talent in his own relatives, when he fell in love he actually preferred a doll." The "doll," of course, was Isabel Arundell. "On the whole he preferred the Eastern ideal of a wife . . . a dog-like being whom no Englishwoman, clever or stupid, could possibly imitate."

Meanwhile, the "doll," the "dog-like being" who was to become Burton's wife, had appeared in Boulogne. Burton could be fatalistic at times, but Isabel Arundell was even more so. "Destiny" was a common word in her vocabulary, and it could mean almost anything. In Boulogne it was to signify nothing but Burton himself.

Isabel Arundell, when Burton met her, was nineteen, and

judging from the descriptions of her at that time and the few rare early portraits, an amazingly beautiful woman. Moreover, in a milieu of middle- and upper-class English, where the women, like the men, ran to types, she was unclassifiable. In fact, she was probably one of the few women who could fit into Burton's ideal of what was to be cherished in a wife—beauty, and affection, with brains, talent, and moral and physical courage.

Isabel was the oldest of a very large family of prominent Roman Catholics with a long and distinguished pedigree that included warriors, noblemen, and prelates. Isabel could leap over obstacles in the family tree with ease to find the knightly, the romantic, the saintly ancestor. She traced the Arundells back to the misty generations of the ninth century—the first Arundell (then Harundell) was mentioned in A.D. 877. And a doggerel in old Sussex tradition said: "Ere William fought and Harold fell, / There were earls of Arundel."

To claim descent from these ancient earls was a vanity of Isabel's. She believed, on better grounds, that her family could be traced back to Roger de Arundell, who was listed in the Domesday Book of William the Conqueror as having estates in Dorset and Somerset.

When the Reformation touched the royal court, the Arundells remained staunchly loyal to the Pope as the Crown fluctuated between ecclesiastical independence and submission to Rome. Still, the Arundells were closely tied to the ruling family. Isabel's direct ancestor, Thomas Arundell, was first cousin to Henry VIII, and he married Margaret Howard, a member of the Norfolk family and sister to Catherine Howard, the fifth of Henry's wives. Thomas was also related to Anne Boleyn, the king's second wife. But in that turbulent, suspicious age, when relatives could be more dangerous than strangers, Arundell was named in a plot against the Earl of Northumberland, and though he may have been innocent, he went to the block on Tower Hill.

Like the rest of the Catholic nobility in England, the Arundell family suffered persecutions by Anglicans and non-Conformists alike. These English Catholics, upholding beliefs often derided, took pride in their ancient roots. This was heady stuff for young Isabel, and she never got over it. Not only was she an Arundell, but she was related as well to the Howard and Norfolk families, who at that point were still solidly Roman Catholic.

She was above all a romantic. "She paid great attention to her pedigree," wrote her biographer, W. H. Wilkins. "She regarded her forefathers with reverence, and herself as their product." Isabel wanted to be worthy of her ancestors with a "roving, adventurous spirit," fortified by the qualities of "bravery, daredevilry, and love of conflict," and "tenacity and devotion." Such characteristics gained her enemies, who were likely to charge that she lacked common sense and possessed an unfortunate tendency to fantasize, even to lie. To many who knew her, Isabel's Catholic heritage was not a blessing but an impediment.

Isabel Arundell was born on Sunday, March 20, 1831, at ten minutes to nine in the morning, at Great Cumberland Place, near London's Marble Arch. "Unlike most babes," she wrote in her autobiography, "I was born with my eyes open." She was also born into a new freedom—just two years earlier legal restrictions against Roman Catholics had been abolished with the Catholic Emancipation Act, although popular prejudice against Catholics continued.

Georgiana Stisted, who was usually vitriolic in her comments about Isabel, dismisses Isabel's father, Henry Raymond Arundell, as "a wine merchant" and "not very prosperous, and, as often happens in such a case, had a numerous family." There were fourteen children, of whom ten died early, leaving Isabel and three sisters as survivors.

Mr. Arundell was genuinely liked by everyone, but of her mother the usually charitable Isabel had mixed feelings. "My mother was one of the best and cleverest of women—a woman queenly in manners and appearance . . . she had a noble heart and disposition, was generous to a fault," but she was also "still a worldly woman of strong brain, of hasty temper, bigoted, and a Spartan with the elder half of her brood. We trembled before her, but we adored her."

"I can remember distinctly everything that happened to me from the age of three," said Isabel. "I do not know whether I was pretty or not," she adds, but she did know, for she was always quite aware of her looks and the impression she made on people.

Isabel and the other children were brought up strictly. "We children were little gentlemen and ladies, and people of the world from our birth; it was the old school." At the age of ten she was sent to a convent school founded by an earlier generation of Arundells for children of upper-class Catholics. Isabel spent six years there and then was brought home by her parents, who wanted her company. This, Isabel complained, was at the time when she was just beginning to appreciate her studies. "My leaving school was a misfortune."

The Arundells now lived on an estate in Essex. The main house was a straggling old building, half country cottage, half farmhouse, buried in bushes, ivy, flowers, and creepers; there were stables and kennels and fifty acres of woods and fields. Isabel was an extremely active young woman, as physically active as any boy. She learned to skate, and she roamed the fields with her brothers and sisters, acquiring the physical strength and dexterity that were to serve her well in South America and the Levant. But she also liked to be alone. She had "a great deal of solitude," passing a lot of time in the woods "reading and contemplating." The "contemplating" seemed to be daydreaming rather than anything of depth. She read a lot, she said, but her reading was centered mostly on one book.

> Disraeli's "Tancred" and similar occult books were my favorites, but "Tancred" with its glamour of the East, was the chief of them, and I used to think out a fashion of my future life, and try to solve great problems. I was forming my character.

Tancred was "the book of my life"—"my second Bible." She carried it everywhere and claimed to know it by heart, and referred to it often in her writings. What was this "book of my heart"? Unfortunately it defies easy synopsis and analysis. It was one of those works vaguely heard of and rarely read, a mishmash of half-baked philosophy, theology, romance, travel and adventure, exotic peoples and places, through which runs a vague scheme for a utopian world based on a religious revival. *Tancred* came out of a trip its author, Benjamin Disraeli, had made to the Middle East to get over a state of depression. At the age of twenty-six he had set off for a sixteen-month tour of the East, the supposed birthplace of eternal truths, in search of answers to certain religious and philosophical questions that had troubled him. The hero, Tancred—Disraeli—finds fulfillment in "the great Asian mystery," but what that mystery was is not clear, for the author was vague about what he saw before him. He was fascinated by the desert but hazy about its people ("Arabs are only Jews on horseback"), and in the desert he saw salvation: "The decay of a race is inevitable unless it lives in deserts and never mixes blood."

Isabel spent two years in the garden reading *Tancred*. How much of the book's high-blown theology and philosophy penetrated her young mind is unclear. She was more attracted by its romantic settings, its colorful characters, and its hodgepodge of religion and adventure. *Tancred* "inspired me with all the ideas and yearnings for a wild Oriental life. . . ." In fact, this odd and peculiar book so sunk into her subconscious that when she went to Damascus with Burton as his wife, "I felt as if I had lived that life for years."

It was her love of the Oriental inspired by *Tancred* that led her to the Gypsies who were encamped nearby, though her parents had forbidden her to associate with them.

I was enthusiastic about gypsies, Bedawin Arabs, and everything Eastern and mystic, and especially a wild and lawless life. Very often instead of going into the woods, I used to go down a certain lane; and if there were any oriental gypsies there, I would go to their camp and sit for an hour or two with them. . . . My personal friend was Hagar Burton, a tall, slender, handsome, distinguished, refined woman, who had much influence in her tribe. Many an hour did I pass with her (she used to call me "Daisy"), and many a little service I did them when any of her tribe were sick, or got into a scrape with the squires anent poultry, eggs, or other things. The last day I saw Hagar Burton in her camp she cast my horoscope and wrote it in Romany [the Gypsy language]. . . . The horoscope was translated to me by Hagar. The most important part of it is this:

You will cross the sea, and be in the same town as your Destiny and know it not. Every obstacle will rise up against you, and such a combination of circumstances, that it will require all your courage, energy, and intelligence to meet them. Your life will be like one swimming against the waves; but God will be with you, so you will always win. You will fix your eye on your polar star, and you will go for that without looking right or left. You will bear the name of our tribe, and be right proud of it. You will be as we are, but far greater than we. Your life is all wandering, change, and adventure. One soul in two bodies in life or death, never long apart. Show this to the man you take for your husband.

It is impossible to tell if there were a Hagar Burton or not, and if there was, if indeed she cast Isabel's horoscope, and if she did, if what Isabel reported is what the Gypsy said. The meeting with Hagar Burton smacks somewhat of creative autobiography. Richard Burton, too, visited Gypsies, and what her Richard did, Isabel often liked to echo. The entire passage suggests not an anecdote about Gypsies secretly met down a country lane but the effects of her husband's life upon her own thoughts and yearnings.

One of the most significant lines in Hagar Burton's prophecy as Isabel reported it is this: "One soul in two bodies in life or death, never long apart." This may be Isabel's way of emphasizing that her Jemmy, as she often called him, was a Roman Catholic. But where did the theme of one soul in two bodies originate? It is, for one thing, a popular Sufi concept, and it appears in various forms in Sufi mysticism but on a far grander scale than that of man and woman, usually stressing the relationship between Allāh or God and the mystic. Burton, having studied the Sufi poets so thoroughly in Sind, probably quoted them often to Isabel from time to time in their frequent discussions and arguments over his Islam and her Catholicism.

Gypsies or no, Isabel was going through all the pains of growing up. She left a portrait of herself during this crucial period of sixteen, somewhat denigratory but intended to be contradicted. "This was the ugliest time of my life," she said of that year. "I was tall, plump and meant to be fair, but was always tanned and sunburnt. I knew my good points. What girl does not. I had large, dark blue, earnest eyes, and long, black eyelashes and eyebrows which seemed to grow shorter the older I got. I had very white regular teeth, and very small hands and feet and waist." But she fretted that she was too fat to fit into stock-size clothes. "From my gypsy tastes I preferred a picturesque toilette to a merely smart one."

When Isabel was seventeen, her parents decided to move to London. It was time to introduce her to society. She wrote how she made farewell pilgrimages to every spot connected with the bright reminiscences of her youth, how sad it was to have one's animals destroyed, and, what seems like another excuse for her later behavior, "to make a bonfire of all the things one does not want desecrated by stranger hands." And so the Arundells, having cried over the old retainers, who in turn cried, too, broke up their home in Essex and went off to London.

The pleasures of London quickly erased the pain of leaving Essex. Pretty dresses for the Arundell girls, calling cards dropped at strategic homes, and "we were all ready for the season's campaign." Isabel made her debut at Almack's, a famous club and assembly room where over a twelve-week period a series of weekly balls was given, managed by "a committee of ladies of rank, and admission was exceedingly difficult." The Arundell girls were sponsored by the Duchess of Norfolk, a relative and one of the ancient nobility.

Isabel was immediately popular. Her dances were overbooked. "One may think how vain and incredulous I was, when I overheard someone telling my mother that I had been quoted as the new beauty at his club. Fancy, poor me!"

Then came the opera and dinner parties, and more balls, shopping, visiting new friends. Sometimes there were two or three parties a night. She was "tired-proof" and "dancing mad." But she had a keen eye—or thought things through in later years—for the contradictions, the naive young men and the fortune hunters of both sexes, the rouged, desperate old peeresses "with one foot in the grave, almost mad with excitement over cards and dice, and every passion except love, gleaming in their horrid eyes." When she came to London, said Isabel, she was not aware of the matrimonial market. "Mothers considered me crazy, and almost insolent, because I was not ready to snap at any good *parti*; and I have seen dukes' daughters gladly accept men that poor humble I would have turned up my nose at." She had a poor opinion of many of the suitors. "I sometimes wonder if they are men at all, or merely sexless creatures—animated tailors' dummies. Shame on them to disgrace their manhood!" She thought it was man's work to do great deeds. "The young men of the day passed before me without making the slightest impression. My ideal was not among them."

She was quite specific about her "ideal." He was

about six feet in height; he has not an ounce of fat on him; he has broad and muscular shoulders, a powerful deep chest. . . . He has black hair, a brown complexion, a clever forehead, sagacious eyebrows, large black wondrous eyes—those strange eyes you dare not take yours off from them—with long lashes. He is a soldier and a *man*. . . . His religion is like my own, free, liberal, and generous-minded. . . . He is a man who owns something more than a body: he has a head and heart, a mind and soul.

This was supposedly written while Isabel was still in London and had no knowledge of her future husband. It is so clearly Burton that one might well question her statement that "this is the creation of my fancy." But whenever it was written, Isabel was sure that "such a man only will I wed." And if she should meet such a man and he marries someone else, "I will become a sister of charity of St. Vincent de Paul," a religious order that worked primarily with the poor.

Isabel had but a single season in London. In the late summer of 1850, Mr. Arundell decided to move the family out of England to less expensive and demanding surroundings. "Change of air, sea-bathing, French masters to finish our education, and economy was loudly called for," wrote Isabel. But there was something else in the air to influence her father. Anti-Catholicism had arisen again. By 1848 the revived Catholicism and the influence of the Oxford converts who had interested Burton alarmed Protestants. Papal aggression seemed manifest, especially when the Pope, Pius IX, announced that he was restoring the English hierarchy, with Dr. Nicholas Patrick Stephen Wiseman as the new Cardinal Archbishop of Westminster. Protestant England, as the historical clichés put it, was "aflame."

How much of this unrest alarmed the Arundells is hard to tell. In August, Mr. Arundell chose Boulogne as a refuge; there were relatives already there. When Wiseman arrived in London, "No-Popery" riots erupted. Tensions between the Catholics, the Anglicans, and the powerful Evangelicals increased, and to cross the gulf, as Burton and Isabel Arundell were to do, took courage and conviction; few among Burton's friends and relatives would ever forget that his wife was a Roman Catholic and proud to be one.

Isabel was not happy about leaving England. "I loved society and hated exile," she wrote. But Boulogne on first sight was "a most picturesque town," an opinion she changed the next day: "Boulogne looked like a dirty pack of cards, such as a gypsy pulls out of her pocket to tell your fortune with." The streets were "irregular, narrow, filthy, and full of open gutters, which we thought would give us cholera. . . ."

The Arundell girls were placed at the convent of the Sacré Coeur to learn French and were kept at it all day, along with music and other subjects suitable for young women. There was not much social life for them. Mrs. Arundell escorted them on walks from one end of the town to the other, and at certain times, they were allowed the luxury of strolls along the Ramparts. In general, "mother kept us terrible strict."

And then the great event happened. One day early in the fall of 1850, Isabel and her sister Blanche, still in their school uniforms, were walking along the Ramparts, unchaperoned, when a handsome young man—Burton, of course—was seen approaching from the other direction.

> The vision of my awakening brain came toward us [said Isabel]. He was five feet eleven inches in height, very broad, thin, and muscular; he had very dark hair, black, clearly defined, sagacious eyebrows, a brown weather-beaten complexion, straight Arab features, a determined-looking mouth and chin, nearly covered by an enormous black moustache. . . . But the most remarkable part of his appearance was, two large, black flashing eyes with long lashes, that pierced you through and through. He had a fierce, proud melancholy expression, and when he smiled, he smiled as though it hurt him, and looked with impatient contempt at things in general. He was dressed in a black, short, shaggy coat, and shouldered a short thick stick as if he were on guard.

Burton, accustomed to meeting girls from any culture and not at all shy, stared at them. It was Isabel who caught his eye. He saw before him a tall, willowy, independent, honey-blond, blue-eyed young woman of much self-assurance. "He looked at me," she wrote later, "as though he read me through and through in a moment, and started a little. I was completely magnetized, and when he had got a little distance away I turned to my sister and whispered to her, 'That man will marry *me*.'"

The next day they happened to cross paths again—why and

how at this particular moment and place Isabel does not say. "He followed us," she wrote. Burton scribbled on the Ramparts wall with a piece of chalk, "May I speak to you?" and put down the chalk. Isabel picked up the chalk and wrote beneath Burton's question, "No, Mother will be angry." Later, Mother found the scribblings and *was* angry, again an unexplained question as to how and why Mother recognized these chalk marks as pertaining to her eldest daughter. At any rate, said Isabel, "after that we were stricter prisoners than before."

Both Burton and Isabel Arundell had highly developed senses of the dramatic, as if throughout their lives they were writing a scenario not for some gaslit Victorian drama but for a motion-picture serial not yet invented. Shortly after the encounters on the Ramparts, despite Mother's prohibitions—it was clearly impossible to imprison Isabel—she was out for a walk with her cousin Louisa when Burton appeared. Burton and Louisa knew each other. But—"Agony!" thought Isabel when Burton began to flirt with Louisa. However, "We were formally introduced, and the name made me start." She had met her destiny, as Hagar Burton had predicted.

Then came a long, strange courtship, ritualized as if the two participants were a pair of exotic birds engaged in some kind of long-delayed prenuptial dance, whirling about each other in slow, graceful movements, so slow that final consummation promised never to come. It was Isabel who experienced the deepest anguish from the courtship, felt it most intensely. Burton left no record of his thoughts and emotions. Isabel did, in her diary, which has been the primary source of information about ten years of grand passion, frustration, and final fruition.

I did not try to attract his attention; but whenever he came to the usual promenade I would invent any excuse that came to take another turn to watch him, if he was not looking. If I could catch the sound of his deep voice, it seemed to me so soft and sweet that I remained spell-bound, as when I hear gypsy-music. I never lost an opportunity of seeing him, when I could not be seen, and as I used to turn red and pale, hot and cold, dizzy and faint, sick and trembling, and my knees used to nearly give way under me, my mother sent for the doctor, to complain that my digestion was out of order, and that I got migraines in the street, and he prescribed for me a pill which I put in the fire.

At that point all seemed hopeless. "All girls will sympathize with me," said Isabel. "I was struck with the shaft of my Destiny, but I had no hopes." She was "nothing but an ugly schoolgirl," and Burton had become involved for the moment with a "dashing creature, with whom he was carrying on a very serious flirtation," a girl who was "very handsome and very fast."

Finally, two years had passed, and it was time for the Arundells to quit Boulogne and return to England. "We were sorry to leave our little circle," Isabel wrote. But she was delighted at the prospects of seeing England and, most importantly, "impatient to be relieved of the restraint I was obliged to impose on myself about Richard." Still, she dreaded leaving "his vicinity." Riddled by doubts, she wondered, should she say good-bye to him? On May 9, 1852, the Arundells embarked on the channel steamer for home. Isabel had decided that when she left destiny would bring Richard to go one way and her another. "To see him again would be only to give myself more pain."

Isabel was not to see Burton for four years. She had gone to Boulogne, said W. H. Wilkins in *The Romance of Isabel Burton*, "an unformed girl, she had left it a loving woman," and what was to be true, "She had met her other self in Richard Burton. He was her affinity."

Meanwhile, the Arundells, ignorant of their daughter's burning passion for the outcast, controversial officer, were attempting to get her married, preferably to a man from one of the old Catholic families. The more malleable Blanche was soon married off to a young gentleman named Smyth-Piggot, while Isabel, strong willed, impetuous, liberty loving, confined herself to her diary, rejecting the wealthy, dull aristocrats dredged up by her mother. "Advantageous offers of marriage" fell into desuetude before the reality of her dreams. She asked her diary, "Where are all the men who inspired the *grandes passions* of bygone days? Is the race extinct? Is Richard the last of them? Even so, is he for me?"

She took a hard view of the fate of the English woman, "breeding fools and chronicling small beer." Meanwhile, Burton was preparing to set off for the holy city of Mecca.

16

The Road to Mecca

Through the years in England and France, in what was a kind of exile, Burton had kept in mind the idea of a pilgrimage to Mecca, which would be the finale of a great three-year exploration of Arabia. He returned to London shortly after the Arundells had left Boulogne, determined to carry out this project he had so long been mulling over, "to study thoroughly the inner life of the Moslem." On the surface, a trip through the vast, unknown, and unexplored deserts of Arabia alone was an impractical venture, almost madness. Burton wanted to start at Muscat, a town on the easternmost tip of the Arabian peninsula, and work his way westward, ending in Mecca. To make the venture sound feasible—for he had to get permission from both the Company and the army—he had to offer cogent reasons for going. He wanted three years' leave. Through a friend, General Monteith, he offered his services to the Royal Geographical Society of London. The Directors were heartily in support, for Burton had proposed his trip "for the purpose of removing that opprobrium to modern adventure, the huge white blob which in our maps still notes the Eastern and Central regions of Arabia." This was the famed "Empty Quarter" that was to challenge adventurers well into the twentieth century. "Its horrible depths swarm with a large and half-starving population," Burton had heard, but "the land is open to the adventurous traveller." He wanted to make some ethnological studies of the people "to warrant our questioning the common origin of the Arab family." Even more to the point for certain of the officials he was petitioning for help was this: He was desirous

> to find out if any market for horses could be opened between Central Arabia and India, where the studs were beginning to excite general dissatisfaction. . . .

Burton had some personal reasons, too, one the question of nerve, which he mentioned after his return. He wanted to "prove, by trial that what might be perilous to other travellers was safe to me." And underlying all the other reasons was the matter of his Muslim duty. "Every Muslim is bound," he wrote in *Personal Narrative of a Pilgrimage to El-Medinah and Meccah*, "under certain conditions, to pay at least one visit to the Holy City. 'Abu Hanifa [an early Muslim theologian] directs every Moslem and Moslemah to perform the pilgrimage if they have the health and money for the road and for the support of their families. . . ."

The pilgrimage was known as *hajj*—"The word Hajj is explained by Moslem divines to mean 'kasd,' or aspiration and to express man's sentiment that he is but a wayfarer on earth wending towards another and nobler world." He added, "This explains the origin and belief that the greater the hardships the higher will be the reward of the pious wanderer."

Although the Royal Geographical Society "liberally supplied" Burton "with the means of travel" so that in this venture at least he was not to be financially handicapped (except through his own extravagances), as he was to be on others, the grand scheme was nevertheless to be severely curtailed. Napier's old enemy, Sir James Hogg, the Director of the Honourable East India Company, so easily identified as "that Hogg," turned down Burton's proposal. In the first edition of his *Personal Narrative of a Pilgrimage to El-Medinah and Meccah*, Burton said Hogg alleged "as a reason that the contemplated journey was of too dangerous a nature." It was difficult to argue with Hogg on that point. By the time the Memorial, or fourth, edition of the *Pilgrimage* had appeared, Burton was in no mood to spare that Hogg's sensibilities. The reason Hogg had opposed the trip, Burton now claimed, was his "much disliking if fact must be told, my impolitic habit of telling political truths (in 1851 I had submitted to the Court of Directors certain remarks upon the subject of Anglo-Indian misrule; I need hardly say that the publication was refused with many threats)."

One cannot believe that Burton would be naive enough to think that Hogg would favor his schemes. But a compromise was worked out, saving face in true Oriental style for two men well grounded in Eastern niceties. In compensation for his disappointment, Burton was given a single year of furlough "in order to pursue my studies in lands where the language is best learned."

Burton tried to foresee any crisis that might arise. He even apprenticed himself to a blacksmith in order to learn how to shoe horses, for he might well have become involved in the horse trade if the right studs were found. In April 1853, dressed as a "Persian prince," Burton set off for Egypt aboard a steamer from Southampton, accompanied by a friend, Captain Henry Grindley of the Bengal Cavalry. Burton had not said farewell to his family, for he hated tearful partings, but he had made several last-minute visits to his parents and to Maria and disappeared without a formal good-bye. He left for his mother a letter outlining his plans—rather dangerous, he had to admit—with instructions that should he be killed, his small stock of valuables was to be divided between her and his sister.

Burton had let his hair grow long in the Shī'a Persian style.

He is not at all clear in the *Pilgrimage* just what his disguise was during his first weeks; in the *Pilgrimage* volumes he appears as both an Irani nobleman and a wandering dervish. It was not until he was well established in Egypt that he resolved the ambiguities in his mind and settled on a characterization that offered as little challenge as possible. It had been Grindley's suggestion that Burton should from the very beginning of the trip pass as an Oriental, a fortuitous step, for he was "thoroughly tired of 'progress' and 'civilization' " and wanted to see rather than hear about "Moslem inner life in a really Mohammedan country." Noting that "the vagrant, the merchant, and the philosopher, amongst orientals, are frequently united in the same person," he had resumed his old character of a holy wanderer that had served him so well in Sind. There were lacunae to fill, however. "Many things oriental had faded from my memory," and aboard the steamship *Bengal* "a fortnight was profitably spent in getting into the train of oriental manners." He had to learn again all the minutiae of eating and drinking, of sitting, of urinating and defecating, of sleeping, and above all, of praying, for it seems that despite his fervent commitment to Islam in India, he had let his Muslim practices lapse.

When he landed in Alexandria, the beggars took him for an Oriental, the bystanders were convinced that "the sheepskin covered a real sheep," and he was at last on his way into "Moslem inner life."

Burton was to stay with a friend, John F. Larking, but to avoid suspicions that this Muslim was in reality an Englishman, his host put him in an outbuilding. The servants accepted Burton as an Ajami, a Persian Shī'a, though they themselves were Sunnīs; they thought he was "a kind of Mohammedan, not a good one like themselves, but, still better than nothing." He immediately got himself the services of a shaykh and "plunged once more into the intricacies of the Faith; revived my recollections of religious ablutions, read the Koran, and again became adept in the art of prostration." His leisure hours were passed in the baths and coffeehouses, and in the bazaars. And he had to visit prostitutes. "Nor was an opportunity of seeing 'Al-nahl,' the 'Bee-dance,' neglected, for it would be some months before my eyes might dwell on such a pleasant spectacle again." The dancers were the famous Walid Nahl women, who were to be found all across North Africa and into Egypt. They were, actually, Gypsies, though at the time Burton was not aware of the fact. Not until later, in his unfinished work *The Gypsy*, did he describe them more fully—"arch-seductresses whose personal beauty makes them dangerous; the young women were dancers, the older women spae-wives or fortune tellers." One of Burton's prede-cessors and early rivals in Arabic affairs, Edward William Lane, observed that "their dancing has little of elegance; its chief pe-culiarity being a very rapid vibrating motion of the hips, from side to side."

In Alexandria the sheer joy of life entranced Burton. "Now we are sitting silent and still, listening to the monotonous melody of the East—the soft night breeze wandering through starlit skies and tufted trees, with a voice of melancholy meaning." It is, he said, what the Arabs call "*kayf*," a form of intoxication. It was, he said, "a savouring of animal existence," and it "argues a facility for voluptuousness unknown to northern regions. . . . No won-der that 'kayf' is a word untranslatable in our mother tongue."

Burton would not be the first European to enter the sacred city of Mecca, and in the *Pilgrimage* he was scrupulous about mentioning previous travelers, mostly men who had been cap-tured by the Turks and made slaves and brought, often against their will, to Mecca, after which they escaped captivity.

Of the dozen or so predecessors and contemporaries who had visited the sacred city, the man whom Burton admired most and the only one who could be ranked with him as an explorer, adventurer, and scholar was Johann Ludwig Burckhardt, a Swiss, whom he quoted often and praised by saying, "Homage to the memory of the accurate Burckhardt." Burckhardt was born in 1784 and, after attending universities in Germany, moved to

England, where he studied science and Arabic. In 1808, with
the blessing of the Africa Association, he set off for the East,
intending, after gaining enough experience, to penetrate the
heart of the darkest continent. He reached Aleppo the next year
and settled down to study. Disguised as an Arab and calling
himself Sheikh Ibrahim ibn Abdallah, he lived in extreme poverty, a poor man among the poorest, mastering Arabic, learning
the Qur'ān, and studying the commentaries and Islamic law. He
was challenged as being a secret Christian, but a court of Muslim
elders accepted him as a learned doctor of Islam. After that, in
adventures too numerous to detail, he ascended partway up the
Nile—like Burton later on, Burckhardt entertained the notion
of discovering the river's source—but was forced to abandon his
trip. Now disguised as a Syrian trader, he crossed the Nubian
desert to the coast of the Red Sea. From here, in early 1815,
Burckhardt made the pilgrimage to Mecca but could stay only a
week. He returned later, to spend three months in the city,
finding a room in a quiet quarter, where he could live undisturbed
and make notes of every detail of the life there. "His description
of Mecca is final," wrote a later scholar, Augustus Ralli. "Burton
admits it cannot be improved, and transforms it entire to his
pages." Quite true, and Burton quoted Burckhardt's description
of the Ka'aba, the Bayt Ullah or "House of Allāh," in full as an
appendix in his *Pilgrimage*.

Burton had brought with him a large supply of medicines in
phials and pill boxes, and when inquisitive neighbors saw his
stocks, they assumed that he was some kind of doctor from India.

> Men, women, and children besieged my door, by which means I
> could see the people face to face, and especially the fair sex, of which
> Europeans, generally speaking, know only the worst specimens.

For his "patients" he drew magic diagrams, mandalas, and had
with him a "Magic Mirror," which made his visitors believe that
he was "a holy man, gifted with supernatural powers, and knowing everything." He admitted that "from my youth I have always

been a dabbler in medical and mystical knowledge." Here was a wonderful opportunity to combine both in a single discipline—healing people who weren't actually sick.

He was in Alexandria a month—"a month's hard work," he said—during which time he had polished and redefined his character as a Muslim. He was no longer a Persian, having come to the conclusion that in this predominately Sunnī land it was an error to pose as a Shī'ite. It was a mistake that in truth he should never have made. At times Burton showed a peculiar insensitivity to certain hard facts. Not to have realized, despite his many years among Muslims in Sind, the general dislike of the Shī'a by other Muslims, his failure seems unaccountable. Appearing originally in Egypt as a Persian, he said, was to have "uncomfortable consequences." "Although I found out the mistake and worked hard to correct it, the bad name [of Ajami, Persian] stuck to me: bazar reports fly quicker and harder than newspaper paragraphs." By the time he left Alexandria, he was not a Persian *mirza* but a Sunnī "Shaykh," making the most of his skill as a doctor and a magician, his guise as a dervish, and his Sufi diploma, which he had with him and would show from time to time to impress people. "No character in the Moslem world is so proper for disguise as that of the Darwaysh [dervish]." He can, said Burton, be of any social station, rich or poor, nobleman or peasant, of any age, and he can go anywhere he wishes. He is a "chartered vagabond," and no one may question his origins or his destination. He is a member of the Mystic Path, the *ṭarīqa*, "which leads, or is supposed to lead, to Heaven."

Burton suddenly decided to quit Alexandria because he was bored. He had sensed "a paroxysm of ennui coming on by slow degrees. . . . The man wants to wander, and he must do so, or he shall die."

But leaving the city was not so easily accomplished as he had expected, for he was a "native," and where foreigners, especially the English, might go as they pleased, the natives were bound by a complicated system of passports controlled by the Turks,

Egyptians, and the English. Strangers, Burton complained, "know absolutely nothing of what unfortunate natives must endure." And in the *Pilgrimage*, he gives, out of sheer exasperation, several accounts of how he was treated by Egyptian and foreign officials alike because he was a "native." He was forced to pay the British consulate a Spanish dollar for a certificate establishing his identity as someone from British India. Burton appeared before the consul speaking broken English and could never have gotten his papers if Larking had not been along to "help." "Indignation!" Burton fumed. Then, after going to the police magistrate for a countersignature, he was sent on to the governor's office, "at whose gate I had the honour of squatting at least three hours," until he was sent to another office, where, after being ignored at first, he was called "a dog!" and dismissed. And so it went, through office after office, days being wasted until he got his proper papers. Why didn't he present himself as an Englishman converted to Islam going to Mecca? he knew the reader at home would ask. It was a matter of both pride and disguise. As an Englishman, he could have carried matters "with a high hand," but as a native, "you must worm your way with timidity and submissiveness; in fact, by becoming an animal too contemptible for man to let or injure." And he had to appear as a born believer, for "my spirit could not bend to own myself a *Burmá*, a renegade—to be pointed at and shunned and catechised, an object of suspicion to the many and of contempt for all."

Finally, his papers were in order—at least in Alexandria— and he had his kit—a few toilet articles necessary for carrying out his ablutions, a change of clothing, a waterskin, a coarse Persian rug that was to serve as "chair, table and oratory," a pillow, a blanket and sheet, and an amazing huge, bright yellow umbrella against the sun. He also had a dagger, a brass inkstand and pen holder, "a mighty rosary, which on occasion might have been converted into a weapon of offense," a box of medicines, and for public purchases, some small gold coins in a purse, plus twenty-five gold sovereigns in a heavy leather belt strapped around his waist, under his clothing.

Finally, "Not without a feeling of regret I left my little room among the white myrtle blossoms and the rosy oleander flowers with the almond smell." In true Oriental fashion, Burton the native, "with humble ostentation," kissed the hand of the white man, Larking, his host, in the presence of his servants. Then he went off to the Nile steamer for the voyage to Cairo.

It was now the end of May 1853 and the heat was becoming oppressive. Burton had little to say in praise about the trip up the Nile to Cairo: "It seemed to be Sind all over again—not only the heat, dust, sand, turbid waters, hot winds, fierce sunsets, sand-banks and silt-isles," but "here and there mud villages, solitary huts, pigeon-towers, or watch turrets, whence little brown boys shouted and slung stones at the birds, peeped out from among bright green patches of palm-trees, tamarisk, and mimosa, of maize, tobacco, and sugar-cane." Beyond was "the glaring yellow Desert," and the "boats, with their sharp bows, preposterous sterns, and lateen sails, might have belonged to the Indus." So might

> the chocolate-skinned, blue-robed peasantry; the women carrying progeny on their hips, with the eternal waterpot on their heads; and the men sleeping in the shade or following the plough. . . . The lower animals, like the higher, were the same; gaunt, mange-stained camels, muddy buffalos, scurvied donkeys, sneaking jackals, and fox-like dogs. Even the feathered creatures were perfectly familiar to my eye—paddy birds, pelicans, giant cranes, kites, and wild water-fowl.

On the crowded little steamer, much as he tried to avoid people, Burton made friends with two men, one a Muslim from India who insisted that Burton stay with him at Cairo and the other a man named Haji Wali, a merchant originally from one of the Muslim areas of Russia, who was going to Cairo to settle a lawsuit. Burton stayed with the Indian Muslim a fortnight, until he could no longer stand the English airs his host was putting on: "Was I not flying from such things?" Escaping from the man's unctuous hospitality, Burton found refuge in a room in a *wakála*, or caravanserai, a large, rambling building that was part hotel, part lodging house. Burton's *wakála* was in the Greek quarter of Cairo, not much to his liking, but unexpectedly he met Haji Wali again. "The Haji and I became fast friends." They went to the mosque together, smoked hashish—"this fascinating drug . . . [Egypt] will one day supply the western world with 'Indian hemp,' when its solid merits are duly appreciated," he said in a note in the *Pilgrimage*. Haji Wali advised Burton not to travel as an Ajami, for "you will get yourself into trouble." So Burton became a Pathan, born in India of Afghan parents who had settled in that country. He was to claim that he had been educated in Burma, and any errors in his Persian, Hindustani, and Arabic were to be excused by his long residence in Rangoon. But he was still a "doctor" and continued to practice medicine. Soon he had a wide following, first among the poor, then among the wealthy. His first patients came from across the hall at the *wakála*, where an Arab slave dealer had a group of Abyssinian girls who were suffering from homesickness. "Abyssinian, mostly Galla, girls [are] so much prized because their skins are always cool in the hottest weather," said Burton. They can bring high prices—"they seldom sell for less than £20 [in Arabia], and they often fetch £60"—and were worth more elsewhere. The ailments were usually minor; he had to cure half a dozen "of the pernicious and price-lowering habit of snoring" but didn't explain his method of treatment. Naturally, he flirted with them, and they would ask him to buy them. Burton became an unwilling friend of the slave dealer's, "whose brutal countenance and manners were truly repugnant. The dealer explained certain mysteries in his trade. . . . Little did he know who his interrogator was."

The question that now troubled him was that of servants for the pilgrimage. The sad fact was that much as he importuned against slavery (it was a lifelong crusade), as a respectable native, he was expected to have slaves. He summoned a shaykh ("there is a Shaykh for everything down to thieves in 'the East' ") and made known his wants. The first slave he bought soon stabbed the second he bought and was dismisssed, the police giving him "400 blows on the foot." Burton bought and sold several more slaves and finally settled on an Indian boy named Nūr, who was to remain with him throughout the pilgrimage.

Much of Burton's time in Cairo was spent in refreshing his knowledge of Islam. With the help of Haji Wali he found an old shaykh named Moḥammed al-'Aṭṭár, a once-famous scholar who had fallen upon hard times and was trying to maintain himself as a druggist in a tiny hole in the wall, from which he dispensed a few medicines and taught a few students.

The shaykh's little shop was "a perfect example of Nilotic queerness," a hole about five feet wide and six feet deep. "How does he manage to say his prayers, to kneel down and to prostrate himself upon that two feet of ragged rug, scarcely sufficient for a British infant to lie upon?" The shaykh admitted that he knew nothing about pharmacy, but "his great pleasure appears to be when the Haji and I sit by him for a few minutes in the evening, bringing with us pipes, which he assists us to smoke, and ordering coffee, which he insists upon sweetening with a lump of sugar from his little store." He made Burton read from the Qur'ān and various religious works. "He becomes fiercely sarcastic when I differ from him in opinion, especially upon a point of grammar, or the theology over which his beard has grown grey. I sit admiring to see him." The shaykh remarked often with asperity Burton's habit of taking notes—"Thou art always writing," he complained. "What evil habit is this? Surely thou has learned it in the lands of the Franks. Repent!"

When Burton would catch the shaykh in a difficulty or confusion over an obscure passage and pretend to lose his temper, the old shaykh "looks at me, and with passing meekness whispers—'Fear Allah, O man!' "

That year, 1853, Ramaḍān, the Muslim month of fasting, fell, in the rotating Islamic calendar, in June. "A fearful infliction was that 'blessed month,' " said Burton, for it made the Muslims "unhealthy and unamiable."

> For the space of sixteen consecutive hours and a quarter, we were forbidden to eat, drink, smoke, snuff, and even to swallow our saliva designedly.

The fast put people into frightful tempers.

> The men curse one another and beat the women. The women slap and abuse the children, and these in turn cruelly entreat and use bad language to, the dogs and cats. You scarcely spend ten minutes in any populous part of the city without hearing some violent dispute.

The mosques were crowded with sulky, grumbling people making themselves offensive to one another, and in the bazaars and streets people with pale, long-drawn faces looked "intolerable cross." But Burton, like the others, followed the Ramadān fast scrupulously. Half an hour after midnight a warning gun would alert the faithful that it was time for their last meal of the day. Prayers followed, and then about half past two the order to refrain from food was sounded. This was the period between dawn and dusk when good Muslims abstained from food and drink; the fast was observed as long as there was sufficient light to distinguish between a white thread and a black thread. During the early daylight Burton would say his prayers and sleep until morning. Then his patients would visit him, and afterward he would go off with Shaykh Moḥammed to the mosque to pass three hours in studying before the midday prayers. In the afternoon he was visited by his more affluent patients. Then he would wander through the streets and browse among the bookstalls. In the late afternoon the heat was oppressive. A wind wafted dust and the furnace-heat of the desert through the city. Not a cloud broke the empty skies. At last "the sunset hour approaches—and how slowly it comes!—[and] the town seems to recover from a trance." Night fell, and it was permissible to eat again.

Though he was forced by the shortage of housing to stay in the city's Greek section, Burton preferred to pass his time in the Muslim quarters, where life was much more interesting. "Everyone talks, and talk is always in extremes, either in a whisper, or in a scream." All was exciting in the crowded streets among the storytellers, singers, and itinerant preachers. People thronged the open-air cafés, listening to Greek and Turkish bands or eating cakes, toasted grains, coffee, and sugared drinks. Then there were "certain ladies whose only mark of modesty is the Burká, or face-veil." Though the face had to be covered, many women left their breasts bare without shame. There was an air of excitement everywhere: The donkey boy beat his mount with a cudgel, there were "beggars, intensely Oriental," and blind women rapping two sticks together and singing, "The grave is darkness, and good deeds are its lamp." Burton and the shaykh would often sit on a wall outside the Muḥammad 'Alī Mosque, or they would walk into the wilderness outside Cairo to the City of the Dead, a vast Muslim cemetery, with hundreds of thousands of graves, "where lies the Swiss Burckhardt." Often he and the shaykh would visit a Sufi oratory, a *tarīqa*, to pray and study. Burton preferred, he wrote, "that called the 'Gulshani,' near the Muayyid Mosque outside the Mutawallī's sacred door."

> There is nothing attractive in its appearance. You mount a flight of ragged steps, and enter a low verandah enclosing an opened stuccoed terrace, where stands the holy man's domed tomb; the two stories contain small dark rooms in which the Darwayshes dwell . . . a curious medley of men they are, composed of the choicest vagabonds from every nation of Al-Islam.

"Beyond this," he emphasized, "I must not describe the [*tarīqa*] or the doings there, for the 'path' of the Darwaysh may not be trodden by feet profane."

As so often, Burton was engaging in *taqīya*, concealment, in the matter of his religious beliefs and practices. Why should he not engage in dissimulation?—those who understood, would. This rather mysteriously described oratory was related to his own brotherhood, the Qādiris. He avoided giving specific information about the Cairo *tarīqa*, although the Gulshani oratory was the embodiment of his Sufi training in Sind. "Gulshan" (or Gul-i-stan) means rose garden, a popular term for a dervish convent, and the rose was at the heart of the practices here, as it was in Sind, and had been since the founding of the Qādiris. The rose was the symbol of mystery as it represented the enigma of God, the Absolute, Who was "so nakedly apparent to Man's sight that [He] is not visible," said the popular Sufi handbook, Sa'd-ud-din Mahmūd Shabistari's *Gulshan-i rāz*, "The Secret Rose Garden." But to achieve ecstasy, *hālat*, more than the red-hot sword was often employed. The dervishes at Cairo's Gulshani oratory went much further than those in Sind. Burton's skeptical predecessor, Edward William Lane, said members of the *tarīqa* "pretend to thrust iron spikes into their eyes and bodies without sustaining an injury. They also break large masses of stone on their chests, eat live coals, glass, &c., and are said to pass swords completely through their bodies. . . ." Other Sufis "handle with impunity live venomous serpents, and scorpions, and partly devour them."

But there was more than strange rites and whirling dances in the dervish oratory. Behind "the Mutawalli's saintly door" was the embodiment of one of the most arcane of Sufi doctrines, the *qutb*, the secret "axis" or pole of all the Sufis, in fact, of the entire world. The *qutb*, or *mutawalli*, was a mysterious personage who was chief of all living saints, imbued with strange powers, who could move with the speed of light from one sanctuary to another ("from Mekkah to Cairo in an instant," said Lane, who approached the *mutawalli* with an English caution, giving many details and much folklore but missing the esoteric meanings). The *qutb* was the "Seal of the Saints," who, in groups of three, four, seven, forty, or three hundred, maintained the world order, a concept that postulated a kind of supernatural bureaucracy that ruled the universe. The *qutb* was the point upon which the world revolved, the virtual center of spiritual energy, resting in perfect tranquillity, grounded in God.

Burton spared his readers such details—why should he tell outsiders the secrets of the Sufi oratory? If he had not been, at least at the time, a serious believer, he might have offered some sharp, if not condescending, remarks, ignoring the sensitivities of the dervishes, which would have been a sign that he had merely been posing as a Muslim and a Sufi alike.

At last Ramaḍān was over, and as in the case of Easter in Europe after the fasts and rigors of Lent, the Cairenes appeared in new clothing. "So strong is personal vanity in the breasts of Orientals, men and women, young and old, that from Cairo to Calcutta it would be difficult to find a sad heart under a handsome coat," said Burton. Festivities filled the city. One of the most popular places for celebration was the great cemetery, now "a scene of jollity." It was filled with "singers and musicians . . . jugglers, buffoons, snake-charmers, Darwayshes, ape-leaders, and dancing boys in women's attire. . . . The men swaggered, the women minced their steps, rolled their eyes, and were eternally arranging, and coquetting with their head veils."

Burton was able to visit a harem, and he attended an Armenian wedding. ("After the sameness of Moslem society, nothing could be more gladdening than the unveiled face of a pretty woman," he wrote.) He met other people who were to make the pilgrimage, and eventually a small party was formed to travel the first stage together to Suez.

During Ramaḍān, Burton laid in supplies for the pilgrimage, for he would often be traveling far from towns and villages and each pilgrim had to be self-supporting until he left Arabia. He had also to solve the problem of how to take and keep notes. He got what appeared to be a small Qur'ān, which was slung on a cord over his shoulder, to hang on the right side. But the case had, rather than its Qur'ān, three compartments, one for his watch and compass, the second for ready money, and the third for penknife, pencils, and numbered slips of paper that he could conceal in the hollow of his hand when he wanted to take notes. These were for writing and drawing, after which he planned to copy the material into his diary-book, a "long thin volume fitting into a breast-pocket, where it could be carried without being seen." But the traveler in the desert

> must, however, beware of sketching before the Bedawin, who would certainly proceed to extreme measures, suspecting him to be a spy or sorcerer. Nothing so effectively puzzles these people as the Frankish habit of putting everything on paper: their imaginations are set at work, and then the worst may be expected from them.

He had, also, to arm himself. Besides his public arms—"a good pair of Turkish barrels and stocks, fitted up with locks of European manufacture"—he had a small pistol in a secret pocket "upon which dependence could be placed" in an emergency.

There was one more important item, the special garb of the pilgrim, called the ihrām, which was to be put on at a certain point outside Mecca. The ihrām, which was the male garment, was "nothing but two new cotton clothes, each six feet long by three and a half broad, white, with narrow red stripes and fringes." One, the izar, was tied around the waist in the common manner of the lungi, lava lava, or sarong; the other, the rida, was "thrown over the back [across the left shoulder], and exposing the right arm and shoulder, is knotted at the right side." Women pilgrims were to wear a simple form of their ordinary dress; it had to be plain and clean.

Burton got his ihrām from a new acquaintance, a young Meccan named Mohammed al-Basyúni, whom he was to call thereafter "the boy Mohammed" to distinguish him from all the other Mohammeds he encountered. "He was a beardless youth, of about eighteen, chocolate-brown, with high features, and a bold profile; his bony and decided Meccan cast of face is lit up by the peculiar Egyptian eye, which seems to descend from generation to generation." The boy Mohammed was short and fat, covetous and greedy, and had "a taste for Anacreontic singing, and female society of the questionable kind." Burton was immediately nervous about him, for "he showed signs of over-wisdom," having been in India where he had seen Englishmen, and Burton was afraid that this inquisitive, parasitic young man would guess at too much. He also sold Burton a "Kafan or shroud, with which the Moslem usually starts upon such a journey as mine," and then he disappeared, much to Burton's relief. But later he turned up to dog Burton's footsteps.

Burton had to obtain more visas, again a humiliating experience, for he had to go to the police and then to the British consul, who refused to honor this apparent native as a British subject from India. But with the help of Haji Wali he went to the Persian consul, expecting that he might be a temporary subject of the Shāh's in exchange for a passport. Again he was humiliated by the clerks and refused papers. He was next brought by Haji Wali to the Afghan consul. Here at last he was successful, being certified as "one Abdullah, the son of Yusuf (Joseph [his father's name]), originally from Kabul."

Burton's departure earlier than planned from Cairo was hastened, he said, by "an accident." At the caravanserai he inadventently got into a brawl with a drunken Albanian soldier named Captain Ali Agha and aroused the whole building. After the captain and Burton made peace over a few drinks and a pipe or two, exchanging experiences in a mixture of Albanian, Turkish, and Arabic, they got into a drinking bout that rang through the *wakálá*. Ali Agha called for girls, broke into other people's rooms, and assaulted several strangers before he was overpowered. The respectable Indian doctor had disgraced himself. He had drunk a substance forbidden the pious Muslim, and throughout the caravanserai people gossiped about his hypocrisy. Haji Wali advised Burton to leave as soon as possible.

Burton pulled his equipment together, made arrangements to

join a party of Bedawin going to Suez, and said good-bye to his friends and patients. Haji Wali and the Shaykh escorted him to the city gates. Even with people he had come to know, Burton concealed his true route and gave a false one. " 'Conceal!' says the Arab's proverb, 'thy tenets, thy Treasure, and thy Travelling,' " he wrote.

Burton had hired two dromedaries from a Bedawin, one for himself and one for his Indian servant, Nūr. He planned a forced march to Suez, where he could get a boat to the Arabian port of Yambu'. He asked himself, "How much a four years' life of European effeminacy had impaired my powers of endurance . . . there are few better tests than an eighty-four mile ride in midsummer, on a bad wooden saddle, borne by a worse dromedary, across the Suez Desert." As he left his friends, he said, "I will not deny having a tightening of heart as their honest faces and forms faded in the distance."

He was traveling with a small party of rough nomads. "This is no time for emotion." Burton kicked his dromedary, and off they went at full speed. "Above us [is] an atmosphere, like a blast furnace." Presently they slowed down—"the sun began to tell on man and beast." Complaints aside, Burton was enjoying the ride. After an exchange of pipes, the Bedawi began to ask him questions to pass the time—"they are never satisfied until they know as much of you as you do of yourself." Then they talked about food—"with this hungry race, food, as a topic of conversation, takes the place of money in happier lands." This subject exhausted, the Bedawi began to sing. "Monotonous and droning as it is, their Modinha has yet an artless plaintiveness, which admirably suits the singer and the scenery." They traveled on through the night, and Burton remarked that his companions were "the most good humoured and sociable of men. . . . I have always found them [the Bedawi] pleasant companions, and deserving of respect." The landscape was another matter. Above was "a sky terrible in its stainless beauty, and the splendours of a pitiless, blinding glare, [while] the Samun [the 'poison-wind'] caresses you like a lion with flaming breath." It was "a haggard land infested with wild beasts and wilder men." But he could also call it "the glorious Desert," saying "once your tastes have conformed to the tranquillity of such travel, you will suffer real pain in returning to the turmoil of civilization."

As the skies began to darken, Burton turned off the road to say the evening prayers and was unexpectedly hailed by a figure saying, "As Salamu 'alaykum," the common Muslim salutation. "I looked at the speaker for a moment without recognizing him." It was the boy Mohammed. In Cairo, Burton had rejected his company. Here, in the desert, though he invited Burton to supper, Burton realized that Mohammed had "an utter want of money" and that he himself had been trapped. The boy Mohammed took Burton's food, insulted the Bedawi camel men, and from then on, right to Mecca, made himself a member of Burton's pilgrimage.

Finally, the group reached Suez, then an obscure town, and Burton and the Bedawi found a *wakálá* after much searching— the port was filled with pilgrims on the way to Mecca—and Burton, bone-tired and spurning company, retired to an empty room. "My eighty-four mile ride had made every bone ache; I had lost epidermis, and the sun had seared every portion of skin exposed to it."

Burton's room was a miserable place. He complained that the walls were clammy with dirt, the rafters smoky, and the floor black with cockroaches, ants, and flies. Pigeons nested on the shelf, and "cats like tigers" crawled through a hole in the door. Even a goat and a jackass had the habit of wandering through his quarters. He was able to find some pilgrims who were forming a group "into which fate threw me." They were to be his close companions for the next weeks. One of them was named Shaykh Hamid al-Samman, "the clarified-Butter seller," who was returning to Medina, a descendant of a celebrated Qādiri Sufi. The shaykh was a dirty little man who would not say his prayers because that would mean performing the ritual ablutions and putting on clean clothing. All of the party lost no time in immediately asking Burton for loans. "It was a lesson in Oriental metaphysics to see their condition," Burton said. They had a twelve-day voyage and four days' journey through the desert to Medina before them, "yet the whole party could scarcely, I believe, muster two [Spanish] dollars of ready money." His possessions were discussed and envied—his clothes, his medicine chest, and his pistols. The group noticed his sextant, and when Burton was out of hearing, they consulted one another over it and wondered if he might not be a sahib from India. Finally, they decided that "the light of Al-Islam" was on his countenance. But Burton thought it wise to leave the sextant behind, and he made a point of ostentatiously praying the prescribed five times a day. However, an important tool of his work had been discarded, and he would be unable to check Burckhardt's measurements.

Again Burton had difficulties with his papers. His new companions had warned him that visas signed by the Turkish authorities at Cairo would delay his passage, not help. Again he was forced to face insolent officials, and his request for new papers was refused. In desperation he went to the British consul at Suez, who had been secretly informed of his plans. The consul brought his influence to bear on the Turks, and finally Burton received the proper signatures.

All was now in order. The party had booked passage to sail down the Red Sea to the Arabian port of Yambu', aboard the sambuk *Silk al-Zahab*, "the Golden Wire." The ship was crowded with pilgrims; there were ninety-seven aboard a vessel meant for sixty, and a violent battle over places broke out, a few pilgrims were stabbed in the melee, but Burton —so he wrote—restored order by dumping a large earthenware water jar over the crowd, and at last, about three in the afternoon on July 6, 1853 (Burton carefully noted the time and date of each phase of his journey), the sambuk shook out its sail and bellied into the wind. The pilgrims recited the customary Fātiḥah and Burton experienced "the heartbounding which prospects of an adventure excite." They were now sailing in "classic waters," for it was near this point where the Hebrews crossed in escaping from the Egyptians. At dusk the ship anchored for the night, since the waters were too dangerous to sail in the dark, and in the morning Burton lamented that he had carelessly buried his box of provisions in the hold—"worse still, my opium . . . was perfectly unapproachable"—and he had to breakfast on something popularly called "Mare's Skin," a sheet of dried apricot paste, and hard biscuits.

By the next midday, "men are not so much sleeping as half-senseless; they feel as if a few more degrees of heat would be death." In this frightful heat that drove men to the edge of insanity, Burton could note how kindly his companions on board ship treated each other, how they cared for the children, how they aided a Turkish woman whose baby was dying, how they shared their food. They had a "genuine politeness—kindness of heart."

At sunset everyone recovered. "We arise, still faint, and dizzy, calling for water . . . and pipes and coffee, and similar luxuries." Then, on a primitive stove in a clay box they would prepare "a little rice, a few dates, or an onion which will keep a man alive in our position."

So the days and nights passed. At an anchorage known as Wijh Harbour they were able to buy some foodstuffs—mutton, rice, baked bread, and "luxuries"—"a druggist sold me an ounce of opium at a Chinese price," that is, cheaply. Burton made more friends, prayed, suspected that his disguise was sometimes quietly questioned, but a true Afghan accepted him as a countryman, and he felt secure. At one point the ship was almost wrecked due to a short anchor cable—"We applied ourselves to the grateful task of beating the Rais [the captain] and richly he deserved it." It was for the most part an uneventful voyage, the days being passed in indolence, prayer, and chatter, the only problem being the relentless sun, "a fierce enemy, a foe that will force every one to crouch before him."

Now there came an accident that affected Burton's ability to perform the pilgrimage properly. At sunset on the fifteenth the ship anchored at a spot known as Marsa Mahár. No one had been ashore for forty-eight hours. Burton was restless.

> Wading ashore we cut our feet on the sharp rocks. I remember to have felt the acute pain of something running into my toe; but after looking at the place and extracting what appeared to be a bit of thorn, I dismissed the subject, little guessing the trouble it was to give me.

Burton had stepped on what he later believed to be a spine of the "egg-fruit," or sea urchin (*Echinus*), commonly supposed to be poisonous. He found it impossible to cure his foot. "Every remedy seemed to make it worse."

They were now a short sail from their goal, the port of Yambu'. But the captain was lazy, and "having duly beaten him," they anchored off the coast. Twelve days after leaving Suez, they were safely in the creek that led to Yambu' harbor. Burton's foot was by this time so infected that he "could scarcely place it upon the ground." At Yambu', he and his group had to bargain for camels for the overland ride to Medina. Burton had to buy a *shugduf*, or litter, in which to ride, for he could not walk. He was now among strict and very suspicious people, and he feared that some of the local people suspected he was not actually a Muslim. ("I observed them narrowly watching during *Wuzu* [the ritual ablutions] and prayers.") His companions cautioned him not to speak any language but Arabic, even to his Indian servant, and to dress as an Arab. Burton and his group were able to ally themselves with a caravan heading for Medina. The road was not safe for solitary pilgrims, for bands of nomads plundered and murdered strangers. Burton's group had twelve camels; there were two hundred pilgrims in all and an escort of seven irregular Turkish cavalry. Burton himself had two camel men, miserable-looking little Bedawi—"contemptible small chocolate-coloured beings, stunted and thin, with mops of coarse bushy hair burned brown by the sun, screaming voices, and well-made but attenuated limbs." They wore burnooses, or kufiyahs, "in the last stage of wear," and each had "a tattered shirt, indigo-dyed, and girt with a bit of common rope." However, "these ragged fellows . . . had their pride," and so Burton liked them, although they were lazy and often angered him by being obstinate.

On July eighteenth, about seven in the evening, the caravan passed through the city gate and took a due easterly course in the direction of Medina. "The moon rose fair and clear, dazzling us with light as we emerged from the shadowy streets. . . . My companions, as Arabs will do on such occasions, began to sing."

They traveled until three in the morning, when they stopped to sleep, awakening at nine, once more "in the 'dear Desert,'" exhilarated and hungry, and had a simple breakfast—how Burton liked to talk about his meals!—a biscuit, a little rice, and a cup of milkless tea. Burton took a look at the landscape while the others returned to their sleep. Before him was "an iron plain producing naught but stones and grasshoppers . . . the furious heat was drying up the sap and juice of the land, as the simmering, quivering atmosphere showed. . . ."

At two everyone awakened and had a simple meal—this, too, Burton had to describe—boiled rice with clarified butter, *samn* or ghee, a soft biscuit known as *kahk*, stale bread, pressed date-paste, and "a vile-tasting but wholesome drink called Akit," which seems to have been the common Middle Eastern drink of yogurt and water with spices. Finally, after suffering through a sandstorm, they were off again, traveling at night, Burton making notes on virtually everything he saw, thought, encountered, and heard, asking the names of mountains and streambeds, noting dialects and words, villages and the people who inhabited them, abandoned forts, the cost of provisions ("I bought a moderately sized sheep for a dollar"). He had looked forward to encampment at a certain well, which he envisioned as "pastoral scene, wild flowers, flocks and flowing waters" but "with jaundiced eye" saw that it was nothing but "a deep hole full of brackish water" and not a house in sight.

Meanwhile, Burton's wound became worse. "My sore foot had been inflamed by a dressing of onion skin which the lady Myryam [another pilgrim] had insisted upon applying to it." Burton had wanted to wash the wound with water, but his companions insisted that water would poison it.

Near Medina the caravan was attacked as it passed through a mountain gorge. Shots were fired down from the rocks above. It was a serious battle, though Burton tried to be blasé about it, but "the result of the affair was that we lost twelve men, besides camels and other beasts of burden."

On the night of July twenty-sixth the caravan stopped for the last time, El-Medina was a few miles away, and in the morning, before sunrise, they started off again, crossed a basalt ridge, "and after a few minutes a full view of the city opened upon us."

> We halted our beasts as if by word of command. All of us descended, in imitation of the pious of old, and sat down, jaded and hungry as we were, to feast our eyes with a view of the Holy City. . . . In all the fair view before us nothing was more striking after the desolation through which we had passed, than the gardens and orchards about the town.

"But . . . the traveller returned strong upon me." And Burton drew a rough sketch of the city in the distance, asked questions about the buildings, and made some notes.

17

The Prophet's Tomb

At last Burton had achieved part of his goal. Here was the second most important city in Islam (the first was Mecca, the third Jerusalem). In Medina was the tomb of the Prophet Muhammad—not in Mecca, as many Europeans supposed. "How often this gross mistake is still made," said Burton in the *Pilgrimage*. He had been invited to stay with Shaykh Hamid, who had hurried ahead, and when Burton arrived at the house of his host, he found that the shaykh had abandoned the dirty robes he wore on the journey and, having bathed and been shaved, was dressed in silk and fine cotton, elaborately fringed, of plaids and flowery patterns, and embroidered with gold. Soon Burton could observe that all his companions metamorphosed in an equally remarkable manner, appearing in tatters when necessary on a journey and fine linen where the world would judge their prosperity by their attire.

A morning of greeting people now followed, strangers who

came to visit the shaykh and meet his Afghan guest, so many that Burton called them "a plague," for he was hungry, tired, and thirsty and it was only with an effort that he was able to gain "the society I most desired—my own." Shaykh Hamid had wanted to set out immediately upon arrival to visit his father's grave and the tomb of the Prophet, but he deferred to Burton's exhaustion. In the afternoon, after a ritual ablution and dressed in white ("which the Apostle [Muḥammad] loved"), everyone was ready to visit the shrines. Since Burton's foot was as painful as ever, the shaykh sent for a donkey. "A wretched animal appeared, raw-backed, lame of one leg, and wanting an ear," and off they went.

A ride through muddy streets brought them to the Gate of Pity, and suddenly there was the mosque where the Prophet was buried. "I was astonished at the mean and tawdry appearance of a place so universally venerated in the Moslem world." It was not like the great Ka'aba at Mecca, "grand and simple, the expression of a single sublime idea." The longer Burton looked at the mosque, "the more it suggested the resemblance of a museum of second-rate art, an old Curiosity-shop, full of ornaments that are not accessories, and decorated with pauper splendour." A troup of beggars surrounded Burton and the shaykh, who had to fight their way to the entrance. Hamid asked Burton if he were "religiously pure," and in the formal position required, their hands at the left side of the waist, they entered. "In this Mosque, as in all others," Burton pointed out, "it is proper to enter with the right foot, and to retire with the left." The shaykh walked a few steps ahead of Burton, saying prayers for him to repeat, which he secretly wrote down in full. They had walked through various gardens, ending in one called the Rauzah, where Burton said the afternoon prayers, including "the usual two bows in honour of the temple," and finished with "the hundred and ninth and hundred and twelfth chapters of the Koran," both being short affirmations of Muslim unity and faith, the last of which he translated.

"Say, He is the one God!
The eternal God!
He begets not, nor is he begot!
And unto Him the like is not."

In the *Pilgrimage* volumes, Burton tried to emphasize that Muslims are not pagans, as so many Christians, including those of Victorian England, often charged. "It is only just to confess that Moslems have done their best by all means in human power, here as elsewhere, to inculcate the doctrine of eternal distinction between the creature and the Creator." That God might have issue, as the Christian doctrine of the Trinity implies, in the Muslim view is abhorrent. Jesus was not the Son of God but one of the Prophets and would come again as the Messiah at the end of time.

Having performed his prayers, Burton was besieged by beggars. Not wishing to be distracted by them, he had given some coins for alms to the boy Mohammed before leaving the shaykh's house. Now he turned his pockets inside out to show he had no money and let his servants distribute the alms. This allowed him to observe the famous garden where the Prophet himself had walked and prayed. "Little can be said in its praise by day," he remarked curtly, "when it bears the same relation to a second-rate church in Rome as an English chapel-of-ease to Westminster Abbey." He thought it was "tawdrily decorated," and its columns adorned "with gaudy and unnatural vegetation in arabesque." But at night "the eye, dazzled by oil-lamps suspended from the roof, by huge wax candles, and by smaller illuminations falling upon crowds of visitors in handsome attire . . . becomes less critical. Still, the scene must be viewed with a Moslem bias. . . ."

He prayed wherever told—at the tomb of the first khalīfs, Abu Bakr and 'Umar, and at the tomb of Fāṭima, the Prophet's daughter, and at the still-empty tomb of 'Isā—Jesus—for the Messiah was still expected. He was determined to find the exact location of the Prophet's burial place, and he devoted several pages in the *Pilgrimage* to speculation about its location, but he had to give up in frustration, baffled by not being able to solve a question that sensible people might have found an answer to by looking into one of a half-dozen or so unmarked graves, any one of which might have contained the sacred remains.

Prayers without end seemed to have been demanded wherever he went, and Burton was not at all lax in saying them. It seems to have been with reluctance that he finally wrote,

> Lastly, we returned to the Garden, and prayed another two-bow prayer, ending as we began, with the worship of the Creator. . . . Lastly, I was beset by beggars. . . . Some were mild beggars and picturesque . . . angry beggars . . . nosy and petulant beggars . . . pretty beggars, boys who held out the right hand on the score of good looks; ugly beggars, emaciated rascals whose long hair, dirt, and leanness entitled them to charity, and lastly, the blind, the halt and the diseased. . . .

The tomb of Muḥammad was the goal of the first part of the pilgrimage, although he could not say exactly which of the supposed tombs he had prayed before was the true one. The visit to Medina bestows the title of *Zair* upon the pilgrim (that to Mecca makes him or her a *haji*), and now Burton had time to wander about the city, observe its peoples, and make notes about the minutiae of daily life. Nothing seems to have escaped his notice: He gives a page to describing the dogs that roam the streets in packs ("stronger and braver than those . . . at Cairo") and how they fought and which dog would win. He did not overlook the mixed races that thronged the city, the various family clans, the outcasts and honored ones, dialects and words, the schools of Islamic philosophy, the types of animals (including three breeds of sheep), marriage customs, and dowries. Illnesses occupied his thoughts for a few pages: The "yellow wind"— Asiatic cholera—had visited the city, "sometimes carrying off whole households." Smallpox was especially "fatal to children." His own special affliction, ophthalmia, was "rare." "Low fevers," jaundice, bilious complaints, "dysenteries," hemorrhoids were all common, but *Filaria Medinensis*, the frightful swelling of the limbs caused by a worm in the bloodstream, had died out.

In his constant search for the new, the unusual, and the mere factual, Burton came across material that had interested him from his earliest days in Sind, where, he wrote, female circumcision is *not* practiced. In Medina there was ample evidence of the practice, which he wrote about at length in the *Pilgrimage*. Burton was in Bombay when the manuscript of the book was prepared for publication. His editor was John Gardiner Wilkinson, a man of some fame but minor talents and little competence to edit Burton, being an Egyptologist, not an Arabist. Wilkinson deleted some passages as "unpleasant garbage" and reduced others to footnotes in Latin, a language so common among educated Englishmen (and women) that it might as well have been left alone. Burton's material in a popular book was new and important as a revelation of an age-long battle that continues even today in the East.

Circumcision of both sexes is a very ancient custom among the Arabs. Theologians say that the inventor of this religious mutilation is Sarah, Ibrahim's wife, who, moved by jealousy, in order to lessen Hagar's love [for Ibrahim] tore out the sleeping girl's clitoris by the roots. Then, at Allah's command, Sarah and Ibrahim, both cut off part of their sexual organs with a little knife. Now, the cause of this practice in a man is cleanliness and health, in a young woman, it seems to be a preventative for unchastity. Asiatic peoples . . . all consider sexual desire in woman to be ten times greater than in man. (They cut off the clitoris because, as Aristotle warns, that organ is the seat and spring of sexual desire.) The philosopher could not figure out how great and powerful are the effects of this mutilation. The feelings, love, and desire of women grow less. The trickery, cruelty, vices, and insatiable extravagance of women increase. . . . Among the Somali, an African tribe, the cutting out of the bride's labiæ is accompanied by the cutting off of the clitoris. "Female circumcision is the universal custom in Egyptian Kahira and El Hejaz.

The Bedouin tribes do not wish to marry a whole [i.e., uncircumcised] wife."—Shaykh al-Nazawi. . . .*

Medina's legends and folklore were not overlooked; there was "the belief that an angel sits in each of its ten main streets, to watch over the town, and to prevent 'Antichrist' from entering therein." And what did a slave cost in Medina? A black slave girl for domestic use cost from $40 to $50 (Spanish), while "a little black boy, perfect in all his points, and tolerably intelligent, costs about a thousand piastres; girls are dearer, and eunuchs fetch double that sum." But a white girl from Circassia was too expensive for Medina, for one would "fetch from £100 to £400 prime cost, and few men in Al-Hijaz could afford so expensive a luxury."

In the affectionate, familial Orient Burton found it difficult to get isolation and silence. After the noonday meal, the major repast of the day, he would plead the necessity of a siesta or give the excuse of being a person of melancholic temperament and have a rug spread in the dark passage behind the big room where the family gathered to receive visitors. He would lie there, reading, dozing, smoking, or writing, stripped down for coolness.

Though he apparently thought of himself as a good and pious Muslim, at least for the present, there were certain things he could not give up. He noted that the Turks were "by no means remarkable for sobriety" and that even at Medina the local Turks made araki and other intoxicating liquors, though only they offended Islamic custom by drinking. Publicly he accepted custom but drank secretly. "During the whole time of my stay I had to content myself with a single bottle of Cognac, coloured and scented to resemble medicine."

---

* Although the onus for the practice is laid upon men, it is usually the women of the family, especially the older ones, like a grandmother or aunt, who insist that a young female child be so mutilated, an act of great barbarity performed at an early age without anesthesia. In Egypt, as elsewhere, even the Coptic Christians still practice female circumcision.

Burton spent over a month in Medina, revisiting the tombs and mosques and searching out the place in the Saint's Cemetery, Al-Bakia, where are interred "all the Prophet's wives" except for the first, Khadījah, who is at Mecca. Prayers were said everywhere, libraries visited for rare manuscripts, beggars fended off, notes made without end.

He was conscious of his prolixity in the *Pilgrimage*. "I have now described at wearying length I fear, the spots visited by every Zair [pilgrim] at Al-Medinah," but he could not omit adding a list of mosques mentioned in the Arabic guidebooks, "most of which are now unknown even by name to the citizens." But then he could not resist describing fourteen tombs of saints. One cannot overlook the fact that he had every moment risked his life to gather and record each scrap of information on tiny, square, numbered pieces of paper, to be reassembled in some strange puzzle that only he could solve.

18

The Holiest City

Finally, it was time to set out for Mecca. The Damascus caravan, which had been gathering pilgrims along the route from the city that gave it its name, was to depart on September first. Burton had hoped to leave by another caravan—the "Flying Caravan"—which was to leave later but arrive in Mecca at the same time, but it was canceled. It followed an inland route no other European had ever taken, but the desert tribes had suddenly gone to war with each other. "A splendid comet, blazing in the western sky," had aroused predictions of the usual disasters— "war, famine and pestilence"—and some subfamilies of the Benu-Harb "began to fight about this time with prodigious fury." This desert war put an end to Burton's secret hope that he could have defied Hogg's orders and proceeded not to Mecca but to Muscat, one of the easternmost areas of Arabia, and then doubled back the next year, thus enabling him to see the mysterious Empty Quarter. It would have been a trip "dangerous to the extreme" of some fifteen or sixteen hundred miles. He had been ordered to return to Bombay by March the next year under pain of losing his commission, but he believed that the successful accomplishment of this rash but important venture would have excused him. Now he had but one choice, the Damascus Caravan, and he immediately pulled his kit together. He had to repair his waterskins, chewed by rats, and he packed up enough "wheatflour, rice, turmeric, onions, dates, unleavened bread of two kinds, cheese, limes, tobacco, sugar, tea and coffee" for himself and his camel men for eleven days and to compensate for spoilage and pilfering by fellow pilgrims.

Burton had hired two Bedawi, an old man and his son. They called him Abu Shawarib, the "Father of Mustachios," because he was not shaved according to their religious precepts. Burton's foot still pained him. He had the *shugduf*, the litter, repaired and put on his camel, and they were ready to go. He could congratulate himself "upon having passed through the first danger," the trip to Medina.

> The next risk to be run was the journey between the two cities, where it would be easy for the local officials quickly to dispose of a suspected person by giving a [Spanish] dollar to a Bedawi.

The appearance of the caravan as it slowly crossed the plain was "striking."

> To judge by the eye, the host was composed of at fewest seven thousand souls, on foot, on horseback, in litters, or bestriding the splendid camels of Syria. . . . I include in the 7,000 about 1,200 Persians.

The caravan had departed suddenly on a mere hour's notice on the morning of August thirty-first and traveled all day. In the desert heat, problems immediately arose.

> After the long and sultry afternoon, beasts of burden began to sink in numbers. The fresh carcasses of asses, ponies, and camels dotted the wayside: those that had been allowed to die were abandoned to the foul carrion-birds, the Rakham (vulture) and the yellow

Ukáb [unidentified]; and all whose throats had been properly cut [according to Islamic law], were surrounded by troops of Takruri pilgrims [a Negro tribe from the Sudan]. These half-starved creatures cut steaks from the choice portions, and slung them over their shoulders till an opportunity of cooking might arrive. I never saw men more destitute. . . . I fancied death depicted in their forms and features.

The caravan pushed on, in long forced marches that tried to make the most of the cool hours of the early morning; often it rested until an hour after midnight, and then the wakening gun to strike the tents (for those fortunate enough to have them) would sound, and shortly "a second bids you move off with all speed." There were brief halts of half an hour each, at dawn, noon, the afternoon, and sunset, for the Islamic prayers. Then at night a three-gun warning denoted the station of rest.

It was a monotonous journey, under trying conditions—thirst was a constant problem—but Burton did not neglect to gather information, scribbling down notes about the landscape, the possibility of gold, the superstitions of the Arabs, new words, and the pilgrims with whom he was traveling.

He tried to reach a conclusion to the interesting subject he had broached in London, the origin of the peoples of Arabia, but he had to state that in his opinion there was not in Arabia " 'one Arab face, cast of features and expression,' as was formerly supposed to be the case," and he was forced to admit that the picture of "The Pretty Bedawi Girl" in the *Pilgrimage* is not of a Bedawi; the dress is Arab, but it was worn by "a fairy of the West."* His failure to place the true source of the Arabs, however, did not prevent his filling an entire chapter on "The Bedawi of Al-Hijaz," in which he not only analyzed the various races and described some genealogies (always important to Arabs) but

---

* One might wonder if this was Isabel Arundell posing for the drawing, but the face, being heavily koh'l'd in the Arab manner, is impossible to identify.

also gave a census of various subdivisions, and *their* subdivisions, and *their* subdivisions, along with a detailed accounting of their manner of living, pastimes, and methods of war, information that half a century later was appreciated for its accuracy and detail by other travelers.

When a Turk disemboweled an Arab camel man in an argument, Burton asked the condition of the wounded man. He was not yet dead.

> I was assured that he had been comfortably wrapped up in his shroud, and placed in a half-dug grave. This is the general practice in the case of the poor and solitary, whom illness or accident incapacitates from proceeding. It is impossible to contemplate such a fate without horrors; the torturing thirst of a wound, the burning sun heating the brain to madness, and—worst of all, for they do not wait till death—the attacks of the jackal, the vulture, and the raven of the wild.

They passed through wild landscapes, small villages, and then a desolate plain. "This day's march was peculiarly Arabia. It was a desert peopled only with echoes,—a place of death for what little there is to die in it,—a wilderness where, to use my companion's phrase, there is nothing but He [that is, Allāh]." At last, after "nature scalped, flayed, discovered all her skeleton to the gazer's eye [and] the horizon was a sea of mirage," they descended to land that was thickly wooded, where mist and dew filled the air. The caravan pitched tents, and after a sound sleep, the pilgrims underwent the ceremony of Al-Iḥrām ("literally meaning 'prohibition' or 'making unlawful,' " Burton explained), the putting on of the special pilgrim dress, the *iḥrām*, after a ritual purification, in which the male pilgrims had their heads shaved by a barber, their nails clipped, and their mustachios trimmed. The women, too, had their nails cut and their hair shampooed. Both male and female pilgrims were required to remove pubic and underarm hair. The men's *iḥrām* was simple and unsewn; in theory, the shoulder piece, the *rida*, should not even be knotted to keep it from slipping, but, remarked Burton, "in spite of this interdiction, pilgrims, generally, for convenience, knot their shoulder-clothes under the right arm." Women were allowed sewn clothes, white or light blue (but not black); however, the face veil had to be kept from touching the face.

By midafternoon the caravan was ready to set off again. By now it was close to the Ḥaram Sharīf, the sacred area that included Mecca. "A wondrously picturesque scene it was," with the pilgrims dressed in white and crying out, "Labbayk! Labbayk!"—"Here I am!" A group of Wahhābīs, a much-feared sect of fundamentalists who were noted for their violence and puritanical beliefs, fell in with the caravan, "by no means pleasant companions," Burton wrote. But early the next morning they were instrumental in fighting off an attack by brigands.

After the battle, the caravan continued through the evening and early night, until at one o'clock in the morning they found themselves entering Mecca. It was Sunday, September 11, 1853—"the 7th Zu'l Hijjah," wrote Burton, using the Islamic calendar. Threading their way through the dark streets "in places crowded with rude cots and dusky figures," they arrived an hour later at the house of the boy Mohammed, who kicked the porter awake. Mohammed, formerly "boisterous and jaunty," was now "grave and attentive"—Burton had become his guest. The shuffling of slippered feet in another room told Burton's "hungry ears" that food was being prepared, and soon there appeared "a dish of fine vermicelli, browned and powdered with loaf-sugar. The boy Muhammed, I, and Shaykh Nur, lost no time in exerting our right hands. . . ." Then it was time for a brief rest before beginning the pilgrim rites.

"There at last it lay," wrote Burton in a mood of exaltation, "realizing the plans and hopes of many and many a year." Before him was the huge square catafalque, the Ka'aba, the Sacred House of God, the Bait al-Allāh. He reflected that it had none of the beauty or greatness of the architecturally famous buildings of ancient Egypt or Greece, Italy or India, "yet the view was strange, unique—and how few have looked upon the celebrated shrine!"

> I may truly say that, of all the worshippers who clung weeping to the curtain, or who pressed their beating hearts to the stone, none felt for the moment a deeper emotion than did the Haji from the far-north.

He added, "Few Moslems contemplate for the first time the Ka'abah, without fear and awe," but he had to qualify this statement by saying, "To confess the humbling truth, theirs was the high feeling of religious enthusiasm, mine was the ecstasy of gratified pride," an admission that cast some doubt on the sincerity of his commitment to Islam.

The boy Mohammed left Burton alone for a few minutes before leading him to various sacred places in the great square in which the Ka'aba was centered, allowing him to start his notes, piling up detail upon detail—again those scribbles on tiny numbered squares of paper! Burton began with the Bāb Benu Shaybah, the "Gate of the Sons of the Old Woman," one of the twenty-four gates leading to the Ka'aba, and going to the famous well Zamzam. ("The word Zemzem has a doubtful origin," concluded Burton after several pages that try the reader's patience.) Zamzam was the sacred well of Hagar, the Prophet Ibrāhim's slave girl. Ibrāhim (or Abraham), sacred to Muslims as well as Jews and Christians, had abandoned Hagar and Isma'īl (Ishmael), their boy-child, in the desert with nothing but some dates and a jug of water as sustenance. After a frantic search for water, Hagar found it gushing from the very spot where the child's feet had touched the earth. The pool soon attracted nomads, and eventually a town, then a city—Mecca—developed around the site. Ibrāhim returned later from Canaan and with Isma'īl, now a grown man, built the first earthly Ka'aba, the original having come down from heaven. *

"The produce of Zemzem is held in great esteem," Burton wrote. "It is used for drinking and religious ablution, but for no baser [sanitary] purposes. . . . It is apt to cause diarrhoea and boils . . . the flavour is salt-bitter, and much resembling an infusion of a teaspoon of Epsom salts in a large tumbler of water. . . ."

> Religious men break their lenten [Ramaḍān] fast with it, apply it to their eyes to brighten vision, and imbibe a few drops at the hour of death, when Satan stands by holding a bowl of purest water, the price of the departing soul. . . . Everywhere the nauseous draught is highly meritorious in a religious point of view.

With devotions at the well completed, the pilgrims now turned their attention to the Ka'aba itself. It was a huge cube of masonry and was the holiest center of Islam, in fact, the "center of Earth." Set in the southeast corner, at a height that allowed it to be touched only with difficulty, was the Black Stone, a mysterious object that Burton later tried to analyze. At the moment, because of the crowds, he could get no closer than ten yards, but he raised his hands and said the customary prayer of praise to "Allah alone."

After this came the ceremony of Tawāf, the circumambulation of the Ka'aba, in imitation of the Prophet Muḥammad when he returned to Mecca as a conqueror after his exile in Medina. Muḥammad and his warrior-elders had run around the Ka'aba for three circuits but became so exhausted that they could finish the final four only at a walk, a practice followed by Muslims ever since.

---

* Genesis 21, 1–20, has a different version of the story of Abraham, Hagar, and Ishmael, and the locale is Beer-sheba in the Negeb, not Mecca. "God was with the lad," destining him to be the ancestor of the Bedawin of the southern wilderness.

As he made his circumambulations, and immersed in the religious meanings of the rite, Burton could not help noticing that the pilgrims went in the opposite direction to that followed by other cultures. "The Moslem in circumambulation presents his left shoulder," going widdershins or counterclockwise, while "the Hindu's Pradashina [circumambulation] consists of walking with the right side towards the fane or idol . . . and our processions round the [Christian] parish preserve the form of ancient rites, whose life is long since fled."

Burckhardt had already described the Ka'aba in detail, and Burton, in his book, found it simplest to honor his predecessor with "an extract from his pages," making corrections as he saw fit.

The Ka'aba was indeed an impressive though simple structure, standing in an oblong square, the Harām, enclosed by a great wall. Burckhardt had measured the Ka'aba as "18 paces in length, 14 in breadth, and from 35 to 40 feet in height," but Burton in remeasuring got different figures: "My measurements give 22 paces or 55 feet in length by 18 (45) in breadth, and the height appeared greater than the length." When one realizes that each man made his calculations at the risk of immediate violent death at the hands of angry guards, one wonders if the difference of a few feet is at all important.

From time to time Burton continued to differ from the illustrious Swiss. "This I believe to be incorrect," he says of Burckhardt's statement that there is a stone in Mecca upon which the Pharaoh had stood, leaving the mark of his feet, but he was unwilling to bribe the guards to view it, and a minor point remained unclarified.

Burton finally had a chance to see the Black Stone. The boy Mohammed, aided by half a dozen fellow Meccans and roundly cursing the other pilgrims, beat a path to the Stone through a crowd of angry worshipers.

After thus reaching the stone, despite popular indignation testified by impatient shouts, we monopolized the use of it for at least ten minutes. Whilst kissing it and rubbing hands and forehead upon it I narrowly observed it, and came away persuaded that it is an aerolite [other travelers, including Burckhardt, had thought it "volcanic" in origin].

In every spot where Burton prayed, he was careful to observe the rite to its most minute detail, and he seemed to have prayed with sincerity and conviction, but finally, about ten in the morning, "thoroughly worn out with scorched feet and a burning head,—both extremities, it must be remembered were bare—" Burton left the mosque and returned to his quarters. That evening, in the company of the boy Mohammed and his slave, Nūr, Burton returned to the Ka'aba. He spread out his prayer rug before it, "this time aesthetically to enjoy the delights of the hour." The moon was almost full, and its beams were reflected on the surrounding buildings, drawing from him a comment of appreciation.

> One object, unique in its appearance, stood in view—the temple of the one Allah, the God of Abraham, of Ishmael, of their posterity. Sublime it was, and expressing by all the eloquence of fancy the grandeur of the One Idea which vitalized Al-Islam, and the strength and steadfastness of its votaries.

He had wanted to visit Isma'īl's grave, but the crowds kept him away until late; then he saw an open spot but had a fight over it with another pilgrim. Eventually, his two companions dozed off. Burton went up to the Ka'aba "with the intention of 'annexing' a bit of the torn old Kiswat or curtain, but too many eyes were looking on." The cloth was considered both sacred and a source of good luck and was much desired by pilgrims (later, Burton was given a fragment by Mohammed). Despite this minor frustration, "the opportunity, however, was favourable for a survey with a piece of tape, and the simple process of stepping and spanning. I managed to measure all the objects concerning which I was curious."

The next morning Burton and his companions, on camels,

began the first of the formal rites of the pilgrimage, the visit to the sacred mountain of 'Arafāt, a few miles from the city, where the Prophet had been accustomed to speak to the faithful. The road was filled with white-robed pilgrims, many on foot, some on horses, camels, or asses. "Dead animals dotted the ground," Burton wrote. It was a slow trip, about six hours for most pilgrims, although Burton's party, pushing their camels, arrived in a shorter time. The heat wearied the animals, but "human beings suffered more."

I saw no fewer than five men fall down and die upon the highway; exhausted and moribund, they had dragged themselves out to give up the ghost where it departs to instant beatitude. The spectacle showed how easy it is to die in these latitudes; each man suddenly staggered, fell as if shot; and, after a brief convulsion, lay as still as marble.

The normally empty fiumara, the dry riverbed below the hill of 'Arafāt, now had become a city. A main street of tents and booths, huts and shops, a bazaar, had suddenly appeared and was crowded with people. Burton estimated the number of pilgrims at fifty thousand, but the Arabs believed that the crowd could never be counted and "if a fewer than 600,000 mortals stand upon the hill to hear the sermon, the angels descend and complete the number." Burton noted the usual drunken Albanians and "knots of Egyptians . . . noisily intoxicating themselves with forbidden hemp." The boy Mohammed lent Burton a fine red cashmere shawl to replace the upper portion of his pilgrim's garb, which was "way-soiled," and had tents pitched for the party; they were forced to defend their space against grave diggers who wanted to "bury a little heap of bodies within a yard or two of our tent." Nearby, an old Muslim chanted all night, keeping Burton from sleep. "The coffee-houses too, were by no means silent; deep into the night I heard the clapping of hands accompanying merry Arab songs, and the loud shouts of laughter from the Egyptian hemp-drinkers."

The next morning Burton inspected the holy hill of 'Arafāt, a projection of stone in the heart of a broad, barren valley, with traditions going back to the hoary past. "This is the site where, banished from Paradise, lost in the wilderness and wastes of a strange world, Adam and Eve found one another after two centuries' separation," stated one of the pilgrim guidebooks.

Now it was time for the major ceremonies to begin. Thousands of people had assembled, "all in a state of excitement." Guns sounded incessantly, horsemen dashed about, the women and children wandered restlessly. Burton was soon unpleasantly surprised by the arrival of a Meccan he had met, Ali bin Ya Sin Zemzemi, who had lost his mule and, seeing Burton's party, attached himself to it. "He was far too curious and too observant to suit my tastes," Burton wrote.

Finally, in the middle of the afternoon—the noonday and the afternoon prayers had been said by this time—the ceremonies began to take shape. A procession of warriors and Bedawins, armed slaves, the Sharīf of Mecca and his family and courtiers took up positions on the hill. The crowd fell into silence, and the khatib, the preacher, began the rites for the Wuqūf, or Standing. The pilgrims, if they were physically able, were to stand throughout the entire afternoon until the sun passed the horizon. "From my tent I could distinguish the form of the old man [the preacher] upon his camel, but the distance was too great for ear to reach," Burton wrote. "But how came I to be at the tent?" he asked rhetorically, for the sermon on 'Arafāt was the central point of the pilgrimage for which he had risked so much. Why was he not at the side of the preacher memorizing his words? He even had a square of paper in his hand on which he had intended to write down the salient points, but there was

a tall girl, about eighteen years old, with regular features, a skin somewhat citrine-coloured, but soft and clear, symmetrical eyebrows, the most beautiful eyes, and a figure all grace. . . . The shape was what the Arabs love, soft, bending, and relaxed, as a woman's ought to be.

Instead of the customary heavy veil, she wore one of transparent muslin, and she began to flirt with Burton, who was quite noticeable in the boy Mohammed's red cashmere shawl.

> By the usual coquettish gesture [she] threw back an inch or two of head-veil, disclosing broad bands of jetty hair . . . and soon a dimpled mouth and a rounded chin stood out. . . . Seeing that my companions were safely employed in listening to the sermon, I entered the dangerous ground of raising my hand to forehead. She smiled imperceptibly, and turned away. The pilgrim was in ecstasy.

The sermon lasted three hours. Burton did not hear a word of it as he flirted with the young woman. He may have been experiencing unresolved and vivid memories of the aristocratic Persian girl in Sind—this young Meccan woman and her family were also "fair" and "apparently belonging to the higher classes." Finally, the preacher gave the signal to depart—no one was allowed to leave earlier—and the race to quit 'Arafāt began. All was confusion. "Every man urged his beast with might and main; it was sunset . . . litters were crushed, pedestrians were trampled, camels were overthrown . . . here a woman, there a child, and there an animal was lost; briefly, it was chaotic confusion."

Burton was attempting to make a sketch of 'Arafāt while keeping an eye on the girl and at the same time avoiding the questions of the inquisitive old man from Mecca. Frustration! "The charming face that smiled at me from the litter grew dimmer and dimmer . . . a string of camels crossed our path—I lost sight of the beauty." Burton's only consolation was that he was able to make a "rough drawing of the Mountain of Mercy."

The following day—the party had made a three-hour ride at night to escape the crowd at 'Arafāt—came the next major rite, the ceremony of the stoning at a village called Minā. There is here, as Burton described it, "a dwarf buttress of rude masonry, about eight feet high by two and a half broad." This was the Shaytan al-Kabir, the Great Devil, the first of three similar monuments that mark "the successive spots where the Devil, in the shape of an old shaykh, appeared to Adam, Abraham, and Ishmael, and was driven back by the simple process taught by Gabriel, of throwing stones about the size of a bean." The Shaytan al-Kabir was located in a narrow defile, and it was filled with the faithful, who were each to throw seven stones at it, "all struggling like drowning men to approach as near as possible to the Devil. . . ."

"Avoiding being trampled on by a judicious use of the knife, I lost no time in escaping from a place so ignobly dangerous," Burton wrote. Is he telling his readers that he had to wound, perhaps kill, someone to save himself from the crushing mass of pilgrims? Or is he merely being dramatic? Finally, he and the boy Mohammed were able to throw their stones while shouting, "In the name of Allah, and Allah is almighty! [I do this] in hatred of the Fiend and to his Shame," after which they said a verse in praise of Allāh.

This was the formal ending of the pilgrimage. Now Burton would be free to resume normal clothing—his Arab robes—and to bathe. "The barber removed all my hair," he wrote, meaning not only the hair on his head but his pubic and underarm hair as well. There was a prayer for this, too: "O Allah, make unto me every Hair, a Light, a Purity, and a generous Reward!" Burton could then cover his head from the sun with the end of his *ihrām* until he could get back to Mecca and get his regular clothing.

He rushed to the city as quickly as possible to bathe again and visit the Ka'aba before the other pilgrims arrived. The boy Mohammed had found that the Ka'aba was for the moment empty of pilgrims, and Burton went off still in his *ihrām*. As a man who was now a *haji*, Burton wanted to enter the shrine. The door of the building is not at ground level but some seven feet above it. He was lifted up by the guards, and then he was inside, being questioned by "several officials, dark-looking Meccans." Having satisfactorily answered them about his name, nation, and other particulars, he was allowed to continue.

> I will not deny that, looking at the windowless walls, the officials at the doors, and the crowd of excited fanatics below . . . my feelings were of the trapped-rat description. . . . This did not, however, prevent my carefully observing the scene during our long prayers, and making a rough plan with a pencil upon my white Irham.

There was nothing more simple than the interior of this celebrated building: It was constructed of slabs of fine marble; the floor was made of white-and-colored marble in a checkerboard pattern. It was considered disrespectful to look at the ceiling— "unsafe for a pilgrim," Burton remarked—but he did, noting the cross beams and their size and the type of wood. "Perspiration trickled in large drops, and I thought with horror what it must be when filled with a mass of furiously jostling and crushing fanatics."

Finally, after the customary prayers, he was passed through the door by the brawny Meccan guards and felt free. "Wallah, Effendi!" said Mohammed ambiguously, "thou has escaped well! Some men have left their skins behind."

Burton rushed back to his lodging, exhausted, "and washed with henna and warm water, to mitigate the pain of sun-scalds upon my arms, shoulders, and breast" and was served "a pipe, coffee, cold water, and breakfast."

He was supposed to have sacrificed an animal at Minā but had put it off: his funds were running low, and he was hoping to avoid further expenses. Now he had to return. He got into a conversation with some Meccans, a foolish move, for "I afterwards learned from the boy Mohammed, that all pronounced me to be an Ajami," a Shī'a. Perhaps he was getting careless from exhaustion and the heat, but this was an unfavorable sign.

He "feared the pestilential air of Mina," for "literally the land stank." Five or six thousand animals had been slaughtered and cut up. "Considering the meagre condition of my purse, I could not buy a sheep, but contented myself with watching my neighbours. . . . The surface of the valley came to resemble the dirtiest slaughter-house." Burton worried that his "prescient soul drew bad auguries for the future," but nothing untoward happened to impede his leaving Minā, which was now coming to resemble "a volcanic crater, an Aden." The next day he completed the rites of the stoning. All the obligations of a pilgrim had been met, and as a *haji* he could wear the green turban that denoted a man who had been to Mecca and had fulfilled his sacred duty.

He had a few days of rest among his friends, and he consulted them about the possibility of continuing eastward to Muscat. He had been complaining about his lack of funds but the trip across the Arabian peninsula would have involved considerable expense, and he failed to say how he would have financed it. However, the desert tribes were still at war and such a trip would be unsafe. "Briefly I saw that my star was not then in the ascendant, and resolved to reserve myself for a more propitious conjuncture by returning to Egypt."

In concluding his account of his travels, to forestall criticism for having participated in "pagan" rites, knowing that the English in general viewed Islam as hardly better than the rank Hinduism, with its millions of deities, he wrote forcibly about the Faith. "Of the pilgrimage ceremonies I cannot speak harshly," he wrote, noting that Christianity in Europe still retained elements of earlier paganism—"the English mistletoe, the Irish wake, the pardons of Britanny, the [pre-lenten] Carnival, and the worship at Iserna—what nation," he asked, "either in the West or in the East, has been able to cast out from its ceremonies every suspicion of its old idolatry? . . . At Mecca there is nothing theatrical, nothing that suggests the opera"—he was here comparing Islamic to Roman Catholic rites, especially at Rome—"but all is simple and impressive . . . tending, I believe, after its fashion, to good." He even tried to reconcile the Muslim belief that Ībrāhim and his son Isma'īl built the Ka'aba with the account in Genesis of the Great Patriarch by remarking it "has been suggested to learned men the idea of two Abrahams."

At last, every mosque having been seen, every holy spot prayed at, the Ka'aba visited over and over again, secretly measured and examined, the Zamzam water tasted and speculated about—at last it was time to pack up and leave. Rejecting the idea of returning by the Medina route, a most dangerous venture, Burton hired two camels and sent his possessions ahead with the slave Nūr and followed on donkeys with the boy Mohammed. Other pilgrims joined them—it was the foolish man who journeyed alone in Arabia—and without incident and without recording details—Burton seems to have been truly exhausted at this point, tired of traveling, tired of a torturous and dangerous venture, and tired of making secret notes—he pushed ahead and in eleven hours of overnight riding arrived in early morning at Jeddah, passing through the mass of hovels, coffeehouses, cemeteries, and sandhills that formed the eastern approach to the port. He found a room, had it swept clean, and made it as comfortable as possible. "At Jeddah I felt once more at home," he wrote. "The sight of the sea acted as a tonic."

Now he was truly strapped for money. He had camels and donkeys to pay for and servants to settle with. Still dressed as an Arab, he went to the British consul, a Mr. Charles Cole, but the dragoman refused to admit him. In desperation, Burton scrawled a note saying he was "an officer of the Indian army," and "an exclamation of astonishment and a hospitable welcome followed." Burton and Cole quickly became friends, financial problems were resolved, and Burton patiently awaited the ship to Cairo, intending to pass on quickly to Bombay from there. Weariness is evident now. "Jeddah has been often described by modern pens," he wrote in a lame excuse for not treating the port with a chapter—Burckhardt and Edward William Lane among others had devoted considerable space to this "unhappy capital" of the Hijazi lowlands.

There was one minor religious duty to fulfill, a visit to the grave of Eve, "The Mother of Mankind." The grave was rather remarkable, for it was of unusual length: Burton measured off a hundred and twenty paces from head to waist—there was a small square stone at this point—and eighty from waist to heel. He remarked to the boy Mohammed that if our first parent were of such an odd shape, "she must have presented the appearance of a duck." The Mother, he added, "is supposed to lie, like a Moslemah, fronting the Ka'aba, with her feet northwards, her head southwards, and her right cheek propped by her right hand."

"It is not easy to pass the time at Jeddah," he complained. He had now become careless. Tired and enervated, his foot still paining him, he made some slip or other that aroused the suspicions of the continually suspicious boy Mohammed, who had asked for a large amount of money in order to buy grain and had then disappeared. The slave Nūr told Burton that Mohammed had said, "Now I understand. Your master is a sahib from India [that is, a white man]. He hath laughed in our beards."

"For a time my peregrinations ended," Burton wrote in conclusion in the *Pilgrimage*. "Worn out with fatigue, and the fatal fiery heat, I embarked (Sept. 26) on board the 'Dwarka'," now as an Englishman rumored to have gone to the Holy City and "wondering the while how the Turkish pilgrims who crowded the vessel did not take the trouble to throw me overboard." In due time he arrived at Suez, and in the final paragraph of the *Pilgrimage* he concludes with the words of another traveler, the famous Chinese voyager Fa-Hian.

> I have been exposed to perils, and I have escaped from them; I have traversed the sea, and have not succumbed under the severest fatigues; and my heart is moved with emotions of gratitude, that I have been permitted to effect the objects I had in view.

Burton might have returned to London a hero—his pilgrimage had now been reported in the English newspapers, and his success was hailed as an outstanding example of British daring, though

Burton himself, however pleased that he had accomplished what so few had before him, had to see it in a different light: He was a Muslim, and it was both his Muslim duty and his Muslim privilege to go to Mecca. However, those born Muslims who learned that a Frank had violated their most sacred sanctuary considered it neither daring nor duty nor privilege but blasphemy. There were other considerations also: Burton had to be back with his regiment in Bombay by March 1854, there was not enough time for a trip to London, and if he were late in returning to his regimental duties, he was in danger of losing his commission, though on the basis of his new fame—notoriety, perhaps—he might have been able to override red tape and regulations and get his leave extended. He settled down briefly at the famed Shepheard's Hotel in Cairo to piece together his notes and to begin work on his account of the pilgrimage.

He was in an ambiguous position about what role he should, wanted to, play. He may have again become an English officer in good standing, but he retained his Arab dress, not as a disguise but because he had virtually become an Arab. Religion is to some extent cultural. Christian converts in India (and elsewhere) were forced to wear Western dress; it seemed logical that a convert to Islam would wear some form of dress identified with Islam. The result was that numerous anecdotes about Burton appearing as an Arab have come out of this period. One day he saw a group of familiar officers sitting on the veranda of Shepheard's. Striding up and down in the characteristic loose-limbed stride of the desert Arab, his burnoose flowing behind him, Burton "accidentally" brushed against one of the officers. "Damn that nigger's impudence," said the officer. "If he does that again, I'll kick him."

Burton wheeled about and said, "Well, damn it, Hawkins, that's a nice way to welcome a fellow officer, after two years' absence."

"By God, it's Ruffian Dick," said Hawkins as the officers crowded about Burton.

Also he went back to the Gulshani oratory (or to another

ṭarīqa) to participate in the rites. The anecdote that is told about his part in the rites is undated: it may have happened in the fall of 1853, after his return from Mecca; it was published in a London newspaper after the appearance of the sixth volume of his *Arabian Nights*.

> How completely he is at home with his adopted brethren [the Muslims] he showed in Cairo, when, to the amusement of some English friends who were looking on at the noisy devotions of some "howling" Dervishes, he suddenly joined the shouting, gesticulating circle, and behaved as if to the manner born. He has qualified as a "howler," he holds a diploma as a master Dervish, and he can initiate disciples.

There were other reasons for passing himself off as an Arab. From time to time he visited the Oulid Nahl women or other prostitutes. At some point during the pilgrimage, either when he was in Alexandria or on either of his stays in Cairo, he contracted syphilis. The army physician who treated him two years later, after his fight with Somali maurauders, noted that besides the wound to his face, Burton also "has recently suffered from secondary syphilis."

Burton soon moved from Shepheard's to the more congenial house of an Italian revolutionary named Galeazzo Visconti. A young man named Fred Hankey was also staying there. Hankey, a notorious libertine, had been traveling on the Barbary Coast of North Africa. In a letter to Dr. Norton Shaw, the Secretary of the Royal Geographical Society, on November 16, 1853, Burton wrote that Visconti's house was "a center of depravity, showing what Cairo can do at a pinch, and beating the Arabian Nights all to chalk—that, too, when the Pasha [Visconti] has positively forbidden fornication."

But more serious matters than Sufi dancing and romps with Gypsy prostitutes were on his mind. He sought out a man newly arrived in Cairo, a missionary named Johannes Ludwig Krapf, a linguist and explorer, who in the 1830s had worked among the

Abyssinians and then, in the company of another missionary, Johannes Rebmann, among the Gallas of Somaliland. Krapf and Rebmann had gone into Central Africa to set up a chain of mission posts—an "Apostle's Street"—but, wrote Burton, "never made enough converts to stock a single house," a failure that brought his scorn. However, Krapf possessed information that intrigued Burton. He and Rebmann had repeatedly heard reports of "a vast inland sea in the direction where the Nile sources were said to be, from 0°30′N to 13°30′S." Burton was now mulling over expeditions to almost anywhere rather than return to garrison duty in India.

He informed Shaw that Krapf had come "with discoveries about the source of the White Nile, Killamanjaro, and Mts of the Moon which reminded one of a de Lunatico." The source of the Nile was a mystery that had intrigued, puzzled, and baffled mankind since the age of Herodotus. In Burton's time there was much speculation about the river's headquarters due to the numerous reports gleaned from the Arab slavers and traders who had penetrated the depths of Africa's eastern coast. Periodically, Europeans had attempted to search out the source but had been repeatedly turned back by impassable jungles and hostile natives.

With the success of his Meccan pilgrimage and the fame it had brought him, Burton was looking forward to another trip of equal daring. Why not search for the Nile? It would take him into parts of Africa where no white man had ever set foot before. In his letter to Shaw he had mentioned the prospects of an expedition to Zanzibar, a small, semibarbarous island lying five degrees north of the equator. Burton informed Shaw that the island was "one of the headquarters of slavery"—a subject that always angered him—and that it was "the Americans [who] are gently but surely carrying off the commerce of the country [which] has vast resources still undeveloped." By now Burton more and more had come to favor an expedition to Africa rather than a return to Arabia, for though he remarked that traveling there was a joy and little would please him more than several years passed in exploring the vast eastern coast of Arabia, still virtually unknown, "nothing except more discovery of deserts, valleys and tribes would come of it."

Burton's plan now was an expedition that would begin on the Somaliland coast of northeastern Africa, the so-called Horn of Africa, and proceed into the interior to Harar, a legendary city whose rulers had barred it to whites and even to African Christians, and then turn south, hoping on the way to locate the source of the Nile. After that he would proceed east to Zanzibar. At least the first part of his proposal was of interest to the powers in London. Exploration of the Somaliland coast had been suggested only in 1850 by a Dr. Carter of the East India Company. The Royal Geographical Society had not put its weight behind Carter because it was more interested in the interior and there was some information already about the coastal areas. Carter made a cautious probe of the Somaliland shores, a venture that brought Burton's sarcasm. "Carter, not relishing the chance of losing his cods—that misguided people [the Somali tribes] are in the habit of cutting them off and hanging them as ornaments around their arms—refused to explore the interior," Burton remarked in his letter to Shaw.

The penetration of the Somali coast offered an immediate goal that was as exciting as the pilgrimage to Mecca. The exotic and mysterious city of Harar, some two hundred miles inland from the coast, was perched five thousand feet above sea level, barely known but forbidding, dangerous, and enticing—the very thought of it made an adventurous man's hair stand on end. Harar, wrote Burton in *First Footsteps in East Africa; or, An Exploration of Harar*, was "a counterpart of the ill-famed Timbuctoo in the Far West."

It was a holy and forbidden city. No white man was ever believed to have gone there, though many had tried, among them Dr. Krapf. All had "attempted in vain. . . . The bigoted ruler and barbarous people threatened death to the Infidel who ventured within their walls." There was a superstition that if foreigners once entered the city, it would decline and fall.

> It [was], therefore a point of honour with me . . . to utilize my title of Haji by entering the city, visiting the ruler, and returning to safety after breaking the guardian spell.

Burton could linger in Cairo no longer. Still very much the *haji*, in Arab dress, and wearing the green turban that was the privilege of those who had made the *hajj*, he boarded the *Dwarka* at Suez, not at all distinguishable from any born Arab. One of the passengers was a Father William Strickland, a cousin of Isabel's, who had never met Burton. When Strickland sat on the deck reciting the breviary, a five-times-daily chore for Roman Catholic priests and other clerics—the office is said aloud—Burton would spread his prayer rug on the deck near Strickland and chant the *ṣalāt*, the five-times-daily Islamic prayers, also said aloud, much to Strickland's annoyance. "At last one day," Isabel wrote in the *Life*, "Strickland got up, saying, 'Oh, my God, I can't stand this much more.' " Afterward, he and Burton became friends. Also on board was James Grant Lumsden, the senior member of the Bombay Council, returning to duty. Seeing Burton at prayer, Lumsden remarked to a companion, "What a clever, intellectual face that Arab has!" Burton, rather pleased that he was not only thought an Arab but an intelligent one, made a joke in English and introduced himself. He and Lumsden became fast friends, and Lumsden invited him to stay with him in Bombay while he was finishing the account of his pilgrimage.

In Bombay, for the first time, Burton moved in higher circles than when he was a young lieutenant—the outrageous Napier's entourage had not aided his career—and with other powerful friends, among them the Scottish peer John Elphinstone, the thirteenth baron, who had just become Governor of the Presidency, he was now among the inner cliques. Dr. John Steinhauser had also returned to Bombay, and he and Burton talked endlessly about doing a full translation of the *Arabian Nights*, there being only partial versions in English. And it was probably on his return to Bombay (the date and circumstances are not clear) that Burton met Foster Fitzgerald Arbuthnot, a young India-born civil servant, a member of a leading Anglo-Indian family. "A man of quiet and amiable disposition," said Wright of him, Arbuthnot had been possessed early by the absorbing idea of seeing as much attention paid to the literature of India, Persia, and Arabia as to that of ancient Greece and Rome, which then (as even now) formed the heart of a "classical" education in the West. Burton and Arbuthnot naturally found they had common interests in Oriental literature and out of this friendship were to grow the imaginative though only partially realized plans to publish a large corpus of Eastern works.

Burton seems to have been able, to the best of his abilities, to shirk his ordinary regimental duties. He was "popular in his regiment when he returned," said Wright, and "he disliked the routine." Burton used his time to work steadily away at the manuscript of his account of his pilgrimage—it was entitled *Personal Narrative of a Pilgrimage to El-Medinah and Meccah*—and in less than a year had the first two of three projected volumes ready to send off to his publisher, Longman, Brown, Green, and Longmans, in London; they were published in 1855. The third volume did not appear for another two years.

After each of his works was published, Burton invariably wanted to revise it, but the *Pilgrimage* was the first where he was given the opportunity. There was some slight tampering with the manuscript when it was prepared for publication. Burton was at a safe distance, and Longman, Brown entrusted the first two volumes to John Gardiner Wilkinson, who not only deleted objectionable material or put it into Latin but scrambled some of the Arabic, for example, confusing *taqīya*, dissimulation, with *tarīqa*, Sufi convent or the mystical path. The work was to pass through many editions, four in Burton's lifetime and four later, each edition showing many variations over its predecessors and some major changes. Pictures and maps were shifted about, the appendixes moved to the final volume, and more added, including one by a noted Orientalist, Aloys Sprenger, correcting some minor geographical errors Burton had made.

The *Pilgrimage* has remained a classic in its field. It is often grouped with *Arabia Deserta* by Charles Montagu Doughty, a man whom Burton respected but who set himself apart from Burton. Doughty was extremely critical of Burton (and Burton mildly of Doughty). There may never have been a quarrel if Doughty, a young geologist and archaeologist, and a very strict Evangelical Christian, had not disapproved of Burton's traveling as a Muslim. Doughty had spent two years, 1876–78, among the Bedawin. As an openly professed Christian, he did not go to Medina or to Mecca; even so, his trip through the Arabian peninsula was courageous and dangerous in the extreme. His volumes on his travels were published ten years later, written in a rich but tortured prose that still wins him admiration but few readers. Doughty never understood Burton's commitment to Islam and always made a point of not reading him. In Arabia, Doughty suffered hardships that Burton escaped, from heat, the desert, and Bedawin cruelty. But in the end it was not Burton's success that angered Doughty but his acceptance of Islam— turning Turk.

Burton's magnificent achievement was not without other detractors, invariably men who envied him, did not have his courage and fortitude, lacked his fluency with languages, but felt that their own ineptitudes had to be paralleled by similar failings in Burton. One enemy was Francis Palgrave, who made a famous trip through Arabia and published an account of it in 1865 as *A Narrative of a Year's Journey through Central and Eastern Arabia*. Palgrave made the mistake of impugning Burton's character and honesty.

Passing one self off for a wandering Darweesh, as some European explorers [that is, Burton] have attempted to do in the East, is for more reasons than one a very bad idea. It is unnecessary to dilate on that moral aspect of the proceeding which will always first strike unsophisticated minds. To feign a religion which the adventurer himself does not believe, to perform with scrupulous exactitude, as of the highest and holiest import, practices which he inwardly ridicules, and which he intends on his return to hold up to the ridicule of others, to turn for weeks and months together the most sacred and awful bearings of man towards his Creator into a deliberate and truthless mummery, not to mention other and yet darker touches—all this seems hardly compatible with the character of a European gentleman, let alone that of a Christian.

It was a savage attack, and Burton's riposte was just as savage, and perhaps unfair. He pointed out that Palgrave, born a Protestant, of Jewish descent (his grandfather was Meyer Cohen, a Jewish stockbroker in London), having become a Jesuit priest, had, though a British officer, served the French as a secret agent, had posed as a Syrian "quack," and "by return to Protestantism violated his [priestly] vows." It was, Burton added, "Satan preaching against Sin." But the heart of the matter was that Burton had made a mockery of Islam. To this Burton replied,

> What is there, I would ask, in the Moslem Pilgrimage so offensive to Christians—what makes it a subject of "inward ridicule"? Do they [the Muslims] not also venerate Abraham, the Father of the Faithful? Did not [John] Locke and even greater names, hold Mohammedans to be heterodox Christians, in fact Arians who till the end of the fourth century represented the mass of North European Christianity?
>
> The fact is . . . Al-Islam, in its capital tenets, approaches much nearer to the faith of Jesus than do the Pauline and Athenasian modifications which, in this our day, have divided the Indo-European mind into Catholic and Roman, Greek and Russian, Lutheran and Anglican. . . . The Moslem may be more tolerant, more enlightened, more charitable, than many societies of self-styled Christians.

He continued fairly much in the same vein. Palgrave's account of what he had seen and done in Arabia—the geography, climate, waterways, oases, towns and cities, the people, and his forays into unknown areas—had been quietly questioned by certain men experienced in the East, but to challenge a man so clearly the lion of the moment, as Palgrave was in 1865, was not to be done, and it was not until later that much of what he had claimed as personal experience was found to be the retelling of information he had gleaned from the Bedawi or had read in Arabic works.

During the time of Burton's return to Cairo and then to Bombay, Isabel Arundell was languishing in London, with little interesting company except for her diary—how dull the young men were! The feelings she poured into this secret book were not always profound, perhaps, but they expressed strong, direct emotion and intense, undying love for Richard. And she had a keen perception of English society as it was.

> One always pictures the "proper man" to be a rich, fat, mild lordling, living on his estate, whence as his lady, one might rise to be a leader of Almack's. . . . I could not live as a vegetable in the country. I cannot picture myself in a white apron, with a bunch of keys, scolding my maids, counting eggs and butter, with a good and portly husband (I detest fat men!) with a broad-rimmed hat and a large stomach.

She ruled out country squires, doctors, lawyers ("I hear the parchments crackling now"), parsons, clerks in London offices.

> God help me! A dry crust, privations, pain, danger for him I love would be better. Let me be with a husband of my choice to battle, nurse him in his tent, follow him under fire of ten thousand muskets. I would be his companion through hardship and trouble, nurse him if wounded, work for him in his tent, prepare his meals when faint, his bed when weary, and be his guardian angel of comfort—a felicity too exquisite for words!

She feared her "Ideal Lover" would never accept her. "Shall I never be at rest with him to love, and understand me, to tell

every thought and feeling, in far different scenes from these—
under canvas before Rangoon—anywhere in Nature?" She believed that a woman should not marry a man "for liking, esteem,
gratitude for his love but from the fulness of her own love." And,
"If Richard and I never marry, God will cause us to meet in the
next world; we cannot be parted; we belong to one another."
She thought she was destined for Burton alone—and she was
probably absolutely correct—"How worthless I should be for any
man but Richard Burton!"

But for the moment these grand passions were to remain in a
romantic limbo. No one knows what thoughts of Isabel Arundell
were entertained in Burton's mind. He was compelled, almost
driven as if by forces beyond his ken or control, to the kind of
acts that so engaged Isabel. Plans for one daring adventure after
another absorbed all his energies. There seemed to be no relaxation.

With a touch of bravado and stoicism, Isabel could note in
her diary that "Richard has just come back with flying colours
from Mecca; but instead of flying home, he has gone to Bombay
to rejoin his regiment. I glory in his glory. God be thanked!"
But this was followed by an understandable wave of self-pity,
desolation, and hopelessness.

> But I am alone and unloved. Love can illumine the dark roof of
> poverty, and can lighten the fetters of a slave; the most miserable
> portion of humanity is tolerable with its support, and the most
> splendid irksome without its inspiration. . . . Is there no hope for
> me? . . . I can laugh, dance, and sing as others do, but there is a
> dull gnawing always at my heart that wearies me.

19

"City of Evil Fame"

From Bombay, Burton bombarded the powers in London—the East India Company and the Royal Geographical Society—for permission, and backing, for his grand trip into the heart of Africa to search for the sources of the Nile. But the Directors had more specific goals in mind. They preferred a penetration of Somaliland only, along with a survey of the coastal ports. There were practical reasons for this decision. In 1839, after a dispute with a local shaykh, the East India Company had taken the tiny port of Aden, an ancient and previously unimportant harbor at the southern tip of the vast Arabian Peninsula, and had turned it into a significant stop on the route between Suez and India. Aden itself was a small spit of land, three miles in depth and five miles in width, and consisted chiefly of a mass of barren and desolate volcanic rock, a sun-baked cinder heap of no charm. Aden had many faults. It was not the most satisfactory port of call, being somewhat out of the way for shipping on the Suez-to-Bombay route, and its anchorage was not of the best. The climate, as Burton complained, was torrid. But across the Gulf of Aden, on the Horn of Africa, was Berbera, the chief port of Somaliland and one of the safest and best on the western side of the Indian Ocean. It was therefore natural that John Company's directors learn more about the port and the strange and fearful country that lay behind it. But the Company, as always showing its customary mixture of caution and greed that characterized its dealing with those of its servants who stepped out of what Burton referred to as its "quarter-deck routine," gave only part approval to the plan. In 1849 it had said, "If a fit and proper person volunteer to travel to the Somali country, he goes as a private traveller, the government giving no more protection to him than they would to an individual totally unconnected with the service." However, "they will supply him with all the instruments required, afford him a passage going and returning, and pay the actual expenses of the journey."

After Carter's cautious and ineffectual probe of the coast, Somaliland remained in abeyance until Burton saw it as the first step into the heart of unknown Africa. He had three equally eager companions ready to accompany him, Lieutenant G. E. Herne, of the 1st Bombay (European) Fusileers, Lieutenant William Stroyan, of the Indian navy; and Dr. J. Ellerton Stocks, his old friend from Karachi. All were eminently qualified for an expedition as daring and as dangerous as the penetration of the East African coast proved to be. Herne was distinguished by his skill as a surveyor and as a master of the recently developed science of photography and for skill with machinery. Stroyan, too, was an able surveyor and an artist. Stocks, besides being Assistant Surgeon of the Medical Establishment in Bombay, was also a botanist, a seasoned traveler in primitive areas, and a "first-rate man in all ways."

That year, 1854, East Africa was not a prime subject in the minds of Burton's compatriots at home. In January, England, in conjunction with France, its recently hated enemy, had joined the Turks in their war against Russia. While his country was absorbed in the war, Burton went ahead with his plans, suffering barely more than the usual inconveniences from superiors in Bombay. In May, anticipating a favorable reply for his plans from London, he sailed to Aden in an East India Company ship, along with Herne and Stroyan. The Company had extended itself far enough to give them all free passage. Stocks, on leave in London, was expected to join them in Aden, but shortly news came that he had died unexpectedly of apoplexy. This left the expedition short one man. The atmosphere at Aden, both physical and political, was not conducive to the final planning and preparation of the venture, and a general air of foreboding hung over it, beginning with the oppressive climate and topography. The "Eye of al Yemen," as the port was known, was, Burton remarked, a mountain of misery, with "outlooks only into desolation, sand, salt water, and despair." The English camp was a "Devil's Punch-bowl," stifling hot nine months of the year and subject to alternations of sandstorms and simoom winds, "unproductive for want of rain." Burton complained that "not a sparrow can exist there, nor will a crow thrive"—an attempt had been made to bring the birds from Bombay; the sparrows died, and the crows failed to reproduce.

The Company officials at Aden opposed Burton's plan, and that was to result in disaster. First, the Political Agent there, Captain Stafford B. Haines, R.N., had just been removed from his post on the charge of embezzlement. A "dark chapter in the history of the Bombay Government," said *Allen's Indian Mail* six years later, for the case against the agent seemed inspired not by criminal activities but by the political infighting that occupied so much of the Company's servants. The tragedy for Burton was that Haines, having served fifteen years at Aden since its capture, knew the Somali tribes well, could deal with the Arabs, was highly respected by the various native peoples, and understood the Oriental mind as Burton did—he handled the Arabs with their own tactics "by quietly letting them know you perceive their intentions, before they are prepared to carry them out and that you are prepared to counter their designs." As his replacement, Colonel James Outram was sent out in July. Outram and his aides were to change the entire cast of the Somali Expedition. Long-dormant feuds got second winds: hostilities that had their roots in the dark days of Sind, between Napierists and Outramists, the military and the politicals, still unresolved and smoldering, now burst into the open. Outram was in poor health and was to hold the post at Aden only until December, but long enough to affect Burton's plans. The tension began immediately.

> I had no reason to like him [said Burton in the *Life*]; in his younger days, thirsting for distinction, Outram was ambitious to explore the Somali country, then considered the most dangerous in Africa, but when I prepared to do so, he openly opposed me.

Outram called upon his friends far and wide for support against Burton. In Bombay, the famous Dr. Buist, the editor of the Bombay *Times*, turned his pen against Burton. After the expedition ended, Buist wrote in an editorial:

> In Aden, in August last, Col. Outram, then only a fortnight in office, but basing his views on those of the oldest and most experienced residents on the spot, pointed out to us most emphatically the extreme unwisdom of the so-called Somali Expedition and the tragedy that in some shape or other was almost certain to follow the wild adventure of a set of reckless young men, who, whatever their talents . . . did not seem likely to add greatly to our scientific knowledge.

Buist added that Burton had replied "with his usual ability . . . expressing views opposed as much as possible to those we had advanced." By now the colony was divided, as Sind had been, into two camps. Outram expressed the opinion that the expedition was a tempting of fate. Burton was bitter in his denunciation, pointing out that "the European degenerates rapidly . . . in the hot, enervating and unhealthy climates of the East"—his compatriots had lost their nerve. "The rough manners, the fierce looks, and the insolent threats of the Somal . . . had prepossessed the timid [English] colony at the 'Eye of El Yemen' with an idea of extreme danger. . . . The writer and his comrades were represented to be deliberately going to their deaths. . . ."

Outram "refused to countenance the scheme proposed" and insisted that the expedition be split up, each member taking a different route for exploration. This was a major error. Even now it is not clear if this decision was originally Outram's or Burton's or jointly arrived at after much argument, with Burton willing to accept almost any compromise in order to get to Somaliland. "The human head once struck off does not regrow like the rose," said a member of Outram's staff to Burton. But the new plan now offered three human heads as a bouquet.

To complicate the tensions between Burton and Outram, a third party appeared on the scene, a man who was first to serve Burton's plans and share in the work and then to become a kind of nemesis, an enemy disguised as an associate and friend. This was John Hanning Speke, who unexpectedly arrived from India in September. Speke was six years Burton's junior but already a captain. He had gone to India at the age of seventeen as a protégé of the Duke of Wellington and got a commission in the 46th Bengal Native Infantry. In the five years before he had come to Aden, he had spent his leave time in exploring the Himālayas and had crossed into Tibet, traveling alone except for the usual complement of native bearers. He was known as being cold, priggish, and calculating. Tinges of controversy had touched him in India and had lingered on. But it was controversy of a rather innocuous sort, unlike the dark whisperings about Burton. Even by the cruel standards of nineteenth-century England, Speke was a ruthless hunter, almost a murderer of animals rather than a sportsman, and spared no effort, no matter how demanding or dangerous, in seeking out game. He prided himself as a collector of fauna and flora, and now, having amassed three years' leave, he planned on spending most of it in Africa, where he assumed that he could find much to hunt. Speke had saved his money like a miser and thought he would devote the next two years to collecting specimens. Clearly, at the time, he was interested only in hunting. Later, he claimed that the primary purpose of his trip was to search for the sources of the Nile, thus trying to establish *a posteriori* precedence over Burton, a claim that he made quite explicitly in his book *What Led to the Discovery of the Source of the Nile* (published in 1863 and dedicated to Outram). Speke claimed he had come to Aden to organize the expedition into wildest Africa and that when he had found the Nile head-waters he would sail down the river to Egypt.

Originally, Speke had planned on going to Africa alone, a most unsound idea. He was not a linguist, speaking only the most rudimentary form of military Hindustani, and worse, unlike Burton, who might complain and rail about the natives but in the end had an appreciation and love for them, Speke thought little of the indigenous races, calling them "simple-minded negroes."

When Speke laid out his plans before Outram, he was surprised to find them opposed. The agent not only refused to help him but stated that he should not venture into Africa at all, "as the countries opposite Aden were so extremely dangerous for any foreigners to travel in." Moreover, the Somali were "of such a wild and inhospitable nature that no stranger could possibly live amongst them." This was a strict and firm prohibition, but then Outram allowed that Speke might replace the much-lamented Ellerton Stocks, upon whom Burton had counted so much for so many skills.

Of all the people who passed through Burton's life, Speke is, more than anyone, subject to the hazards of twentieth-century amateur psychoanalysis. Born in 1827, he was the second son of rural gentry who traced themselves back to an old Yorkshire clan, the Especs. Speke was tremendously jealous of his older brother and even remarked upon this in print. He had but a smattering of education; he hated "book-learning" and preferred pastimes like bird nesting. He read little because he was subject to serious ophthalmic attacks, an ailment that was to affect him frequently in later life. He may also have had a touch of dyslexia, and his medical problems led him to seek the company of his mother. Thus, he might be regarded as an almost textbook case of the "little brother" who must spend his life trying to prove himself, which he did with some distinction in India. He served in the Sikh wars, battles that had been denied Burton by circumstance, and won medals in several major engagements. Throughout his military career he was a loner, a "good soldier," who spent his free time by himself. His career was, in a way, exemplary. By military standards he was the ideal soldier, hardworking, brave in battle, a perfectionist always trying to please his commanding officer, never getting into trouble. He stayed away from native women (and from the wives of fellow officers), and he did not drink or gamble.

As Burton was to observe, Speke was by no means modest and was prone to make the kind of boast that was palpably ridiculous. Fortunately for his self-esteem, he was never challenged until later, and then by Burton, who knew the facts. Speke claimed, for example, that he had "shot over three quarters of the globe," though his hunting experience was confined to an infinitesimal area—the British Isles, some of the Indian states, then a few places in Africa. More serious, because it was advanced to establish his claim as an expert cartographer, he boasted that he had explored and mapped Tibet: "I was the first [white] man who penetrated into many of its remotest parts, and discovered many of its numerous animals." In fact, Tibet had seen a steady stream of hardy European souls, among them Jesuit missionaries, "writers" sent by the East India Company (including William Moorcroft, who was believed to have lived in Lhasa for twelve years), various Frenchmen, and most recently the brothers Henry and Richard Strachey. Consequently, the circumstances of Speke's life, his fantasies and desires and a jealousy of Burton, were ample reason for his subsequent behavior. He wanted to be known as *the* man who found the source of the Nile, an honor he would not share with anyone, particularly Burton.

Burton's immediate reaction to Speke was favorable and friendly. The newcomer appeared experienced, courageous, strong, and interested in the expedition. Later, Burton attempted to make a fair and reasonable assessment of Speke. This was after Speke's death, when Burton felt the need to offer some explanation of the differences that almost immediately arose between them. He was appreciative of Speke's physical attributes: "A man of lithe, spare form, about six feet tall, 'blue-eyed, tawny-maned, the old Scandinavian type, full of energy and life,' with a highly nervous temperament, a token of endurance, and long wiry but not muscular limbs, that could cover the ground at a swinging pace. . . ."

However, by this time, it was difficult for Burton to hide his true feelings and remain neutral. He tried to make it plain that "I do not stand forth as the enemy of the departed," as he wrote after Speke's tragic death by a gunshot.

> No man can better appreciate the noble qualities of energy, courage, and perseverance which he so eminently possessed, than I do, who knew him for so many years, and who travelled with him as a brother, before the unfortunate rivalry respecting the Nile Source arose like the ghost of discord between us, and was fanned to a flame by the jealousy and ambition of "friends."

Burton claimed "only the right of telling the truth and the whole truth." It was a truth that in retrospect was not pleasant. Speke, Burton wrote, "had no qualifications for the excursion. . . . He was ignorant of the native races of Africa. . . . He did not know any of the manners and customs of the East. . . . I saw that he was going to lose his money and his 'leave' and his life. Why should I have cared? I do not know." By taking Speke as a full member of the Somaliland Expedition, Burton saved Speke's money and furlough but said, "You would now think, that the case was reversed—that he had taken me, not I him." A serious problem was Speke's claim to have "surveyed Tibet," which turned out to have been merely boasting. His knowledge of that country came through his friend, the well-known Captain Edmund Smyth, an adventurer of Burton's type, who apparently had entered Tibet on a secret mission in 1851 and again in 1853. In fact, Speke seemed strangely vague about Tibet despite his boasts. What appalled Burton and the other officers was that Speke said he liked to eat the meat of the fetuses of the game he killed. "He had acquired a curious taste for the youngest of meat, preferring it even when unborn," wrote Burton in *Zanzibar.* Speke himself unwisely referred to his penchant later after he had been in Africa several years.

> On once shooting a pregnant Kudu doe, I directed my native huntsman, a married man, to dissect her womb and expose the embryo; but he shrank from the work with horror, fearing lest the sight of the kid, striking his mind, should have an influence on his wife's future bearing. . . .

Speke had other serious defects in the light of the dangers to be faced by the Somaliland Expedition. His ignorance was surpassed only by his blind ambition. "Without knowing even the names of the harbour-towns [of East Africa], he proposed to explore some of the most dangerous parts of Africa," said Burton, appalled that Speke could so blithely risk disease, hunger, and the natives' spears. There was a reason for this casualness. "Before we set out he openly declared that being tired of life, he had come to be killed in Africa—not a satisfactory announcement to those who aspired to something better than the crown of martyrdom." Yet, despite Speke's unnerving admission, Burton had to say, "When the opportunity came he behaved with prudence as well as courage." However, "Lieut. Speke was uncommonly hard to manage. Having been for years his own master, he had a way as well as a will of his own."

But for good or ill, Speke was needed to replace Stocks, and Burton continued with his preparations.

Meanwhile, the first of Burton's reports to the Royal Geographical Society in London about the Meccan pilgrimage had been received and commented upon. The Society praised his "boldness and sagacity" and the accomplishing of a dangerous journey "with complete success." Despite this, the Directors of the East India Company showed their usual pusillanimous skill in avoiding definite support for the Somaliland Expedition. In October, when Burton was about to depart for the African coast, Outram received a letter that the expedition was not to be official

. . . but undertaken by Lieut. Burton as a private traveller. . . . Lieut. Burton must be positively enjoined not to encur any immoderate risk. . . . He should carefully feel his way, and not proceed onwards, unless he has reasonable grounds for believing that his own life and those of his companions will not be seriously endangered.

The cruel fact was that Outram's opposition to the expedition and his insistence that if it should take place the members proceed separately endangered the lives of four officers and the natives who would accompany them. It was decided that in November Herne would go to Berbera after the opening of the famous annual trade fair, which attracted merchants from all over Africa's eastern coast. "It was judged that the residence of this officer upon the coast would produce a friendly feeling on the part of the Somal," Burton wrote.

Herne stayed at Berbera from November 1854 to the following April, being joined by Stroyan on January first, both waiting in this relatively safe port city where white faces were not unknown. Their mission was to inquire into the state of commerce, the slave trade, and the caravan routes, to explore and map the maritime mountains, and so far as was possible, to keep records of the weather. But the assumption that the presence of British officers at Berbera would "produce a friendly feeling" was a naive and grave error, and one that Burton should not have made. Speke was directed to land at Bunder Garay, a small harbor in the Ara al-Aman, or "Land of Safety," whence, after picking up local guides and bearers, he would search out and map a celebrated valley and stream, the Wady Nogal, and buy horses and camels for use on future expeditions. He was also to collect specimens of a certain reddish earth that was widely believed to contain gold dust.

And what of Burton?

Burton had reserved the most interesting, the most daring, and the most dangerous role for himself. "The author, assuming the guise of an Arab merchant," he wrote, "prepared to visit the forbidden city of Harar. . . . I proceeded, more, it must be confessed for curiosity and for display of travelling savoir faire than for any other reason." "I could not suppress my curiosity about this mysterious city," said Burton in an article in the Royal Geographical *Journal* when he returned home.

Harar was a goal worthy of Burton at his best, his most daring, his most fearless. It was a city whose walls no European had ever penetrated, and it was hostile to others as well, among them the Abyssinians, who were Christians. It was an ancient metropolis, inhabited by a strange, once powerful race who spoke a language no other spoke (what a challenge that was to Burton!) and was famed as a seat of Islamic learning equal to Mecca (another challenge!). Moreover, it was notorious as a center of the slave trade, through which blacks captured elsewhere were brought by Arab caravans on the way to the coast—that made it a target of Burton's rage. And to justify his interest in Harar, Burton could point out to the Directors of John Company that there were many commercial advantages to the city, with its lucrative coffee and cotton trade. In short, Harar offered Burton a challenge he could hardly ignore. And a reconnaissance of Harar might give some clues to the way to the headwaters of the Nile.

There was no doubt of the danger. "A tradition exists," said Burton, "that with the entrance of the first [white] Christian Harar will fall."

All therefore who have attempted it were murdered. It was therefore a point of honour with me to utilize my title of Haji, by entering the city, visiting its Ruler, and returning to safety, after breaking the Guardian's spell.

Burton was to travel as one Haji Mirza Abdullah, falling back into the role he had assumed on the Mecca pilgrimage, except that he was now someone special, a man who had made the *hajj* and was to be respected. He would wear Arab clothing, and he suggested—in fact, ordered—that the others wear it, too, not so much as an act of dissimulation but merely for convenience and because Arab clothing would give a certain protection since they would not be immediately recognized as Europeans. That Burton would appear before the Somalis as anything but a British officer infuriated Outram. He thought that such a disguise denigrated the British in the eyes of the natives. Speke, also, was not pleased. He wrote that Burton

> thought it better that we should appear as his disciples, in according with which Herne had already purchased his dress, and now I bought mine. It was anything but pleasant to feel. I had a hot turban, a long close-fitting gown, baggy loose drawers, drawn at the ankles, sandals on my naked feet, and a silk girdle with pistol and dirk.

Though he was forced by circumstances to pass the entire summer in Aden's stifling and oppressive atmosphere, Burton was anything but inactive or given to the type of lassitude that so easily overwhelms a man in the tropics. He had taken a suite of rooms in an old hotel at Steamer Point, away from the British colony. Steinhauser was also there, and he and Burton talked endlessly about both a joint expedition into Central Africa and a collaboration on a translation of the *Arabian Nights*, "that wonderful work." And Burton threw himself into what he could of Somaliland and the people and their language. It was at first not an easy task, for aside from Outram's prohibition against the expedition, the British at Aden had set firm boundaries between themselves and the natives. So Burton, as was his wont, associated with the people who would know the most, in this case the Somalis living in Aden and the Arabs. He was started in his language studies by a paper by Christopher P. Rigby, his old rival in the semiannual language examinations in Bombay. Rigby had turned out a valuable essay, *Outline of the Somauli Language, with Vocabulary.* The rivalry continued: Rigby claimed that Somali had "not the slightest similarity to Arabic in construction." Burton took the contrary point of view. But there was a better and more pleasurable means of learning Somali than by a paper of arguable merit. It was more useful to follow the ancient and proved adage that the best way to acquire a language was in bed, and so Burton took up with some of the Somali prostitutes in Aden and quickly attained proficiency in their tongue. But the women were not quite prostitutes.

> There are no harlots in Somaliland [Burton observed in *First Footsteps in East Africa*]; but there are plenty of wives who, because of the inactivity of their husbands, prostitute their bodies without scruple. The man makes his intention clear by nods, smiles and shameless finger gestures. If the woman smiles, Venus rejoices. Then the fornicator indicates with his fingers the sum he is prepared to pay. . . . The Somalis have only one method of making love. Both parties lie on their sides, never, as is our custom, the man on the woman. The woman lies on her left side, the man on his right. . . .

The ease of obtaining Somali women led him to a judgment he might not have made as a younger man. "As regard their morals," he did not find them in a "golden state. . . . As a general rule, Somali women prefer *amourettes* with strangers, following the well-known Arab proverb, 'The newcomer filleth the eye.' " Who but Burton was the "newcomer"? He praised the Somali women's "rich brown complexions and round faces." "One of their peculiar charms," he wrote in *First Footsteps in East Africa*, "is a soft, low, and plaintive voice. . . . It has an undefinable charm. I have often lain awake for hours listening to the conversations of the [Somali] girls, whose accents sounded in my ears rather like music than mere utterances."

Despite his liking for them, he had to add, "Generally, Somali women are of cold temperament, the result of artificial as well as natural causes. . . ." He found that Somali women, without exception and like the women of Egypt and Arabia, had been subjected to infibulation, the sewing together of the labia. In an appendix to *First Footsteps* entitled "A Brief Description of Certain Peculiar Customs," which dealt with excision (or "circumcision") of the clitoris and infibulation, he pretended to derive the material from two earlier explorers, W. G. Browne, who, in 1802, mentioned excision of the clitoris among Abyssinian Christians and Egyptian Muslims, and Ferdinand Warne in 1842, in an account of his travels along the Blue Nile. But Burton's information was hardly secondhand.

> There is a most remarkable method regularly practiced by the Somalis, as it is also among the Abyssinians, Nubians and Gallas, of preserving the chastity of their women. They sew up the lips of the girl's private parts either with a leather lace, or, more often, with one of horse-hair. A female slave, whom the Arabs call Kadimah and the Somalis Midgan, cuts the girl's clitoris and nymphae with a large knife; when the excision has been made she takes a needle and sews up the lips with a continuous series of large stitches. A small passage for passing water is left with the lower part, and the pudendum thus loses its natural shape and becomes circular. They heal the girl's wounds by fumigation with myrrh, bandaging her thighs and placing her over a fire which gives off the fumes; the cure takes ten or twelve days. All the upper classes among the Somalis use the sewing-up method. In the towns quite young girls are so treated; in the country districts it is not done until they are fifteen.

He was to spare the reader no detail of "this barbarous guarantee of virginity and chastity," which is supposed to preserve the girl until marriage.

If a man wishes to fornicate with a girl, and she is shameless enough to permit it, he unpicks the stitches; a husband, on the other hand, will take great pains to increase and amplify his physical strength by a meat diet, and at night when he goes to bed with his newly-wed bride will strain to break through the blockage with his sword of love. Generally he is unsuccessful; then he will attack this artificial membrane with his finger. If he cannot overcome its defence by this method, he opens the pudendum from the lower end with a knife and immediately thrusts his penis up through the bloody opening. The pain is so intense as to cause the woman to shriek; to counteract this, male and female musicians drown the cries of the bride by singing; older girls, however, restrain their cries for shame. Some in their lust for pleasure summon a slave girl who enlarges the wife's pudendum to suit the size of the husband's penis. For about a week husband and wife stay in the same hut and devote themselves night and day to the act of love. Those who suspect their wife's fidelity, when they go on a journey will sew up again the aperture of the pudendum; but a woman who is so minded will break the suture with the greatest ease and sew it up again when her desires are satisfied. They say that in a single year twelve bastards were born in Zayla [a Somali coastal town].

Time seemed to move slowly in this airless, forsaken furnace. England's attention was on the war with Russia. The campaign in Bulgaria had wound down, and England, along with France, saw the opportunity of striking a crippling blow at the Czar by attacking the great Russian naval base at Sevastopol in the Crimea. Aden might never have existed so far as the home country was concerned. What was there to do in the interminable hours and days while the Somaliland Expedition was assembled?— women, languages, arguments with Outram, suspicions of Speke. It was an enervating life for a man who found that

literature is confined to acquiring the art of explaining yourself in the jargon of half-naked savages; where the business of life is comprised of ignoble official squabbles . . . where social intercourse is crushed by gossip; where . . . it is scarcely possible to address fair dame preserving at the same time her reputation and your own.

However, Burton found a drug to help alleviate the tedium. This was the narcotic known as khat (Kat or Cat, said Burton in *First Footsteps*), the tender leaves of a common shrub, *Catha edulis*, found all over East Africa.

> Europeans perceive but little effect from it—friend S[teinhauser] and I once tried in vain a strong infusion—the Arabs, however, unaccustomed to stimulants and narcotics, declare that, like opium eaters, they cannot live without the excitement. It seems to produce in them a manner of dreamy enjoyment. . . .

But despite his mild disclaimer about the weak effect *khat* had on him, Burton, during his Somaliland period, was a regular user. It was a popular drug. The Islamic clergy called *khat* "the Food of the Pious," and "literati remark that it had the singular properties of enlivening the imagination, clearing the ideas, cheering the heart, diminishing sleep, and taking the place of food." *Khat*, according to cognoscenti, was "comparable to the effects of the cacao of Peru." It also had pronounced priapic effects, and addicts could boast of unsurpassed vigor and endurance.

It was now late in the summer, and the Somali Expedition was ready. On the nondescript Sunday of October twenty-ninth, at the very hot and languid hour of four o'clock in the afternoon, Burton gave the order for his boat to cast off, and they sailed down the "fiery harbour." Steinhauser had thrown "the slipper of blessing" at Burton's back, and good luck seemed to be in store. When the boat reached the open sea, Burton and the crew said the *Fātiḥah* in honor of the legendary Shaykh Najud, who the Arabs believed invented the mariner's compass. Almost immediately the native crewmen and Burton's servants shed whatever pretense of civilization they had shown at Aden, removing their turbans and robes—all their clothing down to their breechcloths, anointing what Burton called their "dark morocco" with an "unguent redolent of sheep's tail."

Burton had hired three Somalis in Aden who were to serve

as guides and bodyguards. The head man was Mohammed Mahmud, a sergeant in the Aden police. He was called al-Hammal, or the Porter. He was "a bull-necked, round-headed fellow of lymphatic temperament, with a lamp-black skin, regular features, and a pulpy figure." Burton added, "He cannot read or write, but he has all the knowledge to be acquired by fifteen or twenty years of 'knocking about'" Egypt and India. "He is an excellent mimic and delights his auditors by imitations and descriptions of Indian ceremony, Egyptian dancing, Arab vehemence, Persian abuse, European vivacity, and Turkish insolence."

The second man was another policeman from Aden named Long Gulad, "one of those long, live skeletons, common amongst the Somali. . . . He is brave enough, because he rushes into danger without reflection . . . but he cannot bear hunger, thirst, or cold." The third man was called End of Time. He was a kind of hedge priest, illiterate but with a smattering of religious knowledge. His name, Burton said, alluded "to the prophesied corruption of the Muslim priesthood in the last epoch of the world," and he was "an individual of 'many words and little work,' infinite intrigue, cowardice, stupidity, and endowed with a truly evil tongue." Then there was also a one-eyed boy called the Kalendar.

The voyage across the Gulf of Aden was uneventful, and on the morning of the thirty-first the boat entered Zayla creek and by noon made her way to the coral reefs outside the port. As Burton's party prepared to anchor, they got the news from the crew of another boat that the road Burton had intended to take to Harar was closed. Fighting had broken out between the forces of the governor of Zayla, al-Haji Sharmakay bin Ali Salih, and those of the Amīr of Harar, over profits from the very lucrative slave trade. Sharmakay's son had been killed; numerous atrocities had been inflicted, mainly on the helpless; a slave caravan had been plundered, the females carried off and sold; and three hundred "wretched boys" were castrated so they could be employed as eunuchs.

Burton and his servants waded ashore and put on fresh clothing. Having heard the worst accounts of Zayla, Burton was "pleasantly disappointed by the spectacle of white-washed houses and minarets, peering above a long line of brown wall. . . ."

The town, an important export center, was under the control of the Turks, who ruled through Sharmakay. Burton had met him in Aden, and they had become fast friends, but now, to preserve his disguise, they had to pretend not to know each other and went through the ritual of a first meeting at the palace, a building to which Burton applied his customary derogatory description of "cow house." Sharmakay, however, was "rather a remarkable man." Now about sixty, blind in one eye and white with age in the other, "with one foot in the grave, he meditates nothing but the conquest of Harar and Berbera," conquests that would make him master of the seaboard and extend his powers even to Abyssinia.

After his brief meeting with the Governor, Burton was taken to a house in which he was to reside for the next few weeks and was left alone.

> The well-known sounds of Al-Islam returned from memory. Again the melodious chant of the Muezzin—no evening bell can compare with it for solemnity and beauty—in the neighbouring mosque, the loudly intoned Amin [Amen] and Allahu Akhbar [God is Great]— far superior to any organ—rang in my ear.

Soon the sunset gun sounded, and then, later, the curfew drum. "Nightfall was ushered in by the song, the dance, and the marriage festival . . . and muffled figures flitted mysteriously through the dark alleys. . . . After a peep through the open window, I fell asleep, feeling once more at home."

Now followed what Burton terms in *First Footsteps* "twenty-six quiet, similar, uninteresting days" while he went through "all the wearisome preliminaries of African travel." But he was "too much of an Arab to weary of the endless preparations of forming a caravan," he said in the *Life*. At the earliest dawn he would arise and repair to the terrace to perform his devotions. But his time seemed to be engaged in flirting with two young women, sisters by different mothers, one an Indian with "chocolate-coloured skin, long hair," who drew Burton's attention by "combing, dancing, singing, and slapping the slave girls," the other an Abyssinian, whose face was heavily tattooed, a vivid line extending from her brow to the tip of her nose; there were a tattooed *fleur-de-lis* between her eyebrows and tattooed beauty spots everywhere on her face. Burton liked the Abyssinian, and "We soon made acquaintance. . . ."

Breakfast came at six, when the day's heat was just beginning to break forth, and Burton had to tell his readers about it, a heavy meal of sour-grain holcus cakes and roast mutton—"at this hour a fine trial of health and clean living," eaten squatting on the uncarpeted floor around a stool. Visitors joined in, and Burton was scolded when his appetite flagged. Then a nap and after that visitors "by the dozens—no man having apparently any [other] business to occupy him." But it was a time to establish himself as a man of integrity and piety among the Somalis. He had many books with him, mostly religious, among them a Qur'ān and some Sufi works, and he had to show at opportune moments his murshid's diploma to establish his Sufi credentials should his Islam be questioned. So far as anyone but Sharmakay knew, he was an Arab merchant, a man of distinction, who had made the pilgrimage to Mecca. He could speak about religious matters with ease, but often he preferred to tell stories from the *Arabian Nights*, to the delight of his visitors. Most of them were Somalis, "who talk in their own tongue, laugh, stretch their legs, and lie like cattle upon the floor, smoking the common hookah, clean their teeth with sticks and eat snuff 'like Swedes.' " Burton would sit on a low couch, reading, telling stories, or explaining points of religion. "It argues 'peculiarity,' that I own, to enjoy such a life," he wrote. He stood in risk, he said, of being convicted "of being an 'amateur barbarian,' " a self-description he repeated often. In the afternoon he wrote his journal, and when the air began to cool, he went off with friends and attendants for a walk to the ocean. On the shore was a tiny mosque where people played a rude form of chess or engaged in rough types of athletics—gymnastics and wrestling and similar sports. Burton boasted, "I soon acquired the reputation of being the strongest man in Zayla," adding, "This is perhaps the easiest way of winning respect from a barbarous people, who honour body and degrade mind to mere cunning."

On Fridays, the Islamic Sabbath, Burton attended the jāmi, or cathedral mosque, "an old barn rudely plastered with whitewash," with a low roof and a "dreary length unpleasantly hot." As always aware of the need to impress, Burton would enter the mosque with a servant carrying his prayer rug and walk past "the stare of 300 pairs of eyes, belonging to parallel rows of squatters," to the front of the mosque, where he would recite the customary two-bow prayer. He then placed a sword and his rosary before him and, taking up a greasy copy of the Qur'ān, recited "loud and twangingly" a chapter from the sacred book. He liked to select for his reading an excerpt from the famous "Cow Chapter" (Sura 2), one of the most noted of all Qur'ānic texts. It deals with the obduracy of the Israelites, who argued with Moses over his prophecy: because the people had disbelieved God and slain his messengers, Moses ordered them to sacrifice a cow. After the reading, Burton would make a commentary. The Sura, with its 286 verses, contains the essence of the Qur'ān and was an ideal basis for explication and a demonstration of his Islamic learning. *

Eventually Burton was able to get his caravan together. No one seemed to be in a hurry, for the journey promised to be both difficult and dangerous—far riskier than the pilgrimage to Mecca.

---

* Because of this display of learning, Burton remained for a long time in the memories of the Somalis and in their oral tradition. Years later, an old Somali told an English visitor, Ralph E. Drake-Brockman, that not only could Burton read the Qur'ān better than any of the mullahs but that he was better learned in the teachings of the Holy Prophet.

In the Somali desert, where raiding parties were frequent, the nomads murdered even pregnant women in the hope that the unborn child might be a male. Slain enemies suffered castration and phallotomy. "The hero carries home the trophy of his prowess," Burton wrote, "and his wife, springing from her tent, utters a long shrill scream of joy" and taunts the other wives with their husbands' failures, the women then abusing their men "with peculiar virulence, and the lords fall into paroxysms of envy, hatred and malice." But whatever the risks before him, he was eager to depart, and by Monday, November twentieth, being so "thoroughly exhausted by delays" that he almost decided to walk, the necessary mules and camels were suddenly on hand, and a week later, escorted by Arab match-lock men, Burton and his caravan set off. Half an hour out of Zayla the Arabs fired a final salute, and Burton replied by emptying his six-shooter, and he was on his way.

His entourage had expanded considerably since he left Aden. One of the most important members was the *abban*, or guide, a man named Raghi, from the ferocious Īsa tribe.

[In Somaliland] the Abban acts at once as broker, escort, agent, and interpreter, and the institution may be considered the earliest form of transit dues. In all sales he receives a certain percentage, his food and lodging being provided at the expense of his employer, and he not infrequently exacts small presents for his kindred. In return he is bound to arrange all differences, and even to fight the battles of his client against his fellow countrymen. . . . According to the laws of the country, the Abban is master of the life and property of his client. The Traveller's success will depend mainly upon his selection. . . .

In Raghi, Burton had found himself a good, reliable *abban*, and the success of his ride to Harar was ensured. (Speke had naively taken as *abbans* the first two Somalis he encountered, two young donkey boys with no authority at all, and he was to suffer consequently throughout his search for the Wady Nogal.)

Burton had also taken on several women servants to cook and act as beasts of burden. Burton remarked that they "look each like three average women rolled into one." They were enormously strong, could carry as much as a mule, pitch tents, fetch water, make tea and coffee, and speak of "vulgar subjects" in "soft voices." A few other undefined Somalis made up the rest of the caravan, and at the end trudged a ragged Bedawin woman driving a donkey. The most magnificent of all was Burton himself.

> I follow them mounting a fine white mule, which with his gaudily *galonné* [beribboned] Arab pad and wrapper cloth has a certain dignity of look; a double-barrelled gun lies across my lap; and a pair of holsters . . . contains my Colt's six shooters.

Because the tribes that lay directly between Zayla and Harar were in a state of war, Burton had to take a detour southeast along the coast and then turn inland toward Harar. In *First Footsteps* he seems to have noted every moment, every hour of the day, every bush, bird, tribe, impoverished settlement, and every danger. Across hard, stony alluvial desert they went, over boggy creeks, warty flats of black mold, through patches of thorn bush and masses of somber granite and rock. Even though it was now December, Burton was burned wretchedly by the sun. They were now entering a land of paganism, perhaps of no religion; the strictness of Islam had disappeared. They were among savages untouched by the refinements of the Saving Faith. The scenes faded one into another, long marches over unfriendly land, villages suspicious of strangers; heat, dust, burning winds, importunate herdsmen begging for food and tobacco. Running almost unnoticed among the mélange of information is that Burton was ill and every day was a trial. He had picked up an unrelenting, nagging case of diarrhea in his last week at Zayla, and nothing he did to ameliorate it was effective. In the tropics, even under ordinary conditions of rest and comfort, colic, as Burton called it, was enervating. Now he was riding muleback through rough terrain under conditions that demanded his full strength.

From time to time marauding nomads were seen in the distance, but an attack never came. A foreboding of disaster, of death, haunted everyone. The very nervous hedge priest, End of Time, would take refuge in quoting fragments of poetry, the melancholy odes known as Belwo among the Somalis.

> Man is but a handful of dust,
> And life is a violent storm.

Ever since his days in Sind, Burton had been taken by such sad and melancholy statements. The Belwos were very much like the verses of the Afghan poet 'Abdu'r-Raḥman, whom he admired so much (and quoted in *First Footsteps*). Another Belwo said:

> Your body is to Age and Death betrothed
> And someday all its richness they will share.
> Turn not away in scorn:
> Someday a grave will prove
> The frailty of your face
> And worms its grace enjoy.
> Let me enjoy you now—and
> Turn not away in scorn.

Only an "amateur barbarian" could feel at home in the scenes that were encountered day after day. They were traveling among people almost as wild as the animals that either threatened to attack or ran away, and desperately poor, worse off than the desert and forest creatures. The men from the Īsa tribe were as "wild-looking as open mouths, staring eyes, and tangled hair could make them [and] gazed with extreme eagerness upon my scarlet blanket . . . the inviting texture was pulled and fingered by the greasy multitude."

The Somalis, though warriors, were not impressed by guns,

and from time to time remarks were made about Burton's. The warriors believed that the true test of manhood was ability with spear or sword, javelin or dagger. To silence his critics, Burton would shoot down a bird on the wing. After the men at one kraal had muttered the "ominous term 'Faranj,' " or foreigner, he took aim at a vulture.

> A bullet through the bird's body caused a cry of wonder. . . . Then loading with swan shot which these Bedawin had never seen, I knocked over a second vulture flying. Fresh screams followed the marvellous feat. . . .

While Burton was wending his way across the desert, Isabel Arundell was still with her diary. She had heard that he had gone to Harar, "a deadly expedition. . . . I am full of sad forebodings. Will he never come home? How strange it all is, and how I still trust in fate!" As she was writing these lines, Burton was entering the first of the highlands, and among the Gudabirsi who inhabited the hills

> was the first really pretty face seen by me in the Somali country. . . . Her skin was a warm, rich nut-brown, an especial charm in these regions, and her movements had that grace which suggest perfect symmetry of limb. . . . A cloth imperfectly covering the bosom, and a petticoat of hides, made no great mystery of forms.

As a tribute to the girl's beauty, Burton gave her some cloth, tobacco, and a bit of his rare supply of salt. It was now early December, and as he pushed farther inland, he found that his skin color was attracting attention, and he became increasingly anxious about his disguise. Moreover, his diarrhea was getting worse. "The bad water, the noonday sun of 107°, and the cold mornings [51°] had seriously affected my health." Native remedies did not help. Lions prowling around the camp at night, the bitter cold after sunset, and Burton's illness all combined to make a difficult journey even more so.

This time Christmas in the field went unnoticed. There was

no nostalgia for past scenes, for family, friends, for Isabel. By now Burton was far into the highlands, and the villages and people had a strong look of Central Africa. A few days later he entered a town called Wilensi, which was to serve as the last resting place before the push into Harar. Burton had expected to find the local ruler, the Gerard Adan, but the Gerard—the term means prince or sultan—had gone off, leaving his wives to care for the stranger. Burton was given space in a rough cottage and settled down to nurse his ailments and prepare for the final stage of the journey. The Gerard was an important man, and his help was needed. He was a relative of the Amīr of Harar, and Burton expected him to guarantee safe passage to the city. Meanwhile, all Burton could do was make notes about life among the clan and complain about the food—"always flesh and holcus; these people despise fowls and consider vegetables fit for cattle." As usual there was no privacy. "Men, women, and children enter in crowds, and will not be driven away." At night the people got drunk on millet beer—"detestable," said Burton, having tried it several times. "It flies directly to the head, the consequence of being mixed with some poisonous bark."

Finally, word came that the Gerard Adan was in another village not far away. Burton was now forced to break up his caravan, for he was to pass through country that was even more difficult and dangerous. The women servants and most of the men were told to stay behind. Taking only the most necessary objects, Burton packed everything into a pair of small leather saddlebags, which could be carried on a single mule, and set off. The date was now December 29, 1854, and the road led through beautiful country where fragrant dog roses grew in abundance. "The scenery around us was remarkable . . . the beds of waterfalls shone like sheets of metal . . . and in the distance was a mass of purple peak and blue table in long vanishing succession." The primeval forests, untouched by the ax, resounded with the cries of guinea fowl and apes. Finally, at a village called Sagharrah, they came upon the Gerard Adan, "a strong wiry Bedawin . . .

about forty-five years old, at least six feet high . . . a tricky smile. . . . In character he proved to be one of those cunning idiots so peculiarly difficult to deal with."

The Gerard wanted help in building a fort by which he could control the countryside and threaten Harar. He demanded numerous presents, and Burton gave him a sword, a Qur'ān, a turban, a gaudy satin waistcoat, about seventy robes, and much indigo-dyed cloth, a fraction of what was demanded. But it was clear that not only was he not going to extend himself to help Burton reach Harar, but he was afraid of the Amīr. "We remained six days under the roof of the Gerard Adan, one of the most treacherous and dangerous Chiefs in this land of treachery and danger," Burton was to write in his report to the Royal Geographical Society. His men "saw with horror that preparations were being made to enter the city of evil fame . . . but the unfortunates little knew the persistence of a Haji."

It was clear that Burton was in a precarious position. The Gerard Adan feared to guarantee Burton's safety. The best he could do was to allow his son to go with Burton. Audacity seemed the only course. "Throwing all forethought to the winds," Burton decided "to rely upon what has made many a small man great, the good star." He had realized that his guise as an Arab was harming rather than helping him. "My white face converted me into a Turk, a nation more hated and suspected than any Europeans, without our prestige." The wisest move appeared to be to show himself openly as an Englishman. Not having any credentials to prove his true identity, he wrote a letter in English from the Political Agent—purportedly from Outram—to the Amīr of Harar that he would deliver in person as the envoy of Her Majesty's Government.

But the anguish and turmoil over what course to take, what role to play, had been experienced under distressing conditions. For the entire period at Sagharrah he felt too ill to rise. He lay under a tree virtually helpless. In fact, he seemed likely "to die under a tree. . . . Nothing indeed, would have been easier than such [an] operation: all [it] required was turning the face to the wall, for four or five days.

"But to expire of an ignoble colic!"—he wrote—"the thing was not to be thought of." His iron will beating his colic, Burton now tried to negotiate with the Gerard. The prince wanted a fort; Burton, safe passage into Harar. Neither seemed likely. Then five strange men appeared, two Harari, the others Somali. After suspiciously inspecting Burton and his party, they informed the Gerard that Burton was in no way a peaceful Arab merchant but a spy and wanted to send him as a prisoner to Harar, a request the Gerard refused, as Burton was his guest. It was this incident that finally led Burton to proclaim that he was an English officer. The five strangers left, and the next day, Burton felt sufficiently strong to set out for Harar. The *Fātiḥah* was said for a safe journey, but the villagers assured him "that we were dead men."

Despite his continual show of bravado, Burton was very much aware that he might be killed, and killed in a very excruciating manner. But he was determined to conquer Harar. He cut his baggage to the minimum—"a change of clothes, a book or two, a few biscuits, ammunition, and a little tobacco." In the light of the dangers ahead he wrote a note to Herne "directing him to act in case of necessity" and entrusted it to End of Time, whom he was leaving behind. His escort now consisted only of Long Gulad and the Hammal and three men of the Gerard's, one of them the prince's son. He was like a man riding to certain death, but his mind was clear, and amazingly he soaked up as usual the details of the land about him.

> High up on our left rose the perpendicular walls of the misty hill, fringed with tufted pine, and on the right the shrub-clad folds fell into a deep valley. The cool wind whistled and sunbeams like golden shafts darted through tall shady trees. . . . The ground was covered with dank grass, and around the trunks grew thistles, daisies, and blue flowers, which, at a distance, might well pass for violets.

At this point he hardly dared take notes. For the next ten days everything he saw and experienced was stored in his memory—the landscape, the look of the people, the clans and tribes, the flora and fauna, meteorological observations, the kind of information that might be useful to the unappreciative John Company and its worried and worrisome Directors.

At last

> about thirty miles distant, and separated by a series of blue valleys, lay a dark speck upon a tawny sheet of stubble—Harar.

After an afternoon of riding through forests and rough passes, Burton took shelter in a village of the Migdan tribe, whose people greeted him hospitably. But his rest was soon spoiled by the arrival of the two Harari he had met previously, the same men who wanted to take him prisoner. They offered to escort Burton to Harar. He replied that they could do so the next morning. During the night the Migdan elders informed Burton that the Harari had acted as if they were about to attack him. He left his remaining papers—his journals, sketches, and other books—in the care of an old Migdan and asked that they be forwarded to the Gerard and early in the morning—it was now January third—he left quickly, carrying only his arms and a few presents for the Amīr, having escaped the attentions of the Harari, and pushed on to the city. Along the way he encountered a group of Galla peasants. "All wondered at the Turk, concerning whom they had heard so many horrors." He was now close to the city, and then he could see it, only a few miles away. "The spectacle, materially speaking, was a disappointment." Harar was "a long sombre line strikingly contrasting with the whitewashed towns of the East. . . . Many would have grudged exposing three lives to win so paltry a prize."

> But of all that have attempted, none ever succeeded in entering that pile of stones; the thoroughbred traveller, dear L. [he was addressing Lumsden], will understand my exultation, although my two companions exchanged glances of wonder.

It was midafternoon when Burton reached the city gates. He was forced to wait, surrounded by curious crowds, who "scrutinized, derided, and catechized" the strangers. After half an hour he and his two companions were taken to the courtyard of the palace, which earned the description of "a mere shed, a long single storied windowless barn of rough stone and reddish clay." Again Burton was forced to wait, this time in a huge courtyard filled with idling Galla warriors. But he was not being received cordially. The warder who had brought him from the city gates to the palace was surly and angry. In Harari, a language Burton did not yet speak (although he easily got the drift), he ordered Burton and his companions to give up their weapons. Burton refused: "By dint of obstinacy we retained our daggers and my revolver."

> The guide raised a door curtain, suggested a bow, and I stood in the presence of the dreaded chief.
>
> I walked into a vast hall, a hundred feet long, between two long rows of Galla spearmen, between whose lines I had to pass. They were large half-naked savages, standing like statues, with fierce movable eyes, each one holding . . . a huge spear, with a head the size of a shovel. I purposely sauntered down them coolly, with a swagger, with my eyes fixed upon their dangerous-looking faces. I had a six-shooter concealed in my waist belt, and determined, at the first show of excitement, to run up to the Amir, and put it to his head, if it were necessary to save my own life.

The most dangerous man in this part of East Africa was not prepossessing. "His appearance was that of a little Indian Rajah, an etiolated youth twenty-four or twenty-five years old, plain, thin-bearded, with a yellow complexion, wrinkled brows and protruding eyes."

Burton entered the room with a loud "Peace be upon ye" in Arabic, to which the prince unexpectedly replied graciously. Two chamberlains stepped forward and, taking Burton's arms, forced him to bow low over the Amīr's extended fingers, "which I did not kiss, being naturally averse to performing that operation upon any but a woman's hand." Now followed a few moments of polite palaver according to Eastern etiquette, and then the Amīr asked Burton the purpose of his visit. Burton, in Arabic, said he was bringing the compliments of the governor of Aden and that "we had entered Harar to see the light of H. H.'s countenance." This was the type of exchange that Burton always enjoyed; here it was one of those risks that could turn either way. How would the prince react?

"The Amir smiled graciously."

"This smile, I must own," said Burton, "was a relief." He had been prepared for the worst. The interview was now ended, and after a repetition of the entry formalities, Burton and his attendants were taken to a house where they were to reside for the next ten days, being fed three times a day from the ruler's kitchen.

Now Burton met other officials, each encounter being fraught with uncertainty, for

> I was under the roof of a bigoted prince whose least word was death; amongst people who detest foreigners; the only European that had ever passed over their inhospitable threshold, and the fated instrument of their future downfall.

How true and tragic this statement was Burton did not know at the time. He was indeed the instrument of the city's downfall. The "Guardian Spell" had been broken, and within a generation Harar's most superstitious fears had come true. The city was, twenty years later, little more than an exotic, faded town rapidly succumbing to colonization.

The occasional meetings with the Amīr during the first days were formal and cautious. The Amīr, who might so easily have had Burton killed in small stages, showed but faint signs of friendship. He was, however, interested in propitiating the British, who had such large ships and were so well known for taking over other people's countries. Moreover, the Amīr feared that England's friend Sharmakay at Zayla would carry out his dream of seizing not only Berbera but Harar as well. The Amīr needed the English as friends, but how was friendship to be accomplished without losing his country? To confirm his worries, the amazingly effective native grapevine had brought word that "three brothers," whites, were in the country and aimed to seize it. "Two of them [Herne and Stroyan] were anxiously awaiting at Berbera the return of the third [Burton] from Harar, and that, though dressed like Moslems, they were really Englishmen in government employ." Speke's ineffectual wanderings in search of Wady Nogal had apparently not been noticed. (So accurate was the native transmission of information that Burton reported that the Somalis knew even of the war in the Crimea.) What also concerned the Amīr was the fear that the English were likely to interfere with the slave trade, which brought him so much revenue. Consequently, Burton was a "dangerous guest," and it was necessary that he be sent away with the minimum of fuss. But, Burton realized, they were not to let him go easily; delays began to multiply.

He spent ten days in a kind of limbo, during which he was free to wander about but not see too much or to write or sketch. Because of the precariousness of his position he did not dare write out notes even in the privacy of his quarters, nor could he draw up what was foremost in his mind, a grammar of the Harari tongue. He had to estimate the altitude (about 5,500 feet, he thought—it was actually 6,000), and he worked out the longitude and latitude quite accurately. Later, he was able to give a fairly precise description of the city and its surroundings, to turn out several pages of history, and to describe the fortifications in some detail, should John Company want to invade it. Harar was not an inviting city, however, and he quickly dismissed its "artless construction," its lack of trees and gardens, its narrow lakes "strewed with gigantic rubbish heaps, upon which repose packs of mangy or one-eyed dogs."

There were always women available. Burton passed some time with the Galla slave girls, including "one Berille, an unlovely maid, whose shrill voice and shameless manners were a sad scandal to pilgrims and pious Moslems." Then there was "Aminah, the pert, [who] would insist on extinguishing the fat-fed lamp long ere bed-time, or would enter the room singing, laughing, dancing and clapping a measure." The women were invariably beautiful to Burton.

> They have small heads, regular profiles, straight noses, large eyes, mouths approaching the Causasian type and light yellow complexions. . . . Stars are tattooed upon the bosom, the eyebrows are lengthened with dyes, the eyes fringed with Kohl, and the hands and feet stained with henna.

Unfortunately, "the female voice is harsh and screaming, especially when heard after the delicate organs of the Somal. . . ." Burton found the Galla slaves adept at a technique popular in East Africa and Egypt and was to mention it often in his erotic writings.

> Amongst some races [especially the Galla women] the constrictor vaginae muscles are abnormally developed. In Abyssinia, for instance, a woman can so exert them as to cause pain to a man [is not Burton speaking from personal experience?], and, when sitting upon his thighs, she can induce the orgasm without moving any other part of her person. Such an artist is called by the Arabs 'Kabbazah,' literally meaning 'a holder,' and it is not surprising that the slave dealers pay large sums for her. All women have more or less the power, but they wholly neglect it; indeed there are many races in Europe which have never heard of it.

He could praise the women, but of the men he wrote, "I did not see a handsome face: their features are coarse and debauched," and from there he descends to a general denigration of a people he considered "highly unprepossessing."

It was a cruel city, in a part of the world where cruelty was commonplace. "The government of Harar is the Amir. These petty princes have a habit of killing and imprisoning all those who are suspected of aspiring to the throne." The dungeon was said to be beneath the palace, and "he who enters it, lives with unkempt beard and untrimmed nails [a disgrace to Muslims] until the day when death sets him free." The prince was judge and jury.

The punishments, when money forms no part of them [as fines], are mostly according to Koranic code. The murderer is placed in the market street, blindfolded, and bound hand and foot; the nearest kin to the deceased strikes his neck with a sharp and heavy butcher's knife, and the corpse is given over to relatives for Moslem burial. . . . Theft is visited with amputation of the hand. . . .

Often Burton would engage in other pastimes enjoyable to him as an amateur barbarian, taking *khat* and talking religion. He noted that the people of Harar eat *khat* ("here called 'Jat' ") "every day from 9 a.m. till near noon," when they dine.

Religion was a subject that always interested him, and Harar offered many opportunities. "I need scarcely say that Harar is proud of her learning, sanctity, and holy dead. . . . The city abounds in mosques, plain buildings without minarets, and in graveyards stuffed with tombs. . . ." The city "inundates the surrounding districts with poor scholars and crazy 'Widads' [hedge priests]. . . . None but the religious sciences are cultivated."

Soon Burton had a much-desired opportunity of impressing the Harari officials with the depth of his religious learning. The elders were entertaining themselves with *khat* and religious talk one day, and one of them, who was reading from the Qur'ān, misled by a marginal note in the text, read out, "Angels, Men and Jinnis." It should have been "Men, Angels, and Jinnis," Burton was quick to explain, for "human nature, which amongst Moslems is *not* a little lower than the angelic, ranked highest, because of it were created prophets, apostles and saints. . . . My theology won general approbation and a few kind glances from the elders."

The audience with the elders and the minor theological victory had been a preliminary to an interview with the Amīr, in which serious issues were apparently at last about to be discussed. Burton was granted the honor of sitting near the Amīr, who now produced the forged letter Burton had presented on the day of his arrival. The Amīr "looked upon it suspiciously and bade me explain its contents." Did Burton intend to "buy and sell Harar?" "We are no buyers or sellers," Burton replied emphatically. "We have become your guests to pay our respects to the Amir—whom may Allah preserve!—and that the friendship between the two powers may endure."

This slight exchange seemed to satisfy the prince—was this all that Burton's most dangerous journey had come to?—but Burton, too, was satisfied that he had the personal satisfaction of breaching Harar's gates, and stored away in his memory was information for John Company that would justify the Somaliland Expedition.

The problem now was to get out of Harar. Burton was aware that two or three months might elapse before the Amīr felt like releasing him. He importuned the prince, and later, alone, various court officials, for permission to go and begged provisions and water. Finally, in an uneventful last meeting with the Amīr and his senior officials, Burton and the prince exchanged mutual compliments and wishes for the success of each other's nations, and it was clear that he had permission to leave. There were some delaying moments; he had to have a long talk on Sufism with a Shaykh Jāmī, whose library he inspected ("The only truly valuable MS. in the place was a fine old copy of the Koran"), and he said his final farewells to the various minor officials. An auspicious day, Monday, was urged upon him for departure, but "the people of Harar are famously fickle; we know not what the morrow might bring forth from the Amir's mind" and long before dawn on Saturday he was able to escape, knowing that

all these African cities are prisons on a large scale, into which you enter by your own will, and, as the significant proverb says, you leave by another's.

Suddenly my weakness and sickness left me—so potent a drug is

joy!—and, as we passed the gates loudly salaaming to the warders
. . . a weight of care and anxiety fell from me like a cloak of lead.

Burton had escaped Harar with his cods and everything else
intact, except, perhaps, his honor. With the "Guardian Spell"
that had kept the city inviolate now broken, Harar would never
again present a formidable, impenetrable barrier to Europeans,
its gates would be breached, and within a generation a totally
unexpected enemy, the Egyptians, would occupy it and open it
up to anyone who might wish to enter, one of them being Arthur
Rimbaud, poet, slaver, and gun-runner. The sickly Amīr died
the year after Burton's visit, although the English had sent an
Arab doctor to treat him, not a trained physician but a holy man
"with some slight medical skills." It was "important for the Somali Expedition and for the future opening out of the African
trade that this Chief be conciliated."

A day after leaving Harar, so quickly did Burton and his two
companions travel, they reached the relative safety of Wilensi,
where the Gerard Adan and the remainder of Burton's party were
waiting. Rumor had already spread that Burton had been put to
death—there could be no other ending to so rash a venture—
but now he was safe. He collected his books and papers. A week
was passed in Wilensi preparing for the demanding trip across
the desert to Berbera. Burton spent his time working on a vocabulary of the Harari tongue with a Harari who had been banished from the city and a Somali poet "celebrated for his wit,
his poetry and his eloquence. . . . His linguistic sagacity enabled
me to perform a feat of no ordinary difficulty, that of drawing
out a grammatical sketch of the language."

Our hours were spent in unremitting toil; we began at sunrise,
the hut was ever crowded with Badawi critics, and it was late at
night before the manuscript was laid by. On the evening of the third
day my literati started upon their feet, and shook my hand, declaring
that I knew as much as they themselves did.

This was a major and substantial achievement considering the shortness of time. Only when Harar was opened up to foreigners did further work in linguistics get done, some of it not until 1936, when the Italians occupied the land.

Now there was a mad, almost insane ride to the coast under the guidance of a man named Bubayr, the Donkey, a man unable to endure fatigue, and, "lately married, he was incapacitated for walking." It was dangerous country. "In the land we were to traverse, every man's spear would be against us." There were reports that one of the tribes was incensed that Burton had not gone through its territory on the way to Harar, and thus it missed the tribute he would have paid, and now it was about to attack. Another rumor came that a hundred cows had been offered for Burton and his servants, dead or alive. Still, Burton, with his usual thoroughness, could amass notes on the country—the look of the desert, the ancient ruins, the impoverished villages, the misty mornings, the "horrid hills," and the "uniform and un-interesting scenery." Half-starved from lack of adequate provisions, the party finally reached grassy uplands and felt some rain. But as they descended to the coastal plain, they ran out of water. "Repeated requests for aid at various villages were refused." Men and mules became faint from thirst. When the caravan reached the coast, where there were wells, Burton found the villages were those of enemies of his servants. On the last day of January 1855, after a forced march of forty miles, Burton reached Berbera and the hut where Herne and Stroyan were waiting. It was two o'clock in the morning. Burton thought he had a ride that "will live in local annals for many and many a year." The ill-starred Jack Speke had not yet arrived, having had difficulties on his own excursion, it being his fate now, as later, always to trail the formidable Burton.

In the daytime, when Burton saw Berbera, "it was with ex-citement that I reflected upon the impolity of having preferred Aden to this place."

The Emporium of Eastern Africa has a salubrious climate, abundance of sweet water—a luxury to be "fully appreciated only after a residence at Aden"—a mild monsun [monsoon], a fine open country, an excellent harbour, and a soil highly productive. It is the meeting place of commerce, has few rivals, and with half the sums lavished in Arabia upon engineering follies of stone and lime [at Aden], the environs might at this time have been covered with houses, gardens and trees.

But Aden had been chosen, and to that "mountain of Misery," to "that coal heap," he must now return. On the fifth of February, accompanied by the Hammal, Long Gulad, and End of Time— they "could scarcely believe their departure from Berbera with sound skins"—Burton went on board a coastal sailing ship and, after a brief voyage of reconnaissance along the Somaliland coast, was safely arrived at Aden, where "I had the pleasure of seeing the faces of friends and comrades once more."

At Aden, Burton received the news that his mother had died. He had arrived on February 9, 1855, and Speke appeared a week later, calling his own trip a failure and blaming everyone but himself. "He was thoroughly disgusted with his journey," wrote Burton, "and he brought back a doleful tale of trouble." Speke thought that "one of the reasons for his failure was his dressing as an Arab." He was convinced that there was no such feature as the Wady Nogal, though its existence was a matter of common knowledge.

> He began at the very landing place with a serious mistake, which might have led to the worst consequences. Meeting the first mop-headed Somalis who spoke broken English, he told them his intentions, and he actually allowed two donkey boys to become his Abbans—guides and protectors.

Not only did Speke suffer at the hands of natives; he did also at Burton's, who showed no sympathy for his companion's misfortune.

He had recorded his adventures in a diary whose style, to say nothing of its sentiments and geographical assertions, rendered it, in my opinion, unfit for publication, and I took the trouble of rewriting the whole. Published as an Appendix to "First Footsteps in East Africa," it was in the third person, without the least intention of giving offense, but simply because I did not wish to palm upon the reader my own composition as that of another person.

Speke was furious about this rewriting of his work, and his friends supported him, at least one attacking Burton in print for the outrage. Later, in Africa, when Speke was delirious with fever, he poured out his grievance, to Burton's surprise, "that his Diary had been spoiled." Throughout this period Burton had completely misunderstood Speke's character. Whatever manifestations of ill will, of anger and jealousy, that appeared in Speke, Burton tried to explain away as the result of understandable stresses that often arose in the execution of a difficult task. That Speke found fault with virtually everything hardly mattered to Burton. Burton did, too, but there was a difference. Burton's complaints were not personal, and it was obvious that even when things got on his nerves—the succession of "cow sheds" and "dog houses" that passed as palaces and the screeching native girls, for example—he was in fact enjoying himself. But Speke took virtually everything as a personal affront, part of a huge conspiracy to lead him to failure.

Meanwhile, Burton had much to do at Aden, writing out a series of reports, secret in character, to the government at Bombay and preparing for a return to Somaliland. In his reports and in his private writings Burton had to walk a fine line. Every trip, every adventure, from his earliest days in Sind, had been turned into a book, in which he was not remiss in making personal criticism of official policy; often he was forced to soften his words in a second edition, as he did in the *Pilgrimage*. The appearance of any of his works was a source of anxiety to Government. Now he had to assure John Company that his book about Somaliland and Harar would be "a mere narrative of adventure. . . . That all political allusions will be carefully avoided." But such promises could hardly deter his pen, and he was critical of both the Court of Directors of the East India Company and the Governor-General of India. He spared no one he thought stood in need of correction. In his secret reports he recommended that the English establish themselves in Berbera but not advance into the interior. Harar need not be taken. He thought that the natives in Somaliland would prefer the British "to that other alternative—the Turks."

Unfortunately for the immediate future of British imperialism, the rich Horn of Africa was soon snapped up by other powers. No matter what one thinks of Burton's politics at this point, it was the nineteenth century, and the native world was there for the exploitation. Two rivals appeared unexpectedly from inland to take parts of Somalia, Abyssinia from the west and Egypt from the north. In 1884, Britain appropriated the northern coast of the Horn, and a few years later, France found a nice piece around the port of Djibuti. At the end of the century, Italy squeezed herself into the vacant land on the bottom of the Horn, to the south of the British.

More than territorial aggrandizement occupied Burton's mind. The issue of slavery rather than of making a rich empire even richer troubled him, and in his reports he spoke eloquently of the question.

It is no Quixotic theory against slavery which urges me to recommend its extinction. But where slavery flourishes commerce declines. It is far more satisfactory for a barbarous people to fire a kraal and sell the fugitives than to sow some cotton and grow coffee. I have ever spoken favourable of domestic thralldom amongst the Moslems [of Arabia and Egypt], but the practice of slave-driving must be abominable to a philanthropic people. My report might be adorned with pictures of horror—children left to be destroyed by wild beasts, women whose persons are subject to the extreme of brutality and men whose spirits must be tamed by diabolical tortures.

After the reports were out of the way, he turned to the central issue in his mind, the search for the source of the Nile, for which he needed government support. Not averse to flattery if it would help him, he proposed that a great Agency building be constructed at Berbera, to be called "Elphinstone." He suggested that he and Speke return to Berbera, where Herne and Stroyan, having collected mules and camels, were waiting for them, to start the second phase of the Somaliland Expedition. In April, the monsoon season, they would head straight inland into the Ogaden, a fierce desert that otherwise supported little life, for at that time "the wells are full, grass for the cattle abounds and the land flows with milk." He pointed out that fully adequate time must be allotted to the journey, for the natives were dilatory in giving help because they were feeding off the travelers' supplies; they do not want him to leave. He warned on his own behalf that "nothing increases the perils of sickness, and the fatigue of man and the elements so much as haste." Consequently, he asked for another year of leave, and to relieve the government of responsibility, he offered to sign any document required stating that he would not "incur an immoderate risk in carrying out the object in view, so that my own life and that of my associates will not be seriously endangered." He closed by saying that he feared "little from the Somali beyond our being gradually stripped in the most friendly way of all our goods— excepting our arms." This to Burton was part of the game; he knew the rules and was willing to play by them. To strengthen his own hand, he had one more request: the local rank of major in East Africa to impress the natives. He received permission to make the expedition to search out the sources of the Nile, but for the rank of major, no. Other men of lesser or no ability would outrank him constantly, but Burton was never to be more than a captain in John Company's native armies.

To Norton Shaw, Burton did not underestimate the dangers of the expedition. "Our difficulties will be principally amongst that penis-cutting people," he wrote, referring to the Somalis, "but by day we need not fear for a host," for the expedition would be heavily armed.

Next he had to deal with the petulant Speke. Speke had clearly been taken advantage of by the natives during his time on the mainland, but "his life was never in real peril," Burton wrote. Speke had no understanding of the people—"savages cannot believe that a man wastes his rice and cloth to collect dead beasts and to ascertain the direction of a stream." Speke had also offended native religious sensibilities: he was obviously a Christian and was "ignorant of the Moslem faith." A major, irreversible gulf was slowly developing between Burton and Speke. That there were differences Speke, from all the evidence, well realized. But Burton seemed insensitive to Speke's susceptibilities, and if he were at all aware, he consistently ignored the arising tensions. Perhaps he thought they would be bridged over and healed by the common work before them. For Speke, however, there was no forgiving, no turning back. Every slight, every injury or argument, would be magnified and hardened into a mortal hatred that even in the seemingly peaceful atmosphere of Aden was savaging the success of the coming expedition.

Despite the problems, Speke was now an important factor in Burton's plans. No one else rash enough to risk his life in East Africa had appeared, and Speke had to be relied upon. Burton found him a completely trustworthy *abban*, and he was sent back to the Somali coast to collect camels for the expedition; he arrived late in March. On the coast there were numerous problems; rumors, possibly quite true but always to be denied, were afloat that the English intended to take Berbera, or give it to their ally Sharmakay, and that they planned on stopping the slave trade. When some Somalis at Berbera argued that the English would be halted halfway, before they had made any deep advance into Somaliland, Speke's *abban* translated the conversation for him.

If the Somalis came down to fight [one of the elders had said], and then ran away back into the fastness of their hills, what would the English do then, who cannot live a day without drinking beer and eating meat? Whereas the Somali can do very well without anything, seldom requiring even water, and not more than one morsel of meat, for a whole week together.

Native boasting, obviously. But Burton, if he had heard it, would have known the elders were speaking the truth. The fault for such native confidence could be rightly ascribed to Outram, for his having broken up Burton's original plan for a force in strength, even though small, had revealed to the Somalis that the English were vulnerable to being picked off one by one. Outram had now left Aden, being replaced by Colonel W. W. Coghlan, who was no friendlier to Burton than his predecessor. In Somaliland, Speke, aided by his new *abban*, easily got camels together and returned to Berbera on April third, to join Herne and Stroyan. The trade fair was in its last days. A huge caravan of three thousand men and as many cattle had come to town with the purpose of gathering eight months' supplies for resale in their own territories, mostly the Ogaden desert. Speke thought quite correctly that the Somaliland Expedition should have joined it. "Had we gone straight from Aden without any preliminary fuss, and joined the Ogaden caravan at Berbera just as it was starting, I feel convinced that we should have succeeded."

Burton arrived on the seventh aboard John Company's schooner *Mahi.* The ship anchored offshore to give support and protection to the expedition as final preparations were made.

The camp was pitched upon a rocky ridge about three-quarters of a mile from the town, near the site of Burton's proposed Agency. The site had been selected because it was within range of the *Mahi*'s guns. The English camp was composed of forty-two men, the four English officers and a mixture of Egyptian, Nubian, Arab, and Negro servants, and twenty Somali warriors from different, rival tribes, under rival chiefs, each of whom vied to be the guide for the expedition. Coghlan had refused Burton police from Aden; hence, the somewhat makeshift guard. A key figure was the *ras*, or captain, of the expedition, a Somali, who was responsible for the day-to-day activities. He was called al Balyuz, or the "Envoy." "He had the reputation of being a shrewd manager, thoroughly acquainted with the habits and customs, as well as the geography, of Somaliland," Burton wrote of the *ras*, who was obviously the most reliable and responsible of all the natives attached to the expedition.

The English tents were pitched in a line. Stroyan's was at one end; in the center, about a dozen paces away, was a large "Rowtie," occupied by Burton and Herne, and at the other end was Speke's tent. The Rowtie was a type of tent commonly used by sepoys, a large "pent-house" shape, with one end higher than the other—what Americans might call a lean-to—supported by a single transverse pole on two uprights and open at one of the long ends. The baggage was placed between Speke's tent and the Rowtie; the camels were tethered in front on a sandy bed below the ridge, and in the rear were the horses and mules. During daytime everyone was alert, and at night sentries were posted; they were visited at times by the English officers or by the *ras* and were regularly relieved. Though there were rumors of marauding parties, the natives seemed friendly, including the two groups of rival Somalis who formed the guard. Minor disputes over the hire of horsekeepers and camel drivers had been settled amicably. "Briefly," Burton wrote, "we had no grounds of apprehension." The expedition was almost ready to leave, but Burton wanted to see the end of the trade fair, and he was waiting for instruments and other necessities to arrive by the mid-April mail from Europe. On the afternoon of the ninth the first shower fell, signaling the beginning of the Gugi, or Somali, monsoon, and the merchants began to leave. The next day, the town was virtually deserted. On the fifteenth, the last vessel sailed out of Berbera creek. The *Mahi* had been called to other duties, leaving the expedition without the protection of its guns. On the eighteenth, a small native ship from Aden entered the creek, carrying about a dozen Somalis who hoped to go to the Ogaden with Burton. The captain had expected to sail that evening, but "fortunately . . . I had ordered our people to feast her commander and crew with rice and the irresistible dates," said Burton.

That evening, about sunset, three strange horsemen approached the camp. Burton questioned them and received noncommittal answers, and the warriors rode away. Sentries were posted as usual, and the camp seemed quiet and safe.

Sometime after two o'clock the next morning Burton was awakened by shouts that the camp was under attack. What happened after that has always been a matter of dispute. "Hearing a rush of men like a strong wind, I sprang up, called for my sabres and sent Lieut. Herne to ascertain the force of the foray," Burton wrote. The officers were to learn later that Somalis from various clans were the attackers. Herne found the enemy everywhere and learned that the guards had run away. Meanwhile, Burton roused Stroyan and then Speke. No one saw Stroyan alive after that; he was cut to pieces by the Somalis.

Speke at first thought the sounds of firing were a false alarm to scare away pilferers but then realized the attack was real. He joined Burton and Herne in the Rowtie, and the three men each tried to fend off the attackers from a different point. The marauders meanwhile were trying to enter through the opening of the Rowtie and the space between the walls and the ground, throwing javelins and stabbing out with their long, heavy daggers. Burton was armed with only a sabre, but Speke and Herne had their Colts, which they used "with deadly effect." But soon the chambers were emptied, and unable to reload easily, they had to use the revolvers as clubs. Finally, a Somali broke through the rear.

At this time, about five minutes after the beginning of the affray, the tent had almost been beaten down, an Arab custom with which we were all familiar, and had we been entangled in its folds we should have been speared with unpleasant facility. I gave the word to escape, and sallied out, closely followed by Lieut. Herne, with Lieut. Speke in the rear. The prospect was not agreeable. About twenty men were kneeling and crouching at the tent entrance, whilst many dusky figures stood further off, or ran about shouting the war-cry, or with shouts and blows drove away our camels. Among the enemy were many of our friends and attendants, the coast being open to them, they naturally ran away, firing a few useless shots and receiving a modicum of flesh wounds.

Burton thought he saw Stroyan lying on the ground and cut his way toward him through a dozen Somalis. He heard a sound at his side and thinking it one of the attackers, turned. It was the *ras*; Burton had almost cut him down.

He cried out in alarm; the well-known voice caused an instant's hesitation: at that moment a spearman stepped forward, left his javelin in my mouth, and retired before he could be punished.

Burton escaped "as by a miracle." The *ras* reappeared and led him to a spot where he thought the other officers had gathered, and disappeared. Though overpowered with faintness and pain, Burton spent the interval before dawn wandering in search of his comrades. As day broke, he found himself at the head of the creek, where he was picked up by the crew of the native vessel he had entertained the night before and carried aboard. He still had the javelin in his jaw, and it was now removed. Burton sent some of the crew to search for his comrades. Herne had gained the safety of the boat shortly before Burton, having suffered no serious damage but stiff blows from war clubs. Stroyan's corpse was found and brought aboard. Speke, even more than Burton, had suffered numerous wounds, and in his case it was a miracle that he survived. Separated from his fellow officers, he was attacked, seized from behind and thrown on the ground, and tied with his hands pinioned at his back. He suffered the alarm that overwhelms Europeans caught by natives. "Whilst I was pinioned," he wrote, "they felt my private parts. . . . I felt as if my hair stood on end, and not knowing who my opponents were, I feared that they belonged to a tribe called Eesa, who are notorious, not only for their ferocity in fighting, but for the unmanly mutilations they delight in." But the warriors were only trying to find if Speke, Arab fashion, was carrying a dagger concealed between his legs. Speke was now alternately treated rather kindly, considering the situation, by some of the Somalis, and beaten and attacked by others as he lay on the ground.

Eventually he worked his hands free, and when he rose to his feet, he was assailed several times, being beaten by war clubs and stabbed by spears and knives. He managed to escape—the attackers were more interested in plundering the camp—and ran and walked three miles, severely wounded—he had eleven wounds in all, two of which had pierced his thighs—until he was rescued by the shore party from the native boat. Stroyan's body, which had been savagely mutilated, was buried at sea the same day, and two days later the remnants of the Somaliland Expedition arrived in Aden with the news of the unexpected disaster.

At Aden, Burton and Speke were treated for their wounds. The military surgeon noted in his official report that the javelin had entered the left side of Burton's face and had come out the right, knocking out two molars and splitting the palate. Also noted was that Burton suffered a secondary stage of syphilis. The surgeon recommended that Burton be spared Aden's hot weather and be returned to England to recuperate. Speke's wounds were far worse. He was too severely injured at the moment even to move. His arms and legs were described as "contracted into indescribable positions." He began to suffer from a partial blindness, and when he was at last able to move, he was sent home to England.

The news of Burton's trip to Harar, his stay there, and his return to Berbera and then to Aden, followed by the fight at Berbera, had all been reported in England and was closely followed by Isabel, who feared "it was doubtful whether Richard would recover."

Doubtless this is the danger alluded to by the clairvoyant, and the cause of my horrible dreams concerning him about the time it happened. I hope to Heaven he will not go back! How can I be grateful enough for his escape!

In the moribund, gossipy society of Aden, the battle at Berbera became a dominant topic of conversation. Those who had warned of disaster for the Somaliland Expedition were now proved right. Moreover, certain prejudices were confirmed: The natives were not to be trusted, and Burton had presumed too much by associating with them and believing he could outwit them. It had been a magnificent battle, fought by brave men against overwhelming odds, but Burton's enemies wondered that it had been allowed to happen at all, and there was now a well-supported attempt to hang the blame on him. Colonel Coghlan, Outram's successor, did not want Government held responsible in any way for the disaster. He had inherited all of Outram's prejudices against Burton and allowed them to flourish. After Burton's departure, secret investigations were initiated of which Burton had no knowledge—the papers lay in Government files until the 1960s. Even the exchange of public documents was acrimonious, and the three surviving officers did their best to exonerate themselves.

First, from Speke's report:

We have been condemned for not putting on more sentries to watch; but had the whole camp been in a state of ordinary preparation for war, with such cowardly hearts as our men had [he is referring to the native servants], we should have been signally defeated.

Herne put the emphasis on the size of the enemy force:

Had any of the guard, or Somali, stood we should have resisted the attack, but under such overpowering numbers we had no chance.

Burton, like Speke, was scornful of their own native soldiers:

The officers under my charge fought coolly and with energy, but of our twelve men armed with swords and muskets, Saad, a black slave, only is severely wounded; there are also three slightly hurt . . . the others behaved with the vilest cowardice . . . they threw down their weapons and ran after firing only three shots in the air.

Burton felt beleaguered by the accusations. He tried to point out that this "melancholy occurrence was the act of a troop of Bedouin brigands . . . in every way opposed to the custom of the country and a flagrant infraction of the people's code of honor." In his own defense he said, "I cannot refrain from remarking, that as I took upon myself the responsibility of the expedition, so I have discharged it to the utmost of my ability." He had been led to believe "that the coast about Berbera was as safe as Bombay itself," and he had been forced to wait for mail from Aden, which had not been forwarded "within a moderate time."

But Coghlan did not accept Burton's excuses. "It may seem harsh to criticize the conduct of these officers who, to the grief of their wounds and the loss of their property, must add the total failure of their long-cherished scheme," but, he emphasized, "their whole proceeding is marked by want of caution and vigilance," and, in short, he had nothing good to say about them but to praise their bravery in an attack that he thought might have been prevented by "common prudence and forethought." The exchanges continued and grew more bitter. Burton was soon back in London, followed by Speke, and Coghlan took advantage of their absence to gather statements from certain of the Somalis attached to the expedition. Naturally, they did not want to be blamed for the disaster and threw the fault to Burton, saying they had warned him not to camp where he did—in short, that Burton had been well warned. Their statements, so injurious to Burton, were taken at face value—though Coghlan, like most of his compatriots, always assumed that natives were not likely to tell the truth—and these statements stood in sharp contrast to those by the three officers. In answer to these particular accusations, Burton charged that the native chiefs had falsified their reputed conversations with him. He was not informed of all the papers drawn up against him, and he could only rail against "this shuffling procedure [by which] a man's character [is] stabbed in the back." This latest file, like others before it, grew to impressive proportions and finally was forwarded to Lord Dalhousie, the Governor-General of India.

In Bombay, Elphinstone, though a friend of Burton's, had come to accept Coghlan's views but hoped to find some means of blunting the attacks. Only Lumsden supported Burton fully. Shortly, Coghlan himself was under fire for his lack of understanding of the very delicate situation. Dalhousie, rejecting Burton's recommendation that the British occupy Somaliland, stated that he "deprecated" a policy that would involve the government in India with "a nook of Africa at a distance of 1,600 miles from its resources," and Burton was an old man before he saw his dream come true.

20

"Rotten Heads"

Severely disabled by wounds that might have put another man in the grave, Burton returned to London for treatment. Not only had four teeth been knocked out by the Somali's spear thrust into the upper jaw and part of the palate damaged, but both cheeks had been pierced. Burton could barely speak. He put himself under the care of a surgeon and a dentist and recovered with remarkable ease, although the left side of his face—the one he liked to exhibit, as in the portrait by Frederick Leighton, in which he appears in an ambiguous position between English gentleman and Oriental despot, though a despot of great sensitivity and intelligence—was disfigured. Napier, who had received a similar wound years earlier, spoke of the "almost intolerable agony" it gave him.

Burton had another touch of his customary bad luck in gaining recognition after an expedition. His daring work in India had resulted only in secret denunciations in his dossier; he had failed to capitalize on his pilgrimage to Mecca by not returning home when he might have received all sorts of acclaim; and after the two expeditions into Somaliland, the glory of the first was lost by his going to Bombay, that of the second was overshadowed by his country's war with Russia in eastern Europe and the Crimea, and his savage fight for life meant little when in a previously unknown land, the Crimea, British lads and even a few generals were expiring daily before the Czar's guns or from cholera and other diseases, the cold, and from Allied intrigues and inefficiency.

When, shortly after returning to London, Burton read a paper at a meeting of the Royal Geographical Society about Harar, his expedition seemed like a trivial exploit. And when he tried to call attention to the importance of Somaliland, especially ports like Berbera, he had to suffer through an annoying and ignorant attack by "an ancient fellow" who had never been to Somalia but was convinced that Burton had crossed a major river on the way to Harar and wanted to know why Burton had not mentioned it. Merely a stream, Burton tried to reassure the Fellows, but without success.

"Wounded and sorely discomforted" by his experiences, though he had the satisfaction of seeing *Personal Narrative of a Pilgrimage to El-Medinah and Meccah* already in print and had begun the manuscript of what he was to entitle *First Footsteps in East Africa; or, an Exploration of Harar*, he turned his attention to the great diversion of the moment, the Crimean War, in which the Czarist naval base at Sevastopol was under seige.

Russia and Turkey had gone to war against each other in October 1853 along the vast borders held in common in eastern Europe and the Danube delta. It was to England's advantage to support the Turks, for always present was the threat of Russian expansion into Central Asia and south to the Indian Ocean, areas that were of prime concern to the British Crown. Some dissidents in England favored Russia, and thirty years later, reversing his earlier commitment to the Great Game, Burton was to write that "this disastrous blunder lost to us forever the affection of Russia, our oldest and often our only friend among the continentals of Europe." What happened, he wrote, was that Russia was diverted from Europe to focus more strongly on India and especially "at the same time doubling her extent by the absorption of Turcomania," that is, Central Asia, so long one of Britain's own goals. Britain and France, suddenly allies, sent a fleet to Constantinople in token support of Turkey. After the Russians crushed the Turkish fleet, the two European allies were forced to take an active role and in January 1854 declared war on Russia and sent ships and troops to the Danube area and eventually brought the Czar to surrender in eastern Europe. The new allies, the Napoleonic Wars having become ancient history, now found a chance to cripple Russia and, with the Turks, attacked the great Russian naval base of Sevastopol on the western Crimean coast in September 1854, thus initiating one of the most disastrous and tragic wars of the century. Burton saw the conflict as "an unmitigated evil to England." And the manner in which it was fought appalled him. To the young officers of the British units it was an opportunity for glory; in fact, it ostensibly offered all the traditional military values that men of certain classes sought: wild cavalry charges, hand-to-hand skirmishes, artillery duels, naval encounters, and heroism under the most frightening conditions. But men who were magnificent on the parade grounds were ineffectual on the battlefield, and the officers with experience in war, the Indian officers, were denied commissions because the India services were looked down upon. The supreme commander, Lord Raglan, was "exactly the man *not* wanted," wrote Burton. Then there was Lord Cardigan, the man in charge of the Light Brigade made famous by Tennyson's elegiac, and his brother-in-law, Lord Lucan, whose feuding brought the death of so many men. The Light Brigade, some seven hundred men, had ridden straight into the mouths of Russian guns, only two hundred survivors returning. "It is magnificent but it is not war," Burton quoted a French general as saying.

In London, Burton obtained a few letters of introduction to various commanders—he was in effect a true free-lance mercenary—packed his gear, and hurried through France and found a boat to Constantinople. He spent a few days in the Turkish capital greeting old friends and then proceeded to the Crimea, landing at Balaklava ("Fish Town," he noted), where the siege was taking place against the Russian fortifications. He visited various commands, a man in search of a commission, or a job, but no general would take him, there being so much prejudice against officers from the Indian army. Finally, he returned to Constantinople, where he met an officer friend from Boulogne, General W. F. Beatson, a wild, independent man of thirty-five-years' service in Bengal, and was immediately given a commission. Beatson was assembling a cavalry unit of Turkish irregulars who operated independently of ordinary military channels. They were known as "Beatson's Horse," but the popular name was Bashi-Bazouks, "Rotten Heads" in Burton's free translation. The Bashi-Bazouks were mostly men from the Turkish Balkan provinces, mainly village toughs and delinquents who were feared as being undisciplined, even criminal. They were not paid but survived by plunder and were notoriously difficult to control. Beatson was a brave but impassioned and undiplomatic old veteran who wore "a gorgeous uniform blazing with gold" to impress the Turks. The Bashi-Bazouks wore similar uniforms—the only way to impress an Oriental, Burton remarked on several occasions, was with such show. "An eastern judges *entirely* by dress."

His account of his days at Constantinople is filled with the minutiae of gossip about men once important politically whose names are barely remembered today, some of them men after his own tastes, like Percy Smythe, Lord Strangford, a linguist who "seemed to take a language through every pore, and to have time for all its niceties and eccentricities." Strangford and Burton could talk to each other about Sufism with complete understanding. Burton also came across Fred Hankey, his old friend from Cairo, whose interests were largely erotic and pornographic. Then there was Alison, later minister at Tehran, who knew "Romaic [demotic Greek] perfectly, Turkish well, Persian a little, and a smattering of Arabic." Burton moved in the highest circles in the Turkish capital, but the fact remained that he was an Indian officer serving in a native contingent commanded by a man who was as undisciplined as his soldiers.

The Bashi-Bazouks were stationed at Gallipoli at the mouth of the Dardanelles. The situation there was a cobra's nest of intrigues. Not only was there a rivalry between the regular officers and the Indian officers, but between some of those serving under Beatson as well, "black sheep" who schemed for themselves. The officials at the capital looked down on the men in the Dardanelles, and the Turkish regulars resented Beatson's Turkish irregulars. The Greeks preferred the Russians to the English, and Burton accused the powerful Jewish merchants also of being pro-Russian. The local Turkish pashas feared that the Allies were attempting to take over their country, a fear encouraged by the German engineers working on the fortifications. And the French resented the English, their recent conquerors.

"But our deadliest enemies," Burton said, "were of course those nearest home." A party within the English opposed the Bashi-Bazouks and were able to gain the support of the British ambassador, Lord Stratford, who had taken a dislike to Beatson. The general had scandalized his superiors by his frankness in proposing "to hang the Military Pasha of the Dardanelles, if he continued to intrigue and report falsely concerning his forces."

The general paid no more attention to regulations than did his Bashi-Bazouks, and Burton, having been made Chief of Staff, "overhauled his books and stood aghast to see the style of his official despatches." Beatson, Burton wrote, "was presently persuaded, with some difficulty, to let me mitigate their candour under the plea of copying." However, on one occasion when Burton had thought he had made an agreeable copy, he looked in the envelope and found a formal challenge to Lord Stratford.

> Fancy the effect of a formal challenge to combat, "pistols for two and coffee for one," upon the rancorous old man of Constantinople [the Ambassador] whose anger burnt like a red-hot fire, and whose revenge was always at a white heat! I took it out, but my General did not thank me for it.

Shortly, with the experience on the parade grounds of Baroda still fresh in his memory, Burton got the Bashi-Bazouks into military shape, with a strong inculcation of discipline. Now, what was to be done with these men, some four thousand strong, wild and eager for action and capable of heroic deeds? But the corps sat idly at Gallipoli; the British high command had no role for irregulars. Mulling over the situation and talking endlessly with Beatson and the other officers, Burton got the idea of relieving the garrison at Kars, an ancient citadel in eastern Turkey not far from the Russian border. Kars had been under siege for a long time: The garrison was composed of Turks but commanded by an Englishman, General Fenwick Williams Pasha, who had fired off eighty "officials" requesting help from Lord Stratford without receiving a single reply. In England the relief of Kars became an issue. Karl Marx, then a "war correspondent" for the *New York Tribune*, a radical, populist, socialist newspaper, although he had never left London, wrote frequently about Beatson's plans to relieve the city, not knowing that Burton was the instigator. The saving of Kars seemed obvious to many among the British. Its fall would not only harm the Turks but also make easier the Russian advance on Persia, Mesopotamia, Afghanistan, and western India. The Bashi-Bazouks themselves had petitioned to go to the aid of Kars, Marx reported. Finally, Burton went to plead with the Ambassador and was allowed an interview with Stratford's chief aide, General Robert J. Hussey-Vivian, "a man redolent of pipe-clay and red tape, and servilely subject to the

Ambassador." Stratford had used as an excuse for not relieving Kars the fact that there was no transport.

So I felt the game was in *my* hands, and proceeded in glorious elation of spirits to submit my project for the relief of Kars to his Excellency. We already had 2640 sabres in perfect readiness to march, and I could have procured *any quantities* of carriage [as transport]. The scene which resulted passes description. He shouted at me in a rage, "You are the most impudent man in the Bombay army, Sir!" But I knew him . . . and did not mind. It ended with, "Of course you'll dine with us to-day?"

Frustrated and puzzled, Burton returned to Gallipoli.

It was not until some months afterwards that I learnt what my unhappy plan proposed to do. Kars was doomed to fall as a makeweight for the capture of half of Sebastopol, and a Captain of Bashi-Bazouks (myself) had madly attempted to arrest the course of *haute-politique*.

At Gallipoli the irregulars had gotten themselves into trouble. There had been some rioting—"sky-larking," Burton called it, explaining that "only one woman was dishonoured." However, Turkish regulars had surrounded the camp and allied warships stood offshore ready to fire; the Bashi-Bazouks were about to attack their "enemy." But Beatson issued firm orders and "restrained the natural anger of his much-suffering men." The incident was apparently ended, but the general's enemies in Constantinople carried on the battle, sending "note-takers," among them a Mr. Skene, to dredge up information against Beatson and his officers, including Burton. Beatson meanwhile had suffered an injury in falling from a horse and was unable to carry out his duties, and to make matters worse, General Vivian replaced him with another man, Major-General Richard Smith, who arrived at the camp not with English troops in support but French. Burton and the others tried to lay the case before Smith, but he refused to listen. "After an insult of this kind, we felt that we could no longer serve with self-respect. It was this proceeding, I suppose, which afterwards gave rise to a report that I had done my best to cause a mutiny."

Meanwhile, Stratford, as a sop to Burton for not being allowed to relieve Kars, had offered him another chance to see some action. In the Caucusus there was a famous Muslim tribal chief, Schamyl (Samuel), who ruled over most of the tribes in the area and was considered an imām of special qualities, second only to Muḥammad in the eyes of the faithful. For almost a quarter of a century he had been preaching and waging a *jihād*, a holy war, against the infidel Czar. His long struggle against the Russians, his adroitness and daring (which included many hairbreadth escapes from encircling enemy troops) gained him the admiration of all of Europe. Burton called Schamyl a "brigand" in the *Life* and said that he had "lately been accused, amongst other atrocious actions, of flogging Russian ladies whom he had taken prisoners." To the British high command it seemed like a sound idea to send the troublesome Captain Burton with his Muslim sympathies to the imām, to enlist him actively on the side of the Allies. "I could not understand how Lord Stratford, who had an unmitigated horror of all Russian cruelties, and who always expressed it in the rawest terms, could [on the other hand] ally himself with such a ruffian."

"There were difficulties and dangers," Burton recalled later, including a long ride through Russian territory, but "the task might have been accomplished." He thought he could rely "greatly upon the ardent patriotism of the Circassian women who then filled the harems of Constantinople. I should not have seen a single face, except perhaps that of a slave-girl, but I should have been warmly assisted with all the interest the fair patriots could make." He thought seriously of the matter, but in the end he realized that Schamyl would expect "money, arms and possibly troops," and if Burton did not arrive with whatever the imām needed, he would "infallibly set me down for a spy, and my chances of returning to Constantinople will be uncommonly small."

It was fortunate that Burton had the sense not to go on this harebrained mission. It was learned later that in another example of *haute politique* the Russians had made a pact with Schamyl that they would not harass him if he did not help the Allies. That Burton would have been seriously compromised and probably killed if he had gone on the mission seems apparent. With Beatson disgraced and his own career in the war ended, Burton returned to London. Here he was called as a witness in the trial that the general brought against his enemies for defamation of character. The chief opponent was Skene, whose lawyers intimated that Burton was one of the culprits in the Bashi-Bazouk "uprising." On the witness stand Burton was sarcastic, even nasty—the lawyers on the other side were ignorant of many military terms, and he made the most of it. In the end Beatson was vindicated, as was Burton. Again he emerged from a difficult situation with a bad reputation. Rumors at best ridiculous, at worst sordid, were circulated about his activities during the war. "A fellow officer," wrote Thomas Wright in his biography, "an unmitigated scoundrel [whom, however, he did not name] whose life has been sullied by every species of vice," began telling rather lurid stories about Burton's escapades in Turkey. The officer "inserted particulars that gave them verisimilitude." The officer himself had a bad reputation—he had "robbed the Post Office at Alexandria" and had attempted unsuccessfully to swindle a Greek heiress. "This sordid and callous rascal tried hard to lead people to suppose that he and Burton were hand in glove in various kinds of devilry." A favorite phrase was " 'I and Burton are great scamps.' " Burton's friend Lord Strangford said in reply, "No, that won't do, ----- is a real scamp, but Burton is only wild."

One story that never died down was that Burton had been caught in a Turkish harem and castrated. ("The usual indescribable penalty" was Wright's euphemism.) This is the only gossip that was ever known to annoy Burton, but, Wright says forcefully, "he most certainly underwent no deprivation." Other rumors "of an even more offensive nature got abroad," Wright added. "Pious mothers loathed Burton's name, and even men of the world mentioned it apologetically."

Crimea had died down but for the recriminations, analysis, and the mourning of the dead. A quarter of a million men had perished on each side: seventy thousand Allied casualties had come from cholera and other diseases. After the Beatson trial, Burton turned his attention to what was called the "Unveiling of Isis," the search for the source of the Nile, which he expected would be found in the lake regions of Central Africa.

A small incident served to distract him. "One summer day in August, 1856," wrote Isabel Arundell, "we [the Arundell family] had not gone out of town, and I was walking in the Botanical Gardens with my sister, Blanche Pigott, and a friend, and Richard was there, walking with the gorgeous creature of Boulogne —then married."

> We immediately stopped and shook hands, and asked each other a thousand questions of the four intervening years, and all the old Boulogne memories and feelings which had lain dormant, but not extinct, returned to me.

Isabel had *Tancred* with her, still "the book of my heart and taste," which Burton now explained to her. They spent an hour together, "and when I had to leave he gave me a peculiar look, as he did at Boulogne." She added that she "hardly looked at him, yet I felt it, and I had to run away." And when she got home, "Fright!"

The next morning Isabel and Blanche went out again into the Botanical Gardens, and Burton was there, too, writing some poetry. He came forward and said, laughing, "You won't chalk up 'Mother will be angry'?" referring to the first meeting on the Boulogne Ramparts. Burton and Isabel walked about and talked over "old times general."

After a third meeting, Isabel noticed a strange change in Burton's previously carefree attitude. "We had begun to know each other. . . ."

21

The Great Safari

With the search for the sources of the Nile, Burton entered upon the most dangerous, demanding, and tragic period of his life. Africa was nothing like the deserts of Sind and Arabia. Even the wild ride to Harar and back seemed more like an escapade fecklessly entered upon compared with the safari* into the African interior. But more than geography, miasmic jungles, disease, and natives of a type he had never before encountered complicated the trip for Burton and turned sour the aftermath. What happened in Africa was to mark him for the remainder of his life. Not only his physical health but his sanity was imperiled. The cause of many of his troubles was not, as so many people suggested, Isabel Arundell but John Hanning Speke and Speke's friends and allies. The tragedy was that Burton, having so often cut himself off from the English world, did not understand Speke.

* It was Burton who introduced the term *safári* (Swahili, from the Arabic *safár*, to journey) into English.

353

Burton did not seem to have the slightest notion of what occupied Speke's mind—his secret thoughts (often obliquely revealed), his ambitions, his greed, his yearning for recognition, and especially his desire for revenge, for he sincerely believed that Burton had injured him quite deliberately.

After the disaster at Berbera, Speke had recovered rapidly from his wounds. "A touching lesson how difficult it is to kill a man in sound health," Burton wrote of Speke in *First Footsteps*. "He has never felt the least inconvenience from the wounds, which closed up like cuts in Indian-rubber." Speke then joined the rush of young officers to the Crimea, where he was somewhat more fortunate than Burton, being assigned to a regiment of Turkish regulars as a captain. He was posted to the front but saw no action. When the hostilities ended, he decided that instead of returning to England he would remain in West Asia and try his hand at shooting and collecting fauna in the Caucasian mountains; he expected to be accompanied by his close friend Captain Edmund Smyth of the Bengal army, "an old and notorious Himalayan sportsman," as Speke described him. They needed passports to enter the Caucasus and wrote to Norton Shaw to ask his influence in obtaining them. Shaw replied that to enter Russia at that time was ill advised and that Speke should consider joining Burton, who was again organizing an expedition into Africa. "By the next mail I received a communication from Captain Burton himself, inviting me to join him once more in exploring Africa." Burton wrote that the Home and Indian governments had each promised to contribute £1000. "This settled the matter." Speke returned immediately to England to prepare for the trip.

Why had Burton asked Speke to join him?

> I was anxious again to take Lieut. John Hanning Speke, because he had suffered with me in purse and person at Berberah, and because he, like the rest of the party, could obtain no redress.

Apparently Burton thought that there would be enough profit, both financially and in terms of acclaim, to make up for the losses taken in Somalia. But the Court of Directors would not grant Speke leave once he had arrived in London, and it seemed that Burton would have to proceed without him, relying on others already committed to the expedition.

With his usual thoroughness in laying plans for a grand venture, Burton had proposed to the Royal Geographical Society and John Company alike "an exploration of the then utterly unknown Lake regions of Central Africa." He was also—an echo of the Mecca pilgrimage—to correct certain geographical errors (of which there were many) concerning the Dark Continent and to survey as fully as possible the resources of Central and intertropical Africa. He had researched the literature of the past with his customary energy, reading accounts of the Nile and its sources in Strabo, Pliny, Ptolemy, and other classical authors in the original Greek and Latin as well as the many works in Arabic. He had examined old maps and had investigated the legends of the fabulous "Mountains of the Moon," the Jebel Kumri (as the Arabs knew them), the "Lunatic Mountains" in his own mind because of the myths and legends that told how men were driven to madness in seeking them out. He also studied the later literature, the accounts of the Portuguese, Dutch, English, and French explorers (none of whom had ventured far beyond the coast but were reporting hearsay and myth), and he collected the papers of the missionaries, like Johannes Ludwig Krapf, who had actual experience in Africa.

By this time Burton had the trip fairly well worked out, his announced destination being the village of Ujiji (pronounced "Ooweewee"), about a thousand miles inland, on the shore of the relatively unknown Lake Tanganyika. Ujiji was said to be inhabited by Arab traders, and Burton thought they would be useful in the search. His true goal seems to have been purposely kept unclear—perhaps *taqīya*, dissimulation, was operating here—and he did not make it public that he intended to keep going until he found the river itself as well as its source.

Who might join him was a worrisome question. An important

member of the expedition was to be Steinhauser. It was necessary that a medical man accompany the expedition, for it was to enter a land where disease, fever, tropical sores, and other malignancies of the most destructive nature were rampant. Since Steinhauser and Burton knew each other well, understood each other's idiosyncrasies, and had common interests (including the *Arabian Nights*), they would be able to cope with the pressures of exploration under extremely trying conditions and would balance and complement each other's natures. Steinhauser was also a linguist, unlike Speke, speaking Arabic and other Oriental tongues.

Burton had also been in touch with the German missionary Johannes Rebmann, who had accompanied Dr. Krapf ("one of the better known Abyssinian travellers," according to Burton) and with him had seen the snow-covered Mount Killma-njaro (as Burton spelled it). Rebmann was then living in a mission outpost about eighty miles inland from Mombasa, the former Portuguese colony north of Zanzibar, and was working under the auspices of the London Missionary Society. Burton got a letter from the Society releasing Rebmann of his missionary duties should he want to join the expedition.

And then there was Speke as the fourth man, if he could get permission from the army. It seemed as if he would be a positive and valuable member of the expedition, and he was welcomed as the man who rounded out the staff.

However, at the moment there was only one assured member, and that was Burton himself. Though he and Steinhauser had been corresponding, the doctor was then in Aden, and Rebmann would have to be approached in person. He was written to but the letter never arrived. Speke was eager, it seemed, but he would have to travel to Bombay to apply for permission from the East India Company officers for an extended leave.

At this time—the late summer of 1856—Burton's work on Somalia, *First Footsteps in East Africa*, had appeared, being rushed through the writing and publication. It made no money for its author, though a second edition was issued, and after Burton's death there were various reprints. It was a massive work; the first edition ran almost seven hundred pages, with maps and illustrations, some in color, but two of its five appendixes caused trouble. Appendix IV was omitted by the publisher, Longman, Brown, Green, and Longmans, at the last minute without explanation. Actually, it was a four-page note in Latin about the practice of infibulation among the Somali, the only clue to its content coming from Burton's introduction to the book, in which he referred to "certain peculiar customs . . . under the name of fibulation [female circumcision]."

But it was Appendix I—Speke's journal as rewritten by Burton—that caused the most controversy. In his own text Burton had insinuated that Speke, given an important but easy assignment, had nevertheless failed, had not even reached the Wady Nogal, the object of his mission, and had come back "determined that no such feature . . . existed." To compound the slights was the matter of his journal, so painstakingly written in a rather flat and unimaginative style. Burton did not fully address the problem of Speke in print until the publication of *Zanzibar* in 1872, when he listed his reasons for rewriting the journal in the third person, adding that "an article from a well-known pen" in *Blackwood's* magazine lamented that Speke was not allowed to appear under his own words. This article, which was likely inspired by Speke, "kindled a fire which did not consume the less fiercely because it was smothered." Then Speke felt further injured because he had received no income from the book, although Burton, too, had earned none, for the book did not sell until after Burton's death. These slights, along with others real and imagined, were to smolder in Speke.

The Royal Geographical Society gave Burton the funds he had requested, but as he probably expected, John Company slipped out of what it had promised, and so he set off underfinanced and relying on nerve, courage, and ingenuity to make the most difficult of his journeys. It was already the fall of 1856 when he left London. He was now thirty-five, an age that might have encouraged him to less strenuous adventures. Accompanied by Speke, who was hoping that in Bombay the officials of the East India Company would take a more favorable view of his request for leave than did the Directors in London, Burton went first to Boulogne to see Edward, then on furlough before returning to India. Burton and Speke arrived in Cairo on November sixth. There Burton found waiting for him an order from the Court of Directors of the East India Company summoning him to return to London immediately to testify "at some wretched court-martial." He ignored it on the excuse that it was not clearly worded and that it was also impossible to get a boat at the moment. He and Speke continued to Suez and down the Red Sea. His sharp eye and keen ear had led him to see that trouble was coming. Political, social, and military conditions arising from "Anglo-Indian mismanagement and . . . Arab temper" would soon result in "some terrible disaster." This brought him to fire off "a long memorandum, showing the true state of affairs to the home branch of the Indian government." He added, "Again that zeal!" As a matter of prudence, he was to realize later, he should have reported "all things couleur de rose," but he had sniffed trouble in the air, and with his years of experience in the Orient, knew trouble would break out and had warned of it.

> The result was a "wig" [rebuke] received in the heart of Africa, and—curious coincidence!—accompanying that sheet of foolscap was a newspaper containing news of the Jeddah massacre [of] nearly the whole Christian community.

Burton and Speke reached Bombay on November twenty-third and were welcomed by Lord Elphinstone and James Grant Lumsden, Burton's old friend from Cairo, now an important member of the Bombay Council. Speke was granted the necessary leave by Elphinstone, and in great haste he and Burton got their equipment together. They also hired two Goan "cook boys" named Valentine and Gaetano as servants, "scions of that half Pariah race which yearly issues from Goa, Daman and Diu," Burton commented. They were indispensable for their job but were also vain, boasting, petty thieves, and gluttons, with "a deficiency of bodily and constitutional strength." Elphinstone, "knowing how much importance Orientals attach to appearance," made a sloop of war available so that the two explorers could land at Zanzibar with the full weight of the Government behind them. Lumsden saw his friends aboard. "On December 2, 1856 . . . we bade adieu to the foul harbor of Bombay the Beautiful, with a single sigh," Burton was to write in *Zanzibar* sixteen years later. "No phantom of the future cast a shadow upon our sunny path as we set out, determined to do or die."

As always, such an adventure was tremendously exciting for Burton, for the Amateur Barbarian was always lurking beneath his European skin. "I find my journal brimful of enthusiasm," he wrote.

Of the gladdest moments in human life, methinks [he had written on sailing], is the departure upon a distant journey into unknown lands. Shaking off with one mighty effort the fetters of Habit, the leaden weight of Routine, the cloak of many Cares and the slavery of Home, one feels once more happy. The blood flows with the fast circulation of childhood. . . . A journey, in fact, appeals to Imagination, to Memory, to Hope,—the three sister Graces of our moral being.

"Somewhat boisterous, but true," he added. But for the moment, "the sudden sense of freedom adds a cubit to the mental state . . . and the glorious face of nature gladdens the soul."

The sloop was impeccably clean, the food was good, the trip without incident, the officers honored Burton and Speke as brave men going out on a brave adventure, and "of course we had no adventures." On the evening of the eighteenth, they were forced to stop at a pinpoint of land called Tumbatu lying offshore from Zanzibar. Never wasting time, Burton collected several pages of ethnological information on the inhabitants. "We stood in the presence of another and new race," he observed. Apparently he saw a death in his few hours ashore, for much of his material is about funeral customs. Early the next morning they were in Zanzibar channel,

> awed by our first view of the then mysterious island of Zanzibar, and set off by the dome of distant hills, like solidified air. . . . Earth, sea, and sky, all seemed wrapped in a soft and sensuous repose, in the tranquil life of the Lotus Eaters, in the swoon-like slumbers of the Seven Sleepers, in the dreams of the Castle of Indolence.

Captain Burton, again very much the amateur barbarian, immediately fell in love with Zanzibar.

> . . . all was voluptuous with gentle swellings, with the rounded contours of the girl-negress . . . every feature was hazy and mellow, as if viewed through "woven air," and not through vulgar atmosphere.

Over all hung the spicy perfume of the clove plantations. Burton had been ordered to report to the British resident, Lieut.-Colonel Atkins Hamerton, of the Indian army. The colonel was the epitome of the white man ground down by the tropics.

> I can even now distinctly see my poor friend sitting before me, a tall, broad-shouldered and powerful figure, hair and beard prematurely snow-white, and a complexion once fair and ruddy, but long ago bleached ghastly pale by ennui and sickness. Such had been the effects of the burning heat of Maskat and 'the Gulf,' and the deadly damp of Zanzibar, Island and Coast. The worst symptom in his case—one which I have rarely found other than fatal—was his unwillingness to quit the place which was slowly killing him. At night he would chat merrily about a remove, about a return to Ireland; he loathed the subject in the morning. To escape seemed a physical impossibility, when he had only to order a few boxes to be packed, and to board the first home-returning ship.

With Hamerton's illness hampering his work, Burton found also that since the death of the sultan seven weeks earlier events in Zanzibar had become chaotic. There was now a battle between the sultan's two sons, one in Maskat, who was notoriously anti-British, and the younger son, who had taken the Zanzibar throne and was now preparing for war with his brother. Smallpox had recently devastated the island, and a severe drought had reduced the southern coast to a state of famine.

Hamerton was not in favor of the trip into Africa and told Burton of the fate of a young French naval officer who had been the last European to attempt a march into East Africa. Taken prisoner by the warriors of the Mzungera tribe, the officer had been tied to a tree, various parts of his body were lopped off, and finally his head. The murderers escaped except for the drummer who had beaten the death roll; he was caught and spent ten years bound to a tree in Zanzibar prison. Hamerton, perhaps influenced by his own poor health, suggested that Burton "had better return to Bombay. But rather than return to Bombay, I would have gone to Hades on that 20th December, 1856."

Meanwhile, Burton made the most of the island. Zanzibar was a dismal place for whites. "What with bad water and worse liquor, the Briton finds it hard to live at Zanzibar," Burton observed. In the air around him was disease so palpable that one could almost touch it, see it. Native physicians were unknown, and the full range of tropical illnesses proliferated without check.

Urinary and genital diseases were prevalent—"Gonorrhea is so common that it is hardly considered a disease"—and even a simple matter like turning up the soil for planting led to strange illnesses. "Syphilis spreads wide . . . and presents formidable symptoms." The Arabs called it the "black lion," Burton wrote. It "will destroy the part affected in three weeks; secondaries are to be feared; noses disappear, the hair falls off, and rheumatism and spreading ulcers result." He described elephantiasis of the legs and arms, "and especially of the scrotum," which affected twenty percent of the native inhabitants. Heat, disease, bad food, the rains, "depressing insomnia with alternations of lethargic sleep . . . the burning day and breathless night"—there was little that did not affect native and white alike.

Zanzibar City was as rank as any he had ever encountered. "Corpses float at time upon a heavy water, the shore is a cesspool." In the streets "as on the odious sands [where people defecated], the festering impurities render strolling a task that requires some resolution, and the streets are unfit for a decent (white) woman to walk through."

It was not black skin that irritated Burton but the lack of culture and civilization. Not even a veneer existed, and Burton was not slow in complaining about the very primitive manners and mores of the natives. Several times he complained about "Negro insolence," and he made the broad statement that the blacks were "an undeveloped and not to be developed race." But it was to the black world that he kept returning despite his snarls and anger, exploring "the native town—a filthy labyrinth, a capricious arabesque of disorderly lanes and alleys. . . . It would be the work of weeks to learn the threading of this planless maze, and what white man would have had the heart to learn it?" But it was Burton who spent endless hours probing its mysteries, so baffling to a man who thought he understood the Oriental world. He would go out early in the morning "before the black world returns to life . . . through the foul mass of densely crowded dwelling places where the slaves and the poor 'pig' together." Quickly compassion overcomes anger. "The pauper classes are contented with mere sheds. . . . The meanest hovels are of palm-matting, blackened by wind or sun . . . hardly less wretched than the west Ireland shanty."

Besides the Arabs and the blacks there were "the Dollar-hunters from Europe . . . a mere floating population" and the Banyans from western India, the Cutchis, "with placid, satisfied countenances, and plump, sleek, rounded forms, suggesting the idea of happy, well-to-do cows." And to remind him of his experiences with the Āghā Khān, he found "half a dozen pale-skinned 'Khojahs,' tricky-faced men with evil eyes, treacherous smiles, fit for the descendants of the 'Assassins.' . . ."

After almost two decades of military service and wandering in the Eastern world, Burton, now almost forty, married Isabel Arundell, ten years younger, and settled down to his version of domestic life. These are the wedding portraits by the fashionable society artist Louis Desanges. From Isabel Burton's *Life*.

Speke's Search for the Nile

In a heroic but controversial second search for the source of the Nile, Speke (*standing*), having avoided a commitment to Burton, set off with Captain James Augustus Grant, and, without actually having seen the source, was able to report to the world that he had found it.

The ferocious King Metesa of Uganda, who walked with lionlike strides in imitation of the king of the beasts

Speke's dalliance with what he referred to as his "water carriers" brought him ridicule and led to doubts about his claims to the Nile. After he had used the women he gave them to his bearers.

Speke presents rhinoceros heads to King Rumanika.

Speke spent much of his time in Uganda in the royal harem. Here he introduces Grant to the Dowager Queen, who is at the same time being given a cup of banana beer.

Isabel Burton at the height of her mature beauty and powers. The *Edinburgh Review*, usually hostile to the Burtons, said that at her best she was "a clever, capable woman, self-reliant in difficulties, with a pretty sense of humour. . . ."

Two views of Burton, showing different sides of his character—one brutal, the other romantic. The painting is by a society artist, Madame Gutmansthal de Benvenuti, and shows him at the age of fifty-eight.

The Burtons at Home

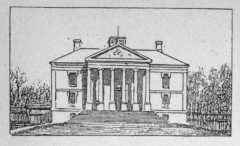

The last residence of the Burtons, outside Trieste, a huge, rambling palazzo. Here Burton translated such masterpieces as the *Arabian Nights*, the *Kama Sutra* and *The Perfumed Garden*. It was here that he died in October 1890.

The Burtons on a holiday at Folkestone with Dr. Frederick Grenville Baker. The doctor was Burton's private physician for the last years of his life.

The Burtons at dinner, in a dining room chock-full of typical Victorian clutter

Isabel Burton, in a photograph by Baker
that is only half humorous, nagging her
husband over some trifle or other

Burton at his desk where he
translated the *Arabian Nights*. He
had eleven desks in all, one for
each of his current projects.

These are supposedly the last
photographs of Burton, made from
cracked negatives. They are believed to
have been made the day of his death.

The Burton tent tomb at Mortlake, a London cemetery, where the bodies of
both Burtons lie

Complete the group by throwing in a European—how ghastly appears his blanched face, and how frightful his tight garb!—stalking down the streets in the worst of tempers, and using his stick upon the mangy "pariah dogs" and the naked shoulders of the "niggers" that obstruct him.

Then he turned to the subject that was almost an obsession. "Slavery was rampant," he reported. Hamerton had brought his influence on the late sultan, and "sundry floggings and confiscations of property installed into slave-owners the semblance of humanity," Burton said in the *Life*. But despite such measures, slavery continued, for Zanzibar was a clearing house for the import and export of human beings. Since the sultan extorted a tax on each slave to pass through the island, "wretches were thrown overboard when sick, to prevent paying duty; and the sea-beach before the town, as well as the plantations, presented horrible spectacles of dogs devouring human flesh."

Even more important to Burton than his explorations of the city was the pursuit of languages, here Swahili, the great lingua franca of the East African coast, which Burton called Wasawahili. In Zanzibar, Burton did not find many women who served formally as prostitutes, his favorite teachers of a language, but there were many married women whose husbands tolerated extramarital activities; the local whites preferred to keep as concubines the cool-skinned penis-clutching Abyssinian and Galla girls as mistresses but were not generous in sharing them. Burton eventually found the *lāl bāzār* in the Malagash quarter, a foul, muddy, miasmic slum, "the very centre of prostitution." All the women were Wasawahili. A mixture of Arab and black, they were, however, not congenial companions. "Their faces like skinned apes, and lean legs enclosed in red silk tights, make their appearance as revolting as their society is dangerous."

Burton gave the Wasawahili an inordinate amount of attention in the pages of *Zanzibar*, with an extended discussion and analysis of every detail of the tribe, a mélange of Arabs and Persians with blacks, speaking at length about their social structure, history, physical types—the shape of the skull, the jaw, eyes, skin colors ("a chocolate brown, varying in shades, as amongst ourselves"). He stated that from the Arabs the Wasawahilis "derive shrewd thinking and practice to conceal their thought: they will welcome a man with the determination to murder him . . . truth is unknown . . . honesty and candour are ignored even by name."

His spleen over the people may in part have been due to his difficulty in learning their language, because Swahili (and the other tongues he tried to absorb immediately) did not fit the linguistic patterns he was accustomed to. After a long harangue on the Kisawahili tribe he stated, "The most interesting point connected with these coast negroes is their language. . . . Oral tongues are essentially fluctuating; having no standard, the roots of words wither and die, whilst terms, idioms and expressions once popular speedily fall into oblivion and are supplanted by neologisms." And he goes on to give an analysis of the tongue, and of kindred tongues, which seems like a basic introduction for even the most accomplished linguist.

Kisawahili is at once rich and poor. . . . It abounds in names of sensuous objects; there is a term for every tree, shrub, plant, grass, and bulb, and I have shown that the several ages of the cocoa-nut are differently called. . . . Abounding in vowels and liquids, the language admits of vast volubility of utterance; in anger or excitement the words flow like a torrent, and each dovetails into its neighbour until the whole speech becomes one vocable.

Finally, he could state, after much discussion and analysis, that "the dialect is easily learned . . . it is a lazy language which well suits the depressing climate."

He made a full study of the wide variety of tribal marks, the beauty slashes, lumps and scars, tattoos, and the "tribes and tribes of women who enlarged their lips with disks of bamboo, ivory, wood and tin." He noted with apparent pleasure, probably having had some erotic satisfaction from stroking, that "the Zanzibarian slave girl shaves her head smooth, till it shines brown and shiny like a well-polished cocoa-nut."

Burton's ethnological and linguistic researches and his exploration of Zanzibar town were interrupted by a sudden decision to set off on what he called a "tentative expedition" to visit Dr. Rebmann, who, he expected, would join him on the search for the Nile.

Burton found a half-Arab named Said bin Salim el Lanki to be guide and caravan chief. Though he derided Said's courage and fortitude—"he cannot bear hunger or thirst, fatigue or want of sleep"—still Burton liked him and made him the head of the native section of the expedition when it ventured inland, for despite Said's many faults, Burton also found him "full of excellent gifts, courteous, thoroughly good-tempered and apparently truthful, a bright exception to the rule of his unconscientious race."

It was to be a voyage carried out under penurious conditions, being insufficiently financed and supplied. There was one minor luxury, an iron boat, which Burton named the *Louisa*, leaving future biographers to wonder why it was not called the *Isabel*. The *Louisa*, an American invention, was made of iron and came in seven parts, which could be bolted together. Burton had expected that the boat could be carried disassembled by porters to Tanganyika, but it soon became apparent that because of its weight the *Louisa* was a luxury, not a necessity.

He had hired "an old Arab Beden," the *Riami*. "She was a fine specimen of her class; old and rotten, the boards and timbers of the deck were breaking up . . . the sails were in rags; the ropes and cables broke every half hour, and the awning leaked like a cheap waterproof." Ants swarmed over their instruments, cockroaches dropped on them during the day, "and the rats made marriage," as Said remarked, "during the live-long night."

Burton and his entourage set sail on the evening of Sunday, January 4, 1857, towing the *Louisa* behind. It was a voyage of minor importance and not to be an easy one. Its significance to Burton and Speke was that it served to temper them for hardships to be encountered on the mainland. Burton showed his usual enthusiasm in recording the voyage up the coast, describing the people, languages, the heat, the flora and fauna, living expenses, tribes, landscapes, and even aromas, as they headed toward Mombasa, once an important Portuguese colony, where Camões had passed some unfortunate months.

Stopping briefly at Pemba, an island group under the control of the sultan of Zanzibar, Burton and Speke went ashore in the *Louisa*, landing at Chak-Chak, the chief port, fort, and town.

> The complicated entrance . . . has that silent, monotonous, melancholy beauty, the loveliness of death, which belongs to the creeks and rivers of these regions. . . . We heard not a voice, we saw no inhabitant—all was profoundly still, a great green grave. A chain of islets forms the approach to a creek, below all mangrove and black vegetable mud, which stains the water, and bears roots upsticking like a system of harrows; above all on both sides are rounded hillocks crowned with the cocoa and the clove. Near sunset we anchored in the outer port, four or five miles distant from the town. On a wooded eminence rose the white walls and the tall tower of Fort Chak-Chak, standing boldly out from its dark green background . . . while the spars of an Arab craft peered above the curtained trees. With the distinct remembrance of Indian rivers, my companion and I could not but wonder at the scene before us.

Pemba had little to interest Burton aside from its scenery, which he described at length in poetic and imaginative terms, and he ordered his party on to Mombasa. "The run into Mombasah was truly characteristic of Africa," Burton wrote. The men shouted from afar for news, while "we were unmercifully derided as Whites by the black nymphs bathing in the costumes of Camoens's Neirids. . . . Sunning themselves upon the white sands, [they] shouted the free-and-easy Muzungu—'Europeans!'" Muzungu was a word that he and Speke were to hear often, and Burton realized later that the jungle people, likely to name their children anything that struck their pleasure, were already calling some of them Muzungu, though he and Speke were the first whites they had encountered. One of the first things Burton did at Mombasa was to search out the tomb of a fellow Englishman, Lieut. John James Reitz, who had been buried there in 1822. The site "has been turned into a cattle-yard by the Banyans," he noted with some sadness over the fact that an English grave could be so desecrated by cow-worshiping Hindus.

Burton had now put on "an Arab dress—a turban made of portentous circumference, and a long henna-dyed shirt." He noted with a touch of asperity that Speke was trying to harden himself by going without shoes. "The heat of the ground made my barefooted companion run forward to the shade, from time to time, like the dogs in Tibet." Though Speke might try to go shoeless, he had a dislike and a contempt for the practice of Englishmen wearing native clothing. Later, when he was searching out what he was to call Lake Victoria, the local Arab traders advised him to put on Arab clothing

> in order to attract less attention: a vain precaution, which I believe they suggested more to gratify their own vanity by seeing an Englishman lower himself to their position, than for any benefit that I might receive by doing so.

"At any rate, I was more comfortable and better off in my flannel shirt, long togs, and wide-awake [a soft felt hat], than I should have been, both mentally and physically, had I degraded myself, and adopted their long, hot, and particularly uncomfortable gown."

After a brief survey of the town, Burton set off to see Rebmann, who was stationed eighty miles inland. Burton found the missionary and his wife a most extraordinary couple; they were surrounded by natives, who seemed of a strangeness that astounded him.

> One of the attendants had that in his face and manner which suggested the propriety of having a revolver ready. "Do not mind him," said Mrs Rebmann, "he is a very dear friend,—one of our

oldest converts." "Yes," pursued her husband, "Apekunza was mentally prepared for Christianity by a long course of idiocy, poor fellow!"

At first, Rebmann was eager to join Burton and Speke. "But presently cool reflection came." As a missionary, Rebmann wanted to engage in proselytizing whatever natives he met. But Hamerton, carrying out a promise he had made to the new sultan at Zanzibar, had asked Burton not to engage in any such efforts—not that he would—so a man who would have made a significant contribution to Burton's work was refused him. Rebmann "thought that we relied too much on the arms of flesh—sword and gun," and he did not want to risk his own health on an expedition in which he would be denied the very reason for his being.

After his meeting with Rebmann, Burton showed a perhaps understandable pique with missionaries. Rebmann was the sole survivor of the original ten members of the Mombas Mission, and Burton remarked about "the delusions in which even honest men can live," believing the missionary effort was a failure. "Religion is the mental expression of a race, and it cannot advance without a corresponding intellectual improvement on the part of its votaries," for he thought that the Africans were incapable of higher religious beliefs.

He had hoped to continue inland from Mombasa, "but everything combined to oppose the project." The land was parched, provisions were not to be had, and plundering parties of Masai warriors were close by. "Such is the normal state of East Africa, from the Red Sea to the Cape." Later he was to write with annoyance about a German cartographer who "could not resist the temptation of taunting me with having hesitated to face dangers through which missionaries had passed, 'weaponed only with their umbrellas.' "

Mombasa having been adequately explored and various tribes visited and described—the Warimango were "a perfect picture of savagery . . . their eyes were wild and staring, their voices loud and barking, and all their gestures denoted the 'noble savage' "—Burton decided to return by stages to Zanzibar.

He sailed south in a small native craft, past Pemba, to the Pangi-ni River, where he and Speke set up camp in a town at its mouth. Here they made "sundry excursions," and Burton searched out abandoned cities of long-lost civilizations, complaining constantly about the cost of the trip, how the natives of every race were trying to cheat him, the endless pilfering, the difficulties of traveling, but inevitably there seems not a fact that escaped him—the scarification on tribal faces, the vegetation, the composition of the soil, the price of vegetables. Pangi-ni was a miserable little town dominated by Hindu traders, and Burton came to dislike them as much as anyone despite his long association with Indians. He went up the river with Speke, through high mountains, to see the falls; rain fell constantly. At one village they gathered an entourage of Baluchi mercenaries, some of the fifteen hundred that were serving in garrisons under the sultan of Zanzibar. Their forebears had been brought over a few generations earlier from India as soldiers. They were, Burton said, "a rabble rout of Arabs and Afghans, of Sidis [blacks] and Hindostan men. The corps spoke some half-a-dozen different languages, and many of the members have left their country for their country's own good—a body of convicts, however, generally fights well."

There was one unusual man among the Baluchis. "The gem of the party, however, is one Sidi Mubarak, who has taken to himself the agnomen of 'Bombay.' " Sidi Mubarak had "sooty skin" and filed-down teeth. He had been captured as a youth and sold into slavery to a Banyan, who took him to India, where eventually he was freed. He worked his way back to Africa and joined the Baluchis. He was short, black, and ugly, but an exceptional man, and Burton appreciated him.

He works on principle and works like a horse, candidly declaring that not love of us but his duty to his belly makes him work. With a sprained ankle and a load quite disproportionate to his chétif [puny] body, he insists on carrying two guns; and after a 30 miles' walk he is as fresh as before it began. He attends us everywhere, manages our purchases, carries all our messages, and when not employed by us, is at every man's beck and call. Speaking a little broken Hindostani, he has for all 'jungli niggers' an ineffable contempt, which he never attempts to conceal.

Burton thought so highly of Sidi Bombay Mubarak that he got him detached from the Baluchi squad, paid off his debts, and persuaded him "to follow our fortunes." Since he had a smattering of Hindustani, he was assigned to Speke. "On our march to the lakes he was the confidential servant and interpreter of my companion, the only man with whom the latter could converse," Burton wrote.

By this time Burton's antiblack feelings had begun to abate, and he accepted Sidi Bombay Mubarak as a man to be respected. Speke accepted him, too, but when the chance came to let Bombay know his rank in the hierarchy of human beings, he did not hesitate to explain why blacks experienced the "cruel destiny of being slaves of all men."

I related the history of Noah, and the dispersion of his sons on the face of the globe; and shewed him that he was of the black or hamitic stock, and by the common order of nature, they, being the weakest, had to succumb to their superiors the Japhetic and Semitic branches of the family. . . .

After a walk up the Pangi-ni and back to the coast, Burton and Speke, with a week to wait before their dhow was to pick them up, decided on a hippopotamus hunt. They set out in a forty-foot canoe with the Baluchis and Sidi Bombay "at early dawn, when wild beasts are hungriest and tamest." They came to a pool where they found their prey.

The mise en scene is perfect: the bright flush of morning, the cool, clear air, the river, with its broad breast swelling between two rows of tall luxuriant trees, and, protruding from the mirrory surface, the black box-heads flanked with small pointed ears, and, not a little resembling the knight in old chessmen. . . .

My companion, a man of speculative turn, experiments upon the nearest optics with buckshot and two barrels of grape. . . . The eyes, however, are obliquely placed: the charge scatters, and the brute, unhurt, slips down like a seal.

Finally, Speke was able to make a successful hit.

There is a splash, a struggle, the surface foams, and Behemoth, with open mouth like a butcher's stall, and bleeding like a gutter-spout, plunges above the surface. . . . At last a coup de grace, speed-ing through the ear, finds out the small brain; the brute sinks, fresh gore purples the surface, and bright bubbles seethe up from the bottom. Hippo has departed this life: we wait patiently for his reap-pearance, but he reappears not.

The slaughter continued.

Whenever a head appears an inch above water, a heavy bullet "puds" into or near it; crimson patches marble the stream: some die and disappear; others plunge in crippled state; while others, disabled from diving by holes drilled through their snouts, splash and scurry about, with curious snorts, caused by the breath passing through the wounds.

Speke sees a baby hippo. "Off flies the crown of the little kid's head." The mother attacks the canoe, Speke sends a ball through her sides, and the mother "funks and bolts till nothing is visible but a long wavy line of gore." Speke lands to shoot from the shore, firing at an old rogue male. "A cove from the Colt strikes him full in the front; his brain is pierced, he rises high, he falls with a crash upon the wave, and all that hulking flesh cannot keep in a little life. Sultan Mamba [the hippopotamus] had for-ever disappeared . . . shall never he bully canoe-men, never shall he break nigger's leg again."

Perhaps Burton was being ironic about the slaughter. Normally he no longer hunted, and he did not seem to engage in the hippo hunt, but there was a certain excitement to his words. "By 10 A.M. we had slain six besides wounding I know not how many of the animals." He had found "the massacre monotonous . . . little more than pheasant shooting."

Back at Pangi-ni, he and Speke were struck by fever, along with the Goan cook boys and Sidi Bombay. The dhow returned. Burton was so ill that he "was obliged to be supported like a bed-ridden old woman" and was carried aboard. Shortly, the expedition arrived back at Zanzibar port, and "we found ourselves once more within the pale of eastern civilization." They had spent three months in wandering, with little to show except some hard-won experience of the "real" Africa and what was popularly called a "seasoning fever."

It was still not time to enter the interior. The southwest monsoon, "which came in like a lion, had improved my health," Burton wrote, but it further delayed the expedition. Massive doses of quinine, recently discovered as a cure for fevers, had aided his recovery. Burton began gathering supplies and taking care of "the hundred impediments which pertain to African exploration. . . . I was possessed by a nervous impatience to be up and doing."

Steinhauser was detained at Aden—cholera had broken out —and when the epidemic abated, there was at the moment no boat to Zanzibar. So he went over to Berbera "with the gallant project of marching down country to join us in the south." But the doctor could not reach Zanzibar in time and gave up hope of joining Burton.

> The absence of Dr Steinhauser lost the East Africa Expedition more than can be succinctly told. . . . Lieut. Speke would have escaped deafness and fever-blight, I paralysis and its consequent invalidism.

With Rebmann also unavailable, that left Burton with only Speke to carry on the heavy burden of exploration. What was he to do now? Though the search for the Nile was a popular and romantic dream enjoyed by many, in fact few men were actually prepared to risk their lives for that improbable adventure. And to find those brave souls would have meant delays of up to, perhaps, a year. Consequently, Burton had to rely on Speke and hope for the best.

Now he pushed preparations in a rush. To travel as far as Ujiji and back would require tremendous amounts of equipment and supplies. In *The Lake Regions of Central Africa* Burton gives a detailed list ("for the benefit of future travellers") of what the well-furnished expedition required, beginning with what was a very personal need.

> 1 dozen brandy (to be followed by a dozen more); 1 box cigars; 5 boxes tea (each 6 lbs.) [and so on, including curry and spices, pickles, soap, vinegar and oil, etc.]

Next came arms and ammunition for the two officers, including "100 lbs. gunpowder" and "20,000 copper caps," shields, swords, daggers, and knives for the Baluchi guards. There was camp furniture—tents and bedding, chairs, tables, mosquito nets, mats, carpets, and whatever else was needed for a proper English home in the field; mapping and surveying instruments, including several types of compasses, thermometers, a chronometer, sundial, rain gauges, and numerous other pieces of scientific equipment, virtually all of which was either broken in transit, lost by the porters, or damaged by Speke in use. There were numerous writing materials and blank diary books, packets of paper, pencils, inks, meteorological tables, maps, star charts, account books, watercolors and other drawing materials, atlases, grammars of African languages, manuals of surveying and mapmaking. One necessity, the medicine chest, Burton said, was "vilely made." He had to send back by an Arab caravan to Zanzibar for quinine, morphia, citric acid, chiretta root, and a preparation known as Warburg's drops, a cure-all that was a mixture of quinine with opium, flavored with sloe plums. There were also numerous miscellaneous items, scarlet broadcloth for presents for important chieftains, and various other types of cloth for lesser individuals, umbrellas and knives, penknives, 200 fishing hooks, a sewing kit, toilet articles, and a Union Jack for flying at opportune moments. There was also a well-stocked carpentry shop, with everything from fifty pounds of nails, grinders, augers, and bits to various saws and chisels. What was skimped on was clothing. "Not looking forward to so long a journey, we left Zanzibar without a new outfit; consequently we were in tatters before the end."

Such was the well-stocked African expedition, European style. In a sense it would eat itself up. Its successful march would mean that it had lightened itself of much of what it carried and part of the ownership of beads, cloth, and wire would pass on either as gifts along the way or as salary to the *pagazis*, the men who carried such materials, who in turn would trade it for other items, either different types of cloth or beads, or especially for slaves, a practice that annoyed Burton and that he tried to prevent, if possible. Even slaves owned slaves, much to his disgust. Cloth was an especially popular item as a kind of tariff demanded by the local chiefs—the more showy pieces were "invariably demanded by the more powerful Sultans for themselves and their wives, whilst they divide the Merkani [American] and Kaniki [Indian], which composes their hongo—'blackmail' or dash— amongst their followers."

Suddenly, on June fifth, the rains stopped, and it was time to depart on the Great Journey. Hamerton appeared to be dying, though he felt strong enough to accompany Burton and Speke to the coast. They had a ragtag caravan, a new Baluchi escort of seven men picked up at the bazaar, "nine ruffians" obtained from a Banyan, Ramji, a slave owner, who charged Burton more for the hire of his men than they would have cost on the slave market. It amused Burton to refer to them as "the Sons of Ramji." The caravan leader—the kafilah-bashi—was Said bin Salim, the man who had led the trip in search of Rebmann; he now wheedled an exorbitant sum out of Burton before he would consent to joining the expedition. Said had his own entourage, four slave musketeers as guards and a boy and two girls for his own pleasures. The Sultan lent a ship, and the party was carried over to the mainland.

Africa lay before them, a giant, cruel, fetid, miasmic, challenging continent whose mysteries lay wrapped in enigmatic myths and legends. "In writing our adventures," said Burton in the *Lake Regions* volumes, "I was careful not to make a sensation of danger . . . but future travellers will do well not to think that when about to explore Central Africa, they are setting out upon a mere promenade." Many men had died in the attempt without traveling far from the coast, and Burton's famous contemporary Dr. Livingstone had been held prisoner by a chief. As Burton had stated to the Royal Geographical Society, his goal was the village of Ujiji, on the shores of a great lake, Tanganyika. Here there were Arab settlements and a sultan who was said to be favorably inclined to traders. The route to Ujiji was well known and well traveled, having been opened as early as 1825 by an Arab slaver and ivory merchant, and since then the tribes along the way had become accustomed to caravans, out of which they made a profit. The frequency of Arab caravans would also enable Burton to request more supplies and to send reports and letters to Zanzibar for forwarding to London.

Burton had hoped to hire sufficient porters on the mainland —he had estimated that he needed 120—but all he could obtain were thirty-six, the Arab traders having taken most of the available men. He bought thirty pack animals but needed many more. Thus, he was forced to leave valuable supplies behind, hoping that the Arabs would bring them up at a later date.

There were portents of disaster. Rumors spread among the Banyans that he was responsible for certain unnamed misfortunes befalling the local people and that therefore he would never reach the halfway point. That night, on the mainland, "in the solitude and silence" of the dark native hut in which he was lodged, he felt himself "the plaything of misfortune."

Assessing the situation later, he realized that he was now alone with "a companion and not a friend, with whom I was strangers yet," and a motley crew of natives, cowardly, lazy, rapacious, and, as he soon found out, inclined to desert with whatever could be pilfered from the expedition. Burton and Speke spent two weeks in final preparations at the village of Kaole, at last setting out for the interior on June twenty-seventh. Hands were shaken all around, with Arabs, with half-caste Arabs, with Hindus and Indian Muslims, with black chieftains. At four o'clock —such expeditions usually begin late the first day—after innumerable delays and quarrels—"everyone and every thing, guide and escort, asses and slaves, seemed to join in raising up fresh obstacles"—Burton was able to give the signal to leave, and the caravan started off in a shuffling, straggling fashion. Though the rains had ended on Zanzibar island, they were beginning in full force on the mainland. The caravan marched an hour and a half before stopping. Not only did the first march start late; it was always brief, serving merely to get on the trail and away from the base. But things did not go easily. Three days later the Baluchis mutinied—"another forced halt, when I tasted all the bitterness that can fall to the lot of those who explore regions unvisited by their own colour." The guards wanted more pay, trinkets, tobacco, beads; the donkey drivers complained of the indignity of their work, and the local villagers threatened to attack. The departure, when matters were settled, "was like driving a herd of wild cattle."

The Baluchis seemed continually mutinous, taking any forbearance on Burton's part as a sign of weakness, and became daily more insolent and threatening.

One day as he was marching along, gun over shoulder and dagger in hand, he became conscious that two of his men were unpleasantly near [wrote Thomas Wright], and after a while one of them, unaware that Burton understood his language, urged the other to strike. Burton did not hesitate a moment. Without looking around, he thrust back his dagger, and stabbed the man dead on the spot. The other, who fell on his knees and begged for mercy, was spared. *

Later, there was another attempt on his life—again Wright is the source. Burton heard some of the Sons of Ramji discussing killing him. To put some fear into them, he placed a canister of gunpowder in the earth under the spot where they would make their campfire. When the wood was stacked and the fire lighted, up went the intended murderers in the explosion. †

Almost immediately both Burton and Speke came down with malaria, but they forced themselves to continue, covering 118 miles in eighteen days despite their illnesses and other problems that seemed inevitable and unavoidable. These marches, or stages, were by their nature short and, because of the heat, began early.

> At 3 A.M. all is silent as the tomb. . . . About an hour later a rooster's crowing lets it be known that dawn is approaching. I have been lying awake for some time, longing for the light, and when in health, for an early breakfast.

The Goans would build a fire, trembling with the cold—it was 60°F, Burton said—and prepare food. He and Speke had tea or coffee, rice-milk gruel and yogurt-raised flat cakes or a porridge. In the background the Baluchis chanted their morning prayers. (Burton apparently was not practicing Islam on the sa-

---

* Says Wright, "This story appears nowhere in Burton's books. I had it from Mr. W. F. Kirby, to whom Burton told it." *The Life of Sir Richard Burton*, 1: 154.

† "We tell these tales just as Burton told them to intimate friends. The first may have been true, the second, we believed, simply illustrates his inveterate habit of telling tales against himself with the desire to shock." Ibid.

fari, but he was referred to as "Haji Abdullah," his pilgrimage to Mecca being commonly known and respected.)

By 5:00 A.M. the camp was "fairly roused." This was a critical moment: "The porters have promised overnight, to start early, and to make a long wholesome march." Now arguments began: the *pagazis* were cold, still tired, lazy, rebellious; they importuned for more pay. "We return to our tents," wrote Burton, in this manner ignoring them and thus implying a loss of pay—for some kind of haggling on his part seemed to be the only way to force the porters to work. Then, in a rush, the *pagazis* would pick up their loads and start the march. "My companion and I, when well enough to ride, mount our asses, led by the gunbearers . . . when unfit for exercise, we are borne in hammocks, slung to long poles, and carried by two men at a time."

When all was ready, the chief guide, dressed in animal skins, raised a furled blood-red flag, "the sign of a caravan from Zanzibar," and set off, followed by a *pagazi* beating a kettle drum. The *pagazis* would pour out of the kraal "in a disorderly mob" and wait a few hundred yards away for stragglers; the huts would be fired either by accident or mischievousness, and finally the caravan would be on its way, accompanied by "mindless noise." "The normal recreations of a march are, whistling, singing, shouting, hooting, drumming, imitating the cries of birds and beasts, repeating words which are never used except on journeys . . . and abundant squabbling," all in all a scene that delighted Burton no matter what he said in derogation.

Having recovered somewhat from his malaria, Burton came down with marsh fever. He was now ill for twenty days while they passed through wretched land where "the water was bad, and a mortal smell of decay was emitted by the dark, dank ground." Annoying and enervating as these attacks were, they may have served to cure Burton of his syphilis, for it was known that fever will kill the spirochete. Whatever it was, these fevers or others later, Burton came out of Africa recovered from syphilis, disabled as he was by other ailments. But it was a wearying experience.

> . . . the alternations of damp heat and wet cold, the useless fatigue of walking, the sorry labour of waiting and re-loading the asses, the exposure to sun and dew, and last, but not least, the morbific influences, the wear and tear of mind at the prospect of imminent failure, all were beginning to tell heavily on me.

Meanwhile, Speke fell ill with fever, which he quickly shook off, only to be hit again. "Jack was in worse shape," Burton wrote. "My companion suffered even more severely, he had a fainting fit which strongly resembled a sun-stroke, and which seemed permanently to affect his brain."

Later, Speke made similar charges, that Burton was somewhat touched in the head. "My companion complained of the shock his nerves had received since the Somali encounter [at Berbera], and this appeared to effect him during the whole of the campaign." He was also to remark that Burton, ill with a fever, was "occasionally wandering in his mind." Such mutual suspicions did not serve the smooth functioning of the expedition. In his weakness Speke was repeatedly thrown from his mount—"as often as twice in two hours," wrote Burton. Meanwhile, the pack animals began to drop dead from overwork.

Struggling under appalling conditions, two sick men, handicapped by insufficient resources, a shortage of porters and animal transport, lack of equipment, and a rebellious caravan, pushed ahead into an Africa that no European had ever seen and which even the long-experienced Arab slavers and traders approached with caution and fear. Still, neither Burton nor Speke thought of turning back to the safety and solace of Zanzibar. They pushed on, through villages that were "nothing but filthy heaps of the rudest hovels," peopled by "miserable inhabitants." Because of the continuing loss of animals and the desertions by porters, the trip was turning into a nightmare. "The grounding of the Expedition appeared imminent and permanent," Burton wrote. "The result was a sensation of wretchedness. . . ."

On July fourteenth the caravan entered a small trading post called K'utu, where Burton was able to find a cottage and "enjoyed for the first time [on the march] an atmosphere of sweet, warm smoke." Speke, trying to prove that he was too rugged for such self-pampering and despite Burton's orders, "remained in the reeking, miry tent, where he partially laid the foundation of the fever which [later] threatened his life in the mountains of Usagara." They had reached "a fine park country, peculiarly rich in game." Large gnus, hartebeest and other antelopes, partridge and guinea fowl abounded. But the weather was "a succession of raw mist, rain in torrents, and fiery sunbursts, the land appeared rotten, and the jungle smelt of death."

Then they reached a major resting place, "that hot-bed of pestilence, Zungomero, where we nearly found 'wet graves.' " Burton and Speke were lodged in an African hut. "The roof was a sieve, the walls were systems of chinks, and the floor was a sheet of mud." Outside, the rain poured "pertinaciously." Meanwhile, the Baluchis looted the village, and the Sons of Ramji tried to rape the women. But more porters were found, and finally "the whole party [reached] a total of 132 souls," and they set off again, leaving Zungomero, that "acme of discomfort." The delay had seriously affected the health of many of the caravan. "We were martyred by miasma," Burton wrote. He and Speke were so feeble that they could scarcely sit on their mounts, "and weakness had almost deprived us of the sense of hearing."

The trails they were now taking were well worn and thoroughly charted by the Arab traders and slavers. The tribes along the way were shrewd about charging tolls and demanding baksheesh or *hongo* and in overcharging for supplies, fresh water, milk, and bearers. And the frequent Arab caravans could be counted on to bring up more supplies, ammunition, beads and cloth for trade, and additional *pagazis*, and they would carry mail and reports in both directions.

Continually, both Burton and Speke were ill, pursued by illnesses, as if illness had become a permanent member of the expedition, an unseen, unfriendly companion who nagged, teased, struck down, and even paralyzed. When Burton threw off his latest fever, his mouth became ulcerous, and he was unable to talk. At the same time, he could not walk. The bad food, the climate, the jungle, and the nagging illnesses turned his mind into two split sections. He experienced insomnia, depressions, delirium,

> a queer conviction of divided identity, never ceasing to be two persons that generally thwarted and opposed each other; the sleepless nights brought them horrid visions, animals of grisliest form, haglike women and men with heads protruding from their breasts.

The native members of the caravan fared little better, and they deserted steadily, pilfering what they could. The very coin—the cloth, wire, and beads—needed to pay daily expenses was stolen by men eager to make their way back to the coast and better health. Burton and Speke were now so ill that they could not control their men. Burton wrote that he and Speke were "physically and morally incapacitated for any exertion beyond balancing ourselves upon the donkeys."

Still, under conditions that would have turned other men back, Burton insisted on pushing ahead. Much to Speke's annoyance, he would not allow time for hunting except to shoot game for the bearers' food. During the first year there was some friendship and camaraderie between these two very incompatible men. In their periodic illnesses, fevers, and partial blindness, each nursed the other. Burton wrote that he treated Speke "as a brother." To while away the dismal hours of illness and boredom or when waiting out the arrival of porters or for propitious times in which to travel, they read Shakespeare and other works from their limited library aloud to each other. In the beginning, Speke showed Burton his journals, but perhaps irked by the nagging memory of the fate of his Somali diary, he stopped the practice.

Africa—and Burton—began to get on his nerves. He could talk to no one except Burton and Sidi Bombay, while Burton chatted away in his vast polyglot manner with anyone who came along. Even the hunting Speke was allowed was becoming monotonous, and by the second year he was complaining that there was no game to shoot except elephants. Africa had turned into "one vast senseless map of sameness." But Africa was not "sameness" to Burton. His complaints about the natives subdued as he traveled farther inland. He saw them in a greater variety than in the simple caricatures he wrote of in his first year in Africa, though it was a variety that leaned to rascality, stubbornness, stupidity, and greed.

And there were always the women. One gets the impression that for much of this period in Central Africa, at each stop, fever or no, Burton was passing his time in a village bedding a woman, while Speke sat morosely in his tent writing letters to his mother or filing complaints with Norton Shaw. Women were so available that his readers find Burton making comments about lax morals, a notion not often common in his earlier writings.

Nothing was going well for either man. Speke, despite his later boasts of good health, was many times so ill that he had to be carried in a hammock, but often the *pagazis* refused the burden, and Burton was forced to "that sweet speech which, according to Orientals, is stronger than chains, and administered 'goose's oil' in such quantities that I was graciously permitted to make an arrangement for the transport of my companion."

Getting Speke carried was but one of many problems. In mid-September Burton realized that "the outfit, which was expected to last a year, had been half exhausted in three months." He called Said bin Salim for an explanation and was told that "Allah is all-knowing" and that a caravan would come with porters and cloth. "Such fatalism is infectious," Burton wrote. "I ceased to think about the subject."

The matter of supplies and bearers could be left up to providence; the loss of instruments was another matter. Continually, the numerous compasses, watches, chronometers, and other necessary means of measurement and mapping broke down, malfunctioned, were stolen, or suffered from some other mishap. The only pedometer failed to give proper measurements. When carried by Speke, "it gave a steady exaggerative rate," but when transferred to Sidi Bombay, "it became worse than useless, sometimes showing 25 for 13 miles." Two weeks after the expedition set out, the three pocket chronometers "failed in their ratings and became useless for chronometric longitudes." For a while the compasses were of service despite the fact that their pasteboard faces curled up in the damp and heat. One was stepped on by Speke; the other, by a native. A ship's compass also failed and had to be discarded. Improvisation and informed guessing had to supplant accurate measurements.

On November 7, 1857, having traveled 134 days, they entered Kazeh, a settlement centered around a fine well. The town was better known to foreign cartographers as Tabura, a fact that led some of Burton's critics to assume that he did not know where he was. He had traveled six hundred miles, and many of the expedition were ill and exhausted, but Burton ordered everyone to put on his best clothes so as to impress the Arabs and the villagers, who in turn put on their finery to welcome the caravan. "Such luxury my eyes had long been unfamiliar [with]," wrote Burton. And what a change it was from the previous Negro settlements! Here was a civilized Arab village, of slavers, it was true, but clean, with well-constructed mud houses, spacious courtyards, and pleasant gardens with fresh vegetables, and the food proved to be palatable.

The Arab merchants greeted Burton as a friend, and he immediately became close to them, especially to a trader named Snay bin Amir, "one of the wealthiest ivory and slave-dealers in Eastern Africa." Snay was to serve as Burton's agent at Kazeh, enlisting porters for him, finding him a house, and supplying food. The Arabs were men Burton knew and understood, intelligent, educated, clean, and practicing a religion he himself was partial to and at times had followed faithfully. Though he railed endlessly against slavery as "a flight of locusts over the land," for the present he could separate the men from their trade. Despite the Arabs, however, Burton complained that Kazeh was "one long trial of patience."

The caravan remained at Kazeh for five weeks while Burton reorganized his men, got additional porters, and talked to the Arabs about the land that lay ahead. Conflicts with Speke that had their genesis as far back as Somalia and had been exacerbated along the trail into Central Africa were now beginning to harden, though their full expression was not to be visible until later. Whatever Burton did during this period, Speke eventually tried to take credit for in his two books on the search for the Nile. Perhaps Burton was being selfish and Speke telling the truth when he wrote, "Captain Burton got desperately ill, whilst I picked up all the information that I could gather from the Arabs, with Bombay as interpreter." That Burton was unable to learn any of the African tongues in time was a theme that Speke harped on in his own writings.

> To save repetition, I may as well mention the fact that neither Captain Burton nor myself were able to converse in any African language until we were close to the coast on the return journey.

Whatever Speke learned about unknown lakes and rivers through Sidi Bombay was not to his liking. The Arabs were telling him things he did not want to know, and it appears that he did not rely on Burton to translate from the Arabic. Speke was adamant about what kind of information he wanted: "I made them confess that all these rivers ran exactly contrary to the way they first stated." Speke insisted, without evidence, that one river, the Jub, "must flow out of the lake instead of into it, as they had said." To humor Speke, the Arabs agreed: if he insisted the river flowed the opposite to what they knew, then, so it flowed.

Illness among the men continued. The Sons of Ramji went

on strike, and delays multiplied. Burton came down with fever again. He had "distressing weakness, hepatic derangements, burning pain, and tingling soles, aching eyes, and alternate thrills of heat and cold, [which] lasted, in my case, a whole month." Snay bin Amir had been serving as the caravan's doctor, being "an adept in the treatment, called by his countrymen, 'camel-physic,' namely, cautery and similar counter-irritants." Camel physic, however, did not cure Burton, and the shaykh called in a local witch doctor, an old woman with "greasy skin, black as soot," who doused him with what he suspected was bhang mixed with water, which also failed to cure, though he had paid her handsomely with cloth, and eventually he recovered of his own resources.

On December fourteenth, Burton and Speke set out for Ujiji; they had been in Africa almost a year. Burton hoped that at Ujiji he would find some clues to the mystery of the Nile. Speke claimed later that he was opposed to the march. He was "so sure in my own mind that the Victoria N'yanza* and not Lake Tanganyika would prove to be the source of the Nile, I proposed going to see it at once, instead of going on to Ujiji." But he admitted that they had been informed that "the route to the N'yanza was dangerous" and Captain Burton preferred going west. Speke emphasized that Burton was in no condition to travel: "I thought Captain Burton would die," adding repeti-tiously, "He begged me to take account of his effects, as he thought he would die." That Burton was near death was a state-ment Speke made several times. Some of the native guards, told to go ahead by Speke at one leg of the march, "found Captain Burton lying on the roadside prostrated with fever, and taking compassion on him, brought him into camp." A few weeks later, Speke thought "Captain Burton would die if we did not make a move, so I begged him to allow me to assume the command *pro tem*, and I would see what I could do to effect a move."

---

* The lake was not so called until later, when Speke made a trip alone.

The issues became magnified in Speke's mind. He stated that Burton was envious of his health and energy and tried to prevent his succeeding in the search for the lake that supposedly flowed into the Nile. "Captain Burton threw obstacles in my way at first. . . ." Again and again, to show that Burton was incapable of performing his duties, Speke referred to Burton's health: "Both Captain Burton and I contracted fevers. Mine occasionally recurred at various intervals, but his stuck to him throughout the journey, and even lasted till sometime after he came home." He made these points over and over, trying to imply that he was the *de facto* leader. When one day the natives "struck for food . . . an altercation took place which I had to settle, as was invariably the case when difficulties arose in camp."

That both men were constantly ill is not to be questioned. Burton did not hide the problems, medical as well as other, but that Speke was the driving force cannot be but doubted.

Whatever Burton's condition at this time, near death or very much alive, he set out filled with energy for Ujiji, seeing it as the culmination of a very hard year and filling his notebooks about the area; no succeeding ethnologist with more time and better resources ever matched his insight, detail, and curiosity in recording the very heart of African village life with unchallenged accuracy: social structure, custom, rite and ritual, slavery (or the lack of it—"They rarely sell one another," he said of one tribe)—and of course languages. ("Their language is copious but confused . . . they are immoderately fond of simple and meaningless syllables used as interjections.")

Christmas in the jungle passed virtually unnoticed, with the usual problems unabated: there were more desertions among the porters, the going was difficult, and eye problems seemed to strike almost everyone, an "unpleasant phenomenon," as Burton called the affliction.

My companion . . . now began to suffer from "an inflammation of a low type, affecting the whole of the interior tunic of the eyes, particularly the iris, the choroid coat, and the retina;" he described it as "an almost total blindness, rendering every object enclouded as by a misty veil."

The Goan cookboy Valentine suffered a similar problem, and Burton did, too, "for a few days webs of flitting muscae obscured smaller objects and rendered distant vision impossible." Speke and Valentine continued to be afflicted, but Burton "escaped by the free use of 'camel-medicine.' "

They crossed rugged and rolling ground, divided by deep swamps of mire and grass, the weather alternating between "the full break of the rainy monsoon, and the frequent outbursts of fiery sun." Burton now came down with what he called "an attack of 'paraplegia,' " meaning he was paralyzed in all four limbs and had to be carried. But shortly his bearers deserted, and he had to mount an ass. His sight was failing—he was not sure what he saw. Speke, suffering from constant ophthalmia, was virtually blind and could not travel unassisted. He was in great pain, and a porter had to lead his ass. He seemed like a man barely alive. Small disasters continued to plague the march. One day Burton's Rowtie was lost, along with his bedding, and porters still absconded whenever they could. The path was broken and slippery and pitted with deep holes. The jungle now showed extensive clumps of bamboo and rattan, plantains, sarsaparilla vines, and wild grapes "of diminutive size and of the austerest flavour."

On February 13, 1858, they were in different terrain, passing through tall grass and up a stony hill spotted with thorn trees. Speke's mount collapsed and died. Burton called a halt at the top of the hill to rest. Though still partially blind, he caught a glimpse of something shining below. "What is that?" he asked Sidi Bombay.

"I am of the opinion," said Bombay, "that is *the* water."

Burton's failing sight showed him what, through the mass of trees, appeared to be nothing more than a very small lake. Immediately he thought of returning to Kazeh and starting afresh.

He advanced a few yards farther, however, and found the view very different. He stared with "admiration, wonder and delight." Shimmering in the gorgeous tropical sunshine was Lake Tanganyika. "Truly it was a revel for soul and sight!"

But think of poor Speke!

"You may picture to yourself my bitter disappointment," he wrote, "when . . . I found on approaching the zenith of my ambition, the Great Lake in question was nothing but mist and glare before my eyes."

Now Burton was able to see it clearly.

Nothing . . . could be more picturesque than this first view of the Tanganyika Lake, as it lay in the lap of the mountains, basking in the gorgeous tropical sunshine. Below and beyond a short foreground of rugged and precipitous hill-fold, down which the footpath zigzags painfully, a narrow strip of emerald green, never sere and marvellously fertile, shelves towards a ribbon of glittering yellow sand, here bordered by sedgy rushes, there cleanly and clearly cut by the breaking wavelets. . . .

In the distance was "a high and broken wall of steel-coloured mountain." To the south was the Malagarazi River, which discharged red loam in a violent stream, and all about were villages, cultivated lands, and the canoes of fishermen on the water. It was a scene, he thought, that could "rival, if not to excel, the most admired scenery of the classic regions." The next day they reached Ujiji, the farthest goal of the expedition, having been on the trail seven and a half months.

As soon as he and Speke were safely bivouacked, Burton got hold of a solidly built Arab boat belonging to an absent merchant. It was capable of holding thirty-five men and was said to be the second largest craft on Tanganyika. They set out on a brief voyage of exploration, but both men were too weak for an extensive survey. Then they settled down for a stay that was as uncomfortable as a march through the jungle. The damp pervaded everything. Books rotted, writing became illegible from stains and mildew, botanical specimens collected by hard labor perished. Around them the natives showed continued hostility. Demands for *hongo*, payment, became exorbitant. The two surviving asses were repeatedly wounded by spears. Thieves stole the clothing of some of the Baluchis. The old woman who had been selling milk to Speke now demanded so much cloth that he had to stop buying.

"At first the cold damp climate of the Lake Regions did not agree with us," said Burton, speculating that the fish diet was "over-rich and fat" and that he and Speke had gorged themselves on vegetables, here freely available. "All energy seemed to have abandoned us."

I lay for a fortnight upon the earth, too blind to read or write, except with long intervals, too weak to ride, and too ill to converse.

Speke was in even worse shape. "My companion . . . was almost as 'groggy' upon his legs as I was [and] suffered from a painful ophthalmia, and from a curious distortion of face, which made him chew sideways, like a ruminant."

The Goan cookboys and the Baluchis were also seriously ill. The mercenaries and the *pagazis* were paid in cloth for their services, and various presents were given the local natives, who were headed, wrote Speke, by a man named Kannena, "a very ill-disposed chief . . . tyrannical, and, as such savages invariably were, utterly unreasonable."

Despite the illnesses, "work remained to be done," Burton wrote, his will conquering sickness and lethargy. He had been told of a large dhow across the lake; it was reported to be the only respectable vessel on Tanganyika, and he ordered Said bin Salim to get it so that the northern waters could be explored; there was said to be "a large river flowing northwards" from the lake. The kafilah-bashi "shirked so artistically" that Burton "directed my companion to do his best about hiring the dhow, and stocking it for a month's cruise." Burton, still weak, had decided to send Speke alone to learn about the upper end of Tanganyika;

letting the near-blind, monolingual Speke explore alone was a chance he had to take. Eighteen days were spent in negotiating for the dhow and getting a crew together. There are, at this point, as in so many instances after this, two different versions of what happened. Speke said that Burton was too ill to move; Burton said he ordered Speke to go. Speke wrote that "Captain Burton threw obstacles in my way at first" because the voyage did not seem safe. Whatever, Speke, still quite blind, set out with a party of twenty-six, including Sidi Bombay and one Goan, two Baluchis, and the rest, local natives as paddlers.

It was mostly an uneventful voyage, along shores empty of people, empty of villages, and empty of signs of civilization. How much this "emptiness" was due to Speke's inability to see clearly cannot be guessed. He complained of the "unceasing monotony . . . of green trees, green grass—green grass, green trees—so wearisome in their luxuriance." He was soon at odds with his crew. He had offended the paddlers by asking the names of places, for they feared "a vitiating of their uganga or 'church,' by answering a stranger any questions whilst at sea." Once, he had thrown the remnants of his dinner overboard, and that the paddlers thought presaged ill luck. The weather was tempestuous and rains frequent. When a violent storm broke out, Speke took refuge on an island. He lay in his tent musing on his life and the problems with the captain while the winds and rains tore unmercifully at him. When the storm ended, he lit a candle to rearrange his kit.

As though by magic, the whole interior became covered with a host of small black beetles, evidently attracted by the glimmer of the candle. They were so annoyingly determined in their choice of place for peregrinating, that it seemed hopeless my trying to brush them off clothes or bedding, for as one was knocked aside another came on, and then another; till at last, worn out, I extinguished the candle, and with difficulty—trying to overcome the tickling annoyance occasioned by these intruders crawling up my sleeves and into my hair, or down my back and legs—fell off to sleep.

Then came a serious accident. "One of these horrid little insects awoke me in his struggles to penetrate my ear, but just too late." In trying to extricate the beetle, Speke pushed it farther inward. "He went his course, struggling up the narrow channel, until he got arrested by want of passage-room."

This impediment evidently enraged him, for he began with exceeding vigour like a rabbit in a hole, to dig violently away at my tympanum. The queer sensation this amusing *measure* excited in me is past description. . . . What to do I knew not.

Speke tried pouring melted butter into his ear to flush out the beetle. "That failing, I applied the point of a penknife to his back, which did more harm than good." He had killed the beetle but the point of the knife wounded his ear "so badly, that inflammation set in, severe suppuration took place." His face became contorted, and boils broke out. For several days he was unable to chew his food and had to live on broth alone.

For many months the tumour made me almost deaf, and ate a hole between the ear and the nose, so that when I blew it, my ear whistled so audibly that those who heard it laughed. Six or seven months after this accident happened, bits of the beetle—a leg, a wing, or parts of the body—came away in the wax.

He added, "It was not altogether an unmixed evil," for "the excitement occasioned by the beetle's operations acted towards my blindness as a counter-irritant, by drawing inflammation away from my eyes."

In constant pain, Speke explored part of the lake. One mission was to find the dhow, which was owned by a Sheikh Hamed bin Sullayin. The Arab welcomed Speke cordially and treated him like an honored guest. Yes, he could have the dhow, but what puzzled Speke was that Hamed said nothing about payment, and from what Sidi Bombay could learn from a Hindustani-speaking servant of the sheikh's, none was expected. But why this generosity? What were Hamed's secret motives? None could be fathomed. He promised to find a crew, too, and Speke patiently waited to set off in this magnificent craft, with its white swanlike sails. Each day Hamed repeated his promises and brought Speke provender—cows and goats for meat, oil, ghee, Muscovite ducks, fowl, eggs, plantains, and other foods. Finally Speke came to the unhappy conclusion that Hamed was deliberately delaying him. When Speke pressed him for an answer, the trader said he would sail with Speke and Burton but that they must wait three months. So Speke was compelled to give up all hope of getting the dhow and returned to camp to give Burton "the mortifying intelligence of my failing to procure the dhow." This news appeared "doubly distressing to Burton."

Burton stated rather flatly, "I was sorely disappointed: he had done literally nothing." Burton had been enjoying the relative calm of "this African Eden," disturbed by nothing more than the quarrels of the natives, when, announced by the firing of matchlocks, Speke returned to camp.

> I never saw a man so thoroughly moist and mildewed; he justified the French phrase, "wet to the bone." His paraphernalia were in a similar state; his guns were grained with rust, and his fire-proof powder-magazine had admitted the monsoon-rain.

Burton later consoled himself, he said, by "supplying certain deficiencies as regards orthography and syntax in [Speke's] diary, which [later] appeared in Blackwood [magazine] of September, 1859. . . . I must confess my surprise." Speke had placed "the vast horseshoe of lofty mountains" in the very heart of what was called "Sir R. Murchison's Depression." It was a "wholly hypothetical, or rather inventive feature . . . which my companion gravely published, with all the pomp of discovery, in the largest capitals." Speke had written, "This mountain range I consider to be THE TRUE MOUNTAINS OF THE MOON." Burton was annoyed at this misunderstanding: "Thus men *do* geography! and thus discovery is stultified."

There was not much to be done at this point except to investigate the lake in common canoes. There was very little time left, supplies were running low, and trade goods were in short supply. "I was sorry for it," Speke wrote, "as my companion was still suffering severely, so severely, that anybody seeing his attempt to go would have despaired of his ever returning. Yet he would not be left behind." So Burton and Speke set off, Burton in a large canoe with forty paddlers and the surly chief Kannena; Speke, in a smaller craft. Kannena was accompanied by his harem and his sailors and their women, playing crude oboes and beating on sheets of iron "with painful perseverance." The sound, Burton added, "still lingers and shall linger in my tympanum." The yells and shouts of delight, "the bray and clang of the horns, shaums [a reed instrument], and tomtoms, blown and banged incessantly . . . last through the livelong day."

Kannena would not allow the paddlers to take the boat too far north. The presumed outlet of Tanganyika, which might have been the beginning of the Nile, was never seen. The wily Hamed had earlier assured Speke that the river ran into the lake. "Had I thought of it, I should have changed the whole course . . . on my map, and made it run out of the lake, but I did not," wrote Speke on the sometimes correct theory that the natives invariably said the opposite of the truth or of what they actually believed. But that was not quite the answer. Sidi Bombay now confirmed to Burton that Speke had misunderstood the conversation with Hamed, who, it appeared, had never been to the end of Tanganyika.

"I felt sick at heart," said Burton later in *Zanzibar*. "The African's account of stream-direction is often diametrically opposed to fact," he continued, "seldom the Arab's—in this point I differ totally from Capt. Speke." Meeting three young Arabs, the sons of a local sultan, "the subject of the mysterious stream which all my informants, Arabs as well as Africans, had made to issue from the lake, and which for months we had looked upon as the western head-stream of the Nile, was at once brought forward," and they, too, "declared (probably falsely) that they had visited it; all asserted that the Rusizi river enters into, instead of flowing from the Tanganyika." And he had to conclude—this was in 1872—that "the mystery remains unsolved. . . . The fact is, we did our best to reach it [the probable source of the Nile], and we failed."

The voyage back to Ujiji saw frustration piled upon frustration. The boats leaked constantly and were "disgracefully crowded," the shipping of water spoiled the tents, wetted the salt, and soddened the grain and flour; the gunpowder was damaged, and the guns became honeycombed with rust. "By degrees [Kannena] introduced in addition to the sticks, spears, broken vases, pots, and gourds, a goat, two or three small boys, one or two sick sailors, the little slave-girls and the large sheep."

Violent storms broke out. "Heavy showers fell almost every day and night, and the intervals were bursts of burning sunshine." Burton developed ulcers of the tongue so severe that he could not speak. His hands became so paralyzed he was unable to write—what a trial that was!—and the rains continued. How bad things had become between Burton and Speke and the rest of the crowded expedition came in a cryptic remark Burton made, that he sheltered himself "under my then best friend, my mac-intosh." The bearers were again mutinous and boldly slaughtered and ate the three goats intended as provisions on the return to the base. But nothing ever seems to be wasted in Burton's travels. There are always observations to make, curiosities to uncover, and now he came across a miserable little tribe of cannibals living in an area where "the malaria, the mosquitoes, the crocodiles, and the men are equally feared." The men were the Wabembe, "who are correctly described in the 'Mombas Mission Map' as Menschenfresser-anthropophagi." They were an apathetic peo-ple, "who devour, besides men, all kinds of carrion and vermin, grubs and insects. . . . They prefer men raw, whereas the Wadoe of the coast eat him roasted. . . . Among cannibals one always fancies oneself considered in the light of butcher's meat." How-ever, he added, "the poor devils, dark and stunted, timid and degraded, appeared less dangerous to the living than to the dead."

In the more remote districts, as the boats sought out places not even the Arab slavers had dared visit, the villagers

were even more troublesome, noisy, and inquisitive. . . . We felt like baited bears; we were mobbed in a moment, and scrutinized from every point of view by them. . . . They were pertinacious as flies, to drive them away was only to invite a return; whilst, worst grief of all, the women were plain, and their grotesque salutations resembled the "encounter of two dog-apes."

"Their eyes . . . seemed to devour us" in the constant staring. But, "curious to say, despite all these discomforts our health palpably improved." They returned to their base as the monsoon broke up. "The climate became truly enjoyable," said Burton. Now a "strange inexplicable melancholy" overcame him. He added that such a melancholy "accompanies all travellers to tropical lands." However, such a simplistic answer as he was to give did not explain his depression. "I never felt this sadness in Egypt and Arabia; I was never without it in India and Zanzibar." In the lushness of tropical Africa, where "nature is beautiful in all that meets the eye" and where "all is soft that affects the senses," he sighed "for the rare simplicity of the desert." But it was not nature that overcame him. "Want began to stare us in the face." The expedition did not have sufficient funds to return to Kazeh, a march of two hundred and sixty miles, requiring seventy-five porters and guards, plus *hongo* for the sultans along the route. "One thousand pounds does not go very far, when it has to be divided amongst a couple of hundred greedy savages in two and a half years."

On the twenty-second of May gunshots announced the un-expected arrival of an Arab caravan—"after a dead silence of eleven months"—with "boxes, bales, porters, slaves, and a parcel of papers and letters from Europe, India, and Zanzibar." For the first time Burton heard of the Indian Mutiny, and later he was to learn that in the uprising Edward Burton had suffered the final illness that would make him an invalid for the rest of his life. The new porters were the worst to be sent, and Burton had to give up any hope for further exploration of Tanganyika. He could go back to Kazeh, but he still lacked men and supplies for returning to the coast by a long southern march to Nyassa Lake and Kilwa.

"We have done with the Tanganyika Lake," Speke wrote in his journal, with no reference to the problems the expedition was suffering, the bad health of the principals, and the shortage of trade goods. Burton ordered the return to Kazeh and the civilizing surroundings of the Arabs. "I shall long remember the morning of 26th May [1858], which afforded me the last sunrise-spectacle of the Tanganyika Lake," said Burton with some sadness. "The charm of the scenery was perhaps enhanced by the reflection that my eyes might never look upon it again." And he recalled the mists as the sun rose—

> the internal living fire shed forth its broad beams, like the spokes of a huge aerial wheel, rolling a flood of gold over the light blue waters of the lake.

By the time the caravan reached Kazeh, everyone's health was even worse. "Again I suffered from swelling and numbness of the extremities, and strength returned by tantalizing slow degrees. My companion was a martyr to obstinate deafness and to a dimness of vision, which incapacitated him from reading, writing, and observing correctly."

> But, under the influence of narcotics, tonics, and stimulants, we presently progressed towards convalescence; and stronger than any physical relief, in my case, was the moral effect of success, and the cessation of ghastly doubts and cares, and of the terrible wear and tear of mind which, from the coast to [Ujiji], had never been absent.

In somewhat better health, Burton delayed a return to the coast. In his numerous conversations with the Arab traders, they had told him not only the details of the countries lying to the north and to the south of the expedition's line of march but also of their discovery of a large *bahr*, a sea or lake, lying fifteen or sixteen marches to the north. Burton saw at once that "the existence of this hitherto unknown basin would explain many discrepancies promulgated by speculative geographers [in Europe], more especially the notable and deceptive differences of distances caused by the confusion of the two waters." It seemed advisable "to ascertain if the Arabs, had not, with the usual Oriental hyperbole, exaggerated the dimensions of the Northern Lake."

Speke, now rested and in better health, "appeared a fit person to detach upon this duty." Burton thought that if either he or Speke saw the unknown *bahr* much would be clarified. There was no need for both men to make the journey. There were other reasons, too. "His presence at Kazeh was by no means desirable," and "I was afraid to leave him behind at Kazeh," for Speke was prone to anger the Arabs.

> It was very difficult to associate with Arabs as one of themselves. Jack was an Anglo-Indian, without any knowledge of Eastern manners and customs and religion, and of any Oriental language beyond Hindostanee. Now, Anglo-Indians . . . often take offence without reason; they expect extreme civility as their *due*, they treat all skins a shade darker than their own as "niggers".

That was Burton's version. Speke was to write that Burton did not want either one to go to the northern lake. This brought a final break between the two men, and ever afterward there were to be contradictory versions of events. Speke was to write that Burton was "unfortunately quite done up" and "unable to move without the assistance of eight men to carry him in a hammock." "This is far from being the fact," snapped Burton in *The Lake Regions of Central Africa*. "I had more important matters to work out." In his journal of July second Speke had also written, "I have proposed to take a flying trip to the unknown lake, while Captain Burton prepares for our return homewards."

Whatever the truth—each man may have been partly right—one is inclined to side with Burton. So Speke was ordered, or requested, or volunteered, to go on a search to the north. Said bin Salim was instructed to accompany him but refused; even the usually cooperative Sidi Bombay also refused, as did many of the guards and *pagazis*. In the end, after much argument, shouting, and bullying and promises of higher pay and ample rewards, Speke was able to assemble a small caravan and left Kazeh on July tenth.

Burton, blissfully rid of Speke for a few weeks, settled down to regain his health and to gather as much information as he could from the Arabs about the northern lake and the princes Speke might be expected to encounter on the route. He also "collected specimens of the multitudinous dialects" and got ready for the journey down to the coast.

In such matters as ethnographic, linguistic, and geographical information, Burton was always careful about his sources. He noted that the information he gathered about the lakes was culled from "a mass of Arab oral geography. All the vague accounts noted down from casual information were submitted to them for an imprimatur." He thought it wrong to collect information and to attempt to strike a happy medium between conflicting accounts—the result could only be error. "It is the explorer's unpleasant duty throughout these lands to doubt everything that has not been subjected to his own eyes," he wrote.

Getting a grasp of the languages was a more specific problem. He had learned Kisawahili "after some months of desultory work," and "once mastered, it renders its cognates as easy of acquirement as Bengali or Maharatti after Hindostani." The principal obstacle to the African tongues was "the want of instructors and books." But with the help of Snay bin Amir and "the Sons of Ramji and other tame slaves," he collected some 1,500 words of the three principal dialects. Then he found some "wild slaves" at Kazeh "with whom I began the dreary work of collecting specimens."

The work was not a labour of love. The savages could not guess the mysterious objects of my inquiry into their names for 1, 2, and 3; often they started up and ran away, or they sat in dogged silence, perhaps thinking themselves derided. The first number was rarely elicited without half an hour's "talkee-talkee."

But once started, "their tongues . . . often hobbled on without halting," but with all the slaves, wild or tame, "the glazed eye [and] the irresistible tendency to nod and snooze, evidenced a feeble brain soon overworked."

Meanwhile, Speke pushed northward. No doubt he was a brave man, or perhaps merely a foolhardy one. Here he was alone in a completely strange land, strange even to the slave traders, among people who were as likely to kill him as to feed him, not knowing what anyone around him was saying except what was passed to him in broken Hindustani by Sidi Bombay Mubarak, the only man with whom he could have even a smattering of conversation. His escort was sullen and mutinous, and worst of all, he was still almost blind, and the remnants of the beetle in his ear kept him near deafness.

Both Burton and Speke left accounts of this safari into the unknown. Burton—could it have been otherwise?—even in this instance can give a better version of the safari than the man who made it. But Speke's own words will suffice. He had made "a dreary beginning." As soon as they came to a village, the *pagazis* got hold of *pombe*, banana beer, and got drunk. Everyone was sullen, but Speke could not help remarking that "these curly-headed bipeds," even after a hard day's work, would spend the night dancing and singing—"singing the same song over and over again, and dancing and stomping with their legs and arms flying about like the wings of a semaphore" to the accompaniment of the village drums. But these were minor inconveniences. Speke had brought the wrong types of beads as currency, "and

I cannot buy those little luxuries, eggs, butter, and milk, which have such a powerful influence in making one's victuals good and palatable." He had brought white beads, when with colored beads "I might purchase anything."

"Misfortunes continued anew," he remarked when a sultana, the only woman ruler to be encountered, not only did her best to delay the first white man she had ever seen but also to divest him of his clothing.

On August first, following a small creek that grew in breadth as it flowed northward, Speke was pleased to see that it finally attained "very considerable dimensions" and "many little islands." "Would that my eyes had been strong enough to dwell unshaded upon such scenery!" He had been wearing gray spectacles against the light, and these attracted swarms of natives, who came within inches of his face to peer at his double eyes. He was forced to remove his glasses. Two days later, on the third of the month, the caravan wound its way up a long hill, "which, as it bears no native name, I shall call Somerset." This practice of dropping English names upon native geography infuriated Burton and other purists, but the names were to survive. But more than a name was at hand. At the summit of the hill

the vast expanse of the pale-blue waters of the N'yanza burst suddenly upon my gaze. It was early morning. The distant sea-line of the north horizon was defined in the calm atmosphere between the north and west points of the compass.

Bestowing more foreign names upon nameless native terrain, Speke labeled a distant string of islands the Bengal Archipelago, and the lake itself: "This magnificent sheet of water I have ventured to name VICTORIA after our gracious sovereign." In the distance Speke could make out the smoke from cookfires and here and there partially concealed villages and hamlets. "But the pleasure of the view," he wrote, "vanished in the presence of those intense and exciting emotions which are called up by the consideration of the commercial and geographical importance of the prospect before me."

> I no longer felt any doubt that the lake at my feet gave birth to that interesting river, the source of which has been the subject of so much speculation, and the object of so many explorers.

So Speke had found it, the source of the Nile! But had he? Arguments that would affect men's careers and lives and lead to his own death would come out of this statement. He felt utterly confident of his discovery, though he had seen nothing but one small fragment of the largest lake in Africa (and the second largest in the world, surpassed only by the Caspian). The map he had drawn from "Arab testimony"—Burton and Sidi Mubarak would have had to gather that information for Speke—"was so substantially correct that [of] its general outlines I had nothing whatever to alter." He had already passed the map on to the Royal Geographical Society.

Burton had heard from some of his Arab friends at Kazeh that there was at the lake a certain Mansur bin Salim, an impoverished rogue who depended on the goodwill of the local sultan, a cruel and untrustworthy man named Mahaya. Speke found the Arab immediately. Speke gave him some small items from his own larder, and in return Mansur led him about the shore on brief rambles, during which a number of wild fowl fell to Speke's guns. He still had no accurate or precise information about the lake and the presumed river that formed its outlet and became the Nile. Where was this so important river? How long was the lake? Speke asked Mansur. The trader had no sensible information, and a man he brought to Speke—"the greatest traveller of the place"—turned out to know very little. Speke's account of the conversation brought him ridicule when he returned to London.

> On my inquiring about the lake's length, the man faced to the north, and began nodding his head to it; at the same time he kept

throwing forward his right hand, and making repeated snaps of his fingers, endeavoured to indicate something immeasurable. . . .

The native added that nobody knew the extent of the lake but that "it probably extended to the end of the world." Speke had already managed to offend the sultan, Mahaya, to the point that Mahaya had forbidden his people to give the caravan any food. Accepting apologies from Said bin Salim and Sidi Bombay (Speke does not say what the offense was), the sultan got his court together for Speke's benefit, "but not a soul knew anything about the northern extremity." Even one of the sultan's wives ("a pretty crummy little creature"), who came from the north, said that "she had never heard of there being any end to the lake." After three days at Victoria N'yanza, believing he had learned all that was to be learned and convinced that he had found the legendary source of the Nile—how simplistic and naive his observations are as he reports them in *What Led to the Discovery of the Source of the Nile!*—he now decided to return to Kazeh, a hero, having at last bested Burton in something important. He thought "but a little more time, and a few loads of beads" would have enabled him to settle "every question which we had come all this distance to ascertain," but the matter did not seem to concern him deeply—what would Burton have done under the same circumstances?—and planning "to do everything that lay in my power to visit the lake again," he got his caravan together and without delay set off to the south.

The return to Kazeh went without incident. Speke found time for some shooting: "I bagged a fine young male hippopotamus . . . by hitting him on the ear when standing in shallow water." He made simple notes in his journal: "The natural laziness and ignorance of the people is their own and their country's bane." He complained of the natives' "dreadful sloth" and thought that "morally and physically they were little better than brutes." He recommended that missionaries enter the land to Christianize and civilize and that England take it over for economic development and the benefit of the people. The black man's heart, once gained, "can easily be turned in any way the preceptor pleases, as is the case with all Asiatics; they soon learn to bow to the superior intellect of the European, and are as easily ruled as a child is by his father."

His caravan reached Kazeh on the twenty-fifth, and the Arabs rushed out to meet it. "Captain Burton greeted me on arrival," Speke wrote, "and said he had been very anxious for some time about our safety"—there had been reports of tribal war in the areas where Speke had traveled.

> I laughed over the matter, but expressed regret that he did not accompany me, as I felt certain in my mind I had discovered the source of the Nile. This he naturally objected to, even after hearing all my reasons for saying so, and therefore the subject was dropped.

That the subject was dropped is all that Speke and Burton could agree upon. Speke, said Burton, had not broken the news of his discovery until after breakfast the following day. The delay in passing on this interesting piece of information—the chief reason for the expedition—Speke never explained. Why had he withheld it and then dropped it unexpectedly on Burton?

"Jack changed his manners to me from this date," said Burton in the *Life* with a touch of sadness. "His difference of opinion was allowed to alter companionship," and "after a few days it became evident to me that not a word could be uttered upon the subject of the lake, the Nile, and his *trouvaille* generally without offence." By tacit agreement the two men avoided this very controversial matter.

> Now, for the first time [added Burton], although I had pursued my journey under great provocations from time to time, I never realized what an injury I had done the Expedition publicly, as well as myself, by not travelling alone, or with Arab companions, or at least with a less crooked-minded, cantankerous English.

Speke's book, *What Led to the Discovery of the Source of the Nile*, ends abruptly with his return to Kazeh "in a state of high spirits and gratification," but Burton filled another half volume—after all, there was as much to see going down to the coast as coming up—and the reader is the beneficiary. Still, it was not an easy march. Hardly had the caravan left Kazeh when Speke became ill, racked with pains that ran through his entire body, and he suffered nightmares and wild dreams in which he was "haunted by a crowd of hideous devils, giants, and lion-headed demons." Burton called the fits "epileptic" and said they "more closely resembled those of hydrophobia than aught I have ever witnessed." Said bin Salim claimed that it was a comet in the skies that had made Speke ill.

On March 4, 1859, Burton and Speke finally reached Zanzibar, where they learned that war had broken out between claimants to the sultanship. And worse, Captain Christopher Rigby, Burton's rival from the Bombay language examinations, had replaced Hamerton as consul—again Burton found an enemy in a position to do him harm—and Rigby was implacable as an enemy. Even ten years later, in a memoir answering Speke's claims to "the 'settlement' of the Nile," Burton adapted as a footnote a passage from what he humorously termed Dickens's *Nicholas "Rigby"* to underline his anger at the consul: "Ah! that harsh voice, that arrogant style, that saucy superficiality which decided everything, that insolent arrogance that contradicted everybody: it was impossible to mistake them!"

Burton again fell into a state of depression. The native members of the expedition were clamoring for pay, for rewards and bonuses, and endless arguments broke out, although the men had been paid along the way and were now asking for more than they deserved. Speke immediately became friendly with Rigby, as he had with Outram at Aden, while the old antagonisms from India between Burton and these men persisted and perhaps had deepened. Outram had tried to throw the blame for the disaster at Berbera on Burton, and on Burton alone; now Rigby did his part in harming him. Burton's two-volume journal on Zanzibar, which he had completed in 1857 before going into the interior, was "lost." It had been neatly wrapped in a package addressed to the Royal Geographical Society in London—Norton Shaw should have received it in due time—but somehow the clerk in the consulate at Zanzibar, whom Burton described in pique as a "Eurasian apothecary," had sent it to the Bombay branch of the Royal Asiatic Society, where it had languished unnoticed for years. Why no one had recognized the package so plainly addressed and passed it on to London is not clear—were Burton's enemies deliberately thwarting his work, or was it mere bureaucratic incompetence? But the journals were not the only material from Zanzibar to be mislaid. His official Letters on his early excursions along the coast were temporarily lost; the meteorological observations made on the African shore and during the discovery of the lakes were "mislaid for years hidden in deep recesses in certain pigeon-holes at Whitehall Street." *Zanzibar; City, Island, and Coast* (into which the other lost material was incorporated) consequently was not issued until 1872. By then Burton had served as consul in West Africa, Brazil, and Damascus and had had numerous other adventures. Speke had made his second glorious but ultimately controversial expedition into Central Africa and had suffered a tragic death back in England. In those years Burton had ample time to place events into a better, though caustic, perspective.

Speke seemed "uncommonly eager" to return to London, and he managed to do so ahead of Burton. They left Zanzibar together on March twenty-second for Aden. "The cloe-shrubs and cocoa-trees of Zanzibar again faded from my eyes," Burton wrote. The English doctor at Zanzibar had warned both men that their health was precarious, and at Aden, Steinhauser "also recommended a lengthened period of rest." By chance. H.M.S. *Furious*, with the noted diplomat James Bruce, Lord Elgin, aboard, was in port on its way home from a mission in the Far East. Speke immediately boarded the *Furious*, preferring to stay there than ashore in the Aden garrison. Steinhauser had talked to Speke alone and had warned Burton with some alarm that he was not to be trusted.

Whether or not Burton had the opportunity to sail with Speke is a controversial point. He had reasons for not leaving immediately; his health and the desire to discuss the *Arabian Nights* with Steinhauser were among them. It is also likely that he was not invited to sail with Elgin. Speke quickly got his papers together and went off to England. "He left Aden in such haste that he did not take leave of his host," said Burton. "Still we were, to all appearances, friends."

> Before parting with me, Capt. Speke voluntarily promised when reaching England, to visit his family in the country, and to wait my arrival, that we might appear together before the Royal Geographical Society. . . . From Cairo he wrote me a long letter, reiterating his engagement, and urging me to take all the time and rest that broken health required.

On board ship, Burton wrote, Speke "was exposed to the worst influences." He was "persuaded to act in a manner which his own moral sense must have afterwards strongly condemned, if indeed it ever pardoned it."

Burton was not to mention the "worst influences" in print, but everyone knew. Aboard the *Furious*, serving as Elgin's secretary, was a strange but attractive and popular young man, Laurence Oliphant, then twenty-nine. Flamboyant, outrageous, vain, amoral, and opportunistic, a seeker of mystical experiences and in the forefront of the latest social, political, and literary fads of the time, Oliphant was an eccentric in the grand style of nineteenth-century England. He immediately set about turning Speke against Burton.

"He got hold of and poisoned Speke's mind against Richard," wrote Isabel Burton in the *Life*, telling Speke that Burton "would take all the glory of Nyanza. . . . Speke resisted at first, but his vanity prevailed, and carried him along until one thing after another was piled up against the unconscious absentee." In a footnote she elucidated: "Speke told me of this, and after his death I taxed Laurence Oliphant with it, who said so simply, 'Forgive me—I am sorry—I did not know what I was doing.' "

Burton wrote, "Hardly had [Speke] reached London before he had appeared at Whitehall Place to give his own views of important points [on the source of the Nile] still under discussion."

Speke became the lion of the hour; he gave lectures on his discovery, and almost immediately the Society gave him charge of a second expedition to Central Africa, to be amply funded. And what of Burton? "I reached London on May 21st, and found that everything had been done for, or rather against me. My companion now stood forth in his true colours, an angry rival." All the slights, the injuries real or imagined, the fantasies that the expedition owed its success to him and not to Burton (or to their combined efforts), had by an alchemy Burton understood been permuted into an anger that was meant to crush. "No one is so unforgiving, I need hardly say," said Burton, "as the man who injures another."

To compound the hurts, Speke immediately rushed into print with two articles, each of which contained errors that Burton thought nullified much of the success of the expedition. He had made mistakes in geography and in reporting information received from the Arabs. "Though the many-headed may think little of such matters, a man who has risked his life for a great discovery cannot sit tamely to see it nullified," Burton wrote. His friend from his Oxford days, Alfred Bate Richards, said, "Burton, shaken to the backbone by fever, disgusted, desponding, and left behind in the spirit and in the flesh, was . . . 'nowhere.' "

22

"My Earthly God and King"

But what of Isabel Arundell, now aging, now weary of her parents' unceasing efforts to get her married to a respectable, plump, financially secure English Catholic gentleman during the thirty-three months in which Burton was absent? How strange a relationship that was! Burton is said to have written her but four letters—four!—during this period and, when he got out of the jungle and arrived at Zanzibar, a poem of but six lines. No message, just six lines of poetry of a typical Victorian cast.

To Isabel
That brow which rose before my sight,
   As on the palmer's holy shrine;
Those eyes—my life was in their light;
   Those lips—my sacramental wine;
That voice whose flow was wont to seem
   The music of an exile's dream.

"I knew then it was all right," Isabel wrote in her journal. But it had been a bad period, those last few days. Speke had arrived, but where was Richard? Then she read in the press that Burton was returning momentarily. She had been thinking again of becoming a nun, but then the news of his return was published, news she read with a mixture of anticipation and anxiety. "I feel strange, frightened, sick," she scribbled in her diary on May twenty-first, "lest, after all I have suffered and longed for, I should have to bear more."

The next day, Isabel went to visit a friend, not knowing that Burton had arrived in London the previous day. The friend was out, and Isabel decided to await her return. The doorbell rang, and she heard a familiar voice asking of the maidservant:

> A voice that thrilled me through and through came up the stairs, saying "I want Miss Arundell's address." The door opened, I turned around, and judge of my feelings when I beheld Richard! For an instant we both stood dazed. . . . We rushed into each other's arms. I cannot attempt to describe the joy of that moment. He had landed the day before, and come to London, and had called here to know where I was living, where to find me. . . .

Tea with Isabel's friend was forgotten about, and Burton led Isabel downstairs and into a cab "and told the man to drive about—anywhere."

> He put his arm around my waist, and I put my head on his shoulder. I felt quite stunned; I could not speak or move, but felt like a person coming to after a fainting fit or a dream; it was acute pain. . . . But it was absolute content, such as I fancy people must feel in the first few moments after the soul has quitted the body. When we were a little recovered, we mutually drew each other's pictures from our respective pockets at the same moment, to show how carefully we had kept them.

But was this a man worth waiting for? Many women (it might be said without denigration) would have turned away from this once-handsome, once-dashing figure of a man. Now he was a tragic sight.

> I shall never forget Richard as he was then. He had had twenty-one attacks of fever—had been partially paralyzed and partially blind. He was a mere skeleton, with brown-yellow skin hanging in bags, his eyes protruding, and his lips drawn from his teeth.

"But never did I feel the strength of his love as then," Isabel hastens to assure the world, and it was a love that would not wane, no matter how ill Richard was, or how battered and besmirched he might be by the world.

> He returned poorer and dispirited by official rows and every species of annoyance; but he was still—had he been ever so unsuccessful, and had every man's hand against him—my earthly god and king, and I could have knelt at his feet and worshipped him. I used to feel so proud of him; I used to sit and look at him, and think, "You are mine, and there is no man on earth the least like you."

What Burton needed at that moment more than anything was love, love from a warm, uncritical, noncompetitive person, and Isabel gave him what was to nourish and invigorate him. "I think that but for me he would have died," she said simply. It seemed then as if it were a likely time for them to marry, but Mrs. Arundell was firmly opposed to any union, for reasons both Isabel and Burton knew only too well. Mrs. Arundell fought Burton with all her strength, continually emphasizing what to her were his two major faults: "He is not a Christian, and he has no money." That he was a Christian, even a Roman Catholic of sorts, became one of Isabel's campaigns throughout their lives, and as for money, Burton had inherited on his father's death the considerable sum of £16,000. * Burton was ready to marry: he agreed to marry in the Roman Catholic faith, he would promise in writing to raise their children as Catholics, and he was willing

---

* Perhaps as much as $300,000 to $400,000 in today's purchasing power.

to settle down, possibly in a diplomatic post—the consulship at Damascus was a prime interest.

Sadly, that incredible encounter in a friend's house, so theatrical as were so many between Burton and Isabel, was to produce nothing but frustration, for dealing with the Arundells was hopeless. Mr. Arundell liked Burton, but his wife was adamant against a marriage. "Dick Burton is no friend of mine," she would say to the end of her life.

Between quiet, clandestine meetings with Isabel, Burton migrated back and forth from London to Dover, where his sister and brother were staying. Maria's husband, Colonel Henry Stisted, had recently returned from India, followed by Edward Burton, now on an extended medical leave. Both men had gone through the frightful carnage of the so-called Sepoy Mutiny of 1857. The colonel had escaped injury, but poor Edward, having "served with distinction," had reached the end in India. The overwhelming heat, the scenes of blood and chaos, the atrocities committed by both sides, had finally struck him down: his brain was somehow damaged—addled—by sunstroke or some other undefined calamity. "His mind slowly gave way and never recovered," wrote Georgiana Stisted. Eventually he was put into the Surrey County Lunatic Asylum, immobile and speechless, a tragedy that affected his older brother as much as any in his life. Hopelessly mute and passive, Edward was not to be coaxed into speaking for the rest of his life, until shortly before his death in 1895, when a cousin, Dr. E. J. Burton, as a test, accused him of not paying a certain minor debt. "Shabby," said Dr. Burton to Edward of the incident. At which, Edward replied, "Cousin, I did pay you, you must remember that I gave you a cheque." But except for that exchange there was only silence.

Burton was still not in good health. He took long walks with Maria, the family had pleasant dinners together, and he worked steadily away on the manuscript of his book on the search for the headwaters of the Nile, but, wrote his niece years later, "everybody remarked that he looked ill and depressed. The sweets of success were mingled with many bitters. Speke's strange breach of faith affected him more than he would confess to. . . ."

Miss Stisted, as was her wont, refuses to bring in the name of Isabel Arundell, that awful name that she does not mention for pages to come in her biography of Burton. He was driven to desperation at this time trying to placate the implacable Mrs. Arundell, who was regularly intercepting and burning his letters to Isabel, further affecting a nature that so easily slipped into melancholy. In the early fall the family went over to France, visiting Paris and staying longer in Boulogne, one of their favorite cities, a town that Burton, as he wrote to friends at home, found ideal for working. Another trip took them to Vichy, where Burton tried the waters for his aches and pains.

But walks with his sister, chats with Colonel Stisted, waters for his physical ailments, secret visits to Isabel, did not heal. How Burton managed to write during this period is a mystery, but write he did, and well. Perhaps writing was an anodyne for the misery and pain he experienced, not only from the Arundells but also from Speke, who was doing his best to denigrate his former commander. The attacks had started as soon as Speke had landed, and then, under Oliphant's direction, had come in a deluge, with certain others, friends of Speke's or enemies of Burton's, joining in a widespread campaign of vituperation. Speke might have let heroic facts speak for themselves, but he was eager for the world to know of his discovery. Why did he not let his magnificent accomplishment stand out as done? He had found the source of the Nile, and that simple announcement should have been enough. Why must he destroy Burton? By the time Burton had arrived home, the second expedition had already been decided upon, with Speke in command and £2,500 promised in support. Speke had asked for £5,000, but that seemed like too much, since the first expedition had set out with only £1,000. Sir Roderick I. Murchison, the president of the Royal Geographical Society, had not even bothered to wait for Burton's arrival. When he learned of the new expedition, so as not to be shut out completely, Burton had suggested that there be two expeditions, one led by Speke, the other by himself, to meet further inland and join in a great venture of discovery. His proposal was abruptly rejected.

Oliphant's influence on Speke continued for many years. He had been born in 1829 in South Africa, a member of a distinguished Scottish family. "The boy's education was of the most desultory kind," wrote his junior contemporary, the Right Honourable Montstuart Elphinstone Grant Duff, who had no use for Oliphant. As a young man, Oliphant wandered around Ceylon, India, and Nepal and wrote a book about his adventures. After trying the English and Scottish bars, he went off to Russia—another book. His support of Speke might have come in part from a then-unrecognized competition with Burton, for Oliphant claimed to have been the first person, not Burton, to suggest the relief of Kars during the Crimean War and the mission to the bandit-imām Schamyl in the Caucasus. His travels in obscure places hint at a role in the Great Game. When he was in the Crimea before the war, he poked about the Russian naval base at Sevastopol. The Russians expelled him, but he had formed an opinion about the size and placement of the fortifications, and he was able to offer pertinent observations about the Russian railway system and the difficulty of transporting troops south should it be necessary in a war.

Oliphant's hold over Speke was hard to define. His intellectual brilliance, though erratic, is obvious. He had connections in England that were beyond Speke. He continued to work upon Speke, telling him that Burton had taken advantage of his efforts and discoveries, that it was he, Speke, not Burton, who was the leader, the directing force, of the expedition, and that no time should be lost in making it clear to the public. Moreover, Oliphant encouraged Speke in the idea that Burton was not even English but some kind of "European" (Speke is said to have stated that Burton was a Corsican, a reference to England's not-too-long-dead nemesis, Napoleon Bonaparte) and that only an

Englishman—that is, Speke—was entitled to the discovery of the Nile. Oliphant, whom Duff called "only partially sane," was persuasive, calculating, and he could manipulate Speke as he willed.

While Burton had suddenly found himself a diminished figure, Oliphant had been taking Speke about London to meet influential people, among them the Blackwood cousins, William and Robert, the younger generation of an important Glasgow publishing house founded in 1804. The Blackwoods were known as shrewd, intelligent, and successful publishers with an eye for the popular and the unusual, and their publication, *Blackwood's Edinburgh Magazine*, was both successful and respected. Speke immediately was signed as a *Blackwood's* author. That his articles on the search for the Nile, as he submitted them, were virtually illiterate and even incomprehensible was no problem. The Blackwoods polished and edited as necessary, and Oliphant steered him through the perils of writing, meanwhile fanning the resentments that consumed his protégé day and night. Speke, in letters to various people, produced a barrage of accusations, half-truths, and fabrications damaging to Burton. One of his favorite correspondents was Rigby, who was certain to repeat his charges. When Burton's own cautious denial that the Victoria N'yanza was the source of the Nile was ignored or dismissed by scholars and public alike, Speke gloated in a letter to Rigby that "Burton has got the dumps, and is cutting himself at every turn."

Burton was also suffering from Rigby's accusations that he had cheated the porters when he returned to Zanzibar. Speke, who had originally sided with Burton in the matter, now reversed himself and accused Burton of not paying the men as he had promised. Again, as had happened after the fight at Berbera, the English officials took the unproved word of natives against the sworn testimony of one of their own men, and Rigby informed India House that Burton's intransigence was making the government lose face. That England might be concerned about its standing with semibarbarian natives was a cruel farce. Never a man to avoid a fight, Burton got into a terrible row with Rigby, and in mid-January 1860 found himself rebuked by India House. It was suggested that he alone would be responsible for paying the alleged debts. The result was more angry letters, which produced no satisfactory solution. Speke, having made the most of the situation, wrote to Rigby, "They listen at India House with great pride when I tell them the way in which you govern at Zanzibar . . . you are the father of Zanzibar and the Sultan is your eldest son."

The bitterness that had broken into the open when the two men arrived home continued unabated through 1860, each man becoming more and more formal when they corresponded, for they had to exchange notes in settling the affairs of the expedition, their salutations going from "Dear Jack" and "Dear Richard" to "Dear Speke" and "Dear Burton," and finally, for each, to "Sir." Throughout, Burton tried to be gentlemanly and proper, but formally and icily so. By November 1859, Burton had become so frustrated with the situation that he wrote Norton Shaw, "I don't want to have any further private or direct communication with Speke. At the same time I am anxious that no mention of his name by me should be made without his being cognizant of it." Shaw heard both sides of the argument over the pay for the porters and also that Burton had advanced a considerable sum out of his own pocket to keep the safari on its feet and had lent Speke money. Burton's contribution was £1,400, and he thought Speke could reimburse him with £600, a request that was not to be honored. "The debt was contracted unconditionally by you in Africa," Burton had written to Speke. "Had I known you then as well as I do now I should have required receipts for what was left a debt of *honour*. I must be content to pay the penalty of ignorance." With this, Speke wrote not to Burton but to Shaw, saying that Burton had found further correspondence "distasteful." At about the same time, he also wrote to Burton with profound insensitivity about the situation, "You appear *desirous* of shunning me." By this time it was clear that Burton *was* shunning Speke, for a rational exchange of views over their now numerous differences was clearly impossible.

Even Burton's having used his own money to keep the expedition going and having lent some to Speke was turned about. Speke began to insist that Burton was so desperate to have him for his special skills and strengths that "he even gave me money for my passage out to Bombay rather than *lose my services*. Oh what humbug!!! . . ."

If one were not directly involved in the battle, some of Speke's attacks might be considered high comedy. He expressed the opinion that the publication of his articles in *Blackwood's* would "have the effect of reforming Burton; at any rate it will check his scribbling mania, and may save his soul the burthen of many lies." He also told the Blackwood cousins that he would rather die a thousand deaths than have a foreigner take from Britain the discovery of the source of the Nile. That Burton was "not one of us" Speke continually tried to make plain with his intimations that Burton was not even an Englishman; his dark Gypsy looks proved that. But worse than such infantile accusations were Speke's crude slanders in which he mentioned darkly the notorious report about the male brothels in Karachi. W. H. Wilkins thirty-five years later tried to stem the rumors that still circulated by writing that "Speke had spread all sorts of ugly—and I believe untrue—reports about Burton. These coming on top of certain other rumors—also, I believe, untrue—which originated in India, were only too rapidly believed." There was never any clear-cut, tangible evidence that Burton was a homosexual. This was undoubtedly the most damaging of all the unfair accusations against Burton and one that has not yet died out. For Speke to accuse Burton of homosexual proclivities was hardly an adequate defense of his claim to be the great discoverer of the sources of the Nile.

Still, not everyone supported Speke wholeheartedly and without question. In a savage society—upper-class Victorian England—where men and women were prepared to believe the worst about each other and where gossip often prevailed over fact or truth, Speke, too, had his detractors. Burton had many friends, some of them powerful and distinguished, and support was not lacking; when he was not likely to defend himself publicly or criticize Speke before others, his friends spoke out. The gossip about Speke's not paying his debt to Burton, a heinous offense in the eyes of many upper-class Englishmen, had become widespread, and Speke's young brother, Benjamin, wrote to Norton Shaw in October 1860 (Speke himself was then in Africa): "I hear from my mother that there was much talk about it in London rather derogatory to my brother." Six months earlier, prior to his departure for Africa, Speke had written Burton saying that he had directed Benjamin to pay the debt on his behalf, but it was never paid.

The eminent and highly respected Dr. David Livingstone was soon to add his voice. He is said to have disliked Burton personally, but as a fair man he thought that Speke, with whom he corresponded, had erred in his geography. Later, he was to say so publicly. One of Burton's most fervent and outspoken supporters was James Macqueen, a Scotsman who had spent his youth managing sugar plantations in the West Indies and had collected the slaves' accounts of their homelands. Though he had never visited Africa, Macqueen was extremely knowledgeable in its geography and customs, and he attacked Speke's articles not only for their errors but with some maliciousness for their pomposity and boasting.

During his first, hectic, controversial months back in England, Burton began to receive invitations from the elite, the powerful and influential. Speke, wrote Georgiana Stisted, "became the annual lion necessary to the London season," but "in literary and bohemian circles" her uncle "was very much sought after and feted." Among the people Burton visited after his return were the Duke of Somerset, Lord Palmerston, Lord Derby, Lord Stanley, and Richard Monckton Milnes, later Lord Houghton.

All were valuable friends, well respected and connected to the inner circles of government and finance. Of this group the wealthy and influential Milnes was one of Burton's closest friends. Burton and Milnes had like interests of a sort, and Milnes was able to help Burton through many difficult passages in his career. He was among those who persuaded the Royal Geographical Society to finance the first expedition to Central Africa.

Also, Milnes was not the ordinary bluff fox-hunting lord. An amateur poet of some proficiency, he was a friend of the literati and a quiet and generous patron of writers in need. He was an early enthusiast of the Brontë sisters. Touched by Charlotte Brontë's comparative poverty and "loneliness mid her fame," he quietly had the Reverend Arthur Nicholls's annual stipend increased so that he could marry her. Milnes himself had wanted to marry young Florence Nightingale, but after he had courted her for five years she slipped away to go on to greater things as a humanitarian; she always liked Milnes because he unobtrusively supported the juvenile reformatories and other charities dear to her heart. Milnes did not marry until he and his fiancée, the beautiful, intelligent, neurotic, artistic, reclusive Annabel Crewe, were well into their forties. The well known and the unknown of England's poets and writers flocked to the Milnes homes, especially the country estate, Fryston, a large, decrepit mansion in the Georgian style, which Tennyson called Freezetown. Milnes's gatherings were famous: Carlyle, Disraeli, and later Swinburne were frequent guests. Milnes had a then-odd liking for Americans, usually made fun of because of their accents and bad grammar. Nathaniel Hawthorne and Henry Adams were among those welcomed at Fryston.

Much of what is known today of Milnes and his circle has unfortunately been given an overly lurid cast by later writers to his detriment, so that he appears as hardly more than an aging man who liked pornographic books. A French writer of a later generation, Georges Lafourcade, thought Fryston "a sinister Yorkshire mansion filled with sadistic literature and presided over by a 'feline' and malicious host." Such a doleful view of Milnes has rubbed off on Burton as a member of the Fryston salon. Among those to denigrate Milnes and thus Burton was the noted critic and scholar Mario Praz, who said that Milnes was a man of "Mephistophelian malice" who used his friends as "instruments in order to put together some strange cruel comedy."

During the late summer of 1859, Burton made several visits to Fryston. The great libraries intrigued him: There were books everywhere, in room after room. The mansion itself was a disaster. Plaster fell from the ceiling, and Milnes would not let his wife decorate as she pleased, but he built more and more bookshelves. The library was orderly and cataloged by subject and language and represented European literature over four centuries, from English poetry, the French Revolution, theology, magic and witchcraft, and crime to Milnes's unique collection of erotica, for which he was notorious.

The erotic material came mostly from Fred Hankey, Burton's acquaintance from his days in Cairo after the Mecca pilgrimage. Hankey was now living in Paris, a prominent center of pornography. He had a French mistress without whom he would not travel. He was not welcome in Fryston when bringing erotica— what a commentary that was on the double standards of the Victorians!—and so he sent books over either in diplomatic pouches or strapped to the back of a Mr. Harris, the manager of Covent Garden, a frequent visitor to France on business.

Hankey may have been as wicked as the stories that circulated about him claimed, stories that some writers have attempted to connect to Burton. The famous French novelists and historians, the brothers Edmond and Jules Goncourt, were taken to see Hankey at his apartment in Paris. "His conversation seemed to them so evil and disgusting that they could scarcely believe their ears," wrote Milnes's biographer, James Pope-Hennessy. Hankey had expressed the opinion that Paris was rather tame—in London there was a house where not only could young ladies be whipped but one could stick pins in them (and he indicated the length of the pins with his thumb and forefinger). Hankey claimed that he and a friend had rented a room opposite the public execution ground in Paris from which they could observe a woman being guillotined for murder, meanwhile having two prostitutes "do their thing" as they watched; unfortunately for Hankey and his friend, this exquisite frisson was denied them when the Empress pardoned the murderess. Hankey was reported to have every sexual object known to man decorating his apartment. His notoriety as a sadist made him the stock figure of the English sadist that turned up in French and Italian novels in the last half of the century. Hankey, well exhausted by his erotic mania, disappeared eventually, but he is believed to have died toward the end of the century "perhaps . . . in a Paris lunatic asylum."

While he was staying with the Stisteds, Burton made several visits to Paris, presumably to see Hankey. He met Hankey in the late fall of 1859 and again the next January, and possibly on other occasions. There has been some discussion of Burton's so-called bipolarity—his attraction to young innocents like the very virginal Isabel Arundell as opposed to his interest in exotic sexual practices—but perhaps this dichotomy is stretched too far. Isabell Arundell was hardly naive, though surely a virgin, when she was "engaged" to Burton; she could assume the customary Victorian airs, and she was probably the only white woman with whom Burton was either romantically, emotionally, or physically involved, despite his teenage crushes on other middle-class English girls, his affairs with the whores of Italian cities, and his flirtation with Louisa. As in so many situations where Burton has been accused of violations of ordinary human decency, there is no real evidence of anything untoward to charge against him. Milnes had written some perverse lines dealing with flagellation, and Burton commented on them, politely. From time to time, in Africa or elsewhere, Burton would write to Milnes to ask, "Anything of Hankey?" or, "Any news of Fred Hankey?" and finally, a decade later, "Fred Hankey must nearly have been burned out."

Hankey had shown the Goncourt brothers a folio that he wanted bound in the skin of a Negress flayed alive. It seemed that he asked Burton to get him one, and a great amount of opprobrium has fallen upon Burton because of the request, but the Goncourts wrote that it was in fact someone else, Dr. Heinrich Barth, also an African explorer, who had promised to get him the skin. Barth was a German, Burton's age, who had traveled in North and Central Africa under the auspices of the British government; he was a member of the Royal Geographic and Asiatic Societies and had published a major work in three volumes of his experiences; it was advertised in Burton's *City of the Saints* (published in 1861). There could have been no confusion in the minds of either Hankey or the Goncourts. Dr. Heinrich Barth was not Capt. Richard Francis Burton. Hankey had known Burton for years and possibly knew Barth as well, and the Goncourts were too knowledgeable to confuse the two men. But even if Hankey had seriously asked Burton to bring him the skin of a black woman flayed alive, Burton was not one to honor such a request, though he might have let himself humor Hankey from time to time. Considering the distaste with which he viewed the abuse of human beings in primitive lands (and in his own) and the manner in which he railed against the cruelty of Africa— slavery, ritual slaughter, human sacrifices, and torture—it was not likely that he would have had a Negro woman skinned for the benefit of a half-crazed, sadistic Englishman who babbled constantly about sexual matters.

Despite his bad health and the frustrations with the Arundell family, Burton seems to have passed a very active year after his return from Central Africa, shuttling back and forth to London for secret meetings with Isabel, his vacations with the nobility at their country estates, and the completion of the manuscript of his book on Central Africa. He also continued to go to Vichy, a favorite haunt, where he regularly took the waters in an effort to correct his tendency to gout. He ransacked libraries wherever he was, but more than anything else, the situation with Isabel

Arundell occupied his thoughts. He wanted to elope with her, but she refused. She hoped and prayed that her mother would consent to a proper Catholic marriage, and she was willing to work out the details and nuptial agreement. In the October of Burton's return, she had written her mother a long, pleading letter about her desire to marry Burton and no one else. The letter runs to almost five pages of small type in the *Life*, where it is reprinted, and it is a most moving, well-reasoned, and impassioned appeal. "My dearest Mother," the letter begins. "I feel quite grateful to you for inviting my confidence. It is the first time you have ever done so, and the occasion should not be neglected."

> I am rather ashamed to tell you that I fell in love with Captain Burton at Boulogne, and would have married him any time between this and then, if he had asked me. The moment I saw his briganddaredevil look, I set him up as an idol, and determined that he was the only man I would ever marry; but he never knew it until three years ago, before he went to Africa.

Then she detailed his various trips and expeditions. On his return from the Crimea in 1856, she wrote that he then "fell in love with me and asked me to be his wife, and was perfectly amazed to find that I had cared for him all that time." She recalled to her mother that when she had told her "that I had found the Man and the Life I longed for, [you had replied] that he was the *only* man you would never consent to my marrying; that you would rather see me in my coffin." And so she continued, detailing her life and Burton's, his military services and his fame. ("Look at his writings, his travels, his poetry, his languages and dialects!") Burton stood first in Europe in languages; he was the best horseman, the best pistol shot. And she wrote emphatically about his qualities and her love for him. Now, what about her mother's side? "You have said that 'you do not know who he is, that you do not meet him anywhere.' " But saying the first makes her mother out "illiterate," and the second is merely that the kind of society Mrs. Arundell frequents in order to get her daughters married Burton considers "boring." As far as religion is concerned, though Burton may scoff, "he leads a good life, has a natural worship of God, innate honour, and does unknown good." He will be married in the Catholic Church and will bring up their children as Catholics. She begged her mother to discuss the question together and to let Burton go to Mr. Arundell to make a formal request for her hand. She wanted "a kind word" from her mother. She warned that "we shall never marry any one else, and never give each other up. . . . If you drive me to it, I shall marry him in defiance." There will be no one but Burton for her; if he should give her up, "I will go straight into a convent." She begged her mother not for rejection but "a blessing!" But it was to no purpose. "The only answer to this letter was an awful long and solemn sermon." Again, Burton was not a Christian; he had no money. And that was the end of the matter for the moment.

In retrospect, years later, Isabel could concede—unfairly to herself, one might think: "Of course I can see *now* what an aggravating letter it must have been to a woman whose heart was set on big matches for her daughters." Burton remarked that Isabel and Mrs. Arundell were "both gifted with the noble firmness of the mule." The impasse remained, fortified by all the barriers that English society could erect around a couple—class, religion, money, ancestry, snobbism, obstinacy, pride, and self-ishness.

In an incredibly concentrated and productive period of writing, despite the many interruptions and distractions, Burton finished his manuscript, the massive two-volume *Lake Regions of Central Africa*, and on April 10, 1860, sent it off to the publishing house of Longman, Green, Longman, and Roberts. He had also written a 460-page account of the expedition that was published late in 1859 in the *Journal* of the Royal Geographical Society (it was reissued a year later as a paper-covered book), and there were also brief accounts and letters by both Burton and Speke in at least five issues of the Society's "Proceedings." Burton also contributed to *Blackwood's* a twenty-four-page article, "Zanzibar; and two months in East Africa." An immense amount of writing that any other man might have spent a decade on was completed in less than a year. Still, he felt it necessary to apologize for his tardiness in completing the manuscript of the book—"the impairment of my health, the depression of spirits, and worse still, the annoyance of official correspondence, which to me have been the sole results of African exploration, may be admitted as valid reasons for the delay."

A great piece of writing had been published, a name made and perhaps lost. Speke was momentarily about to depart without Burton but with another officer, James Augustus Grant, on a second, possibly even more significant search, and the Arundells were firmly opposed to Burton's marrying their daughter.

Now what was to happen?

> One day in April, 1860, I was walking with two friends [Isabel wrote], and a tightening of my heart came over me that I had known before. I went home and told my sister, "I am not going to see Richard for some time."

The sister tried to reassure Isabel, but "a tap came at the door, and a note with the well-known writing was put in my hands. I knew my fate, and with deep-drawn breath I opened it." Burton had disappeared without a word. "I was for a long time in bed," wrote Isabel, "and delerious [*sic*]."

> For six weeks I was doctored for influenza, mumps, sore throat, fever, delerium, and everything that I had not got, when in reality I was only heartsick, struggling for what I wanted, a last hard struggle with the suspense of my future before me, and nothing and nobody to help me.

Burton's action might have been precipitous, but it was not without its reasons. An impasse had been reached, he was desperate for a solution, and none was in sight. He seems to have been drinking heavily, something he did in excess from time to time when under pressure. He had been corresponding with Steinhauser, who had written to Burton to "come with me and drink through America." The doctor had written:

I'll drink mint-juleps, brandy-smashes, whisky-skies, gin-sling, cock-tail sherry, cobblers, rum-salads, streaks of lightning, morning glory, and it'll be a most interesting experiment—I want to see whether after a life of 3 or 4 months I can drink and eat myself to the level of the aborigines—like you.

Drinking throughout America was not a bad solution to the Arundell and other problems. "So I replied in the affirmative," wrote Burton.

The trip to America contains many unsolved mysteries. At first it was not known that Burton had someone with him at least on part of the trip, but a fragment of a journal that escaped destruction mentions the invitation, and the publication of *Zanzibar* in 1872 reveals that his companion was Steinhauser—"generally he exists upon bottles"—by then deceased.

Burton had quietly obtained an extension of his leave—Milnes might have helped him—and so made the unlikely and unexpected decision to go to the States. The subject of America had not previously appeared in Burton's published thoughts; there was no long foreshadowing of such a journey as there had been of those into Arabia and Africa, no Mecca or Nile to discover. North America was hardly an exotic land for the English. Immigrants still flooded the continent from all over the British Isles, and many visitors had returned to publish their experiences, observations, and judgments. Not even the lure of the primitive could claim Burton. The Indian tribes that survived were either in a dispirited, impoverished condition or were in a state of war against the federal government and the settlers. Burton was to show little interest in their tongues, though he was fascinated by Indian sign language. He later announced that he had wanted to see the Mormons, who a few years earlier, after being hounded across America, from upstate New York to Utah, had settled around Great Salt Lake.

That Burton was frustrated, angered, dejected, and depressed by events at home clearly was a major factor in his decision to escape to another environment. The arguments with Speke had sapped his energies. Speke would shortly be in Africa without him but profiting by his work. Dr. Livingstone was also in Africa and had turned down Burton's request to join him. Perhaps there was more in this strange voyage to the New World than appears on the surface. Burton's motivations, aside from his desire to drown his sorrows, are far from clear. That he hoped to see one more exotic religion—Mormonism—*in situ* is hardly an excuse for a long and tiresome, sometimes dangerous journey. Like the time spent during the Crimean War, Burton's months in the States are but an interlude, time passed, to be forgotten except for the expected—and superlative—volume of experiences.

He boarded the S.S. *Canada* sometime in April, not even waiting to see proofs of the *Central Africa* volumes. His journal begins on the twenty-first, aboard ship, and mentions fleetingly some encounters with other people. He did not seem to be languishing in sorrow after his departure from Isabel—the first morning he awoke to see "a beautiful face opposite me . . . a lovely glow upon her!" But other relationships were hardly amicable. He immediately disliked the captain ("a liar"); another man with whom he had been friendly at first he soon disliked—perhaps the man refused to drink with him. Tension and melancholy seemed to infuse him. He was drinking, and continued to do so. But where was Steinhauser? It is possible that the doctor was already in the States or met Burton later and left early. The *Canada* landed at Halifax, and here Burton found the people friendlier than on board ship. He was feeling not only disappointment and frustration but his years, a mere thirty-nine, and complained that "after 40 a man should eat and live, after 60 he hasn't any pleasure in life but to eat. As for the other excitements, 'twixt 60 and 70 it's all dead weight."

He seems not to have lingered in Halifax but immediately went down to New York, where he spent a few days talking to publishers—Harper and Brothers were to issue *The Lake Regions of Central Africa* later in the year—and then he went south to Washington. Here he saw John B. Floyd, a Virginian who was Secretary of War. Burton asked Floyd for letters of introduction to various military commanders in the West, hoping to be allowed to join a battle against the Indians. Then he continued on his southward journey, an excursion that lacks documentation. His time in the South is virtually a blank. He did not write about it for publication; letters, if he wrote any (he was normally a prolific correspondent), are either buried in obscure official files or private collections or lost. Isabel is silent in the *Life* about these vanished weeks or months. Was he drunk all the time, so drunk he was unable to communicate with anyone? Was he passing his time in brothels?—New Orleans was notorious for the number and variety of its houses. Was Steinhauser on the scene during this period? In *The City of the Saints and Across the Rocky Mountains to California*, there is no mention of the New Orleans period or of a companion; and the available records of the year, especially the Salt Lake paper, the *Deseret News*, of August 29, 1860, noted his arrival and, on October third, his departure without mention of a traveling companion or even of a Germanic military doctor during the same period.

There is another aspect to those lost days in the South. The year of 1860 was one of approaching crisis in the United States. The Union was on the verge of splintering: long-seething quarrels over states' rights, slavery, even agriculture and industry, were bringing the nation to the brink of civil war. Many Englishmen favored the South—cotton among other raw materials was basic to the British economy. It might be assumed that Burton was on a secret mission arranged by influential friends in London to certain southern leaders. Milnes, who was to favor the North when war broke out, still might have played a role in backing the mission. That so many of Burton's trips had multiple purposes rarely became apparent until years later. Whom Burton saw during his weeks in the Deep South, where he stayed, or what he did remain even more obscure than certain vacant periods in Sind when he was working for Napier.

On August seventh, having been in the States for over three months, Burton surfaced unexpectedly at St. Joseph, a ragged frontier town on the Missouri River, having, he said, just come from St. Louis. St. Jo's (as Burton liked to call it) was a staging point for emigrants bound west. There Burton boarded a coach headed for Salt Lake City. He wrote that he paid $175 for his passage, a staggering sum. Aboard also were a federal judge, Mr. Flemmikin, a state marshal, Mr. Grice, and the Danas, an army family of father, mother, and daughter.

With this start, Burton shed the melancholy that had plagued him at the beginning of the trip, as he had so often when the prospect of a voyage into the unknown was before him and elevated his frequently depressed moods. He immediately began to record his impressions in a notebook. American slang entranced him, particularly common expletives like "God damn," which he realized had lost its meaning. He was soon dropping elements of this fascinating version of his native tongue into his speech and writings. "Getting liquored up" was a favorite, as indeed he was so often in such a state.

Burton never embarked on a trip without careful preparation and a study of suitable texts. He had put together a small library dealing with the States that would tell him something about American character and customs. He had bought some recent American literature, including Moby-Dick and The Scarlet Letter. Burton liked Melville's religious opinions ("astute") but dismissed Hawthorne's great work as "unreadable." He also had the works of early western explorers—Frémont, Stansbury, and Gunnuson—and a collection of "the most violent Mormon and anti-Mormon polemicals." He was to warn that in the States there was much anti-Mormon sentiment: the writings by anti-Mormons and apostate Mormons were "venomous" and "thoroughly untrustworthy."

More important were Bartlett's *Dictionary of Americanisms* and Captain Randolph B. Marcy's *The Prairie Traveller*. This latter work, a guide for immigrants by an American army officer who had explored some of the westward trails and had also fought Indians from Minnesota to Texas and Mexico, was never far from his pocket. Burton was so enamored of it that he prepared a European edition for later emigrants to the West.

Burton had followed Marcy's advice about dress; in fact, he resembled one of the illustrations of the well-accoutered frontiersmen in *The Prairie Traveller*. He wore a heavy English shooting jacket that resembled those worn by westerners, a flannel shirt, trousers strengthened by buckskin and tucked into heavy boots, and a large brown felt hat. He also wore a broad leather belt into which he stuck a pair of Colt six-shooters. He had a bowie knife—an Arkansas toothpick, he liked to call it—tucked into his boot. For formal moments to be spent among the Mormons (and perhaps also worn in the South in meeting various leaders) he had a silk hat and an umbrella. He had brought some simple surveying instruments, a pocket sextant, compass, and a telescope, sketching materials and notebooks, and for his private pleasures, the inevitable cognac, pipe tobacco, and opium, plus as medicine, quinine and Warburg's drops.

The coach passed along the famous Emigrants' trails over which thousands of newcomers had ridden or walked, through settlements, villages, and across fords and rivers that bore names of great romance—Troy, Kennekuk Station, Big Grasshopper, Kickapoo, Uncle John's Grocery, the Little Sandy and the Big Sandy, West Turkey, the Omaha, Little Kiowa, and Horse Creek. Burton recalled Bleeding Kansas, Sweet Rock, and Devil's Gate. But he was distracted from these fascinating nomenclatures by minor discomforts. The food was a standard complaint: "The eternal eggs and bacon" for breakfast were a regular annoyance. He saw covered wagons, "those ships of the great American Sahara." At Fort Kearny he hoped to join the cavalry in a battle against the Indians, but "the Commanches, Kiowas and Cheyennes had lately been defeated." He had some hope that the stage would be attacked along the way, but encounters with Indians were minimal. He picked up local prejudices against them. He saw nothing of Indians at their best and found little but poverty and dirt, and he complained about the inevitable lying of the type that enraged him in India and the Middle East. But whites lied, too, though their lying seemed more a picturesque sport than patently devious.

His notebooks quickly piled fact upon fact, discovery upon discovery. Many of his remarks often compared previous sights and experiences in India, Arabia, and Central Africa. He had hoped to see a scalping, but none was performed at the propitious moment. At Alkali Lake he tried through sign language to persuade a warrior to demonstrate the art, but the brave was reluctant to perform this most popular pastime. Burton was apparently transferring his notes to a finished manuscript as he traveled—how one always admires his industry!—and his view of America is fresh, lively, sharp, and pertinent. *The City of the Saints* is one of his best works but is sadly overlooked. How many English-speaking readers were interested in one more account of a trip to the New World by still another Englishman? Still, the book is a rare account by an experienced traveler who was alert to every detail, to language, to the nuances of a dynamic developing nation that showed high civilization on its eastern coast and progressive barbarism as one traveled westward. Here are emigrants, soldiers, desperadoes, wanderers, frontier women, Indian tribes, government officials, rascals and saints, the inevitable pretty girls (white and Indian alike). Social conditions, perceptions about democracy, advice to the army about dealing with the aborigines (the Indians were like a sort of Bedawin to Burton), lists of routes and way stops, the legal system and frontier justice, analyses of raw materials and alkaline waters, the sources of rivers, the weather, soil conditions—it is mid-century America in five hundred pages and appendixes and rarely dull.

At last, on August twenty-fifth, having "accomplished not less than 1136 statute miles," the stage arrived at Salt Lake City. There was only one hotel, the Salt Lake House. "In the Far West one learns not to expect much of the hostelry," Burton wrote, though it was the first decent accommodation he had encountered since leaving St. Jo's. "We looked in vain for a bar on the ground floor . . . the usual tempting array of bottles and decanters was not forthcoming." What a blow to a drinking man! Worse, the rooms were separated by thin partitions only. Burton might as well have been back in a Parsi-run hotel in Fort Bombay. As in India, there were compensations: a language teacher appeared to instruct him in Ute, but the effort seems to have been merely routine, for he passed by the usual learned digressions on the language and its structure, cognates, and vocabulary.

He was now in the midst of strange religionists for whom, contrary to expectations, he had strong sympathies. Though their doctrines were of a sort that ordinarily would have aroused his most outspoken hostilities, criticism, and sarcasm, he was most tolerant, and for an outsider, very understanding. Of the strange and mysterious work known as the *Book of Mormon*, on which the doctrines of the Church of Jesus Christ of Latter-day Saints are based, he had a most charitable and uncritical view, and his summary of its history is most objective. As is widely known, the Mormons state that the work, in the form of a mysterious script on golden tablets, was revealed to an upstate New York farm boy, Joseph Smith, who "translated" the writings with the help of certain mysterious spectacles believed to be from the breastplate of the high priest Aaron. Whereas skeptics like Mark Twain could damn the scripture with irony, sarcasm, and ridicule, Burton saw it as a valid religious testament—had he not enough experience in exotic religions to appreciate genius and inspiration when he saw them? Quickly he came to know as much and more of Mormonism as the average Mormon. He had to acknowledge, however, that there was, as with certain other faiths, "an inner life into which I cannot flatter myself or deceive the reader with the idea of having penetrated." What a sad admission, however honest, after the successes of India and Mecca!

Burton had asked for a meeting with Brigham Young, the successor to the martyred Joseph Smith, and one was granted. Burton found Young to be a vigorous, highly intelligent man, clearly in control of the church and its people, and what to Burton was most impressive, "He shows no signs of dogmatism, bigotry, or fanaticism, and never once entered—with me at least—upon the subject of religions."

This "affable and impressive, simple and courteous man" showed a "want of pretension [which] contrasts favorably with certain pseudo-prophets that I have seen [apparently in India and Arabia], each and every one of whom holds himself to be a 'Logos' without other claim save a semi-maniacal self-esteem." Young's life was "ascetic; his favorite food is baked potatoes with a little buttermilk . . ." and he abstained from hard liquor and tobacco. "He has been called hypocrite, swindler, forger, murderer." But, Burton added, "no one looks it less." Of Young's secular powers, Burton compared him with the head of the Assassins, "the Old Man of the Mountain." Young "stood up to fight with the sword of the Lord, and with his few hundred guerillas, against the mighty power of the United States."

Young knew of Burton's travels in Africa and could point out the area of exploration on a wall map, much to Burton's delight and pleasure. "The Prophet is no common man," he concluded.

It was inevitable that Burton look into the practice of polygamy, then so common among Mormons and so widely criticized by outsiders. He thought polygamy among Mormons came down to two issues: There were more women than men among them, and "servants are rare and costly: it is cheaper and more comfortable to marry them." There was so much heavy manual labor in the western household that a single woman could not do it all. However, though he could understand the practical reasons, Burton seemed to find aspects of Mormonism and of polygamy not to his liking.

> At Great Salt Lake City there is a gloom like that which . . . the invading Moslems [cast] over the innocent gayety of the primitive Hindoo. The choice egotism of the heart called Love . . . subsides into a calm and unimpassioned domestic attachment; romance and reverence [are] transferred . . . from love and liberty to religion and the Church.

But because of the Mormons, the "Utah Territory has been successful in its colonization." The emigrants, largely from the British Isles, have gained much by going to the Far West, he thought, and he expressed a touch of compassion for the lower levels of English society notably lacking in his earlier works.

> Mormonism is emphatically the faith of the poor, and those acquainted with the wretched condition of the English mechanic, collier, and agricultural laborer—it is calculated that a million of them exist on £25 per annum—who, after a life of ignoble drudgery, of toiling the year from morning to night, are ever threatened with the work-house, must be, of the same opinion. Physically speaking, there is no comparison between the conditions of the Saints and the class from which they are mostly taken. . . . When wealth shall be less unequally distributed in England, thus doing away with the contrast of excessive splendor and utter destitution, and when Home Missions have done their duty in educating and evangelizing the unhappy pariahs of town and country, the sons of the land which boasts herself to be the foremost among the nations will blush no more to hear that the Mormons or Latter-Day Saints are mostly English.

It was time to leave the Saints. Burton's traveling companions from St. Jo's were to join him on the journey to Carson City and San Francisco. After much haggling with the local drivers, not unlike that with camel drivers in Arabia, the party found "a

Ras kafila," a Mr. Kennedy, who was driving a herd of horses and mules and some wagons to San Francisco and who agreed to a fee of $150 per passenger.

Ahead, Burton noted with some anticipation, lay possible trouble with the Indians. "It was the beginning of the hungry season, when the Indians would be collecting their pine nuts and be plotting onslaughts upon the spring emigrants."

He forestalled a possible scalping by having his head shaved but regretted not having wigs, as when he went to India. He had a last round of drinks with newly made friends—"a cocktail whose aroma still lingers in my olfactories"—and "a *café au lait* as good as the *Café de Paris* affords," and said farewells all around. "All my adieux were upon an extensive scale, my immediate future being somewhat dark and menacing."

The stage bivouacked at Frogtown, then passed five days at Camp Floyd, an army post, where Burton learned "that in former times in Western America as in British India, a fair [female] aborigine was not infrequently the copartner of an officer's hut or tent." And conditions were not dissimilar. "The Indian squaw, like the Beebee, seldom looked upon her [man] in any other light but her banker." And, as in India, the officer had to support all her relations and friends and even her tribe. On the other side, "officers who were long thrown among the Prairie Indians joined, as did the Anglo-Indians, in their nautches and other amusements," and, as Burton had done, became Indian. "The skin was painted white, black and red, the hair was dressed and decorated . . . and a skin shirt, broadcloth blanket, legging and moccasins completed the costume." But now, in the 1860s, as in India, improved communications and "the frequency of marriage" with white women had changed the situation, rendering it unfashionable, but such a life had had its day and, as in British India, had sunk "many a fathom deep, in the general Anglo-Saxon gloom."

The party had now acquired some apostate Mormons, some fleeing for having violated Mormon rules of sexual conduct.

The stage passed through sites whose names Burton was pleased to recall—Lost Springs, Fish Springs, The Devil's Hole, Willow Creek, Deep Creek, Robber's Roost, Ruby Valley—into cold and snow. They found a burned-out house, some charred posts, and a lone chimney, the remnants of an Indian attack in revenge for the slaughter of seventeen Utes by an army detachment. Everyone was sure the Indians would attack again, but after a night in severe cold and snow, no attack came, and the wagons set off. This brief view of Indian warfare served to light Burton's insatiable curiosity, and shortly he had a well-researched chapter—his sources were his fellow travelers—about the Indians in the areas they had passed through, broken down into tribes and families, with his opinions formed, sadly, not by experience but by the prejudices of his companions.

"Chokop's" Pass, Dry Creek, Simpson's Park, and other settlements came and went—the names were not so interesting now—and then they were in Carson City. "Three murders in three days," Burton noted, and full of "legal vultures—attorneys, lawyers, and judges. . . . In and about Carson City a dead man for breakfast was the rule."

By now a certain weariness has overcome him; in fact, his book is too long for some readers and has become so for the author, knowing that he has overloaded his manuscript with details, facts, opinions, advice, statistics, charts, and tables. "I trespass on the reader's patience for a few pages more," he writes in apology. Carson City is soon disposed of. He tried his hand at panning for gold and went on to Sacramento and San Francisco, where he spent "ten pleasant days." Here at last he felt truly exhausted. He did some sightseeing, "but in truth I was aweary of the way," and the best he can do is give a list of the people who had entertained him. He was indeed aweary, for he refused to lecture on Mecca and El-Medina. On November fifteenth he boarded the *Golden Age*, and steamed out of San Francisco and down the Mexican coast to Acapulco, "where any lurking project of passing through ill-conditioned Mexico was finally dispelled." On December fifth he debarked at Panama for three days; here he found another hotel reminding him of Bombay in this "horribly wet, dull, and dirty" town, where, however, he met "a charming countrywoman, whose fascinating society made me regret my stay there could not be protracted." But he was eager to return to Isabel. By the ninth of December he was aboard ship again, passing through the islands of the West Indies, and at last he reached England, where a gale and pea-soup fog kept the ship from anchoring for three days. But he had returned in good health and fine spirits, presumably having worked out in his mind what to do about Isabel and the Arundells. Still, nine months had passed, time was afleeting, and the impasse had to be broken, forcibly if necessary.

23

Victoria's Lake

Meanwhile, the great Nile drama moved into a second and ultimately tragic act. Speke had quickly mapped out the broad plan of his expedition. He had arranged to have John Petherick, the honorary vice-consul at Khartoum, a strange town in the Sudan, meet him on the northern side of Uganda at a place on the Nile called Gondoroko, a thousand miles south of Khartoum. Petherick would wait for Speke with fresh supplies, medicines, and some of the comforts of England. Speke had no money for Petherick, so a popular subscription of £1,000 was raised for supplies. With his new wife, Kate, and an adventurous young Scottish doctor, James Murie, Petherick set off for Khartoum, from where, at the proper time, they would go south to Gondoroko. At Khartoum, awaiting the arrival of the consul, was an American, Clarence Brownell, also a doctor, who had vague plans of walking "across" Africa. Brownell soon died of a fever, virtually unknown.

Along with his new partner, Captain James Augustus Grant,

Speke left Southampton on April 27, 1860, for Zanzibar. He had originally hoped that Edmund Smyth would be his partner, but Smyth, for whatever reasons, did not join him. He may have been alarmed by the battles with Burton, or he may have preferred to return to Tibet. With Smyth's refusal, Speke had turned to Grant, a Scot, who had little said about him other than that he was "dull." Grant was a tireless traveler, was Speke's age, and had served in the Indian army since the age of nineteen, fighting, as Speke had, in the Sikh wars; he was wounded in the relief of Lucknow in the Mutiny of 1857 and was invalided out of the army. His dullness implied absolute loyalty to superiors: he did not question orders, but the more aggressive and intelligent Smyth might have been a better and more resourceful partner. Speke found Grant an ideal subordinate, but Grant would have driven Burton into continual rages.

Much as Speke counted on Grant's sterling qualities, he may have made a serious error; with the lessons of the first expedition behind him, he should have expanded the personnel of the expedition for both safety and efficiency and to share the many burdens. It had been only bad luck that prevented the first expedition from having four whites as officers. Speke had learned nothing from not having a doctor on the first safari, and an officer with some knowledge of African languages would have been invaluable. But he believed that nothing was impossible for him. He was still weak in languages, not having Arabic and being confined to his barracks Hindustani and a smattering of Swahili he picked up late on the first expedition. Still, off he went, blithely, confidently, basking in the acclaim he had received in London. Was he not the discoverer of the source of the Nile?

Because direct transportation to Zanzibar was not available at the time Speke chose to leave, the two explorers had to take a roundabout route through the South Atlantic. They stopped first at Rio de Janeiro, then crossed to Capetown, South Africa. Here Speke, having decided that the Baluchis on the first trip had not been reliable, hired to replace them a detachment of Hottentots. At Zanzibar, where Rigby was still consul, Speke and Grant assembled their expedition, some two hundred men as porters, including the faithful Sidi Bombay Mubarak. Speke and Grant set out in October, reaching Kazeh (Kase in Speke's attempt to stand apart from and correct Burton) on January 24, 1861. All along, the expedition had been plagued by the usual problems of illness, demands by the villagers and the chiefs for *hongo*, strikes by the *pagazis*, and constant pilfering and desertion. But Speke and Grant moved doggedly ahead, and by October 1861 had reached the southwest shore of the Victoria N'yanza. Speke, having thought out the problem with some care, had decided to go up the western shore of the lake. Before them was a vast, cruel, and enigmatic land, the kingdom of Uganda. Whereas Burton might have moved on with a full appreciation of the dangers to be encountered, Speke plunged on very much the Englishman, the white man among natives he considered inferior. The mysterious lands ahead had never before seen a white face: in fact, they had rarely been visited even by Arab slavers, and the three major kingdoms on the western shore of the N'yanza—Karagwe, Buganda, and Bunyoro—and the smaller tribal areas were greatly feared by other Africans. The three kingdoms, especially Buganda, were rich and far advanced in contrast to other sections of black Africa. They had developed in isolation and were governed and ruled with unmatched cruelty. The great territory of Uganda, wrote a later British administrator, Sir John Gray, had a history like "a crime to which there are no witnesses." Still, unlike so much of black Africa, they bore a certain patina of civilization that was to astound Europeans later, with well-organized bureaucracies, statesmanship of a superior order, finely developed arts and architecture, and unusual handicrafts—baskets woven of rushes and reeds were so finely made that they could hold water. But the kingdoms had no alphabets, no means of counting, no calendar. Their high level of culture had a dark side: for generations, as far as the genealogists could recount, they had been ceaselessly and unnaturally cruel and barbaric, traits that were taken as a matter of course by rulers and subjects alike. In Buganda, the biggest and wealthiest of the three, the recently crowned King Mutesa killed his own people as casually as one might step on an insect. He had attained the throne early in 1860 and to ensure his own survival had burned his brothers alive—there were sixty in all. But any of them would have done the same. Despite his cruel nature, Mutesa was intelligent, charming, and a statesman.

Speke and Grant first entered Karagwe, on the southern shore of the Victoria N'yanza. The king, a large, friendly man named Rumanika, was anxious to avoid trouble with his more powerful neighbors to the north and ruled with an eye to their pleasure or displeasure. At Karagwe, Speke came across an interesting custom, one that more than others attracted his attention and was to bring some ribald comments when he described it in *Journal of the Discovery of the Source of the Nile*. What was to intrigue the public was not the author's accounts of Africa and its flora and fauna and his hunting exploits but—in his second work—his sexual interests. Burton needed only to hint obscurely, and the public understood. Speke, having presented himself in almost virginal terms, now felt compelled to show himself as something of a rake, and it was these passages that got him remembered, denounced, and ridiculed.

In Rumanika's harem the women were force-fed with milk until they were so fat they could no longer stand; if they resisted food, they were whipped into eating. It occurred to Speke that in the interests of science—though his critics doubted that scientific observation was foremost in his mind—he measure the girth and height of the queen and one of her maids. The queen's chest, Speke recorded, was four feet two inches, her thigh two feet seven inches, and her calf one foot eight inches. Accompanying the queen was her daughter, stark naked. Speke always seemed to have been prudish about the nude body, but "I got up a bit of flirtation with Missy, and induced her to rise and shake hands with me. Her features were lovely, but her body was as round as a ball."

While Speke was measuring the royal beauties, Grant developed a massive ulcer on his leg and was confined to his hut. Rumanika had warned Speke that he must not proceed into Buganda until King Mutesa had formally invited him. Speke waited three months for his messengers to return with the invitation. It arrived on January 8, 1862. Grant's leg had not healed, and Speke set off without him, though he might have had his companion carried in a hammock, as was done for himself and for Burton on the first safari, but he sensed that something important lay ahead and he was reluctant to share it. Alone he went into the most murderous of Central African kingdoms, with only the most rudimentary information about it, to meet the dreaded Mutesa.

During the six weeks' march to the king's court, Speke came within sight of the Victoria N'yanza. He felt more certain than before that the lake was a vast inland sea and that, more important, it was the source of the Nile. Still, he did nothing to explore the lake or to confirm it as the body of water whence the great river flowed.

On February nineteenth he arrived at the Buganda capital. To impress the Bugandans, he put on his best uniform and had his men dress in red blankets. He assembled a collection of gifts for the king and proceeded to the palace. But rain fell, and the reception was canceled. The next day, he set forth again for the palace, with his bodyguard carrying the Union Jack. At the palace Speke was informed that another delegation had been given precedence. In a rage, he turned about, refusing to wait in the burning sun, and returned to his own hut, about a mile away. Such behavior had never before been seen in Buganda. Normally it would have brought torture and death, but the king's courtiers came running after Speke to say it had been a mistake. Mutesa would see him immediately, and what was more, he would be allowed to *sit* in the king's presence on his own chair.

At the palace there was a flurry of activity. A royal band of five-stringed harps and shawms was playing, and Speke was brought into the august and very imposing presence of the king. Speke had his chair set before Mutesa and sat down. What was to happen next?

Nothing happened. Speke and the king sat facing each other for an hour, each man staring at the other without a word passing between them, though from time to time Mutesa made comments to his courtiers about the white man, or his umbrella, and occasionally took a sip of banana beer. At last a courtier approached Speke and asked, had he seen the king? "Yes," said Speke, "for one full hour." When this was translated, Mutesa got up and walked away from the royal chamber on his toes, in a stiff-legged stride that was supposed to resemble the gait of a lion. The king had delayed eating that day until he had seen his visitor, and now he ate alone—an act of courtesy, it was explained to Speke—and then, as the sun was setting, he returned and he and Speke exchanged presents. The king gave his distinguished and somewhat puzzling guest cattle, goats, fish, fowls, and some Buganda delicacies—porcupines and rats. In exchange, Speke presented the king with several rifles, ammunition, a gold watch, an iron chair, beads, silk cloth, knives, spoons, and forks, and a telescope. That was the end of the day, and Speke went back to his hut, tired but self-satisfied. At another meeting there came an incident that was disturbing to Speke as well as to his readers. To demonstrate his "magic," Speke shot four cows with his pistol. (One was merely wounded and charged him; he finished it off with a second shot.) The king now gave a loaded carbine to a page and told him to shoot a certain man in the outer court, which he did. "The affair created hardly any interest," remarked Speke. But every day he had to shoot a cow, or the king would shoot vultures and other creatures and a human or two.

Speke, who seemed the height of Victorian respectability (he called his trousers "unmentionables"), now showed a prurient interest in the Bugandan women. He was to say that Mutesa "detained" him from proceeding on his quest for the Nile. Speke was but a few miles from the Victoria N'yanza, he seemed to have freedom of movement, but not once during his stay in Buganda did he make an effort to explore further. His failure to do so was to bring criticism later. What was he doing with his time? One reason, and perhaps the most important, for not looking for the sources of the great river was that at this point in his life he had begun to "dally" with native girls. Mutesa sent him a woman to "carry his water." Speke sent her away because she was ugly. He was sent a prettier girl, and then another, and eventually he would turn them over to the most favored members of his safari. Speke described the women in offhand terms, as if he were being forced into the relationships. "Young virgins" were "stark naked, and smeared with grease . . ." he wrote. "For decency's sake" they would often carry a small square of bark cloth, the *mbugu*, in their hands to cover the pelvic area. The queen mother, "fair, fat, and forty-five," took to Speke, and there seems to have been some kind of romance between them. The queen, a woman of power and importance, had her own palace apart from Mutesa's, where she led a happy but dissolute life, being rarely sober, drinking *pombe* in great quantities, and smoking and dancing the day away. She complained to Speke of pains in her stomach and of bad dreams. Speke gave her medicines from his own stock and advised her to give up *pombe*, advice the queen ignored, and one day Speke found her and her attendants on all fours swilling *pombe* from a trough. Speke was unable to keep himself from the orgy—that perhaps was understandable—but that he should write about it was something many of his readers could not comprehend.

The queen mother, too, sent Speke women to "carry his water"—how that phrase must have entertained Victorian England!—among them two quite attractive young teenagers. The queen, it seemed, was interested in knowing what color the offspring would be if the white man fathered a child. It was a most delicate situation, and Speke becomes quite evasive about it in his writings, acting the prim Victorian but hinting that he fulfilled his manly, even fatherly, duties, after which he turned the girls over to Sidi Bombay. Speke indeed had fathered a child—how pleased the queen mother must have been to see its color! Among whites in colonial lands "everyone" had native girls rather openly (and some white women had native men, very secretly); that Speke was so crass about the matter was embarrassing to his readers, and to abandon them, once used, to his porters was most un-British. Such information, gratuitously dropped into his book, seems as if he were attempting to counter the very disturbing rumors that circulated about his friendship with Laurence Oliphant.

Three months after Speke had settled down in Buganda with the drunken queen mother and his nubile young women, Grant arrived, limping slightly from his leg infection but ready to push ahead. Mutesa was not eager to let his visitors go, he liked having two white men at hand to entertain him. He stalled and lied before he would release them—they would next visit a rival, King Kamrasi in Bunyoro—but on July seventh, Speke and Grant were able to set out, heading east to the shores of the great lake, at last free of Mutesa—if the chief were ever a true warder: we have only Speke's version of the situation. Speke and Grant now had knowledgeable guides and porters, thanks to the king's generosity. However, the guides led them farther north than they had anticipated. The lake, with its promise of the sacred Source, was said to be to the southeast. Speke and Grant conferred, and the decision they made has always puzzled geographers, historians, friends, and biographers. Grant, it was decided, would go to the court of King Kamrasi at Bunyoro, while Speke would look for the river that was said to flow from the lake and could only be, in his mind, the true source of the Nile. But there was in fact no need to send Grant away except to deprive him of a share in the final discovery. On July twenty-eighth Speke found the river he had been told about. It was running out of the lake, and Speke assumed—correctly, it was realized later—that the stream would become the Nile. But it was a discovery without documentation, without scientific study, without proof. Speke and Grant then headed north with the intention of following the "Nile" to the Mediterranean, but to save time and their limited strength, they cut across vast sections of jungle far from the river. When they once again came to flowing water, they confidently assumed it was the same river they had followed earlier, the upper reaches of the Nile. But was it? Intuition, not proof, was their only standard, and intuition, as Burton, Macqueen, and other skeptics would point out, was no substitute for fact.

24

Santa Isabel

Speke's Great African Drama was being matched by an equally fascinating romantic drama at home. Burton, health restored, mind clear, heart burning with love, had come home from the States determined to marry Isabel Arundell no matter what. It was now Christmas, 1860. Isabel was spending the holidays with relatives in the country.

> There was a large party in the house, and we were singing; someone propped up the music with the Times which had just arrived, and the first announcement that caught my eye was that "Captain R. F. Burton had arrived from America."

Isabel could no longer concentrate on the carols. She retreated to her room. What to do? She "sat up all night, packing, and conjecturing" how to get away. Two letters arrived. One had been opened and read by somebody else and been "burked at home before forwarding." How to get to Richard? She was with twenty-five relatives and friends, and she had "heaps of luggage."

The roads were blocked with snow, and the house was nine miles from the station. "It was not an easy matter," but she managed to have a telegram sent her ordering her home. "What a triumph it is to a woman's heart, when she has patiently and courageously worked, and prayed, and suffered, and the moment is realized that was the goal of her ambition!"

"As soon as we met, and had our talk," she said in the *Life,* Burton said to her,

> I have waited for five years. The first three were inevitable on account of my journey to Africa, but the last two were not. Our lives are being spoiled by the unjust prejudices of your mother, and it is for you to consider whether you have not already done your duty in sacrificing two of the best years of your life out of respect to her.

He gave Isabel an ultimatum: If she let him go, he would never come back, "because I shall know that you have not got the strength of character which *my* wife must have." She had to choose between her mother and him. If they did not marry, he would go back to India and on other expeditions. "Is your answer ready?" he asked. "Quite," said Isabel, "I shall marry you this day three weeks, let who will say nay."

There were still difficulties of a type that two intelligent but very superstitious people encounter. Isabel wanted to marry on Wednesday, the twenty-third, "because it was the espousal of our Lady and St. Joseph," but Burton would not, because "Wednesday, the 23rd and Friday, the 18th, were our unlucky days; so we were married on the Vigil, Tuesday, the 22nd of January."

Isabel went straight to her parents to tell them. Mr. Arundell said, "I consent with all my heart, if your mother consents." Mother said, *"Never!"* The brothers and sisters said they would welcome Burton with delight. Mrs. Arundell offered a compromise of sorts: The Arundell men might attend the wedding; she and her daughters would not. Isabel thought it was a slight not only upon Burton but upon his family and hers. She refused. She went to see the very understanding Nicholas Cardinal Wiseman and explained the situation. The Cardinal asked her if her mind was "absolutely" made up. She replied, "Absolutely!" He then called Burton in and asked that he give three promises in writing: that Isabel should be allowed the free practice of her religion, that their children be brought up Catholics, and that Burton and Isabel be married in the Catholic Church. Burton remarked later, "Practice her religion indeed! I should rather think she *shall.* A man without a religion may be excused, but a woman without a religion is not the woman for me." A special dispensation for a mixed marriage was immediately obtained from Rome, and Isabel set about the preparations for her wedding.

During this period Mrs. Arundell was indulging in histrionics. She feared she would be struck with paralysis should the marriage take place; she must have "no shocks, no agitation." A family council decided that to spare her, no one of them should attend the ceremonies, only friends, and that Mrs. Arundell would not be told of the marriage during her lifetime or until it seemed safe.

> I made a very solemn religious preparation, receiving the sacraments [wrote Isabel]. Gowns, presents, and wedding presents had no part in it, had no place. Richard arranged with my own lawyer and my own priest that everything should be conducted in a strictly legal and strictly religious way. . . . A very solemn day to me was the eve of my marriage.

It was not a marriage of great or even of moderate fortunes that might be expected in this upper stratum of English society. "I regret that I am bringing you no money," said Isabel, for she had no dowry under the circumstances. "That is not a disadvantage as far as I am concerned," said Burton, "for heiresses always expect to lord it over their lords."

Burton refused to have a showy wedding. "A grand marriage is a barbarous and an indelicate exhibition," he said.

On the morning of the ceremony Isabel was supposedly going to visit a friend in the country for a few weeks. At nine o'clock a cab arrived for her.

> I had to go and wish my father and mother good-bye before leaving. I went downstairs with a beating heart after I had knelt in my own room, and said a fervent prayer that they might bless me, and if they did, I would take it as a sign. I was so nervous I could scarcely stand. . . . Mother kissed me and said, "Good-bye, child, God bless you." I went to my father's bedside, and knelt down and said good-bye. "God bless you, my darling," [he said,] and put his hand . . . on my head. I was too much overcome to speak, and one or two tears ran down my cheeks, and I remember as I passed down I kissed the door outside.

The cab took Isabel to the home of close friends, Dr. George Bird and his sister Alice. Here she changed her clothes—"a fawn-coloured dress, a black-lace cloak, and a white bonnet." With the Birds, she drove off to the church of Our Lady of the Assumption on Warwick Street, popularly known as the Bavarian church because it served the Bavarian embassy. Burton was standing at the doorstep, wearing a rough shooting coat and nervously smoking a cigar. Papers had to be signed before the registrar—this was to be an important point in arguments over whether or not Burton was a Catholic, for if he were, there would have been no need for a secular registration. Then the wedding party walked through the church. There was rather a large crowd attending the ten-thirty daily Mass, many of whom knew both Burton and Isabel. As he entered the church, Burton took holy water and "made a very large sign of the Cross." The party went into the sacristy and learned that during the night Cardinal Wiseman had been taken ill and the vicar-general, Monsignor Hearne, would perform the Catholic matrimonial rites. As the Burtons left the church, Isabel recalled to mind Gypsy Hagar and her couched eyes and her prophecy that she would bear the name "Burton." The breakfast party at the Birds' was a happy, jolly event, and everyone was relaxed. Burton was coaxed into recounting some grisly tales of his adventures in the Nejd and Somaliland, including the account of the fight at Berbera. Dr. Bird chaffered with him about what was true and what was not. "Now, Burton, tell me, how do you feel when you have killed a man?"

"Richard looked up quizzically," wrote Isabel, "and drawled out, 'Oh, quite jolly, doctor! how do you?' "

After the wedding luncheon the newlyweds walked down to Burton's apartment, where Isabel's boxes had been sent. Burton immediately wrote a note to Mr. Arundell in his fine, delicate hand: "My dear Father, I have committed a highway robbery by marrying your daughter Isabel, at Warwick Street Church, and before the Registrar. . . . It only remains to me to say that I have no ties or liaisons of any sort, that the marriage is perfectly legal and respectable. I want no money with Isabel: I can work, and it will be my care that Time shall bring you nothing to regret."

After forty years of independence, roving in primitive lands, and enjoying sexual freedom wherever he went, Burton seems to have been uneasy, even shy, about letting the world know of his marriage. "There is one thing I cannot do," he said to Isabel, "and that is, face congratulations, so, if you are agreeable, we will pretend that we have been married some months." But such matters were not easy to conceal. A few days later, his cousin, Dr. Edward J. Burton, said to him, "I am surprised to find that you are married."

"I am myself even more surprised than you," Burton answered. "Isabel is such a strong-willed woman, she was determined to have her way and she's got it."

"For the first days of our marriage," Isabel admitted, "Richard seemed to be worried about being stared at as a bridegroom . . . but that sort of annoyance wore off, and then he became rather proud of being a married man."

They were both transformed by marriage, each in a different

way. Burton worried, chafed, but Isabel was ecstatic. "To say that I was happy would be to say nothing; a repose came over me that I had never known." She was in "a bewilderment of wonder at the goodness of God, who almost worked miracles for me."

The marriage was kept from Mrs. Arundell, but rumors began to circulate, and at last Mr. Arundell told his wife, Isabel "was married to Dick Burton, and thank God for that."

"My mother behaved like a true lady and a true Christian," wrote Isabel. "She kissed us both, and blessed us." When she took Burton to her parents' home

> they received Richard in the nicest way, and then mother embarrassed us very much by asking our pardon for flying in the face of God, and opposing what she knew to be His Will. My husband was very much touched.

Such was Isabel's optimistic, romantic memory: "She loved him as much as her own sons." However happy the principals of the marriage were, critics invariably had their say. People like Thomas Wright and Georgiana Stisted said in print what many people believed and what was often passed as gossip. Wright did not care for Isabel, and he was not hesitant in saying so rather obliquely. Isabel Burton, though "a dream of beauty," was "of larger build than most women. . . . Her beauty, however, was of a rather coarse grain, and even those most attached to her remarked in her a certain lack of refinement." That Isabel was a Roman Catholic was a general criticism—the Catholic Emancipation Act of 1829 had not dissolved Protestant prejudices— and Isabel was always a fervent Catholic.

> The religious question [said Wright] often made unpleasantness between Mrs. Burton and Lady Stisted and her daughters—who were staunch Protestants of the Georgian and unyielding schools. . . . The trouble originated partly from Mrs. Burton's impulsiveness and want of tact. She could not help dragging in her religion at all sorts of unseasonable times. She would introduce into her conversation

and letters what a moment's reflection would have told her could only nauseate her Protestant friends. "The Blessed Virgin," or some holy saint or other was always intruding on the text.

Married . . . The first months, years, were strange, if not rocky. There were initially some seven months of relative normalcy imposed on a man who had rarely passed a month in any one place since early childhood except when confined by duty, prostrated by fever, or immersed in study and writing (and even then he was likely to pass from spot to spot like some restless bird unable to find a comfortable roost). Kipling in his short story "Miss Youghal's Sais" was shrewd in analyzing the situation through the means of his character Strickland, who had married

> on the strict understanding that [he] should drop his old ways, and stick to Departmental routine, which pays best. . . . Strickland was far too fond of his wife . . . to break his word, but it was a sore trial for him; for the streets and the bazars, and the sounds in them, were full of meaning to Strickland, and these called him to come back and take up his wanderings, and his discoveries. . . . [Now] he is forgetting the slang, and the beggar's cant, and the marks, and the signs, and the drift of the under-currents, which, if a man could master, he must always continue to learn.

And what would not be normalcy for a woman who has spent the last eleven years yearning, pining for her "earthly god," living in a kind of dream world that had suddenly come true? These first months are filled, in the various accounts, with the trivia, though often interesting trivia, about a couple trying to adjust to each other and to a society that did not quite know how to place them. It was trivia of a sort that served to highlight the vagaries of the newlyweds, and if people like Wright had not recorded them, these tidbits of information would long ago have disappeared. Isabel generally called her husband "Dick," but often, especially in letters, he was "The Bird," and, "Often, however, for no reason at all, she called him 'Jemmy.' " (This last name may have been Isabel's identification of Burton with the Sufi poet Jāmī.) Of their domestic habits at the time Wright can add only this:

> Burton took a pleasure in sitting up late. "Indeed," says one of his friends, "he could talk all night in preference to going to bed, and, in the Chaucerian style, he was a brilliant conversationalist, and his laugh was like the rattle of a pebble across a frozen pond." "No man of sense," Burton used to say, "rises, except in mid-summer, before the world is brushed and broomed, aired and sunned." Later, however, he changed his mind, and for the last twenty years of his life he was an early riser.

On his return from the States, Burton had been invited to a breakfast by Monckton Milnes in London. It was a bachelor affair, a not uncommon event; Mrs. Milnes had taken the children to the country. Among the guests were Algernon Swinburne and Coventry Patmore. This was the first time that Burton had met Swinburne, then twenty-three. Swinburne had just published some remarkable dramas, *The Queen Mother* and *Rosamond*, which had already made his reputation.

The young poet was a strange creature, and he made an impression on everyone he met. Henry Adams, who was a year younger than Swinburne, met him at Fryston in 1862 and thought at first he was a young boy. It was a strange group at the breakfast— Oliphant with his arm in a sling after being wounded in an attack on the British legation in Japan, the oddest of all being Swinburne, whom Adams was to describe as resembling "a tropical bird, high crested, long-beaked, quick-moving, with rapid utterance and screams of humor quite unlike an English lark or nightingale. One could hardly call him a crimson macaw among owls, yet no ordinary contrast availed." What Adams quickly learned was that Swinburne was a nonstop talker, "quite original, wildly eccentric." He added, "The idea that one has actually met a real genius dawns slowly on a Boston mind, but it made its entry at last." Mrs. Milnes did not particularly care for the young poet: he had the habit of outstaying other guests and could stay on at Fryston even after the Milnes family had returned to London. "Left Mr. Swinburne at Fryston with Aunties," wrote Annabel Milnes on one occasion.

It seemed inevitable that the rake of the Orient be connected—in gossip, at least—with a younger man of Swinburne's notoriety, and such was done, much to the further harm of Burton's reputation. James Pope-Hennessy lamented "the melodramatic light in which Milnes' introduction of Burton to Swinburne has been placed by the imaginative biographers of the poet." Supposition led to gossip as "fact." That Swinburne had an immediate and deep crush on Burton is well known. The poet disliked traveling (and actually hated the Mediterranean, that favorite haunt of the English), and here before him was a man who had lived and traveled "everywhere." That Swinburne and Burton got drunk together is hardly a surprise. Burton was a heavy drinker, and Swinburne got tipsy on a single drink.

Milnes, now Lord Houghton, took in the Burtons and formally introduced them to English society. Lord Palmerston gave a party, at which Isabel was "the bride of the evening." Lady Russell presented her at Court, and the Burtons' position in society was settled.

> We passed delightful days in country houses, notably at Lord Houghton's [Isabel wrote], and at Lord Strangford's house in Great Cumberland Place, we met all that was worth meeting of rank and fashion, beauty and wit, and *especially* all the most talented people in the world.

Madame Mary Mohl, an Englishwoman by birth married to a Frenchman, and a follower of Florence Nightingale's, told of a great weekend party at Fryston attended by the painter Holman Hunt, Swinburne, Francis Turner Palgrave—one of Burton's special dislikes—and various unattached women. The Burtons arrived after the party was well under way, and they fascinated everyone. Madame Mohl left a simple macaronic, unpunctuated impression of them.

> se sint distribues les roles he acts a ferocious musselman [Muslim] to her lovely oppressed and impassioned slave and I suspect they chuckle over our simplicity instead of fighting in their secret compartment and if she told you he had beat her I would believe it unhesitatingly.

One of the occasional guests at Fryston was the Hungarian linguist and adventurer Arminius Vambéry, a man as brave and as inquisitive as Burton, a master of obscure languages and fearless in traveling in parts of the world where a white face could bring death. As a young man, he had wandered throughout Turkey and into Central Asia, seeing and recording scenes of wild barbarity. Burton's rivalry with Vambéry was not friendly, despite Isabel's blasé statements.

> I can remember Vambéry telling us Hungarian tales, and I can remember Richard sitting crosslegged on a cushion, reciting and reading "Omar el Khayyam" alternately in Persian and English, and chanting the call to prayer, "Allahu Akhbar."

Vambéry not only knew Omar Khayyám's quatrains as well as Burton—the Edward FitzGerald version of the *Rubáiyát* had recently appeared, and the poet was an immediate Victorian favorite—but both men had read and studied the Persian manuscripts years earlier, Vambéry being as well grounded in Sufi mystical works as Burton. However, Burton saw in Vambéry not a fellow scholar but a rival in exotic fields, and the two men remained cool toward one another in all their meetings.

Burton had hoped, even expected, that because of his exceptional service to the Crown over some nineteen years, during which his trips, expeditions, books, and secret reports had helped bring vast areas of Asia and Africa to the attention of his government, he might be given a challenging diplomatic post somewhere. He had always been interested in serving as consul at

Damascus, but the only post open at the moment was that at Fernando Po, an isolated, forsaken island in the Bight of Biafra on the African west coast, one (of many) known as a "white man's grave." The previous consul had just been dismissed for "irregularities." There were no other applicants. "Everyone admitted his immense brain power," wrote Thomas Wright, "but those mysterious rumours due to his inquiries concerning secret Eastern habits and customs dogged him like some terrible demon."

Isabel would not be stopped by such stories. She was adamant, unbending, and insatiable in the defense of her husband. She wanted the public to see Richard Burton as she saw him, and to some extent she succeeded, writing letters to everyone who mattered, to friends, to the press, to high officials, even to enemies, wheedling, bullying, threatening. "She was often woefully indiscreet," remarked Wright. Damascus was impossible; it had to be Fernando Po. Some of Isabel's friends persuaded Lord Russell, the Foreign Secretary, to give Burton the post. The consulship carried with it a salary of £700 annually and the promise of fevers and death. Fernando Po was, in truth, no great honor. With some luck it would finish off Burton, for like so many similar posts, it was a place where a man's energies were consumed in keeping himself alive. "They want me to die," said Burton with bitterness, "but I intend to live, to spite the devils."

He got himself together, books, writing materials, tropical clothing, medicines, a stock of drugs, including opium and War-burg's drops, brandies, and all the other paraphernalia that experience had taught him was necessary for life in a primitive land. He made rounds of farewells, gave speeches, and attended social gatherings, but the somewhat ambiguous partings, cheerful and saddening, were marred by a great tragedy, the loss of his priceless collection of manuscripts put together over the years in India, Sind and the Punjab, the Arab countries, and East Africa. They had been stored at Grindlay's warehouse in London: a fire destroyed everything, along with numerous mementoes and artifacts, Oriental clothing, and dozens of other treasures. One special loss was a Turkish edition of the *Arabian Nights*, which he had treasured for the day when he could begin his translation of the great Middle Eastern work. When the Grindlay clerk learned that no jewels or rare metals were lost, he remarked that the loss was apparently minor. Burton appeared calm on the surface, but from time to time a great sigh would come forth. What a tragedy!

There was another blow, also. In 1861 the Indian army passed from control of the East India Company to that of the Crown; the events of the Mutiny had brought major changes in the administration of the subcontinent. It had been common in the past that Indian officers be allowed to accept Foreign Office appointments and still remain on the cadre of their regiments. Burton, when he accepted the post at Fernando Po, had not taken the sensible precaution of ascertaining whether or not he might retain his commission. He was summarily dropped from the army lists without a hearing. That he had done great deeds and was likely to do more meant nothing. His was a household name, but the men he had antagonized could not forgive him. Burton's rank would be permanently "captain," as lesser men outdistanced him. What more crushing blow could there be for the man who had spied out Sind and the Punjab, had successfully penetrated forbidden Mecca and secret Harar and survived the heart of blackest Africa, who had—as he so often boasted—mastered twenty-nine languages, than to strip him of his future in the army as he went off to moulder in a tropical outpost?

There was no doubt that conditions at Fernando Po were disastrous for whites. Though Isabel had gained the post for her husband, the price was that she could not accompany him.

They went to Liverpool together, where he was to take ship, and on August 24, 1861, after "a heart wrench" and a tight embrace, Burton boarded the *Blackbird* and was off to the wilderness of West Africa. It was the kind of parting that Burton, outwardly so bluff and unsentimental, had never before experienced. Whereas in the past he had slipped away quietly, he now had all the sorrows of a parting in public with a woman he loved with all passion. "Unhappily," wrote Burton, "I am not one of those independents who can say *ce n'est que le premier pas qui coûte.*" But he seems to have been shattered. He could not, would not, take his bride with him to entombment in the tropics. Isabel went off to her parents, and Burton was left with his memories. That Isabel had truly become part of his life was obvious in a statement he made about the women of Teneriffe—the ship was to stop at twenty-four ports on the way south—and Burton went ashore at each for some sightseeing and "wandered about the streets seeking *l'aventure.*"

> For those who admire black everywhere except "in the skin" there is nothing more enchanting than the women of Tenerife. . . . I will confess that one soon wearies of black eyes and black hair, and that after a course of such charms, one falls back with pleasure upon brown, yellow, or, what is better than all, red-auburn locks and eyes of limpid blue.

That he remained more or less faithful to Isabel seems likely, even possible, for the records of the African years show him obsessed with intellectual pursuits as a distraction from sexual encounters.

The African period reveals Burton at his most truculent. He was bitter, angry, black mooded, and he poured out his fury on the Africans wherever he encountered them. It was very much the age of white supremacy, and the darker a man's skin was, the lower he was supposed to be in God's creation. Burton's forte was using his talents to express vitriolic prejudices. He had little good to say about the black people of West Africa—"No humane Englishman would sell his dog to a negro"—and those that escaped his bile were those converted to Islam; the Christians were to him more rascally and rapacious than the simple animists. He fulminated regularly at Negro "insolence" and was incensed to learn that at Accra it was against the law to call a man a "nigger."

After seeing the Juju or sacrifice houses at the Grand Bonny River, he wrote:

> There is apparently in this people a physical delight in cruelty to beasts as well as to men. The sight of suffering seems to bring them an enjoyment without which the world is tame; probably the wholesale murderers and torturers of history, from Phalaris and Nero downwards, took an animal and sensual pleasure in the look of blood, and in the inspection of mortal agonies. I can see no other explanation of the phenomena which meet my eye in Africa. In almost all the towns on the Oil Rivers, you see dead or dying animals in some agonizing position.

Though he had shared his meals with the *pagazis* on the safari through Central Africa, he was incensed when blacks were allowed to eat in the first-class cabin of the *Blackbird*. "A ruling race cannot be too particular about these small matters." He thought, also, that it was a mistake to work for the betterment of the Negro. He despised the blacks who had gone to England for education or for business reasons and had become Anglicized. Of the Muslims, particularly a group called the Mandengas, he said, "The honest and manly bearing of these Moslems—so wonderful a contrast with those caricatures in pork-pie and peg-topped broadcloth—had prepossessed me strongly in their favour."

The *Blackbird* plodded onward, halting at steaming ports to unload and load again, taking on passengers and discharging Negroes Burton was happy to see go ashore, stopping at ports seemingly without end. But he loved to record their names with his accustomed touch of the romantic—Bathurst, Sierra Leone, Monrovia, Grand Bassam, Cape Palmas, Half Jack, Grand Baltam, Axim, Elmina, Cape Coast Castle, Salt Pond, Winnebah, Accra, Addah, Quitta, and so on. Sierra Leone, the British settlement for freed slaves, was filled with "litigious niggers." At Lagos he found that his reputation as a Muslim had preceded him. He seems to have returned in part, if not fully, to Islam at this point, although he may not have been openly practicing the full ritual of ṣalāt, the prayers, in public. This focusing on Islam again may have been some kind of solace for his difficulties with the pestiferous bureaucracy at home and his separation from Isabel. The *Blackbird* annoyingly steamed past Fernando Po to Old Calabar and then returned on September twenty-sixth. The island was "the very abomination of desolation." It was a hell-hole. The consulate building was falling down. Burton's vocabulary fails: He cannot describe his mood except in terms he has used before—he felt "uncommonly suicidal" that first night at Fernando Po. He had arrived in the rainy season, and the climate was terrible—from May to November the rain fell "as a sheet of solid water," often accompanied by unnerving bursts of lightning and deafening peals of thunder.

There was a grave here of an Englishman—Burton still had that strange passion for visiting the resting places of deceased countrymen—Richard Lander, a Cornishman who had died there in 1834. Standing before the untidy grave, Burton meditated upon death, wondering if he, too, would perish in this dismal post.

In the capital, Santa Isabel, an unprepossessing town, the name of which did not seem to strike a sympathetic response, ennui consumed the populace. The whites were mostly Spaniards, pallid and enervated, who sat listlessly with their chairs propped against the walls of buildings or lolled about the verandas of their houses. The streets were white-hot. An air of pestilence floated everywhere. Burton had disliked the blacks encountered on his voyage south, but here he took a liking to the local people, the Bubes, who lived in wall-less sheds and went naked except for broad-brimmed hats worn as protection against falling tree snakes. Still, he often complained about their "insolence." When "a nigger dandy" entered the consulate and slapped him on the back with what he thought was overfamiliarity, he called his canoe men and said, "Hi, Kroo-boys, just throw this nigger out of the window, will you." The Kroo-boys threw the man headfirst into the street.

It was Sind and half a dozen other torrid, dismal lands again. If Burton was faithful to Isabel, we cannot tell; we must assume his fidelity, though there were occasions on the mainland that raise questions. But there was no hint of live-in búbús or bíbís of any race or color at Fernando Po. He seems to have been drunk all the time. How else was a man to pass the hours in such a place? In Sind he had sat under his worktable with wet sheets over it. Here he solved the problem of concentration with alcohol. Wright found a description of Burton at Fernando Po, thanks to a Reverend Henry Roe, a missionary.

> When night fell and the fire-flies began to glitter in the orange trees, Burton used to place on the table before him a bottle of brandy, a box of cigars, and a bowl containing water and a handkerchief and then write until he was weary; rising now and again to wet his forehead with the handkerchief or to gaze outside at the palm trees, transmuted by the sheen of the moon into lucent silver. . . .

Romantic but not quite accurate: a light at night would have attracted insects beyond toleration. But perhaps the brandy helped.

He could rationalize his drinking easily. "In dangerous tropical regions, where there is little appetite and less nutritious diet, when exertion of mind and body easily exhausts vitality . . . he dies first who drinks water," he was to write in *Two Trips to Gorilla Land*. The light drinker will also die, while "the survivor is the man who enjoys a *quantum suff.* of humming Scotch and Burton ales, sherry, Madeira, and port, with a modicum of cognac," and he referred back to the lesson learned in India, when the surgeon suggested "a dozen good port" after a fever, to which Burton had replied, "Why not drink port before the fever?"

He settled down to work. The consulate building was in shambles. "Scarcely habitable," Burton complained to the Foreign Office. He had it repaired. The cost was £344, but London would not recognize the bill, and Burton wrangled over it for the next three years.

He had an assistant, an acting consul, E. Loughland, who was actually a trader and was more concerned with his own interests than those of Her Majesty's Government. But Burton's own consular duties were minor, and he passed what he could onto Loughland. The chores were routine—the ships that called at Santa Isabel, the mails, invoices, manifests. Were there slaves hidden in the holds? Was there other contraband? One of Burton's major accomplishments in West Africa was the reform of the Equity Courts, the only legal institutions for the hearing of grievances between natives and whites. In the various "British" ports Burton was able to set up courthouses where monthly meetings were run by equal numbers of native chiefs and white supercargoes under an elected chair to fix fines, duties, and rents and to oversee the protection of lives and property, a major achievement in the chaos of West Africa; however, in some places, as Burton complained to the Foreign Office, "all signed the agreement but no one adhered to it."

Fernando Po had long been under British influence, and for decades it was understood that the British consul would aid and side with the British traders—Burton's predecessors had, and the French consuls were notorious for their support of the monopoly held by the firm of Victor Régis of Marseilles—but Burton remained completely impartial. He had too many private interests of his own to investigate rather than champion the interests of the Liverpool traders.

Much has been made of the fact that Burton did not seem to be paying attention to consular duties, that he wandered all over the coast of West Africa and spent very little time at Fernando Po—he was able to get a ride aboard a ship going to Lagos a week after arriving in Santa Isabel but was back at his post within five days and then went off again. In fact, he was carrying out his work in his own manner, casually but highly efficiently. The entire coast was suffering vast changes, changes that would destroy the ancient fabric of native society, weaken the kingdoms, and leave them open to seizure by Europeans. The export of slaves—a trade that had been profitable for four hundred years —was nearing an end due in part to the effectiveness of the British warships that patrolled the seas and in part to the American Civil War, which had resulted in the end of an important market. Everywhere the market for human beings was shaken. Another crop, palm oil (and to some extent cotton), became a major substitute for the slave trade, but the price fluctuated wildly, and Burton, in a series of private letters to the Foreign Office, reveals a profound understanding of the complexity of the issues. He believed that competition from petroleum and tallow in the States was harming the palm-oil market, causing the price to drop, and that attempts by traders, mostly whites, and local merchants to withhold palm from the market in the hope of driving it up was not working. The lack of ready cash money was also hurting the native kingdoms; some princes had been advanced huge sums of money and could neither deliver export items nor repay the loans. Dynastic struggles, blood feuds, and wars were increasing as the princes tried to keep their kingdoms afloat. The West African lands, with their promise of vast natural resources and cheap labor, presented great temptations to the Europeans. The area was by white standards a frontier world in which Europeans were lawless and resented efforts by their own consuls to establish control. Other factors also affected the well-being of the Coast. There was no standard system to convey unconvertible native currencies to a common exchange, and the merchants of all races still employed archaic weights and measurements.

Burton felt a certain optimism about West Africa and his role. Places like the newly discovered Niger River, he wrote Lord Russell, though at the moment of little value, offered "vast future profits." He felt that the British faced fierce competition from the French, who had monopolies with certain of the princes, exchanging European guns and powder, cloth, tobacco, and rum for slaves, gold, ivory, and above all, palm oil. There was more competition from the Brazilian creoles, who wanted slaves for Brazil and Cuba. As the slave trade began to dwindle, indentured labor was then sent out to the French Antilles and other West Indian islands and to other parts of West Africa. Burton was dichotomous in his thinking: He always condemned slavery, but he thought that indentured labor—which could be as cruel and as degrading—was a benefit for man and employer.

The British seemed alone in the struggle to stop the trade in human beings. The French, though officially against slavery, did not meddle in the trade, and the American slavers lurked offshore, to dart past the British blockades. The French and the Americans were quick to go to court when their ships were seized, and the endless litigation served merely to divert the British ships. Burton noted the various conflicting interests: the British government; the missionaries (mostly Wesleyan, though French Catholic priests were now entering fields once the province of the Portuguese and the Spaniards); the traders, white, black, and Creole; and the diverse native kingdoms. Her Majesty's representative—Richard Francis Burton—had his hands full, and he was scrupulous about doing his assigned job, though he managed to pass on much of the routine work to the untrustworthy Loughland.

Burton's private papers to Lord Russell reveal his concentration on his duties: On the surface he seemed to be a consul in absentia, rarely staying at Fernando Po but wandering wherever he willed on the mainland in order to gather material for his books. The reports to the Foreign Office—the official papers on trade, economies, raw materials, local conditions, problems with the supercargoes, and similar matters—are rarely exciting, though such information sometimes resulted in later British acquisition and colonizing of various sections of the African West Coast.

At the end of October, having been in Fernando Po barely over a month, Burton got transport aboard H.M.S. *Prometheus* to the coast with Commander Bedingfield and then traveled inland to see a native chief, Abeokuta, to get his mark on a treaty. Onshore Burton fell from his horse in an accident he might have expected—it was a Friday. Burton and Bedingfield did not get along. Burton disliked the commander's dog, which had the mange, barked incessantly, jumped overboard from the ship ("exciting different emotions amongst those in it"), and finally got lost.

Everywhere Burton found that polygamy was a common practice. It was the "foundation stone of Yoruban society," and he took the opportunity to affirm that marriage to but one woman was "the most curious delimitation of human liberty ever forced upon mankind." Tender thoughts about Isabel remained vague. He had another mishap with a horse, the day being Friday, and after getting the chief's signature, the party sailed downstream toward Lagos. They stopped for the night at a village where they had "a right merry evening," with singing, feasting, and dancing. On this "soft and balmy evening," Burton found the women beautiful—"*superbae formae*," he wrote in Latin, as if using another language would excuse his acts. "Our hosts were perfectly civil and obliging, and so were our hostesses—rather too much so I could prove, if privileged to whisper into the reader's ear. But what would Mrs. Grundy say?" In summary, he could state, "Upon the whole, our trip was decidedly 'jolly.' "

At Lagos, Burton got a cabin aboard the H.M.S. *Bloodhound* and was off to the Brass and Bonny rivers, landing at Victoria, Nigeria, a missionary station. Here he met a young botanist, Gustav Mann, who was planning to ascend the Cameroon mountains. Burton urged Mann to wait a few days, as he wanted first to visit the Cameroon River—probably he saw the possibility of a report for the Foreign Office that would excuse his wandering—and when he returned to Victoria, he found that Mann had left. Burton had now acquired some other friends, among them a Spanish judge from Fernando Po and a missionary, Dr. Alfred Saker. With his servant, Selim Aga, Burton and the others set off to follow Mann, only to meet him returning. Mann claimed that he had already scaled the mountains. Burton was hurt, and, remembering similar bitter experiences with Speke, he calculated that Mann could not have actually done so, but Mann stuck to his claim. Mann, knowing of the quarrels with Speke, wisely decided not to argue with Burton. Now the entire group ascended the mountains together, Burton communicating with the tribes along the way with the American Indian sign language he had learned in the States.

On their return to the base camp, Burton erected a whipping post for unruly natives, giving as many as thirty-six lashes to the most troublesome. The party now indulged in a practice Burton had previously condemned, giving the geography European names. The two highest peaks in the mountains were called Victoria and Albert. Three others Burton named Mount Isabel, Mount Milnes, and Mount Silenes, and Saker and Mann remembered loved ones with Helen, Arthur, and Leopold. In explanation, Burton had to say that "even strict geographers cannot blame the act in a place which has no terminology."

From the base camp they ascended various peaks. Burton and the judge climbed the solitary splendor of Mount Milnes. "We were the first Europeans, perhaps the first men, who ever stood within gunshot of that tall solitary pile." They broke the silence with a cheer.

Burton and Mann then decided to ascend Mount Victoria, the tallest and the peak Mann had claimed to have conquered earlier. Burton, at forty, was less agile than Mann, but he managed to reach the summit first. A cairn of stones was erected containing a small sheet of lead on which everyone's name was inscribed and inserted in an empty bottle along with some sixpence and a few pages from *Punch*. The cairn was found in 1886 by the explorer Sir Harry Johnston.

At the base camp, after so much violent exercise, Burton found himself so exhausted that he did not bother to remove his boots when he went to sleep. The next morning, he had cramps in his knees, and his feet were inflamed; he had severe ague and fever. He was to spend the next month in a state of disrepair, studying the Kru tongue, collecting botanical specimens, and flogging natives. Mann, too, was ill with dysentery; he cured himself with a tonic of iron rust in brandy and arrowroot with chalk. When the party was well again, they made a second ascent of Victoria. On February 4, 1862, Burton returned to Fernando Po, that hated island, feeling as if he were in prison; he was to recommend, unsuccessfully, that the island was an excellent site for a convict station. Yellow fever broke out shortly afterward; seventy-eight of the 250 white men at Fernando Po died, the black deaths not being tabulated. "This 'lofty and beautiful island' [as Camões had called it] had become a charnel house, a 'dark and dismal tomb of Europeans.' " Burton was not to escape "the bitterness of death" until another ship, the *Torch*, appeared offshore at the end of July and he could escape again.

He now began to wander incessantly, as if constant motion would ease whatever secret pains racked his mind and body. Loneliness, despair, rejection underlie the books, reports, and letters to friends. But there was always something exotic, strange, challenging on the horizon. In March, having been back at his post only a month, he went off to look for gorillas in the Gaboon. The animals had suddenly become a special quest for Europeans after a Frenchman, Paul du Chaillu, had written about them. But Burton's search ended in failure. After many adventures, including being struck by lightning, and numerous mosquito bites, he had to give up, though he had shown villagers pictures from the du Chaillu book and had offered a reward for a live specimen. The best he could get was a skin sent him after he returned to the coast; it was likely a large chimpanzee rather than a gorilla. Though he had not seen a living animal, Burton had gathered a rather accurate picture: "The gorilla," he said in a matter-of-fact way, "is a poor devil ape, not a hellish dream creature, half-man, half-beast."

He returned to the Gaboon again, to visit a tribe called the

Fans, who were reputedly cannibals. Though Burton spent only a week among them, he gathered an immense amount of material and tried, with some success, to understand the motivations behind their customs and religion. Then there were as always those special themes of polygamy and circumcision. "The operation is performed generally by the chief . . . the thumbnails are long, and are used after the Jewish fashion: neat rum with red pepper is spirited from the mouth to 'kill wound.' " He wrote that circumcision here is "purely hygienic and not balanced by the *excisio Judaica*," that is, excision of the clitoris.

> Some physiologists consider the latter a necessary complement of the male rite; such, however, is not the case. The Hebrews, who almost everywhere retain [male] circumcision, have, in Europe at least, long abandoned excision. I regret that the delicacy of the age does not allow me to be more explicit.

His primary purpose was to investigate cannibalism, a practice whose motivations he understood and did not condemn.

> Anthropophagy can hardly be caused by necessity, and the way in which it is conducted shows that it is a quasi-religious rite practiced upon foes slain in battle, evidently an equivalent of human sacrifice. If the whole body cannot be carried off, a limb is removed for the purpose of a roast. The corpse is carried to a hut built expressly on the outskirts of the settlement: it is eaten secretly by the warriors, women and children not being allowed to be present, or even look upon a man's flesh; and the cookingpots used for the banquet must all be broken.

It was a society marked by "ghost-existence and veneration of material objects, places and things." He understood, but did his fellow Europeans? He thought not. Whites did not understand natives—"the main obstacle . . . being the almost insuperable difficulty of throwing off European ideas and modes of thought. . . ." He noted, also, as elsewhere, the special, very unpleasant character of the European. "Even in Asia, whenever I spoke contemptuously to a Moslem of his Jinns, or to a Hindu of his Rakshas [demons] the rejoinder invariably was, 'You white men are by nature so hot that even our devils fear you.' "

He made an endless effort to get to the very roots of the motivating forces of the African mind, attempting to find the key to fetishism. He worried incessantly that he was not actually finding out what men believed. He denied the missionary view that fetishism was "a degradation of the pure and primitive (Adamical) dispensation," but he himself had a different opinion: "I cannot but look upon it as the first dawn of a faith in things not seen."

> And it must be studied by casting off all our preconceived ideas. For instance, Africans believe, not in soul nor in spirit, but in ghost. . . . They have a material, evanescent, intelligible future, not an immaterial, incomprehensible eternity; the ghost endures only for a while and perishes like the memory of the little-great name.

Despite his eternal scoffing at religion, it was a subject that captured Burton and held him prisoner. He queried the natives and the missionaries and white officials about the people's thoughts, but a missionary with twenty years' experience who had worked diligently to collect tradition and religious beliefs had to admit that he had found that "no two men thought alike upon any single subject," and Burton reported a conversation a missionary had had with one of the Niger kings on the difference between "the Christian religion and heathenism."

> "*Herr Schön.* There is but one God.
> King Obi. I have always understood that there were two," etc.

It was a search into roots, into primitive sources, into the archaic past, as if he were trying to find his own primitive roots, his Ur-soul. He was finally able, after much petitioning, to enter a fetish house, "one of these rude and embryonal temples" so carefully shut against outsiders. It was a disappointment, being decorated with crude statues, musical implements, basins smeared with colored chalks and adorned with beads and ribbons, and held no clues to whatever he was searching for.

Despite his constant reviling of blacks who presumed too much in the company of whites, of "negro insolence" and other sins, Burton's opinion of blacks changed radically after four years among the tribes of West Africa, and he had a warning for the natives.

> They would do wisely to decline intercourse with Europeans; but this, of course, is impossible—there is a manifest destiny for them as for their predecessors. The vile practice of the West Coast is to supply savages with alcohol, arms and ammunition: to live upon the lives of those they serve. The more honorable Moslems of the eastern shores do not disgrace themselves by such greed of gain.

Polygamy in West Africa was as common as sunrise and sunset, and Burton could never resist its praise, although he had his own standards. One of the princes "hospitably offered me his daughter-in-law Asizeh, Forteune's second wife. . . . Forteune then hinted that perhaps I might prefer his daughter-in-law—'she be all same woman.' " But Burton had become a middle-aged moralist: "Both offers were declined with *Merci, non!*" When he encountered the Mpingwe on his search for gorillas, he noted that polygamy is "a necessity to the men, and even women disdain to marry a 'one-wifer.' " It was easy to find practical, sensible reasons for polygamy. In Africa it was "rather a political than a domestic or social institution."

> A "judicious culture of the marriage tie" is necessary amongst savages and barbarians whose only friends and supporters are blood relations and nuptial connections. . . .

He added, without much hope, "I should try vainly to persuade the English woman that there can be peace in households so constituted: still, such is the case."

Was he trying to persuade his wife to agree to such an arrangement? "As amongst all pluralists, from Moslem to Mormon, the senior or first married is No. I.; here called 'best wife:' she is the goodman's viceroy, and she rules the home-kingdom with absolute sway." Did Burton, in his secret, somewhat barbarous heart, believe that life in England would be better for him as a polygamist than life with one woman? Would Isabel tolerate being Best Wife as a series of slippery, nubile young women, their skins oiled and scented, took their allotted turns in the Great Man's bed? One can only surmise that the other women would have been Persian, Indian, Arab, Somali, Bedouin, African, in exotic dress, in chaddars or saris, salwars, churidars, pantaloons, pareus, lungis, lava-lavas, or nothing at all, their skins greased with palm and rare perfumes, eyes rimmed with koh'l. He tried to reassure Isabel that "everywhere, moreover, amongst polygamists, the husband is strictly forbidden by popular opinion to show preference for a [younger] favourite wife; if he do so, he is a bad man." The endless sounding of the theme throughout Burton's works finally led Isabel to an explosion. In his absence later on, after their stay in Brazil, she had been entrusted with supervising through the press *The Highlands of Brazil* (published in 1869), in which Burton again advocated polygamy. She added her own preface, partly in rebuttal of ideas she did not like. She warned the reader "to steer through these anthropological sand-banks and hidden rocks as best he or she may" and denounced her husband's upholding of "that unnatural and repulsive law, Polygamy, which the Author is careful not to practice himself, but from a high moral pedestal as he preached to the ignorant as a means of population in your countries."

Throughout Africa, Burton had observed the tremendous physical strength of the women, noting their "masculine *physique*, enabling them to compete with men in enduring toil, hardship, and privations." At one village in Dahomey he noted "the size of the female skeleton" compared to that of the male "and the muscular development of the frame . . . in many cases femininity could be detected only by the bosom." The tremendous physicality of the women was probably a factor in his yearning for polygamous marriage—how strong, supple, and agile were native women compared to the typical Englishwoman, housebound, rather pampered, soft in muscle, and confined in types of clothing he thought demeaning and physically harmful.

When Burton encountered Amazons by the hundreds, they never failed to interest him. Women were commonly used as soldiers—King Gelele was reported to have a corps of them, and other rulers used them as well for troops. They were invariably big, athletic, though often ugly women, finely dressed and magnificently drilled and undoubtedly braver in war than the men. Still, there was always that one great unanswered question: What were they like in bed? The younger Burton would have made every effort to find out—the women were notoriously celibate, but bastards were still common—but the aging Burton seemed to have left the matter to speculation and fantasy, and if he did try and the results went into his diaries, they were likely among the casualties in the great burning of his papers by Isabel.

At home, Isabel was ever anxious about her husband's health, well-being, and his career. She was able to get him home leave of four months. Burton arrived in England in December 1862, having been absent some sixteen months, months long enough for a newlywed marooned in a pestilential land. Burton was filled with suggestions for the Foreign Office. He had looked into the mining of gold, and he told Lord Russell that if he were made governor of the Gold Coast he could send home "a million a year." Gold was becoming too common, Russell told him. "Burton's comment was an explosion that terrorized everyone near him," wrote Thomas Wright.

Burton celebrated Christmas with Isabel and the Arundell family at Wardour Castle, the home of his wife's uncle. The principal event of his leave was the founding on January 6, 1863, of the Anthropological Society of London in company with Dr. James Hunt; there were initially eleven members, and in two years, five hundred. Burton had founded the Society chiefly as a means of getting his more outrageous material before the public—the Society, he wrote, offered "a refuge to destitute truth. There any man, monogenist, polygenist, eugenistic or dysgenistic, may state the truth as far as [it is] in him."

> As a traveller and a writer of travels I have found it impossible to publish these questions of social economy and those physiological observations [such as female circumcision], always interesting to our common knowledge, and at a time so valuable.

He started a magazine, the *Memoirs of the Anthropological Society* (later incorporated as a quarterly with *The Anthropological Review*), in which to publish "certain subjects." Nine years later the Society merged with the Ethnological Society to form the Royal Anthropological Institute of Great Britain. Still another group, under Burton's aegis, founded the London Anthropological Society and issued a periodical called *Anthropologia*. "My motive," said Burton, "was to supply travellers with an organ which would rescue their observations from the outer darkness of manuscript and print their curious information on social and sexual matters. . . ." But it was not an easy path, this venture into basic levels of mankind. " 'Respectability' that whited sepulchre of all uncleanness, rose up against us." The "brazen, blatant voice" of propriety was raised, and "the weak-kneed brethren fell away."

Soon it was time to return to his post. Burton and Isabel had decided to spend some weeks together in a more salubrious climate and took ship to Madeira. Isabel had been complaining about her lonely state to her husband.

> I told him I could not possibly go on living as I was; it was too miserable, one's husband in a place where one was not allowed to go, and I living with my mother like a girl—I was neither wife, nor maid, nor widow; so he took me with him.

It was not an easy voyage. The ships on the African lines were meant for cargo, not passengers, and visited twenty-two ports. There was no bath, "the conveniences were difficult," and they set out in a storm, the steamer shipping water. "The under berths were full of water, the bird-cages and kittens and parcels were all floating about, most of the women were screaming, many of the men-passengers were drunk, the lights went out, the furniture came unshipped and rolled about at its own sweet will."

Isabel was "sick and terrified," but it was a good introduction to traveling with Captain Burton. Eventually, the storm subsided, and they arrived in Madeira, found old friends, went to parties, and then on to Teneriffe, where there were "no comforts and luxuries" and the yellow fever was raging.

Still, the Burtons, here as they would everywhere, managed to turn misery, difficulties, and unpleasantness into fun. They explored the island, made friends with the people ("The women of Teneriffe were the most beautiful I have ever seen," said Isabel, innocently confirming her husband's earlier opinion), and she wrote her first book, which, however, Burton would not let her publish, as it was not quite professional.

When it was time for Burton to continue to Fernando Po, he let Isabel sail with him, but she was not allowed to stay there, and she returned home, while he settled down again to his consular duties. Teneriffe became a secret rendezvous for the Burtons. How many times Burton slipped away from Fernando Po is not known—often, one surmises—but they had solved in part the problem of being separated.

Not a word had been received from Speke and Grant for over a year; there was much worry over their safety. Various "rescue" missions were being assembled, men and even women who were willing to risk health and life itself to make the ascent of the Nile to find the missing explorers; and John Petherick, as the official government representative, was also to be waiting at Gondoroko.

The most important person among all the volunteers was Samuel Baker, a Scottish gentleman and sportsman, who had entered the quest entirely on his own initiative and without any official support. Baker expected that he would encounter Speke and Grant somewhere near Gondoroko. The town was known only by name to Europeans as a notorious and truly evil settlement of slavers and hostile to outsiders. "A perfect hell," said Sam Baker when he entered it. The temperature ran about 100°, the town stank, and crime was a major pastime. Murders were common, and the most powerful slavers had private armies. Baker, a widower, had with him his mistress (and later his wife), a young white woman named Florence Sass whom he had bought in a slave market in Hungary to keep her from some Turk's harem. Among the other would-be rescuers were three Dutch women, the Tinnes, extremely wealthy and adventurous, who also hoped to await the missing explorers in Gondoroko.

The Pethericks arrived at the town far ahead of the other parties of whites, having made the difficult trip up the Nile by boat under exhausting conditions, but with no notion of where Speke and Grant might be, they went off into the countryside on other business.

It was not until February 13, 1863, that Speke and Grant, escorted by a marching band and a column of Egyptian and Nubian soldiers in the service of the Turks, headed by a trader in both ivory and slaves sent by Baker, who had heard rumors of two white men in the desert, reached Gondoroko. As they approached the town, the two explorers saw the figure of an Englishman coming toward them. To their surprise it was not Petherick but Sam Baker, whom Speke had met in 1854 on the way from India to Aden when he joined Burton on the ill-fated Somali expedition. "My old friend Baker, famed for his sports in Ceylon, seized me by the hand," wrote Speke. "What joy this was I can hardly tell. We could not talk fast enough, so overwhelmed were we both to meet again." The Tinnes, whom Speke did not know, had been overcome with fever and had returned to Khartoum. Three Austrian missionaries soon appeared, but where was Petherick? That the consul had waited a year and then gone about other business was no excuse in Speke's mind. But both he and Grant were in good shape.

> Speke [Baker wrote] appeared the more worn of the two; he was excessively lean, but in reality he was in good tough condition; he had walked the whole way from Zanzibar, never having ridden once during the wearying march. Grant was in honourable rags; his bare knees projecting through the remnants of trousers that were an exhibition of rough industry in tailor's work. He was looking tired and feverish, but both men had a fire in the eye, that showed the spirit that had led them through.

A few days later Petherick arrived with his wife, Kate, and James Murie, but by then it was too late. Speke was in a cold rage at not having been properly welcomed and attended to by the official representative of his government. On the surface, all the whites, joined from time to time by the Austrian missionaries, appeared to be friendly. Privately, Speke raged at Petherick. Kate Petherick tried to smooth over the situation, but Speke would not relent even though in London, before setting out, he had assured the consul that he was free to go about his own affairs while awaiting the arrival of the expedition. Kate wrote of the situation with Speke, "His heartlessness will recoil upon him yet." And even when still at Gondoroko, Speke was still consumed with anger at Burton and wrote a letter to the Royal Geographical Society, to be posted from Khartoum, that Burton knew nothing of cartography despite his own efforts to teach him.

When back in England later, Speke publicly attacked Petherick relentlessly. Macqueen, and Burton when he returned, spoke of "the cruelty of the manner" in which he crushed Consul Petherick with his "ill temper, vanity and jealousy."

Speke refused to accept the boats, well armed and provisioned, that Petherick had waiting for him, and he and Grant sailed down the Nile to Khartoum in Baker's boat. Baker, too, was not spared Speke's anger. Speke soon began to make remarks about Florence and her ambiguous state as a mistress in a place like Africa, where disease was rampant and life so short. Might not she be suddenly left an informal widow?

In the relative civilization of Khartoum, having continued down the Nile—his river!—Speke telegraphed Murchison that "the Nile is settled." It wasn't, of course; that issue would have to be resolved in later years.

The twenty-two natives who survived the safari, including Sidi Bombay Mubarak and three women, among them the two teenage "water carriers" who had entertained Speke at Buganda, accompanied Speke and Grant to Cairo, where they were given tents in a public park. They received three years' wages and much attention and were returned by ship to Zanzibar, where they received more pay and more acclaim. When Speke and Grant returned to England, they were welcomed by Rigby when they landed, heroes and lions, very much the great men of the moment.

They were greeted by crowds everywhere. When Speke spoke before audiences, people outside broke windows to see him. With the invaluable assistance of the Blackwoods, Speke's two volumes of exploration were rushed into print, with almost identical (and thus confusing) titles: *Journal of the Discovery of the Source of the Nile* and *What Led to the Discovery of the Source of the Nile*. The next year, 1864, Grant published *A Walk Across Africa*, the title having been suggested by Lord Palmerston's remark "You have had a long walk." But Burton and Macqueen were quick to attack Speke's works on the Nile question, the latter having reviewed Speke's writings as soon as they appeared and Burton adding his own caustic comments to Macqueen's biting and sarcastic essays in *The Nile Basin*.

25

The Evil Nights

Burton's life abounds in strange, mysterious, dark passages, but the three years in West Africa—three years that must have seemed like an eternity of hell—are among the strangest. Three years in a stinking, malarial, undeveloped, miasmic, ignorant, nasty backwater! And, presumably, with no búbú to comfort him during the black mosquito-laden nights, no búbú, but only the memory of Isabel and those brief encounters at Teneriffe, that quaint but limited island.

That he wrote a lot of books—nine fat volumes—during those three years is a matter of record, books that are pedantically, obsessively entranced with facts, with details, with the layering up of information. As virtually always, any single one of them would have been enough to make another man's reputation, to ensure a safe berth in a university or a foreign office, but again the prolixity of published work tends to smother the individual worth of each. "Obsession" is hardly the word for his writings.

He turned out books (as well as all the other impedimenta of his mind—the articles, official reports, letters, and essays) like some kind of runaway automaton, a computer before its time, that had instant recall for tribes and races, scarification, white rascals and black rascals, the sins of missionaries and slavers alike, types of soils, produce, common and rare plants (the banana receives a better review in Burton's West Africa than in his Central Africa), exports and imports, precious metals (gold was always a major preoccupation), folklore, history (such as it was), geography (longitude, latitude, heights and depressions, distances between river landings, errors of earlier travelers—how he liked to correct his predecessors!), illnesses and diseases, and above all, languages. There is hardly a page or a chapter in which he does not dig into some common or obscure African tongue to explain how words have developed, changed, or lost meaning or to correct earlier linguists. "Mr. Wilson [a missionary] could hardly have had a nice ear, or he would not have written Nchigo 'Ntyge,' or Njina 'Engene,' which gives a thoroughly un-African distinctness to the initial consonant." Wilson and a dozen other earlier grammarians are so worked over in the African books, but there was a reason: Burton loved languages, and he wanted everyone to love them as he did. After disposing of the unfortunate Wilson, he goes on to say:

> Liquid and eminently harmonious, concise and capable of contraction, the Mpingwe language does not deserve to die out. . . . The people have never invented any form of alphabet, yet the abundance of tale, legend, and proverb which their dialect contains might repay the trouble of acquiring it.

But the West African tongues were not easy to learn, for they were distinguished by

> polysyllabism, inflexion by systematic prefixes, and an alliteration, the mystery of whose reciprocal letters is theoretically explained by euphony in many cases unintelligible. . . . I have found the negative past, present and future forms of verbs wholly dependent upon a

change of accent, or rather of intonation or voice-pitch, which the stranger's ear unless acute, will fail to detect.

He could not sit still in Fernando Po. "Little islands are all large prisons: one cannot look at the sea without wishing for the wings of a swallow." He was seized by a kind of demon: he had to travel, to wander, to explore. "Starting in a hollowed log of wood—some thousand miles up a river, with an infinitesimal prospect of returning, I ask myself 'Why?' and the only answer is 'damned fool,' " he had written to Monckton Milnes at the end of May 1863. What had driven him to this point? "The devil drives," he had concluded.

It was true that he had ventured upriver—it was the Congo —in a native canoe, but he was hardly a thousand miles from the coast, but some hundred or so. However, the higher reaches had barely been explored, and only the lower section was well known to Europeans, the Portuguese having posts all along it. Burton thought of going beyond the lower rapids as far as possible, but lack of equipment and the shortness of time prevented him. The river had taken the lives of a brave Englishman, Captain J. K. Tuckey, R.N., and sixteen companions in 1816, and since then no one had reached the town of Isanglis beyond the rapids. A respectful silence had fallen upon the upper Congo, punctuated only by reports of cruel and savage African kings. Burton returned to his island, where shortly he received the welcome news that he was to be permitted—sent, in fact—to visit the notorious King Gelele of Dahomey, a sinister African kingdom, the most sinister of all on that unhappy continent. Europeans visiting Dahomey had returned with stories of the slaughter of two thousand victims at a time, of canoes floating in lakes of blood. Shortly after he had arrived at Fernando Po in 1861, Burton had asked permission of the Foreign Office to visit Dahomey. It had been denied, but he went secretly, staying five days at the capital and meeting the king briefly. He wrote Monckton Milnes at the time that he was "generally disappointed" in the lack of bloodshed. "Not a man killed, or a fellow tortured. The canoe floating in blood is a myth of myths. Poor Hankey must still wait for his peau de femme." He added that the victims were between "one and two hundred a year instead of thousands." He could be unpleasantly cruel in his jokes: "At Benin . . . they crucified a fellow in honor of my coming—here nothing! And this is the blood-stained land of Dahomey!"

Burton had promised Gelele to return someday, and upon his further urging, the Foreign Office had at last given him formal permission to enter Dahomey and to protest not only the ritual slaughters, which were in fact greater in number than Burton had reported to Monckton Milnes, but the slave trade as well. Isabel seems to have had a hand in the Foreign Office's change of heart. She had hoped to use the occasion to visit Richard and to accompany him to Dahomey, where she would show lantern slides of scenes from the New Testament and say a few words in the local language to terrify the king into abolishing human sacrifice and becoming a Roman Catholic. Her Majesty's Protestant government patiently explained to her that the magic lantern might be considered a real work of magic and that she and the Captain would be in danger of being among those to contribute to the purported lake of blood.

Burton was formally made ambassador to Dahomey with the object of protesting both the ritual annual sacrifices, known as "custom," and the practice of slavery. He had little hope that he could force a change in Gelele's practices. The best he could expect was that he might persuade the king not to kill anyone, at least during his visit, though it would be at the time of the yearly custom. Burton would travel in full pomp. The H.M.S. *Antelope* would convey him to Whydah on the coast; he would carry magnificent presents, and he would be accompanied by personal assistants and almost a hundred porters, hammock men, interpreters, cooks, and others necessary for a successful expedition. Besides his servant Selim Aga, he had with him a naval surgeon, John Cruikshank, and the Reverend Peter W. Bernasko, described as a "native assistant missionary."

They landed at Whydah on the Slave Coast on November twenty-ninth and were forced to wait at the town until early December before permission to proceed came from Gelele. But the time was not wasted. Burton found widespread signs of a phallic cult, with priapic clay statues everywhere by the hundreds. On December fifth they set off for Dahomey, passing through villages virtually destitute of adult males, and on the eighteenth reached Kana, the site of the king's temporary palace. The following day, Burton met the king in a "penance of reception"—the usual and inevitable ceremonies and dancing. Burton was impressed by Gelele. "He looks a king of [black] men, without tenderness of heart or weakness of head," he wrote. "His person is athletic, upwards of six feet high, lithe, thin flanked and broad shouldered." The king's eyes were "red, bleared and inflamed," and as a tattoo he had "three short parallel and perpendicular lancet cuts, situated nearer the scalp than the eyebrows."

Though he welcomed Burton with pomp, the king refused to give him a private audience, probably suspecting the true purpose of his visit. Meanwhile, Burton settled down to observing Dahomey, particularly the Amazons. The women were not the glamorous creatures of classical antiquity or even the enticing figures he had fantasized about earlier, but ordinary African women. He wrote Milnes:

> I was looking forward with prodigious curiosity to see 5,000 African adult virgins, never having met with a single specimen. I found most of them were women taken in adultery and given to the king as food for powder instead of being killed. They were mostly elderly and all of them hideous. The officers were decidedly chosen for the size of their bottoms.

As troops of the king, they were supposed to live in chastity, no matter what their previous history, but, wrote Burton, "so difficult is chastity in the tropics" that one hundred and fifty were pregnant. He was not impressed with the Amazons as soldiers. "They manoeuvre with the precision of a flock of sheep, and they are too light to stand a charge of the poorest troops in Europe." Worse, "an equal number of British charwomen, armed with the British broomstick, would . . . clear them off in a very few hours." Still, they had achieved some notable victories over neighboring kingdoms, and he thought whatever defeats they suffered were the result of poor leadership by male officers.

During the long period of waiting, the tension at Kana increased daily as preparations were made for the celebration of custom. Finally, the fateful day arrived. Burton had insisted that no one be killed in his presence, and he demanded the release of twenty victims he saw tied up in a shed. Gelele released ten. Frenzied dancing and drumming commenced: the decapitation rites had begun, directed by the king himself, who led the dancing. Gelele insisted that Burton and Dr. Cruikshank join him; Burton complied with a *pas seul*, to the acclaim of the crowd, and was joined by Gelele, the result bringing a great ovation. The king now toasted his honored guest by drinking from a skull and then presented Burton with two for himself.

It was barbaric and of an unlimited, unmeasurable cruelty. Burton did not see any executions, but in deference to him— or to his Queen—the victims were slaughtered at night—"the evil nights," said Burton—the king cutting off the first head himself. Nine men perished in the first slaughter, the victims being decapitated and castrated after death, "in respect," wrote Burton, "to the royal wives." In all, Burton counted twenty-three male victims. He was told that eighty perished during the five days of the custom, and some five hundred during the year. Women criminals were executed by "officers of their own sex, within the palace walls, not in the presence of men," a fact that he could not resist emphasizing later: "Dahome is there one point more civilized than Great Britain, where they still, wondrous to relate, 'hang away' even women, in public."

We can hardly find fault with putting criminals to death [in Dahomey] when in the year of Grace 1864 we hung four murderers upon the same gibbet before 100,000 gaping souls at Liverpool . . . our last Christian King but one killed a starving mother of seventeen, with an infant at her breast, for lifting a yard of linen from a shop counter.

What was the reason for such cruelty among the Africans? Unlike earlier travelers who had seen or knew of the executions, Burton tried to go beyond ordinary speculation to the heart of the matter. The reason, he believed, was essentially religious, to communicate with the honored dead. The victims were made drunk, "the object being to send them to the other side in the best of tempers. . . . The king wished to communicate with his father." The practice of custom "originates from filial piety."

Burton was at last given a private interview with Gelele. By now he was in something of a rage, and he promised reprisals on the part of his government against Dahomey, especially for the slave traffic. Then he protested the custom.

The king had his answers. It was the English who long ago had initiated the slave traffic; now he needed the revenue— palm oil would not defray the expenses of the custom—and as for the latter, it was an ancient practice, and he slew only male-factors and prisoners of war, who, if they could, would do the same to him. Burton tried to argue from common sense: "Da-homey wanted not deaths, but births. It was like talking to the winds."

It had been a frustrating, disappointing, unsuccessful trip, and psychologically the king had been Burton's master. "You are a good man," the king said, "but you are very angry." Only Burton's magnificent two-volume work on his efforts served to offset his disappointments. The work was called *A Mission to Gelele, King of Dahome*, and its subtitle served to encompass whatever Burton could squeeze into it: "With Notices of the So-called 'Amazons,' the Grand Customs, the Yearly Customs, the Human Sacrifices, the Present State of the Slave Trade, and the Negro's Place in Nature."

The trip to Dahomey was Burton's last major expedition in West Africa. In the late summer he received leave again. His quitting Fernando Po was accompanied by the accustomed flurry of acrimony and controversy. He had been too casual in leaving details of the consulate to Loughland. The latter, when Burton was in Dahomey, sold off the estate of a deceased Sierra Leone trader who owed him some money. The principal item in the estate was a battered schooner, the *Harriet*. Before he left for the coast, Burton had signed the certificate of sale for the ship without having considered fully what he was doing. The trader's heirs sued the British government for £280, and the Foreign Office declared that Burton, not the Crown, was liable. The result was the usual lengthy correspondence over grievances, a minor echo of the battle with Speke over the loan on the Nile safari. Isabel, entering the exchange of charges and counter-charges, worked out a compromise with her friends in Government. The Foreign Office would recognize £275 of the £344 Burton had claimed for repairs to the consulate at Fernando Po, and he was to repay the trader's heirs in full.

Thus, Burton left Africa poorer than when he had arrived, vitriolically accusing "litigious niggers" at Sierra Leone for this ignominious blow.

The denouement of the Nile drama was now about to be played out. Speke's volume on the "successful" conclusion of his search for the Nile was received with acclaim—exploration of the unknown was a popular and romantic subject in the nineteenth century—but to the more astute among the experts there were passages in the book that aroused suspicion and scorn.

Burton had returned from West Africa about the time the book appeared. He immediately spotted discrepancies and errors, for Speke's statements often seemed hardly better than guesses. Speke had seen a large body of water in 1858 in one place on the first expedition and in 1862 another large body in another place on the second expedition and had assumed they were the same huge lake, which was almost the size of England. He had not explored the shoreline and had no information about what rivers fed it or flowed from it. When he found an outlet that he confidently decided was the Nile, he had not bothered to follow it but made shortcuts, marching across country, believing that whatever river he met on the way was the Nile. Burton accused Speke of "an extreme looseness of geography."

Men with less of a personal interest in the Nile question than Burton now entered the controversy, and most of the press, which had previously endorsed Speke, began to indicate doubts, *Blackwood's* being the exception. Then Speke's attacks on Petherick reflected on his charity. (Grant, too, who had been previously friendly to the consul, turned against him.) Petherick was perhaps not the monster Speke and Grant made him out to be.

Burton did not have to speak out openly and forcibly against Speke, for there were others who could express his anger for him, notably Macqueen. What gave Macqueen his best ammunition were the passages about Speke and the native women, his measuring of Rumanika's fat wife and fat daughter, whose body was "as round as a ball." "We believe," Macqueen wrote, "none of our readers ever met with or ever heard of such a piece of 'engineering' as this, and we dare say will never wish to meet with such another."

That Speke was so casual about the atrocities in Mutesa's court brought condemnation, and the affairs with the "water carriers," more scorn. That Speke did not go see the famous lake he claimed was the source of the Nile was a point Macqueen stressed: the Captain was too busy with the native girls.

Captain Speke was all the time mentioned amused and employed in drinking *pombe*, courting the Queen Dowager, shooting cows, reducing to order his rebellious female intimates. . . . It is almost incredible that any man who had come one thousand miles to see the position of the outlet of the Nile, supposed it to be in that spot, should remain five months within eight miles of it, without hearing or seeing something certain about the great object of his research, or have found the means to see it.

Why could Speke have not taken the arm of the beautiful princess Kariana, "slipped on his or her mbugu, and instead of sitting moping and mourning, walked off in a morning walk . . . to the lake or river and so in one forenoon got what he wanted and thus relieved us and the world from all our pain and disappointments?" Speke never was able to explain why he had not gone to see the lake, and the issue was left unresolved.

There was more from Macqueen's acid pen, including a remark about the queen's curiosity about the color of Speke's offspring —"Different colors will flow. Captain Speke is himself a competent witness to the process." But there was also a serious side to the charges. By using Speke's own figures, Macqueen was able to show that he made the Nile flow uphill. "No correct or thinking geographer can find his way in such pages . . . a mass of intelligence, if such it can be called, so muddled and confused in everything that we really believe he himself cannot find his way in it."

Meanwhile, Speke continued his public appearances, so self-assured in his success that he could plan a third African expedition.

In his public statements and his letters Speke was speaking recklessly, and even Isabel complained, in particular of a speech of Speke's in December 1863, "which for vaingloriousness and bad taste was unequalled." Speke's behavior continued to be odd and combative. The next March, accompanied by Laurence Oliphant, Speke went to Paris to try to persuade the French to share the rule of Africa with England. He told the Société de Géographie de Paris that the Africans wanted an emperor, a French emperor, and that England would be well pleased if one were found. Also, that the Africans would benefit by the moral example offered by France. Speke seemed somewhat unhinged, and Oliphant expressed his concern privately to friends, including the Blackwood cousins, to the extent that they had demanded the deletion of a section of Speke's second book in which he had accused Burton of "incompetence, cowardice, malice and jealousy" on the first Nile expedition. In June, one of the Blackwood clan, John, wrote to Oliphant, "Pray speak to him and prevent him from putting his foot in it as much as possible." At the same time, the Blackwoods urged Oliphant to attack Burton's articles on the Nile question.

Death seemed to weigh upon Speke as it had when he arrived in Aden and first met Burton. In Paris, so Oliphant told the Blackwoods, Speke brought up the matter of death.

> He said that since having made the Nile discovery, life seemed so utterly flat and uninteresting to him that after knocking Burton down he felt he should no longer have any object in living. He talked altogether in the most indifferent way of existence and would not have looked on death as a misfortune.

A clash in public between Speke and Burton seemed inevitable, and one was engineered by Oliphant. It was to be an open debate at the British Association Meeting on September 15, 1864, at Bath. Oliphant told Burton that Speke had said that "if Burton appeared on the platform at Bath, he would kick him." Burton replied, "Well, *that* settles it!"

The initial session was set for other subjects; the debate between Speke and Burton was to take place the second day. Meanwhile, having arranged the face-to-face meeting with the two Nile antagonists, Oliphant had gone off to Germany so that he would be spared whatever anger either participant might have shown him had the debate gone the wrong way.

During the first day's session, Speke and the Burtons sat on the same platform with each other. Isabel wrote:

> I shall never forget his face. It was full of sorrow, of yearning, and perplexity. Then he seemed to turn to stone. After a while, he

began to fidget a great deal, and exclaimed half aloud, "Oh, I can't stand this any longer."

Speke left the hall. That was Isabel's recollection, and perhaps her memory is correct.

The next day, a large crowd was assembled for the debate. Out of several hundred people at the hall, Isabel, elaborately dressed, was apparently the only woman present. She wrote that she and Burton seemed to be shunned by the others and that they were alone on the platform, Burton standing with his notes in his hand waiting for Speke to arrive.

> There was a delay of about twenty-five minutes, and then the Council and speakers filed in and announced the terrible accident out shooting that had befallen poor Speke shortly after his leaving the Hall the day before. Richard sank into a chair and I saw by the workings of his face the terrible emotion he was controlling, and the shock he had received.

Still, despite the tragedy, the Council asked Burton to give his speech.

> When called upon to speak, in a voice that trembled, he spoke of other things and as briefly as possible. When we got home he wept long and bitterly, and I was for many a day trying to comfort him.

Other reports state that when the news of Speke's death was announced to the audience in the hall, Burton, as he fell back into his chair, cried, "By God, he's killed himself!"

The circumstances of Speke's death are ambiguous and will remain so. After leaving the hall the first day, he had gone hunting with his cousin George Fuller and a gamekeeper. He had fired twice at partridges from his gun, a double-barreled breech-loader Lancaster with a safety catch. Fuller, about sixty yards from Speke, heard a third shot and looked toward his cousin. Speke was standing on a low stone wall, about two feet high. Then he toppled over. Fuller rushed to him, to find Speke lying on the ground with a gaping wound in his chest. One barrel of the Lancaster had been discharged, the other had not, and the hammer was at half cock. It seemed that Speke had stepped to the top of the wall and had pulled the gun after him and it had gone off.

"Don't move me," said Speke, still conscious. Fuller ran for help, leaving Davis, the gamekeeper, to care for Speke, but by the time he returned with a surgeon, the wounded man was dead. An inquest, held the same day before a jury "of respectable inhabitants of the place," heard the testimony of Fuller, Davis, and the surgeon and concluded that the shooting had been an accident, though it seemed odd that a man of Speke's experience with weapons should have been so foolish as to pull a loaded gun muzzle first toward himself. The obituary in the London *Times* three days later called Speke "a gallant soldier . . . and a sagacious and enterprising traveller" and gave him full credit for discovering the source of the Nile.

Speke's place in history, like his "discovery" and his death, is contradictory. His name seldom appears in print nowadays except in works dealing specifically with the Nile; he is credited as the founder of the source, Burton being given a secondary and inferior role. But the mystery surrounding his death was to continue, and instead of peaceful rest for the dead man, the controversy simmered with new charges. Burton had written a friend, W. Frank Wilson, that "nothing will be known of Speke's death. I saw him at 1:30 p.m. on the first day of the meeting and at 4 p.m. he was dead. The charitable will say that he shot himself, the uncharitable that I shot him." As late as 1921, George Fuller, then an old man of ninety-two, tried to correct the still-persistent belief that his cousin had committed suicide. In a letter to the *Times* he reaffirmed that Speke's death was an accident; moreover, that "Burton could not have seen Speke that day, and the death occurred before 1:30 p.m."

That Burton always felt tremendously hurt by Speke's actions, by his claims, his inaccuracies and misstatements, and especially by his death, so unclear and tragic, is apparent in whatever Burton said or wrote about the years in Africa and the succeeding period. He wrote that he always considered Speke a "brother," and he had the greatest admiration for Speke's accomplishments, much as his errors were to be deplored. For example, in June 1863, when Burton was in West Africa and Speke in England, Burton wrote a fellow officer, "Please let me hear all details about Captain Speke's discovery. He has performed a magnificent feat and now rises at once to the first rank among the explorers of the day." Consequently, Speke's attacks hurt him deeply. He knew Speke's loneliness, anguish, and insecurity. A cloud would forever diminish the luster of Speke's accomplishments. That a brave though often vain and foolish man—but always brave— would die as Speke died would forever trouble Burton.

26

Brazil

Now there came an opportunity for the Burtons to live to-gether. Isabel had, after much effort, gotten a transfer for her husband from Fernando Po to Santos, a Brazilian port town perhaps as hot, malarial, and steamy as any spot in West Africa but accepted as a post where Europeans could live safely. Mean-while, Burton had finished the incredible number of nine books based on his African material: *Wanderings in West Africa* (two volumes), *Abeokuta and the Cameroons Mountains* (two volumes), *A Mission to Gelele, King of Dahome* (two volumes), *Wit and Wisdom from West Africa* (one volume), and *Two Trips to Gorilla Land and the Cataracts of the Congo* (again, two volumes). Thomas Wright was rather caustic about this prodigious amount of work—"Remorselessly condensed, these nine volumes might, with artistry, have made a book worthy to live"—and lamented Burton's "prolixity." Burton dedicated *Abeokuta* to Isabel, with a Latin inscription, which in part, translated, calls her "Light of my night, sweet rest from cares by day." A rather romantic sentiment, to which Isabel wrote in her copy, "Thank you, sweet love."

The Burtons took a vacation in Ireland, and another in Portugal, seeing bullfights in Lisbon and visiting various places of interest, passing two months in a kind of honeymoon with no cares or worries. Then Burton sent his wife back to London "to pay and pack," a phrase that was to be a hallmark of their life together, while he set off for Rio de Janeiro: Isabel arrived a few weeks later; they went down to Santos in October 1865. The swampy, humid port town reminded Burton too much of the scruffy ports along the West African coast. It was not a place where a reasonable man and his wife could settle permanently, so the Burtons found a better home in São Paulo, a few miles inland, on the pretext that both towns needed a British consul. Isabel took over a former convent as their new home. Here Burton had a forty-foot-long room in which to work, and Isabel had a chapel where, with the permission of the local bishop, she could preach to the black slaves, who, she found, had grown up under the impression that since they were black they had no souls, an error she did her best to correct. Burton told her she was being too sentimental about blacks; she would find them untrustworthy. Her only convert was a black dwarf named Chico, who betrayed her faith in him by roasting her favorite cat alive over the kitchen fire. The question of slavery continued to haunt Burton. Brazil was then a slave country, and the only servants the Burtons could get were slaves, though the consul paid them as free men.

Brazil might have been spared the label of "white man's grave," but it was hardly a "safe" country for inexperienced visitors from the Northern Hemisphere. Almost immediately Isabel came down with a fever as rank as any her husband had experienced in Africa. She was overcome by "sickness and vomiting, colic, dizziness, faintness, shivering, heat and cold, delirium, thirst, disgust of food." She was given calomel and other popular preparations; the delirium alarmed Burton, and he resorted to a favorite practice, hypnotism, and she regained her health.

Santos, when the Burtons were forced to visit it, was filled with sand flies and mosquitoes, jiggers, ticks "the size of a little fingernail," spiders "as big as a toy terrier," and ants so large that some people dressed them up as dolls to play with. "Snakes are everywhere," Isabel noted. Storms were a hazard—"often their force broke the windows," and there were "balls of fire flying through the air." But Santos had its beauties, too—orchids, parrots, and gigantic butterflies.

That was the side of life in Brazil that Isabel could write home to her mother about, for she had no close female confidantes to spill out her troubles to. And there were other pleasant events to tell Mother. The Burtons met the Emperor and Empress of Brazil and found themselves favored over more distinguished guests, for the sovereign was an amateur scientist and his wife a very religious woman and each had a lot to say to one or the other of the Burtons. And then there were other interesting people to meet, people from the European colony, and trips to make here and there. It was a rich country, and as he had in West Africa, Burton found himself absorbed in the idea of finding some quick form of wealth that would relieve his ever-increasing poverty, for the post paid only £700 a year. He speculated in coffee and cotton and explored the notion that there might be some easily gained treasure in the rich red Brazilian earth. He took an option on a lead mine, much to the annoyance of his superiors, and he found rubies in a part of a riverbed owned by a poor old peasant woman, but to buy the land from the woman would have meant disguising his purpose, which would have been cheating her, or telling her the truth—and in that case she would have demanded an exorbitant price. But there were, he expected, other ways to find wealth in the earth, either through diamonds or gold. It was gold that always attracted Burton, but in Brazil, or West Africa, it escaped him, and all he had were dreams of sudden wealth, the wealth of sultans and emperors.

What Isabel could not write her mother about was Burton's incessant wandering, alone (unless he had some secret búbús and bíbís that she was unaware of), wandering here and there, often in dangerous places, just disappearing as if he weren't married but were back in Sind or Arabia or East Africa and had no one to answer to except some faraway general of no account.

Often she was left to suffer in silence and if she dared complain to Mother, it was always with the caution not to mention the matter in answering. There were compensations—Chico and the salvation of the blacks and talks with the Empress—but once, when she came down with a case of boils that covered her almost from head to toe ("I cannot sit or stand, walk or lie down without a moan") and needed nursing and sympathy, Burton went off to search for a sea monster said to be 160 feet long. A four-day trip turned into a month's absence; part of the time Burton drifted in the ocean in shark-infested waters after his canoe had capsized.

Still, Isabel had her illusions. After a year in Brazil she wrote her mother, "I have just domesticated and tamed Richard a little." She was being careful, though—she did not want to give him any excuse for wandering. "He requires a comfortable and respectable home, and a tight hand upon his purse strings, and I feel that I have a mission which amply fills my hands."

How hard Burton worked as consul is difficult to assess. He complained that he had to put out an endless number of reports—"Cotton Reports," 32 pages, "Geographic Report," 125 pages, "General Trade Report," 32 pages, and so on—but he also spent days and weeks on his own works. He translated at last *Vikram and the Vampire*, the popular Hindu folk story—"adapted" was his word, for it was greatly altered from the original—worked on his translation of Camões, collaborated with Isabel on some translations from the Portuguese, investigated Brazilian Indian languages, drafted a grammar of the Tupy-Guarani tongue (which was never completed or published), and had someone else translate for him the autobiography of a German soldier of fortune, Hans Stade of Hesse, who had been captured by Indians in eastern Brazil in the middle of the sixteenth century. Burton wrote an introduction for the book and added extensive footnotes and polished the text. Stade was captured by cannibals, who tied his legs together and made him hop through their village—"Here comes our meat hopping along," said the Indians. But he escaped and went on to other adventures. Burton also spent endless time in archaeological exploration. He dug into the ruins of abandoned Indian villages of past centuries and of jungle-covered Portuguese forts.

Even with her problems, the tropical illnesses and the vermin, the loneliness brought about by her husband's absences, Isabel Burton was an impressive individual, and people flocked around her. One of them, a young attaché from the British Foreign Office, Wilfrid Scawen Blunt, then beginning a short career that would bring him to other posts where Burton served, gave his recollection of Isabel in a work written many years later. "She had developed into a sensible and very talkative woman, clever, but at the same time foolish, overflowing with stories of which her husband was always the hero. Her devotion to him was real, and she was indeed entirely under his domination, an hypnotic domination Burton used to boast of."

Ever on the search for gold, Burton heard of a mine in the state of Minas Geraes. After much hesitation he decided to take Isabel with him. The trip had its romantic side, for it meant going up the river São Francisco on a canoe raft. The mine was impressive and dangerous—men were injured or even died daily from accidents in it. But there was nothing for Burton to get involved in. He decided to continue downriver to the ocean, a thirteen-hundred-mile adventure everyone assured him had never been accomplished before and was impossible. Isabel had sprained her ankle, she did not heal rapidly, and there was no choice but to send her home overland with the servants, a fifteen-day ordeal in the company of the cat-burning Chico, relieved only by numerous visits to churches, convents, and hospitals where Isabel hoped to alleviate the sufferings of the black soulless Catholic slaves. Not much positive was accomplished.

Meanwhile, Burton floated downriver with two Brazilian companions, inspecting diamond mines along the way and shooting rapids no man was known to have survived. This was one of the last major excursions without his wife. "I confess to having felt an unusual feeling of loneliness as the kindly faces faded in the distance," and he thought of the Nile, "of the white man paddled by dark Amazons adorned with barbaric gold."

He came out of the voyage alive, in ragged clothing, sunburned and looking very much like an outlaw from the *sertãos*, the backlands. He got two volumes out of the trip, two volumes of no great consequence that were poorly reviewed. By the spring of 1868 he was in bad health, age and the tropics having taken their toll. And he had been drinking heavily. He had hepatitis—what Isabel called "liver congestion"—and a lung infection that grew steadily worse. The doctor prescribed drastic treatment: Burton was given leeches and cupped and a blister placed on his right side. "He lost an immense amount of black clotted blood," Isabel wrote. "The agony was fearful." He appeared to be close to death. "He seemed to be dying," she wrote. Since modern medicine had failed, she tried prayers and holy water, and after a while Burton said, "Zoo, I think I'm a little better," and he recovered, though he was wan and thin, his voice was hoarse, and he looked sixty rather than forty-seven. "It is sad to look at him," his wife observed.

Life in Brazil had come to an end. "Richard told me he could not stand it any longer. It had given him that illness." Burton applied for leave. The doctor told him not to return to England at once but to go down to Buenos Aires for a rest, and Isabel went off to London to see if she might find him another post and to get his Brazilian manuscripts published.

* * *

In August, shortly after Isabel had sailed for home, Burton set off for Paraguay, where one of the most vicious wars of the century was being fought. It had arisen out of a dispute between Paraguay and Brazil over borders. Argentina and Uruguay were soon drawn into the battle on the side of Brazil after Paraguay had violated their territories, and the war had quickly turned into a struggle, as Burton phrased it, among "an obscure nationality," "a palaeolithic humanity," which fought with single-shot rifles, whose navy was largely punts and canoes, and the highly industrialized military machine of the Allies, who had the latest Spencer and Enfield rifles and armored ships. Paraguay had to call to arms every able-bodied man—there were regiments of boys from twelve to fifteen and even battalions of women—and by the time the war ended in 1870 it had lost eighty percent of its population of one and a third million people; there were only 28,700 men among the survivors.

Burton had little sympathy for the Paraguayans. As consul to Brazil, he was compelled for diplomatic reasons to stay with the Allied forces. He attributed the backwardness of the Paraguayans to the Jesuits (who had been expelled 120 years previously)—the Order had produced a "deadening, brutalizing, religious despotism," he wrote. Still, he had some admiration for their courage, though not for their common sense. He noted that Paraguay had "the bulldog tenacity and semi-compulsory heroism of a redskin Sparta" and "a stubbornness of purpose, a savage valour, and an enduring desperation rare in the annals of mankind."

After a month on the battlefield among the Allied generals and troops—he saw no frontline fighting—he visited Montevideo and then went down to Buenos Aires, a town without sewerage (such an expected complaint by now!) whose streets were "long, narrow, and ill ventilated." He was in a depressed state of mind, drinking heavily and expressing open hostility to everyone he met. He was even more haggard, shabby, and unkempt than when he had come out of the Brazilian wilds. Blunt, in Buenos Aires, came across Burton several times during this period and was distressed by his appearance. "He seemed to me then already a broken man." Blunt was never sympathetic to Burton, and his comments may have been tempered by his fears of this strange and powerful man. Sixteen years after Burton's death he recalled some of the time they spent in Buenos Aires.

> His dress and appearance were those suggesting a released convict. . . . He reminded me by turns of a black leopard, caged but unforgiving, and again with his close cut poll, and iron frame of that wonderful creation of Balzac's, the ex-galérien Vautrin. . . . He wore, habitually, a rusty black coat with a crumpled black silk stock, his throat destitute of collar, a costume which his muscular frame and immense chest made singularly and incongruously hideous, above it a countenance the most sinister I have ever seen, dark, cruel, treacherous, with eyes like a wild beast's.
>
> I have sat up many nights with him, talking all things in Heaven and Earth, or rather listening while he talked till he grew dangerous in his cups, and revolver in hand would stagger home to bed.
>
> In his talk he affected an extreme brutality, and if one could have believed the whole of what he said, he had indulged in every vice and committed every crime. . . .

Burton had a few other friends in Buenos Aires, also men who liked to drink. He set off with two of them on an extended exploration of the Argentine pampas and the Andes, disappearing unnoticed into the wilds of Latin America. This period, like his disappearance into the American South in 1860, was a time—six months in all—that has not been documented. He seems to have written few or no letters, and there were no journals, essays, government reports, articles, or digressions on languages. There was not even the customary book about his travels. However, rumors about his escapades were to circulate, the truth of which cannot be affirmed or dismissed. He is said to have been involved in knife fights in the Andes and to have escaped being murdered by brigands on Christmas Day after another battle almost to the death. There was a report of still another fight in which he was badly wounded in killing four men, but this was the kind of story that Burton liked to tell when drinking or even under more staid circumstances at dinner parties to shock the guests.

Eventually, he reached Lima, where there was nothing to do but drink, and drink some more. Burton was now about as far away from home, friends, career, and his wife as he could be, just wandering from bar to bar, drinking, prowling the streets like an enraged black leopard, brooding over the meaning of things. What had *qismet*—fate—wrought in his life?

27

The Emperor and Empress of Damascus

One day in Lima, when Burton was sitting in a run-down café, drinking his way into insensibility, an acquaintance came up and told him he had just been appointed British consul at Damascus.

The tireless Isabel had wangled the post for him; formal notice was on the way to his office in Brazil. Burton pulled himself together—he had been thinking about returning home, anyway—and set out for England in an aimless, roundabout way that was indicative of his confusion at the time. He sailed down the coast of Chile and through the Strait of Magellan to Buenos Aires, where he found a sack of mail awaiting him, including the formal letter from the Foreign Office about his appointment to Damascus. Then, instead of sailing to London, he went off to the battlefields of Paraguay, where he spent the first two weeks of April interviewing various participants in the war and collecting notes for a book. By now, having a project to interest him, he tapered off his drinking and was able to organize himself sufficiently to be able to return to England, arriving on June 1, 1869, haggard and dressed in the same disreputable clothes he had worn while inspecting the mines.

After a visit to his tailor's came innumerable parties and receptions plus several speeches before learned audiences. Before her husband returned, Isabel had been very busy: she had brought home three large manuscripts for which she found publishers. They were *The Highlands of Brazil* (two volumes), *The Lands of the Cazembe*, and *Iraçéma: The Honeylips*, a translation from the Brazilian Portuguese that was her own; it was bound with a work they had jointly translated, a seventeenth-century chronicle named after its author, *Manuel De Moraes*. She had also a moneymaking project of Burton's, which, like all his others, failed. This was the formation of a company to work some of the Brazilian mines, but the scheme never got started. Burton had also brought back drawings for a new type of pistol that he had thought of while on the Paraguayan battlefields. It would not only be ideal in war but useful for travelers in lands where there were constant threats from highwaymen, and even from bar companions. It was patented but never went into production.

Finally, after the inevitable and expected rounds of visits to relatives and friends, lectures, sightseeing in parts of England that amused them, and extensive preparation for life in Damascus, the Burtons set off on a leisurely voyage to the Levant. They went first to Boulogne to visit "old haunts where we had met as boy and girl"—the words are Isabel's. She went back to London, "as usual, to 'pay, pack, and follow,' " while Burton went to Vichy for a month's course of the waters. Vichy, snapped Isabel, was "a dull, small place, full of sickly people with liver complaints." Burton did not think well of Vichy, either, for he wrote Monckton Milnes a scathing note about the town, calling it "a hideous hole," with its "jaundices, gouts and diabetes," adding, "Out of Paris the French are perfect monsters—the Casino of Vichy would disgrace Constantinople. Separation of sexes complete."

Swinburne was also at Vichy, along with Frederick Leighton, an artist, his sister, Daisy, and a retired diva, Madame Adelaide Kemble Sartoris. Burton and Swinburne made several excursions together into the countryside. In a letter to his mother during this period Swinburne referred to Burton as his "older brother," and there has been much speculation about their time together at Vichy. Was it a homosexual interlude in Burton's life, a respite from native women of all colors and cultures and an unusually pious, demanding Anglo-Saxon wife, an episode that would add to the rumors about Burton's "proclivities" as far back as the Karachi days? Nothing was ever proved, but guilt by association was easy to assume, and speculation has run wild, though Burton's name had never been linked definitely to any other male. Swinburne was notorious for his small perversions, especially his penchant for being birched, but that does not establish an intimate relationship with Burton.

Swinburne and Burton went hiking, climbed various peaks, and sat with their feet swinging into formidable abysses. By dusk both would be exhausted, Swinburne by his natural frailty and Burton from his long years of hard living and his advancing age. Swinburne at this time was drinking heavily, on the way to becoming a chronic alcoholic, while Burton had virtually given up alcohol, possibly as a response to the challenge of the forthcoming post at Damascus. Isabel arrived soon; she would not have appreciated Swinburne's letter to Alice Swinburne: "I rather grudge Mrs. Burton's arrival here . . . though we are excellent friends, and I dare say I shall see none the less of him." There was more sightseeing and a lot of jovial fun with the poet and the Leightons and Madame Sartoris. Then the group broke up, Swinburne returning to England and the Burtons going on a pilgrimage to various holy places in southern France. They continued to Turin, where they separated. Isabel had not yet finished packing and returned home while Burton made a leisurely trip to Damascus, traveling lightly except for two bull terriers and a copy of Camões and his fat volume of the Bible, Shakespeare, and Euclid bound together.

Burton's appointment to Damascus had been immediately controversial. Many of the behind-the-scenes negotiations among his enemies were supposedly unknown to him until later. Even before he had arrived home from South America, Sir Henry Elliot, the British ambassador at Constantinople, had written on May twelfth to his home office to state that among the ruling circles in Damascus, "the most fanatical town in the [Turkish] Empire," Burton's appointment was viewed "with apprehension," and he feared "very undesirable consequences."

> By the Mussulman population Captain Burton is regarded either as having insulted their religion by taking part as an unbeliever in their most sacred rites, or else as having, at that time, been a Mohomedan and having become a renegade.

The new secretary of the Foreign Office, Lord Clarendon, had warned Burton personally of the objections to his appointment. A few days later Burton was informed by the Foreign Office that

> very serious objections to your appointment in Damascus have reached [the Secretary] from official quarters, and that, although Lord Clarendon has allowed the appointment to go forward on receiving your assurances that the objections were unfounded, his Lordship has warned you that if feeling started to exist against you on the part of the authorities and people at that place which should prevent the proper performance of your official duties, it would be his Lordship's duty immediately to recall you.

Burton replied in a formal letter, repeating his assurances to Clarendon "to act with unusual prudence, and under all circumstances to hold myself answerable for all the consequences." And he went on to say that he believed that "neither the authorities nor the people of Damascus will show for me any but the most friendly feeling." However, he did not know the power and the extent of the opposition. The key figure in the machinations against him was the Turkish governor of Syria, Mohammed Rashid 'Ali Pasha, the walī, or viceroy. Rashid had heard enough about Burton to know that the new consul at Damascus might easily become a threat to his own rule. But there were other enemies, lesser men who still had a voice in London, enemies, as Burton had learned so many times in other situations, to be found among his own people. S. Jackson Eldridge, the consul at Beirut, who was technically Burton's superior, feared his arrival, and the English Protestant missionaries worried about a man who was known to favor not Christians but Muslims. Attempts to halt Burton en route failed. Rashid 'Ali met Elliot in Constantinople, to be told that although Burton could not be recalled before he had arrived, Clarendon had placed "strict injunctions upon Captain Burton which he would not be likely to neglect."

That Her Majesty's Government, especially the Foreign Office, was ignorant of the talents of its best Arabist and the controversies that might surround him is difficult to accept. The entire Levant was then in the grip of the Turks, now losing the verve that had made them masters of the Muslim world. Czar Nicholas's biting description of Turkey as "the Sick Man of Europe" was even more valid than when he had first uttered it, and in the costly Crimean War, England had done better than its fair share to hold a crumbling native empire together. That Elliot in Constantinople and the Foreign Office in London cared at all about the grumbling suspicions of a dastardly viceroy in Syria—the wily Rashid 'Ali—is doubtful. England wanted to know what was going on in the Levant, what weaknesses and strengths the Turks showed among alien peoples who resented their rule. If Turkey withdrew or was forced out of Syria, Lebanon, and other areas by war or rebellion, how would the local people react? Would the upper-class elites align themselves with England, Russia, or France? Would they try for independence? And how would the different, conflicting sects and minorities— the many Muslim factions, the warring Christians, minorities like the Druzes and Shī'a—respond to a Turkish collapse? Burton himself could hardly have been naive about what was wanted of him, and that perhaps was the true reason for his dawdling return to London and his procrastinations in reaching Damascus—he was likely worrying over the situation, wondering if he should accept a post that promised disaster as much as honor and glory.

Still, the various British officials involved, while making important-sounding statements and issuing cautions that were ostensibly private but quickly known to the public—especially to the Turks—were also careful to isolate themselves from Burton, for if he failed and they could be shown to have had any part in his failure, their careers, too, would be endangered.

Thus, Burton took a post that was pregnant with contradictions, with the promise of disaster. And if he succeeded, the glory of success might not be acknowledged publicly, for he would have again played out another secret chapter in the Great Game, one for which no credit would be given and for which only blame could be attached.

Even on the premise that Burton was taking on an assignment that implied more than routine consular duties, there were factors that would under ordinary circumstances serve to undermine his position. Rashid 'Ali was an obvious enemy; no one had a kind word to say about him. But there were others who would be willing to see him fail and would quietly do their part to prevent the successful completion of his appointment. The machinery was creakingly set in motion for Burton's eventual recall, and no matter what he did, in the eyes of his enemies his consulship could be interpreted as one blunder after another, which sooner or later would lead to his disgrace. So the situation went inevitably ahead like some involved drama out of the *Arabian Nights* or an Oriental passion play in which events, beyond anyone's control, moved inexorably to a final martyrdom, the central figure being not the sainted Khalīf 'Alī, whom Burton admired so much, but Burton himself.

At first all seemed to go well. Burton arrived in Beirut on

October 1, 1869, and was in Damascus two days later. He had been appalled at Eldridge's consulship—"Eldridge does nothing and is very proud of it," he observed. Isabel, well packed—she had an English maid, five dogs, among them a St. Bernard, and enough luggage to last for ten years—appeared six weeks later. Two of her boxes disappeared on the way—one contained £300 in gold, all the money she possessed—but they turned up safely five months later with the money intact. She found her husband ailing; he was "looking very old and ill." Burton had not received a single one of her many letters, which arrived in a heap later.

Life at Damascus promised to be "all labdanum"—an opium dream; for a while it was. Isabel expected the city to be "my Pearl, the Garden of Eden, the Promised Land, my beautiful white City with her swelling domes and tapering minarets, her glittering golden crescents set in green of every shade," but Damascus was far more exotic than she had expected, for she realized she felt herself "six times further away from home than when living in Brazil."

Damascus was one of the world's great mysterious and exotic cities, an ancient city that had been mentioned in Genesis and later became a center of Islamic culture and learning as the capital of the Umayyid khalīfs after they had moved from Medina. It was a city of mystical importance, pregnant with the esotericism of the Sufis. Al-Ghazzālī, the greatest of Islamic theologians and a Sufi, had retreated to Damascus for a period of "retirement, meditation and devout exercises," spending his days and nights in prayer and meditation in the minaret of the Great Mosque. Ibn al-'Arabī, whose birth had been foretold by 'Abdu'l-Qādir Gīlānī, the founder of Burton's Sufi brotherhood, had settled here in A.D. 1216; his contemporary Salāluddin Rūmī had come to Damascus when his family was fleeing the Mongol advance into Afghanistan. Then there was a minor Sufi brotherhood, the Sházlis (or Shādilīs), an offshoot of the Qādiriyyas.

The mosque itself was an important spiritual center; within it was a shrine with the head of John the Baptist, one of the Muslim *nabis*, or prophets. The aura of mystery and mysticism was heightened by the knowledge that it was in Damascus that al-Dajjal, the anti-Christ, was to make his final appearance. Al-Dajjal, said Burton, "will arise in the East and will peregrinate the earth, but he will be unable to penetrate into Meccah and in approaching [el-Medina] he will turn towards his death-place, Al-Sham (Damascus)." The anti-Christ would be one-eyed and marked with the Arabic characters KFR, meaning *kāfir*, or infidel, and would lay waste the earth in a forty-day reign of terror. Then the descent of " 'Īsa [Jesus], son of Maryam," would occur near the white minaret of the Great Mosque. 'Īsa would descend at the time of the afternoon prayers to lead the *salāt* according to the rite of Muḥammad. He would slay the anti-Christ. He would take a wife, beget children, and after forty years on earth would be buried at el-Medina. "Under him there will be great security and plenty," said a Muslim commentator. "Lions and camels, bears and sheep, would live in peace and a child shall play with [poisonous] serpents unhurt." After 'Īsa had prepared the way, the Madhī, the "Expected One," who was now in occultation, would appear to make the Muslims a mighty nation ruling the world.

Damascus was also the land of *Tancred*, and Isabel found recollections of the book everywhere in the rich tapestry of race and religion all around her. There were Sunnī Muslims of the four schools, and many Shī'a sects, including the Isma'īlīs, and Baha'īs and Yezīdīs, the so-called devil worshipers of the Kurds, the puritanical Wahhābīs, five types of Jews and fourteen Christian sects, including Maronite, Greek, Armenian, Jacobite, Copt, and Abyssinian, and a handful of Protestants converted by missionaries from England and the States; French, Italian, and Spanish missions had produced their own handfuls of devout Roman Catholics, each group distinguished by the cultural imprint of its founders. The mixture of races, tribes, and faiths, so intriguing to scholars, was chaotic: Explosions threatened constantly. In 1860 there had been devastating intercommunal riots:

parts of the city were burned, and some two thousand people had been killed or severely wounded. It was generally assumed that sooner or later another riot would occur.

Exciting as the city was, it was not to be the Burtons' home. It was surrounded by walls, and the gates were locked at night, giving the consul claustrophobia. Isabel found a house in the Kurdish village of Salahiyyeh ("of the saints"), a fifteen-minute ride from the Damascus walls, where the Burtons could have "a freer and wilder life": "You could mount your horse, and be out in the desert in ten minutes. . . ." And in Salahiyyeh, Burton could study the Kurdish Yezīdīs, the Peacock Angel cult whose doctrines would someday infuse his strange elegy, *The Kasîdah.* So, the Burtons settled down to live in the grand style, a style that was more Oriental than English.

The house, centered around a larger court with orange and lemon trees, was virtually a palace; outside could be seen the cool white domes of the mosques and the slim minarets and apricot trees and towering palms. The garden, lush with roses, jessamine, vines, and citrus trees, ran down to an ancient river, the "jewel blue Chrysorrhea." The Burtons had stables filled with horses. "I know everything they say, and think, and feel; and they know also what I say to them," said Isabel. The Burtons kept any type of horse but a thoroughbred, for such horses might have led to rumors of corruption. Isabel also had a menagerie. Her special forte was rescuing animals and also trying to convert the natives, of whatever religion, to her kind of Roman Catholicism. She had donkeys and a camel, turkeys, bull terriers, pye-dogs (once as many as fifty), lambs, pigeons and goats, a white Persian cat, a pet lamb, chickens, geese, guinea fowl, a panther so tame it would eat from one's hand, and, as Burton remarked, "other notions." Isabel spent many hours trying to train natural enemies to love each other, but the panther ate the lamb and chased the goats, one of which jumped into the river and drowned; the fowl ate the seeds and flowers in the garden, the cat killed the birds, and the dogs worried the cat, but Isabel noted that the survivors of the menagerie became "a really harmonious family."

The grand manner in which the Burtons lived soon gave them an air of royalty; they were, in fact, a kind of "Emperor and Empress of Damascus," active, powerful, charming, much sought after, with friends in all social classes, racial and religious groups, and sects. They had some of the trappings of royalty, too, like the four *qawwáses*, or consular guards, dressed in bright scarlet coats, who not only protected the consulate but also made themselves noticeable at Isabel's salon or preceded her when she walked through the city's crowded streets. Rumors spread quickly that the *qawwáses* cleared the way for her with whips, but those were rumors, not fact.

On Isabel's reception days, when the elite of Damascus flocked to her salon, visitors, if they were Oriental, sat cross-legged on divans—on chairs if they were European—all smoking cigarettes and pipes of exotic character, drinking sherbet and coffee, and nibbling on baklava, halva, fritters in syrup, pastries like konafa, zalabia, and ma'amounia, and delicate puddings of rice, figs, or bananas.

The visitors ranged from local dignitaries to wandering Europeans, a few of them figures of importance and imposing power. One of the most powerful and most dangerous was the governor, Rashid 'Ali Pasha, already a sworn enemy, a man the Burtons disliked immediately. He was fat and indolent, with pinpoint eyes; he dressed in furs, walked on his toes, purred, and looked like "a well-fed cat," Burton said in the *Life*. "Call him Ra'shid, with the accent on the first syllable," Burton emphasized, "and do not confound him with Haroun al Rashid, accent on the second syllable—'the orthodox,' the 'treader on the right path,' " meaning the famous khalīf of the *Arabian Nights*.

A more congenial friend was the exiled hero of the Algerian wars against the French, Abd el Kadir, a regal-looking man whose fine dark features were enhanced by the snow-white robes he always wore. Abd el Kadir, as his name implies, was a Sufi of the same order as Burton's, the Qādiris. "A conscientiously religious Moslem," Burton said of the shaykh. Abd el Kadir was also affiliated with another Sufi brotherhood, the Shādilīs, an order found all across North Africa and in Damascus. The shaykh was one of the great Muslim leaders of the time. For fifteen years he had led a war against the French occupation of Algeria, finally surrendering in 1847 in the face of a superior military machine. The French promised the shaykh that if he gave up the struggle, he and his family would be allowed to go into exile in the Levant; instead, they were imprisoned. After five years Abd el Kadir was released and eventually found his way to Damascus. When the great anti-Christian riots broke out in 1860, the shaykh gave sanctuary to three thousand refugees, despite the bitter memories of his treatment by other Christians. In his exile, the shaykh, a natural scholar, devoted his time to theology and philosophy. His major work was entitled (in English) "Call to the intelligent, Warning to the indifferent." He also wrote a book on the Arab horse. All these qualities—bravery, intelligence, a passion for learning, the ability to write works of impressive scholarship—made him a favorite of Burton's, for he was that special figure, the warrior-saint, a man impressive in leadership and intellect.

One of the most colorful feminine members of the salon, and the one who interested Europeans, was Lady Jane Digby, "notorious and polyandrous," as Thomas Wright described her. It was true she had married often and always on the highest levels. She was first the wife of Lord Ellenborough, then of Prince Swartenberg, and after that of a number of other gentlemen. Wright says six, but he was relying on gossip, and he overlooked the uncounted affairs, which included interludes with several kings, among them King Ludwig I of Bavaria and Ludwig's son, Otto, when he was king of Greece. After the last few relationships in Greece, one with a Count Spyridon Theotoky and another with an Albanian swashbuckler, General Xristodolous Hadji-Petros, who took her off into the reckless life of the Balkan mountains—the general was over sixty, Jane in her thirties—she left Europe and made her way to the Orient, where, as Isabel Burton wrote, at the age of forty-eight she married "a dirty little black," a true Bedawin shaykh. Despite the color of his skin (which Isabel may have exaggerated), the shaykh, Medjuel El Mezrab, was the leader of an important subtribe of nomads. Isabel had to admit that "he was a very intelligent charming man in any light but that of a husband. That made me shudder." However, it was a marriage that eventually lasted twenty-six years, during which Jane attempted to "tame" her husband—it took her fifteen years to teach him how to use knife and fork.

Whatever Lady Jane's credentials, she and Isabel became close friends, for there were few Europeans in Syria at the time, and Isabel needed a female confidante. Burton didn't like Lady Jane, but Isabel thought her "a most beautiful woman, though sixty-one, tall, commanding, and queen-like." Lady Jane, in Isabel's opinion, was a grande dame to the tips of her fingers, as if she had just quitted the salons of London and Paris.

She spoke nine languages perfectly . . . she lived half the year in Damascus, and half with her husband in his Bedawin tents, she like any other Bedawin woman, but honoured and respected as the queen of her tribe, wearing one blue garment, her beautiful hair in two long plaits down to the ground, milking the camels, serving her husband, preparing his food, sitting on the floor and washing his feet, giving him his coffee, and while he ate she stood and waited on him, and glorying in it. She looked splendid in Oriental dress. . . . She was my most intimate friend, and she dictated to me the whole of her biography.

They were indeed close friends. Nothing was spared in Lady Jane's revelations, and the book that she dictated to Isabel Burton must have been one of the wildest, steamiest narratives ever put on paper, not only the many trysts and unbridled passions but the great dramatic moments, like the time she saw her lover shot down by one of her husbands. Unfortunately, when Lady Jane died, her survivors in England insisted that the manuscript be destroyed, so Isabel burned it.

Both Isabel and Lady Jane were inveterate smokers, and with Abd el Kadir and Burton they passed endless evenings on the terrace of the house with their *nargilehs*, or water pipes. Lady Jane, as Burton sensed, was not to be trusted. He wanted to visit a historic site in the desert, the ruins of Tadmor, an eight-day ride from Damascus. There were only two known wells on the way, and their location was kept secret by Lady Jane's Bedawins, who charged a fee for all travelers, a monstrous £250. Burton was determined to make the trip without paying the tolls. When Lady Jane heard of his plans, she was furious, for if Burton found a way to avoid payment, so would other travelers, and the tribe would lose an important source of revenue. She pleaded and argued with him, but he was determined to stamp out this form of blackmail (and all the others) that so enraged him.

Lady Jane's way of handling the problem was to offer Burton a Bedawin from her tribe as a guide to steer him away from brigands and to show the way to water "if it existed." It was learned later that the guide had been instructed to lead Burton and his party into ambush, to be held prisoner until they could be ransomed. Burton, so long wise to the ways of the Arab world, disarmed the guide as soon they were away from Damascus, took his horse, and kept the man prisoner for the journey while they continued on to visit the ruins—"an imposing sight," Isabel wrote.

Burton had his men do some excavating, a few ancient statues were found, and the party, after a month in the field, returned to Damascus, having outwitted Lady Jane and found water without paying the Bedawin.

Syria, so archaic and filled with esoteric cultures, was of inestimable interest for Burton. Wherever he went there was something to attract him, to engage his scholarly attention. As usual, he ransacked the libraries large and small for copies of the *Arabian Nights*; among other treasures he found an early Greek manuscript of the Bible and a portion of a second-century visionary Gnostic tract, the *Shepherd of Hermas*. Isabel talked her way into Abd el Kadir's harem.

> He had five wives, one of them very pretty. I asked them how they could bear to live together and pet each other's children. I told them that in England, if a woman thought her husband had another wife or mistress, she would be ready to kill her. They all laughed heartily at me, and seemed to think it a great joke.

Isabel got invited to various religious and social functions that were the province of the women and in various harems was able "to note things hidden from mankind." She collected a lot of unusual information, some of which got into Burton's massive notebooks and was later worked into his copious annotation of the *Arabian Nights*. "Wealthy harems," he was to write, basing his material on his wife's researches on lesbian practices, "are hot-beds of Sapphism and Tribadism." In Damascus, "every woman past her first youth has a girl she calls her 'Myrtle' [Venus]. . . ."

Some of the harem material was later put into his translation of an Indian erotic manual, the *Kama Sutra*. "Where there are many women to a single man," he wrote, "they give pleasure to each other in various ways as now described."

> Having dressed the daughters of their nurses, or their female friends, or their female attendants, like men, they accomplish their object by means of bulbs, roots, and fruits having the form of the lingam, or they lie down upon the statue of a male figure, in which the lingam is visible and erect.——
>
> . . . Such are the ways of enjoyment prevalent in Eastern countries, and what is said about the means of enjoyment of the female is also applicable to the male. . . .

The year 1869 ended in a blaze of parties, and the new year . . . well, "It was an excitable year," wrote Isabel with understatement in the *Life*.

At first, Damascus had promised to be an undemanding post for Burton. There were only thirty or so British citizens in the city, but there were complications. Under international custom at the time, the British government took responsibility for Levantine Christians living within that part of the Turkish Empire. Also, some of the other minorities, among them certain of the Jewish community, were under British protection.

One day in July 1870, the Burtons were "surprised" to find some visitors outside their home. They were then in their summer quarters at Bludán, a small Christian village in the Lebanese mountains west of Damascus. Burton seems to have been expecting them, although he feigned ignorance of their coming.

> I suddenly found two Englishmen camping with a gypsy-tent below the garden. They were Palmer and C. F. Tyrwhitt-Drake, brown and sunburnt by travel in the service of the 'Sinai Survey Expedition.' . . . They proved to be the most pleasant of companions. . . .

They were Charles Francis Tyrwhitt-Drake and Edward Henry Palmer. Drake had been born in 1848 and Palmer in 1840. Each had extensive experience in the East, and on their latest excursion they had walked from Suez across Sinai and then through areas—"Biblical" was the general description—that were empty spaces on European maps. Drake had been an asthmatic from childhood and was handicapped even in obtaining an education, yet he had become a skilled ornithologist, going off at the age of twenty to Morocco to hunt and collect natural-history specimens; in this manner he acquired much "valuable knowledge of the Eastern character" and learned Arabic. He later turned up in Egypt, and in the spring of 1869 he went to the Sinai, where he made the acquaintance of the members of the Sinai expedition, one of whom was Palmer. Drake returned to England to prepare for a longer trip into the Levant and in the autumn, with Palmer, went back to the Middle East. The two wandered about the Negeb and parts of Edom and Moab previously unknown to Europeans, discovering new sites and making extensive maps. On his way home Drake passed through Palestine, Syria, Greece, and Turkey, and in the early months of 1870 he returned to Egypt, ostensibly for the Palestine Exploration Fund. Again Palmer was his companion.

Drake was young and only moderately experienced, but a rapid learner. Palmer, more experienced, more intelligent, better educated, and a far more complicated person, seemed, in the light of later knowledge, like an echo of Burton as a young man.

Like Burton's Hindustani mentor, Duncan Forbes, Palmer had been educated at Perse grammar school, where he was in advance of his age in his studies. He was a born student—sixteen hours of study at a time were common for him—and a natural linguist, and though not yet sixteen he distinguished himself by learning Romany, which he picked up at odd times and on half holidays by haunting the Gypsy encampments in the area and spending his pocket money in entertaining wandering tinkers. On leaving school, Palmer got a job with a wine merchant in London. In his free time he took up Italian, learning it as he did Romany, from the people who spoke it as their first language—in this case the political refugees from Italy whom he met in cafés, organ-grinders, music-hall entertainers, and street vendors of Catholic religious articles. He was said even at this time to have "a remarkable vocabulary," and he learned various Italian dialects also. He picked up French in the same manner. Like Burton, Palmer had a mystical side, too, investigating the occult, crystal gazing and wondering about the so-called "philosopher's stone," and experimenting with mesmerism, "in which he exhibited extraordinary powers."

At Cambridge he began a serious study of Oriental languages under various Indian scholars, and shortly his command of Persian, Arabic, and Hindustani was described by one Indian professor as "elegant and idiomatic." Palmer now became deeply immersed in Oriental studies and even contributed articles in Persian and Urdu to journals in India. Meanwhile, his esoteric interests continued: In 1867 he published a small work called

Oriental Mysticism: a treatise on the Suffistic and Unitarian Philosophy of the Persians, an interpretation of a little-known work, 'Afiz ibn Mohammad Afasi's *Maksad-i Aksa*.

In 1869, Palmer was invited to join the small group of officers and civilians surveying the Sinai under the auspices of the Palestine Exploration Fund. His chief duty on this mapmaking expedition was to collect from the Bedawin the correct names of places and to establish an accurate nomenclature of the peninsula. This was his first contact with ordinary Arabs, the nomads and the peasants, and he quickly picked up local dialects and studied peasant life and thought. It was on this expedition that he encountered Charley Drake, and it was then that their joint work in the Middle East began to take on an air of mystery. In London, Palmer and Drake planned another expedition and returned to Cairo. Now they went off into the desert alone, without the customary guides and attended by no armed guards and dragomen. Palmer, like Burton on the Mecca pilgrimage, passed as an Arab, calling himself 'Abdallah Effendi. Both men traveled on foot, walking the six hundred miles from Sinai to Jerusalem, ostensibly—if they were stopped by the Turks—searching for antiquities. They explored for the first time El Tib, the "Desert of the Wanderings," as Palmer translated it, much to Burton's pedantic annoyance, for he claimed that El Tib meant only "a wilderness where man may wander." Whatever the nomenclature, Palmer and Drake visited many areas of Edom and Moab unknown to Europeans and "accomplished a quantity of useful geographical work." It was not only a difficult trip but also a dangerous one. "Numerous stories are related of [Palmer's] presence of mind in moments of danger and difficulty and of his extraordinary influence over the Bedouin, for which, perhaps, his early experiences among the Romany had formed a sort of initiation," wrote Stanley Lane-Poole, who knew Palmer.

Palmer and Drake continued on foot to Damascus, to turn up in the Burtons' garden. Perhaps their long walk was a typical adventure carried out by a pair of courageous and inquisitive young men, but from what is known of certain aspects of Palmer's later career, questions might be asked about whether or not he was just a wandering scholar interested in antiquities of the deserts or involved in the Great Game. Palmer had an extraordinary command of Arabic and its various dialects, he was well versed in Islam, and he could easily pass himself off to the average Middle Easterner as one of themselves. In fact, on the final mission that cost him his life, he called himself El Shámi, the Syrian, and he was carrying an extremely large amount of money for use in a secret-service operation, so one might easily wonder what he was doing in Damascus with Burton, for the appearance of Palmer and Drake at the consulate made it seem likely that the three men were not simply curious scholars investigating buried ruins and lost cities but, as the Walī, Rashid 'Ali Pasha, feared, engaged in anti-Turkish activities that should be stopped.

It was for the moment an idyllic life, with endless explorations into the desert, relentlessly pursuing the "white spots" that the cartographers had ignored, finding them teeming with ruins, broken pillars, inscribed stones, tombs, the remnants of a dozen cultures and civilizations, especially Christianity—"a Fifth Gospel," Burton said—visiting shaykhs, Bedawin chiefs, shrines of all faiths, and most importantly of all, mapping and charting the land. It was this latter activity, almost frantic in retrospect, that aroused the Turks. There had been talk of a railway to India, but nothing definite was done. Burton thought a main railway from Constantinople across Syria and the Euphrates Valley and Persia into India should be constructed. "Syria is fated to become in a few years most important to England," he said in an unintended reference to his activities. If England did not act, then the French would, and worst of all, the Russians. How much of this was Burton's own scheme for imperial annexation and how much was part of his government's playing of the Great Game will not likely ever be known. But there was enough unexplained mapmaking to arouse the suspicions of the very nervous, very suspicious Rashid 'Ali.

Meanwhile, the romantic rides continued. If traveling seemed dangerous, Burton's party had an armed escort. Sometimes, to avoid scandal, Isabel dressed as a boy and posed as Burton's son. It was Romance of a high order—rides at dawn in the desert cool, halts in the noonday sun, simple meals of laban or yogurt, raw onions on pita bread, eggs fried in ghee. Then there were the sounds of the night when the jackals played in the moonlight, "sounding in a distant pack like the war cry of the Bedawi," Isabel wrote.

> I can never forget some of those lovely nights in the desert, mules, donkeys, camels, horses, and some mares picketed about, screaming, kicking, and hallowing: the stacked loads, the big fires, the black tents, the Turkish soldiers, the picturesque figures in every garb, and the wild and fierce-looking men in wonderful costumes lying here and there, singing and dancing barbarous dances. . . . Richard reciting the Arabian Nights, or poor Palmer chanting Arab poetry, or Charley Drake practising magic to astonish the Mogháribehs. . . .
>
> I have seen the gravest and most reverend Shaykhs rolling on the ground and screaming with delight in spite of their Oriental gravity, and they seemed as if they could not let my husband go again.

The nomads called Burton "Brother of the Lion" and made up a song in his honor.

> Marshalla! Marshalla! At last we have seen a man!
> Behold our Consul is our Shaykh! . . .
> Let us follow him all over the earth!

There was no doubt that Burton was on good terms with the local people, in Damascus and in the villages, with the desert tribes and the religious sects. In the summer of 1870 he decided to visit some outlying Druze chieftains. He invited Eldridge to accompany him, to come to Damascus and then go out into the desert. But Eldridge was known never to leave Beirut and did not answer. Rashid 'Ali Pasha heard of the proposed expedition and was vehemently opposed, as the Druzes were strongly antagonistic to the Turks. By this time Burton suspected some kind of trick and wondered if he was to be ambushed and assassinated in the desert, a plan devised by the Walī with Eldridge's implicit consent. Isabel was ill with dysentery, so with Palmer and Drake, Burton set out without her. Rumors reached Isabel of a plot; she sent a messenger after Burton with a warning hidden in a medicine bottle. When the message was received, the three Englishmen hid their horses in a cave. "After a few hours," Burton wrote, "we saw a hundred horsemen and two hundred dromedary riders beating the country, looking for someone in the plains."

Burton and his party escaped the ambush. "I was never more flattered in my life," he wrote, "than to think that it would take three hundred men to kill me."

In the fall of the same year—1870—Drake and Palmer left Damascus, their work finished for the moment. There seemed to have been no suspicions of the men at the time other than Rashid 'Ali's worries about Burton. Drake remained in the Middle East, traveling, exploring, and mapping. He soon returned to Bludán to collaborate with Burton on *Unexplored Syria* (published in 1872 in two volumes, with numerous maps and illustrations). Drake also contributed maps and drawings to Palmer's account of the Desert of Tib and some minor reports and official Letters.

After leaving Damascus, Palmer went to Constantinople and then to Vienna, where he met Arminius Vambéry, one of Burton's most contentious rivals; he then returned to England to marry Laura Davis, his fiancée of many years. After being denied honors and university recognition, Palmer finally was given a modest but not quite financially comfortable post at Cambridge teaching Arabic, Persian, and Hindustani. He compiled Arabic and Persian dictionaries and a Persian grammar that is still in print and translated the Qur'ān and a mystical Kabbālistic work, the *Zohar*, and turned out minor translations from the Finnish, Danish, and German. He had always been especially interested in Ḥāfiẓ and finally made a translation of the poet, which drew some criticism from Burton. But less demanding people saw Palmer's work in a better light, and he was invited to contribute the fine section on Ḥāfiẓ in the *Encyclopaedia Britannica* that was still included in the famous eleventh edition of 1911.

Questions about Burton began to circulate, reaching even the British minister at Constantinople. Almost from the beginning of his consulate Burton had tried to impose his own very strict ethical code of behavior on people who preferred their own. He had more than sufficient experience to know better, but perhaps he was becoming thoughtless and even narrow-minded. Servants who stole or cheated were summarily dismissed. But such acts were minor in the larger scale of events. Burton had protested certain un-Christian acts of the Greek Christian bishop and earned the enmity of the Greek faithful. At Holy Week in Jerusalem, a period of intense excitement among the many Christian sects in the Levant, Burton's servants were stoned by a group from the patriarchate. When Burton and Drake came out of their tents, they, too, were stoned with cries of "Kill them! kill them!" as if St. John's Gospel were being reenacted in real life. Though he was hit several times, Burton stood his ground. To drive off the attackers, he fired a shot in the air. It seemed like a minor incident at the time in a land of endless violence, but it was the first of many unpleasant events to come, a small cloud in an enveloping storm that grew each day.

A major incident erupted in August 1870. A series of religious squabbles had broken out, starting with the beating of a Syrian Christian who was attempting to collect a debt from a Muslim. The Catholic patriarch had the Muslim jailed. About the same time, two young Jewish boys, barely twelve years old, were caught painting the Cross on the latrine of a mosque, an act that was an affront to Muslims and Christians alike. One of the boys worked for a Jewish merchant under the protection of the British government, the other for a French merchant. Both boys were arrested but, being under age, were released. The leading English missionary at Damascus, who had already warned Burton of impending trouble, told him he believed the Muslims were actually the culprits behind the incident; other rumors blamed the Druze community. Then Drake received a report that the Druzes were preparing to attack the Christians. Rumors ran unchecked and spread without refutation. On the minds of the leaders of all communities—the British and other Europeans, the native Christians, the Jews—was the memory of the frightful slaughter of 1860. The Turkish militiamen, all Muslims, threatened the Christians with another massacre. It was a situation that required cool nerves, an iron will, determination, exterior calm, and a profound understanding of the minds of alien peoples. Burton quickly made a public show of his calm by appearing on the streets of the most dangerous quarters in a manner that told the crowds of the foolishness of arousing the anger of British power. From then on, resentment against foreigners, and especially against Burton, increased. Burton, under the rights given the British consul, called in the Jewish boys to question them. Rumors spread that he had the boys tortured and that Isabel insulted a Jewish woman at a party by tearing off her necklace and jewelry and stomping on them, saying they were the blood of the poor. This was merely the beginning of troubles with the Jewish community, who sensed that Burton showed a streak of anti-Semitism. The tensions continued, centered on the activities of three Jewish moneylenders. Under Syrian law, debtors could be sent to prison. If the creditor was under British protection, he had the right to demand that the British consul assist him in collecting the debt. When one of the moneylenders requested Burton's aid in collecting £60,000 owed him by some peasants, Burton refused, saying he had not come to Syria to be a bailiff. The moneylender, Burton charged, had "ruined and sucked dry forty-one villages." The three moneylenders next wrote to friends in London accusing Burton of anti-Semitism. The friends were powerful and active. One was Sir Moses Montefiore, a noted philanthropist who had taken up the cause of the Jews in the Levant and had gained many rights for them; another was Sir Francis Goldsmid, the first English Jewish barrister, who stated that he heard that Burton's wife was "a bigoted Roman Catholic" who was likely to influence him against the Jews.

Montefiore and Goldsmid were but the avant-garde of Burton's enemies. Stories began to circulate in London that Isabel had struck a young Muslim in the face with a riding whip, to be followed by the rumor that she had killed two men and had wounded another because they had refused to salute her. It hurt Isabel that Montefiore, who had been among Burton's friends, believed unsubstantiated reports. That she hit a Muslim was true, but she explained in the *Life* that it was during a period of high tension between Muslims and Christians, when violence was about to erupt. The son of a local shaykh spat at her and tried to pull her from her horse as he was leading a horde of fellow Muslims to burn down the house at Bludán. At the time, Burton was absent on a mission in the desert. Isabel, to assert her control over the situation—for such a personal attack "in the East means volumes"—struck the man in the face with her crop. She learned later from a Turkish officer that it was Rashid 'Ali himself who had ordered the burning of the village of Bludán, which was populated mostly by poor Greek Orthodox Christians. But she persuaded the Turks not to level the village, and the tension abated.

Into this atmosphere of chaos, rivalries, intrigues, suspicion, mysteries, riots, and murders there came one more incident, major in extent and the one that was to finish Burton as consul. Down in the "lower quarter" of Damascus was an esoteric sect of Muslims known as Sházlis, a Sufi brotherhood that, like many such poor and underprivileged groups, was messianic in character. The Sházlis began to congregate at night to study and pray; visions and miracles were reported. One of those sympathetic to the Sházlis was Burton's friend Abd el Kadir. For two years the inner circle of the sect had met at his house to meditate and pray "for enlightenment before the throne of God." Finally, wrote Isabel, "they became conscious of a presence amongst them that was not theirs. They used to hear things and see things they did not understand, and this went on for two or three months before they came to an understanding." "At length," said Burton, "they were assured by a vision that it was the religion of Christ which they were seeking. Yet such was their dread of authority that none could trust his secret with his neighbours."

The movement had begun only in 1868 when a small group of peasants in the city had been initiated by a man calling himself Abd el Matar of Darayya. He was a self-taught mystic, and in his searchings he left his wife, family, clan, and native village to found a center in Damascus, basing it on a Sufi brotherhood established in the thirteenth century by 'Abd al-Ḥusayn Shādilī, a noted Sufi mystic, who had died in Mecca in 1258.

> Presently about forty of them, headed by Abd el Karim Matar, met for their usual night prayers. After prolonged devotional acts, all fell asleep, and our Lord was pleased to appear to all of them separately. They awoke simultaneously, and one, taking courage, recounted his vision to the others, when each responded, "I also saw Him."

"Christ had so consoled, comforted and exhorted them to follow His faith, and they were so filled with a joy they had never known, that they were hardly dissuaded from running about the streets to proclaim that Christ is God," Burton added, "but they were admonished that they would only be slaughtered."

A second collective dream brought a vision of a saintly old man with a long white beard, dressed in a coarse brown garment and holding a lighted candle. The Sházlis searched the city for three months to find such a guide and eventually came across Fray Förner, a Spanish Franciscan monk living in a monastery in the northern section of Damascus, and told him of the visions and mystical raptures they had experienced. Now they questioned their own Islam and wondered if there was not something better. They told Förner that the old man in the vision had said "sweetly," "Let those who want the truth follow me." That the

Sházlis were being led to Christianity seemed apparent, and, rather troubled, Fray Förner confided in the Burtons, for the conversion of Muslims to another faith was a serious matter and usually resulted in the convert's being sentenced to death by both the religious and secular authorities.

What was to be done for these unfortunate people? They would clearly be exposed to the fury of the ruling powers, the 'Ulema, the Islamic judges, and the military, all of whom, going by the laws of Islamic orthodoxy, could punish the Sházlis as heretics.

Förner and the Burtons were not the only Christians to become involved with the Sházlis. Some Protestant missionaries heard of their dilemma and attempted to proselytize the group. The situation was steadily worsening, and Burton, disguised as a Muslim and unknown to anyone but Isabel, mixed with the Sházlis in their quarter and passed much of his time there learning their doctrines and trying to find a solution to the problem. "He saw what he saw," wrote Isabel with some drama. "Fray Förner was the guide who was pointed out to them by that spiritual Presence." Her husband's interest in the sect, she added, "was his ruin. . . . Though he did not mean it, he ended up by sacrificing his worldly career entirely to it." What originally had seemed like no more than a few hundred poor, sometimes wretched Arabs seeking a Saviour to rescue them from their misery quickly assumed the proportions of a major heresy. Some twenty-five thousand Sházlis were now reported ready for baptism, and they would become Roman Catholics, not Protestants. These "secret Christians," Burton wrote later, were "longing for baptism."

Burton's next move was either so altruistic that he failed to see the consequences or was merely part of some involved British maneuvering against the Sublime Porte in the playing out of the Great Game. He proposed to finance the resettlement of the Sházlis outside Damascus. He would buy land, have houses built, and move the Sházlis, all twenty-five thousand of them, and would not expect repayment or taxes.

What raises questions is that a man on Burton's salary would certainly find this a difficult project to finance, even with his wife's three hundred gold pounds. However, Burton's cryptic remark, made later in the *Life* about the disbursement of secret-service funds in Sind, may have some relevance here; he may have had such funds available in Damascus; he certainly was no stranger to the kind of oblique and seemingly nonexistent maneuvering that was involved. That there were ambiguities in the Sházli situation is evident. Burton had little sympathy for Christians and less for converts of any kind, and yet he was willing to see the Sházlis turn into Roman Catholics.

Events now ran out of control for the Sházlis and for Burton. He had expected that he might get permission from the Turks and from the newly installed British ambassador, Lord Granville, in Constantinople, for both a mass conversion and the resettlement of the sect, but forces were at work that would undermine the Sházlis and demolish Burton.

Twelve of the most spiritually favored of the Sházlis, men who had experienced the most intense visions and divine raptures, were arrested by the Turks, put in chains, to suffer a kind of martyrdom, and then Fray Förner died mysteriously. Burton had hoped that the Latin patriarch of Jerusalem, Archbishop Valerga, could baptize the Sházlis en masse, with Isabel standing as sponsor. Granville forwarded Burton's proposal to Valerga, who openly and "clumsily" approached the Turkish authorities—Rashid 'Ali Pasha and his subordinates—at Damascus, and that was the end of the Sházli affair, and soon of Burton, for the accumulation of incidents in which he stood opposed not only to the Turks but also to his own government, to the Protestant missionaries, the Greek and Roman Catholic bishops, the various Muslim sects, the Jewish moneylenders—in short, to anyone he thought was not open, honest, courageous, and moral—undid him. "This is suffering persecution for justice' sake," he said as the attacks on him mounted. He now seemed to have nothing but enemies, and the attacks "broke his career," wrote his wife.

It was *qismet*—fate—working inexorably and as cruelly as anyone might have feared.

The grand plan had collapsed. The British embassy at Constantinople, Archbishop Valerga, the Sublime Porte, and Rashid 'Ali all had a role in betraying him. The Sházlis were to be sacrificed to mysterious British designs, just as Kars had been a few years earlier when Burton's scheme to rescue the beleaguered garrison fell to the necessities of *haute politique*.

One day in mid-August 1871, Burton and Isabel were about to go for a ride in the Anti-Lebanon. Isabel was outside the house waiting for her husband. The horses were saddled, when suddenly "a ragged messenger on foot" appeared. Isabel brought the note inside to Richard. The letter, which was from the vice-consul at Beirut, said that Lord Granville had sacked Burton and another man had already taken responsibility for the Damascus consulate. The entry in Burton's journal for that day was as terse as it was tragic.

> *August 18*th.—Left Damascus for ever; started at three a.m. in the dark, with a big lantern; all my men crying; alone in *coupé* of diligence, thanks to the pigs. Excitement of seeing all for the last time. All seemed sorry; a few groans. The sight of Bludán mountains in the distance at sunrise, where I have left my wife. *Ever again?* Felt soft. Dismissal ignominious, at the age of fifty, without a month's notice, or wages, or character.

Granville had dismissed Burton without the usual courtesies, without a hearing, without an opportunity for explanation or defense. Isabel saw a larger dimension in the tragedy. "From that date," she wrote in the *Life*, "began the ruin of Damascus and the visible and speedy decline of Syria."

Burton rode off to Damascus, leaving Isabel behind without telling her what had happened. A short while later he sent her a note by mounted messenger, "Don't be frightened, I am recalled. Pay, pack, and follow at convenience." Isabel wrote that she was not frightened, "but I do not like to remember what I thought or felt."

Isabel could not rest that night, the nineteenth. Three times she thought she heard Burton calling her. She got up, dressed, saddled her horse, and set off straight across country "over rocks and through swamps" to the coach station nine hours away. Here, "hot, torn and covered with dust and mud from head to foot," she stopped the diligence and climbed aboard and reached Beirut twenty-four hours before Burton's steamer was to sail. From the diligence Isabel saw her husband walking along the road, "looking so sad and serious. . . ." But she was "well rewarded for my hard ride. For when he saw me his whole face was illuminated, and he said, 'Thank you, *bon sang ne peut mentir.*' " They had "twenty-four hours to take counsel and comfort together." Burton was now nothing but a private citizen in misfortune, with not even a *qawwás* to attend him, to see him out with a show of honor and respect. But he was not quite alone. Though the British consul had cut him, the French consul took in the Burtons, now so forlorn and at the mercy of whatever fates might buffet them. Burton sailed off to England, while Isabel returned to Bludán to pay and pack.

Burton had now only the small consolation of listing the major forces that did him in, among them Rashid 'Ali Pasha, who only a month later was arrested by his own government for various crimes, taken to the capital, and imprisoned. Shortly after that, Burton wrote, the Pasha's brains were blown out by a man he had oppressed. Among the enemies who had helped destroy him, Burton listed his own consul general at Beirut, a man distinguished only by "the careful registering of his barometers, and the amount of beer which helped that arduous task."

The major causes, however, of Burton's troubles in Damascus were two: He was honest in his dealings with people, and he got trapped into a secret mission that neither he nor his government would acknowledge. Why should he not have been able to prepare the way for British annexation of the Levant? In fact, large areas, notably "Palestine," Egypt, and Mesopotamia, would within less than half a century fall to the Crown. When he saw injustice, he did his best to stop it. That his government was not the least concerned over the plight of some debt-ridden Syrian villagers or the messianic hopes of the Sházlis or the abuses by the Greek archbishop was a hard fact for its consul to accept. The Foreign Office wanted smooth going, no quarrels with the Turks; it looked to the unobtrusive functioning of its consulates in the Levant and no stirring of perpetually muddy waters. At the same time it wanted information that would be useful should the Turks lose control over the vast areas they occupied. It had been a mistake to appoint Burton to the post—there were always more docile men who could have served in Damascus—but Isabel had brought pressures that could not be ignored, and the men in government assumed that Burton would be the proper person without thinking out the implications of his character. In the end there was total chaos in the Damascus consulate, and Burton had to be brought home.

Burton arrived in London several days before Isabel, who was on her way with mountains of luggage and her Syrian maid, Khamoor, and went directly to the sanctuary of his sister's house, so often his refuge in times of trouble. The Stisteds had been in Canada, where the Colonel had served as governor-general, and had not seen Burton for several years. Burton had not written to warn them of his visit, for he was traveling as quickly as the post. "The pleasure of our long-deferred meeting was sadly spoilt by his dejected, heart-broken mood, a state of things we were quite unprepared for," wrote his niece.

Never had we known him so wretched, so unnerved; his hands shook, his temper was strangely irritable, all that appreciation of fun and humour which rendered him such a cheery companion to old and young alike had vanished. He could settle nothing; he was restless, but would not leave the house ailing, but would take no advice—it was indeed a melancholy spectacle.

Burton had served in what his niece thought of as a "beggarly Consulate," and now it was clear that he would be denied all further promotion. "Morocco, Constantinople would never be for him." Georgiana Stisted blamed all of her uncle's problems on his wife: "Thanks to his wife's imprudence and passion for proselytizing . . . his career was blighted." A visit to the unspeaking, vegetablelike Edward in the Surrey County Lunatic Asylum did nothing to relieve Burton's depression. But after a few weeks his tremendous powers of recuperation won out, and "his marvellously sanguine disposition reasserted itself." That unquenchable spark of intellectual curiosity and creativity ignited his interest in a long-forgotten work. The lost manuscript of *Zanzibar* had surfaced, having made its way from India to England. Burton immediately turned his attention to preparing it for publication. Although it served as a means of coming to terms with his depression and anger, he began with an understandably melancholy view of the distant past.

> I could not believe, before Experience taught me how sad and solemn is the moment when a man sits down to think over and to write out the tale of what was before the last Decade began. How many thoughts and memories crowd upon the mind! How many ghosts and phantoms start up from the brain—the shreds of hopes destroyed and of aims futile, of prizes won, the successes and failures alike half forgotten! . . . How many graves have closed over their dead during these short ten years—that epitome of the past!

Isabel did not arrive until the middle of October. Blame for the crisis was widely attributed to her, and especially to her religion, by Burton's friends and by members of Government alike. But she was never at a loss. She was determined to save Richard. While Government might be able to cope with the Sublime Porte, with the London friends of Syrian moneylenders, with distant bishops of slightly heretical leanings, it could not cope with Isabel Burton. She visited influential friends, relatives, and high-ranking strangers by the dozen to make it clear that the fault for the collapse of her husband's consulate was not his. She besieged the Foreign Office for information about what had actually happened in Damascus, what the secret documents revealed. When she could not reach the officials, she went to their wives. \

Letters began to arrive from Damascus supporting Burton. Leading Muslims wrote crediting him with the downfall of the hated Rashid 'Ali Pasha, who had been replaced by a more liberal man. Some of the missionaries who had been opposed to Burton now came to his defense. Muslim leaders held public prayers to request his return, and eight Muslim *sayyids*, or holy men, wrote, "We saw no bad in him and he loved [the Muslims] and those that were under him. And there never came from him anything but truth, and he always walked with justice and hated none but the liars." Edward Palmer wrote to say: "The Mohammedans, whose 'fanatical aversion to Captain Burton' is the ostensible pretext for his recall, have been holding mass meetings, and even praying publicly in the mosques that God will send him back to them."

Burton had always been a public favorite despite the controversies that so frequently engulfed him, and the press presented him as a brave figure standing alone against injustice, a fantasized Englishman of heroic stature. The Foreign Office, now feeling beleaguered, issued a White Paper on Burton with documents from both sides of the matter but did not apologize. It seemed that the government thought Burton would be better off in an obscure post, so Granville offered him a position as consul at Pará, a small town in northern Brazil near the equator and even hotter than Santos. Burton saw it as a demotion and refused it. He thought he should have a major post like Tehran, which had just become vacant. But to his fury, Tehran was given another man. The anger and hurt continued to smolder, and though he had been attacked by parties representing all faiths—some honest men, some scoundrels—he began to develop a dislike of the Jews, for he felt that he had been betrayed by men like Sir Francis

Goldsmid and Sir Moses Montefiore ("this eminent philanthropist") who did not understand the situation in Syria. In *The Highlands of Brazil*, published in 1869, he had said, "Had I a choice of race, there is none to which I would more willingly belong than the Jewish," and he had already begun an essay on the Jews that had started off with an extremely favorable view, commenting on "the exceptional healthy and vigorous physique of the race" that "points to a remarkable career in times to come. . . . The Jew, like the Gypsy, stands alone, isolated by character, if not by a blessing." The Jewish nation has "a most abundant vitality," and "its indestructable and irrepressible life-power enables this nation without a country" to survive with "strength and pertinacity." He spoke of the Jews' "rare humanity" and lamented "the perpetration upon them by 'Christians' of atrocities almost unequalled for merciless savagery." It was an essay of unbounded appreciation, but toward the end his tone began to shift, and in a final summation, drawing upon certain Talmudic texts and a list of anti-Semitic charges that may have come from a then-popular but scurrilous German novel, *Biarritz*, by Hermann Goedsche (under the pseudonym Sir John Retcliffe), he let loose a series of charges that are irrational and unfair, listing acts of anti-Christian atrocities and ritual murders such as had been circulated since the Middle Ages. He included, according to W. H. Wilkins, who edited the manuscript after Burton's death, an appendix dealing with "the alleged rite of human sacrifice among the Sephardim of Eastern Jews."

Burton worked intermittently on the manuscript over the next few years, finishing it in 1875. However, friends warned him against publication, and in a rare example of good sense, he set the work aside; it was not published (and without the last section) until 1898, along with some other unfinished material on the Gypsies and Islam.

By the end of the year, with no post in sight, having spent the last of the inheritance from his father, Burton was broke. Together he and Isabel had only fifteen pounds left, and she lost one in a railway carriage when they were on their way to visit her uncle, Lord Girard. "I sat on the floor and cried," she wrote, "and he sat down by me with his arm around my waist, trying to comfort me." Still, financial difficulties did not keep the Burtons from enjoying a full social life in the great circles of Victorian England. Names like Lord Houghton, Strangford, the Prince of Wales, Disraeli, and Gladstone are scattered throughout their memoirs.

There were always small hopes. During the lean year of 1872 Burton received an offer from a British mining speculator to explore the sulfur mines in Iceland. He was promised his expenses and £2,000 if large deposits should be found. At that period most sulfur was mined in Sicily, but English industrialists were concerned that a war in the Mediterranean might cut off their sources. In June, Burton sailed from Scotland with the speculators. Iceland was something of a disappointment. He thought the old travelers' accounts were highly exaggerated. The famous great geyser merely hiccupped, and the smaller geysers were even more disappointing. The natives were dirty and unfriendly. And where were "the girls who kiss the stranger on the mouth, who relieve him of his terminal garments, and who place a brandy bottle under his pillow and a bowl of milk or cream by his side"? He complained also about "the chilly women of the north" who "live only by the head" and "gorgonize us into stony statues." There was sulfur aplenty, but it did not seem easily available.

Burton had scarcely left Scottish shores when Isabel's mother died, an event that helped widen the division between Isabel and her husband's relatives. "My darling child," Isabel wrote to Georgiana Stisted. "My dear mother died in my arms at midnight on Wednesday 5th [June 1872]. It was like a child going to sleep, most happy, but quite unexpected by us, who thought, though sinking, she would last till August or October." Isabel added that she had written "pages full of family detail" and had wanted to send them to the Stisteds, "but I thought that our religious views and observances might seem absurd to others, and I felt ashamed to do so." Isabel was at last perceptive about how the Protestant side of the family saw her Roman Catholicism, but two decades of her "superstitions" had already firmly alienated the Stisteds.

During this sad occasion, when she was standing at her mother's coffin, Isabel received a letter from Lord Granville offering Richard the consulate at Trieste, a rather decrepit but lively port city in the Austro-Hungarian Empire at the head of the Adriatic. She had been praying at that moment that the "sombrous [dark] overhanging cloud might pass away," and it did. The salary was £700 a year, much less than the salary at Damascus, but it was a worthy post and better than Pará and the other unmentionable backwaters the Foreign Office had dangled before Burton. "Better than nothing," Isabel decided, and immediately began to pack, assuming that her husband would accept when he returned from Iceland.

The salary was abysmal, but the duties were not demanding: An assistant consul would always be on hand to care for drunken sailors and tourists who had lost their papers or to attend diplomatic functions of a minor sort. Government seems to have posited no great demands at all on Burton. From the viewpoint of a later century it looks as if Trieste might have been a kind of reward for his years of service for the Crown, a minor prize for duties carried out under difficult conditions, without open recognition. He would be given the opportunity to be his own kind of consul without embarrassment. This windy Austro-Hungarian pasture was his to graze in as he wished, and if he spent his time writing, or wandering from his post, or even daydreaming, no one would mind. From time to time the Foreign Office was to give him a mild wigging for being away from Trieste too long, reprimands that no one but Burton took seriously—he had slight tinges of guilt over his absences, and he always worried that he might be relieved, thus ending a sort of working pension.

Before setting off for Trieste, Burton was faced with an operation of some seriousness. Years earlier, after a supposedly playful blow on the shoulder when his back was turned during a cudgel bout with a friend, Burton developed a lump that did not subside but turned into a tumor, opening and discharging. An operation was eventually considered necessary. Early in October, in London, Burton underwent surgery at the hands of his friend Dr. Bird. The operation was performed in a room with a northern exposure, and the procedure tells much about operations of the time, dramatized by a touch of Burton's flair for showing his fortitude. With Isabel in attendance, he straddled a chair, smoking a cigar and talking steadily. In what seemed to be a chore quickly achieved, in a mere twelve minutes, Bird removed a growth two inches in diameter. In the afternoon Burton insisted on taking a trip by rail to Brighton, alone, possibly an attempt to assert his masculinity in the face of Isabel's sometimes overwhelming mothering.

28

Trieste, Sadness

Trieste was hardly unknown, and its geographical position at the head of the Adriatic offered possibilities for extensive travel throughout the Mediterranean and Europe. The previous consul, Charles Lever, had taken a relaxed attitude about his duties, meanwhile writing some thirty-nine books, a production that rivaled Burton's. After a ragged, rather wild life (at one point he had been held captive by North American Indians), Lever had been handed the post of consul in Trieste by Lord Derby in 1862 with the comment (which Burton likely knew), "Here is six hundred a year for doing nothing, and you are just the man to do it." Lever said that at first Trieste was "all that I could desire," but abruptly the city became "detestable and damnable." The demands on poor Lever had not been heavy— he suffered seriously from depression his last years—and Burton could see that Trieste was not likely to engage him seriously, either. Others shared Lever's gloomy view of the port. Georgiana

Stisted had her pertinent comments, which were likely to be the opposite of Isabel's, saying, Trieste, as consulates go, was "not to be despised," but then, "Trieste is not one's beau ideal of a home."

As was their practice, the Burtons set off independently. Burton sailed from England on October 24, 1872, and Isabel, accompanied by Khamoor, left by train about three weeks later. Each thought the other had already arrived at Trieste and wrote to the other at the consulate. The assistant consul, a Mr. Brock, who had been at the post some forty years, wondered why the new consul and his wife were ignorant of each other's plans; letters began to pile up. Mr. Brock began to think "what a funny couple he had to deal with," wrote Isabel. Stories circulated later about the Burtons' odd behavior. He was said to have arrived with nothing—he had lost twelve boxes of clothing en route— but a fighting cock under his arm.

But in fact Burton was accompanied by Isabel. They had met by chance in Venice. The story was told that they had come across each other in the Piazza, had shaken hands "like brothers," and had gone off to their hotels, immediately to sit down to their writing "as if nothing was the matter." But it was not so casual as that, and they landed together in Trieste, a few hours across the gulf from Venice, and settled into a hotel near the waterfront, liking it not at all but staying six months.

Trieste was not a bad city to be exiled in, but Burton thought he was very much an exile and began to identify with another famous exile, the Latin poet Ovid, who had been banished in A.D. 8 to a small port town in the Danube delta for holding unpopular views. Burton and Ovid were about the same age when they went into exile—Burton was fifty-one—and he managed to find a common destiny with Ovid. "I, too," he said, drawing on the poet, "am a neglected book gnawed by the moth" and "a stream dammed up with mud." He was "clapped for nothing in particular, onto the belly of a brazen bull." He began to think of Trieste as *tristia*, sadness. *

Since Burton was perhaps the best Arabic scholar of the time and a linguist unsurpassed by anyone then alive, it seemed a waste of time and talents for the government to send him to Trieste. However, from the government's point of view, it was a spot where he could do little damage with his opinions or his sarcasm, and he could quickly be brought home if he misbehaved. "Looking back dispassionately," his niece wrote, "I can but think that the enormous amount of liberty accorded him during those eighteen years proved that Lord Granville, far from bearing any ill-will against the luckless Haji, made up for the harshness of the recall [from Damascus] by providing him for the rest of his days with what was practically a sinecure." Moreover, Isabel was out of the way. "Isabel could convert whom she pleased; indeed, she tells us in print [in the *Life*] that she stood sponsor to a housebreaker."

For many people, however, Trieste had little but faults. If the Burtons complained, it was in a romantic manner: The consul had seen worse, and for his wife everything was new and an experience. Visitors complained about the winds, there being three, the bora, which could blow like a cyclone, sweeping everything into the sea; the sirocco, which came from the opposite direction and blew the drainage back into the town; and the contradite, when both winds blew at the same time. The bora was so fierce that on occasion it knocked Burton down and was known to overturn trains. Then there were the earthquakes, which were common enough not to be noticed. Burton would often complain about the sewer smells that wafted through the town, but his favorite target was the politics, which were violent, Italians against Austrians in particular, with the Slavs opposing both. And the bombs! "If an Austrian gave a ball, the Italians

---

* After Ovid's own work in exile, *Tristia*.

threw a bomb into it; and the Imperial family were always received with a chorus of bombs—bombs on the railway, bombs in the gardens, bombs in the sausages; in fact, it was not at times pleasant," Isabel wrote.

The winds and bombs were nuisances, but there were compensations, minor pleasures to be appreciated, specifically the women, though by now Burton was feeling his years and he seemed also to have been consistently faithful to his wife. The women of Trieste had a special walk similar to that of "Arab Ladies"—"I have never seen it in Europe except among the trading classes of Trieste, who have a 'wriggle of their own.' " Later, he added Spanish women to his list, explaining that such a woman moves "with the slightly swinging walk of a thorough-bred mare, bending her graceful neck from side to side at objects as she passes."

Eventually the Burtons found a "small apartment," a flat of only ten rooms, in a building close to the sea, situated in a spot that "the smells failed to reach." The flat was on the top floor of the building—the Burtons liked the exercise of going up and down stairs—and the "little old ladies of both sexes" refused to climb so high. The Burtons did not remain housebound for long. There were short trips to Miramar, the palace of the ill-fated Archduke Maximilian, who had been sent to rule Mexico, and most often, to nearby Venice, "our happy hunting ground," and longer trips to France and to Rome, where Burton had spent so much time as a child. As usual, he was filled with schemes for improving the unimprovable—he had a plan for cutting a new channel for the Tiber and for draining and reclaiming the swamps of the Campagna. Wherever the Burtons went, they met old friends or made new ones, usually of high social rank or intellectual qualities or among the local nobility. But there were more serious interests, too. Burton explored and partially excavated some of the mysterious prehistoric castellieri of Istria and visited the "wild People" (as Isabel called them) in the countryside to learn their language, a dialect of old Venetian.

Friends came to visit them in Trieste in a stream, among them Burton's old schoolmate from university days Alfred Bate Richards, who left a detailed description of the couple at home. Isabel had her own suite, the walls of which were covered with holy objects—crucifixes, paintings of the Madonna, and relics of the saints, candles and medals and scapulars.

> Thus far [wrote Richards], the belongings are all of the cross, but no sooner are we landed in the little drawing-rooms than signs of the crescent appear. These rooms, opening one into the other, are bright with oriental hangings, with trays and dishes of gold and burnished silver, fantastic goblets, chibouques [pipes] with great amber mouth-pieces, and eastern treasures made of odorous woods.

Burton collected only handmade objects. "It is so much better than the poor, dull work of machinery," he would say to visitors. Virtually every corner in the flat contained some kind of weapon—guns, pistols, spears, swords of every shape and type. Then there was a cupboard labeled "The Pharmacy" containing Isabel's numerous concoctions for helping the poor. But dominating everything in the flat were the deal (wooden plank) tables, eleven in all, spread with writing materials and sheafs of manuscripts. "Dick likes separate tables for each book," Isabel told Richards, "and when he is tired of one he goes to another." By Victorian upper-class standards this was a small flat. "If I had a great establishment," said Burton to Richards, "I should feel tied and weighed down. With a flat and two or three servants one has only to lock the door and go out." Isabel had her own worktable, at which she would sit in her queenly manner dressed in a gray *choga*, a long, loose Indian gown of soft camel's hair, and a cap of the same material. Richards found his old friend still an impressive figure.

> Standing about five feet eleven, his broad, deep chest reduces his apparent height considerably, and the illusion is intensified by hands and feet of Oriental smallness. The Eastern and distinctly Arab look

of the man is made more pronounced by prominent cheekbones (across one of which is the scar of a javelin cut), by close-cropped black hair, just tinged with gray, and a pair of piercing, black gipsy-looking eyes.

It was a happy, busy, productive life, but Burton was beginning to show signs of increasingly bad health, especially symptoms of cardiac problems. In May 1874, he made an excursion into the Alps with some friends. He always tried to keep himself in top physical condition, and on this climb (as on others), to harden himself, he slept outside in the snow, lightly clad and in thin shoes. A few days later he came down with a fever. An inflammation developed and settled in the groin. A tumor was found there, and the doctor counseled an operation, saying that "it was going to be a long illness." Isabel telegraphed home for "good port wine," Burton's famous self-prescribed medication. The tumor was cut out, but after seventy-eight days of recuperation it was realized that the surgeon had not gone deep enough and the operation had to be repeated. Isabel was taught how to dress the wound.

> I was afraid his life would ebb away, but I kept up his strength with good port wine, egg-flips with brandy, cream and fresh eggs, Brand's essences, and something every hour.

Then the news came that Charley Drake had died of a fever on the very day that Burton had been operated upon. He had been as agnostic as Burton in his conversation, but as death approached, "he wept bitterly," Isabel wrote, then resigned himself and said, "Tell my mother I die in the love of Jesus."

Burton recovered, and Isabel took him to Italy, though he had to be carried in a sedan chair most of the time. She reported that her husband began "to get exceedingly nervous." He thought he would never be able to leave his room alone and fancied he could not swallow. But Isabel got holy relics from her priests, and Burton took the cure at various spas and eventually was back in fair health.

* * *

One of the manuscripts on the deal tables at Trieste was a translation of an Indian marriage manual, the first of a series of erotic (and almost pornographic) works that Burton was to become involved in. He had been corresponding with Foster Fitzgerald Arbuthnot, who had decided to put into English a popular Indian erotic classic, the *Kāma Shāstra,* also known as the *Ananga Ranga.* * The author was a sixteenth-century poet, Kalyana Malla; Burton also credited a sage named Koka Pandit as the possible author, this expert also being known as the author of the *Koka Shāstra,* leading to inevitable confusion over titles and authors. Kalyana Malla drew much of his material from earlier writers on erotic subjects, notably the sage Vātsyāyana, the presumed author of the vaguely known and hard-to-obtain *Kāma Sutra* (which Burton called simply *Kama Sutra*), which was yet to gain a reputation among Westerners.

In Bombay, Arbuthnot placed the Sanskrit and vulgar texts in the hands of an Indian pandit or scholar, Bhagvanlal Indraji, for a rough draft in English. It was Burton's happy task to turn the draft into more acceptable and polished language, which he did with a cheerful abandon that greatly changed the tenor and nature of the original and allowed him to express some very deeprooted opinions about man's duty to please women sexually but not forgetting such pleasure for the man as the wonderful penis-squeezing Galla girls. Thus, many sections of the English version of the *Kāma Shāstra* come not from Kalyana Malla's Sanskrit but from Burton's fertile brain, developing and improving upon a text that some Western scholars believe is poorer and more pedantic than its translation.

The book was significant for the Englishman, Burton thought,

* Burton was not consistent in his spelling (or hyphenation) of *Kāma-Shāstra,* and later *Kāma Sutra,* using such variations as Kama Shastra (Society), *Kama Sutra,* and so on, to the confusion of readers, biographers, and bibliographers alike.

because it had "so much of novelty and of interest on the congress of the sexes," even though its originality "is everywhere mixed up" due to "the peculiarities of Hindu thought" and "the verbosity of Hindu style."

From the introduction to his reworking of the conclusion, one finds that Burton is imposing his own special view of how man must treat woman, and one must always remember that at this time the woman in Burton's life was Isabel Arundell. After a passing reference to the greatest joy in life, which was "derived from knowledge of the Creator," he gets to the point, his own:

> Men, it is true, marry for the sake of undisturbed congress, as well as for love and comfort, and often they obtain handsome and attractive wives. But they do not give them plenary contentment, nor do they themselves thoroughly enjoy their charms, the reason of which is, that they are purely ignorant of the Scripture of Cupid, the Kama Shastra; and, despising the difference between the several kinds of women, they regard them only in an animal point of view. Such men must be looked upon as foolish and unintelligent. . . .

The *Kāma Shāstra* itself, even with Burton's copious annotations, light touches, and inventive passages, is pedantic and pedestrian in the extreme. It possesses charts of how and where the man is to touch the woman, from forehead to big toe (apparently a symbol of both the clitoris and the lingam), all of which are "the touches by which passion is satisfied." There is a lot of scratching and biting, kissing and chewing, and if the Westerner was confused or amused by this kind of lovemaking, it must be remembered, as Burton pointed out, that the couple normally were children when the marriage rites were performed and a gradual process of getting to know each other had to take place before sexual union was consummated.

Burton's deep-rooted cynicism appears from time to time. In a note he asks, "What man in his sense can believe in the 'seduction' of a married woman? As a rule, indeed, the seduction is all on the other side." In a list of the types of women who are easily seduced, he mentions "the woman who has never learned the real delights of carnal copulation," which brings his comment "Which, allow us to say, is the case of most English women and a case to be remedied by constant and intelligent study of the [Kāma Shāstra] Scripture."

But the translation, for all its ethnological interest, sexual curiosities, helpful advice, instructions on positions in great variety in order to avoid satiety, its crankishness and private jokes, its more or less commonsense attitudes toward marriage and sex, and its impassioned pleas to introduce the women of England to pleasures they never imagined existed, was doomed to languish in obscurity for a dozen years. Only four (or possibly six) copies were proofed, for as Burton's friend Henry Spencer Ashbee stated in his *Index Librorum Prohibitorum*, "the printer, on reading the proofs, became alarmed at the nature of the book, and refused to print off the edition."

Was there a way out of the near-poverty that always seemed to hang over Burton? Grand schemes for quick riches obsessed him, with gold the great burning attraction. He had wished for gold in the States, for gold in Brazil, for sulfur in Iceland, for gold in West Africa. For a moment he had the idea of quick riches from a lesser venture: Why not "Captain Burton's Tonic Bitters" for ailing livers? "Liver" was a common complaint among the Victorians, and Burton's was probably in as bad a shape as any. In India he had been given a secret recipe for a tonic by some Franciscan monks, who had obtained it in 1565 from a Swedish physician. Its antiquity guaranteed its efficacy. It was to be "prettily bottled," with Burton's picture on the label. "Many people have made a fortune with less," wrote Isabel, but the Burtons did not, and that was the end of the scheme.

But Burton had a bigger dream, diamonds in India. The year of 1875 was one of restless activity for Burton. He traveled to London in May with "a ton or so of books" and while in England managed to arrange for the publication of his accumulated manuscripts, among them *Etruscan Bologna* and *A New System of Sword Exercise for Infantry*. But his special goal was to get permission for a trip to India, his secret plan being to investigate the Golconda diamond mines.

After Christmas dinner in Trieste, the Burtons set off. The Suez Canal had been completed five years previous and proved to Burton how enlightened rulers brought progress. But more than a canal was important, for Suez brought a rush of memories, of the Bedawi and their camels, the women in blue robes, the smells of the land, the sight of the villages and the desert. He went ashore at various ports familiar from his pilgrimage to Mecca, at Yambu' and Jeddah, where he was greeted enthusiastically. At Jeddah the ship was loaded with some eight hundred pilgrims returning home, a sight that touched Isabel, for when a storm arose and the pilgrims cried in panic and when supplies ran low and twenty-three of them died of hunger and thirst, Isabel wrote later, "They won't ask a Christian for help, but if they see a kind face they speak with their eyes as an animal does." At Aden, Burton inquired after the members of the Somali expedition. The two women who had served as all-around helpers were still alive, but the one-eyed boy, the Kalendar, had been murdered by the Īsas in Somaliland and End of Time had been stabbed to death. Throughout the voyage in idle moments, Burton dictated his memoirs to Isabel, a project that still hung unfinished at his death. The ship landed at Bombay on February 2, 1876, and the first person Burton visited was Arbuthnot, now the Collector of the port. He and Burton immediately plunged into a discussion of plans to publish various Indian and Arab works. One of the participants in their plans was the extraordinary scholar Edward Rehatsek, an Austro-Hungarian. He had been born in 1819, was educated in Budapest, and had gone out to India in 1847 to teach Latin and mathematics. After retiring in 1871, Rehatsek had settled down in a native house built of reeds and lived very much like a middle-class Indian of modest means, dressed in threadbare clothes and doing his own shopping

in the bazaars. But "this strange, austere, unpretentious man"
was one of the great but unrecognized scholars of the period.
The result of the talks was that Arbuthnot, Burton, and Rehatsek
decided to revive the lapsed Translation Fund of the Royal
Asiatic Society and issue a series of Oriental works unknown to
the West.

After a tour of Bombay to the places Burton recalled from his
early army days, the Burtons went on to Karachi, which had
grown from a fishing village of 6,000 to a slum city of 45,000,
alleviated only by some fine new avenues and noble houses.
Memories flooded Burton's mind as he walked the streets: he
could recall where he had set himself up as a merchant on his
missions for Napier and where he had strolled as an English officer
with his bull terrier. He saw again the pond where the Sufi saint
Mango Pīr had turned flowers into alligators, the same beasts
that Burton's messmates had teased and jumped across to show
off their courage.

Burton was becoming more and more sentimental with each
site to be revisited. At Ghara he told Isabel, "None of us died,
because we were young and strong; but we led the life of sal-
amanders." In the desert he found the place where the Persian
girl had been encamped—Oh, what sad memories there! The
Burtons went up the Indus to the Phuleli and to Hyderabad:
"There is the house which fell down, nearly crushing my mon-
shee." The fireplaces were half filled up; the floors, overgrown
with camel thorn. "How small and mean are the dimensions,
which loom so large in the pictures stored within the brain!"
he told Isabel. "There I temporarily buried the 'young person'
[Nūr Jān] when the police-master gave orders to search the
house."

Sentiment engulfed him. "How strange are the tricks of memory, which, often hazy as a dream about the most important
events of a man's life, religiously preserves the merest trifles! And
how very unpleasant to meet one's self, one's 'dead self' thirty
years younger!"

The Burtons visited the battlefield of Mīanī, the turning point in the British invasion of Sind, and went into Jat country to see the Gypsies and up almost to the borders of Afghanistan and back, leisurely, romantically, Burton all the time overcome by memories and yet criticizing changes—the decline of the Indian army, the failure of the government to make needed improvements.

Back in Bombay they went to see the Āghā Khān, now settled there permanently. It seems that it was an encounter entered upon very cautiously by both Burton and the Prince-Imām. It was the month of Muharram, and the Āghā Khān invited the Burtons to attend the 'Āshūrā celebrations, the grand passion of the deaths of 'Alī's son Ḥosayn and his followers. And Burton did not overlook the graves of honored predecessors. On a trip to Baroda to visit his first military post, he took Isabel to see the tomb of Tom Coryat. The Burtons also searched through twenty thousand graves at a Bombay cemetery before they found a very plain stone with the name of Victor Jacquement, a French botanist and naturalist who had died in India in 1832 at the age of thirty-one.

Finally, they reached Golconda, with its abandoned diamond mines. The British resident and the prime minister of the state took them on tours and arranged parties and receptions. They rode through the city on elephants and saw animal fights, and the prime minister arranged an expurgated version of a nautch for Isabel—nothing happened that could not be reported in letters back home. Burton accumulated a lot of information about the mines and concluded that diamond mining in India had been prematurely abandoned. Later, he attempted by letters to the British press and in various reports to enlist the interest of British capitalists. But it was all too vague for the British businessman. Burton released his hopes and fantasies with a long article about the "Nizam Diamond," a stone that was like a "little brother" to the larger, ill-fated Koh-i-noor that Ranjīt Singh had stolen from Shāh Shuja.

Back in Bombay the Burtons visited the famous Towers of the Dead on Malabar Hill, where the Parsis left the bodies of the faithful for the vultures. A final excursion was to Burton's beloved Goa, where his hero Camões had spent so many years and Burton had hoped to recover from the fires and fevers of Sind. But Isabel, like so many tourists, saw Goa in another light. "Of all the God-forsaken, desert holes, one thousand years behind the rest of creation, I have never seen anything to equal it." And that was the end of India. They left it as the heat of April overwhelmed all and reached Trieste on June eighteenth, having been away almost six months.

If Golconda's diamonds could not make Burton rich, there was always gold, and he was not at a loss in embarking upon a search for it with the verve of his youth. His perpetual want of money nagged relentlessly. But dreams and hopes did not overcome the advance of years. He was now fifty-five: pains racked his body; he creaked like some old camel litter that had survived uncounted caravans through burning, trackless deserts. Quick wealth was never far from his thoughts. He was obsessed by gold above all other sources of riches. There was gold, he was certain, still to be found in the Arabian Peninsula, particularly in the Midian in that area known to Europeans as "the Empty Quarter"—had not the rascally Haji Wali, his friend from Cairo on the Mecca pilgrimage, once shown him a secret map of long-lost mines that the Romans had worked?

At this time, the peninsula, along with much of the Muslim world, was under the control of the Turks, who ruled it from Egypt through their governor, the Khedive Isma'īl. The Khedive was considered as a modern administrator of liberal principles with commendable desires to raise the standards of his people, the very model of the progressive ruler. However, he was perpetually on the edge of financial and political disaster, a fact that Burton may have considered privately, and perhaps he saw it as an advantage. Isma'īl's profligacy was notorious—he was rumored to have spent five million pounds on his harem; such extravagances threatened not only his own position but the stability and prosperity of Egypt.

On March 31, 1877, Burton, armed with suitable presentations, left for Cairo to importune Isma'īl for funds for exploration for gold in Midian. An air of romanticism quickly smothered reality. Burton was immediately hailed as "the new Joseph," and he expected that he would make both himself and Egypt rich beyond computation. He enlisted the services of Haji Wali, now seventy-seven; his age "had only made [him] a little fatter and a little greedier."

With his customary caution in such matters, Burton took a "preliminary canter" into Midian to size up the ground and assess the obstacles to be overcome on a full-scale expedition.

Heat, terrible heat. It was the heat of Sind and Aden, of the road to Mecca and the Somali desert again, but now Burton was much older. After two weeks in the field, sketching, planning, and collecting metalliferous specimens and the natives' stories of ruined towns once prosperous with dense populations, of quarries where King Solomon found gold for the walls of the Temple, his drinking vessels, and his lion throne, of turquoise mines, Burton returned to Cairo something of a hero. He had amassed, in truth, not an impressive amount of geological samples but notes, and by April twenty-first he was back in Trieste, to spend the summer and fall writing *The Gold-Mines of Midian and The Ruined Midianite Cities*, a massive work of over four hundred pages that was well received and ran through two editions the next year.

That there was such treasure as the title implied was merely speculation. In October, as cool weather was approaching, Burton returned to Cairo for a serious assault on Midian's secrets. He assembled a suitable entourage, including Haji Wali, and on an Egyptian gunboat he passed through Suez and down the Red

Sea to Moilah, a forsaken port on the western shore of the Arabian Peninsula. He landed on December nineteenth. Long experienced in making impressive first appearances among semi-barbarous peoples, Burton went ashore amid a flurry of cannon shots and musketry, followed by a guard of twenty-five men from the Khedive's army and his workers. His first move was to hire three shaykhs as guides and 106 camels and dromedaries and their drivers. The excitement of the desert and the penetration of unknown lands enlivened his spirits, as so often in the past. He had planned three expeditions into different parts of Arabia, using Moilah as his base. The work promised to be difficult. He himself knew nothing of engineering, so he had hired a practical engineer, a Frenchman, one M. Marie, and he had some artists for on-the-spot recording, but foolishly he did not include either a practical prospector or a metallurgist. His solution for such an oversight was to carry a divining rod. Haji Wali soon got an attack of "indigestion" and returned home, never to be seen again. Still, Burton was in a state of high excitement. "The Power of the Hills" was upon him.

It was a wasted journey. At Maghair Shu'ayb, once the capital, he passed "a silly fortnight, searching for gold"—his hopes had been raised by the discovery of the remains of furnaces and some old coins. The best that could be found was the catacombs, the tombs of long-forgotten kings, in which were scrawled graffiti that may have dated to the time of Christ.

The expedition then worked its way north, passing "the Praying Place of Jethro" and a shallow clay basin reported to be Moses's wells. At 'Aqaba, now an important port in southern Jordan, there was nothing but shadowy legends of a biblical past, where Solomon's ships landed en route from Sheba and India. Back at Moilah on February thirteenth, Burton spent four days in reorganizing and getting fresh provisions. His next destination, The Hasma, could best be described as "arid." A third trip, far down the coast, started at el Wijh, whence the expedition marched to the ancient mines of Abul Maru; this, too, was equally futile, and Burton saw no choice but to give up the quest. By April 20, 1878, he was back in Suez, where Isabel had been waiting for him, working hard on finishing her own "AEI"— *Arabia, Egypt and India*—and shooting off endless telegrams to Burton's publishers in London about the delay in publishing his first Midian book. Isabel had spent a week in Cairo, where she had been talking to General George Gordon, who had for several years been unsuccessfully trying to persuade Burton to take the post of governor of the Sudan. The general had expressed his grave doubts about the possibility of finding gold in Midian; more important, he tried to impress upon Isabel the need to have her husband take the post in the Sudan. Seven years later Gordon was killed in a native uprising.

In Cairo, Burton put on a brave and smiling face. He had returned with twenty-five tons of minerals—"returned triumphantly"—argentiferous and cupriferous ores and numerous archaeological objects. However, the results were shabby, and all Burton got out of the venture was still another book, *The Land of Midian (revisited)*, a two-volume opus of nearly seven hundred pages. He put on a magnificent exhibition in Cairo, attended by the Khedive, a great display of specimens, maps, graffiti, sketches, and tons of rocks of little commercial value. The English papers gave Burton a lot of publicity, and there was no doubt that despite his faults he was a popular and heroic figure.

But when a cantankerous Englishman and a semibarbarous, profligate Khedive enter into an agreement, it can end only in a tangle of charges and countercharges, and Burton found himself in unresolved litigation over unpaid natives that brought him nothing but personal debts, not the gold of Midian.

Aches and pains beset him; he was growing old. He was crippled by gout, and his responses were slow. Worse, there was the eternal poverty—his purse, he complained, was "full of cobwebs."* On a trip to Egypt again in December 1879 to try to get the damned rascally Egyptians—Isma'īl had been replaced by a son, Tewfik—to finance still another attempt into Midian, Burton was set upon by thugs one night in Alexandria.

In the old days he would have knocked his assailants' heads together, or even better, killed them (was he not an initiate into the Assassins?), but now he collapsed on the street and was left for dead. As the morning sun burned its way into the dusty streets, Burton arose, and bruised, bloody, and in pain, returned to his hotel. That was the least of the disasters. Tewfik refused to honor his father's debts—not that Isma'īl was scrupulous in honoring them, either—and Burton was forced to return to Trieste. If any lessons came out of the episode with the robbers, with Tewfik, it was that he was getting too old for excursions into dangerous and now-strange worlds.

Whatever his personal problems, Burton became more and more of an attraction to the public. The lean young "Arab" of the Sind days, however, was gone, buried by easy living and encroaching health problems. Still, Burton's contemporaries could find much of that exotic appearance. Arthur Symons, a poet and critic who had been a young editor at Bernard Quaritch's, a firm that published several of Burton's books, wrote that Burton was

> Arab in his prominent cheek-bones. He was gypsy in his terrible magnetic eyes—the sullen eyes of a stinging serpent. He had a deep bronzed complexion, a determined mouth, half-hidden by a black moustache which hung down in a peculiar fashion on both sides of his chin. His face had no actual beauty in it. It revealed a tremendous animalism, an air of repressed ferocity, a devilish fascination. There is an almost tortured magnificence in his huge head, tragic and painful, with its mouth that aches with desire, with those dilated nostrils that drink in I know not what strange perfumes.

* A phrase he likely borrowed from the Roman poet Catullus, whom he was then reading.

Ouida, a fashionable romantic novelist of the period and a friend of both Burtons, thought that he "looked like Othello and lived like the Three Mousquetaires blended into one." The writer Frank Harris, describing Burton at the age of sixty, found "there was an untamed air about him."

He was tall, about six feet in height, with broad, square shoulders; he carried himself like a young man, in spite of his sixty years, and was abrupt in movement. His face was bronzed and scarred, and when he wore a heavy moustache and no beard he looked like a prize fighter; the naked, dark eyes—imperious, aggressive eyes, by no means friendly; the heavy jaws and prominent hard chin gave him a desperate air.

But it was not just physical appearance that impressed Harris.

His intellectual curiosity was astonishingly broad and deep rather than high. He would tell stories of Indian philosophy or of perverse negro habits or lust and cannibalism, or would listen to descriptions of Chinese cruelty and Russian self-mutilation till the stars paled out. Catholic in his admiration and liking for all greatness, it was the abnormalities and not the divinities of men that fascinated him.

Beyond this was still another aspect. "Deep down in him lay the despairing gloom of utter disbelief," said Harris. "Burton's laughter, even, deep-chested as it was, had in it something of sadness."

His head seemed to increase in size over the years, and his mustaches drooped more fiercely than ever. The portraits from the last third of his life show him truculent, brooding, and sardonic, a man one did not trifle with. The well-known portrait by Sir Frederick Leighton, painted in 1876 (Burton was then fifty-five), shows him in a better light than most, at worst as an Oriental despot of thoughtful mien, his face scarred by the Somali spear that had entered his jaw at Berbera.

He was always an interesting character, and not only did the famous and near famous want to meet him; so did the press find him a fascinating subject—his life, his house, his strange wife, the books he was writing or might write, how he lived and what he did, and whatever was occupying his mind at the moment and what was on his eleven worktables, which always gave an air of mystery and exoticism. He was now concentrating primarily on translations, most often adaptations, improvisations, and improvements on the originals. In the flood of "translations" that was to pour out of the Trieste years, there was one, *The Kasîdah*, that was not a translation at all but a highly creative, though puzzling, summary of his thought. *The Kasîdah* was ostensibly the work of a Persian Sufi, Hâjî Abdû El-Yezdi, and was "translated and annotated by his friend, F.B." Both the Haji and F.B. are none other than Burton, anonymous for whatever obscure reasons obsessed him at the time.

The Kasîdah appeared a few years after Edward FitzGerald's very popular and romantic *Rubáiyát of Omar Khayyám*, a "translation" that FitzGerald labeled a "transmogrification"— corruption—and which knowledgeable critics saw as a perversion of the original. It has been commonly assumed that Burton's work was merely a copy of FitzGerald's, and a not very successful one at that. That both works are "Persian" and in verse makes one seem original and the other an imitation, but the differences are greater than the similarities.

The history of the writing of *The Kasîdah* is vague. Burton's friends, and especially his wife, claimed that he began it after coming out of Mecca in 1853, during his recuperation at Cairo, Aden, and Bombay. He let it lie more or less dormant (with perhaps some minor additions and development) until after the appearance of the FitzGerald *Rubáiyát* in 1859, when the success of that book led him to take up *The Kasîdah* again. It did not appear in final form, however, until 1880. It was a small work of thirty-eight pages, bound in stiff yellow paper, with the title in English and Arabic; however, because of the extreme length of the lines, the page was an outsized 8 × 10 ⅝ inches (later editions after Burton's death cut the lines in half to fit smaller pages). The quantity of copies was limited—not more than two hundred were run off, possible proof that Burton did not intend *The Kasîdah* as a commercial rival to the *Rubáiyát*—and was distributed among Burton's friends. Only one hundred copies went to bookstores, and not many of them were sold. Reviews were virtually nonexistent, and it seemed that *The Kasîdah* would be listed among Burton's failures, but after his death it was reprinted over and over again, in various formats, to the extent that the bibliographer finds it difficult to assemble an accurate record of the many editions.

The silence that greeted *The Kasîdah* may have been due to Burton's using a pseudonym, Hâjî Abdû El-Yezdi, as the author and the initials F.B. as the "translator." "F.B." stood for Frank Baker, a pseudonym Burton sometimes used (Baker was his mother's name), but the work itself was of a complexity that few people cared to face. Burton had followed a standard Sufi poetic form, the *qasîda*, and his work should be approached in that context. A *qasîda*, an Arabic term also used in Persian, is a monorhymed poem, which, among the Arabs (and the Persians, Turks, and other Muslims), is used to express the poet's own experiences and emotions, often mystical, and might also be a means of displaying his eloquence and erudition, filled with obscure allusions and complicated antitheses. The earlier Sufi poets employed the *qasîda* as a meditation on God. Burton, who came across the form in Sind and in his Persian studies, used his as a meditation on "non-God."

> Unknown, Incomprehensible, whate'er you choose to call it, call;
> But leave it vague as airy space, dark in its darkness mystical.

Whereas the Sufi poets have attempted to portray the divine qualities, the mystery of God's beauty and majesty, His grace and love, the marvels of creation, His beauty and anger, Burton wrestled agnostically with a God, incomprehensible and fathomless, Who he suspected did not exist.

Behind the surface tangle of seemingly undeveloped ideas,

overexamined premises condensed into insensibility, and blows at the incomprehensible First Cause, there are deeper layers, as is the Sufi wont, of arcane knowledge, esoteric mysteries casually referred to, and private jokes, all cloaked, perhaps, with a strong touch of *taqīya*, concealment. None of the people who knew Burton best, his wife and sister and niece, friends like Alfred Bate Richards and his early biographer, Francis Hitchman, or even Thomas Wright and W. H. Wilkins, who had access to Burton's surviving relatives and friends, gave any hint of the various puzzles in the work or even of the name of the supposed author, Hâjî Abdû El-Yezdi. Hâjî is, of course, the honorific given a man who has made the pilgrimage to Mecca, and Abdû is Burton himself, the Abdullah of the pilgrims. The brief semi-fictional reference in the Notes describes the author as "A native . . . of Darâbghirid in the Yezd Province [of Persia]. . . ." Darâbghirid is a small provincial center in the Irani desert and is believed to have been founded by the great world conqueror Darius himself, for the Persian name, *Darâb-gherd*, means "Darius-town." One might ask why Burton identified himself with the great Persian. He also referred to Abdû Hâjî as El-Hich-makâni, which he said meant the man "Of No-Hall, Nowhere," as if effacing himself from the ideas presented in *The Kasîdah*. At the same time, there may be another identification: the wily Odysseus, the great wanderer, was also from "Nowhere." More important was his calling himself Nabbianâ, "our Prophet," but in the end Nowhere and Prophet failed to attract critical analysis. Yezd is the province in which Burton placed Darâbghirid, and on the surface these two names suffice as a geographical locus for Hâjî Abdû. But Yezdi—that is, someone from Yezd—has another meaning. The Yezdis (or Yezīdīs) are a peculiar sect of mystics, now reportedly debased, founded in the fourteenth century by the Sufi shaykh 'Adi ibn Musafir.

The shaykh was a conventionally orthodox Muslim with vague ties to the Qādiris. His teachings, as his followers practiced them, with many borrowings from other sources, developed along strange paths, leading other Muslims to reject the sect as heretical and even diabolical. The central symbol was the peacock—the sect is often called the Peacock Angel (as the Arabic name, *Malak Tauus*, is translated)—followed by that of a black snake, symbolic of the wisdom of Life. Romantic historians have had great enjoyment with the Peacock Angel cult, and numerous misconceptions have run rampant, leading its members to refuse any information whatever about themselves to outsiders. And the ordinary Muslim is likely to reject the Yezīdīs with horror, as did the man Burton had met so long ago at Mango Pīr's alligator shrine in Sind.

Burton did not spell out the significance of "Yezd"—that was left for the reader to puzzle over, if he were so inclined—but there was clearly some sort of connection in his mind to *The Kasîdah*. He may have first met Yezīdīs in Sind; there were certainly Yezīdīs among the Kurds in Damascus and Salahiyyeh, and their doctrines would have interested him.

Many clues to the inner meaning of the work lay only half-concealed. The cover of *The Kasîdah* bore three lines of Arabic, which, translated, said, "Abdû Hâjî Al-Kasîdah, or The Lay of the Higher Law by Abdû The Traveller," which adds another connection to the Yezīdīs, for the name of the founder, 'Adi ibn Musafir, means "Son of the Traveller." But Burton himself was also a son of a "Traveller," Colonel Joseph Burton.

Throughout the work there were echoes not only of the Peacock Angel cult and other heretical and orthodox forms of Islam but Buddhism, Confucianism, Hinduism, and Christianity, as if Burton were trying to wrestle each to an understanding. But it was the Peacock Angel cosmogony that underlay the work, whether in the more extreme beliefs or those that resemble more conventional themes. The Yezīdīs believed that God had withdrawn Himself after Creation, as Burton suggested also, His rule being taken over by Malak Tauus, the Peacock Angel, a benign being who intended the best for the world even though mankind did not always understand his plans and so considered him evil.

The Yezīdīs believed themselves the highest of mankind: they were the descendants of twins who had been born out of a jug nine months after insemination by the seed of Adam. The jar-born individual, deity or human, was a doctrine common among the early inhabitants of Central Asia and the Indian subcontinent. Burton's hodgepodge of religion in *The Kasîdah* reflects other Yezīdī doctrines: The cult believed in the transmigration of souls; they consulted oracles and engaged in sacred dances like the Sufi *samā'* in which Burton himself had been a frequent participant; they believed that Christ was an angel in human form; Muḥammad and Abraham and the patriarchs were prophets; the faithful looked forward to a future life (Burton was doubtful) and practiced both baptism and circumcision as initiatory rites. In short, the sect was a mixture of the wilder beliefs of West Asia—archaic Hinduism, Zoroastrianism, Manichaeism, Nestorianism, Islam, and strange forms of heretical Christianity.

From this amalgam Burton tried to derive "a faith of his own . . . an Eastern version of Humanitarianism blended with the skeptical, or, as we now say, the scientific habit of mind." He considered that "a world without God is horrible," but he thought of himself as "Agnostic." He could not agree with the Yezīdīs about the afterlife, regretting "the excessive importance attached to a possible future state: he [that is, Burton] looks upon this as a psychical stimulant, a day dream, whose revulsion and reaction disorder waking life."

Like many searchers for the truth, Burton considered himself not only a pilgrim in the body and a Wanderer like Odysseus but also a pilgrim in the soul. "The pilgrim's view of life is that of the Soofi," he wrote, "with the usual dash of Buddhist pessimism." He described himself as "weary of wandering over the world and of finding every petty race wedded to its own opinions. . . ."

Throughout, in the manner of the Sufi master, or *murshid*, who teaches in contradictions—"There is no heaven, there is no hell," "There is no Good, there is no Bad"—he seemed to be trying to resolve the problems that apparently haunted him throughout his mature life. He called upon Ḥāfiẓ, Omar Khayyám, the Sufi Christ figure al-Ḥallāj, and the Islamic Elijah figure, Khiḍr, as guides along the way. Throughout, Sufi mystical concepts appear—wine as a symbol of mystical intoxication, the Potter and his pot, and "Death who in Arabia rides a Camel, not a pale horse." And at the end of life, there is, in the Muslim phrase, nothing but "the whispers of the desert-wind; the tinkling of the camel's bell."

So, in conclusion, he seemed like some wise old Sufi (the apothecary in Cairo he liked to visit, for example) who knows too much and has gone beyond worldly categories and definitions into another existence while still alive, in which all below is dross and chaos and perpetually unfinished, "The unripe grape, the ripe and dried; all things are changed into nothing, but into that which is not at present." The pilgrim's sole consolation is to conclude that "the highest ideal of the highest" is lived in obedience to the "inner law which cannot alter," a law that Burton had enigmatically wrapped in *taqīya*, leaving for the seeker to question and understand with only himself as guide.

> Mine eyes, my brain, my heart are sad,—sad is the very
>   core of me;
> All wearies, changes, passes, ends . . .
> Cease, Man, to mourn, to weep, to wail; enjoy the shining
>   hour of sun;
> We dance along Death's icy brink, but is the dance less
>   full of fun?

One day in the fall of 1882 there came disquieting news. Edward Palmer had disappeared on a mission in the Arabian desert. Palmer had been called out of the tranquillity of Cambridge to undertake a secret, desperate assignment for the government, an undercover mission too well publicized, and had disappeared. He had gone to the Sinai with two other Englishmen, Gill and

Carrington, and a small party of Arab guides, ostensibly to buy camels for the English army. That the party may have been after camels is possible, but there was a more important side to the mission. Some of the Bedawi tribes were in revolt against the Egyptian government. The English had established a "Protectorate" in the Nile Valley on the pretext that the Ottoman Empire was no longer effective there, and it was in British interests to keep the tribes pacified. Palmer had with him £3,000 in gold, about $200,000 in late-twentieth-century purchasing power—some reports said he had as much as £20,000 (a figure given also by Stanley Lane-Pool and Wilfrid Scawen Blunt). He was "to bribe the Bedawi" to oppose the expected tribal uprising against the Egyptian government. Disguised as an Arab, Shaykh Abdullah el Shámi (the Syrian), Palmer and his two companions, both army officers who spoke Arabic and were experienced in the East, landed at Gaza. "A fatal series of mistakes seems to have begun," Burton wrote. The party cut the telegraph wires linking Egypt to Syria and then set out into the desert, fully confident of reaching and bribing the Bedawin. However, Palmer had not hired the right kind of guides. He got not influential chieftains but a Christian Arab from Beirut and a young Jew of no standing, and as his *ghafir*, or "protector," a no-account Arab named Matr Nassar, "light-headed and half-witted," as Burton described him, without tribal connections. And the worst mistake of all was that Palmer's secret hoard of gold for bribes was no secret at all, and shortly Matr Nassar led the party into an ambush. Though Palmer was an excellent Arabist and had "brotherhood" with many Bedawi, the party was held prisoner for the day and then—the accounts differ—was taken to the edge of a precipice, where the Bedawi shot Gill and Carrington and gave Palmer the choice of being shot or jumping over the edge. Native gossip said that Palmer covered his eyes and jumped. The bodies of the two officers were found, but not Palmer's at first.

The government thought that Palmer might still be alive—

there was a report of a white man wandering forlornly about the desert—and requested Burton's help in searching for him.

"Ready to start by first steamer," Burton cabled the home office and left for Gaza. "A miserable, God-forsaken hole," he was to write of Gaza. He had an immediate antagonism for the officer in charge of the search, a Colonel Charles Warren, who had been a director of the Palestine Exploration Expedition but did not speak Arabic despite many years in the East. Burton thought there was something strange about the entire incident. "To Richard, who knew the Bedawi," wrote Isabel, "it was a puzzle; certainly they [the three Englishmen] were slain, but there was always something we shall never know; it was not Bedawi ways." The Bedawi would have killed the men immediately, not after a day's wait. Burton's private surmise was that the Turks had been the instigators.

But Palmer was indeed dead. The three Englishmen had been slaughtered and their bodies thrown down the precipice but were not buried, the expectation being that the birds and jackals would devour them and destroy all traces of the crime.

Palmer's remains and those of his companions were not collected until the following March, by Colonel Warren. Burton wrote a long account of the incident, and of the state of Egypt, but could not get it published. He was away over six weeks, during which time Isabel went into a retreat at the Convent della Orsilini at Gorizia, Austria. She had "long felt the need" of a period of prayer and meditation. "My life seems to be like an express train, every day bringing fresh things which need to be done." And: "I am here, my God, according to thy command, Thou and I, I and Thou, face to face in the silence." This last sentence smacks of Sufi forms of meditation, the "Thou and I, I and Thou," which Burton specifically mentions in the Nights, and the seeking of the Face of the Invisible, an advanced stage in the mystic's approach to the Divine. It is likely here that Isabel, far from being strictly Roman Catholic in her spiritual life, had picked up, probably subconsciously, Islamic meditative practices from her husband.

Burton returned to Trieste embittered by his treatment by Warren. From this point on there would be no more travels in the desert. The desert would exist in his mind alone, but in forms so tangible that he could almost touch them. Now he was deep in a wide variety of translations, not only the *Arabian Nights* but also, at the same time, Indian, Arab, and Latin erotica. And after the erotic translations had been completed, he had on his various worktables drafts, outlines, and nearly completed manuscripts on a wide variety of subjects—the Gypsies, Uruguay, Istria, the eunuch trade in Egypt, the Congo, the Passion Play at Ober Ammergau, several on the sword, four more volumes in his study of Camões—the list is almost inexhaustible in its expression of one of the most fertile and creative minds of the century.

In 1883, the year after poor Palmer's death, the Burtons found a house that suited them. It was outside Trieste, on a promontory that gave them a view not only of the city but of the Adriatic, on a site where the air and light were "delicious." The house was a mansion of twenty rooms in the old palazzione style, built by an English merchant, with an entrance big enough to drive a carriage into, with fine gardens and walks and all the luxurious space that the Burtons demanded. Burton took a large room on the north side of the house in which he slept and worked, which the sun did not touch but which was prone to the bora. Isabel was certain that this damp and unhealthy room contributed to her husband's gout, which was steadily worsening; she eventually convinced him—how she must have nagged!—to move to a sunny room on the south side of the house, smaller but conducive to good health.

This was to be the Burtons' last home together, where they would pass seven years amid their work, their visitors, their separate shrines to two of the world's greatest religions, their games and pageants of being people of another age, another world—fantasies perhaps in the eyes of visitors but in fact the extension of what had been so real in Burton's past and in Isabel's dreams.

Despite space, time, and comfort, moments of despair could intrude. Depression was rarely absent. Later the same year, on December sixth, Burton made a sad entry in his journal, which, said Norman Penzer, "fills the heart of an Englishman with pity and a feeling of resentment against the authorities of that day." Burton had written to the home office in the hopes of a better post, to be answered with silence. In the journal, in red ink, was

To-day, eleven years ago, I came here; what a shame!!!

In his final years at Trieste his wandering was incessant, a repetition, an echo of the wandering he had experienced as a child. There was barely a spot in Europe that the Burtons did not visit. Sometimes Burton went alone—Isabel said it was lack of money that often kept her from accompanying her husband —or she would return to England to see relatives or friends or talk to publishers about a new manuscript of his. And the friends that they both knew were on all levels of society and of intellect. The royalty alone read like excerpts from *Burke's Peerage* and the *Almanach de Gotha*. Isabel was especially good at tossing off names—Lord and Lady Amberly, Robert Browning, Lady Louisa Ashburton, the Emperor and Empress of Austria, the Crown Princess Frederick of Germany, the Grand Duke and Duchess of Baden, the theosophist Mme. Helena Blavatsky, the poet-diplomat Edward Bulwer-Lytton, Thomas Carlyle and John Ruskin, Benjamin Disraeli, the Prince of Wales. The list is virtually endless, and everyone was "our dear friend."

Each trip away from Trieste was organized like a major expedition into lands unknown, as if a hundred *pagazis* were ready to carry the immense amount of luggage, trunks and trunks of clothing and souvenirs, trunks and trunks of Burton's library, which he might need at a crucial point in his writing. There were servants, too, some exotic like the Syrian girl Khamoor, who got to be too Westernized in her ideas, and a more docile Austrian woman, Lisa, and dogs of all sorts and at times even a fighting cock.

They were a strange couple. Both wore koh'l around the eyes to keep off the sun and the dust, as if foggy London or the snows of the Alps were the same as the scorching deserts of the Levant. Burton dyed his hair an intense black, and he did look younger until the final years when his illnesses had stripped away his strength and vitality. Isabel's beauty was spoiled by her increasing weight, which, over-fleshing her naturally large frame, made her a somewhat grotesque figure not at all hidden under her loose Oriental robe. Both Burtons were intensely athletic—fencing and a daily swim in the Adriatic were part of their regime, and Burton would wear the lightest possible clothing in winter to keep himself hardened.

Odd as their appearance was, their interests were far beyond those of the ordinary educated Englishman and woman. They became involved for a period in the doctrines of the ancient Egyptian sage, Hermes Trismegistus, and then in Theosophy and spiritualism. In his quest for Gnosis, Burton never stopped searching and spoke and wrote often about the latter subject—to him the world owes the invention of the term ESP, which he described as "extra-sensuous perception."

Burton's discussions with Arbuthnot and Rehatsek in Bombay in 1876 eventually resulted in a definite project, the translation of various Oriental works, primarily erotica, which were to be released under the guise of an Oriental publishing house known as the Kama Shastra Society. In the Indian vernacular tongue *Kāma* was the love god, a type of cupid, and *śāstra* meant scriptures or chapter. In working on the translation of the *Kāma Shāstra*, or *Ananga Ranga*, Burton had noticed the references to

Vātsyāyana, who was so well versed in the science of erotics; the sage's own writings were embodied in a text known as the *Kāma Sutra*, or "Love Verses," a manual of erotic instruction dating back to a period in India previous to the fourth or fifth centuries A.D.

Arbuthnot had recently come back from Bombay, had married an admiral's daughter, Eleanor Guthrie, the widow of a country gentleman, and had settled down in a great estate in Guilford for a leisurely pursuit of Oriental (and erotic) literature. He had already published *Early Ideas* (1881), "a group of Hindoo stories," "Collected by an Aryan." Besides Indian erotica, Arbuthnot was working on other projects, among them *Persian Portraits* (published in 1887) and *Arabian Authors* (1890). He also contemplated a massive biography of Honoré de Balzac but the work, though eventually finished, never saw publication.

Arbuthnot envisioned a series of translations of Indian love books more or less known to the general Indian public and to some English officers stationed in India. They were to be the *Kāma Shāstra* (or *Ananga Ranga*), which was still languishing in proof form, the *Kāma Sutra* of Vātsyāyana, and eight others, including three medieval Persian Sufi mystical works. Two of the Sufi texts were translated rather woodenly by Edward Rehatsek; except for the *Kāma Shāstra* and the *Kāma Sutra*, the other Hindu books remained untouched. The Persian translations were not truly erotic, although Thomas Wright suggested "a snip or two with the scissors" so that they might "be read aloud in almost any company."

The Kama Shastra Society was composed of Arbuthnot and Burton, but they had a circle of friends as supporters, among them Monckton Milnes, who probably helped with the financing. The men on the periphery might be thought of as "typical" readers for the Society's publications, educated, affluent, and scholarly. One of the most significant was Henry Spencer Ashbee, a successful businessman, said by Thomas Wright to be experienced in the low life "from the sordid purlieus of Whitechapel to the bazaars of Tunis and Algiers." Ashbee's hobby was the compiling of bibliographies of pornography—he had done three in all—for which he used the pseudonym Pisanus Fraxi (Bee of an Ash); these works give details of the Kama Shastra Society upon which biographers have drawn.

A virtually unknown but very supportive figure was the shadowy Dr. Steingass, an immigrant who arrived in England in 1873, a self-taught linguist of fourteen languages, who, following the popular trend among scholars of the time, was to produce an *Arabic Dictionary* (1884) and later a *Persian Dictionary* (1892).

The actual proceedings of the Society, the rendering into English, the financing and printing, were at first shrouded in mystery: the translators were not identified until later, and then by their initials only and reversed—A.F.F. and B.F.R. The preliminary drafts of the *Ananga Ranga* and the *Kama Sutra* were done by the Indian pandit Bhagvanlal Indraji, whom Arbuthnot had commissioned to work up a translation in English. The *Ananga Ranga* was freely available in various languages in the bazaars—in fact, a Maharatti version was published in 1842, the year Burton had arrived in Bombay—but for the *Kama Sutra* Indraji had to call upon the Sanskrit libraries at Benares, Calcutta, and Jaypur for manuscript copies and then made a collation. How reliable his reconciliation of texts was and how accurate was his rendering into English are a matter for scholars. Rehatsek is said to have had a hand in the first drafts, after which Arbuthnot and then Burton took over. From the tone of the finished *Kama Sutra*—authoritative, witty, polished, and thoroughly annotated—one can surmise that Burton had the dominant role of all four men.

Burton and his collaborators approached the publication of the *Kama Sutra* with understandable caution, though he was ready—and eager—for a battle in court should there be any attempt at censorship. To publish erotic and pornographic works was a daring and risky undertaking. Victorian England had strict standards of morality and at the same time an unbridled underground licentiousness such as few ages have seen. As early as 1802, Dr. Thomas Bowdler had reworked Shakespeare to remove whatever might offend tender minds. The Protestant churches, particularly the Methodists, were relentless in their attacks on "Vice," but millionaire whores rode their carriages in the most fashionable parks with rich and titled lovers and associated with certain members of the royal family. Some streets were compared with Oriental bazaars, "Bhendi bazaars" in London. The delicacy of words and sentiment, however, ran to strange forms of self-censorship. Traditional English names were changed. James Balls became James Woolsey; the *Times* published a list of other changes, among them Holdwater, Prick, Poopy, Maydenhead, and so on. Even simple household words like breeches, petticoat, and smock became "inexpressibles" or a similar euphemism. Pornography flourished, and raids on bookstores were ineffectual. A bookseller could make more from the sale of a single pornographic volume than he would lose in the confiscation of another five.

Such was the atmosphere in which Burton and his friends entered upon the publication of works that were sure to arouse the anger of the puritans. The pretense was to be that the books were printed and published elsewhere—Benares or some other Oriental city—then to pretend that they were meant only for "scholars," males, who wished to study the great unknown literature of the East, a respectable discipline begun by Sir William Jones and the pandits of Fort William College in Calcutta. These erotic works, Arbuthnot pointed out, were, in one form or another, in the hands of two hundred million Orientals—surely, a few grave, bald-headed, bespectacled, happily married English gentlemen might read them without moral injury. They had to be wealthy, too. Each work was offered at the staggering price of £2 10s,* which eliminated virtually everyone but rich "scholars" as readers.

---

* At least $50 to $200 today.

The *Kama Sutra* appeared in 1883. The first edition was issued in seven parts, each bound in paper of varying tints of gray and fawn. Conspicuously on the cover was the legend "For Private Circulation Only." The first section bore the dateline "London," but the other six parts said "Benares." Two different printers were used on the chance that the authorities might descend on the project and try to stop it, and only 250 sets were printed. Shortly afterward Burton issued a second edition in which all the sections were bound into one volume. Unscrupulous publishers quickly pirated the work, and copies were run off in Paris and Brussels and possibly in the English Midlands. During Burton's lifetime only his two "legal" but nevertheless uncopyrighted editions were published; the pirated editions ran into many more, and should anyone have been able to keep an accurate record, his *Kama Sutra* is probably one of the most popular best sellers of all time.

The *Kama Sutra* is a curious, cynical work, even dangerous for those who might take it as a kind of Indian Gospel that allowed a license to crime. It was originally written for the amusement and instruction of hedonistic and well-to-do young Indians of the better classes at a period when Indian society was open and free. The "erotic" chapters, which form the central portion of the text, have diverted attention from its general purpose, which is the use of others, specifically women, for material and social gain and personal advancement and power. There is little cant or ambiguity in the work. In tone and purpose the *Kama Sutra* echoes its contemporary, the lesser-known *Artha Śāstra*, one of the world's earliest works devoted to the art and science of ruling, which is considered a distant predecessor of Machiavelli's *The Prince*. Here morality and ethics in government are moot questions. What is important in the *Artha Śāstra* is employing the most effective techniques for gaining the upper hand over one's subjects and the establishing of a monolithic, totalitarian state. Power, naked or concealed, is the goal. Spies, *agents provocateurs*, false accusations, and psychological manipulation, including setting friends against each other, are some of the means advocated in the *Artha Śāstra* and are similarly found in the *Kama Sutra*, by which the man can possess and control the women he desires, using them for his own purposes.

Certain types of women may be used. By making

this woman my [sexual] friend, I shall gain the object of some friend of mine, or shall be able to effect the ruin of some enemy, or shall accomplish some other difficult purpose.

In another instance:

By being united with this woman, I shall harm her husband, and so obtain the vast riches which I covet.

In an alliance with a woman of wealth, the man is advised to act on the principle that "I am very much in need. I shall therefore obtain her vast riches . . . without any difficulty."

In yet another example, "the husband of this woman has violated the chastity of my wives. I shall therefore return that injury by seducing his wives."

The *Kama Sutra* assumes that women are easily obtainable—detailed instructions for seduction are given—but there are always those who will not succumb. In that case

the man should, with his friends, fall upon her guards, and having killed them, or frightened them away, forcibly carry her off.

But Burton and Arbuthnot were most likely interested in the erotic sections, not the preliminary chapters. The sexual act itself was divided into a series of stages, acts, and embraces that some Westerners, among them Burton, thought pedantic and foolish. There were instructions to the point of boredom on the types of embraces, types of kisses, on scratching and biting and pressing with the nails, and on the methods of making love to women of different physical characteristics and different "countries." What has challenged the foreigner are the instructions for intercourse in various positions, lying down, sitting, standing (including one partner upside down), and various methods of wrapping the limbs about the other person. Burton commented that one has to be an athlete to engage in some forms of congress. The *Ananga Ranga* was to ignore the instructions for gaining power over women and the naked aggression of the earlier work, but the *Kama Sutra* cannot leave the matter alone, and after disposing of sexual congress—there is nothing about variant forms, like sadomasochism and other practices, though a short section treats of oral sex—returns to the matter of getting women for whatever purposes they may be needed. But then, in the kind of balance and symmetry so dear to the Indian mind, the work ends with some thoughts about how the woman may use men— "On the Means of Getting Money, of the Signs of the Change of a Lover's Feelings, and of the Way of Getting Rid of Him." The instructions are direct and unsentimental, and the woman, like the man, is taught the techniques of "Subjugating the Hearts of Others."

The success of the *Kama Sutra*, not only its acceptance by a small number of select readers but in escaping the censors, led Burton and Arbuthnot to salvage the *Kāma Shāstra* they had attempted to publish in 1873, and in 1885 they were able to issue it in three successive editions. Burton retitled it *Ananga-Ranga; the Stage of the Bodiless One*; it was published in the same format as the *Kama Sutra* but never achieved the success and notoriety of that work.

29

Arabian Nights

Though the little-read "Camões" volumes, the Sind volumes, and the early African books can stand alone as great works of their type, and the *Pilgrimage* ranks high on the list of any form of great world literature, it is the translation of the *Arabian Nights* that is most often identified with Burton. It is due to him that the work in general, and especially certain of the stories like "Aladdin" and "Ali Baba and the Forty Thieves," became such a standard item in the early reading of Western children.

The Arabic title was *Alf laylah wa laylah*, which Burton translated as *The Book of a Thousand Nights and a Night*. The work was a huge collection of stories, and stories within stories, told by a young woman in the hopes of keeping a very suspicious king, Shahryár, from having her beheaded in the manner of some thousand women before her. In general, the tone and construction resemble some of the parrot books Burton discovered early in India in which stories were told night after night to delay the unfolding of some threatening event. The *Nights* was a massive work, found in both oral and manuscript form, varying greatly in shape, content, and quality. In Burton's hands the translation is unsurpassed, though others had tried their versions of the Arabic: his text is unrivaled and the poetry superb. The notes and annotations that fill the volumes would alone make the reputation of many other men, and the final essays, dealing with the *Nights* and the social and religious conditions in which they appeared, are masterpieces of their kind.

Burton had long entertained the idea of translating the *Nights*, starting, he claimed, from his earliest days in India and the Middle East. He got to know the stories by heart—they could be heard almost anywhere in the Islamic East—recited by the *rāwis*, the professional storytellers, in the bazaars and souks and coffee houses, and they were collected in various manuscripts, sometimes fully, sometimes in fragments. By the time Burton had come out of the pilgrimage to Medina and Mecca, he was ready to start a translation, passing the summer of 1854 at Aden, where he "put up" with Steinhauser.

> When talking over Arabia and the Arabs, we at once came to the same conclusion that, while the name of this wondrous treasury of Moslem folk-lore is familiar to almost every English child, no general reader is aware of the valuables it contains, nor indeed will the door open to any but Arabists.

Before parting, Burton and Steinhauser agreed to collaborate on a translation and "produce a full, complete, unvarnished, uncastrated copy of the great original." Steinhauser was to do the prose, Burton the poetry, of which there were some ten thousand lines. Steinhauser's early death ended the collaboration, but Burton continued to mull over the idea, collecting material (often oral), searching out manuscripts, and telling the stories when he had a sympathetic Arabic-speaking audience, as he did in the Arabian desert, Somalia, and Damascus. He must have been the *rāwi par excellence*, the storyteller who loved his subject, was thrilled to have an audience, who not only knew the traditional texts by rote but could also add his own embellishments, developing characters, spinning out themes, and keeping his hearers enthralled with the natural music and poetry, the high drama, and the earthy anecdotes of the stories. The freedom offered in the Trieste consulate afforded him the time to return to the *Nights*, which he did in his haphazard fashion of juggling many works at the same time on his deal tables. The *Nights*, he was to write, "laborious as it may appear, has been to me a labour of love, an unfailing source of solace and satisfaction."

During my days of official banishment to the luxuriant and deadly deserts of Western Africa, and to the dull and dreary half-clearings of South America, it proved itself a charm, a talisman against ennui and despondency. Impossible even to open the pages [of the Arabic manuscripts] without a vision starting into view. . . . From my dull and commonplace and "respectable" surroundings, the Jinni bore me at once to the land of my predilection, Arabia, a region so familiar to my mind that even at first sight, it seemed a reminiscence of some by-gone metempsychic life in the distant Past. Again I stood under the diaphanous skies, in air glorious as ether, whose breath raised men's spirits like sparkling wine. . . . Then would appear the woollen tents, low and black, of the true Bedawin, mere dots on the boundless waste of lion-tawny clays and gazelle-brown gravels, and the camp-fire dotting like the glow-worm the village centre. . . .

After Steinhauser's death, "his valuable MSS, left at Aden, were dispersed, and very little of his labours came into my hands." Burton proceeded with the translation "fitfully amid a host of other obstructions." In the spring of 1879 "the tedious process of copying began and the book commenced to take finished form." Then he was jerked to a halt by an unexpected announcement.

. . . during the winter of 1881–82, I saw in the literary journals a notice of a new version by Mr. John Payne, well known to scholars for his prowess in English verse. . . . I wrote to the "Athenaeum" (Nov. 13, 1881) and to Mr. Payne, who was wholly unconscious that we were engaged on the same work, and freely offered him precedence and possession of the field till no longer wanted.

Payne accepted Burton's offer. There were further delays. Burton had meanwhile gone off to the West African Gold Coast to search for gold, and when he got back to his own translation, he had some fears that his "literary labours, unpopular with the vulgar and the half-educated, [were] not likely to help a man up the ladder of promotion," for there was a "despotism of the lower 'middle class' " that presented a formidable obstacle for the man "who dares to think for himself. . . ."

Payne issued a prospectus offering nine volumes in which the entire known body of the stories would be published, though certain "indelicacies" would be omitted. Burton's years of planning, of daydreaming, of haphazard translation had been dashed.

Payne had expected that he might sell five hundred subscriptions; to his surprise he received a thousand orders. As an honest man, he allowed only the five hundred sets to be printed and distributed. He had also promised that there would be no reprinting, and that seemed to be the end of a popular version of the complete *Nights*. Burton wrote Payne that he would be happy to take over the edition and issue it under his own auspices, the profits going to Payne, but that was not suitable to the other man's sense of fairness, and after the five hundred sets were distributed, Burton felt free to continue with his own *Nights*. He sat down at his worktable to complete a version that he hoped would not only equal Payne's but perhaps be better. He had several advantages. He did not expect to surpass Payne in the text portions but believed his own poetry—the ten thousand lines of verse ran from doggerel to high literature—would surpass Payne's, and he was certain that his notes, which would be copious and detailed, coming out of his unequaled experiences in the Eastern world, would be of greater value than Payne's inadequate and inexperienced annotations.

Burton's correspondence with Payne was carried out mostly

not from Trieste or London but en route to the Gold Coast and from various ports along the way. The insatiable yearning for wealth—gold, as usual—had propelled him into an expedition to Africa to search out mines he believed contained the riches that would solve his financial difficulties. Backed by "a private speculator," John Irvine, a Liverpool merchant who held mining rights in West Africa, and in the company of Commander Verney Lovett Cameron, who had spent five years crossing Central Africa from one coast to the other, the first man to engage in that dangerous venture, Burton set off at the end of November 1881. Burton and Cameron were to have all expenses paid and were to receive shares in Irvine's company. From Lisbon, Burton wrote Payne saying he had hoped to be back in London in April to talk about the *Nights* and suggested the name of an expert who might be useful in helping translate Persian and Arabic dialectical terms. However, Payne's first volume was already in type and was about to go to press, but he offered to let Burton see future volumes. It was mid-March 1882 when Burton, writing from Axim, Gold Coast, had to admit that since he was setting off into the bush country, he did not have time for collaborating with Payne on the *Nights*; he offered "any assistance in my power," but added, "I must warn you that I am a rolling stone." Which indeed he was. He also told Payne, "I am working on a scheme for Chinese immigration to the West Africa coast, and this may take me next winter to China."

Burton's reactions to China would have been interesting, but the trip was never made. His reactions to the people of West Africa were more predictable. Whatever prejudices he had developed in earlier years had been honed to a sensibility that was almost erotic. He was infuriated to find that the ship on which he had sailed took blacks as first-class passengers. "A ruling race," he fumed, "cannot be too particular in such matters, and the white man's position on the Coast would be improved were the black man kept in his proper place." He admired the French attitude: "Its imperious, warlike, imperial attitude is what Africa wants: it reverses our Quaker-like fad for peace!" And he denounced "the petting and pampering process, the coddling and high-strung sentimentality" engaged in by his fellow English.

Throughout her husband's absence Isabel was in a state that bordered on black depression. She thought "*entre nous* Cameron is not very solid." She felt Burton's absence deeply: "As I go on getting older . . . I dread fever for him. . . . I fear natives and beasts." What added to her depression was that she had cancer—the type is not known—a slow cancer that sapped her energies and will but which she would not reveal to anyone, particularly to her husband. She once "dreaded my empty home without children or relatives, but I have braved the worst now."

Burton and Cameron were able to report that "there was plenty of gold, and that the mines could easily be worked." In fact, however, the expedition was not a success, and both men were back in London in mid-May 1882, having spent six months in an unproductive search for a dream. It was Brazil and Iceland and Golconda and Midian repeated. "I ought to go down in history as the man who rediscovered one Gold Country and rehabilitated a second, and yet lost heavily by the discovery," Burton wrote Payne when he had time to assess his wasted efforts. But not all was lost. As usual, he had a book out of the trip; this, in collaboration with Cameron, was the two-volume *To the Gold Coast for Gold,* hardly one of Burton's better works but still the record of a man who could become passionately absorbed in whatever he was engaged in, even a search for gold among people he despised.

Perhaps the "reviving of a host of memories and reminiscences which are not the common property of travellers" kept Burton from slipping into some kind of insanity, an emotional collapse so often threatened by his frequent bouts of depression and his often justified anger at the world. Not only visual memories flooded his mind as he worked on the *Arabian Nights* but so did

the recollection of sounds—"the wild weird song" of the shepherd children, "the measured chant" of the warriors, the muezzin's call to prayer, the jackal's cries, the music of the palm trees
answering "the whispers of the night breeze with the softest tones
of falling water." And then he could recall the shaykhs and old
men sitting around the campfires "whilst I reward their hospitality
and secure its continuance by reading or reciting a few pages of
their favourite tales." And so he worked away in transports of
creative energy that seemed almost mystical, as if he were again
in the baking sands of the desert or the dusty streets of ancient
cities.

As with a few of Burton's other writings—*The Kasîdah* is a
notable example—the question of when he began to work and
what and from whom he borrowed—his influences and his
sources—developed into a public argument. Some of his enemies
and critics used the *Nights* as a means of attacking him, of impugning his honesty and his scholarship, of denigrating his creative energies, claiming that he had borrowed wildly, if not stolen
outright, from others, particularly Payne. However, there is little
doubt that Burton had become interested in the *Nights* at a very
early period and that he knew many of the stories and had told
them not only on the Meccan pilgrimage but in Somalia and
elsewhere.

Determined not to make the same error that Payne had in not
offering enough sets of the *Nights*, Burton proposed an edition
of one thousand sets of ten volumes, each at a price of ten guineas
the set. With the six volumes of the *Supplemental Nights*, he was
to earn 16,000 guineas, out of which 6,000 were paid for printing,
binding, and other expenses. Isabel sent out prospectuses to
36,000 people and was swamped with returns. Her role in the
project has always been underplayed. It was a strange fiction
maintained by both Burtons that she did not see the text, that
its indecencies and indelicacies were not to be read by the Englishwoman, yet she helped prepare the index for each volume

and later edited and published a "family" edition, though she could not give a convincing explanation of how she was able to condense, delete, and edit without actually reading the text.

To the surprise of both Burtons, they received not a thousand but two thousand subscriptions to the *Nights*. Again, as with Payne, there was a dilemma about possible profits and unfilled subscriptions. Burton felt that he had to draw the line at one thousand; to make up for the misjudgment in the obvious popularity of the *Nights*, he almost immediately set about translating a *Supplemental Nights* in six volumes (later reprinted in seven). After his death, innumerable editions were issued by pirates, as there was no proper copyright on the work.

Burton had been apprehensive about his work. Victorian moral codes were stricter than ever, though licentiousness was common. He had his defenses prepared. He would appear in court with the Bible and the Urquhart-Motteux translation of Rabelais under his arm, along with the Latin and Greek classics that every English public schoolboy was expected to know. However, to his surprise, the first volume of the *Nights* appeared to public acclaim, not censorship by the police. The complaints dealt with literary quality primarily. "Mr. Payne is possessed of a singularly robust and masculine prose style," said the reviewer in the July 1886 number of the *Edinburgh Review*. "Captain Burton's English is an unreadable compound of archaeology and slang, abounding in Americanisms, and full of an affected reaching after obsolete or foreign words and phrases."

The Payne and Burton translations were not the first to appear in Europe. The major English version from the Arabic was by Burton's predecessor, Edward William Lane, a man he disliked intensely. "Lane," said Burton, did not "score a success. . . . He had small score of Arabic . . . and his pages are disfigured by many childish mistakes. Worst of all, the three handsome volumes are rendered unreadable . . . by their Anglicized Latin, their sesquipedalian English words, and the stiff and stilted style of half a century ago when our prose was, perhaps, the worst in

Europe." Throughout his own version of the *Nights*, in footnotes, annotations, and commentaries, Burton attacked Lane whenever possible, and when Lane could not be a target, he attacked Lane's grand-nephew Stanley Lane-Poole. But of Payne he said, "His version is most readable. . . . He succeeds admirably in the most difficult passages, and he often hits upon choice and special terms and the most exact vernacular equivalent of the foreign word, so happily and so picturesquely that all future translators must perforce use the same expression under pain of falling short." This last sentence is an apparent excuse for the frequent charges that Burton borrowed from others, notably Payne. Wright, who also did a biography of Payne, accused Burton of making "his translation very largely a paraphrase of Payne's," and added, "He takes hundreds, nay thousands—of sentences and phrases from Payne, often without altering a single word." Wright states in summary that "Payne is concise, Burton diffuse." To add to his sins—and this is one of the obvious faults—he "spoils his version by the introduction of antique words that are ugly, uncouth, indigestible and yet useless." Burton indeed overexerted himself in trying to find English equivalents of what may have been at times archaic and difficult forms of Arabic. In "Tale of the Wolf and the Fox," we find such phrases as "O rare! ab but swevens [dreams] prove true," "Sore pains to gar me dree," "A garth right sheen," "Follow not frowardness," and so on, to the reader's discomfort and confusion. But in the long run it is Burton's *Nights* that the world now reads, remembers, and quotes, not Payne's.

The very earthy, bawdy, and outspoken tone of the *Nights* continued to haunt Burton despite his plans for a dramatic defense. He would not condescend to bowdlerize the text for the public, and he was critical of those who did. The long story called "The Queen of the Serpents," "containing sundry episodes" and occupying fifty-three nights, was "wholly omitted by Lane because [Lane considered it to be] a compound of the most extravagant absurdities. He should have enabled the readers to form their own opinions." As with his other translations, especially of the Indian erotica, Burton adopted the fiction that the volumes were printed by the Kama-shastra Society in Benares (or some other Oriental city) and were for "scholars," men who presumably did not respond to the graphic descriptions of sexual behavior or erotic stories. But it was the general public that bought the *Nights*.

The structure of the *Nights* is that so common in Oriental works—some of the parrot books, the *Pancha Tantra, Vikram and the Vampire*, and *The Fables of Pilpay*—in which a series of stories is told within a frame of a larger story, a story that leaves the listener or the reader in continual suspense. Will the parrot, by spinning out his story, be able to prevent the princess from cuckolding the prince? Will the wazir's daughter keep the king from sending her to the headsman? It is a simple yet dramatic device, and the *Nights* makes full use of it. Here the king, Shahryár and his brother, King Shah Zaman, have each been betrayed by his wife. Zaman, returning unexpectedly, "found the Queen, his wife, asleep on his own carpet-bed, embracing with both arms a black cook of loathsome aspect and foul with kitchen grease and grime." Zaman drew his scimitar and cut "the two in four pieces with a single blow."

The indignity forced upon King Shahryár was even worse. Not only the queen but his ten favorite concubines cuckolded him en masse every day, the queen with "a big slobbering blackamoor with rolling eyes which showed the whites, a truly hideous sight." The slave girls meanwhile were similarly engaged with white slaves, "kissing and clipping, coupling and carousing. . . ." Shahryár had the queen and her attendants beheaded, solving the problem of woman's infidelity by taking a new queen every night for three years, until his people protested and his wazir could find no more young women willing to sacrifice themselves for a night as queen. The wazir then offered his own daughter, Shahrázád. It was she who began the ruse of entertaining the king with a different, unfinished story every night, so that his curiosity about hearing the ending delayed his ordering her death.

The ruse was successful, and three years later, after bearing Shah-ryár three children and entertaining him for a thousand and one nights, the young woman was accepted as the new queen, about whom there would be no suspicion.

The stories gave Burton every opportunity not only to draw upon his vast and lifelong experience in the East but also to indulge in all his favorite intellectual pursuits as well as to unload his almost boundless store of prejudices that spared neither sex, race, religion, nor skin color. The first story has barely begun when he is off on linguistics and chastising the editors of various Arabic editions of the *Nights* for their sloppy work, denouncing Lane and others, giving Payne some praise, and indulging in graphic footnotes that must have sent England into states of both amusement and shock. A discussion of the correct spelling and pronunciation of the word *wazir* and a digression on the spirits known as *jinni* and the origins and misuse of the term are harmless and informative, but almost immediately he becomes involved in a type of bawdiness that is unpleasant, even offensive. "De-bauched women prefer negroes on account of the size of their parts," he wrote in a note on page six of the first volume. "I measured one man in Somaliland who, when quiescent, num-bered nearly six inches. . . . These imposing parts do not increase proportionately during erection. . . . In my time no honest Hindi Moslem would take his women folk to Zanzibar on account of the huge attractions and enormous temptations there and thereby offered to them."

He let his prejudices run free. He picked and chose from the various Arabic manuscripts at his disposal, and he made the most of such episodes, letting ethical and racial prejudices insert them-selves into what is otherwise an exceptional work. Still, this was Burton at his best, witty, erudite, caustic, earthy, handling com-plicated images and strange desert rhythms like a master juggler but becoming sometimes pedantically stuffy in explaining obscure matters of history or language. The prose rolls along with the easy cadence of a bazaar storyteller, the *ráwi*, at home with his material and his audience, and the poetry is superb in an age that knew and respected good verse.

Not all the stories are bawdy and raunchy like the introductory episode. Some of them are of a sweet delicacy that charms; some are religious parables, and some are fantasies that offer hope to the impoverished listeners—accounts of strange caves with unexpected wealth or secret doors that open into unknown worlds, of palaces and fortresses, tunnels that bring one to mountains of gold or silver or rare jewels. There are cruel kings and kind kings, rascally holy men, shrewd traders, adventurous sailors, nubile young women who seduce the stranger, khalīfs, judges, and rajas, maidens who wait to be futtered by innocent young men, lecherous old women of unsurpassed ugliness and unsatisfied lust, exotic animals, intrigues and plots; there are Muslims, Jews, Christians, and Zoroastrians and gems, golden rings, magic talismen, charms, and spells. Burton could recall that when he recited the stories to his listeners in the desert, they were "breathless with attention; they seemed to drink in the words with eyes and mouths as well as ears."

Great as the translation is, it is the famous, or notorious, "Terminal Essay" that many readers turn to first, an essay that stands out as one of the most important products of nineteenth-century scholarship. Though it was written in a few months, it embodies the studies and experience of a lifetime, in which Burton not only lays out the history, manners, morals, mores, and religion of the Arabic and Persian peoples and their rulers but places all in relation to the rest of the world, to the other peoples of the Middle East, the classical ages, the Egyptians, Greeks and Romans, the Mesopotamians. The "Essay" has the reputation of treating only and solely with homosexuality but that subject is but a part of the the whole, some two hundred pages divided into four sections, all reflecting deep scholarship and an unparalleled ability to analyze complex subject matter.

Virtually every scholar and student of the *Nights* has had his or her own views about the origins and the dates of the stories as well as of the compilers or authors. In the "Terminal Essay," Burton derided Lane for believing that one or two men had written the *Nights*, and from an analysis of the internal matter —the types of clothing and costumes, the weapons or lack of them (the gun and the cannon, for example), the use of certain foods (wines, ciders, and barley beer and the lack of coffee and tobacco), the types of diseases that afflicted some characters (certain forms of Asiatic cholera were mentioned, and smallpox was known, but not syphilis), and references to various historical figures—Burton was able to state that "the body of the work, as it now stands, must have been written before A.D. 1400." The framework was "purely Persian," some stories may date from the eighth century, some from the tenth, but the major part of the work was put together in the thirteenth century, with some tales added as late as the eighteenth century. "The author is unknown for the best reason: there never was one," for the *Nights* are the work of compilers and editors unknown.

Whatever the qualities of the "Terminal Essay," however, the most read and quoted section is that on pederasty, in which Burton discusses homosexuality. By way of explanation he said that the section was the "éclaircissement des obscénités." He is detailed but hardly sympathetic, referring to it as the "excrabilis familial pathicorum," "Le Vice," "abomination," "pathological love," "sotadic debauchery," and so on. He noted that "Pederasty is forbidden by the Koran" (and gives several references), "though Mohammad seems to have regarded [it] with philosophical indifference."

It was probably the first such discussion to appear before the general public, and it was a daring venture (as was the frank translation of the stories), considering the mood of Victorian England. Burton might have ignored the subject—it served in the minds of many to taint him and confirm the ever-present rumors—but he had been outspoken about heterosexual practices in his annotations throughout the *Nights* as well as in his translations from the Indian sex and marriage books, and he treated other sexual matters such as circumcision, excision, and eunuchism with the same openness. One gets the impression that not only is Burton showing off his vast erudition in the section on pederasty—there is hardly a classical or contemporary text or ethnological fact that is not mentioned—but he also makes the most of the section to include some very bawdy anecdotes that he could not work into other writings and which would amuse some readers and shock others.

Shaykh Nasr, the Governor of Bushire, "a man famed for facetious blackguardism," wrote Burton in an anecdote that sounds as if it came from his earliest days in Sind when he was associating with Persians,

> would ask his guests if they had ever seen a man-cannon (Adami top), and, on their replying in the negative, a grey-bearded slave was dragged in blaspheming and struggling with all his strength. He was presently placed on all fours and firmly held by the extremities; his bag trousers were let down and a dozen peppercorns inserted suo ano; the target was a sheet of paper held at a reasonable distance; the match was applied by a pinch of cayenne in the nostrils; the sneeze started the grapeshot and the number of hits on the butt decided the bets.

However, the "Terminal Essay" offers more than an exposition of al-Islam, discussions of pederasty, Middle Eastern literary history, and an examination of Arabic metrical composition (this section being written by Dr. Steingass). Burton uses the essay to indicate—rather obliquely, as he had in *The Kasîdah*—his very private commitment to mystical experience, taking for an exegesis of his own Sufi beliefs the very story that Lane had omitted as being unfit for the general reader, the long and complex "Queen of the Serpents," which covers fifty-three nights in the telling and is in fact a series of stories within stories, the underlying theme being the search for the Self. Woven into "The Queen of the Serpents" are themes that bore directly upon Burton's own mystical pilgrimage—the nāga kings and queens of India, patronymics of the Nāgar Brāhmins of which he had become an initiate so long ago; the "old serpent" of Genesis, symbol of his brush with Roman Catholicism; Zoroastrian and Magian dualism that influenced the Yezīdīs and the Peacock Angel cult. In some of the stories there is a guide, a kind of *murshid*, or teacher, the popular Islamic saint el-Khiḍr "whose eye shall see" where good begins and evil ends. The name, said Burton, means "the Green One," the color denoting the saint's eternal youth. In the Qur'ān, el-Khiḍr is equated with the Prophet Elijah; in Sura XVIII el-Khiḍr initiates Moses into the inscrutability of divine justice: he aids the weak and unfortunate, corrects the unjust, and guides the pilgrim on his mystical search. The story led Burton into a deep analysis of mysticism and offered an opportunity for him to explicate what is in fact his primary interest, the great Persian Sufi epic the *Manṭiq uṭ-ṭayr*, which he translated as "The Colloquy of the Fliers" (others call it "The Conference [or Parliament] of the Birds"). In a short, very arcane two pages that stand apart from the rest of the "Terminal Essay" and reveal a rare expression of Burton's private religious beliefs, a momentary abandonment of his long-practiced *taqīya*, Burton set down a very special and esoteric aspect of Persian Islamic mysticism only partly hidden by his normal dissimulation in such matters. His words are brief, cryptic, strange, and unless his readers were initiated into that special form of mystical discipline, confusing and not at all helpful. Yet he had a purpose and a message, and since this passage does not resemble any other in his works, one must assume he had a reason for including it.

The *Manṭiq uṭ-ṭayr* is by the Persian mystical poet Farīduddīn 'Aṭṭār. Like the old man Burton enjoyed visiting in Cairo in his youth, 'Aṭṭār was a pharmacist—his surname means "chemist" —and he was a repository of both popular and mystical knowledge. Before his death at a respectable old age in 1220 (he is believed to have been murdered by the Mongols at the age of 110), he had written 115 works, some of them of epic length, many dealing with the search for Divine Union, often in terms that defy logical analysis. His repeated theme was "the perpetual movement of the soul" toward its origin and goal. The Manṭiq says

> Everyone's journey is toward its perfection—
> Everyone's proximity [to the goal] is according to his "state."

Life was one long, endless pilgrimage, the theme so common in Sufi writings and one that was picked up in the West—the search for the Holy Grail, *The Romance of the Rose*, and Chaucer's pilgrims going to Canterbury are said by Western scholars to be influenced by the Manṭiq uṭ-ṭayr.

In the true Sufi manner of teaching—elliptical and subtle—Burton lays out the clues to be followed by those who will. The themes are complex and elusive. Burton weaves together the Qur'ān, the *Arabian Nights*, and the Manṭiq in a few sentences. In the Qur'ān Solomon is the King who has been instructed in the secret language of the Birds and can talk to them about the mysteries of God—"Bird" is a common Sufi metaphor for the human soul, and Solomon is equated with the soul in its transfigured state. In the *Nights* the lengthy "Queen of the Serpents" relies heavily on alchemical and magical symbols, among them the Ring of Solomon, long a sign of the ultimate goal. But the central focus is the search for the tomb of Solomon in the sacred mountain Kaf (properly Qāf), which Burton referred to as "the encircling mountain . . . a later [version] of the Persian Alborz." Alborz is where the Zoroastrian redeemer Prince Pesh-o-tan awaits the end of the world, to return in the Second Coming. Solomon's coffin, Burton reminded his readers, was transported not to Jerusalem, as the pious believe, but across the Seven Mystical Seas, where it rests as the goal in the quest for the final union with the Divine. In the Qur'ān a mysterious bird, the hoopoe, comes to Solomon to tell him that he has visited the land of Sheba, where a woman rules. The queen is a metaphor of the soul awaiting the wealth that only Allāh can bestow through the True Religion, that is, Islam. In the Manṭiq (as in other Islamic esoterica) the hoopoe is the symbol of the realized Sufi and will lead thirty birds—that is, souls—on the quest for the greatest of all birds, the Simurgh, who lives on Mount Kaf. Nothing is as simple as it looks—Burton explained that "Simurgh" means thirty birds—"Si = thirty and Murgh = bird"— and the reason soon becomes apparent as his exegesis reveals at last the meaning of the sacred journey as he saw it in the declining years of his life. He was a pilgrim like the birds, a "traveller"— as he had identified himself in The Kasîdah—a wanderer, for whom little matters except the mystical goal.

"Our eyes are blind though the world is lit by a brilliant sun," says the Mantiq. "If you succeed in glimpsing him, you lose your wisdom; if you see him entirely, you lose yourself." Burton was always doubtful about God, but the secret quest was never far away. His final remark on 'Attār's great work was as follows:

> So in the Mantak al-Tayr . . . the Birds, emblems of souls, seeking the presence of the gigantic feathered biped Simurgh, their god, traverse seven Seas . . . of Search, of Love, of Knowledge, of Competence, of Unity, of Stupefaction, and of Altruism (i.e. annihilation of self), the several stages of contemplative life. At last, standing upon the mysterious island of Simurgh and "casting a clandestine glance at him they saw thirty birds in him: and when they turned their eyes to themselves the thirty birds seemed one Simurgh; they saw in themselves the entire Simurgh; they saw in the Simurgh the thirty birds entirely." Therefore they arrived at the solution of the problem "We and Thou;" that is, the identity of God and Man; they were forever annihilated in the Simurgh, and the shade vanished in the Sun.

Now we can see the reason for Burton's endless pilgrimages to the tombs of honored forefathers buried in strange lands, to Mecca, to the steamy Asian and African ports where his predecessor, the one-eyed adventurer Camões, had lived and languished. In a kind of oblique revelation Burton was telling his readers what went on behind the doors of his Islamic shrine in the endless rooms of apartments and houses, while Lady Isabel honored the Virgin, the faithful saints, and the Good Lord Jesus. He had come at last to the solution of the question of "We and Thou." They were "forever annihilated in the Simurgh, and the shade vanished in the Sun."

He was the perpetual wanderer, the Son of the Wanderer (had not his father also been a wanderer?), guided by el-Khiḍr, "the Green One," symbol of Elijah, whose "eye shall see" where good begins and evil ends.

30

Perfumed Gardens

There had been rumors that Burton might be shifted to Morocco, and early in 1886 he took Isabel to Tangier in a restless search, for what he did not know. Morocco was not a country he enjoyed. "It is not a pleasant place for an English," he wrote in his journals, for in heat and general atmosphere it was Suez before the building of the Canal.

Then came an unexpected surprise.

> On the fifth of February, 1886, a very extraordinary thing happened [wrote Isabel in the *Life*]—it was a telegram addressed to "Sir Richard Burton." He tossed it over to me and said, "Some fellow playing me a practical joke, or else it is not for me. I shall not open it, so you may as well ring the bell and give it back again."

But the telegram was for Burton, and he had been knighted, being given the Knight Commander of St. Michael and St. George, a grudging gesture on the part of his government for his services. Isabel had had a hand in getting the honor for her husband, but she did not tell him that. From this moment on he would be Sir Richard Burton, K.C.M.G. It was not the K.C.B. that Isabel had worked for, but still an honor, and despite the rumors, Morocco was not to be Burton's, either—someone in the government had made a joke about not wanting the Burtons to be "Emperor and Empress of Morocco," and so they returned to Trieste.

The following January they went to Paris, where Burton had the pleasure of meeting a German scholar who had found an Arabic original of "Aladdin" and another story; then they went south to Cannes. The state of her husband's health now gave Isabel great uneasiness. "I saw him dipping his pen anywhere except into the ink," she wrote. "When he tried to say something he did not find the words."

The French doctors who were called in believed that he had a fit of "epileptiform convulsions" and thought he would not recover; they turned the responsibility of treating him over to a young English doctor, Frederick Grenville Baker, who was at the resort because of his own health. Baker entered the sickroom with the painful task of passing on the diagnosis of the French physicians.

"Then you suppose I am going to die," said Burton.

"The medical men who have been holding a conversation are of that opinion."

Shrugging his shoulders, Burton said, "Ah, well!—sit down."

He told Baker a story out of the *Arabian Nights*. Baker remained at Cannes another two weeks, then left. Burton, realizing the very precarious state of his health, got another physician to come from England, Dr. Ralph Leslie, who met the Burtons in Trieste. Burton was now working on the supplemental *Nights*, though prostrated by illness. Friends helped him in various ways, getting him Arabic originals or making rough translations from the Hindustani when Arabic texts were not available. Burton's health continued to cause grave anxiety; still, he went off for a summer vacation in Germany. Dr. Leslie moved to another post, and Grenville Baker was invited to replace him.

Baker remains something of an unknown. He was the kind of man one tends to overlook, but he had his role in the Burton household. His chief value, aside from helping prolong the life of a very difficult patient, was that he was the source of some important information about Burton's last years, and he was a good amateur photographer—his snaps show the Burtons in a most sympathetic and human light.

Baker had been born in Lahore, the capital city of the Punjab; his father was a colonel in the Indian army, and Baker and Burton had a lot to talk about. He was educated "privately" in England, then went to Germany for further studies. After spells with different hospitals and a few years of private practice, he became Burton's traveling physician.

Baker was a low-keyed individual. He never married, and his interests ran to fishing, gardening, and photography. After Burton's death, he was to lead a rather aimless life, traveling and studying in Europe, Africa, and America, a life possibly inspired by his most famous patient but one that lacked productivity. He wrote a few pieces about Burton; his major effort was to found the Richard Burton Memorial Lecture Fund in collaboration with the brilliant young academic and scholar Norman Penzer; Baker outlived all the others who knew Burton personally by twenty-five years.

Baker took the post with the Burtons on the condition that his patient follow his instructions about diet and rest. Burton often skimped his meals in order to get back to his work, and —a sin to Victorians—failed to drink even a normal-sized glass of whisky as a stimulant and relaxant. Baker became an integral part of the household and accompanied Burton on the few remaining travels he could enjoy, mainly jaunts to spas here and there in continental Europe. Meanwhile, Burton worked steadily away on various projects, though weary, ill, and depressed. Almost daily he received reports of the deaths of old friends, one of them Matthew Arnold, who had enjoyed a Civil List pension of £250 a year. Arnold's death was barely announced when Isabel petitioned the Government—unsuccessfully—to ask that the pension now be given to her husband, a step "credible to her heart but not to her head," Wright commented. Isabel had committed such indiscretions "frequently."

Arbuthnot arrived in Trieste in May, and about the same time there appeared another of the Kama Shastra publications, Burton's translation of *The Perfumed Garden of the Cheikh Nefzaoui*, a curious piece of eroticism, raunchy and at times funny, which had given him both pleasure and relaxation in translating.

The original version of *The Perfumed Garden* was credited to a fifteenth-century Tunisian scholar, Shaykh Nefzawi, who is said to have assembled the work for the pleasure of his bey, basing it on earlier manuals, notably Indian, and drawing widely upon stories and anecdotes similar to the wilder parts of *The Book of a Thousand Nights and a Night*. Its tone and approach is different from the Indian erotic books. Here woman is not a partner in sex but more of an object, to be used as desired. But not only pleasure was derived from woman; so was disease, treachery, and deceit. The book had been found in manuscript form by some French army officers in North Africa and was translated into French, some thirty-five copies being run off on the crude duplicating machine in the post headquarters. The French version—titled *Le Jardin Parfumé*—was reprinted in France, where Burton soon discovered it; he set about making a translation into English that was issued under the auspices of the Kama Shastra Society, coincidental with the publication of the tenth of the *Arabian Nights* volumes.

Not having the Arabic text, Burton gave the French-into-English version his own usual flourishes, but he was not satisfied with the result and immediately began to search for an Arabic original.

Bawdy and even humorous at times, *The Perfumed Garden* is

still a work in which man uses woman, though in turn she often takes advantage of him. The approach to sex is rather heavy-handed compared to the entwining, acrobatic maneuvers of the *Ananga Ranga* and the *Kama Sutra*, even though the types of the sex acts the book describes (which in fact are mostly drawn from Indian positions) have a certain piquant interest—frog fashion, he-goat fashion, the screw of Archimides, the somersault, the tail of the ostrich, fitting on of the sock, reciprocal sight of the posteriors, driving the peg home, the fitter-in, the one who stops in the house. But sex was a battle for these Arabs. "There takes place between two actors wrestlings, intertwinings, a kind of animated conflict . . . the arena of conflict resembles the head of a lion. It is called vulva. Oh! how many men's deaths lie at her door? Amongst them how many heroes!"

To Burton's annoyance, the French version was not complete; it had twenty chapters, and there was said to be a twenty-first, part of it about "a certain subject" and, in all, as long as the first twenty. A second, slightly improved, version of Burton's *Perfumed Garden* was brought out immediately, and immediately the work was pirated "by a bookseller, whose Committee, as he calls it, appears to be the model of literary pirates, robbing the author as boldly and as openly as if they picked his pocket before his face."

In the summer of 1888 the Burtons returned to England on a formal visit. Burton had importuned Government for sick leave, a permission not given gracefully, for he wrote his sister, Maria, that it was "accompanied by some disagreeable expressions which will be of use to me when retiring." He thought "the prospect of leave makes me sleep quite well," though he complained that "the dreadful dull life of England accounts for many British madnesses." "When he landed in June," wrote Georgiana Stisted, "we were horrified at the change in his appearance. . . ."

We knew of course that he had been ill . . . but he had not prepared us for the utter breakdown in health. . . . By the autumn his loss of strength was yet more startling. His eyes wore that strained look which accompanies difficult respiration, his lips were bluish white, his cheeks livid; the least exercise made him short of breath and sometimes even he would pant when quietly seated in his chair. . . . Heart disease, a hereditary malady, was making rapid strides.

Miss Stisted thought her uncle "seemed to live on by sheer force of will" but was constantly fighting a "distressing melancholy" brought on by his health. Much of Burton's time in England was passed with cronies like Arbuthnot, Payne, and Ashbee. When not with friends, Burton and his wife wandered all over England. He was restless, ill at ease, and sightseeing did not avert his increasingly poor health and physical distress. He oversaw the publication of the last of the *Supplemental Nights*. These final volumes lacked the verve and the élan of the first ten, though they brought to the public some of the stories that more than others are identified with the *Nights*, among them "Aladdin" and "Ali Baba." In his weariness Burton had not exerted himself, drawing upon Payne when necessary. "I confess that I could not have made it without your previous version," he wrote to Payne. He was faulted by some of the reviewers for poor scholarship, but in fact he could not always get Arabic originals and had to rely on the Hindustani versions of his friends.

At last he had to return to his post. "The end was approaching," Miss Stisted wrote. Burton was increasingly restless, and "it seemed that he must travel or die." On October fifteenth, a gusty morning enlightened by a pale gleam of sunshine, Burton left his native land to return no more. Now his wandering became incessant, as if movement would forestall the dreaded approach of death.

Noise, fatigue, hours spent in changing trains or boarding or disembarking from steamboats did not deter Burton. Geneva, Venice, Naples, Brindisi, Malta, Tunis, Algiers, the Riviera, the Alps, with a dozen stops in between, were visited and complained about. He was forced at times to return to his consular duties, having been reminded by the Foreign Office that he had a job to perform.

Late in November 1889 the Burtons set off on a winter vacation through the Mediterranean, stopping at Brindisi, where they saw Virgil's house, then going on to Malta, and finally landing in Tunis, the home of Shaykh Nefzawi, the author of *The Perfumed Garden*. Here Burton hoped to find Arabic manuscripts of the work. He ransacked the bazaars, but there were no manuscripts. "Nobody had ever heard of it," he complained. The Burtons continued on to Algiers. Burton was excited about the city and said he wanted to live there, but after a few weeks he was ready to leave. No manuscripts here, either. He thought Algiers "a Paris after Tunis and Constantine, but like all France (and Frenchmen) in modern days dirty as dishwater. . . . I have found these French colonies perfectly casual and futile." He stayed a full month and at last found an incomplete copy of *The Perfumed Garden*. It lacked the twenty-first chapter. But his time in North Africa had not been entirely wasted. He began to work on another translation, this of the *Carmina of Caius Valerius Catullus*, of which he did the verse portions, the prose being done by a new friend in England, Leonard C. Smithers, who was primarily a printer and who was to issue various "Memorial" editions of the *Nights* after Burton's death. Burton decided at last that he liked French North Africa but for the way in which animals were treated, for the donkey drivers and camel men beat their beasts unmercifully.

By autumn 1890, back in Trieste, Burton's physical condition was deteriorating rapidly. His eyes had sunk into the cavities of his skull; he had lost weight, and his hands seemed transparent; sometimes his voice was so inarticulate he could not speak. Small attacks of gout, not serious enough to prevent his daily walks, bothered him. The climate of "this penitential seaport" again began to annoy him. Dr. Baker noted that Burton's heart was weakening and that he suffered from flatulence. By this time death was always in his thoughts. His memory was failing, and small objects he put in "safe" places so he could find them again would easily be lost and he would have to call upon Isabel for help. On the last trip to England a clairvoyant had told Burton that he was "bad in the head, eyes, down the back of the neck, stomach, feet, and legs" and that Isabel had cancer but that she had "healing powers, powerful light from heaven, a red cross above [her], a large protection, and light from above, with troops of friends and patrons." Burton was upset by the prophecy of cancer in his wife, but she ridiculed the idea, and he accepted her denial.

The Foreign Office wanted Burton to be visible in Trieste, and he thought he had to stay there, believing that if he could survive the remaining months of 1890 and as far as March the next year, he would have completed his servitude to the government. By then he would be seventy. Meanwhile, his work was spread out before him in the rambling palazzo, on the eleven tables, each with its own project. It was a question now of survival, of having the strength to get through the day until the Nirvana, the paradise of March, liberated him. He spent the early autumn months on his new translation of *The Perfumed Garden*, which he had now retitled *The Scented Garden*. He worked diligently, rapidly, as if this would perhaps be his last effort.

There is much confusion about the final manuscript. It was known that Burton finished the first twenty chapters of the book, having found a complete Arabic text. The French translation had omitted a lot. Burton had learned that the Arabic text of chapter twenty-one had been five hundred pages long, the length of the previous twenty. The question of the twenty-first, dealing with what was likely homosexuality, is unclear. Did he finish this, too, or was he about to start on it? Arguments would arise after his death and continue for decades. At any rate, there was a massive new translation, thoroughly annotated, and possibly a twenty-first chapter, even more than thoroughly annotated.

There is little doubt that, twenty-first chapter or not, the manuscript included a long section somewhat similar to the "Terminal Essay" of the *Nights*.

Burton still kept early hours, rising at five-thirty and working steadily throughout the day, until dusk, taking time, often grudgingly, for his exercise and his meals. His only diversion would be a sip of whisky, and often that would be forgotten. This final manuscript seemed, to Burton, to be his greatest work. One day, as he and Baker were walking through the garden, he stopped abruptly and said: "I have put my whole life and life blood into that Scented Garden, and it is my great hope that I shall live by it. It is the crown of my life."

Baker had a serious and sensible question. "Has it ever occurred to you, Sir Richard, that in the event of your death the manuscript might be burnt? Indeed, I think it not improbable."

"Do you think so?" said Burton, turning to Baker. "Then I will write to Arbuthnot and tell him that in the event of my death the manuscript is to be his." Burton wrote to Arbuthnot the same day. Several letters were exchanged on the matter, but no one knew later if Isabel was aware of the arrangement.

A man is dying, one tidies up. Other arrangements were also in progress. Isabel now returned to a favorite topic, the matter of her husband's religion. Was he a Catholic, converted by the berry-brown priest from Goa? Did he convert later, before the trip to Africa, when he carried a letter from Cardinal Wiseman in his pocket describing him as a Catholic gentleman? His Islam, his Sufism, were not considered. That he might be Sufi and Catholic together was not within Isabel's comprehension. Or was he to make a declaration of faith now? Whatever, it seems that perhaps within three months before his death, Burton had written and signed a letter about his faith. The English publisher T. Douglas Murray reported the contents.

About a year before her death, Lady Burton showed me a paper of considerable length, *all of it in Sir R. Burton's writing and signed by himself*, in which he declared that he had lived and died a Catholic, adhering to all the rites and usages of the Church.

Lady Burton may have acknowledged that if her husband was not a good Catholic, he was at least *a* Catholic. During the last two years of his life Burton had the habit of locking the doors of the palazzo and engaging in private prayer. Isabel would prefer us to believe that her husband was reciting Catholic prayers, but most likely he was performing the Islamic *salāt*, or at least a simplified form of the ritual, since his aged and pain-racked body could no longer make the bows, prostrations, and special "sitting" that are entailed. Still, he could easily say the *dhikr*, the Remembrance, which anyone can recite aloud or silently, "*La ilāha illā-Allāh*," "There is no God but God," after which comes the phrase "*Muhammadun rasūlu*," "Muhammad is His Prophet." This is all that is required for salvation.

One afternoon in mid-October, an English friend, Daisy Letchford, whose brother Albert had done some illustrations for the *Arabian Nights*, came with her young sister for tea with Burton. He was in a good mood and joked and chatted with Daisy and the child. It was Burton's practice to say, "*Au revoir*," when people left after a visit. Now he said, "Good-bye, Daisy."

"I was so startled," she said, "by that 'Good-bye' that a shiver passed over me. I felt at the moment that I should never see him again." Albert Letchford saw Burton two days later and found him complaining that the good he had gotten out of a recent excursion to Switzerland had ended.

With the completion of the translation of *The Scented Garden* in sight, Burton was looking forward to retirement and a spring vacation in Athens, where he planned on meeting Professor Heinrich Schliemann, the discoverer of Troy. Baker had been watching anxiously over his patient. On the last full day of his life, Sunday, October nineteenth, Burton seemed better than usual, and the household remarked on his good spirits. Isabel went to the eight A.M. Mass, and when she returned home, she found that Burton had finished the last page of the new version of *The Perfumed Garden*. In no one's account is it clear whether this meant he had completed merely the first twenty chapters or the controversial twenty-first. He remarked to his wife, "Tomorrow I shall have finished this, and then I will begin our autobiography."

"What happiness that will be," Isabel replied, not quite concentrating on what he said, for at that moment one of those strange events that both Burtons put so much—superstitious—emphasis upon had happened. A bird had pecked for the third time at a window that was never opened. Burton remarked, "This is a symbol of death." "Bird," as Burton well knew, was the great sign of the soul seeking God. In fact, in Turkish, there was a phrase, *can kuşu uçtu*, "his soul-bird has flown away," meaning that someone has died, and similar images could be found in Persian and other tongues.

It was a beautiful day, and Burton took a two-hour walk with Dr. Baker, his usual practice when the weather suited. On the way through the garden, Burton noticed a robin drowning in the basin of the fountain. Baker rescued the bird, and Burton put it under his vest to warm it, then carried it inside to be cared for by the porter. In the afternoon he wrote some letters and discussed the proposed visit to Greece with his wife and Dr. Baker. They dined at seven-thirty, a cheerful, chatty meal, though Burton seemed tired. However, he was in a joking mood and teased Isabel about scapulars and other pious objects. Much of the conversation centered upon General Booth's scheme for helping the poor in England, the "Submerged Tenth," a project that Burton was very much in favor of. "When you and I get to England and are quite free, we will give our spare time to that," he told Isabel.

His typist, Mrs. Victoria Maylor, had come in during the day with the manuscript of *The Scented Garden*, which she had just finished typing for the printer. She was a Catholic, and as such did not seem to be included in the rubric that "nice" women did not read such works as Burton had been translating—she had typed the entire manuscript of the *Nights*. At nine-thirty, Burton, aided by Dr. Baker, went upstairs to his room. When he was undressed and in bed, Isabel came to say her night prayers at his side. While she was praying, "a dog began that dreadful howl which the superstitious regard as the harbinger of death." When the prayers were finished, Burton asked for some "chou-chou," light reading. Isabel gave him *The Martyrdom of Madeleine*, by Robert Buchanan.

After Burton had read and dozed for a while, he began to feel uncomfortable; at midnight he complained about a pain in his foot, believing it a touch of gout. Isabel wanted to call Baker, but Burton told her to let him sleep; the doctor had gone off with a migraine headache, and Burton said he needed his rest. At four in the morning Isabel called for Baker, who saw no cause for alarm; he gave Burton something to relieve the pain. But half an hour later Burton complained that there was no air in the room. Now thoroughly alarmed, Isabel again called Baker. Her husband was clearly dying. Burton said, "Poor chap, don't disturb him." Baker, when he entered the room, realized that the situation was grave. Isabel aroused the servants and sent them off for a priest. With Baker, she tried every available medicine at hand to save her husband. "Oh, Puss," cried Burton, "chloroform—ether—quick!"—medicines that were then given internally in a crisis. "My darling," said Isabel, "Dr. Baker says it will kill you. He is doing everything possible."

Burton's breathing was labored, and after a brief struggle for air, he cried, "I am dying, I am dead!" Isabel took him in her arms, but he seemed to get heavier and presently became insensible. Baker applied an electric battery to the region of Burton's heart. Isabel, on her knees at the bedside, holding her husband's hands, prayed her "heart out to God to keep his soul there (though he might be dead in appearance) till the priest arrived."

Burton seemed now indisputably dead. A priest did not arrive until six-thirty. He was a Slavonian, Pietro Martelani, described by those inimical to Isabel as "a country priest." "We may regret what followed," said Wright, "but no one will judge harshly the actions of an agonized woman." Georgiana Stisted called what followed "an awful farce." Martelani looked at the great wasted figure on the bed. Burton seemed to be dead, though the body was still warm. The priest asked if there might still be life in it. There were no heartbeats and no pulse. Isabel admitted this later to her family but believed that life still continued in the brain. She told Martelani, "He is alive, but I beseech you, lose not a moment, for the soul is passing away." Martelani knew enough about the Burtons to pose a sensible objection. "If he is a Protestant, he cannot receive the Holy Sacrament [of the last rites] this way."

Isabel declared that Burton had "abjured the heresy and belonged to the Catholic Church." Martelani administered the last rites. Georgiana Stisted gives a less favorable view of the scene.

> Isabel would listen to no arguments [about Burton not being a Catholic], would take no refusal; she remained weeping and wailing on the floor, until at last, to terminate a disagreeable scene . . . he consented to perform the rite. Rome took formal possession of Richard Burton's corpse, and pretended, however, with insufferable insolence, to take under her protection his soul.

It was a view shared by many of her contemporaries at home. As soon as Burton's death became known in Trieste, the public came in great numbers to pay tribute to the English consul. "An inquisitive mob never ceased to disturb the solemn chamber," wrote Burton's niece.

> Other priests went in and out at will, children from a neighbouring orphanage sang hymns and giggled alternately, pious old women recited their rosaries, gloated over the dead, and splashed the body with holy water, the widow, who had regained her composure, directing the ceremonies.

While Burton was dying, Daisy Letchford had an unsettling experience. At home, she experienced "a strange case of telepathy."

> My brother had gone out, and I waited alone for him. Suddenly I fancied I heard footsteps in the passage and stopping at the door of the room where I was reading. I felt drops of cold sweat on my forehead. I was afraid, yet I knew that no one was about at that time of the night. The door opened slowly, and I felt the impression of some one looking at me. I dared not raise my eyes. The footsteps seemed to approach. In a fit of fear I looked up and saw Sir Richard standing before me. He started, waved his hand, and disappeared. Early in the morning came a ring at the bell. I jumped out of bed and burst into tears, as I said, "This is to tell me that Sir Richard is dead." At that moment the maid brought in the letter for my brother from Dr. Baker. I ran with it to his room. "Albert, Albert," I cried, "Sir Richard is dead." He opened the letter. It was only too true.

When the undertaker stripped down Burton's body for embalming and burial, it was "found to be covered with scars, the witness of a hundred fights"—so Thomas Wright reported. More mystery, for in all the literature involving Burton—his own writings and various biographies by relatives and friends, essays, and letters—there is (aside from the encounter at Berbera) no authentic evidence of the kind of fights, obviously knife or sword, that would have resulted in so many wounds. The likely cause of the wounds was Burton's ecstatic involvement in the samā' and the dance of the swords in the Sufi khānqāhs, the convents, in Sind and possibly in Cairo.

The body was embalmed, laid out in uniform, and surrounded by candles and flowers. Behind the bed was a large map of Africa. On Burton's chest Isabel placed a crucifix. He still wore the steel chain and medal of the Virgin that she had given him for his protection when he went into Central Africa.

The Trieste press echoed with obituaries about the famous explorer, and in London, Burton's death was a major topic in the news. Swinburne wrote an elegy: "A fame outshining Raleigh's fame." It was a great event, a national celebration, the sorrow and joys of which were marred only by the mutterings of the Protestants, the agnostics, and the profane—and a single, denigratory letter from James Grant to the *Times* on the subject of Burton's mistreatment of Negroes and his trying to take credit for Speke's discoveries.

The Masses said in Trieste were not for the final burial. That would take place in England. The ceremonies in Trieste were medieval—three separate High Masses, of elaborate pageantry and ritual. Georgiana must have been driven into a fury over Isabel's letter.

> I did not have him buried, but had a private room in the cemetery consecrated (with windows and doors on the ground floor) above ground where I can go and sit with him every day. He had three church services performed over him, and 1,100 masses said for the repose of his soul.

For a man who thought of himself as an "amateur barbarian," it was, for the proper people back in England, as barbaric as one could get. Burton's body would eventually rest in the Catholic cemetery at Mortlake in London. Meanwhile, there was the tremendous task of cleaning out eighteen years at Trieste and a lifetime of work that did not overlook India and Arabia—souvenirs, manuscripts in several dozen languages, Qur'āns and Bibles, weapons of all sorts, maps and sketches, human bones, uniforms and native costumes from various places, geological specimens. What had Sir Richard not left behind! He had left, among other things, journals, manuscripts of his books, notebooks, poems, letters, essays, reviews, clippings, and . . . erotica. To the great problem of her husband's papers, Lady Burton addressed herself with an almost mystical passion.

31

The Widow's Burning

Isabel now commenced the famous "bonfire" in which the heart, the very soul, the spirit of Captain Sir Richard Francis Burton, Ḥaji and K.C.M.G., was consigned to the flames, in some strange kind of *satī* in which the widowed soul is sent as an offering to the deities. For sixteen days she shut herself up in the palazzo in order to go over her husband's papers and classify them, to pack up his library and "carry out his instructions." People had often acknowledged her "goodness, sweetness and character" and her devotion to her husband, but there was another side, which some critics saw as dominant, saying she was "indiscreet, illiterate, superstitious and impulsive," and possessed of a colossal self-assurance.

The Letchfords moved in to give Isabel some company and to assist her in various tasks. Daisy was asked to help with the papers. Isabel would let no one else in the room where she had assembled them. She believed that Daisy was too young and innocent to understand their content. "She did not suspect that often when she was not near I looked through and read many of those MSS, which I bitterly repent not having taken, for in that case the world would not have been deprived of many beautiful and valuable writings," said Daisy. One of the writings was a long poem in the style of "The House That Jack Built," which was a sarcastic and ironical satire mentioning the names of many leading Englishmen. "I begged Lady Burton to keep it, but her peasant confessor [Martelani] said, 'Destroy it,' so it was burnt along with a hundred other beautiful things."

Burning irreplaceable papers was not an act that gave Isabel any qualms. She had destroyed Lady Jane Digby's autobiography when asked to; she burned her own book of spiritual meditations—

> . . . a book called "The Sixth Sense," and [I] was vain enough to think it was clever; but I was afraid it would do harm and I took the courage to burn it.

And as a most impressive precedent, she pointed out that "Turner's executor burned a few of his last pictures under similar circumstances to leave his reputation as a painter at its zenith. I acted from the same motive." Here Isabel is quite inaccurate or is dissembling. It was John Ruskin who, in 1852, burned a large collection of J. W. M. Turner's art—sketches, drawings, and oils, work, said Ruskin, "of a most shameful sort." Ruskin had been appointed executor of Turner's work by the National Gallery and, to his horror, found work in the legacy that was "inexcusable, inexplicable"—drawings and oils of prostitutes "in every sort of abandonment." Ruskin anguished for weeks over his discovery.

> I put myself in Tune with the Highest, till suddenly it flashed on me that perhaps I had been selected as the one capable of coming, in this matter, to a great decision. I took the hundreds of scrofulous sketches and paintings and burnt them, where they were, burnt them. . . . I am proud of it, *proud*.

Isabel could also quote with approval an account of a burning of a manuscript she had been told about in India. A Mrs. Hough, who used to party with Sir Arthur Wellesley (later the Duke of Wellington), had died the year before the Burtons arrived in Bombay. The editor of the Bombay paper regretted that Mrs. Hough had burned all her memoirs, but Isabel noted in her journal, "I dare say she knew why she burnt them. I dare say thousands of people's descendants have cause to bless her for it."

So, Isabel burned. . . . But what was in those pages? The common assumption is that they—journals, manuscripts, letters, whatever—were filled with sexual information, often of a very personal and even degrading nature—accounts of affairs, descriptions of intercourse, bestiality, experiences with native women, pederasty, drawings of such subjects as clitoridectomies or unusual forms of circumcision, of mutilations, of eunuchs— and perhaps there was such material, but Burton's range of interests was so vast that everything from personal opinions to political judgments would have been possible. And since he had been involved at times in various aspects of the Great Game there was likely in the private journals material of a compromising nature on the actions of his government. Much of the sexual information (but far from all of it) had been introduced either into the main text or the annotations of *The Thousand Nights and a Night* and the Indian, Arab, and European erotica. What had not yet been published was the far more dangerous material about Government policies, his superiors in the Foreign Office, even personal friends—the "many great people still living" that Daisy Letchford said were in the poem (and Burton seems to have written several such works)—material that Isabel knew was more dangerous to the memory of her husband than accounts of long-ago seductions in Sindhian and African villages or descriptions of brothels, lupanars, and harems.

As if saving the best for last, like some kind of pyromaniac's dessert, Isabel had set aside the manuscript and typescript of *The Scented Garden* and a few other papers. By this time she had discovered that Daisy was not so ignorant as she thought. Daisy begged her not to destroy *The Scented Garden*. Isabel promised not to destroy it. Daisy went out for the evening, and for the moment Isabel was closeted with that challenging work. She began to examine it. Apparently Burton had not allowed her to read this latest version, though its character was no secret. Fifteen hundred subscriptions had already been received, and she was said—this has not ever been confirmed—to have been offered 6,000 guineas for it by an English publisher. Isabel sat down on the floor with the piles of manuscript and typescript and started to peruse them. She was "perfectly bewildered and horrified." The text alone was more explicit than Burton's previous translation from the French, but it was the annotation that upset her—"notes of a certain character." She tried to reassure herself that the book was written only for scholars and mainly for Orientalists and that her husband "never wrote a thing from an impure point of view."

What to do? . . . The issue was settled with the apparition of Burton himself standing before her, "just as he had stood in the flesh."

Burton's apparition pointed to the manuscript and said, "Burn it." Then he disappeared.

To burn or not. The apparition returned to command a second time that the manuscript be burned. Still Isabel was not sure what to do. Burton's apparition returned a third time and spoke in an even more commanding voice, and now, as Isabel wrote, she saw no choice but to follow instructions. The manuscript went into the fire page by page. When Daisy Letchford returned, all she saw were a few pages smoldering in the fireplace.

Should Isabel have burned this most controversial work? What was in it? Who else had read it? Well, for one, Mrs. Maylor had read it and typed it. Grenville Baker was quite familiar with the contents as the result of many chats with Burton at meals and as they strolled about the gardens, and he was to pass his opinions on to Norman Penzer many years later, who published them in

1923 in his *Annotated Bibliography*. "It is, of course, most dangerous and wrong to burn unpublished MSS, of an author, even if the person doing so be the man's own wife."

Penzer immediately negated his own position by wondering "whether the reading world missed much by the burning of this manuscript. . . ."

> I have a very good notion of what exactly was in the MS owing to the fact that my friend, Dr. Grenville Baker, during the time Burton was writing this edition of the "Perfumed Garden" daily heard and discussed its content with Sir Richard himself.

Baker had told Penzer that it was "merely a greatly annotated edition of that issued in 1886" and contained "a large amount of material that Burton had not been able to include in the 'Nights,' " and that the " 'Perfumed Garden' offered a good opportunity for putting on record what remained partly in Burton's private note-books and partly in his great brain." In conclusion Penzer said:

> I can definitely state that the work was one which would only have been of value to a small circle of genuine scholars of the East.

There was another manuscript set aside. This was the translation of the Latin poet Caius Valerius Catullus, which Isabel undertook to edit, removing "improprieties." The retyped manuscript was sent to Leonard Smithers in London for publication. The typist had made innumerable errors, and Smithers was puzzled with what had been given him, yet the work was finally published in 1894 in a private edition of 1000 copies.

Fortunately, still other manuscripts—innocuous in character to Isabel—escaped the flames, along with some small notebooks and a few other fragments. Then there were letters in the hands of others, friends or acquaintances, and in government files— material for the large part still not available to the public; hundreds, perhaps thousands, of letters seem to be permanently entombed in private collections and official archives, despite efforts by biographers and scholars to pry them loose. Among the surviving material were quite a number of books in manuscript form, like *Uruguay*, translated by both Burtons from the Portuguese, the *Pentamerone* (which was to be published in 1893), five books on Latin America, four more dealing with Camões, extensive notes for books on Greek proverbs and Slavonic proverbs, and so on, mostly material that would not arouse the fastidious. After the burning, Isabel's friend and secretary, Miss Minnie Plowman, drew up a list of eighteen other manuscripts, all on noncontroversial subjects (A *Study of the Wali*, A *Trip to the Congo*, *Syrian Proverbs*, *Four Cantos of Ariosto* are typical), but after Isabel's death, her sister, Mrs. Fitzgerald— "the very last kind of woman who ought to have been allowed to have touched Burton's papers and books," said Penzer— burned most of the surviving material except for what had already been published by Isabel. "Of the above lists nearly everything was flung into the fire in a mad fit of wantonness." Miss Plowman tried to halt the burning as Daisy Letchford had earlier of other manuscripts; Mrs. Fitzgerald even attempted to burn books by Burton that had already seen print.

When the burnings of the papers, journals, manuscripts, diaries—most of what Burton had left—was known, outrage swept over England, but the damage had been done, or the sacrifice performed, and no amount of civilized anger would undo the terrible deed. To a few people Isabel was a saint; but for most, a monster.

Trieste was finally at an end. Isabel was "packing and paying" for the last time. She said good-bye to the vast circle of friends, to the servants, to the children at the orphanage, to the animals at the shelter, and set off for home by train. Burton's body was being sent by steamship. There was a report that his remains had been crated in a piano box, but that was not so.

Isabel reached London in early February 1891. Her first mission was to visit Maria and Georgiana Stisted. They were not happy to see her. Isabel had hoped that her husband might be interred in Westminster Abbey, or St. Paul's, but such honors were immediately denied, and she went to the Catholic cemetery at Mortlake to buy a plot for a grave. The ship with the coffin landed at Liverpool on the twelfth, and Isabel, though feeling ill, went to meet it. The weather was chilly and rainy, and she caught cold and had to take to bed. It was not until the end of April that she was able to carry on with her duties. But even during her illness she was not idle, reading and answering two thousand letters of condolence and making plans for the funeral. A public subscription raised nearly seven hundred pounds for the proposed tomb. It was quickly built, of two shades of dark stone and white Carrara marble, and was in the shape of "an Arab tent"; the general opinion was that it was magnificent. It is of course not quite a true Arab tent but more that of an English army officer, not unlike the Rowtie at Berbera, where Burton was so severely wounded.

Burton's coffin was placed inside on trestles. There was room for Isabel when she died. The tent was so realistic, Isabel said, that people often asked why the canvas was not taken off so the coffin could be seen.

Isabel spent a short time at her convent, the Canonesses of the Holy Sepulchre, and then took a house in Baker Street. (Sherlock Holmes lived nearby, at 221B.) Here she settled down to being The Widow. During the last decade she had become (to use her own words) "coarse and rather unwieldy," but in her widow's cap, with its long white streamers, she still maintained an air of dignity. Eventually, she bought a small house at Mortlake so she could visit Richard every day. Triumphs were balanced by embarrassments. When she sent out invitations to the opening of the Tent at Mortlake, five hundred people accepted, but there were "another 450 influenza refusals."

Then Isabel got to work writing the official *Life*, a job that took a mere eight months, although the finished book ran to two volumes totaling over thirteen hundred pages. "That she was quite unfitted for the task, must be clear to all who have any knowledge of Burton," snapped Thomas Wright, having reached the breaking point over Lady Burton's vagueness, prevarications, and confusion and the book's "frequent offense against good taste." But just as Burton had appeared to his wife at Trieste to order her to burn, he now stood by her side to assist her with the task of writing his life.

Isabel's "Catholic" version of the world-renowned explorer, writer, linguist, and consul brought a rejoinder from the other side of the family. Georgiana Stisted soon rushed to print with a corrective, *The True Life of Capt. Sir Richard F. Burton,* which was as much an attack on Isabel as a biography of her husband and defense of his character. But Isabel had already died, and revenge was taken upon a woman who never saw the accusations. The mysterious illness—the unidentified cancer—that had plagued Lady Burton for so long finally took her in March 1896. She was sixty-five, a respectable age at the time, and had lived as exciting, challenging, and adventurous a life as most men, except, of course, her husband.

And shortly, Burton's world was erased, and fourteen years after his death, his family was extinct. Henry Stisted had died of consumption in 1876, and Burton's younger niece, the retiring, unmarried Maria (or Minnie) Stisted in 1878; Burton's sister, Maria, died in 1894 and Edward Burton in the fall of 1895, and lastly, Georgiana Stisted, who also never married, in 1904. And if Burton's line survives at all, it is obscurely through those mysterious Anglo-Indian Burtons in western India, descendants of an English officer and "sir" and an unnamed nautch girl from the Baroda bazaar, whose "infallible recipe" to prevent maternity may have failed her, for the family, aside from name and tradition, has, as was written earlier, an uncanny resemblance to Richard and Maria Burton in the portrait by Jacquard.

Just as he had often made pilgrimages to the tombs of his spiritual and intellectual ancestors or had found descriptions that also might be applied to himself, Burton left an epitaph behind in—

of all works!—the *Kama Sutra*. There is a passage not in the original, and not in all the English language versions, that Burton, one must surmise, meant as his own epitaph; it comes in the final paragraph.

In a beautiful verse of the Vedas [Gospels] of the Christians, it has been said of the peaceful dead, that they rest from their labours, and that their works follow them. Yes indeed, the works of men of genius follow them, and remain as a lasting treasure. And though there may be disputes and discussions about the immortality of the body or the soul, nobody can deny the immortality of genius, which ever remains as a bright and guiding star to the struggling humanities of succeeding ages. . . .

Notes and Major Sources

Sources other than books by Burton (for which, see Bibliography A) are given by the name of the author. For their titles, see Bibliography B. *Life* is the Isabel Burton biography.

1. *The Gypsy Child*

Major sources are the Isabel Burton *Life* and the Georgiana Stisted and Thomas Wright biographies.

2. *Dark and Sooty England, Sunny France*

Again, Isabel Burton, Stisted, and Wright.

3. *Among the Grocers*

Isabel Burton, Stisted, and Wright. Also see Leslie on the Oxford Movement; Burton's *Vikram and the Vampire* and *Goa, and the Blue Mountains*, both of which contain references to Oxford. See Vesey-Fitzgerald on the English Gypsies. For Burton's esoteric interests: Rudolph on Gnosis; and Scholem and Schaya on the Kabbālah, Hermes Trismegistus, the parrot books, and Zadkiel.

4. *The Great Game*

Isabel Burton, Stisted, and Wright. Also, Alexander Burnes, James Burnes, Eastwick, Elphinstone, Fredericks, Furber, and Osborne. Rudyard Kipling's *Kim* gives an excellent picture of the playing of the Great Game at a later period.

5. *The Griff*

Isabel Burton, Stisted, and Wright. See Richardson for life in Bombay's English colony in the 1840s. On the Bombay brothels as Burton experienced them, see the *Kama Sutra, passim*. Sushma Kumar furnished information on the Grant Road houses. On the Goans: personal information given the author by members of the Goan community and others. Yeats-Brown, though of a later date, is excellent in setting the mood of British India, as is Fraser in *Flashman*.

6. *The Black Wife*

Scinde; or, The Unhappy Valley and *Scind Revisited* discuss the búbú system; also, the *Life*, Stisted, and Wright. See Balhatchet on sexual relations between Europeans and Indians. Cyrus Jhabvala explained the role of the *hawaldār* (personal conversation). Various members of the Anglo-Indian community, among them Frank Anthony (New Delhi), Foy Nissen (Bombay), and Mr. Nix-James (Byculla), were helpful in giving details of the union of Europeans and Indian women and their descendants. See 'Ruswā, the semiautobiographical *Courtesan of Lucknow*, for material on the life of the common prostitute of Burton's time in India; its heroine was born in Baroda in 1842, the year of Burton's arrival. The Reverend Father Suria, S.J., contributed information about the Catholic church in Gujarat; unfortunately, the parish records for 1843 are missing, as are those of the Anglican parish. A thorough search of the Anglican records in Bombay (which now has all those for western India from Burton's time) revealed neither marriage nor baptismal records for Burton or for an offspring. In Bombay, Denzil and Mercy Burton and their sister-in-law Mavis Burton reluctantly revealed information that shows a possible connection to Richard Francis Burton (several conversations, February 1980). The author is indebted to female members of the Simoes family of Panjim and Igatpuri for information on preindustrial and primitive forms of contraceptive practices; also, to R. Simoes for material on female circumcision.

7. The Snake Priests

Isabel Burton, Stisted, and Wright (and later biographers) all refer to Burton's joining the Nāgar Brāhmins but fail to understand their importance. Various people in Baroda were helpful in giving information (but cautiously—the Nāgar Brāhmins are not popular). Hastings's *Encyclopedia* has very accurate information on the caste. For Burton's Tantric practices, see *Vikram and the Vampire*, *passim*. Also Daniélou, Woodroffe, Moor, Dubois, and Thomas; the author is also indebted to the Deb family (Bengali Brāhmins) and Jyoti Gupta for details on caste. See also the author's own *Eastern Definitions* and Pagal Baba's *Temple of the Phallic King*. The author was fortunate in being present in India in 1980 during an eclipse of the sun when Tantrics celebrated the event openly while orthodox Hindus (and Muslims and Christians) remained in the safety of their homes.

8. Young Egypt

Isabel Burton and Stisted. Burton's Sindh books form the core of this chapter. See also Alexander Burnes, James Burnes, and Lambrick. Some incidental information is derived from the author's own experiences in Sind and the Punjab.

9. The Assassins

Burton's *Sindh* contains his views of the Āghā Khān and the Assassins. For the peregrinations, aspirations, and machinations of the Āghā Khān in vivid detail, see Algar. Lewis's work on the Assassins is essential.

10. The Royal Court

Burton's *Sindh*; also the *Life*, along with Algar and Lewis. See Williams on Shī'a sects and esoteric doctrines.

11. *The Smell of Death*

See Burton's Sindhi works. The paragraph on Muslim customs comes from Burton's *Pilgrimage*. Circumcision was a running topic in all of Burton's works. See also Sharif, Hastings under *Circumcision*, and Bryk. Al-Ghazzālī is invaluable in discussing required and optional Muslim observances and practices. Goan and Anglo-Indian sanitary practices are ribald chitchat among Indians. Snelling gives some aspects of the Great Game, and of course *Kim* cannot be overlooked. Brodie quotes Burton's poem about the Persian girl but erroneously believes she was also the same person as his pariah inamorata.

12. *The Secret Path*

See the "Terminal Essay" in the *Nights* for Burton's undercover work in the male brothels of Karachi and the unfortunate result. His undercover work for Napier in Sind was described in broad outline in *Falconry in the Valley of the Indus*. See Chapter VIII of *Sindh* for his comments on Ḥāfiẓ and other Sufi poets. See also 'Abdu'l-Qādir Gīlānī, Burckhardt, Khan, al-Ghazzālī, Nicholson, and Arberry.

13. *Searching for Camões*

The primary source for this chapter is *Goa*. See also Panter-Downes, Burton's translation of *Os Lusiadas*, and his biography of Camões. The poem to "fair Margaret" is quoted in Brodie. See Burton's *Sindh* and *Religious Hinduism* (a compilation by Jesuit scholars) for Sikh practices.

14. *The Mystical Rose*

Burton has left an excellent description of the training and initiation into a Sufi brotherhood in Chapter VIII of *Sindh*. The popular Sufi manual of instruction, Suhwawardī's *'Awārif-u'l-Ma'ārif*, tells in detail the rites of Burton's own order, the Qādiriyyas, including the ecstatic sword dance, the *samā'*. See also Brown's *The Darvishes*. References to 'Abdu'l-Qādir Gīlānī are found throughout literature dealing with Islamic esoterism (see, for example, Sharda and Schimmel). On the Jesus prayer which is related to the Sufi *dhikr*, see Kalistos. Burton's Sufi diploma was called into question (personal interview, 1980) by Shaykh Hasan Saani Nizami, scion of one of the most revered of Indian Muslim saints, the thirteenth-century mystic and philosopher Niẓāmuddīn 'Au-liyā'* (see Baba and Schimmel, *passim*). Trimingham also questions the diploma most vociferously.

15. *Daisy*

Isabel Burton's autobiography (see W.H. Wilkins, *The Romance*) and the *Life* are the basis for this chapter. See also Stisted, *passim*, for critical views of Isabel.

16. *The Road to Mecca*

Primary source is Burton's *Pilgrimage*. For details of the pilgrim's life, see Husain; also Muhammad Ashraf on *salāt*. Lane describes life in Cairo about the time of Burton's visit but often fails the esoteric meanings. For non-Muslim visitors to Mecca, see Ralli.

17. *The Prophet's Tomb*

The *Pilgrimage*, Husain, Muhammad Ashraf, Ralli. Burton repeated the material on male and female circumcision in the *Nights*.

18. *The Holiest City*

The *Pilgrimage*, Husain, Muhammad Ashraf, and Ralli. See the *Life* and *The Romance* for Isabel Arundell's reactions during Burton's absence in Arabia.

19. *"City of Evil Fame"*

Primary source is *First Footsteps*. Burton's *Zanzibar*, published sixteen years later, puts the Somali Expedition into a full perspective and presents a balanced and fair picture of Speke. Speke's two volumes state simply his early adventures in Africa. Snelling has some brief

* Note: *'Auliyā'*, saints (pl.), not *walī*, saint (sing.), in token of his great sanctity.

material on Edmund Smyth; Snelling informed the author that he found no record of Speke in Tibet. See Hastings for circumcision and infibulation, which supplement Burton's researches. See Enid Starkie on Rimbaud in Aden, Somalia, and Harar.

20. *"Rotten Heads"*

The *Life*, Stisted, and Wright give the outline of Burton's service in the Crimean War. See also Taylor in reference to Oliphant. *The Romance* brings the scene back to Isabel.

21. *The Great Safari*

Zanzibar and the *Central Africa* volumes form the basis for this chapter. See also Morehead. Emil Ludwig's massive work mentions Speke but, curiously, not Burton. See Taylor on Oliphant, Speke, and Burton.

22. *"My Earthly God and King"*

The *Life*, Stisted, *The Romance*, *The City of the Saints*, and Pope-Hennessey on the Milnes circle.

23. *Victoria's Lake*

Speke's works; Hall; the *Life* tells of the Burton-Arundell marriage. Stisted gives a negative view, Wright some gossip. See Pope-Hennessey for society's reaction to the union.

24. *Santa Isabel*

The *Life* and *The Romance* start off the chapter; Burton's West Africa volumes bring us into his exploration of the heart of African life. Wright adds details here and there. See Hall on Baker and the plans to rescue Speke and Grant.

25. *The Evil Nights*

A Mission to Gelele is the basis for this chapter. On the battles with Speke over the Nile, see *The Nile Basin*, particularly the chapters by Macqueen. Also Taylor for Oliphant's role in the matter.

26. *Brazil*

The *Life*, *The Romance*, Stisted, Wright. Burton's books from this period are not among his best. The author's own experiences in Brazil and Argentina a century later were invaluable in giving clues to the Burtons' life in Latin America.

27. *The Emperor and Empress of Damascus*

The *Life*, *The Romance*, Stisted, Wright. Works by al-Ghazzālī, Rūmī, and other Sufis give valuable incidental material on the character of the city. See the *Pilgrimage* on al-Dajjal and the Second Coming. The author's own visits to Damascus (and time spent in the Great Mosque) helped him appreciate the mystical aspects of the city. Lesley Blanch's chapter on Jane Digby has been invaluable. Stisted gives a good picture of Burton after his recall and the dejection he suffered.

28. *Trieste, Sadness*

The *Life*, *The Romance*, and Stisted are starting points. Penzer's bibliography fills in the background of the *Kāma Shāstra* (later called the *Ananga Ranga*). See also the Alex Comfort introduction to Kokkoka, *The Koka Shastra*. Schimmel discusses the *qasīda* form of devotional poetry among Arabs and Persians, *passim*. For Yezīdīs, see Lady Drower. *The Kasîdah* should be read against FitzGerald's version of the *Rubáiyát*. The *Life* includes Burton's report on the Palmer affair.

29. Arabian Nights

Burton's own great work, *The Book of a Thousand Nights and a Night*, including the introduction, annotations, and "Terminal Essay," is the primary source of this chapter. Wright gives details of the sales campaign and of Payne's version. A reading of certain *suras* (chapters) of the Qur'ān is essential for an understanding of Burton's exegesis of the Simurgh (especially those dealing with Solomon), and also 'Aṭṭār's *Conference of the Birds*.

30. *Perfumed Gardens*

The *Life*, *The Romance*, Wright, Stisted, and Burton's own *The Perfumed Garden*. Penzer adds bibliographical details.

31. *The Widow's Burning*

The *Life*, *The Romance*, Wright, and especially Penzer, who grapples with the problem of burning irreplaceable and valuable manuscripts but fails to resolve the issue. Stisted gives a Protestant view of the funeral rites. Of the several popular editions of the *Kama Sutra*, that issued by George Allen & Unwin Ltd. (London, 1963) contains Burton's epitaph.

Bibliography

A. Burton's Works

Original works, translations, etc., by Burton. This bibliography is based on *An Annotated Bibliography of Sir Richard Francis Burton* by Norman Penzer. Works are listed chronologically. Minor writings, such as articles, pamphlets, reviews, letters to magazines and newspapers, are not listed; the reader is referred to Penzer.

Goa, and the Blue Mountains; or, Six Months of Sick Leave, two volumes. London: Richard Bentley, 1851.

Scinde; or, The Unhappy Valley, two volumes. London: Richard Bentley, 1851.

Sindh, and the Races that inhabit the Valley of the Indus., London: W. H. Allen & Co., 1852.

Falconry in the Valley of the Indus. London: John Van Voorst, 1852.

A Complete System of Bayonet Exercise. London: William Clowes and Sons, 1853.

Personal Narrative of a Pilgrimage to El-Medinah and Meccah, three volumes. London: Longman, Brown, Green, and Longmans, 1855, 1857.

First Footsteps in East Africa; or, an Exploration of Harar. London: Longman, Brown, Green, and Longmans, 1856.

The Lake Regions of Central Africa: A Picture of Exploration, two volumes. London: Longman, Green, Longman, and Roberts, 1860.

The Lake Regions of Central Equatorial Africa, with Notices of the Lunar Mountains and the Sources of the White Nile; Being the Results of an Expedition Undertaken under the Patronage of His Majesty's Government and the Royal Geographical Society of London. London: W. Clowes and Sons, 1860.

The City of the Saints and Across the Rocky Mountains to California. London: Longman, Green, Longman, and Roberts, 1861.

The Prairie Traveller, a Hand-book for Overland Expeditions. By Randolph B. Marcy. Edited (with notes) by Richard F. Burton. London: Trübner & Co., 1863.

Abeokuta and The Cameroons Mountains: An Exploration, two volumes. London: Tinsley Brothers, 1863.

Wanderings in West Africa From Liverpool to Fernando Po, two volumes. London: Tinsley Brothers, 1863.

A Mission to Gelele, King of Dahome. With Notices of the So-called "Amazons," the Grand Customs, the Yearly Customs, the Human Sacrifices, the Present State of the Slave Trade, and the Negro's Place in Nature, two volumes. London: Tinsley Brothers, 1864.

The Nile Basin (part one by Burton; part two by James M'Queen). London: Tinsley Brothers, 1864.

Wit and Wisdom from West Africa; or, A Book of Proverbial Philosophy, Idioms, Enigmas, and Laconisms. London: Tinsley Brothers, 1865.

The Guide Book: A Pictorial Pilgrimage to Mecca and Medina. (Including Some of the More Remarkable Incidents in the Life of Mohammed, the Arab Lawgiver.) London: William Clowes & Sons, 1865.

Stone Talk: Being Some of the Marvellous Sayings of a Petral Portion of Fleet Street, London, to One Doctor Polyglott, Phd. London: Robert Hardwicke, 1865.

The Highlands of Brazil, two volumes. *The Aboriginal Indian (Tupy) of Brazil,* vol. 1. *Exploration of the Highlands of The Brazil; with A Full Account of the Gold and Diamond Mines; Also, Canoeing down 1500 Miles of the Great River of São Francisco, From Sabará to the Sea,* vol. 2. London: Tinsley Brothers, 1869.

Vikram and the Vampire, or Tales of Hindu Devilry. London: Longmans, Green, and Co., 1870.

Letters from the Battlefields of Paraguay. London: Tinsley Brothers, 1870.

Unexplored Syria: Visits to the Libanus, The Tulul el Safá, The Anti-Libanus, The Northern Libanus, and the 'Alah, two volumes (in collaboration with Charles F. Tyrwhitt-Drake). London: Tinsley Brothers, 1872.

Zanzibar; City, Island, and Coast, two volumes. London: Tinsley Brothers, 1872.

The Lands of Cazembe. Lacerda's Journey to Cazembe in 1798. Translated by Burton; includes other material. London: Royal Geographical Society, 1873.

The Captivity of Hans Stade of Hesse in A.D. 1547–1555. Among the Wild Tribes of Eastern Brazil. Translated by Albert Tootal and annotated by Burton. Printed for the Hakluyt Society, London, 1874.

Ultima Thule; or, A Summer in Iceland, two volumes. London and Edinburgh: William F. Nimmo, 1875.

Etruscan Bologna: A Study. London: Smith, Elder & Co., 1876.

A New System of Sword Exercise for Infantry. London: William Clowes and Sons, 1876.

Two Trips to Gorilla Land and the Cataracts of the Congo, two volumes. London: Sampson Low, Marston, Low & Searle, 1876.

Scind Revisited: With Notices of the Anglo-Indian Army; Railroads; Past, Present, and Future, two volumes. London: Richard Bentley and Sons, 1877.

The Gold-Mines of Midian and The Ruined Midianite Cities: A Fortnight's Tour in Northwestern Arabia. London: C. Kegan Paul & Co., 1878.

The Land of Midian (revisited), two volumes. London: C. Kegan Paul & Co., 1879.

The Kasîdah. Privately printed. London, 1880.

Os Lusiadas (The Lusiads), two volumes. London: Bernard Quaritch, 1880.

Camoens: His Life and His Lusiads. A Commentary, two volumes. London: Bernard Quaritch, 1881.

A Glance at the "Passion Play." London: W. H. Harrison, 1881.

To the Gold Coast for Gold: A Personal Narrative (in collaboration with Verney Lovett Cameron), two volumes. London: Chatto & Windus, 1883.

The Kama Sutra of Vatsyayana. Printed for the Hindoo Kama Shastra Society, London (later editions: Benares), 1883.

The Book of the Sword. London: Chatto and Windus, 1884.

Camoens: The Lyricks (part one); *Sonnets, Canzons, Odes, and Sextines* (part two). London: Bernard Quaritch, 1884.

Kāma-Shāstra or The Hindoo Art of Love (Ars Amoris Indica), Translated from the Sanskrit, and Annotated by A.F.F. and B.F.R. For Private Use of the Translators Only in Connection With a Work on the Hindoo Religion, and on the Manners and Customs of the Hindoos. Privately printed, 1873 and 1885. Later edition retitled *Ananga-Ranga; the Stage of the Bodiless One, or, The Hindu Art of Love (Ars Amoris Indica)*.

The Perfumed Garden of the Cheikh Nefzaoui: A Manual of Arabian Erotology. Kama Shastra Society of London and Benares, 1886.

The Book of the Thousand Nights and a Night: A Plain and Literal Translation of the Arabian Nights Entertainments, Now Entitled The Book of the Thousand Nights and a Night, With Introduction, Explanatory Notes on the Manners and Customs of Moslem Men and a Terminal Essay upon the History of the Nights, ten volumes. Printed by the Kama-shastra Society, Benares, 1885. *The Supplemental Nights*, six volumes (later seven), 1886–88.

Iraçéma: The Honey-lips: A Legend of Brazil, by J. De Alencar. Translated by Isabel Burton; and bound with *Manuel De Moraes: A Chronicle of the Seventeenth Century*, by J. M. Pereira Da Silva. Translated by Richard F. and Isabel Burton. London: Bickers & Son, 1886.

Priapeia or the Sporting Epigrams of Divers Poets on Priapus. Anonymously translated [by Burton and Leonard Smithers]. Cosmopoli: Privately published, 1890.

Marocco and the Moors: Being an Account of Travels, with a General Description of the Country and its People, by Arthur Leared. Second edition revised and edited by Burton. London: Sampson Low, Marston, Searle & Rivington, Limited, 1891.

Il Pentamerone; or, the Tale of Tales, two volumes. Translated by Burton. London: Henry and Co., 1893.

The Carmina of Caius Valerius Catullus. "Englished" by Burton, with prose portions and notes by Leonard C. Smithers. London: Privately printed, 1894.

The Jew, the Gypsy and El Islam. Edited by W. H. Wilkins. London: Hutchinson & Co., 1898.

Wanderings in Three Continents. Edited by W. H. Wilkins. London: Hutchinson & Co., 1901.

Note: Some of these works were reissued in various editions by Burton or, after his death, by Isabel Burton. Burton's *Pilgrimage* was popular and immediately went into various reprint editions; after his death there were further editions, "Memorial," library and standard, etc. *The Kasîdah* has been widely reprinted, originally by Isabel Burton and later illegally by various publishers. (There was no copyright.) The *Arabian Nights* went through many editions not only in Burton's lifetime but under the auspices of his wife—"Memorial" editions, illustrated editions, "library" editions, facsimile editions, and so on. The *Ananga Ranga* (otherwise *Kāma Shāstra*), the *Kama Sutra, The Perfumed Garden* have been widely reissued by pirates and legitimate publishers alike. Other of Burton's works, among them *Sindh, and the Races that inhabit the Valley of the Indus, First Footsteps in East Africa, Vikram and the Vampire*, the Central Africa and West Africa volumes, *The City of the Saints, The Book of the Sword*, and so on, are among those reissued, often with introductions and annotations by various Burton scholars.

B. Major Sources Consulted

'Abdu'l-Qādir Gīlānī, Hazrat Shaikh Muhyuddin. *Futuh al-Galib* [The Revelations of the Unseen]. Translated by M. Aftab-ud-din Ahmad. Lahore: Sh. Muhammad Ashraf, 1949.

Acton, Thomas. *Gypsy Politics and Social Change.* London and Boston: Routledge and Kegan Paul, 1974.

Ahmad, M. M. Zuhur-u'd-Din. *Mystic Tendencies in Islam in the Light of the Qur'an and the Traditions.* Lahore: Sh. Muhammad Ashraf, 1932.

Algar, Hamid. *The Revolt of the Āghā Khān Mahallātī and the Transference of the Ismā'īlī Imamate to India*, vol. 29. Paris: Studia Islamica, 1969.

Allen, Charles. *Raj, A Scrapbook of British India, 1877–1947.* New York: St. Martin's Press, 1977.

————. *Plain Tales from the Raj.* New York: St. Martin's Press, 1976.

Altekar, A. S. *The Position of Women in Indian Civilization.* Delhi: Motilal Barnardass, 1938.

Anthony, Frank. *Britain's Betrayal in India: The Story of the Anglo-Indian Community.* Bombay: Allied Publishers, 1969.

Arberry, Arthur John. *Sufism: An Account of the Mystics of Islam.* London: George Allen & Unwin, 1950.

Aresteh, A. Reza. *Rumi the Persian, the Sufi.* London: Routledge & Kegan Paul, 1972.

————. *The Art of Rebirth: Patterns and Process of Self-Liberation in Near Eastern Sufism.* Kentucky: Monks Pond, No. 2, 1968, Monks Pond (Trappist publication).

'Aṭṭār, Farīduddīn. *The Conference of the Birds.* Translated by C. S. Noth. Berkeley: University of California Press, 1971.

Baba. *Holy Commandments of The Saint of Oneness, Hazrat Mehboobi-Ilahi Hazoor Khwaja Nizamuddin Aulia, The Beloved of the Almighty.* New Delhi: Institute for Inquiry into the Unknown, 1967.

Balhatchet, Kenneth. *Race, Sex and Class Under the Raj: Imperial Attitudes and Policies and their Critics, 1793–1905.* New York: St. Martin's Press, 1980.

Barr, Pat. *The Memsahibs: The Women of British India.* London: Martin Secker & Warburg Limited, 1978.

Blanch, Lesley. *The Wilder Shores of Love.* New York: Simon & Schuster, 1954.

Bowley, Arthur L. *Wages in the United Kingdom in the Nineteenth Century.* Cambridge, England: Cambridge University Press, 1900.

Brodie, Fawn. *The Devil Drives: A Life of Sir Richard Burton.* New York: W. W. Norton & Company, 1967.

Brown, John P. *The Darvishes.* London: 1868.

Bryk, Felix. *Circumcision in Man and Woman: Its History, Psychology and Ethnology.* New York: American Ethnological Press, 1934.

Burckhardt, Titus. *An Introduction to Sufi Doctrine.* Translated by D. M. Matheson. Lahore: Sh. Muhammad Ashraf, 1959.

Burnes, Alexander. *Travels in Bokhara, together with a Narrative of a Voyage on the Indus.* London: John Murray, 1834, 1835, 1839.

Burnes, James. *A Visit to the Court of Sinde.* Bombay: Summachar Press, 1829.

Burton, Isabel. *The Life of Captain Sir Richd F. Burton, K.C.M.G.,*

F.R.G.S., two volumes. London: Chapman & Hall, 1893. (For Isabel Burton's uncompleted autobiography, see W.H. Wilkins, *The Romance of Isabel Burton.*)

Burton, Jean. *Sir Richard Burton's Wife.* New York: Alfred A. Knopf, 1941.

Chaudhuri, Nirad C. *The Continent of Circe: Being an Essay on the Peoples of India.* Bombay: Jaico Publishing House, 1965.

Coryat, Thomas. *Coryate's Crudities, "Hastily gobbled up in five Moneths travells . . . and now dispersed to the nourishment of the travelling Members of this Kingdome."* London: James MacLehose and Sons, 1805.

Costello, Louisa Stuart. *The Rose Garden of Persia.* Edinburgh: T. N. Poulis, Limited, n.d.

Daniélou, Alain. *Hindu Polytheism.* New York: Bollingen Foundation, 1964.

Davis, F. Hadland. *Jalalu'd-din Rumi,* published in London, 1922. Lahore: Sh. Muhammad Ashraf, 1967 (reprint).

Dermenghem, Emile. *Muhammad and the Islamic Tradition.* Translated by Jean M. Watt. New York: Harper & Brothers, n.d.

Drower, Lady. *Peacock Angel.* London: 1941.

Dubois, Abbé J. A. *Hindu Manners, Customs and Ceremonies.* Madras: 1823. Translated and revised, Henry K. Beauchamp. Madras: 1905. London: Oxford and the Clarendon Press, 1906.

Eastwick, Edward B. *A Glance at Sind Before Napier, or, Dry Leaves from Young Egypt.* Introduction by H. T. Lambrick. Karachi: Oxford University Press, 1971 (reprint).

Edwards, Michael. *British India, 1772–1947.* New York: Taplinger Publishing Company, Inc., 1967.

Elphinstone, Montstuart. *An Account of the Kingdom of Caubul,* published 1815. Karachi: Oxford University Press, 1972 (reprint).

Enchanted Parrot, The, Being a Selection from the "Súka Saptati, or, The Seventy Tales of a Parrot." Translated from the Sanskrit by the Reverend H. Hale Wortham. London: Luzac & Co., 1911.

Erikson, Joan. *Mata ni Pachedi: A Book on the Temple Cloth of the Mother Goddess.* Ahmadabad: National Institute of Design, n.d.

Fairley, Jean. *The Lion River: The Indus.* New York: John Day Company, 1975.

Fairy Tales of a Parrot, "adapted from the Persian text of Mohamed Qadiri's abridged version of the Tooti-Namé." Paris: 1892.

Farwell, Byron. *Burton: A Biography of Sir Richard Francis Burton.* New York: Holt, Rinehart and Winston, 1963.

Flaubert, Gustave. *Letters, 1830–1857.* Edited by Francis Steegmuller. Cambridge, Mass.: Belnap Press of Harvard University, 1980.

Fraser, George MacDonald. *Flashman: From the Flashman Papers, 1839–1842.* New York: World Publishing Company, 1969.

Fredericks, Pierce G. *The Sepoy and the Cossack.* New York: World Publishing Co., 1971.

Furber, Holden. *John Company at Work.* Cambridge, Mass.: Harvard University Press, 1948.

Gaikwad, Vijay Singh Rameshwar Rao. *The Anglo-Indians: A Study in the Problems and Processes Involved in Emotional and Cultural Integration.* Bombay: Asia Publishing House, 1967.

Ghalib (Mirza Asadullah Beg Khan). *Gazals.* Edited by Aijaz Ahmad. New York: Columbia University Press, 1971.

al-Ghazzālī (Ghazzāllī), Abu Hamid Muhammad. *The Book of Knowledge.* Translated by Nabih Amin Faris. Lahore: Sh. Muhammad Ashraf, 1962.

———. *Mishkat al-Anwar* [The Niche for Lights]. Translated by W. H. T. Gardiner. London: Royal Asiatic Society, 1924.

———. *The Mysteries of Worship in Islam.* Translated by Edwin Elliot Calvery. London: 1925. Lahore: Sh. Muhammad Ashraf, 1977 (reprint).

Guillaume, Alfred. *Islam.* Middlesex, England: Penguin Books, 1954.

Gulati, Kailash Chander. *The Akalis Past and Present.* New Delhi: Ashajanak Publications, 1974.

Hall, Richard. *Lovers on the Nile: The Incredible African Journeys of Sam and Florence Baker.* New York: Random House, 1980.

Hanifi, Mansoor Ahmad. *A Survey of Muslim Institutions and Culture.* Lahore: Sh. Muhammad Ashraf, 1962.

Hastings, James, ed. *Encyclopedia of Religion and Ethics,* thirteen volumes. New York: Charles Scribner's Sons, 1917.

Hermes Trismegistus. *The Divine Pymander: An Endeavour to Systematize and Elucidate the Corpus Hermeticus.* Fintry Brook, England: The Shrine of Wisdom, 1923.

Hitchman, Francis. *Richard F. Burton, K.C.M.G.: His Early, Private and Public Life with an Account of his Travels and Explorations,* two volumes. London: Sampson Low, Marston, Searle & Rivington, 1887.

Husain, S. A. *Guide to Hajj.* Lahore: Sh. Muhammad Ashraf, 1972.

Idries Shah. *The Sufis.* New York: Doubleday & Company, 1964.

————. *The Way of the Sufi.* London: Jonathan Cape, 1968.

————. *Caravan of Dreams.* England: Octagon Press, 1968.

Jacquemont, Victor. *Journey in India; Letters from India, describing A Journey in the British Dominions of India, Tibet, Lahore and Cashmeer during the years 1828, 1829, 1830, 1831, undertaken by Order of the French Government.* London: Edward Churchton, 1835.

al-Kalābādhī, Abu Bakr. *Kitāb al-Ta'arruf li-madbab ahl-taṣawwaf* [The Doctrine of the Sufis]. Translated by Arthur John Arberry. Cambridge, England: Cambridge University Press, 1935.

Kalistos, Bishop of Diokleria (Timothy Ware). *The Power of the Name: The Jesus Prayer in Orthodox Spirituality.* Fairacres, Oxford: SLG Press, 1974.

Khan Sahib Khaja Khan. *The Secret of 'Ana'l-Haqq: Being 300 Odd Irshadat (or Sayings) of Shaykh Ibrahim Gazur-i-Ilahi.* Translated from Persian. Lahore: Sh. Muhammad Ashraf, 1926.

Kipling, Rudyard. *Plain Tales from the Hills.* London: 1899.

————. *Kim.* London: 1900.

Kitab al-Izah fi'llm al-Nikah b-it-Tamam w-al-Kamal [The Book of Exposition]. Translated by "An English Bohemian." Paris: Maison d'Editions Scientifiques, 1900.

Klein, F. A. *The Religion of Islam,* published 1906. Budapest: Humanities Press, 1971 (reprint).

Kokkoka. *The Koka Shastra, being the Katirahasya of Kokkoka.* Translated by Alex Comfort. New York: Stein and Day, 1965.

Koran, The Meaning of the Glorious: an Explanatory Translation, by Marmaduke Picthall. New York: Dorset Press, n.d. (reprint).

Koran, The. Translated by N. J. Dawood. Middlesex, England: Penguin Books, 1956.

Kosambi, Damodar Dharmanan. *Myth and Reality: Studies in the Formation of Indian Culture.* Bombay: Popular Prakashan, 1962.

Lambrick, H. T. *Sir Charles Napier and Sind.* Oxford, England: Oxford University Press, 1952.

————. *Sind: A General Introduction.* Hyderabad (Sind): Sindhi Adabi Board, 1964.

Lane, Edward William. *An Account of the Manners and Customs of the Modern Egyptians*. London: Alexander Gardner, 1895 (reprint).

Lannoy, Richard. *The Speaking Tree: A Study of Indian Culture and Society*. New York: Oxford University Press, 1971.

Lawford, James F. *Britain's Army in India*. London: George Allen & Unwin, 1978.

Leland, Charles G. *The English Gypsies and their Language*. London: Trübner & Co., 1874.

Leslie, Shane. *The Oxford Movement, 1833 to 1933*. London: Burnes Oates & Washbourne Ltd., 1933.

Lings, Martin. *A Sufi Saint of the Twentieth Century: Shaikh Ahmad al-'Alawi*. Berkeley: University of California Press, 1971.

––––––. *Muhammad: His Life Based on the Earliest Sources*. Rochester, Vt.: Inner Traditions International Ltd., 1981.

Loeb, E. M. *The Blood Sacrifice Complex*. Memoir of the American Anthropological Association, No. 10, 1923.

Lewis, Bernard. *The Assassins, A Radical Sect in Islam*. New York: Basic Books, Inc., 1968.

Ludwig, Emil. *The Nile: The Life-Story of a River*. Translated by Mary H. Lindsay. New York: Viking Press, 1937.

McDowell, Bart. *Gypsies: Wanderers of the World*. Washington, D.C.: National Geographic Society, 1970.

MacRitchie, David. *Accounts of the Gypsies of India*. London: Kegan Paul, Trench & Co., 1886.

Mir Valiuddin. *The Quranic Sufism*. Delhi: Motilal Banarsidass, 1939.

Moor, Edward. *The Hindu Pantheon* (c. 1810). Edited 1864 by Rev. W. C. Simpson. Varanasi: Indological Book House, 1968 (reprint).

Morehead, Alan. *The White Nile*. New York: Harper & Brothers, 1960.

Muhammad Ali, Maulana. *Muhammad the Prophet*. Lahore: Ahmidiyya Anjuman-i-Isha'at-i-Islam, 1924.

Muhammad Ashraf. *Salat or Islamic Prayer Book*. Lahore: Sh. Muhammad Ashraf, 1971.

Nicholson, Reynold A. *The Mystics of Islam*. London: George Bell & Sons, Ltd., 1914.

––––––. *Rumi: Poet and Mystic*. London: George Allen & Unwin, 1950.

————— *The Idea of Personality in Sufism.* Cambridge, England: Cambridge University Press, 1922.

Nollau, Gunther, and Arnold Fletcher. *Russia's South Flank.* New York: Frederick A. Praeger, 1963.

Norris, J. A. *The First Afghan War, 1838–1842.* Cambridge, England: Cambridge University Press, 1969.

Omar Khayyám. *Rubáiyát.* "Transmogrified" by Edward FitzGerald. London: Bernard Quaritch, 1859.

Osborne, W. G. *The Court and Camp of Runjeet Sing.* London: Henry Colburne, 1840.

Pagal Baba. *Temple of the Phallic King.* Edited by Edward Rice. New York: Simon & Schuster, 1973.

Palmer, Edward Henry. *Oriental Mysticism,* published 1867. London: Frank Case & Co. Ltd., 1969 (reprint).

Panchatantra. Translated by Franklin Edgerton. London: George Allen & Unwin, 1963.

Panter-Downes, Mollie. *Ootie Preserved.* New York: Farrar, Straus and Giroux, 1967.

Pearl, Cyril. *The Girl with the Swansdown Seat.* Indianapolis: Bobbs-Merrill, 1955.

Penzer, Norman. *An Annotated Bibliography of Sir Richard Francis Burton, K.C.M.G.* London, 1923. New York: Burt Franklin, 1970 (reprint).

Philby, H. St. J. B. *The Heart of Arabia,* two volumes. New York: G. P. Putnam's Sons, 1923.

Pope-Hennessy, James. *Monckton Milnes: The Flight of Youth, 1851 –1885.* London: Constable and Company, Ltd., 1951.

Praz, Mario. *The Romantic Agony.* London: Oxford University Press, 1960.

Qur-an, The Holy. An English interpretation by A. Yusuf Ali. Lahore: Sh. Muhammad Ashraf, 1975.

Rahman, Fazlur. *Islam.* New York: Holt, Rinehart and Winston, 1966.

Ralli, Augustus. *Christians at Mecca.* London: William Heinemann, 1909.

Religious Hinduism: A Presentation and Appraisal, by Jesuit Scholars. Allahabad: St. Paul Publications, 1964.

Rice, Edward. *Eastern Definitions: A Short Encyclopedia of Religions of the Orient*. New York: Doubleday & Company, Inc., 1978.

Richardson, David Lester. *Anglo-Indian Passage; homeward and outward bound*. London: Madden and Malcom, 1845.

Robinson, Harry. *Monsoon Asia: A Geographical Survey*. New York: Frederick A. Praeger, 1966.

Rosenroth, Knorr von. *Aesch Mezareph or Purifying Fire: A Chymico Kabalistic Treatise*. Translated by "a Lover of Philalethes," 1714. New York: Occult Research Press, n.d. (reprint).

Rudolph, Kurt. *Gnosis: The Nature and History of Gnosticism*. New York and San Francisco: Harper and Row, 1987.

Rūmī. *Masnawi*. Translated by Reynold A. Nicholson. Lahore: Sh. Muhammad Ashraf, n.d.

'Ruswā, Mirzā Muhammad Hādī, *The Courtesan of Lucknow: Umrā'o Jān Adā*. Translated by Kushwant Singh and M. A. Husaini. Delhi: Hind Pocket Books (F) Ltd., 1961.

Salik, S. A., *The Saint of Jilan; The Life of Saiyedene Hazrat Mohi-ud-din Saiyed Abu Muhammad Abdul Qadir Al-Baghdadi al-Hasani al-Hussani*. Lahore: Sh. Muhammad Ashraf, 1953.

Schaya, Leo. *The Universal Meaning of the Kabbalah*. London: George Allen & Unwin Ltd., 1973.

Schimmel, Annemarie. *Mystical Dimensions of Islam*. Chapel Hill: University of North Carolina Press, 1975.

Scholem, Gershon G. *On the Kabbalah and its Symbolism*. New York: Schocken Books, Inc., 1965.

————. *Kabbalah*. Jerusalem: Kater Publishing House, 1974.

Shabistarī, Sa'd ud-din Mahmūd. *The Secret Rose Garden*. Lahore: Sh. Muhammad Ashraf, 1969 (reprint).

Sharda, Sadhu Ram. *Sufi Thought: Its Development in Panjab and its Impact on Panjabi Literature*. New Delhi: Munshiram Mancharlal Publishers Pvt. Ltd., 1974.

Sharif, Jafar. *Islam in India*. Oxford: Oxford University Press, 1832.

Snelling, John. *The Sacred Mountain: Travellers and Pilgrims at Mount Kailas in Western Tibet, and the Great Universal Symbol of the Sacred Mountain*. London and The Hague: East West Publications (UK) Limited, 1983.

Speke, John Hanning. *Journal of the Discovery of the Source of the Nile*. London and Edinburgh: William Blackwood & Sons, 1863.

————. *What Led to the Discovery of the Source of the Nile.* London and Edinburgh: William Blackwood & Sons, 1863.

Stark, Freya. *The Valley of the Assassins, and other Persian Travels.* London: John Murray, 1934.

Starkie, Enid. *Arthur Rimbaud.* New York: New Directions, 1962.

Stisted, Georgiana M. *The True Life of Capt. Sir Richard F. Burton, K.C.M.G., F.R.G.S.,* etc. London: H.S. Nichols, 1896.

Suhwawardī, Shaikh Shahāb-u'd-Dīn 'Umar B. Muḥammad. *'A-wārif-u'l-Ma'ārif.* Translated from Arabic into Persian by Maḥmud B. 'Alī al-Kāshānī. Translated from Persian into English by Lieut. Col. H. Wilberforce Clarke. Calcutta, 1891. Lahore: Sh. Muhammad Ashraf, 1979 (reprint).

Taittirīya Saṁhitā [The Veda of the Black Yajus School], two volumes. Translated by Arthur Berriedale Keith. Cambridge, Mass.: Harvard University Press, 1914.

Taylor, Anne. *Laurence Oliphant: 1829–1888.* London: Oxford University Press, 1982.

Thomas, P. *Hindu Religion Customs and Manners: Describing the Customs and Manners, Religions, Social and Domestic Life, Arts and Sciences of the Hindus.* Bombay: D. B. Taraporevala Sons & Co. Private Ltd., n.d.

Tootinameh, The, Tales of a Parrot: in the Persian Language: with an English Translation. Calcutta: A. Upjohn (printer), 1792.

Trimingham, J. Spencer. *The Sufi Orders in Islam.* London: Oxford at the Clarendon Press, 1971.

Vambéry, Arminius. *Travels in Central Asia.* New York: Harper Brothers, 1865.

————. *The Life and Adventures of Arminius Vambéry.* New York: Frederick A. Stokes, n.d.

Vesey-Fitzgerald, Brian. *Gypsies of Britain.* London: Chapman & Hall Ltd., 1944.

Westermarck, Edward. *The History of Human Marriage,* three volumes (5th ed., revised). London: MacMillan and Co., Limited, 1921.

Wilkins, W. H. *The Romance of Isabel Burton,* two volumes. Published in 1897. London: Chapman and Hall, 1906 (reprint).

Wilkins, W. J. *Modern Hinduism.* Calcutta, 1881. Calcutta: Rupa & Co., 1974 (reprint).

Williams, John Alden, ed. *Islam.* New York: George Braziller, Inc., 1961.

Woodroffe, Sir John (Arthur Avalon). *Kundalini Śakti* [The Serpent Power]. Calcutta, 1900. Madras: Ganesh & Co. Private Ltd., 1969 (reprint).

————. *The Garland of Letters: Studies in the Mantra-Śāstra*. Calcutta, 1922. Madras: Ganesh & Co. Private Ltd., 1969 (reprint).

Wright, Thomas. *The Life of Sir Richard Burton*, two volumes. London: Everett & Co., 1906.

Yeats-Brown, Francis. *The Lives of a Bengal Lancer*. New York: Viking Press, Inc., 1930.

Zadkiel's Dream Book. Philadelphia: David McKay, n.d.

INDEX

About the Author

Edward Rice is the author of twenty books, including *The Man in the Sycamore Tree*, a biography of the Trappist monk Thomas Merton; *Margaret Mead*, a profile of the anthropologist; and *John Frum He Come*, a study of the cargo cults of the South Pacific. A former editor for *Collier's* magazine, he was founder and editor of the 1950s and 1960s magazine *Jubilee*, which featured the works of Jack Kerouac, W. H. Auden, and Mother Teresa, among others. He has written documentary movie scripts and hundreds of magazine articles, and has traveled throughout Asia and Africa in his work providing written and photographic medical reports for the United Nations.